Tort and Insurance Law
Yearbook

European Tort Law 2001

Edited by the
European Centre of Tort and Insurance Law

together with the
Research Unit for European Tort Law
of the Austrian Academy of Sciences

Helmut Koziol
Barbara C. Steininger (eds.)

European Tort Law 2001

With Contributions by

Ewa Baginska, Elena Bargelli, Herman A. Cousy, Eugenia Dacoronia, Dimitri Droshout, Michael Faure, Jörg Fedtke, María Paz García Rubio, Ton Hartlief, Heinz Hausheer, Manuel Jaun, Johann C. Knobel, Bernhard A. Koch, Helmut Koziol, Christian Lahnstein, Javier Lete, Olivier Massot, Emanuela Navarretta, Jaana Norio-Timonen, Ken Oliphant, André Gonçalo Dias Pereira, Eoin Quill, Wolfgang Reisinger, Henrik Sandell, Barbara C. Steininger, Luboš Tichý, Bénédict Winiger

SpringerWienNewYork

European Centre of Tort and Insurance Law
Landesgerichtsstraße 11
A-1080 Vienna
Tel.: +43 1 40127 1688
Fax: +43 1 40127 1685
E-Mail: ectil@ectil.org

Austrian Academy of Sciences
Research Unit for European Tort Law
Landesgerichtsstraße 11
A-1080 Vienna
Tel.: +43 1 40127 1687
E-Mail: etl@oeaw.ac.at

This work is published with the financial support
of the Austrian Ministry of Education, Science and Culture
and Munich Re

Printed in Austria

Typesetting: Composition & Design Services, Minsk
Printing and binding: Manz Crossmedia GmbH & Co KG, A-1051 Wien

Printed on acid-free and chlorine-free bleached paper
SPIN: 10876479

With 1 Figure

CIP data applied for

ISSN 1616-8623
ISBN 3-211-83824-4 Springer-Verlag Wien New York

Foreword

It is well known that in the last decades there has been an increasing interest for the approximation and harmonisation of private law in Europe. Although the answers given recently to the *Communication from the Commission to the Council and the European Parliament on European Contract Law*, COM (2001) 398 final, Official Journal (2001/C255/01) show that there is still little support for the enactment of a European Civil Code in the short or in the medium term, most of the governments and groups of legal professionals who have been consulted have shown, by contrast, that there is already strong widespread support for the elaboration of *Principles* of law, a task which is carried out by several international groups of legal academics and professionals.

The task of these groups is difficult and praiseworthy. By using comparative law techniques they have undertaken to point out those *Principles* which are common and, in the case of great differences, to stress, among the various options, which solutions are more in accord with current legal needs. Such *Principles* can be very useful for the legislators of the Member States, since they show the way to approximation and harmonisation of legislations. They can also be very helpful for the courts of the different Member States, as guidance in their search for general legal standards, as well as for citizens when organising their legal relationships. It is long recognized that such *Principles* should not only be developed in the area of contract law, but also for other subject matters, such as tort law and, beyond the realm of the law of obligations, even property law.

Therefore the subject matter that this book deals with is one of the main focuses of attention in this process of Europeanisation. Those who know the rules of tort law in various European jurisdictions will have noticed that, although there are developments and trends that are common, the foundations of tort law in these legal systems, at least to some extent, differ considerably. These differences cannot be analysed simply by drawing a line between common law and continental law. Even within continental countries, such as France, Italy or Spain, the tort law in many respects significantly differs from the approach taken for instance in Austria, Germany or the Netherlands.

The *European Centre of Tort and Insurance Law (ECTIL),* which organises and coordinates the research that is presented in this book, was founded in Vienna at the beginning of 1999, among other reasons, to create a secure institutional basis for the drafting of the *Principles* carried out by the *European Group on Tort Law.* This Group, established in 1993 by Jaap Spier, at that time Professor at the University of Tilburg in the Netherlands and currently Advocate General of the Dutch Supreme Court, has already published six books related to the most relevant aspects of tort liability such as wrongfulness, causation, damage and strict liability. The Group comprises more than twenty experts from EU Member States as well as from other European and non-European countries, who discuss these and other fundamental questions concerning tort law on a comparative basis.

The *European Centre of Tort and Insurance Law* is also involved in other comparative legal research studies, the results of which are published in the series "Tort and Insurance Law" by Springer (Vienna/New York). In 2002, ECTIL initiated an Annual Conference to provide both practitioners and academics with the opportunity to learn of the most significant recent developments in tort law. Experts from all over Europe provide a comprehensive overview of the previous year's court practice and legislation in their respective jurisdiction.

This Yearbook includes the papers presented at the 1st Annual Conference on European Tort Law which was held in Vienna on 5 April 2002.

Angel Acebes Paniagua
Ministro de Justicia de España
May 2002

Preface

A harmonisation of European law presupposes sound mutual knowledge of the jurisdictions involved in the harmonisation process. However, partly due to language problems it is not always easy to obtain information about all these jurisdictions, especially as far as new developments are concerned. Against this background, the European Centre of Tort and Insurance Law decided to publish a Yearbook on European Tort Law containing reports on the most interesting new developments in the field of tort law in different European countries.

The present Yearbook on European Tort law includes reports on EU Member States, Switzerland, the Czech Republic, Poland as well as an overview of the developments in the field of EC law. Additionally, it was decided to include one non-European country in every Yearbook – for this volume South Africa, with its highly interesting mixture of civil law and common law, was chosen. Furthermore, the Yearbook includes a short comparative overview and two essays on key issues of tort law. In next year's Yearbook we intend to broaden the scope of information provided by also covering the tort law systems of Hungary and Slovenia. As non-European country we plan to present a report on the developments in Israel. The essays, as well as the most important results of the country reports and some comparative remarks, were presented and discussed at the 1st Annual Conference on European Tort Law in Vienna on 5 April 2002. The 2nd Annual Conference on European Tort Law will again take place in Vienna and the date has been fixed for 25 April 2003.

In publishing the Yearbook we pursue the idea of providing a comprehensive overview of the latest developments in the law of torts of many European countries and thereby, enabling scholars as well as practitioners from different national backgrounds to keep abreast of questions concerning tort law. Furthermore, we do hope that the Yearbook will enhance and promote a greater understanding of the respective national legal and judicial systems which is essential for a successful harmonisation of European Tort Law.

At this point, we would like to express our gratitude for the support of this project by the Austrian Ministry of Education, Science and Culture; the Austrian Ministry of Justice; the Kulturabteilung der Stadt Wien; Munich Re; the Vienna Convention Bureau and Wiener Städtische Allgemeine Versicherungs AG. Without their support this project could never have been realised. Moreover, we would like to thank the staff of the European Centre of Tort and

Insurance Law, especially Prof. Bernhard A. Koch, Dr. Sabine Gantner, Donna Stockenhuber M.A. and Mag. Lisa Zeiler, for the most valuable assistance in preparing the conference and the publication.

Helmut Koziol and Barbara Steininger
Vienna, August 2002

Table of Contents

Essays

I. Strict Liability: What About Fault?

Bénédict Winiger[1]

A. Introduction

1 For nearly 200 years, fault was a necessary requisite for liability. Since the Code Civil Français from 1804, all the important national codifications have mentioned it as a basic condition for the reparation of damage[2]. Today, fault is sick, overcharged by tasks for which it had not been conceived: Judges have extended its application on new forms of risk typical for industrial societies. The particularity of these new dangers is to come up without the fault of anybody. The result of this evolution is a fault concept 'without fault'[3].

2 One of the main aims of contemporary legislators is to find a remedy to this contradiction in terms. The Swiss draft (SD)[4], for example, introduces a specific norm for strict liability (art. 50 SD)[5] with the declared aim of the drafters

[1] I thank Helmut Koziol and Pierre Widmer for their reading of my paper as well as my assistants Samantha Meregalli and Guillaume Etier for their help. My thanks go also to Donna Stockenhuber for proof-reading my English text.

[2] Art. 1382 CCF, §§ 1294 and 1295 ABGB, § 823 BGB, art. 41 COS, art. 2043 CCI, art. 6:162 BW *etc.*

[3] See Pierre Widmer/Pierre Wessner, *Révision et unification du droit de la responsabilité civile. Rapport explicatif* (2000), p.120.

[4] *Avant-projet de loi fédérale sur la révision et l'unification du droit de la responsabilité civile* (2000), (cited Report).

[5] Avant-projet suisse *Art. 50 Responsabilité pour risque*
1 La personne qui exploite une activité spécifiquement dangereuse est tenue de réparer le dommage dû à la réalisation du risque caractérisé que celle-ci comporte, même s'il s'agit d'une activité tolérée par l'ordre juridique.
2 Est réputée spécifiquement dangereuse l'activité qui, par sa nature ou par celle des substances, instruments ou énergies utilisés, est susceptible, en dépit de toute la diligence qu'on peut exiger d'une personne spécialisée en la matière, de causer de fréquents ou de graves dommages; tel est notamment le cas lorsqu'une loi institue une responsabilité spéciale à raison d'un risque comparable.
3 Sont réservées les dispositions spéciales régissant la responsabilité à raison d'un risque caractérisé déterminé.
Art. 50 Gefährdungshaftung

to give back to fault its initial scope[6]. Other drafts, like the Project of the European Group on Tort Law based in Vienna, could propose comparable solutions.

The present paper will try to draw some possible consequences of strict liabil- 3
ity norms on fault. In my sense, the first and apparently paradoxical consequence could be not a diminution, but a notable revaluation of the fault concept. One means of achieving this could be the differentiation of the fault in *culpa levissima, levis* and *lata*.

B. Concepts of Fault Liability

First let us examine some different forms of fault we meet in our law systems. 4
In the absence of real definitions by the law, certain doctrines propose their own definitions, while others prefer to give general descriptions.

A first, and let us call 'basic notion of fault' is that defined by Austrian doc- 5
trine: "A person is behaving faultily when that person should have acted differently and, furthermore, would have been able to act differently"[7]. A Swiss definition underlines "the blame not to have avoided harm to another person, notwithstanding the fact that one would have been in a position and under a duty to foresee and to avert the damage"[8]. Two elements dominate these definitions: the tortfeasor *should* and *could* have acted differently. This type of definition is the oldest one we know, formulated first by Mucius (2nd century B.C.), saying: *but a fault is what had not been foreseen although it could have been foreseen by the diligent or what had been denunciated when the danger could not have been avoided*[9]. Already here, we have the two elements of prevision and duty.

1 Wird Schaden dadurch verursacht, dass sich das charakteristische Risiko einer besonders gefährlichen Tätigkeit verwirklicht, so haftet dafür die Person, die diese betreibt, selbst wenn es sich um eine von der Rechtsordnung geduldete Tätigkeit handelt.
2 Eine Tätigkeit gilt als besonders gefährlich, wenn sie ihrem Wesen nach oder nach der Art der dabei verwendeten Stoffe, Geräte oder Kräfte geeignet ist, auch bei Anwendung aller von einer fachkundigen Person zu erwartenden Sorgfalt häufige oder schwerwiegende Schäden herbeizuführen; dies ist inbesondere dann anzunehmen, wenn für ein vergleichbares Risiko bereits ein Gesetz eine spezielle Handlung begründet.
3 Spezielle Haftungsbestimmungen für ein bestimmtes charakteristisches Risiko sind vorbehalten.

[6] See Report, p. 120.

[7] H. Koziol, Austrian Report on Fault, in: P. Widmer (ed.), Unification of Tort Law: Fault (cited Fault, forthcoming 2003), no. 3; ibid., Wrongfulness under Austrian Law, in: H. Koziol, (ed.), *Wrongfulness* (1998), p. 17; ibid., Liability Based on Fault: Subjective or Objective Yardstick? [1998] *Maastricht Journal*, 111.

[8] P. Widmer, Swiss Report on Fault, Fault, no. 3.

[9] Paulus D. 9,2,31: "... *culpam autem esse, quod cum a diligente provideri poterit, non esset provisum aut tum denuntiatum esset, cum periculum evitari non possit*".

6 The formulation of Mucius suggests a reasoning in two steps. First, the judge establishes the yardstick of the *diligens*. He asks how would a diligent man have acted in this situation? Second, he compares the model behaviour to the tortfeasor's act. If the author of the damage was not diligent enough, he has to repair the harm, otherwise, he will be absolved. In this reasoning, the yardstick is unspecific in the sense that Mucius does not think of a particularly qualified or unapt, but of an average person. The case which led to his definition of fault concerned a *putator*, a man cutting branches on a tree and throwing them on the ground. Unfortunately, one of the falling branches harmed someone who was passing. According to Mucius the harmdoer is liable if he failed to take the safety measures he should have taken. The question is simply what an average person would have done to avoid the harm. In our contemporary reasoning, we can find traces of Mucius' definition. We still refer to an average man and impose his hypothetical behaviour as a duty to everyone. We will see later what exactly is an average man.

7 If we look at the German doctrine, it apparently neglects the definition of fault[10], focusing more on the terms of negligence and intentional wrong-doing. Despite that, in the German doctrine, the two central elements of fault are the foreseeability of the damage and its avoidability[11]. Concerning English law, it is interesting, but not astonishing, that the definition of negligence is not very far from the Austrian, Swiss and Roman types of fault. In *Blyth v Birmingham Waterworks Co*, negligence is described as "(...) the omission to do something which a reasonable man (...), guided upon those considerations which ordinarily regulate the conduct of human affairs, would do; or doing something which a prudent and reasonable man would not do"[12]. Here as well, the criterion is what a *reasonable* man *would* have done, meaning, in Mucius' terms, what a *diligens* would have foreseen. Note in brackets that, as I said, the proximity of fault and negligence is not astonishing. In fact, originally both had the same argumentative function. Already in classical Roman law, fault and negligence were two parallel arguments to prove the wrongfulness (*iniuria*) of the tortfeasor's act.

8 This leads us to a second notion of fault. The juridical practice showed quickly that the, as I called it, 'basic notion of fault' did not offer enough nuances. The first problem concerned the degree of fault. What if the tortfeasor's behaviour was very close to the standard behaviour of a reasonable man? Should the legal consequence be the same if the act was very far from what a reasonable man would have done? In other words, should *culpa levissima* be treated in the same way as *culpa lata* or even *dolus*? This question concerns the foundation itself of liability and especially the problem who should be protected, the

[10] U. Magnus, German Report on Fault, Fault no. 3: "There is no general statutory definition of fault ("*Verschulden*") in German law. The Civil Code makes it clear, however, that fault is constituted by the two categories *Vorsatz* (intent) and *Fahrlässigkeit* (negligence)". For the definition of *Fahrlässigkeit* as omission of due care, see § 276 BGB.

[11] Magnus, Fault, no. 7a.

[12] Cited by W.V.H. Rogers, English Report on Fault, Fault, no. 3.

author of the damage or his victim? Another fundamental point is whether the main purpose of liability is to repair the harm or to apportion the reparation according to the fault of the wrongdoer. The former option neglects the degree of fault, the latter one underlines it.

The answers to this question are various. In German tort law, generally even the slightest degree of negligence renders the author fully liable, the law requiring only 'negligence'[13]. This is also Ulpian's point of view[14] which respects the originally very rigid *ratio legis* of the *lex Aquilia* to repair damage independently of fault considerations. At the other extreme of the scale, in Austrian law, the degree of fault determines the degree of compensation. Here, the basic principle of reparation is influenced by equity considerations[15]. In between, there is Swiss law where, generally, fault leads to full compensation. But, according to art. 43 COS the judge can reduce it in case of *culpa levis*[16]. **9**

What is the link between the, as I call it, 'basic notion of fault' and the different graduations between *dolus* and *culpa levissima*? In reality, they represent two steps in the same direction. The first step, the basic notion of fault, introduced a new symmetry into tort law. The initial symmetry, as we know it from the *lex Aquilia*[17], was based only on wrongfulness. The harmdoer H inflicted damage D to the victim V. H has to give to V the economical equivalent of D. The first step away from this initial symmetry was Mucius' fault symmetry. It submitted reparation to the condition that there was a fault. H had to repair D if his act was faulty. This new symmetry was a double one, taking in account not only the situation of the victim, but also some specific features of the tortfeasor's behaviour. According to Mucius' initial idea, one cannot be held liable for a harm if one had done everything to avoid it or if it was entirely imprevisible. **10**

The second step brought a fault/degree symmetry. H had to repair V's damage D *proportionally* to his (H's) fault. This second step is a direct consequence of the fault idea. The concept of fault results in an analysis of the behaviour of the tortfeasor (and, in case of contributory negligence, the tort or negligence of V or a third person) with the aim of determining whether his act corresponded to what an average man would have done. For this determination, it was necessary to fix standard scales of conduct. It is obvious that sometimes the difference between the standard of conduct and the real behaviour of the tortfeasor was very important, and that sometimes it was not. These differ- **11**

13 Magnus, Fault, no. 9a: "Generally, the lowest grade of negligence suffices to incur full tort liability. Only few tort provisions require a qualified degree of fault (intent: §§ 825, 826 BGB)".
14 Ulpianus D. 9,2,44 : "*In lege Aquilia et levissima culpa venit.*"
15 Koziol, Fault, no. 9a: "It is generally accepted as equitable that the degree of negligence of the tortfeasor should have an influence on the extent of compensation",
16 "*Allerdings ist der Richter nicht verpflichtet, bei leichter Fahrlässigkeit automatisch eine Reduktion vorzunehmen. Grundsätzlich verpflichtet die Verschuldenshaftung zu vollem Ersatz. Volle Entschädigung bleibt die Regel* (art. 41), *Kürzung die Ausnahme* (...)", R. Brehm, *Berner Kommentar, Obligationenrecht* (OR), VI,1, 3.Tb., 1.Utb., Die Entstehung durch unerlaubte Handlungen, art. 41–61 OR, (2nd edn. 1998), art. 43, no. 76.
17 Gaius, D. 9,2,2pr; Ulpianus D. 9,2,27,5.

ences from case to case suggested a refinement of the scales by introducing degrees of fault allowing one to measure more precisely the difference between the standard scale and the tortfeasor's concrete behaviour. In other words, the differentiation of fault in degrees was first an instrument to evaluate whether there was fault. Only later did it become an independent criterion to fix the extent of compensation.

12 At the same time, the distinction of degrees of fault made one thing evident: to fix the reasonable man's behaviour and to compare it to the tortfeasor's fault was always linked to evaluation. Mostly, these evaluations were not purely objectives but based on subjective preferences. The standard itself cannot depend merely on individual preferences, like the security needs of anxious or fearless people. Also the comparison between standard and concrete behaviour is not always established mechanically, but sometimes by analogy, especially if the tortfeasor had adopted new or inventive behaviour (for example up to that point unknown technical processes). Then, the criteria for the analogy imply subjective choice. In other words, fault and its degrees gave to liability a double subjective turn: the judge took into account subjective elements of the tortfeasor *and* his own judgment contained a certain subjectivity due to his evaluation of the facts submitted to him.

13 Let us now turn our attention to a third notion of fault. If the introduction of fault degrees resolved certain problems, it also created new ones. In fact, there was now a need to define the reasonable man's standard. Lawyers and judges were systematically confronted with the question: Who is the reasonable man? Can the same standard be applied to everybody or are there distinctions justifying an adaptation on the particularities of the tortfeasor? In other words, which person is the model for the standard, the average man, the informed person or the specialist? The different answers seem to go into the same sense, introducing classes of models according to the group the tortfeasor belongs to. For example, under German law, if a doctor causes harm to his patient, he is compared to an average doctor of his competence. If he is a specialist in surgery, the reference will be an average specialist in surgery[18]. The judge also takes in account the particular knowledge and capacities of the person[19]. This means, of course, that the standard of the specialist is higher than the generalist's one and that the specialist is obliged to apply all his extra knowledge. Also Swiss law adapts the yardstick to the tortfeasor's category[20]. The English judge takes into account all the specific circumstances of the particular case. He can, but is not obliged to adopt the particular professional standards when he fixes what is due care[21]. Generally, he will suppose that the average person

[18] Magnus, Fault, no. 6.

[19] Magnus, Fault, no. 6: "... a specialist has to make use of all his extra knowledge and is, therefore, liable for a damage which he personally could have avoided, even if a colleague with average abilities in the respective profession could not be blamed for overlooking the damage-causing detail".

[20] Widmer, Fault no. 6.

[21] Rogers, Fault, no. 7.

will have average behaviour and the professional a professional's abilities. Despite that, he can diminish the standard, for example in case of uncommon circumstances like an emergency situation in which the professional took a 'wrong' decision[22]. Austrian law also adapts the 'reasonable man's behaviour' to the particular situation of the tortfeasor. According to § 1294 ABGB, the actor has to take the due attention and diligence. What is 'due' depends on the concrete situation and, for example, on the particular competence of the tortfeasor. This is the general Austrian solution[23]. Furthermore, the expert and the specialist fall under § 1299 ABGB and are held responsible for the lack of their specific abilities[24].

Retrospectively, it seems obvious that the 'reasonable man standard' could no longer remain a monolith applicable to everybody, as it had been proposed by the 'basic notion of fault'. The evolution from an agrarian to an industrial society led to a diversity of individual competences which differentiated the fault notion. This third notion of fault also introduced a new symmetry in tort law. The fault/degree symmetry was transformed into a fault/degree/class symmetry. The advantage of this new symmetry concerns the equity of the judgment. Independently of the fact whether the systems of law accept to make a difference between *culpa levissima, levis* and *lata*, the judge can take into account the specific situation such as the professional qualifications of the tortfeasor. The nurse is no longer judged according to the same scale as the surgery specialist. **14**

Here again, the evolution to this third notion of fault, sometimes called an objectivated fault (which means: objectivated by classes of persons), has its roots in the 'basic notion of fault' we know from Mucius, because one is attentive not only to the victim and his harm, but also to the particular situation of the tortfeasor. At the same time, this 'objectivated' fault represents an important new step. Further on, law will not impose one single behaviour to everybody. It will differentiate the conditions according to the individual shape of the actors. **15**

This brings us to a fourth – and very controversial – notion of fault. The distinction of classes underlined an old problem which once again became topical. How to form classes? What are the typical elements and criteria? For some of them, the answers are evident as they are already stated elsewhere. One of them is the professional competence. Often, the different professions fix themselves not only criteria of professional behaviour, but also classes and degrees of competence. In medical sciences, the generalist does not have the same formation and skill as the specialist. Consequently, the judge can use this **16**

[22] Rogers, Fault, no. 7.

[23] Koziol, Fault, no. 6a: "According to the predominant opinion in Austria, a subjective standard of fault has to be applied and, thus, the personal abilities are decisive. (...) As a subjective yardstick has to be used, one has to examine whether the abilities of the concrete tortfeasor were sufficient to avoid the damage".

[24] Koziol, Fault, no. 6b.

difference *in concreto* as a criterion to determinate the individual competence asked to the tortfeasor. But, even if there are such criteria from outside, all the problems are not resolved for the judge, because he is independent to apply or not to apply them. If there are foreign elements, his problem will be to filter them. So, the question is still, what criterion he will use. What circumstances justify the creation of a class? Beside generally accepted classes of professionals, should there be also, for example, a class of tired or desperate persons because of matrimonial troubles, health disease or other individual problems? In other words, to what extent should subjective elements influence the liability of the tortfeasor? This question can be developed in two opposite senses. First, in the sense of *exemptions* of liability by personal motives. This would lead to an extremely subjective liability, resulting from all the objective and subjective circumstances of the concrete case. Second, it can be developed in the sense of exclusion of all personal elements. The effect would be a purely objective liability excluding all considerations concerning the tortfeasor's individual situation. The first solution opens the floodgate of exemptions, the second one closes them; or alternatively, the first closes the floodgate of liability, the second one opens it.

17 The recent evolutions show that certain national law systems are restrictive in admitting subjective exemptions from liability. Technically, they increase the standard of due care up to a level nobody can respect, whatever they do. The effect is that the actor is faulty in any case of damage, even if he did not commit a fault. This is the so-called fault liability 'without fault', which is, in fact, a strict liability, where the 'tortfeasor' is liable independently of his particular behaviour; here, the causal link between act and damage is sufficient. Another system we find for example in Austrian law, where fault liability and strict liability are considered as the two ends of an 'unbroken chain'[25]. The degree of due care is increasing with the danger of the activity. The effect is that strict liability is limited to very dangerous activities, less danger allows the tortfeasor the possibility to exempt himself with the argument that he has respected his duty of care. The advantage of this system is that it guarantees a direct relationship between the intensity of the danger and the degree of care imposed on the actors.

18 Between the third and the fourth notion of fault there is not a difference of symmetry, but of degree. They both focus on the tortfeasor's person, but differ in the way in which he is considered . Both, the third (or objectivated) and the fourth notion of fault establish classes of persons. The difference is that the fourth notion of fault takes the person not only as a member of a class, but mitigates the evaluation of his act by considerations concerning his individual features and particularities. Historically, this strong subjectivity is to a large extent an inheritance of the jusnaturalisme of the 17th and 18th centuries. Hugo Grotius, Samuel Pufendorf and, above all, Christian Wolff underlined the importance of subjective rights. A main quality of the individuum was to

[25] Koziol, Fault, no. 1b.

have the titularity of rights and, more particularly, of property rights. The basic instrument to protect these individual rights was liability conceived as an individual obligation to repair inflicted harm. The jusnaturalistic concept of liability was extremely subjective and fault oriented. In order to establish the existence or non-existence of fault, the concept penetrated the subject more and more profoundly and observed even its lightest motivations to commit or omit an act. Without any doubt, the fault that emerged later powerfully in the national codifications, and especially in art. 1382 CCF, is a far descendent of jusnaturalism. The celebration of the individuum by the 18th century philosophers culminating in Kant's theory of liberty had deep and unexpected consequences on liability. The protection of the subjective rights of both sides – of the harmdoer and the victim – overlooked a fundamental lack of respect for the individuum's intimacy.

Today, tort law has to resolve two problems concerning fault and strict liabil- **19**
ity. On the one hand, it has to eliminate the conceptual contradiction of fault liability 'without fault'. On the other hand, it has to develop a new concept to seek an alternative to fault liability 'without fault', or, in other words, to fashion a strict liability concept.

C. Strict Liability Concepts

Let us now turn to a very brief examination of strict liability. Besides the dispo- **20**
sitions in special laws, for example for nuclear plants or for motor vehicles, and besides the unproper strict liability through fault liability 'without fault', I would evoke in the European law tradition three different models. The first model is the Roman *lex Aquilia* (286 ant.C.), saying, in shorthand: *damnum iniuria datum*, which means: If someone has inflicted an unlawful damage, he has to repair it. This form of liability is strict because there is no need of fault. The wrongdoer is liable independently of his particular behaviour if there is a causal link between the act and the damage and if the act was committed *iniuria*, that is to say, in violation of the law and without a juridical justification like self defence. Note in brackets that an even older form of strict liability is the Talion of the XII-Tables (451 B.C.): *si membrum rupit, ni cum eo pacit, talio esto*[26]. The main difference with the *lex Aquilia* is that in the Talion reparation is possible, but not compulsory. First, it is up to the parties to look for a private arrangement (*ni cum eo pacit*). Only if they fail to find a solution can the victim ask the revenge of the Talion. As we have seen , the strict liability of the *lex Aquilia* had been completed by jurisprudence only in the 2nd century B.C., when Mucius proposed for the first time a consideration of the faulty behaviour of the tortfeasor. The Roman model of strict liability with all its advantages and disadvantages had been analysed and discussed not only by the Roman jurisconsults, but also during all the second millenary. It is interesting to see that, at the extreme end of the 18th century, Cambacérès came back to a no-fault liability and proposed in his

[26] XII-Tables VIII,2 (I,13 according to Roman Statutes II, London 1996, 578).

'*Projet de Code civil*' a solution very close to the *lex Aquilia*: "*Celui qui cause un dommage est tenu de le réparer, quel que soit le fait qui y donne lieu*"[27]. This is particularly astonishing because at this time fault liability was clearly the mainstream doctrine eternised seven years later, in 1804, in the pure fault liability of art. 1382 CCF: "*Tout fait quelconque de l'homme, qui cause à autrui un dommage, oblige celui par la faute duquel il est arrivé, à le réparer*".

21 The second model I would evoke is the Italian art. 2050 CCI, entitled as *Responsabilità per l'esercizio di attività pericolose*[28]. I have to state that this is not a real or, at least, not a pure strict liability model. However it is strongly influenced by strict liability. It is not the place here to proceed to a profound analysis of this largely commented article. The point of interest to us is the combination between, on the one hand, dangerous activities and, on the other hand, the possibility for the tortfeasor to prove that he has taken all the adequate measures to avoid the damage. The introduction of a specific norm for dangerous activities is the normative answer to a new technical environment in which accidents are more frequent and of higher gravity. This counter-measure to omnipresent dangers is attenuated by – paradoxically[29] – a reversed burden of proof on the part of the harmdoer. In this model, the main question is not anymore whether the tortfeasor was faulty, but whether there had been possibilities to avoid the damage. If such possibilities existed, the tortfeasor is liable, otherwise he is not.

22 In this concept, there are still traces of Mucius' idea of foreseeability. One has to take all the possible and imaginable safety measures. To this traditional element, jurisprudence often adds a retrospective consideration. Once the damage has been inflicted, the judge can be tempted to consider that the tortfeasor should have foreseen this damage. Practically, the tortfeasor is then in the uncomfortable situation of being liable independently of his behaviour, because the mere fact of a damage can be interpreted as a lack of precaution. In this sense, the Italian judge being free in evaluating the danger of an activity and the measures taken by the tortfeasor[30], the liberating proof of art. 2050 CCI risks to be a priori impossible to be given. In reality, under art. 2050 CCI the tortfeasor could be in a situation comparable to the fault liability regime, where the proof of due care is often impossible to be bestowed.

[27] Cambacérès, *Projet de Code civil*, présenté au Conseil des Cinq-Cents, au nom de la Commission de la Classification des Lois, Paris, An cinquième (edited in Paris 1796; reprint Vaduz etc. 1977), livre III, titre I, § II, 745, p. 262.

[28] Art. 2050 CCI *Responsabilità per l'esercizio di attività pericolose.*
Chiunque cagiona danno ad altri nello svolgimento di un'attività pericolosa, per sua natura o per la natura dei mezzi adoperati, è tenuto al risarcimento, se non prova di avere adottato tutte le misure idonee a evitare il danno.

[29] I say 'paradoxically' because normally the reversed burden of proof is a means to get the situation of the harmdoer *heavier*. Here, we have exactly the opposite situation. The reversed burden of proof is the means to give a second chance to the harmdoer who, otherwise, would be exposed to strict liability without any possibility of exemption.

[30] Franzoni, Massimo, Dei Fatti Illeciti, Art. 2043–2059, in *Commentario del codice civile Scialoja-Branca*, 4 (1993), 495.

Other dispositions comparable on certain points to art. 2050 CCI are in the Albanian Code of 1994[31] and in the Russian Civil Code of 1994. Art. 1079 of the Russian Code, which is more restrictive in matter of proof than the Italian and the Albanian rules, regulates the "responsibility for harm caused by activity creating increased danger for surrounding persons". Conceived for "use of means of transport, mechanisms, high tension electric power, atomic power, explosive substances, virulent poisons etc", it proposes a no-fault liability for risky activities. At the same time, it offers the possibility of exemption if "the harm arose as a consequence of insuperable force or the intent of the victim"[32]. **23**

The third model of strict liability has haunted jurists for more than a century and is finally proposed by some recent law projects. Art. 50 SD focuses on liability for risk[33]: Its central criterion of application is a 'particularly dangerous activity'. If such an activity causes damage, the operator is liable, whether faulty or not. He is responsible not for his specific behaviour in the tort event, but for the fact that he has undertaken such a dangerous activity. He is liable, *nota bene*, even if his activity was authorised by the State. Divergent to the Italian disposition, art. 50 SD does not offer to the tortfeasor a liberating proof. This is a direct consequence of the concept of fault in the Swiss draft. Considered as dangerous are activities which cause 'frequent or serious damage' despite the care of a specialist. In this understanding of dangerous activities, the notion of due care loses the sense Mucius invented and transmitted to us, precisely because in this concept of risk no due care would be sufficient anymore to prevent damage. In a certain sense, one could say that this is the inversion of Mucius' concept. For Mucius as well as for us, the foreseeability of the danger renders liable. But if for Mucius it was basically possible to prevent the damage, the concept of strict liability is justified by the fact that the damage is not avoidable, irrespective of what we do[34]. Other texts, for example the project of the European Group on Tort Law, should confirm the trend towards special dispositions on strict liabil- **24**

[31] Albanian Civil Code of 1994, art. 622 says:
"*La responsabilité par l'exercice d'une activité dangereuse.*
La personne qui exerce une activité dangereuse de par sa nature ou de par les objets utilisés et qui cause par là un dommage à autrui, s'oblige à réparer ce dommage, sauf si elle prouve qu'elle a pris toutes les mesures adaptées et nécessaires pour en éviter la survenance". (Translation by Stiljano Ordolli).

[32] *Art. 1079. Responsibility for harm caused by activity creating increased danger for surrounding persons.*
1.Juridical persons and citizens whose activity is connected with an increased danger for surrounding persons (use of means of transport, mechanisms, high tension electric power, atomic power, explosive substances, virulent poisons etc; effectuation of construction and other activity connected therewith, and others) shall be obliged to compensate the harm caused by a source of increased danger unless it is proved that the harm arose as a consequence of insuperable force or the intent of the victim. (...) Civil Code of the Russian Federation, (2nd edn. 1998), (Translation by W.E. Butler).

[33] Text of art. 50 SD see above, note 5.

[34] The General Code of the civil law of the Popular Republic of China of 1986, art. 123 also contains a form of strict liability, but is less general than the Swiss solution because it gives an enumeration of the activities concerned like work with high pressure, explosives, strong poison, radioactivity etc. Furtheron, the parties may be absolved if the victim has himself caused the damage intentionally.

ity. Concerning the Osnabrück Working Team on Torts, it announces dispositions for a form of liability for dangerous things and risk[35].

D. The Effects of Strict Liability on Fault

25 After this short overview of fault- and strict liability concepts, let us now return to our initial question: What could be the possible consequences of strict liability norms on fault? The difficulty in answering this question is that, today, we lack much practical experience with these new forms of strict liability.

26 In any case, the first and obvious effect should be to no longer use fault liability in genuine strict liability cases. Otherwise nobody would understand why particular strict liability norms are introduced in the new projects. In other words the field of fault liability will be restricted.

27 What will be the new field of fault liability? If we look at the different projects, the definitions of fault or negligence (and concepts with comparable functions as, for example, duty of care) show that fault liability could revert to its original functions. Art. 48 SD[36] enumerates, with the terms 'intention' and 'negligence', two of the traditional criteria known for centuries. In art. 48a,1 the term of negligence is even explicitly defined corresponding to its traditional understanding[37]. The same article indicates how to appreciate the diligence. This text is nothing more than a specification of the old and handsome *diligentia*[38] and simply enumerates different elements which modern jurisprudence currently applies. The Osnabrück draft uses in the basic rule (art. 1:

[35] The text of art. 3: 209 "Liability for dangerous things, activities and processes" has yet to be formulated. The actual wording of art. 3: 210 "Other Cases of liability for damage for which one is accountable by law" is: "*A person is also liable for a damage when it results from the realisation of a risk for which he or she is accountable according to statute or as a matter of judgement from the circumstances*", see the Osnabrück Working Team on Tort, Tort law paper no. 7, 25 July 2001.

[36] Avant-projet suisse *Art. 48. D.Fondements de la responsabilité. I.Responsabilité pour faute. 1.Principe*
La personne qui cause un dommage à autrui par son comportement fautif, soit intentionnellement, soit par négligence, est tenue de le réparer.
Art. 48. D.Haftungsgründe. I.Haftung aus Verschulden. 1.Grundsatz
Die Person, die einer anderen durch ihr schuldhaftes Verhalten Schaden zufügt, sei es mit Absicht, sei es aus Fahrlässigkeit, ist zum Ersatz verpflichtet.

[37] Avant-projet suisse *Art. 48a. 2.Négligence.*
1 Agit par négligence la personne qui n'observe pas la diligence commandée par les circonstances et par sa situation individuelle.
2 La diligence requise s'apprécie suivant l'âge, la formation, les connaissances ainsi que les autres aptitudes et qualités de l'auteur du dommage.
Art. 48a. 2.Fahrlässigkeit
1 Fahrlässig handelt die Person, welche die ihr nach den Umständen und nach ihren persönlichen Verhältnissen obliegende Sorgfalt missachtet.
2 Die erforderliche Sorgfalt beurteilt sich nach dem Alter, der Bildung, den Kenntnissen sowie nach den übrigen Fähigkeiten und Eigenschaften der Person, die den Schaden verursacht hat.

[38] See above, (Mucius, p.2)

101) the expression 'breach of duty'[39], which has its roots in Mucius' obligation for everyone to take into account what a diligent man would have foreseen[40]. The project of the European Group of Tort Law also seems to perceive fault in a traditional way as a violation of the required standard of conduct and of care.

Does that mean that we will simply revert to the fault concept we knew before it had been perverted by the extensions to strict liability? Probably not. As we saw, the Swiss draftsmen have announced in the report accompanying its project the will to render negligence more subjective[41]. This means that the evaluation of fault, irrespective of negligence, will take into account more elements specific to the concrete case. In order to make fault and negligence more subjective, the Swiss draft and especially art. 48s SD, but possibly also the European Tort Law draft, underline the importance of the tortfeasor's individual situation. **28**

But, how can one take better account of these individual situations? As we saw, art. 48a SD offers to the tortfeasor the possibility of exemption by taking his personal indispositions into account. One can invoke a structural or permanent incapacity as well as temporary or problems present at the moment of the harmful event. Art. 48a,2 SD confirms and even strengthens this tendency. The diligence is evaluated according to the age, formation, knowledge, aptitudes and other personal qualities of the harmdoer. In other words, art. 48a SD opens the whole individual field to the appreciation of the judge. In practice, it is likely that the scale of criteria will be very large, going from purely objective elements like age and formation to medium criteria like individual knowledge to – possibly – highly private elements. This authorises the judge a quasi free evaluation. It will be up to him to determine whether he will limit his investigations to objective elements or whether he prefers to penetrate the whole personality of the wrongdoer and to weight also perfectly private circumstances like matrimonial disease, professional disappointment or stress due to bad weather forecast or full moon, which had influenced the wrongdoer. Compared to the present Swiss legislation that simply evokes the "circumstances and the gravity of the fault" [42], the field opened to appreciation seems at first sight not to be much enlarged by art. 48a SD. But in reality, the **29**

[39] Osnabrück Working Team on Tort, Tort law paper no. 7, 25 July 2001, *Art. 1: 101 Basic Rule: (1) A person who suffers legally relevant damage has a right to reparation under this Part against someone who caused the damage intentionally or through breach of duty, or who is otherwise accountable for the damage*" Breach of duty is defined as: "*a behaviour which does not meet the requirements of a statutory provision which aims at the protection of the other from the damage he or she suffered, or which does not amount to such care as in all the circumstances of the case is reasonable*", art. 3: 103.

[40] Paulus, D. 9,2,31.

[41] "Pour les auteurs de l'avant-projet, la dérive que connaît actuellement la responsabilité aquilienne – qui ne s'explique que par le désir d'étendre les droits de la victime – doit être corrigée. Cette correction peut se réaliser en donnant à la notion de négligence un contenu plus subjectif", P. Widmer/P. Wessner (*supra* note 3), p. 120.

[42] Art. 43 COS.

fact to enumerate carefully the criteria for negligence and diligence is an explicit incitement to considerations the judge can ignore under the current art. 43 COS. There is no doubt that art. 48a SD would have as an effect accentuation of the fault and to introduce new nuances to it. In this sense, it is likely that the Swiss draftsmen will not miss their declared aim of giving back to fault its subjective character. In the draft of the European Group on Tort Law, fault will probably also be a central concept, even if the subjectivity could be less extensive. Concerning the Osnabrück project, the role of fault does not seem determined yet. Currently, only art. 6:105 mentions it, labelled as 'Contributory fault'. The general rule has yet to be formulated[43].

30 Let us now see how the judge applies the fault dispositions and to what extent this practice could be modified by the new projects. It is well known that the standard of care is an *ad hoc* model that has to be established for each particular case. In a first step, the judge has to fix a reasonable man standard according to the class the tortfeasor belongs to (see the third notion of fault, *supra* [13] *et seq.*). In a second step, he has to adapt the class-model to the individual personality of the tortfeasor (see the fourth notion of fault, *supra* [16]). This is the traditional means by which our judges proceed.

31 In my opinion, the formulation of the Swiss draft, which strengthens fault extensively, and possibly to some extent also the project of the European Group on Tort Law, should have as a consequence the introduction of a more differentiated way to appreciate fault. I think that there is one historical model with an exceptional potential that has not been exhausted. I am thinking of the distinction between different faults going from *culpa levissima* to *culpa lata* and passing by all the intermediate levels (see the second fault model, *supra* [8] *et seq.*). The distinction between these degrees of fault was, without any doubt, a major evolution opening new possibilities to evaluate exactly the degree of liability of the tortfeasor. With this model, the judge can combine two different elements: On the one hand he holds the qualifications of the tortfeasor according to the class he belongs to (for example professional classes

[43] It is certainly a bit too early for speculations about the exact wording of the projects of the Group on European Tort Law and the Osnabrück Working Team.The results between the three projects will maybe differ very much. However, technically the legislators have different instruments to accentuate the fault. Mostly, they use as basic concept the 'standard of care' or, as the Swiss draft calls it, the 'diligence commanded by the circumstances' (art. 48a SD). A first possibility would be to give few instructions how to build the reasonable man standard combined with an extensive definition of negligence. This is the solution in the Swiss draft. Another possibility would be to give extensive instructions how to establish the duty of care standards; then, one does not need to give an extensive definition of negligence, because the possible extensions are already anticipated in the definition of the duty of care. This could be the solution adopted by the European Group on Tort Law. The effect of each one of the two techniques depends, of course, on what is included in the two definitions of duty of care, respectively of the negligence. But it is likely that the first technique, the one with an extensive definition of negligence, would lead to a more subjective interpretation than the second one, which underlines the duty of care without pushing the jurist to the personal features of the individual person. Anyhow, both offer the possibility of building a fault system with subtle nuances.

like a nurse, average doctor, surgery specialist etc). On the other hand, he can take into account the degree of fault as *levissima, levis* or *lata*, according to the particular qualification of the tortfeasor. This model permits a form of calculation. Graphically, one could represent it in a system of abscissa and coordinate: On the abscissa are located the degrees of fault from *culpa levissima* to *culpa lata*, and on the coordinate there are the different acts imposed on the tortfeasor in a concrete case. If the tortfeasor does not have particular qualifications, the list of imposed acts will be short, if he is a specialist, the list will be long. The addition of the different faults committed indicates as a final result the degree of liability[44]. The result of this calculation corresponds to the average liability of a class. If we take the example of a surgery specialist, the number of acts *imposed on him* would go up to the top of the coordinate, probably near to the maximum (A1-An). The degree of fault would be fixed on the abscissa for each one of the imposed acts. If the actor committed 4 faults, his liability would correspond to the addition of the percentages of the 4 faults (A3=20%; A4=10%; A7=40%; A9=5%; A10=10%; Total liability degree= 85%). This calculation would correspond to what the Swiss draft calls the 'diligence commended by the circumstances'.

In a second step, the judge would have to adapt these different fault-levels to **32**
the individual situation of the tortfeasor. In other words, he should take into account the 'individual situation', as art. 48a,1 SD says. He could diminish the

[44] More precisely, there would be on the coordinate a list of acts (A1-An) imposed in a certain case. The list would go from the simple acts, for example to phone for medical help, to the most sophisticated ones, like the handling of newest surgery techniques. The judge would have to situate the concrete wrongdoer on a certain level of the list, according to his class competence. For a *quidam* who meets a hurt person the list would be short; on the coordinate he would be near 0 (for example A1-A3). For the surgery specialist in the same situation the list would be long and he would go near to An. On the abscissa, the judge would have to indicate the degree of fault of each one of the imposed acts. The addition of the different faults' degrees would indicate the final fault degree of the wrongdoer. The maximum of the final fault degree would, of course, be limited to 100%.

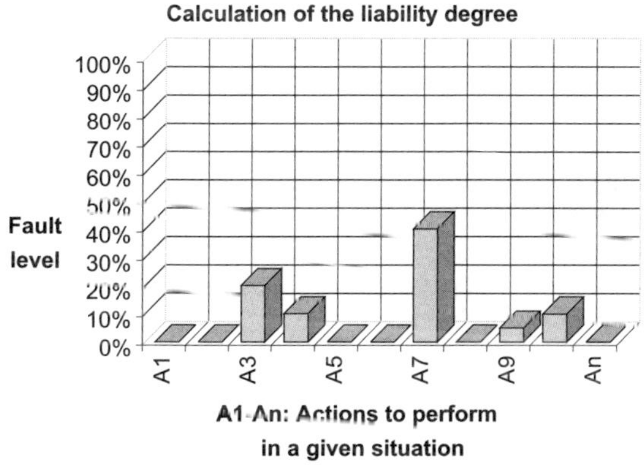

Total liability degree = A1 + A2 + ... +An (max. 100%).

degree of liability if he thought that the specific situation of the tortfeasor justified considering a certain fault as less important. For example, the surgery doctor could benefit from the fact that his equipment was not optimal or, to take a more subjective criterion, that the mistake he made occurred after fifteen hours of an uninterrupted surgery intervention. As I said, the judge would probably have here a very large competence to appreciate what kind of individual situations would permit diminishing the degree of fault.

33 If we look at the current legal systems, we note that this kind of individual appreciation is not totally new. As we saw, Swiss law permits it through art. 43,1 COS and, partly, 44,2. But Austrian law in particular apportions the degree of fault.

34 The advantage of the system presented here would be to establish a direct link between the degrees of fault and of liability. But, there would be a very considerable danger. Though the burden of proof of his allegations would be on the tortfeasor's side, the victim's protection would be reduced by the numerous exemptions the tortfeasor could invoke through his individual situation.

35 Therefore, I think that the 'individual-situation'-argument should be handled with extreme care. The lowering of liability should be submitted to three rules. First, the more the argument for exemption is personal, the greater should be the conditions to accept it be restrictive. For example, a surgery specialist invoking that he was tired when the fault occurred should benefit from reduced liability only in extreme circumstances. Personally, I would even hope that judges never followed such an argumentation, even more so as, in this particular case, the harmdoer would probably have committed a fault by the simple fact of having worked for such a long time. Second, the judge should be attentive to the degree of danger of the activity. The greater the danger is, the stricter should be the conditions to get an exception. This rule is justified by the fact that the probability of the victim to suffer damage increases with the degree of the danger he is exposed to. An increasing danger has to be counterbalanced by an increasing liability not only in order to dissuade the potential tortfeasor, but also in order to offer better protection to the victim in a system that is not particularly favourable to him. This second rule seems to be in contradiction with the basic idea of strengthening fault-liability, because it could open the doors to liability 'without fault'. There is no doubt that this risk could emerge. It would be up to the judge to find the golden way between a too strict and a too latitudinarian handling of this rule. Third, and also with the aim of offering better protection to the victim, the conditions to get an exemption should depend on the gravity of the damage. The judge would have to be more strict for exemptions, the greater is the degree of damage of the victim.

36 To conclude, I come back once more to my initial question: What are the consequences of strict liability on fault? The debate about strict liability is certainly an excellent occasion to eliminate the inconsistent concept of fault liability 'without fault'. With strict liability we would introduce a slightly different logic in our law. Liability would be divided in two fields: a no-fault (strict) and a fault liability. These two fields would be separated by a basic distinction: Fault liability weighs the behaviour of the tortfeasor, while strict liability makes him liable by the mere fact of a damage. This separation would not make sense if the future fault liability failed to offer a better adequacy between fault and liability. This can be obtained by a system in which the degree of liability is directly proportional to the degree of fault. The strict liability, combined with a refined fault concept, would promote the equity of the judgments. Such a system would certainly strengthen the position of the tortfeasor and weaken the victim. In the long term, it could also accentuate the role of insurance in order to compensate the victim's lack of security.

Historically, strict liability would mark a comeback of the first *lex Aquilia* **37**
concept which was also not attentive to the behaviour of the tortfeasor. But this renewal would be only partial, restricted to risky activities. Also the fault would get a certain revival. The introduction of a progressive fault liability system would give late honours to the old idea of fault degrees, rejected already by Ulpian and neglected, since, by a certain tort law tradition. The last decision will be in the hands of the judges who will decide whether or not a real subjective fault will exist. Experience with the actual systems shows that judges are often in favour of high security standards and do all they can to protect the victim. If they adopted the same position under the new system, the role of subjective fault would be minimal. But then, the interpretation of the new fault liability concept could be in contradiction with the inherent logic of the new projects.

II. Tort Liability and Liability Insurance: A Difficult Relationship*

Herman A. Cousy

1 Consider this essay as a critical review of a theatre play. The play is an allegorical one[1] in which the characters represent abstract legal concepts. The plot deals with what is in essence a societal, even political problem, *i.e.* the ancient question how society should react when fate strikes men, or some of them, with unexpected and unearned mishap and harm or, to translate this in more abstract, and modern terms, our play deals with the question to know how society must deal with the allocation of accidental harm to which some of its members are randomly, yet inevitably subjected. To do so, the play concentrates on the role of two characters, and on their complex and at times problematic relationship. "Tort liability" is the lead character and "liability insurance" the antagonist. Both play a leading, yet sometimes competitive role in handling the problem of the allocation of accidental harm. As in a Greek tragedy, there is also a chorus whose members comment on the main action, from the viewpoint of such general values as equity, efficiency, coherence, predictability and certainty. The chorus takes sides in the complex relationship between the two lead characters and even tries to influence their importance and behaviour. The play is purportedly fathered by a disperse and multiple

* This paper holds the slightly updated text of a lecture that was first delivered on 4 November 1999 in the Palais Trautson, Vienna, at the occasion of the inauguration of the European Centre of Tort and Insurance Law (ECTIL) in the presence of Dr. Nikolaus Michalek, Minister of Justice of Austria.
I want to dedicate this publication to the memory of Professor Gary T. Schwartz whose knowledge and wisdom, transpiring both in his writings and his contribution to our discussions in the European Group for the harmonization of tort law, were a shining source of insight and inspiration.

[1] In dealing with the relationship between liability and liability insurance, authors also make use of another allegory, for instance the allegory of the chicken and the egg. Compare Randall R. Bovbjerg, Liability and liability insurance: chicken and egg, destructive spiral, or risk and reaction?, 72 *Texas Law Review* (Tex.L.Rev.), 1655 (a paper delivered in the context of a May 1994 Texas Law Review Symposium on "The law of Bad Faith in Contract and Insurance" and on the subtheme "The Logic of Liability Insurance Purchases"). See also Michael Gill, The expansion of liability and the role of insurance. Who is the chicken? [1999] *The International Journal of Insurance Law*, 27 – 40.

fatherhood (judges, legislators and professors, as is sometimes said[2]) and its plot about the delicate relationship between tort liability and liability insurance has intrigued many of the finest commentators and fascinated a number of them[3].

The play aims first at analyzing the idiosyncrasies of the two lead-characters who are, already by themselves, fairly complicated creatures. To begin with *tort liability*, the problem is that this character is constantly changing roles and is in fact playing, or at least pretending or claiming to play, simultaneously several different, even irreconcilable roles. In other words, the law of tort serves multiple functions, and some of these functions appear to be contradictory (see *infra* nos. [9] *et seq.*). 2

On the other hand there is the character of *liability insurance*, which features the peculiarity that while playing a decisive role in the plot, this character rarely appears on stage, and when doing so, avoids being in the spotlight. There were times when liability insurance policies held clauses forbidding the insured to make the existence of their being covered in liability known to third persons. Even today the liability insurer will borrow his insured's name while appearing in court as a defendant in a liability suit where he must protect the interests of his insured while at the same time serving his own interests. As will be insisted upon hereafter, insurance and insurability very often play a decisive role in the judge's decision to allocate liability, but such will be rarely admitted explicitly, and indeed be demurely kept silent about. Undeniably liability insurance plays an important role, but from a hidden position behind the scenery. What I mean by that in non-allegorical terms is that judges may be induced to motivate their judgments by what are really pretexts, while the true hidden motive (or at least one of them) of their decision often relates to insurance. The presence or even availability of liability insurance at the side of the tortfeasor will prove to be a strong argument for declaring the insured liable, whereas the presence of first party insurance on the victim's side may inspire a decision against liability[4]. It is this role of liability insurance that has led 3

[2] Reference is here made to van Caenegem, *Judges, legislators and professors. Chapters in European legal history*, The Goodhart Lectures, (1987), p. 205. See the paraphrase by W. van Gerven, Community and national legislators, regulators, judges, academics and practitioners: living together apart?, in *Law Making, Law Finding, and Law Shaping: The Diverse Influences. The Clifford Chance Lectures* Vol. II (1997), p. 13.

[3] Just to mention a few of them, to whom I will refer later on, see *inter alia*, P.S. Atiyah, *Accidents, Compensation and the Law* (5th edn. 1993) (P. Cane, ed.); A.A. Ehrenzweig, Assurance oblige. A comparative study, [1995] *Law and Contemporary Problems*, 820–845; J.G. Fleming, *The Law of Torts,* (8th edn. 1993); J. Hellner, Tort Liability and Liability Insurance, *Scand Studies in Law* (1962), p. 129; B.S. Markesinis/S.F. Deakin, *Tort Law* (3rd edn. 1994), pp. 43–54; J. Stapleton, Tort, Insurance and Ideology, [1995] *The Modern Law Review*, 820–845; A. Tunc, *La responsabilité civile* (2nd edn. 1989); G. Viney, *Traité de droit civil. Introduction a la responsabilité* (2nd edn. 1995); W.V.H. Rogers, *Winfield & Jolowicz on tort* (14th edn. 1994).

[4] Compare T. Hartlief, Het verzekeringsargument in het aansprakelijkheids- en schadevergoedingsrecht, [2000] *Aansprakelijkheid en Verzekering*, 93. The author points out that the insurance argument is used in many different directions. For instance, judges will hold someone liable because he is insured, while other courts will declare someone liable because he did not buy insurance.

authors to feel irritated by the hidden and undeclared but decisive role of liability insurance[5].

4 To be sure, the somewhat mysterious "from behind the scene" role of liability insurance is not its only distinctive feature. While compared to the other members of its own kind, liability insurance appears to be a species of its own. Already when looked at from the angle of insurance technique, liability insurance presents the rather special feature that the liability insurer covers the losses of a victim who is not his insured (and whom he cannot control) but a randomly chosen and unknown third person. But liability insurance is also special when looked at from a legal point of view[6]. Liability insurance differs from other and more traditional insurance branches like fire insurance insofar as the risk covered (*i.e.* the chance that the insured person incurs a liability toward third persons) is not entirely independent from the behaviour of the insured person. It is indeed the insured himself who creates the insured event by behaving in such a way as to be rendered legally liable for the harm. To put this in more technical jargon, in liability insurance the risk to be covered is not entirely "aleatory", at the very least the risk is here much less aleatory than it is in the older, less sophisticated insurance branches. Liability insurance is not only less aleatory, it is also a more complex insurance product than, say, the insurance of goods. Such appears from the very simple fact that in liability insurance at least three (instead of two) parties are involved. The (at least) triangular construction of liability insurance (insurer, insured, victim) gives rise to particular legal relationships, especially when the third party victim is given a "direct action" against the liability insurer[7], whence emerge difficult legal issues like the opposability of defences by the insurer against the victim, and the possibility of recourse actions by the liability insurer against his own insured.

In addition liability insurance is also special insofar as the insured event (*i.e.* the insured incurring liability) is not simply a natural fact but a legal process and event which is of such a nature as to constitute a delicate legal issue (tort liability) inside another one (insurance contract)[8]. In liability insurance

[5] The hidden role of liability insurance which appears to be annoying to some, see B.S. Markesinis, La perversion des notions de responsabilité civile délictuelle par la pratique de l'assurance, [1983] *Revue internationale de droit comparé* (Rev.int.dr.comp.), 301; see also W. van Gerven, De invloed van de verzekering op het verbintenissenrecht, [1962–63] *Rechtskundig Weekblad*, 777.

[6] About the origins of liability insurance and the origins of liability insurance, see Picard/Besson, *Les assurances terrestres*, T. I, *Le contrat d'assurance* (1982), no. 352.

[7] As is the case in several national legal systems in the field of automobile liability insurance, and as is now obligatorily imposed upon the EU Member States by the so-called fourth automobile directive (Directive 2000/26/EC of 16 May 2000, *O.J.E.C.*, L. nr. 181, 20 July 2000). In some legal systems the availability of the "direct action" to the victim has been extended to (certain) compulsory liability insurances or even to all liability insurances in general. This last, far reaching step was taken either by the judiciary (as was the case in France since 1926, see M. Cozian, *L'action directe*, Thèse, 1969), or by the legislator (as was the case in Belgium: Loi sur le contrat d'assurances terrestres of 25 June 1992, artt. 86 – 88).

[8] Compare M. Dreher, *Die Versicherung als Rechtsprodukt: die Privatversicherung und ihre rechtliche Gestaltung* (1991) p. 353.

the insured event is in fact a process of some duration, so as to make its precise location in time a delicate decision (see *infra* [74]).

In a Darwinesque view on the origin of the species of insurance, liability insurance is, one may conclude, a more advanced species of insurance[9], and it is definitely a more complicated one.

If the special and somewhat complicated nature of the two leading characters offers, already by itself, fascinating material for further analysis, it is where those two characters get together and interact that the plot becomes truly intriguing and that our play gains "momentum". The reason for this is that the relationship between liability and liability insurance is internally contradictory insofar as they simultaneously support and threaten to destroy each other. We are dealing with one of those ambiguous love-hate relationships. **5**

On the one hand, tort liability is alive and well and flourishes by virtue of and thanks to liability insurance. Liability insurance does indeed support and stimulate the tort liability system, mainly, as will be further explained, by ensuring the actual recovery of damages by the successful plaintiff. **6**

But on the other hand liability insurance also plays a very different role. While being the motor and fuel of the liability system, liability insurance determines at the same time the outer limit of tort law and the borders of its domain. Even if insurance is not the justification for liability in tort, insurability is, in many cases, considered as a condition "sine qua non" for liability. However much this may seem to be contrary to the basic principles of tort law, in practice or, at the very least, in most cases, the limits of liability insurance do determine where the limits of tort liability effectively lie. But there is more and worse! While being strongly supportive of one of the goals of the tort liability system, *i.e.* of the goal of compensation of the victim, liability insurance threatens to destroy other goals or functions of the tort liability system. Indeed liability insurance would seem to destroy much of the repressive or deterrent function of tort law. As the late, and deeply mourned Gary Schwartz, whose writings will be a guide through much of the ensuing analysis, aptly summarizes, it is indeed clear from the outset, that "by removing from the defendant the threat of actual liability, insurance obviously calls into question the ability of tort law to achieve deterrence"[10]. What sense does it make indeed to make someone liable in view of encouraging him to a more damage-preventing behaviour, while at the same time allowing him to escape from the impact of the incurred liability through the coverage of insurance? **7**

[9] I have tried to develop some thoughts about the gradually growing sophistication of insurance products, in my contribution to the forthcoming Mélanges for Professor Madame Y. Lambert Faivre (to be published by Dalloz in the late spring 2002). See also H. Cousy, Losse bedenkingen over de rechtsbijstandverzekering, in *Aspects particuliers de l'assurance protection juridique* (1998), pp. 135–138.

[10] Gary T. Schwartz, Mixed Theories of Tort Law, Affirming both Deterrence and Corrective Justice, [1997] *Texas Law Review*, Vol. 75, 1801–1834.

8 The compensatory effectiveness of the insurance system appears to be so much superior to the (rather poor) compensatory effects of tort liability that at a certain moment and in certain countries the very foundations of tort law were called into question. Some authors have indeed not hesitated to utter the words "the death of tort". As early as in 1948 the American Tort Law specialist James[11] daringly suggested a partial replacement of the law of tort by insurance. A good many years later, echoing Grant Gilmore's essays on "The death of contract"[12], another American tort law specialist John Fleming reintroduced the theme as a question about the possible end of the law of tort[13]. In a recent contribution to the Scandinavian Studies in Law, Professor Bill Dufwa reminds that the very same discussion took place in Sweden, where the potential dissolution of tort law was discussed as early as in the 1940s[14].

A. Act I: The Multiple Functions of Tort Law

9 When I said that tort liability possesses a complex character, this observation refers – in non-allegorical terms – to the discussion about the multiple and sometimes mutually conflicting goals or functions that are assigned to the law of tort. We must give serious attention to this discussion because of its utter relevance to the plot of our play.

From a very general perspective, tort liability can be defined as a mechanism to decide on the conditions and the modalities under which certain losses suffered by a victim will be transferred to one or more other persons who will be legally obliged to compensate for those losses[15].

The discussion is about the reasons why such transfer should take place, in other words, about the reasons why liability should be imposed. Is the goal to punish the tortfeasor and, by the same token, to deter him from further harmful and socially undesirable behaviour? Or is the goal rather to appease the victim or to compensate him for the loss suffered? Or is the goal of tort liabil-

[11] James, Accident Liability Reconsidered. The Impact of Liability Insurance, [1948] *Yale Law Journal*, 549.

[12] G. Gilmore, The Death of Contract (1974), based on a series of lectures, cited by B. Dufwa in his article cited *infra* note 14.

[13] J. Fleming, *An Introduction to the Law of Torts* (2nd edn. 1985), p. 172; also cited by B. Dufwa in his article cited in the next footnote; J.Fleming, Contemporary Roles of the Law of Torts. Introduction, [1970] *American Journal of Comparative Law* (Am. J. Comp. L.), 1.

[14] B. Dufwa, Development of International Tort Law Till the Beginning of the 1990's From a Scandinavian Point of View in *Scandinavian Studies in Law,* Vol. 41, (2001), *Tort Liability and Insurance*, (from p. 86), pp. 91 and 92.

[15] Compare: "Tortious liability arises from the breach of a duty primarily fixed by law; this duty is towards persons generally and its breach is redressable by an action for unliquidated damages" (Winfield, *Province of the law of tort*, (1931), cited in Rogers, *Winfield & Jolowicz on Tort*, p. 4). In continental Europe as well as overseas, the law of torts is, from a legal point of view, a quite separate and indeed clearly distinct branch of the law. Compare the definition by Prof. Ch. von Bar, "Law of delict describes the field of private law which determines whether a person who has sustained damage has a right to compensation (or, where such damage is impending, to injunctive relief) even if the infliction of the damage forms the only legal bond between the two parties" (Ch. von Bar, *The Common European Law of Torts*, Vol. I, (1998), p. 1)

ity rather an economic one like spreading the loss over a large number of people so as to "vaporize" it and reduce its total impact on society's wealth, or is, in the same line of reasoning, the goal to allocate the cost of the losses upon the agent who is best located to spread that cost over a large, or over the right amount of people? Is the goal or function of the law of tort also to implement the respect for certain legal rules and to protect the respect of certain rights, existing rights as well as occasionally new ones, *i.e.* rights which come to be recognized as such by the judge?

We hereby hit the well-known discussion about the functions and goals of tort **10**
law, a discussion which has led to many fine contributions and at times even passionate disputes[16].

At first sight, the long list of the goals and functions of tort law seems to be overwhelming: punishment, vindication, redress of the social order, implementation of legal rules, protection of citizens' rights, recognition and creation of new rights and interests, appeasement of the victim (in the sense of buying off the victim's vengeance[17]), compensation or indemnification of losses, loss spreading, loss shifting, allocation of losses, deterrence (general and specific deterrence), prevention, precaution, reduction of accident costs, justice (compensatory justice, retributive justice, corrective justice[18]).

The richness and variety of meanings and contents of the concept is reflected **11**
in a varied terminology. The French term "le droit de la responsabilité civile" (the law of civil liability)[19] points toward the tortfeasor and to both his legal and moral responsibility for the damaging consequences of his deeds. So do the German "unerlaubte Handlung" and the Dutch "onrechtmatige daad", terms which refer to the unlawful character of the behaviour and to the reprehensible nature of the defendant's conduct. The Anglo-American "tort"[20] has close connections with procedural law insofar as actionable torts can be understood as a form of action through which a claim can be brought before the court[21]. The more modern terminology, using expressions like "the law of compensation of damage", or "Schadenordnungsrecht", radically point toward the victim, to the damages suffered and to their repair. Other contemporary

[16] See the authors cited *supra* note 3. See also P. Cane, *The Anatomy of Tort Law* (1997), pp. 205–238; E. Deutsch, Die Zwecke des Haftungsrechts, [1971] *Juristenzeitung*, 244; J. Fleming, Contemporary Roles of the Law of Torts. Introduction, [1970] *Am.J.Comp.L.*, Vol. 18, 1; H. Kötz, *Introduction to Comparative Law* (translated by T. Weir) (1998), p. 621; A. Tunc, *Torts* Chapter I, Introduction, in *International Encyclopedia of Comparative law*, nos. 154–168; W. van Gerven/J. Lever/P. Larouche, *Cases, Materials Text on national, supranational and international Tort Law* (2000), pp. 13–22.

[17] B.S. Markesinis/S.F. Deakin (*supra* note 3), p. 36.

[18] The terms are explained *infra* [37] *et seq.*

[19] At present many prefer the term "responsabilité extracontractuelle" (a term which is also common in Spain and Italy) to avoid any references which may be associated with criminal law. Nevertheless "law of delict" is also used: see Ch. von Bar, (*supra* note 15), p. 1, no. 1.

[20] Tort appears to mean the same as "wrong" or "crooked conduct" (compare the cover illustration of Rogers, *Winfield & Jolowicz on Tort* 15th edn. 1998) For some more etymology see, Ch. von Bar (*supra* note 15), p. 7, n° 6.

[21] Salmond & Heuston on the Law of Torts (21st edn.), (by Heuston & Buckley), pp. 1 and 2.

terms like "accident law", "le droit des accidents", place the law of torts in a wider and at the same time, in a narrower context, while on the one hand they seem to refer only to cases of physical injury, while on the other hand they encompass all accidental situations covered both by the law of tort as well as by other mechanisms of compensation like (private, and even social) insurance. The very fact that the traditional terms are being engulfed by another broader and differently oriented terminology is probably symptomatic for a crisis, or at least for an evolution in the perception of, and the thinking about, the subject matter.

12 We shall continue to refer to our subject-matter by its curious English name of "tort liability" although, when compared to the other available terms like "civil liability" or "the law of delict", or "non-contractual liability', the word "tort" is by far the most obscure one. "Never", so a famous saying by Wigmore goes, "did a name so obstruct a true understanding of the thing. To such a plight it has brought us that a favourite mode of defining a Tort is to declare merely that it is not a Contract. As if a man were to define Chemistry by pointing out that it is not Physics or Mathematics"[22]. Although the traditional dividing lines between contractual and non-contractual liability may become more and more blurred[23], the distinction is still very much insisted upon. That is why the term of "civil liability" ("responsabilité civile") is perhaps to be avoided since, at least in its French version ("responsabilité civile"), such term refers to both contractual and extra-contractual liability[24].

13 The law of tort, we said, has served multiple functions or goals. Such statement can be understood in two ways. One interpretation is that the law of tort serves and indeed always has served several closely connected functions at the same time[25]. This is the thesis of the "mixed theories of tort law" or of the "multi-purpose function" of tort law, commonly accepted by many commentators[26]. Nevertheless the question arises whether among the different goals and functions, which are assigned to the law of tort, there exists a sufficient degree of reconcilability so as to make their coexistence operable and worthwhile. There exists indeed another possible interpretation according to which the goals pursued by, or to be pursued by, the law of tort have varied with time, place, types of tort and even with the individual circumstances of a given case.

[22] Cited in Rogers, *Winfield & Jolowicz on Tort* p. 1.

[23] Compare M. Beerens/Cornelis, "De aansprakelijkheid van de deskundige in privaatrechtelijke geschillen" in *Deskundigenonderzoek in privaatrechtelijke geschillen* (1999), p. 141 (p. 162).

[24] Compare G. Viney, *Traité de Droit Civil, Introduction à la Responsabilité*, p. 1, n° 1: "l'expression'responsabilité civile' désigne dans le language juridique actuel l'ensemble des règles qui obligent l'auteur d'un dommage causé à autrui à réparer ce préjudice en offrant à la victime une compensation. Elle englobe donc la responsabilité contractuelle comme la responsabilité délictuelle".

[25] A. Tunc, Introduction" in *International Encyclopedia of Comprative Law, Torts* p. 87

[26] E. Deutsch, (*supra* note 16), 244; G. Schwartz, Mixed Theories of Tort Law: Affirming Both Deterrence and Corrective Justice, [1997] *Texas Law Review*, 1324; P. Cane, *The Anatomy of Tort Law* (1997), pp. 244–225.

Most authors will agree with the view that the law of tort presents this particularity that, where its aims are manifold or multiple, none of them has offered a complete justification for the law at all times[27]. The law of tort has tried to simultaneously serve most of the different goals and functions which are assigned to it, be it in different degrees and with varying intensity, through times, places and circumstances. It can confidently be stated that as of late the goal of *compensation of the victim* (taken in the sense of repairing or indemnifying the victim's losses) has played a predominant role in the mind of both legislators and judges. But there were times when the accent lay on the retaliatory effect of the liability system, and since the seventies, and the advent of the "new law and economics" school in legal theory[28], the worry about the *preventive effect* of liability rules has flared up again. The gist of the discussion about the goals and functions of the law of tort lies in the balancing of their relative weight and importance[29]. The discussion is fierce and in some cases even passionate for the reason that value judgments and even ideological positions and visions on society are deeply involved: equity versus efficiency, conservation and protection of vested rights or acquired interests versus freedom of action. **14**

There is a famous dictum by K. Larenz that goes as follows: "*Das Grundproblem jeder Deliktsordnung besteht in dem Spannungsverhältnis zwischen Güterschutz und Handlungsfreiheit*"[30]. The same idea is expressed by John Fleming in his treatise when he writes that the law of torts deals with the tension between two basic interests of individuals: the interest in security and the interest in freedom of action[31]. **15**

In early stages of the development of society, the basic rule governing the handling and the easing of this tension may have been that "a man acts at his peril", so as to make the wrongdoer liable, irrespective of his culpability or state of mind. Fleming explains that while primitive law was heavily concerned with the preservation of the peace and with providing a substitute for vengeance, the simple fact of causation was more important than fault, and was thus considered to be a sufficient reason to create an obligation of the tortfeasor to give some redress or compensation to the victim[32]. Still at the time of the seventeenth century Spinoza's deterministic philosophy appeared to have led to a theory of liability which is not based on culpability or fault[33]. **16**

[27] In this sense B.S. Markesinis/S.F. Deakin (*supra* note 3), p. 35.

[28] Of which we shall have to say a few words, later on, see *infra*, nos. 22 *et seq.*

[29] See however the observation that the discussion about the functions of tort law is unable to answer the question as to when a victim should be compensated or the injurer deterred, or the harmer insured, see W. van Gerven/J. Lever/P. Larouche, (*supra* note 16), p. 19.

[30] The basic problem of each punitive law consists in the tension between the protection of interests and the freedom of action, L. Larenz/C. W. Canaris, *Lehrbuch des Schuldrechts*, Vol. II (13th edn. 1994), p. 350.

[31] J.G. Fleming, *The Law of Torts* (8th edn. 1983), p. 6.

[32] J.G. Fleming (*supra* note 31), p. 9.

[33] See J.E. Fesevur, "Aansprakelijkheid wegens onrechtmatige daad vanuit een Spinozistische optiek. Een metaphysisch-filosofische beschouwing, leidend tot afwijzing van het schuldvereiste en aanvaarding van aansprakelijkheid zonder schuld", in *Tussen de polen van bescherming en vrijheid. Aspecten van aansprakelijkheid* (1993), pp. 3–23.

17 In a further phase, under the combined influence of the Kantian moral philosophy[34], of the economic postulate of "laissez faire", and of the teaching of the church about individual responsibility, the theory about the criteria of liability would become more subjective. "No liability without fault" would become the new rule. The new rule was possibly also inspired by the goal to encourage action by taking away the full burden of damaging consequences from the shoulders of an acting man. Under the new rule tort law looked away from the victim to concentrate more on the injurer. In the course of the nineteenth century the advent of fault liability, knowingly or not, explicitly willing or not, has served the interests of an infant industrial economy by taking away from it the full burden of the many "externalities" it caused to fellow men and to the environment. Instead of nearly automatically placing the burden on those who caused the damage, the new rule would have the losses stay where they happened to strike, unless the wrongful or faulty behaviour of someone would offer a reason for shifting the loss. In the famous words of O.W. Holmes, the new paradigm of the law of accidents appeared to be that "loss must lie where it falls"[35].

18 Today the Holmes paradigm appears to have once more been turned around. As Jaap Spier, Advocate General at the Dutch *Hoge Raad*, pointed out in his recently delivered farewell-lecture at the University of Tilburg[36], people are indeed not prepared any more to bear the weight of the accidental damage that they suffer (and Jaap Spier pointedly added how striking and indeed disturbing it is to notice that such evolution occurs in situations of a wealthy economy). Victims want compensation for all accidentally suffered harms. To satisfy their demand for redress and compensation, victims increasingly revert to the various compensation schemes, but either these or the victims themselves will ultimately look for someone who is liable, since the role of fate is not accepted any more. In other words victims and their first party insurers turn to the tort liability system to obtain (preferably nearly automatic) compensation. The litigation mania may not be everywhere so bad as it is in the U.S., where according to the famous words of Markesinis: "few Americans can tolerate more than five minutes of frustration without submitting to the temptation to sue"[37]. But to a lesser extent, and *mutatis mutandis*, the same phenomenon occurs in Europe. During the post war era, powerful instruments of social security were designed to guarantee a replacement income to those who lost their job because of "social risks", such as illness, old age or unemployment. Besides, instruments of public protection (think of the catastrophe

[34] Kant's moral philosophy is, as is well known, based on the idea that freedom is the essential characteristic of the human being, and that a man's freedom is solely limited by the freedom of other men. In a Kantian approach, liability in tort would find its basis in the fact that a person has transgressed the boundaries of his own freedom and thus trespassed on the freedom of his fellow men.

[35] Holmes's concept appears to be due for a revival: compare Hartlief's essay "Ieder draagt zijn eigen schade (Each one bears his own damage)", (infra note 41).

[36] J. Spier, *Een nieuwe dageraad voor het aansprakelijkheidsrecht?* (1999).

[37] B.S. Markesinis, Litigation mania in England, West Germany and the U.S.A.: are we so different?, Askin Reform Club London, 1989, [1990] *Cambridge Law Journal*.

funds that are designed to alleviate the damage caused by natural disasters[38]) were developed in many European states, and voluntary first party insurance formulas were equally developed to supplement or complement basic compensation. Whereas under such circumstances one would have expected a diminishing importance of the law of tort, the opposite tendency has manifested itself. The post war era and its grand and generous system of social protection have not led to a drying out of the tort liability system but they have witnessed a continuous expansion of it. But here, as so happens in many other cases, growing success breeds dangers of failure. The European doctrine is showing growing apprehension about expanding liability developments[39], while the U.S. legal system has already witnessed a large-scale tort liability crisis[40]. I shall come back to this later on.

The reasons for the growing success of (in the sense of the increasing appeal 19
upon) the tort liability system are manifold. They have often been analyzed. Widening liability has been explained on sociological grounds (diminishing need to protect an infant industry against the threat of increasing liabilities toward workers, consumers and environment), on political grounds (protecting the victims at the expense of the better-off), on economic grounds (the need for "internalising" the costs of accidents caused by a product or an activity), on psychological grounds (the need to compensate the innocent victim against the randomly hitting catastrophes of an anonymous technological society), on ethical grounds (the fairness and justice to spread the loss of an innocent victim over the collectivity which is considered to be responsible for the creation of the risk). In his inaugural lecture held at the University of Leyden[41], Ton Hartlief recently analysed the reasons for the success of the law of tort. At the level of substantive legal rules numerous instances of "strict liability", or "liability without fault", have been introduced by national and international law makers and in some cases even by judges. At the level of procedural law, one must mention the development of the direct action ("action directe") of the victim against the liability insurer and, especially in U.S. law, the creation and the success of the so-called class actions and similar procedural devices for mass tort litigation. An important factor was also the development of legal aid, helping plaintiffs to pass cultural and financial obstacles. Finan-

[38] For an overview see C. van Schoubroeck, Legislation and practice concerning natural disasters in insurance in a number of European countries, [1997] *Geneva Papers for Risk and Insurance*, 238–267.

[39] *Cf.* P. Widmer in J. Spier (ed.), *The limits of liability. Keeping the floodgates shut* (1996), p. 162; See also the paper by O. Haazen/J. Spier for the Dutch lawyers Association: De uitdijende reikwijdte van de aansprakelijkheid uit onrechtmatige daad in [1996] *Handelingen van de Nederlandse Juristen-Vereniging*; M. Faure/T. Hartlief, *Verzekering en groeiende aansprakelijkheidslast. Een juridisch, gezondheidskundig en economisch onderzoek naar ontwikkelingen met betrekking tot de aansprakelijkheidslast en de consequenties voor verzekeraars naar aanleiding van de werkgeversaansprakelijkheid voor bedrijfsongevallen en beroepsziekten* (1995), p. 373.

[40] K. Abraham, Making sense of the Liability Crisis, [1987] *Ohio State Law Journal*, 399; id., The causes of the Insurance Crisis, in *New Directions in Liability Law* (1988), p. 54; Atiyah, American Tort Liability in crisis, [1987] *Oxford Journal Of Legal Studies* Vol. 7, 279 *et seq.*

[41] T. Hartlief, *Ieder draagt zijn eigen schade* (Each one bears his own damage) (1997).

cial barriers are taken care of by such systems as the contingent fee system in the U.S. and the legal aid insurance[42] and state aid elsewhere. The growing awareness and claim-consciousness of consumers and victims is intensified by better information and education and by the background of a very much legalised society in which law-free space ("rechtsfreier Raum") is becoming increasingly sparse, and in which even intimate human relationships (like between spouses, between parents and children, between doctors and patients) are increasingly, so to speak, infected with law. Possible psychological barriers against bringing disputes to court are lowered since liability suits are depersonalised. Litigation is not fought between victim and tortfeasor but between some anonymous (subrogated) first party insurer and some third party liability insurer.

20 One could add that an important role in all this was also played by the effects of the so-called (subjective) "rights revolution"[43]. Reference is here made to an evolution in the Western legal systems whereby "subjective rights" have slowly gained precedence over "objective legal rules". Reference is here made, to say it in better sounding French, to the evolution from a "société de lois" to a "société de droits"[44].

The best-known manifestation and illustration of this evolution is of course encountered in the recognition of implementation of the so-called "fundamental" or "human rights". The "rights revolution" has also led to a dramatic change in the way in which the modern man is aware of and ready to stand up for his (other) rights, and among them his right to compensation of accidentally incurred harm.

21 Legislators and judges are under great pressure to satisfy the demands for redress. The mere existence of liability insurance allows or facilitates legislators to create new liabilities. And judges, although they will readily deny it, are generally thought to be somehow influenced by the actual or even presumed existence or even by the availability of liability insurance both while deciding on the question of liability itself as when deciding on the extent of recoverable damages.

There is no need to insist on the fact that throughout these developments the tort liability system has come to be seen as a legal instrument or technique that serves the goal of compensation at least as much and as well as the other

[42] It is a rather striking observation that the insurance industry is itself helping and indeed encouraging people to bring claims against liability insurers. Whereas such considerations led some legislature, and particularly the German legislator to radically opt in favour of a formula specialized legal aid insurance companies, the European Community has not followed this path while allowing so-called mixed insurance companies, practising both liability insurance and legal aid insurance be it under certain strict conditions aimed at presenting conflicts of interests between the insurer and his insured.

[43] The term was, I think, first used by C. Sunstein, *After the rights revolution. Reconceiving the Regulatory State* (1990).

[44] Compare H. Cousy, "Evolution de la société de "lois" vers une société de "droits": nouveau défi pour l'assurance de protection juridique?", in *Les Mélanges de la protection juridique* (1997), pp. 63–73.

goals which are assigned to it (like deterrence). If it is true that historically tort law was intended to be a surrogate for penal law and that liability was assimilated to a private punishment ("peine privée"), today the compensatory function of the law of tort has come to be considered as being its a primary task.

At this stage, I would like to suggest that, for the purpose of our further discussion about the role and merits of liability insurance, we agree to summarize and reduce the goals or functions of the law of tort to two basic ones, namely *compensation* and *deterrence*. Both concepts must be understood in a broad sense. The goal of *compensation* encompasses appeasement of the victim, repair of the victim's losses, loss shifting from the victim to the tortfeasor and further reduction of the loss through loss spreading by the tortfeasor or by the third party liability insurance. *Deterrence* is also taken in a broad sense and includes such aspects as punishment, discouragement, vindication, prevention of undesirable behaviour, efficient cost allocation and accident cost reduction. **22**

I am well aware that such reduction of the goals and functions of the law of torts to the two mentioned goals of deterrence and compensation is an oversimplification and is otherwise criticisable for several more reasons. **23**

A first critique could be that the reduction of the goals of tort law to the bipolar goal of compensation and deterrence can still be reduced further on to the single one objective of *cost reduction*. It is of course Dean Guido Calabresi who in his seminal book on *The Costs of Accidents* has forcefully explained the view that, apart from the requirements of justice, the (principal) goal of the law of accidents is the reduction of the sum of the costs of accidents and of the costs of handling accident-compensation and of the costs of avoiding accidents[45]. Calabresi uses the concept of costs of accidents in a very broad sense as encompassing three types of avoidance or reduction of costs: the primary, secondary and tertiary cost reduction. These three types of accident cost reduction correspond with three different sub-goals of accident law. Just to freshen up our memories: the primary accident cost reduction refers to the reduction of the number and severity of accidents; the secondary cost reduction sub-goal is concerned with reducing the societal costs resulting from accidents, (in Calabresi's view that is what is really intended by the efforts to compensate victims); and the third sub-goal of accident law is the reduction of the costs of administrating the first two sub-goals, thus the primary and secondary cost reduction. Reducing the tertiary (administration) costs comes down to enhancing the efficiency of the accident law system. It is fair to say that in Calabresi's view the different goals of accident law are indeed reduced to one single goal, which is the reduction of societal costs of accidents. If it may be true that primary and secondary accident cost reduction goals are not always fully consistent with each other, there are also situations in which they do coincide. It can be argued *e.g.* that by introducing a system of strict liability, for instance in the field of product liability, the objective of primary cost avoidance is met by way of forcing individuals to consider accident costs in choosing among activities (the prices of which would

[45] Calabresi, *The Costs of Accidents, A legal and economic analysis* (1970), p. 26

indeed more accurately reflect the accident costs, thanks to the internalization of these costs through a system of strict liability), while at the same time the goal of secondary accident cost reduction is met through the (almost) automatic compensation of the victims and through the spreading of the cost over a large quantity of buyers and sellers through the price mechanism.

24 A second critique is that one should not forget that the law of torts does serve other goals besides those of compensation and deterrence, and indeed even goals other than the reduction of the costs of accidents. Certainly in those legal systems that are based on open-ended general rules (as in the case of the artt. 1382 and 1383 of the French Civil Code), the law of tort also serves other functions besides (even broadly interpreted) compensation and deterrence. For example, especially in the European continent, civil liability law is considered to be a powerful tool in the creation of (new) legal rules, in the implementation of (new) duties and the guaranteeing of (new) rights. A good illustration of this function of the law of civil liability under French and Belgian law is found in the way in which the unfair trade practices legislation (forbidding a number of specifically enumerated unfair trade practices and offering specific procedural devices for fighting them) has developed out of the law of civil liability. The different unfair trade practices can indeed be viewed as specific instances of faulty behaviour, which were gradually identified by the courts as being specific applications of the general concept of fault. Also, by characterizing certain new types and categories of behaviour as wrongful and by sanctioning them with liability for damages, the law of civil liability powerfully contributes to the creation and the refinement of new rights and rules. "L'action en responsabilité civile réapparait en effet comme le moyen d'affirmer certaines prérogatives et de les faire respecter", says Geneviève Viney, who gives other examples such as the emergence in French law of personality rights ("les droits de la personalité") and especially the gradual recognition of the existence of certain so-called "obligations de sécurité", inside as well as outside contractual relationships[46]. Tort law is no good penal law, but like penal law, and sometimes perhaps even better than penal law, tort law induces people to live up to standards of behaviour, and thereby formulates new specific rules of behaviour. We might call this one the "normative function" of the law of tort, being a function which can hardly be reduced to deterrence or compensation.

25 Another example of a rather new function of tort law has been brought into light by the successful cases of "mass tort litigation" (like in the cigarette-cancer cases) where tort law is used by the public authorities as an auxiliary vehicle for carrying out regulatory policies[47].

[46] G. Viney, *Traité de droit civil. Les obligations. Introduction à la responsabilité* (2nd edn. 1995), p. 65.

[47] K. Abraham, Individual Action and Collective Responsability: The Dilemma of Mass Tort Reform, [1987] *Virginia Law Review*, 845; See also Symposium Claims Resolution Facilities and the Mass Settlement of Mass Torts, *Law and Contemporary Problem* (1990), I; G. Casale/R. Ravalk, U.S. tobacco litigation: a lot of smoke, but no fire for the insurance industry, [1999] *The International Journal of Insurance Law*, 2–13.

A third critique against the hereabove suggested reduction of the goals and functions of the law of tort to the basic two functions of compensation and deterrence is that there may be some improprieties in concepts and terminology. It is generally considered that terms like the "goals" and " functions" cover the same content, but our discussion might perhaps gain in clarity if a further distinction were made between *goals or aims* on the one hand and *consequences or effects* on the other hand, or between primary goals and secondary goals or side effects. It is also perhaps improper to state that compensation is the goal of the law of tort, whereas the law of tort has as its only function to decide whether or not compensation for tortious harm shall be given. In the words of Prosser and Keeton: "It is perhaps more accurate to describe the primary function as one of determining when compensation is required[48], or in the words of Kötz "*Das Unfallrecht entscheidet deshalb nicht nur über die Gewährung, sondern genauso über die Versagung von Ersatzansprüchen, und wer behauptet, sein ‚Ziel' sei Kompensation, muss im gleichen Atemzug zugeben dass gleichberechtiges Ziel die Nichtkompensation ist*"[49]. 26

Let us summarize where we stand. Even if compensation is not the goal of the law of tort, tort can be used and is used as an instrument to achieve it. In the same manner was tort law neither conceived nor specifically intended to deter. The foundation of tort law is probably found in some mixed theory, like the one that refers to the idea of corrective justice (see *infra* [39]). Rich as this concept is, tort law can be used as a tool or as instrument for achieving many different goals. For the purposes of our discussion, this multitude can be reduced to two central and main themes: deterrence and compensation. 27

It is here that we hit one of those paradoxes, which are so typical for the law of tort. The utterly amazing observation that countless observers cannot avoid making is that under the prevailing rules, the law of tort appears to be a poor and inadequate instrument with respect to not only one but indeed with respect to both the two major functions (of deterrence and of compensation) which are assigned to this branch of the law. In any event it appears that tort law can only function properly if accompanied and supported by the instrument of liability insurance. 28

Tort liability (without insurance) is a poor instrument of *deterrence*. Historically civil liability was assimilated to a private punishment, a "peine privée". However everybody will agree that tort law is performing simply lousily when considered as being a form or system of penal or punitive law. Not only is such function of the law of tort based on long outdated criminological insights but in addition this branch of the law completely lacks the single most impor- 29

[48] Prosser and Keeton, *The Law of Torts* (5th edn. 1984), p. 18 (also cited by T. Hartlief [*supra* note 41], p. 18).

[49] Kötz, *Deliktsrecht* (7th. edn. 1996), pp. 2–3 (also cited by T. Hartlief, *supra* note 41). Kötz makes the comparison with the law of divorce: "Ebensowenig, wie das Ziel des Ehescheidungsrechts in der Scheidung von Ehe liegt, liegt der Zweck des Unfallsrecht in der Ausgleichung von Schaden" (p. 18).

tant characteristic of any penal law, which is that the sanction must be proportional to the misdeed. The problem lies with the principle of full compensation which makes the amount of the allotted damages entirely dependent on the extent of the losses suffered and entirely disconnected from the gravity of the reprehensible nature of the behaviour which caused the damage. No wonder then that the highest legal authorities have spoken out against any such penal or punitive role. "It is wrong", Lord Devlin said, "to regard the law of tort as associated with the criminal and quasi-criminal law in the work of promoting good standards of behaviour in the community. Its function is to decide how and by whom, in the absence of agreement, damage is to be made good". Apart from the blatant absence of any proportional relation between the fault and the amount of damages to be paid, tort law is indeed infected with other weaknesses. The (tort) sanction of money compensation is generally considered to have less of a deterrent or admonitory effect than the corporal or financial punishment of criminal law. Moreover, as Markesinis and Deakin point out, the deterrent effect is inapplicable "in those numerous cases where the plaintiff's injury is the result of error rather than of blameworthiness", which is, as evidence shows, particularly the case with traffic accidents. Tort law is also ineffective because it gives inappropriate guidance. To prevent undesirable behaviour, criminal sanctions can in many instances achieve a better result than the law of tort. But also when viewed as a system of *compensation*, the tort liability system (without insurance) performs poorly.

30 A first problem lies with the possible existence of a "liability gap". Whether or not the victim will receive compensation depends entirely on the question whether someone was negligent or at fault (or was otherwise fulfilling liability conditions) in causing the harm, which is from the viewpoint of the victim an entirely fortuitous and even irrelevant circumstance. Those victims who are so lucky as to find a liable defendant, against whom they can turn, will still be left without compensation for the sad reason that the liable defendant has empty pockets and thus become victim of a "solvency gap". Even if no such gaps occur, obtaining compensation will be problematic. To obtain compensation, liability of the defendant must be established, which is a long and costly process, even in the European legal order. Indeed, tort liability performs poorly not only as a device for both primary and secondary accident cost reduction, but also from the standpoint of tertiary cost reduction. The implementation of the tort liability system requires much effort, huge costs and sometimes endless duration of time. As the late André Tunc put it in the decisive tone that he was entitled to uphold: "C'est un mécanisme lent, couteux, fondamentalement aléatoire, donc injuste, et qui, s'il fonctionnait mieux, n'aboutirait guère qu'à ratifier les coups du sort"[50]

[50] A. Tunc, in a book review in [1990] *Revue internationale de droit comparé*, 423 (cited by B. Dufwa, Development of International Tort Law Till the Beginning of the 1990's From a Scandinavian Point of View, *Scandinavian Studies in Law*, Vol. 41, p. 93, footnote no. 15).

B. Act II: The Courtship of Tort Liability and Insurance

It is here, in the darkest hour of the examination of the conscience and merits of tort liability, that our second character, *liability insurance*, makes its glorious "entrée en scène". At first sight, it would appear that liability insurance does offer a remedy for several of the major shortcomings of the tort liability system. At their first confrontation, tort liability and liability insurance seem to fit together beautifully and a romance and even true courtship is floating in the air. 31

To be sure liability insurance possesses the charm of youth. This new breed of insurance had appeared rather late on the scenery of insurance, but its usefulness must have been deemed to be so very evident that the contest over the legal validity of this unusual and new type of insurance was of a relatively short duration. Unusual and new indeed because liability insurance was (and still is), as we pointed out earlier, an advanced and sophisticated species in the general genus of insurance[51]. But in spite of these apparent special characteristics, the legal validity of such insurance was rather easily recognized. If it may be true that, as André Tunc wrote that "at the beginning of the nineteenth century, liability insurance would have been unthinkable (and) that it would have been considered ... immoral"[52], the courts both in Europe and America[53] have rapidly done away with such attitude of distrust. In France, the dispute over the legal validity of liability insurance appears to have been settled by a historical decision of the *Cour d'appel de Paris* of 1845 in the affair *Automédon*[54]. In American law the issue was settled by the Missouri Supreme Court's decision of 1909 in the case Breeden v. Frankford Marine Plate Accident & Glass Insurance Company[55]. It is true that there has been some hesitation as to the limits of the insurability of faulty behaviour, especially with respect to the coverage of what in Latin is called the "culpa lata", *i.e.* the shortcoming which is of such gravity as to give the impression that the fault was committed intentionally. Whereas following some Latin precept of obscure origin ("culpa lata dolo aequiparatur": the gross negligence is treated like an intentional fault), many legal systems at the outset considered cases of gross negligence to be uninsurable. More recently modern legislators have not only allowed the coverage of "gross fault", but have 32

[51] See *supra* [2].

[52] A. Tunc, *International Encyclopedia of Comparative Law, Torts* (1983), p. 1.

[53] Purportedly not in the Communist Soviet law where liability was not tolerated on the grounds of fairness and of its undermining the system's deterrence capacity (see A. Erhson Tay., The Foundation of Tort Liability in a Socialist Legal System: Fault versus Social Insurance in Soviet Law, [1969] *University of Toronto Law Journal*, 15, also quoted by G. Schwartz, The Ethics and Economics of Tort Liability Insurance, [1990] *Cornell Law Review*, Vol. 75, (313), 314. See also M. Faure, De grenzen van de verzekerbaarheid rechtseconomisch bekeken, [February 1995] *Welwezen*, 16.

[54] *Cour d'appel Paris*, 1 July 1845, [1848] *Dalloz*, II, 126.

[55] 220 Mo 327, 119 S.W. 576 (1909). The court was divided 5 – 2 on this issue. See further G. Schwartz (*supra* note 7) p. 314.

declared them to be covered, unless the policy decides otherwise *e.g.* by excluding limited and precisely identified cases of gross negligence[56]. In this manner the limit of uninsurability is gradually pushed higher up on the scale of gravity toward the ultimate frontier of the *intentional fault*, which is usually considered to be uninsurable for reasons of violation of "ordre public" and "bonnes moeurs"[57]. It would appear that as of recently, even this ultimate frontier is coming under attack. In life insurance for instance, more and more legislators will allow coverage, or even oblige insurers to cover suicides that take place a given time after the conclusion of the contract[58]. In French law the definition of the "faute intentionnelle" was the object of a judicial "saga" until the *Cour de Cassation* abandoned the battle by leaving the definition of the intentional fault to the appreciation of the trial of fact[59]. In Dutch law equally the *Hoge Raad* limited the effect of the principle of uninsurability of intentional fault by giving a restrictive interpretation of the concept of intentional fault[60].

33 Liability insurance is not only a young (and complex) breed but also a beautiful one and she (let us assume it is a she) has a lot of attractive features. When looked at from the standpoint of the insured, liability insurance is, if the conditions for its full functioning are fulfilled, a powerful and handy instrument to protect the freedom of action of the insured and to fend him against increasingly huge and possibly devastating or disruptive liabilities that threaten the entrepreneur. In this respect liability insurance definitely outweighs other legal instruments or methods serving to protect the acting person or company against the threat of incurring civil liabilities, such as the use of exemption clauses (the validity of which can be contested in court), or the adoption of the form of a company with limited liability (which will not always protect against the impact of professional liabilities incurred by the individual professionals inside the company). Liability insurance enables people to avoid unwanted risks[61]. Whatever the actual degree of risk aversion of people may be, it has been empirically verified that people tend to regard the bearing of a cost (like the cost of an insurance premium) as less unpleasant than the suffering of a "loss"[62] (like the loss of

[56] An example is found in the Belgian 1992 Insurance Contract Act, art. 8.

[57] Compare M. Fontaine, *Droit des Assurances* (2nd edn. 1996), p. 177, nos. 306 *et seq.*

[58] See art. 101 of the Belgian Insurance Contract Act.

[59] Cass. 4 July 2000, no. 98 – 10.744 and the comments, referred to in Lamy Assurances, sous la direction de J. Kullmann, nos. 1163 *et seq.*

[60] H.R. 6 November 1998, [1999] *Nederlands Juristenblad*, 220; and the comments by H. Wansink, De aansprakelijkheidsverzekering en opzettelijk veroorzaakte schade: een Januskop in beweging, [2000] *Aansprakelijkheid, Verzekering & Schade* (AV&S), 14–17.

[61] One will read, I expect with intellectual pleasure and satisfaction, the writings of Peter Bernstein on insurance as an instrument that (a bit like the stock exchange) enables us to make investment decisions "reversible" and thus less risky (P. Bernstein, *Against the Gods, The Remarkable Story of Risk* (1996), p 383).

[62] Compare the interesting empirical findings of D. Kahneman/A. Tversky (cited by Schwartz in his Cornell Law review article, *supra* note 39, and also commented by Thomas Ulen in Law and behavioural Science: Removing the Rationality Assumption from law and Economics, (*supra* note 77). Among their findings: people tend to prefer a guaranteed moderate gain to the possibility of a large gain, (showing risk awareness); people also tend to prefer the possibility of large loss to the certainty of a smaller loss (which rather shows risk-proneness).

incurring a liability). Liability insurance helps to convert possible "losses" into more acceptable "costs".

The principal prowess and attractiveness of liability insurance lies however in the fact that, while being conceived as a mechanism to protect the interests of the tortfeasor (the defendant in a liability suit), liability insurance succeeds in equally protecting and serving the interests of the victim (the plaintiff). That is because liability insurance constitutes a powerful device to fill up the so-called "solvency gap", *i.e.* the absence of protection of the victim that arises out of the liable defendant's insolvency. The existence of liability insurance gives substance to the compensatory function of the tort liability system by ensuring actual recovery to the successful plaintiff. As was explained here-above: in the absence of insurance the tort liability system was the object of scornful and severe criticism since the effective compensation of the victim depends upon the condition that the liable defendant happened to be solvent. Liability insurance fills the solvency gap. **34**

Liability insurance not only mends the problem of a possible solvency gap, it also helps to fill up the so-called "liability gap", that is, by inducing legislators and judges to introduce or recognize more stringent and severe criteria of liability. All of the great lines of development that the law of tort has lived through during the last decades, such as the general move of the criteria of liability from more subjective to more objective criteria, the switch from fault or negligence to no-fault or strict liability, and the trend from stringent to much looser causality requirements, all of them can, to a large degree, be explained by or, at least attributed to the existence or availability of liability insurance.

Insurance has also contributed to make it possible to maintain the rule of full compensation as a typical characteristic of fault liability[63]. We have already noticed that liability insurance also lowers the thresholds to recovery by making actions in tort more accessible to plaintiffs and by depersonalizing the plaintiff-defendant relationship.

The importance of liability insurance is not only that it contributes to the fulfilment of the goals and aims of tort liability, its role is such that in the couple tort liability plus liability insurance, the latter partner occupies the dominant position. This appears from the fact that, in a growing number of cases, liability insurance also determines the limits of tort liability and even its very existence. In a number of cases national and international legislators have felt justified and confident to introduce new liabilities or aggravated liabilities thanks to the availability of liability insurance. Sometimes legislators have even considered it necessary to put caps or ceilings on amounts of compensation that are recoverable in tort because of requirements and limitations of their insurability. Liability insurance is not only the "conditio sine qua non", **35**

[63] In the view of many full compensation of damages is considered as proper to fault liability. In cases where thresholds to liability are lowered (as is the case in the various shades of strict liability) there appears to be a justification for the lowering of the type or amount of recoverable damages.

but constitutes also the outer limit of insurance. No wonder then that in the opinion of some (legislators as well as commentators), liability insurance could even become the "raison d'être" of liability. It is this approach that Ehrenzweig in his famous article so pointedly called the principle of "assurance oblige"[64].

36 Liability insurance is not only a useful tool which supports and fulfils the tort liability system, liability insurance also provides meaningful fairness advantages, no matter what specific explanations or interpretations are given to the fairness concept.

In his seminal article on the ethics of liability insurance in the Cornell Law Review (1990)[65], Schwartz demonstrated that liability insurance is in accordance with all three theories of justice, if at least the insurance premium is "responsive" to the risk behaviour of the insured. In Schwartz's jargon a responsive premium is a premium that is modulated according to the risk behaviour of the insured and is opposed to a "flat" premium where all such modulation is absent (I shall have to come back on these concepts when I shall speak later on about the phenomenon of risk differentiation and premium tariff segmentation). The three theories or arguments of justice that Schwartz refers to are retributive justice, compensatory justice and corrective justice[66].

37 Retributive justice requires that a person, because he acted in an improper way, bears the burden of the liability for the resulting harm[67]. Whereas liability insurance would at first sight appear to be inconsistent with any goal of retribution or deterrence, Schwartz rightly argues that such inconsistency would only exist in the hypothesis that if the insurance were completely flatly priced. If the insurance pricing is perfectly responsive, the extent of the defendant's financial burden is "proportional to the level of improper risks that his conduct occasions", and therefore in accord with retribution theories[68]. We shall have to come back to this line of thought, when we shall have to deal with the question whether liability insurance does not annihilate or destroy whatever deterrent or preventive effect that tort liability (without insurance) may have (see *infra* nos. [46] *et seq.*).

38 With or without differentiation of premium, liability insurance is definitely and clearly in accordance with the argument of so-called compensatory justice, which requires that the defendant, having been involved in the infliction of the plaintiff's injury, is under an obligation to make sure that the plaintiff

[64] A.A. Ehrenzweig, (*supra* note 3).

[65] G. Schwartz, The Ethics and Economics of Tort Liability Insurance, [1990] *Cornell Law Review*, Vol. 75, 313–365.

[66] The following comments heavily draw on Schwartz's articles, cited in the previous notes.

[67] G. Schwartz (*supra* note 66), p. 326.

[68] G. Schwartz (*supra* note 66), p. 328. For a critical view on this, see J.L. Coleman, Moral Theories of Torts: Their Scope and Limits. Part I, [1982] *Law and Philosophy*, Vol. I, (371), 375–376.

receives compensation for that injury[69]. Insurance is not only in accordance with this principle, it actually serves to further and fulfil that principle.

Finally, liability insurance is also in accordance with what some American authors call "corrective justice"[70]. Building on the two previous concepts of retribution and compensatory justice, the concept of corrective justice is concerned with compensation for the victim but emphasizes that the tort defendant, having created risks in a certain way, should serve as the actual source of the compensation payment[71]. Here again, one can argue that liability insurance partially fulfils corrective justice requirements if at least the pricing of insurance is so conceived as to make the defendant bear some significant burden, *e.g.* by way of an increased premium or a raised franchise. It may be true that by taking away a substantial part of the financial burden from the shoulders of the tortfeasor and by installing a sharing of liability, the liability insurance system goes contrary to the objectives of (a strong version of[72]) corrective justice. But this argument is countered by the argument that insurance promotes "corrective" fairness by flattening out the financial burden and by protecting the defendant against the vicissitudes and fortuities of risk. The minimal conclusion is that liability insurance is powerfully supported by arguments of compensatory justice and that, under certain conditions, liability insurance is not inconsistent with theories of retributive and corrective justice. **39**

In more allegorical tunes: tort liability and liability form a handsome couple. **40**
Liability insurance does a wonderful job in its relationship with tort liability.

Life however is never simple, and the rosy relationship between tort liability and liability insurance is, alas, more complicated, and also more troublesome than their early courtship would suggest. After studying the rapture of the early courtship between liability and insurance we must now look at the eye-opening experience of their married life.

[69] G. Schwartz (*supra* note 66), p. 328.

[70] Schwartz rightly warns that the concept of corrective justice, as he and a number of American authors are using it (see R. Posner The Concept of Corrective Justice in Recent Theories of Tort Law, [1981] *Journal of Legal Studies*, Vol. 10, 187; R.A. Epstein, Causation and Corrective Justice. A Reply to Two Critics, [1979] *Journal of Legal Studies*, Vol. 8, 477), does not concide with wider (and more vague) concept used by Aristoteles in The Nicomachean Ethics.

[71] G. Schwartz (*supra* note 66), p. 332. He makes the comparison with the tort theory set forth by George Fletcher, according to whom the proper ground for liability is the nonreciprocal risk imposed on the plaintiff by the defendant: victims of nonreciprocal risktaking have a right to compensation (G.P. Fletcher, Fairness and Utility in Tort Theory, [1972] *Harvard Law Review*, Vol. 85, 537).

[72] For the difference between stronger and weaker versions of the "corrective justice" argument, see the references in Schwartz's article (pp. 332 *et seq.*). Representatives of the "strong version" are D. Smith, The Critics and the 'Crisis'. A Reassessment of Current Conceptions of Tort Law, [1987] *Cornell Law Review*, 765; and E.J. Weinrib, The Insurance Justification and Private Law, [1985] *Journal of Legal Studies* Vol. 14, 681 *et seq*

C. Act III: Marriage, the Eye Opener

41 Marriage, as the pun goes, is a ceremony in which a fellow loses his bachelor's degree without gaining a master's degree. At the very least, married life serves as an excellent eye opener for the partners. At closer look, both of our partners show weaknesses and shortcomings, which threaten to make their union less successful than what would first appear. A number of questions or even problems become apparent.

42 A first problem is well known and concerns the question whether liability insurance, while serving and indeed fulfilling the compensatory function of tort law, does not thwart the other major goals like deterrence and prevention. There is an answer to this problem which, as we shall see, is to be found in the technique of risk pooling and the resulting differentiation of tariff and policy conditions. The problem is however that the application of these techniques in a competitive market structure may lead to an uncontrolled spiral movement which may endanger both the compensatory and the protective function of liability insurance.

43 A second question is whether the tort liability and insurance system is capable of coping with the so-called "new risks", *i.e.* the unknown risks and uncertainties arising out of the application of the new technologies (information and communication techniques, new materials, biotechnology and medicine). In essence the answer of the insurance industry has been to dramatically change its existing system of coverage of liability risks by switching to a system of coverage on "claims made-basis". But here again the question is whether in certain cases the remedy is not worse than the plague.

44 A third question is whether insurance possesses the capacity and the capability to handle the ever multiplying and expanding cases where courts and legislators acknowledge or implement the existence of liability in tort. Are we heading toward an apocalyptic situation, where liability insurance becomes unavailable for a number of (even indispensable) activities or are the insurance techniques apt to "shut the floodgates"? Is the insurance industry indeed capable of adequately responding to the growing public demand for insurance cover and to control the claim-breeding culture?

45 Let us have a closer look at those three questions (*infra*, sub. 2, 3 and 4). But before reaching the first question, we must say a word about the deterrence effect of tort law in general (sub. 1).

1. The Deterrence Effect of Tort Law: A Short Excursion into Law and Economics

46 Does tort law really deter and if so does liability insurance not destroy such deterrent effect? Here again, to treat these questions, I could almost literally refer to two major articles by Gary Schwartz, one titled: "The reality of the

economic analysis of law: does tort law really deter?"[73], the second dealing with "Mixed Theories of Tort Law: Affirming Both Deterrence and Corrective Justice"[74]. But like a pilgrim, I must walk this difficult road by myself.

To answer the question whether tort liability has an effect of ("general") deterrence upon the tortfeasor, which cannot be better achieved by regulation and punitive sanctions (by "specific" deterrence) and whether the supposedly deterrent effect of tort liability is not completely lost when negligence is replaced by strict liability and when liability is covered by insurance, we cannot but turn our attention to the answers coming from a school of legal thought which is known as the "law and economics"[75]. Without deeply engaging in a discussion about this we must at least have a taste of this important source of rational thinking about our problem and tasting the style of the law and economics "discours" is indeed the (limited) object of the following blitz visit to the law and economics site. **47**

A key assumption in such an approach to tort law and indeed in the entire economic theory of tort liability, is the so-called "rationality assumption", the assumption thus that potential victims and potential injurers are rational self-interested decision-makers. It is this "rationality assumption" that is most controversial among old school, classical lawyers, and especially, I would think, among practising lawyers who are daily confronted with the limitless irrationality of human behaviour. People, decision-makers, even the most professional and enlightened ones simply do not think or act along the lines, which the economic theory likes to attribute to them. **48**

Economists are quite familiar with the objection (which is indeed the prime argument against most of their theories) but they are only lightly impressed since – "jusqu'à nouvel ordre" – the rationality assumption is the best they have and the one which brings them closest to the overall pattern of society's behaviour. Nevertheless one cannot but observe – with satisfaction – that among the most alert of economists, the message has been heard, and that some of them are indeed trying to bring their starting points closer to reality by openly addressing the issue of "flaws in rational decision making"[76] and **49**

[73] [1994] *UCLA Law Review*, Vol. 42, 377.

[74] [1997] *Texas Law Review*, Vol. 75, 1801.

[75] As one is well aware, ever since the early 1970's American academic legal literature has witnessed the deployment of this formidable intellectual movement, and of what amounts to a profoundly new legal theory, which is better known as the (new) law and economics or the economic analysis of law.
Starting from the basic Welfare Economics concept that the legal system may be seen as a means of enchanting the efficient allocation of society's resources, the law and economics doctrine elevated economic analysis to a powerful tool for solving societal problems, or as Markesinis said as, "a universal solvent for legal and ethical problems". B.S. Markesinis/S.F. Deakin (*supra* note 3), pp. 22 *et seq.*

[76] See the paper by Th. Ulen, The Economic Analysis of Tort Law and Flawed Decision-Making, commented hereafter.

"beginning the task of amending the economic analysis of tort law to take account of flaws in human decision-making".

50 Rather than trying to make the umpteenth description of the (particularly rich) lines of thought of the law and economics theory in the law of torts, I propose to give brief attention to just one recent statement of the theory because it is one in which the author has tried to meet some of the criticisms that are often raised against the theory's rationality assumption, by taking possible flaws in decision-making into account. My choice fell on an article that Thomas Ulen presented at the ODENSE conference of the European Association of Law and Economics, and in which he dealt with the implications of flawed decision-making for the economic analysis of tort law[77].

51 People who act in society (let us, like Ulen, call them decision-makers) inevitably cause inadvertent harm to society. This harm represents a cost in the sense of a useless spoiling of scarce resources (social cost). Tort law aims at inducing injurers to *internalize* the losses that their actions or failures may impose on others ("external costs"). Tort law does so by charging the wrongdoer with the obligation to pay compensatory damages. To avoid or minimize this price, the potential wrongdoer may invest in preventive precautionary actions, but these will also give rise to costs, which Ulen calls "precautionary costs"[78]. Finally accidents also create the costs of determining who is liable and of handling the compensation system. One recognizes of course Calabresi's three categories of accident costs. Such costs must quite evidently be minimized. Minimization must not be understood too radically here in the sense of a reduction to zero, since such reduction would in its turn give rise to even higher social costs. Instead the social costs of accidents must be reduced to their economically optimal level. Such level will be achieved when decision-makers are induced to take optimal levels of care, or to put it another way, to take the optimal amount of precautionary measures.

52 The assumption is that precautionary measures will make accidents less likely to happen or, when they happen, less severe. Increasing levels of precaution will lead to lowering the probability that an accident will take place and to lowering the severity of possible accidents. As Ulen says, the amount of harm imposed on others in the event of an accident (expected accident costs) is a declining function of the potential tortfeasor's level of precaution (curve A). On the other hand the more precautionary measures are taken, the higher precautionary costs will rise: precautionary costs are an increasing function of the

[77] Th. Ulen, The Economic Analysis of Tort Law and Flawed Decisionmakers, (mimeographed material). See on the same issues, Th. Ulen, Rational Choice and the Economic Analysis of law, [1994] *Law and Social Inquiry*, Vol. 19, 487. See also R. Cooter/Th. Ulen, *Law and Economics* (3rd edn. 2000), Chapter 8. Further reading in law and economics must of course include S. Shavell, *An Economic Analysis of Accident Law* (1989); W. Landes/R. Posner, *The Economic Structure of Tort Law* (1989).

[78] Notice that the term "precaution" is here used in the general acceptance of preventive care, and not in the more restrictive sense (where "precaution" is opposed to "prevention"), that is referred to in the hereafter following comments on the "precautionary principle".

tortfeasor's level of precaution (line B). Costs of precaution plus expected accident costs form "the expected social costs of accidents" (curve C).

Because the expected accident costs decline, and the precautionary costs increase, these "expected social costs of accidents" will first decline and then increase in function of the amount of precaution that is taken by the potential tortfeasor. Evidently the right amount of precaution to be taken by the tortfeasor is that amount where the curve of expected social costs of accidents (curve C) is at its lowest. Additional investments in care would indeed be inefficient.

In the economic approach to tort law, tort liability must be such as to induce potential tortfeasors to take exactly that amount of precaution.

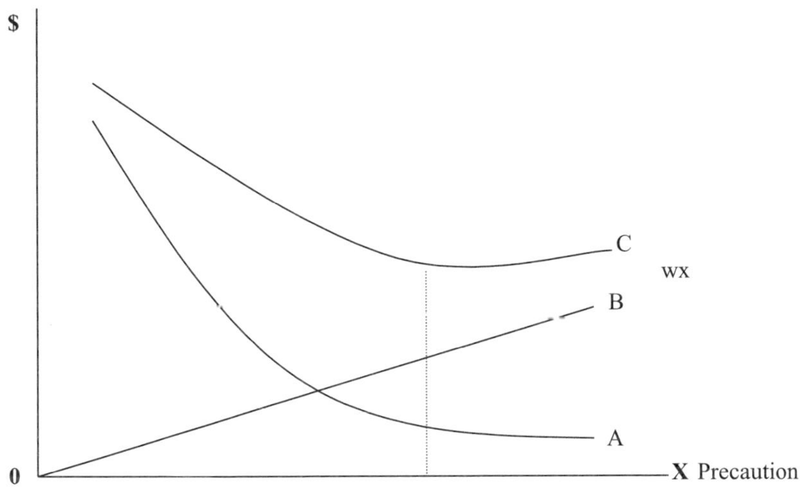

Fig. 1

Ulen goes on by showing that law and economics can help by giving detailed answers to at least three difficult issues of legislative policy: 1. Should the legislator use clear standards of behaviour like speed limits, or quality of pollution, (the "bright-line fault rule") and consider each shortcoming as faulty or should the legislator rather resort to vague rules (like the negligence, or fault rule) which will lead to a case by case of determination of fault[79]? 2. Should the legislator opt for a negligence (fault) criterion of liability or for strict liability? 3. Should one choose for tort liability or rather for safety regulation. At the risk of doing injustice to the finely tuned and superbly elaborated argumentation of the author[80], I limit myself to a few words to situate each of them. 53

[79] French and Belgian lawyers will recognize the two types of the fault, which are distinguished by the courts: the fault consisting in the violation of (any) specific legal obligation and the fault consisting in a shortcoming to the open norm of prudent and diligent behaviour.

[80] And also doing injustice to the mass of thought, which has been consecrated to these issues in the law and economics literature.

54 The first question concerns the fault standard and more specifically, the desirability of a "Bright-Line Fault Rule" – that is the rule where the level of care is once and for all clearly established by the legislator (think *e.g.* of a speed limit rule). The "Bright-Line Fault Rule" is opposed to the case-by-case standard. The advantage of a bright-line rule for determining fault is the saving in information costs for decision-makers. The advantage of the bright-line rule is that no costs are attached to obtaining information about what amount of care should be used. In a case by case approach, the determination of the required degree of care is left to the injurers, but their liability will be judged *ex post* on the basis of the judge's or jury's evaluation of the legal standard of due care. The advantage of this last approach is its flexibility and adaptability to new technologies of precaution.

55 The choice between negligence and strict liability[81] depends upon the unilateral and bilateral nature of the precautions to be taken. In the case of bilateral precaution, where both the parties can take action to reduce the probability and severity of an accident, negligence will be the appropriate liability standard. Indeed, if negligence is the criterion, the potential victim will realize that the other party will not be held liable if this other party has applied the legally required degree of care. To avoid the accident losses, which might thus not be compensated, the potential victim will take whatever precautionary measures he can. Negligence appears to be the appropriate rule in cases where both potential injurers and victims can do something to reduce the probability or severity of an accident, a condition that is usually called "bilateral precaution" or "joint precaution".[82] Strict liability on the other hand will be appropriate in cases which Ulen calls cases of unilateral precaution, *i.e.* cases where the potential victims can realistically do nothing to reduce the probability and severity of an accident (think of an airline crash). It makes no sense here to induce both parties to take precautionary measures, since one of them cannot take any meaningful such measures. In other words it makes no sense to impose a contributory negligence rule (introducing an exonerating level of care for the injurer and exposing potential victims to residual liability). Strict liability[83] of the party who is clearly identifiable as the potential injurer[84] is here the right solution.

[81] We leave aside here the interesting point to what extent strict liability and negligence standards actually differ, the question thus "how strict is strict liability". A parallel question can be raised about the "subjective" degree of fault liability. Compare H. Koziol, Liability based on Fault, Subjective or Objective Yardstick?, [1998] *Maastricht Journal of European and Comparative Law*, 111.

[82] The concept is close to the concept of reciprocal risks, *i.e.* risks where it is not clear *ex ante* who will be the victim and who the injurer.

[83] Note that the economics of tort liability show that, for reasons we will not go into here, the amount of precaution taken by the potential injurer under a strict liability rule and under a negligence rule remains equal. It thus appears that negligence or strict liability both induce potential tortfeasors to the same degree of care. The choice between negligence and strict liability will be determined by the different incentives to take care which are given to the potential *victims* by the one and the other system.

[84] There are many cases where this condition is not fulfilled and where it is not so clear whether one has to do with a unilateral or bilateral precaution situation! Professor Ulen gives the example of product liability cases (*e.g.* the defective chain saw). He argues that in such cases of doubt the challenge is to make the safest choice, that is the system, which leads to the least inefficiency, and that appears to be the negligene standard.

Similar arguments as those pleading in favour of bright-line fault rules and strict liability (transparent rules, free of hindsight bias, possibility of detail and differentiation), plead for substituting safety regulation for exposure to tort law. However such benefits may be neutralized by the additional costs that attend regulations (flaws in group decision-making, disadvantages flowing from overregulation). Although most will agree that a sensible trade-off (between safety regulation and tort liability) must be reached, I suspect that the adherents of an economic analysis of law would have the balance tilt in favour of liability solutions. **56**

2. Liability Insurance and Deterrence

Economic analysis of tort law has always insisted that tort law does (or should?) have deterrence as one of its principal functions[85]. This again is a basic assumption that has been the object of fierce criticisms. Numerous are the scholars who have challenged the deterrence capacity of tort law[86]. And as Gary Schwartz demonstrated on the basis of (the limited available amount of) "real world evidence and observations", "indications of the deterrence efficacy of tort law are not immediately apparent". Even if "some" deterrence effect seems to be achieved by tort liability, the fundamental question arises whether the deterrence effects of tort law are large enough to justify all the costs it imposes on society[87] The question raises the need of confronting the criticisms against "the theory of rational choice". In his (hereabove much cited article on flawed decision-making) Professor Th. Ulen admits that experimental research shows that most people do not make decisions regarding probabilistic outcomes in the manner predicted by rational choice theory. A well-known illustration is the phenomenon of "hindsight bias" *i.e.* the tendency of actors to over-estimate the *ex ante* prediction that they had concerning the likelihood of an event's occurring after learning that it did actually occur. The result of this hindsight bias in tort litigation will be that if jurors are subject to hindsight bias, defendants will be found negligent in situations in which they acted in a socially efficient manner but were struck by bad luck. Such attitude of jurors could provide actors with an incentive to take too many precautionary measures. **57**

While admitting that the theory of hindsight bias does not yet give rise to practical solutions[88], Ulen admits that the theory already argues for some

[85] See *inter alia* M. Faure, Ongevallenpreventie door eficiënte aansprakelijkheidsregels en verzekeringspolissen op competitieve verzekeringsmarkten, [1993] *Verzekeringsarchief*, 3.

[86] See among others R. Abel, A Critique of Torts, [1990] *UCLA Law Review* Vol. 97, 785; P.S. Atiyah, *Accidents, Compensation and the Law* (*supra* note 3), J. Fleming, The System Builders. A Critical Appraisal of Modern American Tort Law Theory, [1980] *Journal of Legal Studies* Vol. 9, 27, and the further enumeration by G. Schwartz in his article in [1994] *UCLA Law Review*, 381 and 382.

[87] G. Schwartz, The Economic Analysis of Tort Law: Does Tort law Really Deter?, [1994] *UCLA Law Review, 377.*

[88] Ulen refers to a suggestion made by Jolls/Sunstein /Thaler (A behavioral Approach to Law and Economics, [1998] Stanford L. Rev, 1471) that juries be shielded from evidence concerning what action the defendantactually took until after jurors have determined what decision would have been reasonable *ex ante*.

reforms like a wider use of strict liability (less *ex post* adjudication of negligence) and a broader use of administrative agency regulations of safety (although the public authorities should be cautious themselves, while enacting new regulations because of the very same dangers linked to hindsight bias).

While such conclusions are not at all intended to entirely abandon the rationality assumption, one cannot but observe that a slow start is made with amending the economic analysis of law to take account of flawed decision-making. And such start may be considered as a breakthrough in a stalemate discussion between traditional legal thinking and the new law and economics approaches.

58 But let us now concentrate on the question whether liability insurance does not undermine whatever preventive or deterring effect that tort liability may have. At least at first sight, the argument appears valid: many indeed fear that the deterrence objective of tort liability is "severely, perhaps fatally undermined" by the prevalence of insurance[89]. Whatever deterrence effect tort liability may have, most of it seems to be neutralized by the effect of liability insurance. Insurance appears to take away from the potential injurer the threat of having to pay high money damages, and thus leads the potential injurer to less precaution than what he would apply if he were to face normal liability judgments.

59 At closer look however, the deterrence undermining effect of insurance may not be as dramatic as would appear at first glance. In fact thanks to liability insurance, the threat of having to bear the consequence may be rendered more precise, more calculable, and therefore finally more convincing and effective. The deterrence, which emanates from incurring liability, is in final analysis not very convincing, because of the absence of any proportionality, and indeed of any limit. The slightest fault may lead to devastating amounts of damages, whereas in other cases the most reckless tortfeasor may get off lightly. Tort liability without liability insurance is as little convincing as a stimulus for (preventive) action a lottery.

60 The effect of insurance upon the preventive deterrence effects of tort law has been looked at from mainly two angles. The first angle is where liability insurance is looked at from the viewpoint of the "moral hazard". The second one (which is in fact partially in coincidence with the previous one) relates to the dangers of "adverse selection". It appears however that these problems are not unsolvable, since there are techniques to avoid or temper the effects of such problems. However as I already announced (see [42]) a further question will arise insofar as the techniques for solving the moral hazard problem threatens to jeopardize the other functions of insurance like compensation and protection.

[89] J.G. Fleming, The Role of Negligence in Modern Tort Law, [1967] *Virginia Law Review*, 815, 823.

Moral hazard is the phenomenon that the behaviour of the insured injurer will change as soon as the risk (in this case the risk of incurring liability) is removed from him[90]. If indeed the risk of incurring liability and of having to face the disagreeable effects were fully removed from the potential injurer, he would lose whatever incentives to prevent such liability that the tort liability system would otherwise (*i.e.* in the absence of liability insurance) give. Theoretically the solution of the problem is easily reached: the insurer must give such incentives to the insured that he comes to behave in the same manner as if he were not insured. The technique to do so is also known. One usually distinguishes between two different methods. The direct method consists in leaving the risk partially on the shoulders of the insured. This vague (and unclear) expression of "leaving the risk partially on the risk uninsured", must be specified. One way to do so is to simply deny insurance for specific risks. Another method would be to leave the risk partially uninsured by excluding certain aspects of the risk, as is *e.g.* the case with the exclusion of intentional harm. A third method is to limit the extent of the coverage of an insured risk by having the insured pay for part of the loss through the use of deductibles, the use of ceilings, recourse actions against the insured, co-insurance and the like. 61

The indirect method consists in differentiating between policy conditions and adapting them to the characteristic of the individual insured.

Let us look at some of the problems which are caused by these techniques and demonstrate how they may have a devastating effect upon the other goals of tort law and liability insurance.

The question when and under what conditions a combination of direct and indirect methods (such as differentiation of conditions and premiums, deductibles, ceilings, self-insurance, etc.) will have an equivalent deterrence effect as a tort liability would have without insurance has not been studied in any systematic fashion. It is usually pointed out that fighting moral hazard is to the insurer's own interest and that they thus know the technique. Such does not show however that they also know how to reach precisely the optimal mix of measures to achieve the right amount of deterrence and precaution. To the contrary, it is quite a hard task for the insurer to know what exactly he must do. I want to demonstrate and illustrate this difficulty by shortly describing the difficulties and problems surrounding risk differentiation or segmentation

Let us have a closer look at the mechanism of risk differentiation which is at the basis of the mechanisms of selectivity and premium differentiation (and other types) of differentiation[91]. 62

First a word about concepts and terminology. Segmentation aims at splitting up the insured population in homogeneous groups (risk pools) so as to enable 63

[90] M. Faure, The influence of insurance on liability issues, in A. McGee/W. Heusel (eds.) *The Law and Practice of Insurance in the Single European Market*, Series of Publications by the Academy of European Law in Trier, Vol. 11, (1995), pp. 179–204.

[91] For an in depth study of the various kinds of segmentation, see N. Depril/J. Dhaene, Rapport du groupe de travail "segmentation", de la Commission des Assurances, in H. Cousy/C. Claassens/van Schoubroeck (eds.), *Competitivité, Ethique et Assurance* (1998), pp. 109–139.

the insurer to apply the tariff conditions and other policy conditions, which correspond with the expected value of the losses which an individual member will cause to the collectivity. We use "segmentation" as the general term, which encompasses both the techniques of tariff-differentiation and of risk-selection. Risk-selection and differentiation take place *ex ante*, at the moment of underwriting (the insurer will refuse to underwrite or differentiate tariffs and other policy conditions by applying different deductibles, profit sharing quota and the like). Risk-selection and differentiation can also take place *ex post*, that is at some later stage in the life of the contract (change of conditions at time of renewal, experience rating, personalisation of premium rates). In the (hypothetical) case where the *ex ante* differentiation would be correct and thus lead to the selection of homogeneous classes of risk bearers, no *ex post* selectivity would be necessary, nor indeed desirable. Segmentation can be both implicit (the insurer is only underwriting in a given risk segment, like *e.g.* outside urban areas) and explicit, and more or less active[92].

64 What is the aim of differentiation and selectivity? Insurance is based on mutuality[93] and this mutualisation involves a certain amount of solidarity (in the sense of transfer of wealth from one person to another without a clear *quid pro quo*). In the context of private insurance, one must distinguish between two types of solidarity which may be at work: the *aleatory or chance solidarity* and *redistributive solidarity.* Ideally each prospective insured should be charged a premium which corresponds to his expected risk (*i.e.* the expected amount of losses that he may cause to the collectivity of the risk bearers). In such a (theoretical) situation of accurate differentiation and segmentation[94], each would pay for the exact risk which he (or she) represents and not for the (higher) risk of his neighbour. No "redistributive solidarity" would take place among the members of such insured population but that does not mean that there would be no solidarity at all, since in any event some transfer will take place from those who are not hit by the risk (although they paid for it) and those who are hit by an actual loss (and who benefit from the premiums which others have paid). This is a form of solidarity or rather "mutuality", which is purely dictated by chance. This is the solidarity between equally prudent and reliable people who only differ from each other in having good or bad luck. We call thus "chance solidarity" or "aleatory solidarity".

If however policy-holders are charged to pay a premium which does not exactly correspond with their exact expected loss value (and that will be almost always the case because of the difficulty of exactly evaluating each and

[92] For some further details, see N. Depril/J. Dhaene (*supra* note 91). For a more condensed description, see my paper prepared for the colloquium on "L'économie du droit dans les pays de droit civil: quelle place pour l'économie dans la construction des règles juridiques?" Law and Economics in Civil Law Countries (Université de Nancy, 28 and 29 June 2000), to be published shortly.

[93] In the sense of the sharing of losses within a group of individuals who are submitted to the same risk: Picard/Besson, *Les assurances terrestres*, T. I, *Le Contrat d'assurance*, Paris (1982) nr. 9.

[94] The term "accurate" comes from K. Abraham, Efficiency and Fairness in Insurance Risk Classification, [1985] *Virginia Law Review*, (403), 405.

every insured) some redistribution will take place between those who pay too much and those who pay too little. This solidarity is truly "redistributive". It so happens that in almost all insurance, a certain amount of such redistributive solidarity is present.

One can safely sustain that the aim of segmentation is to eliminate all kinds of 65
redistributive solidarity and to arrive (ideally) at a situation of homogeneous risk groups whose tariffication is correct, and where the only solidarity is the aleatory one.

If such (ideal) situation of perfectly "responsive" insurance (as opposed to the case where insurance conditions are non-differentiated and thus "flat") is reached, moral hazard problems are eliminated. The insured will indeed be induced to taking all safety precautions, which cost less than the rise of the premium[95]. As Gary Schwartz puts it "tort law deterrence objectives are hence preserved (…). Indeed, in one way liability rules combined with such insurance might produce even better safety results than liability rules standing on their own: for a liability insurer may be able to offer safety advice to an insured that will permit the latter actually to impose the level of safety it provides"[96].

In fact segmentation offers other advantages, especially in a competitive mar- 66
ket environment. Segmentation will allow the insurer to charge less to the good risks and thus allow the insurer to keep those good risks from moving away to join a competitor who by hypothesis charges responsive and thus lower premiums. Segmentation will also act as a counter-measure against the informational asymmetry which exists between insurer and insured, since it will allow the insurer to make his own selection on the basis of his own objective criteria, and will induce the insurer to be inquisitive as far as information about the insured is concerned.

There is however another side to the coin. Segmentation offers not only 67
advantages but also disadvantages, which must be looked at now since they are of such a nature as to jeopardise some other goals of liability and of liability insurance.

There is of course first a number of problems (and "costs") attached to the process of segmentation itself, caused *inter alia* by the inadequate determining of segmentation criteria, the resistance of consumers to the use of some non-transparent segmentation criteria, the difficulties attached to the implementation of both *ex ante* and *ex post* segmentation techniques (the dangers of fraudulent misuse). These problems represent administration costs, which must be weighed against the benefits of the system[97]. In addition there are legal limits

[95] Gary Schwartz gives the following example. Assume a safety precaution would cost a defendant $ 700, but would eliminate a risk whose magnitude is $ 1,000 (*e.g.* a one percent chance of a $ 100,000 injury). In a perfectly operating insurance, the increase in premium for failure to take the $ 700 precautionary measures, will be $ 1,000. The insured will thus benefit from the same precautionary impulses and from some other benefits as well.

[96] G. Schwartz (*supra* note 66), 338.

[97] J.J. Gollier, Vertus et limites de la segmentation, in Cousy/Claassens/van Schoubroeck (eds.) (*supra* note 91), p. 211.

to differentiation, also in insurance. Differentiation may not be discriminatory. But the precise frontier between authorized differentiation and forbidden discrimination is often delicate[98].

There is however a more fundamental problem and that is that segmentation may set in motion a spiral movement which leads to ever better insurance conditions for the better, *i.e.* lower cost risks, and consequently to ever more burdening conditions for the bad, *i.e.* the higher cost risks. This may lead to the economic or actual impossibility for those more expensive risks to obtain any insurance at all. In a truly competitive market, segmentation must end up by leading to the inaccessibility of insurance for a growing number of less good risks. In the field of insurance, segmentation leads to what may be considered to be the main plague of the modern competitive society and characteristic for the new type of social problem, which is usually called under its French name of "exclusion"[99].

68 It is of course salutary and in accordance with sound insurance practice that those bad risks are thrown out or charged a higher premium or more burdening insurance conditions. But whereas it is economically and technically disastrous to let the good risks drop out, it is, in a growing number of cases, equally socially unacceptable to force the bad risks out and deprive them of insurance. In a growing number of cases insurance, especially liability insurance, is a necessary passport to gain access to a growing number of activities in society. If these activities are "necessities", the (liability) insurance becomes a necessity too, and the access to such insurance may even be considered as a (subjective) right especially when the insurance is obligatory or compulsory. France has so introduced a "droit à l'assurance" for motor vehicle liability insurance through the operation of the "Bureau Central de Tarification"[100]. "Droit à l'assurance", a right to obtain insurance, sounds contrary to every sound principle of insurance technique and contrary to the sacrosanct principle of the underwriting freedom of the insurer. But the need for insurance coverage appears to be stronger than the most powerful rationality of economists.

3. Insurance of New Risks

69 Let us now turn to the question whether liability insurance is capable of handling the "new risks". When I speak of new risks, I refer to those risks or dangers which are created by the developments of technology and by the unpredictability of the resulting losses[101].

[98] See W. Wils, Insurance Risk Classification in the E.C.: Regulatory Outlook, [1994] *Oxford Journal of legal Studies*, 449 (concerning the question whether the use of different mortality tables for men and women in life insurance is discriminatory with respect to discriminatory pricing practices automobile insurance, see G. Schoorens, Segmentering en discriminatie, in Cousy/Claassens/van Schoubroeck (*supra* note 91), p. 217.

[99] On different application of traditional social insurance techniques, see P. Rosanvallon, *La nouvelle question sociale*: *repenser l'Etat-providence* (1995), p. 223.

[100] G. Durry, Le Bureau central de tarification, [1992] *Risques. Les Cahiers de l'Assurance* Vol. 12, 89; Y. Lambert-Faivre, *Droit des Assurances* (11th edn. 2001), p. 626.

[101] About what is called the new science of danger, see G.Y. Kervern, L'Ethique cyndinique, [1994] *Risques. Les Cahiers de l'Assurance*, nos. 18, 61.

It is, I think, the French author and distinguished philosopher of insurance François Ewald, whom we can honour as a philosopher of insurance (one of the few), who drew attention to the fact that in our highly technological society, our practical knowledge and capability of achieving practical goals and results are moving ahead faster than our scientific insights[102]. Our highly technologically developed society is capable of providing the planet with heating and air conditioning while scientists have not yet fully mastered the answer to for instance the question what the ultimate consequences of the use of fossil energy sources upon the ozone-layer will be. We are capable of genetically manipulating living organisms but science is not that far as to be able to precisely evaluate the long term dangers and effects. In the words of François Ewald, there is a gap between our "pouvoir" and our "savoir", between our "praxis" and "noesis", between what we are capable of doing and achieving on the one hand and knowing how to do it safely on the other hand. **70**

The consequence is that our present day technological society is creating dangers of which we are not entirely aware and which we cannot entirely master because of our lack of scientific knowledge about cause and effect. Modern technology is creating situations without knowing for sure whether these are really dangerous: such situations are – following the terminology which was introduced by an economist called Knight[103] – not called "risks" but "uncertainties". Uncertainties are situations in which it is not certain whether there is a risk, but where there is only a risk that there is a risk.

Uncertainties give rise to major problems for the insurance industry. Risks are probabilistically foreseeable, and thus calculable and insurable. They can be avoided through preventive action. In the case of uncertainties however, the odds and chances are not calculable because of insufficient (scientific) insight in causal relationships. Uncertainties are uninsurable and they cannot be avoided through preventive measures. The prudent attitude that must be adopted in the face of situations of uncertainty is not prevention but "precaution" (*Vorsorge*)[104]. It is in this sense that the word "precaution" is used in the Rio Declaration and in Art. 130R of the E.C.-Treaty. It is also in this sense that one speaks of the precautionary principle, the "principe de précaution"[105]. **71**

I wanted to briefly remind you of these fundamental concepts and distinctions because I believe that they aptly summarize a number of problems with which the modern insurance industry, and in particular the liability insurance industry, is confronted: the problem of the lack of scientific insight into the long **72**

[102] F. Ewald/F. Chaumet, Petite bibliothèque d'Actualité. Autour de la Précaution, [1992] *Risques. Les Cahiers de l'Assurance*, nos. 11, 99; F. Ewald, Le retour du malin génie, in *Le principe de précaution dans la conduite des affaires humaines*, I.N.R.A., Ed. de la Maison des sciences de l'homme, (1997), pp. 99–126.

[103] F. Knight, *Risk, Uncertainty and Profit* (1921).

[104] About the recognition of the principle beyond the boundaries of environmental law, see G.J.Martin, Precaution et évolution du droit, [1995] *Dalloz Chronique*, 299.

[105] On the concept of precaution: see H. Cousy, A propos de la notion de précaution, [1995] *Risques. Les Cahiers de l'Assurance*, nos. 21, 149; H. Cousy, The precautionary principle. A Status Quaestionis, [1996] *The Geneva Papers in Risk and Insurance*, nos. 79, 158

term effects and risks of our present day highly technological activities. The phenomenon is known under several aspects and denominations. One is well familiar with the problem of the insurability of "development risks", which became famous in the context of product liability. There is also some talk of the so-called "toxic torts", and of creeping damages. It is fashionable to talk about the "new risks" and there is the problem of the so-called "long tail risks". Since the coverage of these last risks confronts the liability insurance with difficulties, which puts its essence into question, we must pay some attention to it.

73 I have already drawn attention to the difficulties which are encountered in the field of liability insurance with identifying the precise moment in time in which the insured event (liability of the insured) is deemed to take place. This problem becomes particularly acute if a long period of time elapses between the successives stages of the process of the insured becoming liable, *i.e.* the original causal event, the first exposure of the victim, the actual occurrence of the loss and the filing of a claim for damages against the tortfeasor or against his liability insurer[106]. Asbestos-cases were typical illustrations of the problem, and so were certain drug cases and especially the sad case of the so-called D.E.S.-daughters. Apart from the problems related to the establishment of causality between today's losses and their decade-old causes and apart from the questions raised by the development of the state of the art between the time of the occurrence of the original damage causing act and the actual incurring of liability, the main problem for the insurance industry is that of identifying the trigger, *i.e.* the event which links the liability to the appropriate insurance policy (*i.e.* the insurance policy which governed the risk "at the right time").

74 To cut a long story short, the prevailing solution that has been applied by the insurance industry to solve possible problems arising out of such long tail risks has been simply to cut off the tail, that is, to conceive a structure of coverage where the policy covers all the claims that are filed during the policy period, regardless of the time when the allegedly tortious activity took place. By virtue of such clauses, the trigger is the filing of the claim: we call them "claims made"-policies, as opposed to "loss occurrence" policies that give coverage for the losses that occurred within the duration of the policy, and as opposed to insurance policies on "act committed" basis, that give coverage if the initial liability creating act or event took place during the time of the policy[107].

75 Claims made policies appear to solve the time-lag problem for the insurer. They offer the advantage, as Kenneth Abraham from the University of Vir-

[106] For an overview of the problem and the fierce debate around the question, see J. Spier/O. Haazen, *Aansprakelijkheidsverzekering op claims-made grondslag* (1996).

[107] For a general situation of the problem and a comparative oversight of the solutions, see H. Cousy/H. Claassens/C. van Schoubroeck (eds.), *Assurance de la responsabilité: couverture dans le temps* (series of Centre for Risk and Insurance Studies, CRIS), (1997), p. 356.

ginia notes in his book on "Distributing Risk" that they can be priced more easily and that the need for long-term provisions is eliminated[108]. They also offer advantages to the insured who benefits from an up to date insurance policy instead of having to fall back upon an old and probably outdated insurance coverage of a long forgotten insurer. But here again the solution (claims made policies) in turn gives rise to yet again other problems.

Claims made policies have met with outright distrust and fierce opposition from certain courts and legislators. An example of a legislative reaction was found in the original version of the Belgian non-marine insurance contract Act of 25 June 1992. According to the (now obsolete) (mandatory) rule of art. 78 of this Act, the insurer is (was) obliged to honour the claims filed after the expiration of the contract, if the "événement dommageable" had taken place during the course of the contract. Under heavy pressure from the insurance and especially the reinsurance industry, the rule was changed in 1994, when the existing mandatory rule was replaced by a rule installing a system of coverage on loss occurrence basis, with an obligatory extension of coverage for claims filed within three years after expiration of the contract[109].

Even more dramatic was the reaction of the French *Cour de Cassation*, that in a series of decisions starting in 1990 declared the so-called "clause de réclamation" illicit and thus void. According to the *Cour de Cassation* civil liability insurance must obligatorily guarantee that the damages which find their origin in an event during the contract period are covered, irrespective of the date when the loss occurs or when the victim files a claim[110].

It is reported that the insurance industry has not submitted to the *Cour de Cassation*'s ruling at least in the sense that a continued use is made of the "clause de réclamation" in a number of liability policies handling the flood of new and increasing liabilities. **76**

And so I come to our third (and final) concern about the uneasy cohabitation between liability and liability insurance. Remember that our first question was **77**

[108] K. Abraham, *Distributing Risk. Insurance, Legal Theory, and Public Policy* (1986).

[109] To be more precise, art. 78 holds a double regime. For – let us say – consumer risks-coverage must be given on loss occurrence basis with unlimited posteriority coverage (coverage of claims filed after the end of the duration of the policy). For all industrial risks, art. 78, § 2 allows the insurer to give coverage on claims made basis but in that case posteriority coverage for a period of three years after termination of the policy must be given, if the loss occurred during the policy period or if the damage causing event was signalled to the insurer before the end of the contract.

[110] For a detailed analysis and critical evaluation of the "jurisprudence" of the French *Cour de cassation*, starting with the seven decisions rendered on 19 December 1990, and references to the (extensive) doctrinal comments, see *LAMY Assurances*, (sous la direction de J. Kullmann), nos. 1292–1312. See also the comments of J. Bigot in [1991] *R.G.A.T.*, 155 and in [1991] *J.C.P.*, II, no. 21656; C. Delpoux, Assurance responsabilité civile et application de la garantie dans le temps, [1993] *Risques. Les Cahiers de l'Assurance*, nos. 14, 72; H. Groutel, L'extermination des clauses limitatives dans le temps de la garantie des assurances de responsabilité civile, [1991] *Responsabilité Civile et Assurance*, Chr. No. 4 and Chr. No. 81; Y. Lambert-Faivre, La durée de la garantie et portée de la nullité des clauses "réclamation de la victime, [1992,] Dall., Chr. 13.

whether liability insurance would not be likely to disturb the deterrence function of tort law. The present question is whether insurance is capable of living up to the other principal goal of tort law which is compensation, given the fact that the realm of tort liability has dramatically expanded over the last decades and that society does make an increasing appeal on tort liability to obtain compensation for accidental harm (*cf. supra* nos. [34]–[35]).

Our previous question was whether liability insurance could live up to the changes in the nature of the insured risks. Our present question is whether insurability can handle the changes in the law of tort[111].

78 And these changes have been manifold and important, as I do not have to explain or illustrate to this audience.

"Expanding liability" refers to the transition from fault to strict liability; it refers to the rising levels of recovery, to the increasing number of tort actions, to the expanding circle of plaintiffs and defendants.

Expansion of liability also refers – more recently and more strikingly – to the relaxation of causal relationship (or of the proof thereof) and to the creation of cases of retroactive liability (cases thus whereby a defendant is declared liable on the basis of today's standards of liability which did not exist at the time when he acted.

79 In their comprehensive and important book on the insurance problems related to expanding liability (in the framework of a research project for the Dutch Insurers' Association)[112], Faure and Hartlief explain how the problem is not as simple that it can be solved by applying some simple cures to the law of tort. Imposing "caps", *i.e.* legally fixed maximum amounts of recoverable damages (*e.g.* for non-economic losses, or for punitive damages) may lead to giving the wrong degree of incentives to preventive action. Moreover there may be other objections from a legal and policy order since full compensation is the traditional privilege of the victim who can prove that the defendant is liable in tort.

80 An even more fundamental critique comes from Priest who sees no cure in lingering with the tort liability system. In his well known article in the Yale Law Journal on the causes of the U.S. insurance crisis in the eighties[113], Priest explains that by artificially expanding tort liability, legislators and courts have induced people to trust on liability insurance and to abandon their own first party insurance coverage. According to. Priest the problem lies with the essential structure of liability insurance. In liability insurance the insurer covers the liability of his clients for losses suffered by third persons. In such a condition it is far more difficult for the insurer to achieve the right degree of differentiation, in other words, to achieve sufficiently narrow risk pools, than is in the

[111] *Cf.* P. Widmer (*supra* note 39), p. 162.

[112] M. Faure/T. Hartlief, *Verzekering en de groeiende aansprakelijkheidslast. Een juridisch, gezondheidskundig en economisch onderzoek naar ontwikkelingen met betrekking tot het aansprakelijkheidslast en de consequenties voor verzekeraars naar aanleiding van de werkgeversaansprakelijkheid voor bedrijfsongevallen en beroepsziekten* (1995), pp. 373.

[113] G. Priest, The Current Insurance Crisis and Modern Tort Law, [1987] *Yale Law Journal*, 96.

case of first party insurance. Because of these difficulties risk pools are too broadly defined in liability insurance, and that means that the risk pools run a danger to "unravel". What is meant by this is that because of the (inevitable) inaccurate risk pooling, the members who represent lower risks, thus the good risks, will drop out, leaving the insurer with the nightmare of an insured population of only bad risks.

Priest concludes that the insurance crisis can only be stopped if substantive standards of liability are redefined in such a way that they do not take compensation into account and exclusively focus on the accident reduction goal.

I am afraid that, in essence, this conclusion comes down to saying that the two **81**
essential goals of tort law, deterrence and compensation, are not compatible and cannot be simultaneously achieved. One of the goals must be sacrificed for the other. For the adepts of the economic analysis of law there is no doubt that deterrence must be the dominant goal. In this view redistributive effects, more generally, redistributive solidarity must be banned from the liability system and the liability insurance system. If a system of redistributive solidarity is to be organised let it be done by the appropriate and transparent mechanism (like taxation). In any event, liability insurance is not the place to do it.

Personally I do not think that it is very realistic to expect such a development given the fundamental lines in the "great expectations" of society and the paradigms underlying our law of tort to which I have referred at the beginning of my lecture.

In addition I do not think that it is very wise to want to totally exclude redistributive solidarity from the mechanism of tort law and liability insurance. It is my impression that a strong societal desire exists that redistributive solidarity is taken care of at the same time as the other goals of the accident law system. I am inclined to think that some degree of (redistributive) solidarity should remain inside the fabric of other important instrument's of justice, like tort law and liability insurance. Must one indeed not fear that when solidarity as a goal is expelled from such mechanisms as accident law, it may be lost altogether, and not be recovered in a sufficient degree by specifically designed redistributive systems?

It would appear to me that successful institutions in society are those that succeed in pursuing several worthy goals simultaneously. In such case compromises are of course inevitable. And compromises are acceptable as long as none of the different conflicting goals is entirely neglected. I think that efficiency, prevention and accident reduction are goals which should be constantly borne in mind in the architecture of the structure of tort law, but I sincerely believe that it is wrong to make them the only or principal goal of tort law.

I finally believe that somehow the corrective justice argument is of perennial value and that it would run against the corrective justice principle to reduce the goals of tort law to its retributive or deterrence aspects.

82 I therefore conclude that both compensation and deterrence goals must be pursued, be it at the cost of the many, largely unsolved dilemma's that I mentioned. In her enchanting collection of early masters commentaries to the great issues of the French law of torts, Suzanne Carval talks in her introduction about the search for replacing "l'équilibre établi par le Code entre réparation et moralisation"[114]. I believe that the combination of liability and liability insurance did, for a long time, constitute such an equilibrum. My conclusion is that the marriage between tort law and liability insurance is a way to achieve the different compromises and that this marriage should stand. What is new is that we may not pretend that this marriage is the only way to achieve the complicated and delicate combination of goals, and it may very well be that marriage must henceforward tolerate the existence of alternative forms of cohabitation.

83 The discussion of the situations in which these alternative formulas of taking care of accidental harm must play a useful role, is the object of another, and probably even longer lecture than the present one. A reflection on this subject could be carried out alongside a critical appraisal of the following alternatives.

First there is the formula of what I would call *insurance without liability.* That would be the solution of generalized first party insurance. Generalized first party insurance for accidental harm comes very close to some of the basic aspects of social security, which follows a philosophy and a dynamic of its own and is the object of another debate than the one we are carrying out now[115].

A second formula is that of *compensation without insurance.* What I mean by that is the compensation fund formula[116]. There is certainly a place for compensation funds perhaps not as a radical alternative to liability insurance, but rather in a complementary or supplementary role to insurance (I am thinking of guarantee funds, advance payment funds). It may also offer a solution in cases where either the damage is collective or where it is impossible to trace the origin of the damage to any one single causal agent[117].

A third formula of *third party insurance without liability,* better known as "direct insurance" ("assurance directe"). What is referred to is a kind of personal accident insurance that is bought by the person or agent who causes the

[114] S. Carval, *La construction de la responsabilité civile* (2001), p. 10.

[115] Although these existing interesting links between the two systems, *e.g.* where the social security institutions are entitled to carry out (subrogatory or other) recourse actions against liability insurers (see M. Faure/T. Hartlief, *Social Security versus Tort Law as instruments to compensate personal injuries: a Dutch Law and Economics perspective*, mimeographed paper, edited by METRO, Maastricht (25 Sept. 2000).

[116] See the extensive Dutch literature on the subject matter, and inter alia L. Dommering van Rongen, *Schade vergoeden door fondsvorming* (1996); M. Faure/T.Hartlief, Een asbestfonds als alternatief voor aansprakelijkheid van de werknemer?, [1996] *Sociaal Recht*, 38.

[117] For some further analysis and some sobering down conclusions (in the sense that in the end compensation funds give rise to similar problems as insurance formulas), see M. Faure/T.Hartlief, Compensation Funds versus Liability and Insurance for Remedying Environmental Damage", [1996] *Review of European Community and International Environmental Law*, 323; M. Faure/T.Hartlief, Een schadefonds als alternatief voor aansprakelijkheid en verzekering?, [1998] *RMThemis*, no. 7, 211 *et seq.*

harm or causes the risk on behalf of the potential victims. One must admit that the formula has a number of attractive features. Direct insurance takes care of compensation, without obliging the victim into a difficult liability suit against a defendant who is either too close (like your doctor), or too far away (like the polluter), to fight against. The formula also avoids the problems that arise where there is no clear liability of any given defendant (like in many cases of environmental damage). The formula also allows a certain degree of deterrence in sofar as the premium can be made responsive to the insured's behaviour.

The formula of "direct insurance" even appears to be in accordance, at least with a broad version of corrective justice, since compensation is financed by the insurance effort of the defendant.

D. Epilogue

Let us not jump too hastily to conclusions and strong statements, not even at a 84
solemn occasion like this one.

The combination of tort liability and liability insurance is still an extremely useful and a powerful institution, with its moments of glory, and its weaknesses.

Bringing the study of the two of them together in one institute for tort law and insurance as was done with the creation of the European Centre of Tort and Insurance Law (ECTIL) is both a very good idea and a challenging undertaking. We do wish the institute the very best of luck.

Reports

I. Austria

Barbara C. Steininger[1]

A. Legislation

1 In the year 2001, there were no major developments in Austrian tort law legislation. Therefore, only a few smaller legislative changes will be mentioned in this section:

1. Abolition of § 866 *Allgemeines Bürgerliches Gesetzbuch* (Austrian Civil Code, ABGB)

2 According to the general rule of § 153 ABGB minors will be responsible for their actions if they have reached the age of 14, but § 866 ABGB provided that a minor, who pretends to have contractual capacity, will only be liable if he has reached the age of 18. The *Kindschaftsrechtsänderungsgesetz* 2001 (Act changing the law of parent and child, KindRÄG) changed the age of attaining majority from 19 to 18 years and in the course of this KindRÄG, § 866 was abolished.

3 On account of the abolition of § 866 it is now unclear if minors will already be liable for *culpa in contrahendo* as from the age of 14.[2] It seems that the legislator did not take this consequence into account.[3] The rules on legal capacity have the purpose of protecting minors. A liability for *culpa in contrahendo* as from the age of 14 would counteract this protective purpose.[4] Thereupon, minors should generally not be liable for *culpa in contrahendo*. A liability of minors for misleading their partners as to their legal capacity should only be possible if § 1310 ABGB applies.[5]

[1] I would like to express my sincere gratitude to Prof. Koziol for all his support.

[2] For this solution compare P. Bydlinski, *Bürgerliches Recht I Allgemeiner Teil* (2nd edn. 2002), no. 2/39; J. Weitzenböck, Die Handlungsfähigkeit Minderjähriger nach dem KindRÄG 2001, insbesondere in Angelegenheiten medizinischer Behandlung, in: S. Ferrari/G. Hopf (eds.), *Reform des Kindschaftsrechts* (2001), p. 4.

[3] Compare the *Erläuternde Bemerkungen* (explanatory commentaries, EB) on art. I subs. 83 of the *Regierungsvorlage* (government bill, RV), 296 *Beilagen zu den stenographischen Protokollen des Nationalrats* (BlgNR) XXI. *Gesetzgebungsperiode* (legislative period, GP).

[4] H. Koziol, Bürgerliches Recht I (12th edn. 2002), p. 60.

[5] Compare H. Koziol (*supra* note 4), p. 60

2. Modification of § 275 *Handelsgesetzbuch* (Commercial Code, HGB): Auditor's Liability[6]

One of the legislative changes to be mentioned is the modification of § 275 HGB on auditor's liability, which entered into force on 1 January 2002. The former version of § 275 HGB provided a cap of ATS 5 million (€ 363,364) for liability of auditors. The new provision does still foresee caps but first, the amounts are now considerably higher and second, a distinction between slight and gross negligence as well as between companies listed or not listed on the stock exchange has been introduced: In cases of slight negligence, damages will be limited to € 2 million and if the company is listed on the stock exchange to € 4 million for one audit. In cases of gross negligence damages are limited to five times these amounts. 4

However, the explanatory remarks of the draft bill[7] explicitly point out that the question of liability towards third persons is not commented on and that a clarification of this question remains for court practice and future legislation. Therefore, it is unclear if § 275 only focuses on contractual liability or if it also concerns liability in tort towards third persons. Still, the text indicates liability towards third persons, as it includes a distinction between companies that are listed on the stock exchange and such that are not. Moreover, the *Oberster Gerichtshof* (Austrian Supreme Court, OGH) in a recent case[8], which however, still concerned the old legal situation, decided in favour of liability towards third persons. 5

3. *E-Commerce-Gesetz* (E-Commerce Act, ECG)

With the *E-Commerce-Gesetz*, which entered into force on 1 January 2002, the Directive 2000/31/EC on certain legal aspects of information society services, in particular electronic commerce, is implemented in Austria. The ECG provides limitations of the liability of service providers. While the Directive only concerns mere conduit, caching and hosting, the ECG also provides limitations of liability concerning search engines and hyperlinks. 6

The ECG almost literally adopts the wording of the Directive: § 13 ECG corresponds to art. 12 of the Directive and states that in case of mere conduit a service provider will not be liable if the provider neither initiates the transmission nor selects the receiver nor selects or modifies the information. Basically under the same conditions § 14 ECG excludes liability of providers of search engines. § 15 ECG corresponds to art. 13 of the Directive and provides an exclusion of liability in case of caching. 7

[6] See W. Dehn, Die Haftung des Abschlußprüfers nach § 275 HGB (nF), [2002] *Österreichisches Bank-Archiv* (ÖBA), 377; S. Kalss, Die Haftung des Abschlußprüfers gegenüber Gläubigern, Gesellschaftern und Anlegern, [2002] ÖBA, 187.

[7] RV 641 BlgNR XXI. GP 97.

[8] *Oberster Gerichtshof* (Austrian Supreme Court, OGH) 27 November 2001, 5 Ob 262/01t.

8 § 16 ECG on hosting is based on art. 14 of the Directive and excludes liability of the provider on condition that the provider does not have actual knowledge of the illegal activity or information and, as regards claims for damages, is not aware of facts or circumstances from which the illegal activity or information is apparent. Upon awareness, the provider has to act expeditiously to remove or disable access to the information. Under the same conditions, § 17 ECG excludes liability of providers for creating hyperlinks. According to § 18 ECG service providers are under no obligation to monitor the information which they transmit, store or make accessible and they will not have to seek actively facts or circumstances indicating illegal activity.

9 The meaning of the provision on claims for damages included in §§ 16 and 17 "if the provider is not aware of facts or circumstances from which the illegal activity or information is apparent" is not entirely clear. Probably this points out that claims for damages are only justified if the conduct of the provider was not only unlawful but also wilfully (grossly) negligent.[9] Moreover, the prerequisites for the exclusion of liability are the same for hosting as for hyperlinks although conditions are quite different: someone who creates a hyperlink deliberately selects the target of the link while host providers do not establish any connection in substance with the respective information.[10]

B. Cases

1. *Oberster Gerichtshof* (Austrian Supreme Court, OGH); 30 May 2000; 1 Ob 48/00s[11]: Official Liability Towards the Creditor in Case of an Incorrect Confirmation Declaring a Certain Piece of Land Building Ground

a) Brief Summary of the Facts

10 A municipality issued an incorrect confirmation declaring a certain piece of land building ground. This confirmation was presented to a bank (the plaintiff) by the purchaser of said real estate. Relying on the confirmation, a bank granted a mortgage loan to the purchaser. Consequently, the bank – *i.e.* a third person – suffered pure financial loss as the purchaser was not able to pay back the loan. The bank claims compensation for this loss from the municipality issuing the confirmation.

9 Compare W. Zankl, Der Entwurf zum E-Commerce-Gesetz, [2001] *Österreichische Notariatszeitung* (NZ), 325; compare also R. Schanda, Verantwortung und Haftung im Internet nach dem neuen E-Commerce-Gesetz, [2001] ecolex, 920.

10 Compare W. Zankl, [2001] NZ, 328; *ibid.*, Verantwortlichkeit für fremde Internetinhalte. Altes und Neues zur Gehilfenhaftung, [2001] JBl, 413, *ibid.*, E-Commerce-Gesetz in Sicht, [2001] *Anwaltsblatt* (AnwBl), 461.

11 [2000] JBl, 729; [2000] *Evidenzblatt der Rechtsmittelentscheidungen* in: Österreichische Juristen-Zeitung (EvBl), no. 198; [2001] *Österreichisches Recht der Wirtschaft* (RdW), 18; [2001] ÖBA, 247.

b) Judgment of the Supreme Court

11 The Supreme Court holds that the confirmation is information according to the *Auskunftsgesetz* (Information Act) of *Niederösterreich* (Lower Austria). Without doubt, the purpose of this act is to provide the person seeking information with correct and complete information to adjust his or her dispositions accordingly.

12 The Court then focuses on the question if persons other than the person seeking the information are included in the protective purpose of the norm. The purpose of the confirmation declaring a certain piece of land building ground is first of all to make sure for the purchaser that the land he is going to buy is building ground. Nonetheless, the confirmation also has the purpose of showing the creditor what kind of property the real estate to be purchased is and the extent to which it can serve as security for the loan. More so, as it is common knowledge that real estate is usually financed via loans.

13 If the bank directly obtains such a confirmation to examine if the land can serve as security, the bank can in any case claim compensation for its pecuniary loss. Therefore, it would be inexplicable if the creditor is not included in the protective purpose of a confirmation obtained by the owner for the same reasons. Especially when taking into account that confirmations declaring a certain piece of land building ground are in most cases demanded from the owner of the land for this purpose.

14 Therefore, according to the Supreme Court, the bank is included in the protective purpose of the norm. The court states that the defendant is liable in principle but that it still has to be clarified if there is any contributory negligence on the side of the plaintiff.

c) Commentary

15 The decision has been met with approval in a review article by E. Karner.[12] In this article Karner first deals with the protective purpose of the norm in the field of official liability and emphasizes that the existence of a subjective public right indicates the inclusion of pure economic loss in the protective purpose of the norm. He then draws a comparison with the general principles developed under § 1300 ABGB (liability for advice and information), which also applies in the field of official liability[13]. As *in casu* the municipality was obliged to provide the requested information, there is a special legal relationship, which means that the more severe liability of § 1300 sentence 1 applies. Subsequently, Karner analyses the particular problem that not the person requesting the information but a third person suffers the loss. He comes to the

[12] E. Karner, [2001] ÖBA, 235.

[13] W. Schragel, *Kommentar zum Amtshaftungsgesetz* (2nd edn. 1985), no. 148; P. Mader in M. Schwimann, *Praxiskommentar zum ABGB VIII* (2nd edn. 1997), § 1 AHG no. 77. OGH in *Entscheidungen des Österreichischen Obersten Gerichtshofes in Zivil- und Justizverwaltungssachen* (SZ) 53/83 = [1980] EvBl, no. 216; SZ 57/172 = [1985] RdW, 244 – [1986] NZ, 62.

conclusion that the third person is included in the protective purpose of the norm: The special legal relationship between the municipality and the person requesting the information also has effects on the third person, this is clear for the municipality and the circle of potentially protected persons is sufficiently restricted.

2. OGH; 25 July 2000; 1 Ob 146/00b[14]: State Liability

a) Brief Summary of the Facts

16 The plaintiff, a German national, was refused authorisation to purchase a real property in Eastern Tyrol by the Tyrolean real estate transactions authority in an individual ruling on the basis of the Tyrolean Real Estate Transfer Act (*Tiroler Grundverkehrsgesetz*) of 1993. The ruling of this authority was confirmed in the second instance and it was upheld by the Administrative Court in its decision of 10 May 1996. On 25 February 1997 the ruling was annulled by the Constitutional Court, which had already declared the Tyrolean Real Estate Transfer Act unconstitutional in a decision of 10 December 1996. The plaintiff argues that the ruling was in breach of EC law and claims compensation from the Republic of Austria (*i.e.* from the Federation) under the regime of EC state liability. After requesting a preliminary ruling of the ECJ[15], the court of first instance set aside the claim and the Court of Appeal confirmed this decision.

b) Judgment of the Supreme Court

17 First, the Supreme Court holds that it cannot decide whether state liability claims for breach of Community law are to be decided by the courts of general jurisdiction or by the Constitutional Court in a proceeding according to art. 137 Federal Constitution (*Bundesverfassungsgesetz*, B-VG). The reason for this is that the lower courts have both explicitly declared legal action to be admissible, which makes their decision concerning this question binding for the Supreme Court.

18 The Supreme Court then goes into the question of capacity to be sued. According to the prevailing opinion, the Austrian Official Liability Act (*Amtshaftungsgesetz*, AHG) has to be applied in analogy to EC state liability even in cases of liability for legislative wrong, as there are no special provisions on state liability for breach of EC law. If a legislative act of one of Austria's autonomous member states (*Länder*) is in breach of Community law, the respective Austrian member state (*Land*) and not the Federation will be liable according to § 1 sect. 1 AHG, which has to be applied in analogy. The Court argues that this is in harmony with principles of Community law as the ECJ[16]

[14] [2001] ecolex, 100 with cmt. by B. Jud = [2001] *Juristische Blätter* (JBl), 181 with review article by P. Schwarzenegger [2001] JBl, 161 = [2001] RdW, 18 = [2001] *Zeitschrift für Verkehrsrecht* (ZVR), no. 34.

[15] 1 June 1999, C-302/97 (Konle).

[16] *Supra* note 15.

stated that "in Member States with a federal structure, reparation for damage caused to individuals by national measures taken in breach of Community law need not necessarily be provided by the federal state in order for the obligations of the Member State concerned under Community law to be fulfilled."

The merits of the plaintiff's argument that the Administrative Court would have had to ask for a preliminary ruling were not further discussed as at the time of the Administrative Court's decision, the Tyrolean Real Estate Transfer Act had to be considered as in conformity with EC law. Therefore, there is no causal link between the damage and the fact that the Administrative court did not ask for a preliminary ruling. **19**

As the Federation is not capable of being sued, the Supreme Court denies a right to compensation. **20**

c) Commentary

The main problem in cases of state liability for violation of EC law is, that there are no special provisions on such liability. Consequently, it is, amongst others, unclear, which court will have jurisdiction.[17] As the Supreme Court is bound by the explicit declaration of the lower courts, it cannot decide the interesting question of jurisdiction for state liability claims. In his review article Schwarzenegger[18] criticises the application in analogy of the AHG for the question of capacity to be sued. He argues that an analogy is only admissible in cases of state liability for administrative acts, not however, in cases of legislative wrong. As there is no liability for legislative wrong under Austrian law, Schwarzenegger doubts if the lack of a rule of imputation constitutes an unintended gap in the law and if the AHG is a suitable basis for an analogy. As there was no causal link, the Court did not go into the question if the failure to ask for a preliminary ruling could form a basis for a state liability claim. According to Schwarzenegger, this question has to be answered in the negative as the parties do not have a subjective right to a preliminary ruling. Further Schwarzenegger supports the jurisdiction of the courts of general jurisdiction and agrees with the use of national law (which according to Schwarzenegger might have to be adapted) as substantive basis of the claim. **21**

[17] Next to the courts of general jurisdiction the Constitutional Court is a possibility according to art. 137 B-VG. *Compare* Verfassungsgerichtshof (Austrian Constitutional Court, VfGH) 6 March 2001, A 23/00 et al. (*infra* case 12).

[18] [2001] JBl, 161.

3. OGH; 5 September 2000; 5 Ob 18/00h[19]: Liability of a Court Expert Towards Third Persons

a) Brief Summary of the Facts

22 At the request of the purchaser the plaintiff, a lawyer, drafted an acknowledgement of receipt of the acquisition price to be presented to the vendor. A few days later the purchaser returned the signed acknowledgement. After some time a criminal trial for fraud was started against the purchaser. In the course of this trial, the plaintiff was called as a witness. The defendant acted as court expert in this trial and in his expert opinion he wrongly stated that the acknowledgement had been manipulated after being signed. The plaintiff therefore was confronted with the suspicion of being involved in fraud. Thereupon, the plaintiff ordered four private expert opinions, all of which failed to confirm the suspicion that the acknowledgement had been manipulated. The expert opinions were presented to the purchaser's lawyer and shortly afterwards, the purchaser confessed the fraud and was condemned. The plaintiff claims compensation for the costs of the four expertises and for his own expenses.

b) Judgment of the Supreme Court

23 First the Supreme Court confirms its opinion that an expert who delivers an incorrect (private) expert-opinion is not only liable towards his contractor but also towards third persons if it was clear for the expert that the contractor, when ordering the expert opinion, also pursued interests of this third person. This liability is based on an objective-legal duty of care in favour of the third person. The answer to the question if interests of a third person are pursued depends on the purpose of the expert opinion. The condition for the liability of an expert towards a third person is that the expert has to reckon with dispositions of this third person on the basis of his expert opinion.[20] A court expert is liable to the parties and in a newer decision[21] the Supreme Court stated that a court expert in a court execution is liable to the acquirer.

24 The court argues that the liability of the court expert towards a third person in the case at hand has to be assessed according to the principles developed for the liability of private experts towards third persons. Therefore, the question if interests of third persons are pursued depends on the purpose of the expert opinion. If the suspicion that someone other than the defendant might be the principal or a secondary offender arises either in the course of a criminal trial from the order given to the court expert or in the course of the taking of evidence, the prosecution of this person can be expected, as criminal offences have to be prosecuted *ex officio*. Therefore, according to the Court, this person

[19] [2001] JBl, 227 = [2001] RdW, 77 = [2001] *Der Sachverständige* (SV), 25 with cmt. by H. Krammer. Compare also P. Rummel, Aktuelle Rechtsfragen für den Sachverständigen, [2001] SV, 101 *et seq.*

[20] OGH in SZ 69/258 with further references.

[21] OGH 13 June 2000, 1 Ob 79/00z = [2000] RdW, 661= [2000] EvBl, no. 206.

will be included in the protective purpose of the order of an expert opinion regardless whether this person acted as a witness in the respective trial or not.

The Supreme Court awards compensation for the costs of one of the private expert opinions. **25**

c) Commentary

It can be met with approval that the Court, when assessing the liability of a court expert towards third persons, goes back to the principles developed for the liability of private experts towards third persons. Taking into account these principles, the inclusion of the plaintiff in the protective purpose of the order of the expert opinion seems to be justified. **26**

The decision is in line with the established practice of the Supreme Court[22] according to which court experts are not to be considered as organs in the sense of § 1 (2) AHG. This means that instead of an official liability there will be a direct liability of the court expert. This established practice of the Supreme Court has, however, been met with broad criticism.[23] **27**

4. OGH; 6 October 2000; 1 Ob 12/00x[24]: State Liability

a) Brief Summary of the Facts

In 1995 the plaintiff, again a German national, purchased a real property with a house in Tyrol which should serve him as principal residence and where he was going to run a trading agency. He notified the Schwaz district administration (*Bezirkshauptmannschaft*) of these facts and declared that the house was not going to be used as a "recreational residence". The district administration informed the plaintiff that the acquisition required authorisation according to the Tyrolean Real Estate Transfer Act (*Tiroler Grundverkehrsgesetz*). In a ruling of 19 October 1995 the district administration refused to grant authorisation to the acquisition and argued that this refusal did not infringe the plaintiff's freedom of establishment, as establishment did not presuppose the acquisition of real property. The plaintiff appealed the ruling and the second instance granted the plaintiff authorisation to the acquisition arguing that the plaintiff had rightly invoked the freedom of establishment. The plaintiff holds that – given a correct interpretation of the law – his first declaration would have been sufficient. He therefore claims compensation for his legal expenses on the grounds of violation of the freedom of establishment and discrimination against an EU national from Austria's autonomous member state Tyrol. **28**

[22] OGH in SZ 28/216; SZ 54/19; SZ 58/42 = [1985] JBl, 628 = [1985] EvBl, no. 125; SZ 60/2 = [1987] JBl, 308 = [1987] EvBl, no. 117 all with further references. OGH 24 April 2001, 1 Ob 1/01f (*infra* case 13).

[23] Compare OGH 24 April 2001, 1 Ob 1/01f (*infra* case 13).

[24] [2001] EvBl, no. 51 = [2001] JBl, 322 = [2001] RdW, 148 = [2001] ZVR, no. 83.

b) Judgment of the Supreme Court

29 On request of the court of first instance, the Administrative Court decided that the ruling is unlawful. This decision is binding for the Supreme Court. The Supreme Court therefore only had to decide if the district authority had acted with fault. The Supreme Court stresses that a legal view is not necessarily unlawful if a higher instance does not share this view; all the less does the conduct of the organs of the public entity have to be faulty. However, according to the Supreme Court, a deviation from a clear legal position or from the established practice of the competent highest court, which does not show that it is based on careful considerations, is faulty.

30 The Court holds that if an organ of the public entity does not apply or only incorrectly applies EC-law directly applicable in Austria, this can give rise to an official liability claim. The conduct creating liability may also be seen to disregard the established practice of the ECJ. In the case at hand the district authority's legal view is contradictory to Art. 44 EC Treaty and, moreover, it disregards the practice of the ECJ. On that account, the Court considers the district authority's legal view as being untenable and therefore, the defendant is liable for the plaintiff's extra legal expenses.

c) Commentary

31 It can be met with approval that the Court awarded compensation on the grounds of official liability for breach of EC law, as the Court's arguments concerning the untenability of the authority's legal view are convincing.

5. OGH; 6 October 2000; 1 Ob 62/00z[25]: Product Liability

a) Brief Summary of the Facts

32 The plaintiff ordered concrete from the defendant in order to repair the terrace of his father's house. In his order the plaintiff, who had calculated the quantity of concrete needed and who had worked with concrete before, indicated that he would personally work with the concrete. When the concrete was pumped onto the terrace the plaintiff and a friend of his, who had also worked with concrete before, were standing barefoot in the ankle-deep concrete. The driver of the defendant's delivery truck asked them if they did not have boots, but the plaintiff answered that they did not need any. After a few minutes the plaintiff and his friend noticed that the skin on their feet started to burn slightly. They washed their feet with water and started working barefoot again. Only after their feet started burning seriously did they stop working without boots. The plaintiff suffered serious cauterizations. He claims compensation for his material and immaterial losses.

[25] [2001] ecolex, 41 with cmt. by G. Wilhelm = [2001] JBl, 177 = [2001] EvBl, no. 50 = [2001] RdW, 79 = [2001] ZVR, no. 84.

b) Judgment of the Supreme Court

The Supreme Court discusses if the defendant has violated his duty of instruction according to § 5 sec. 1 subs. 1 *Produkthaftungsgesetz* (Product Liability Act, PHG): This duty of instruction includes a duty to indicate dangerous properties of the product, although this is only necessary if the consumer is in need of protection. According to the Court, the producer can assume that the consumer has the expertise of an average user of this product if the consumer himself calculates the quantity needed and indicates that he will personally work with the product when ordering. Therefore, the producer is generally under no duty of instruction. However, if it turns out during delivery that the consumer does not have the expertise necessary, the producer does have a duty of instruction, as in such cases the specific danger of the product might materialize. 33

Moreover, the producer is vicariously liable for his agent, the truck driver, who did not warn the consumer although he knew about the consumer's lack of experience. On account of the consumer's contributory negligence, the Supreme Court decides that the damage should be split in the ratio of 1:1. 34

c) Commentary

The consumer's need of protection is decisive for the determination of the duty of instruction. The consumer is in need of protection if the producer has to reckon with the fact that persons not familiar with the product will come into contact with it.[26] A typical user of the product will be the standard of assessment.[27] In the case at hand, the producer could first assume that the consumer knew about the dangerous properties of the product. At that time the producer could not know that the consumer was in need of protection. If however, it turns out afterwards, contrary to the first impression, that the consumer does not know the specific dangers of the product and if this is recognizable for the producer, the latter cannot rely on the first impression of a lack of a need of protection. Therefore, the duty of instruction assumed by the court in this case seems to be justified.[28] 35

6. OLG Wien; 27 November 2000; 14 R 149/00k[29]: Damages for Non-Pecuniary Loss

a) Brief Summary of the Facts

The plaintiff, a woman who was at that time 35 years old, was very seriously injured in a road accident. She now is paraplegic from the 6th cervical segment of spinal cord downwards: the mobility of her arms is severely hampered, her trunk is paralyzed for the most part and her legs, bladder and 36

[26] OGH in SZ 65/149. H. Fitz/M. Purtscheller/P. Reindl, *Produkthaftung* (1988) § 5 no. 9.
[27] OGH in SZ 65/149; SZ 67/105; [1999] ecolex, 315.
[28] See also G. Wilhelm, [2001] ecolex, 42.
[29] [2001] ZVR, no. 43; *Ehe- und familienrechtliche Entscheidungen* (EFSlg) 93.623.

rectum are paralyzed completely. She suffered numerous fractures, a loss of sexual function and a loss of earning capacity. The plaintiff needs a wheelchair but even with this wheelchair her mobility is very limited. She can get from her bed into the wheelchair and *vice versa*, dress herself, have a shower and do uncomplicated tasks like making coffee or spreading butter on bread on her own. For all other daily tasks she is reliant on the help of third persons.

b) Judgment of the Court of Appeal

37 The Court of Appeal awards damages for pain and suffering amounting to ATS 2 million (€ 145,346), the highest amount granted until then. The court argues from the function of damages for pain and suffering: that is to form a satisfaction for all the hardship the victim had to endure because of the injury, to indemnify the victim for all the pain and to put the person injured in a position to gain amenities and facilities as compensation for their suffering and loss of *joie de vivre*. Taking into account this function, the court reasons that the amount of ATS 2 million (€ 145,346) – though higher than the amounts awarded until then – is not too high.

c) Commentary

38 In comparison to other European countries, damages for pain and suffering in personal injury cases are quite low in Austria.[30] The court explicitly takes this into account and referring to the general tendency to raise the amounts of damages for pain and suffering, it awards the amount of ATS 2 million (€ 145,346).

39 In the meantime, the Austrian Supreme Court has confirmed a decision of the Innsbruck Court of Appeal awarding ATS 2,085,778 (€ 151,579)[31] for pain and suffering. Another case on damages for pain and suffering amounting to ATS 4 million (€ 290,691) is pending before the Supreme Court.[32]

7. OGH; 20 December 2000; 7 Ob 271/00d[33]: Legal Duty to Maintain Safety (*Verkehrssicherungspflicht*)

a) Brief Summary of the Facts

40 A municipality – the owner and keeper of a primary school – entrusted the defendant (a legal person) with plumbing work in this school. During their work, the defendant's employees removed the gratings from the cellar windows and leaned them against a freely accessible waste-paper container placed directly in front of the windows. When the plaintiff was disposing of

[30] Compare E. Karner/H. Koziol, Compensation of Non-Pecuniary Loss under Austrian Law in: W.V.H. Rogers (ed.), *Damages for Non-Pecuniary Loss in a Comparative Perspective* (2001), p. 14; W.V.H. Rogers, Comparative Report in: W.V.H. Rogers (ed.), *Damages for Non-Pecuniary Loss in a Comparative Perspective* (2001), p. 269.

[31] OGH 6 September 2001, 2 Ob 201/01z

[32] OGH 2 Ob 237/01v

[33] [2001] JBl, 525.

his waste-paper, he was carrying it in a banana box thereby blocking the sight of the container. Consequently, the plaintiff did not notice the gratings leaning against the container. As the lid of the container was stuck, he had to use more strength to open it and thereby, the container, which was standing on fixed wheels, moved slightly. In consequence the gratings fell down and injured the plaintiff's foot. He claims compensation for pain and suffering, for his travel expenses when seeing a doctor and a small amount for other expenses.

b) Judgment of the Supreme Court

The Supreme Court first stresses that auxiliary contractual duties of care and protection do not only exist in relation to the contractual partner but also towards certain third persons. A building contractor will have duties of care and protection towards the family or the tenants of the contractor, not however towards persons with whom he only gets in contact socially or through general interaction (*e.g.* the postman). In the present case such a general interaction is at hand. The plaintiff is, thereupon, not included in the protective purpose of the contract. 41

The Supreme Court stresses that there are still certain general duties to maintain safety. Whoever creates a source of danger has to take precautionary measures to prevent damage, but these duties of care must not lead to a strict liability. The duty to maintain safety will oblige the proprietor, in case of building works the building contractor. He will be liable for breach of the duty to maintain safety. If he entrusts other persons with the performance of these duties, he will only be liable according to § 1315 ABGB[34]. Legal persons will however be liable in delict not only for their organs but also for all persons acting for them in a fiduciary leading or supervising position. Merely for those persons doing subordinate work the legal person will only be liable according to § 1315 ABGB. But the legal person might be liable if its organs did not properly control the persons doing subordinate work. *In casu* the employees of the enterprise created a source of danger and did not take precautions or warn about the danger. Being the enterprise carrying out the construction work, the defendant has the duty to maintain safety concerning the source of danger created by its workers. The defendant is liable in delict for the breach of this duty, as its organs did not secure by means of instruction or control that no source of danger is created by the workers. However, the plaintiff acted with contributory negligence and will only be compensated partly (in the ratio of 1:1). 42

c) Commentary

The decision outlines the borderlines of the circle of third persons included in the protective purpose of contracts. The Court's remarks on the duty to take 43

[34] According to § 1315 ABGB the principal will only be liable if he appoints an unfit helper or a helper of whom he knows that he is dangerous. Compare H. Koziol/K. Vogel, Austrian report in the Principles of European Tort Law series, Unification of Tort Law, *Liability for Others* (to be published).

precautionary measures to prevent damage in cases where a prior creation of a source of danger is concerned can be agreed with. This duty always lies on the one who actually controls the source of danger.[35] In the actual case this is the enterprise carrying out the construction work. For the acts of persons doing subordinate work the legal person will only be liable according to § 1315 ABGB, but it will have its own duties of control. As the organs of the enterprise did not fulfil these duties, the liability of the defendant is justified.

8. OGH; 21 December 2000; 2 Ob 339/00t[36]: Burden of Proof in Case of a Violation of a Protective Law (*Schutzgesetz*)

a) Brief Summary of the Facts

44 Starting point of this case was a car-crash between a car kept and driven by the plaintiff and a car kept and driven by the first and insured by the second defendant. The first defendant had at the time of the accident a blood-alcohol level between 1.7 and 2.1%. When approaching the place of the accident the defendant repeatedly left his side of the road but he always managed to get back to his side of the road again. It is however, not ascertainable which car had crossed the middle of the road at the time the two cars collided. Both the plaintiff and the defendant suffered serious injuries and their cars were both severely damaged. The plaintiff claims ATS 83,800 (€ 6,090) as compensation for all her damage. The defendant denies the claim arguing that the accident was the plaintiff's sole responsibility, pleading that his own damage amounting to ATS 125,860 (€ 9,147) should be set off with the claim of the plaintiff.

b) Judgment of the Supreme Court

45 The Supreme Court first of all states that generally whoever claims a right has to prove the facts creating the right and who denies a right has to prove the facts hindering this right. On the basis of this the Court argues that the plaintiff would have had to prove that the defendant had crossed the middle of the road at the time of the crash – this could, however, not be ascertained. The court states that the plaintiff did not prove the violation of a protective law. For this reason, its practice in cases of violations of protective laws when the facts cannot be ascertained does not apply.

46 As the first defendant was the keeper of the car, the Supreme Court applies the Statute on the liability of keepers of railways and motor vehicles (*Eisenbahn- und Kraftfahrzeughaftpflichtgesetz*, EKHG) and argues that the strong influence of alcohol on the driver leads to an "extraordinary operational danger". It can however, not be ascertained if this "extraordinary operational danger" was causal for the car-crash. Moreover, it cannot be ruled out that the plaintiff herself caused an "extraordinary operational danger" by jerking the wheel and

[35] H. Koziol, *Österreichisches Haftpflichtrecht II* (2nd edn. 1984), p. 63; C. v. Bar, *Verkehrspflichten. Richterliche Gefahrssteuerungsgebote im deutschen Deliktsrecht.* (1980), pp. 122 *et seq.*

[36] [2001] JBl, 450 with cmt. by C. Bumberger.

thereby bringing her car onto the left side of the road. Because of all these unclarities the Supreme Court argues that neither the plaintiff nor the defendant succeeded in proving irregular conduct of his or her opponent or in bringing exonerating evidence and decides that the damage has to be split in the ratio of 1:1.

c) Commentary

The Supreme Court denies liability of the defendant for the breach of a protective law arguing that a violation by the defendant of the rule to drive on the right side of the road could not be proven for the time of the crash. It is however – as Bumberger[37] points out rightly in her commentary – clear that the defendant violated another protective norm: namely the prohibition of driving under the influence of alcohol. Moreover, the defendant's conduct was in any case causal for the accident. If the defendant had not used his car while under the influence of alcohol, the accident would not have taken place. The only question is, whether the accident would also have happened in case of alternative lawful behaviour *i.e.* whether the accident would also have happened if the defendant had not been under the influence of alcohol.[38] This is, however, a fact to be proven by the defendant, as this is an argument to exonerate him.[39] The decision of the court denying liability of the defendant for breach of a protective norm is therefore not convincing. **47**

9. OGH; 23 January 2001; 7 Ob 273/00y[40]: Liability of an Expert Towards Third Persons and Their Trustor

a) Brief Summary of the Facts

A bank contributed capital to a company as a dormant partner. According to the partnership agreement, the bank was allowed to do so as trustee for third persons. For the settlement, the amount of indemnification (to buy off the partner) should be fixed on the basis of an expert opinion on the company's value. After cancellation of the partnership agreement, the company asked the defendant to deliver an expert opinion, but the defendant assessed the value of the company incorrectly. Therefore, the trustor of the bank claims compensation. **48**

b) Judgment of the Supreme Court

The Court argues that an expert is liable for the correctness of his expert opinion according to §§ 1299 and 1300 ABGB. In accordance with the established practice of the Supreme Court, the expert will also be liable towards third persons if the one who ordered the expert opinion also pursued interests of this third person and if this was recognizable for the expert. The court leaves open **49**

[37] [2001] JBl, 452.
[38] See Bumberger, [2001] JBl, 452.
[39] R. Reischauer in P. Rummel, *Kommentar zum ABGB* (2nd edn. 1992), § 1311 no. 8; M. Karollus, *Funktion und Dogmatik der Haftung aus Schutzgesetzverletzung* (1992), pp. 396 *et seq.*
[40] [2001] ÖBA, 922 with a review article by E. Karner, Haftung des Gutachters gegenüber Dritten und deren Treugebern, [2001] ÖBA, 893 *et seq*

if in such cases there is a contract with protective purpose towards third persons or if the expert has an objective-legal duty of care in favour of the third person. The Supreme Court holds that it depends on the prevailing practice, which persons will be protected in addition to the one who ordered the expert opinion. Thereby, the purpose of the expert opinion will be important. According to the Supreme Court, it was clear from the purpose mentioned in the expert opinion that it should mainly serve as a basis of trust for the dormant partner and that it should protect the latter's interests. On account of this, not only the bank, but also the plaintiff as trustor, are within the circle of protected persons.

c) Commentary

50 In his generally affirmative review article, Karner[41] examines the dogmatic basis of liability towards third persons. According to Karner, the construction of a contract with protective purpose in favour of third person fails especially in cases of opposite interests and he argues that additionally other reasons indicate that the expert has objective legal duties towards the third person. Karner stresses the importance of the expert opinion's contents for the question of liability of the expert. Further, he deals in detail with the delimitation of the circle of protected persons. Thereby he particularly examines the extension of protection to the trustor, which the Supreme Court presumes without giving any reasons. Karner comes to the conclusion that the trustor is included in the liability towards third persons if it was clear for the expert that the trustor will be concerned in the end. The same applies if the expert opinion is project-related and not delimited to a certain circle of addressees. Because in the case at hand, the expert knew the partnership agreement in which the trust was indicated, Karner agrees with the Supreme Court that the expert has duties of care towards the trustors.

10. OGH; 22 February 2001; 2 Ob 79/00g[42]: Mental Shock of Third Persons

a) Brief Summary of the Facts

51 The plaintiff's son was killed in an accident negligently caused by the driver and keeper of a car, insured by the defendant. Because of the message of his son's death in an accident the plaintiff developed a depression; this psychological injury has to be qualified as illness, in other words, as an injury to health. As a result of the depression the plaintiff had to retire two years earlier than he had planned to. He claims ATS 84,000 (€ 6,000) to compensate for loss of earnings and ATS 166,000 (€ 12,000) for pain and suffering. As a defence, among others, the defendant put forward that the plaintiff had not been a direct participant to the accident and, therefore, had only been damaged indirectly.

[41] [2001] ÖBA, 893 *et seq.*
[42] [2001] ZVR, no. 52 with cmt. by E. Karner.

b) Judgment of the Supreme Court

At first, the Supreme Court confirms its opinion[43] that a person who suffers an "emotional shock", *e.g.* by watching a severe accident involving relatives, may have a personal claim for compensation of pain and suffering caused by this injury if the shock amounts to bodily injury.[44] The Court points out that the precedents only had to deal with cases in which the plaintiff was involved in the accident or saw it happen with his own eyes. Since, in the case at hand, the plaintiff was not involved in the accident and did not see it happen, the OGH had to deal with the decisive question whether the same applies if the third person's injury was caused by the mere message of the death of a person with whom there is a strong emotional bond. The Court is of the opinion that in cases of near relatives[45] the way of receiving the information is not decisive as even the mere message is highly suited to cause mental shock. Therefore, the OGH rules that in cases of mental shock of near relatives of the victim it does not make a difference whether they were involved in the accident or only heard about it. **52**

Furthermore, the Supreme Court had to discuss the defence of the defendant that there was a conflict between the plaintiff and his son. The OGH pointed out that such a situation does not remove the danger of a mental shock caused by the news of the death. The Court especially takes into consideration that because of the fatal accident the father was no longer in a position to re-establish the relationship with his son. **53**

c) Commentary

The Court's decision is based on a widespread doctrine[46] and has been met with approval by commentators[47]. Moreover, it is convincing that the way of receiving the information is not to be held as a decisive factor: At any rate, the tortfeasor violates a duty of care in regard of the near relatives of the victim because his behaviour is highly dangerous for the health of these relatives, even if they are not physically nearby. According to common experience, the mere message of the death of one's child is suited to cause a mental shock which can lead to injury to health. **54**

43 See OGH in [1995] ZVR, no. 46; [1997] ZVR, no. 75. *Cf.* also E. Karner, Rechtsprechungswende bei Schock- und Fernwirkungsschäden Dritter? [1998] ZVR, 182 *et seq*; E. Karner/H. Koziol (*supra* note 30), pp. 5 *et seq.*

44 Compare *infra*, case 14.

45 The Supreme Court stresses that the term "near relatives" need not be discussed as at any rate the son is such a relative.

46 K-H. Danzl, Schmerzengeldansprüche für Angehörige der Opfer des Unglücks von Kaprun? [2000] ZVR, 398 *et seq.*; E. Karner, *Der Ersatz ideeller Schäden bei Körperverletzung* (1999), pp. 102 *et seq.*; H. Koziol, *Österreichisches Haftpflichtrecht I* (3rd edn. 1997), nos. 8/47 and 11/11.

47 See E. Karner's cmt. in [2001] ZVR, 206.

11. OGH, 22 February 2001, 2 Ob 33/01v[48] and OGH, 26 April 2001, 2 Ob 133/00y[49]: Liability of the Keeper of a Toll Motorway

a) Brief Summary of the Facts

55 In the first case the plaintiff crashed into a piece of metal lying on the motorway at the end of a tunnel. This piece of metal, which had originally been fixed at the side of the tunnel, had apparently been hit by another car and been thrown on the road. The plaintiff could not evade it as a truck was driving next to him and, as he only saw it when it was about 20 metres ahead, he could not stop. In the second case the plaintiff crashed into the crash-barrier as the road was frozen over, but the state of the road was not visible. For unclarified reasons this part of the road had not been gritted. Both plaintiffs had bought a so-called *Vignette* that is to say they had paid the time-dependent toll to use the motorway and both of them claimed compensation from the keeper of the motorway. The former argued that the fact that said piece of metal could be loosened was a defect of the motorway and that moreover, the piece of metal should have been removed or otherwise the tunnel should have been closed. The latter plaintiff claimed that the defendant ought to have gritted the road.

b) Judgment of the Supreme Court

56 The first question the Supreme Court had to deal with in both cases was if the limitation of liability on cases of gross negligence provided for in § 1319a ABGB was applicable. The Supreme Court argues that the time-dependent toll is not a duty but a civil payment.[50] Therefore, the established practice of the Supreme Court applies according to which the keeper of a toll road is liable in contract for any degree of fault[51]; *i.e.* the limitation of liability provided for in § 1319a is not applicable in case of the time-dependent toll.

57 As long as this is reasonable, the keeper of a toll motorway is responsible for the road safety of the motorway. However, the duty of care of the keeper of a toll motorway may not be exaggerated.

58 As the relation between the plaintiffs and the defendant is qualified as contractual, the reversal of the burden of proof provided for in § 1298 ABGB applies; therefore, the defendant has to prove that he applied the objective standard of

[48] [2001] *Juristische Ausbildung und Praxis* (JAP), 118 with cmt. by S. Kellner = [2001] JBl, 455 = [2001] ZVR, no. 53.

[49] [2001] ZVR, no. 90.

[50] VwGH 27 February 1998, 98/06/0002= [1999] *Zeitschrift für Verwaltung, Beilage* (ZfVB) no. 1048; Stolzlechner/Kostal, Das BundesstraßenfinanzierungsG 1996, [1999] ZVR, Sonderheft 5 A, 17.

[51] Compare OGH in [1974] JBl, 262; [1979] EvBl, no. 61; [1982] ZVR, no. 193; [1983] ZVR, no. 58; [1983] ZVR, no. 83; [1990] ZVR, no. 14; R. Reischauer in P. Rummel (*supra* note 39), § 1319a no. 25; F. Harrer in M. Schwimann, *Praxiskommentar zum ABGB VII* (2nd edn. 1997), § 1319a no. 27; F. Messiner, Die Auswirkungen der Aufhebung des erweiterten Haftungsprivilegs des § 1319a ABGB für Straßensondergesellschaften als Mautstraßenerhalter durch den VfGH, [1997] ZVR, 235 *et seq.*

care. If he cannot prove this, he still has the chance to prove that he cannot be subjectively reproached for the non-compliance with the objective standard.

c) Commentary

The decision is in line with the practice of the Supreme Court[52] and has been met with approval[53]. As the liability privilege of § 1319a is based on the ideas of neutrality of interests and gratuitousness[54], it does not seem to be justified if a road can only be used against payment. According to the Supreme Court, the keeper of the toll motorway and the user of this road conclude an onerous contract. Consequently, the liability privilege of § 1319a is excluded in cases of toll motorways and the general rules of liability law apply. The most important consequence of this qualification is the reversal of the burden of proof, as in practice the burden of proof is often decisive in such cases. The keeper of the toll motorway will be liable for any degree of fault and moreover, he will be vicariously liable for employees according to § 1313a ABGB. 59

12. Verfassungsgerichtshof (Austrian Constitutional Court, VfGH); 6 March 2001; A 23/00 et al.[55]: Jurisdiction in Case of State Liability

a) Brief Summary of the Facts

The plaintiffs are all haulage enterprises having their seat in Austria. They claim reimbursement or compensation for tolls they paid for the Brenner motorway, arguing that these tolls were too high. The plaintiffs base their action on national and EC law of unjust enrichment as well as on EC state liability. In a decision of 26 September 2000[56] the ECJ declared that by the way it handled and raised the tolls for the Brenner motorway, the Republic of Austria violated art. 7 lit. b and h of the Directive 93/89/EEC of 25 October 1993 on the application by Member States of taxes on certain vehicles used for the carriage of goods by road and tolls and charges for the use of certain infrastructures. The plaintiffs go before the Constitutional Court and base their action on art. 137 *Bundesverfassungsgesetz* (Federal Constitution, B-VG). 60

b) Judgment of the Constitutional Court

According to art. 137 B-VG the Constitutional Court decides on pecuniary claims, amongst others, against the Federation if these claims are to be decided neither by the courts of general jurisdiction nor by an individual ruling of an administrative authority. As far as the plaintiffs base their claim directly on the national law of unjust enrichment or damages, the courts of general jurisdiction will be competent according to the Constitutional Court. But the plaintiffs also based their claim on Community law. As there are no 61

[52] Compare note 51.
[53] See P. Schwarzenegger's cmt. in [2001] ZVR, 329.
[54] Compare VfGH in [1997] ZVR, no. 91.
[55] [2001] JBl, 441 = [2001] ZfVB, no. 1922 = [2001] ZVR, no. 49.
[56] C-205/98 (Commission v. Austria).

uniform rules for the realization of such claims, national law applies. The Austrian legislator, however, did not regulate the jurisdiction in case of compensation or state liability claims based on Community law. Thereupon, the Constitutional Court argues, that the question has to be solved according to the general principles of jurisdiction to be found in Austrian law. According to the Constitutional Court, the courts of general jurisdiction will be competent if the act of the state organ leading to the claim for compensation or state liability based on Community law was either an act of civil law or if it happened in execution of the law. The Constitutional Court declares that for the whole time in dispute the levying of tolls has to be considered as an act of "private economic administration"[57] of the state or as a civil act of a disembodied legal entity. This means that courts of general jurisdiction and not the Constitutional Court under art. 137 Federal Constitution will be competent to decide *in casu*. The question if the assignment of the amount was an act of civil law or an act in execution of the law therefore, does not have to be decided by the Constitutional Court but by the courts of general jurisdiction, as this does not affect the question of jurisdiction. Moreover, the Constitutional Court holds that even in cases of legislative wrong, the Constitutional Court will only have jurisdiction under art. 137 Federal Constitution if the act leading to the claim is neither an act of civil law of a state organ nor an act in execution of the law but has to be ascribed directly to the legislator.

c) Commentary

62 In the Constitutional Court's decision, again the controversial question of jurisdiction is at hand. The decision has been reviewed by Koziol[58], who stresses that EC state liability leads to an increased liability in relation to national liability law, as EC state liability can at least partly be considered as strict liability. Koziol then outlines the demarcation criteria developed by the Constitutional Court to determine jurisdiction and gives an overview of the acts potentially giving rise to liability. Next to the liability of the Federation for its organs acting in a civil way, he advocates a liability of the Federation for the legislator. In connection with the fixing of the tariff, there had been two parliamentary resolutions expressing the non-binding wishes of the *Nationalrat* (National Council *i.e.* the 1st chamber of the Austrian Parliament). Koziol argues that according to national liability law the *Nationalrat* has to be qualified as instigator (§ 1301 ABGB) if with its resolutions it provoked acts of its organs being in breach of EC law. Taking this into account the question arises which court will have jurisdiction in cases where both, an attribution to an executive organ as well as an attribution directly to the legislator, is possible. The Constitutional Court's decision is according to Koziol in this respect not entirely clear. Koziol argues that the instigation by the *Nationalrat* forms an independent ground of action. If there are two different grounds of action

[57] *I.e.* if the state does not act with *imperium* but uses the legal forms also available to its legal subjects (R. Walter/H. Mayer, *Grundriß des österreichischen Bundesverfassungsrechts* (9th edn. 2000), no. 560)

[58] [2001] *Zeitschrift für Verwaltung* (ZfV), no. 1563.

there are – according to the prevailing opinion – two different matters in dispute which means that a separate enforcement through a court is possible. According to Koziol in such cases the plaintiff must be at least given the opportunity of a procedure before the Constitutional Court if claiming a wrongful act of an executive organ is less favourable for the plaintiff than claiming a wrongful act of the legislator. Koziol argues that, in accordance with the prevailing opinion concerning the matter of dispute, the plaintiff should always have the choice.

Generally it can be noted that an initiative of the legislator would be highly desirable in order to clarify the various controversial questions arising in connection with state liability claims.[59] **63**

13. OGH; 24 April 2001; 1 Ob 1/01f[60]: No Official Liability for Court Experts

a) Brief Summary of the Facts

The defendant acted as a court expert in a liability trial. Because of his incorrect expert-opinion, the claim was finally dismissed. The plaintiffs of this first trial now claim compensation from the court expert. The court of first instance rejected the claim, arguing that – contrary to the established practice of the Supreme Court – a court expert has to be considered as an organ carrying out sovereign acts according to the *Amtshaftungsgesetz* (Official Liability Act, AHG). The person suffering the damage can claim official liability, but according to § 9 sec. 5 AHG he or she cannot bring a claim against the organ. The Court of Appeal confirmed this decision. **64**

b) Judgment of the Supreme Court

According to the established practice of the Supreme Court, court experts are not to be considered as organs in the sense of the AHG,[61] as they themselves do not decide but only supply the court with evidence through their expert opinion. Although the Court had implied a possible change of this established practice criticised in the literature in an earlier decision[62], the Supreme Court now confirms the established practice. The Court argues, that by creating § 141 sec. 5 *Exekutionsordnung* (Act on the execution of judgments and titles, EO) providing a liability of a court expert in a court execution towards the acquirer and all other persons involved, the legislator supports the established practice. According to the Supreme Court the decisive reason to confirm the **65**

[59] So also H. Dossi, [2000] ecolex, 237. Compare the government programme of the current Austrian government, which contains a provision on the creation of such rules (an English version of the programme is available at http://www.austria.gv.at/e/).

[60] [2001] JBl, 788 with cmt. by P. Rummel; [2001] *Der Sachverständige* (SV), 131 with cmt. by H. Krammer; [2001] ecolex, 834; [2002] RdW, 19.

[61] OGH in SZ 28/216; SZ 54/19; SZ 58/42 = [1985] JBl, 628 = [1985] EvBl, no. 125; SZ 60/2 = [1987] JBl, 308 = [1987] EvBl, no. 117 all with further references.

[62] OGH 19 January 1999, 1 Ob 349/98z = [1999] JBl, 672.

established practice is that the legislator introduced[63] the conclusion of liability insurance as prerequisite for being entered in the list of court experts. The Court states that thereby the legislator has made clear that he approves the court's established practice excluding court experts from official liability, as the liability insurance would otherwise only serve to secure the Federation's claim for regress towards the court expert. The court argues that this is not the purpose of the duty to have liability insurance. The only purpose of this duty is to ensure the protection of persons suffering damage on the ground of incorrect expert opinions of court experts.

c) Commentary

66 The decision has been criticised by commentators.[64] The Court's argument that court experts cannot be considered as organs in the sense of the AHG because they do not decide on their own but only supply the court with evidence, whereas the Supreme Court applies the Official Liability Act (AHG) in case of official experts (*Amtssachverständige*), is not convincing.[65] An incorrect expert opinion of a court expert can only cause damage if the judge adopts this opinion.[66] The state uses experts to substitute the judge's lack of qualification outside his own subject field. This means the court expert acts as an assistant of the judge.[67] Therefore, the court expert has to be considered an organ according to § 1 sect. 1 AHG.

67 The Supreme Court does not deal with these arguments but refers to the recent amendment of two different acts. According to the Court, these amendments clearly show that the legislator supports the established practice of the court. But the intention of the legislator is not as clear as the Court argues. First of all, as the court itself stresses, § 141 sect. 5 EO is not applicable to a medical expert opinion in a civil damage suit like the one at hand. The argument considered as being decisive by the court, namely that if the Official Liability Act applies, the liability insurance would only serve to secure the Federation's claim for regress towards the court expert, cannot convince either. Like Krammer rightly stresses in his commentary,[68] this compulsory liability insurance does not secure the same protection of the victim as an official liability of the court expert: at the time the expert opinion was given in the case at hand there was not yet a compulsory liability insurance for court experts and, moreover, not all persons acting as court experts are registered in the list of court experts. Therefore, not all of them are obliged to take out compulsory liability insurance.[69]

[63] *Bundesgesetzblatt* (Federal Law Gazette, BGBl), I 1998/168: § 2 sect. 2 subs. 1 and § 2a sect. 1 to 4

[64] H. Krammer in [2001] SV 133; P. Rummel in [2001] JBl, 790.

[65] Compare also OGH 27 March 2001, 1 Ob 25/01k = [2001] JBl, 722.

[66] R. Reischauer in P. Rummel (*supra* note 39), § 1299 no. 23.

[67] Compare A. Zechner, [1986] JBl, 417 *et seq.*; R. Reischauer in P. Rummel (*supra* note 39), § 1299 no. 23.

[68] H. Krammer in [2001] SV, 134.

[69] H. Krammer in [2001] SV, 134; P. Rummel in [2001] JBl, 790.

On account of all this, it has to be agreed with Krammer[70], who argues that for the question whether court experts are organs in the sense of the AHG, the fact that part of the court experts are obliged to have compulsory liability insurance and that in case of official liability for court experts their liability insurance would only serve to secure the Federation's claim for regress, is not decisive. 68

14. OGH; 16 May 2001; 2 Ob 84/01v[71]: Compensation for Pain of Grief Which Cannot be Qualified as Illness

a) Brief Summary of the Facts

The first and the second plaintiff are the father and mother of an eight year old girl who was run over and killed by a truck. The first defendant is the truck driver, the second defendant is the keeper of the truck and the third defendant is the keeper's liability insurer. The father of the girl had been informed by a neighbour and found his daughter lying on the street. The surgeon informed him that his daughter was dead and that she had not had any chance of surviving. The girl's mother, who was at that time pregnant with twins, went to the site of the accident with her husband and there, she also saw the dead child. Both plaintiffs grieved considerably and the girl's mother was even further burdened through complications in her pregnancy. Their grief can, however, from a neuro-psychological point of view be qualified as a normal reaction. The plaintiffs claim compensation for pain and suffering. 69

b) Judgment of the Supreme Court

At first, the Supreme Court confirms its opinion[72] that near relatives of an accident victim, who suffer an "emotional shock" may have a personal claim for compensation of pain and suffering. Compensation has, however, only been awarded if the shock could be qualified as an illness. A claim for compensation for mere emotional damage, *i.e.* in cases where like in the one at hand the grief of the relatives cannot be qualified as illness, has up to now been denied.[73] 70

[70] H. Krammer in [2001] SV, 134.

[71] [2001] ZVR, 73 with cmt. by E. Karner = [2001] JBl, 660 = [2001] *Arbeits- und Sozialrechtskartei* (ASoK), 323 with cmt. by L. Stärker = [2001] ecolex, 669 with cmt. by E. Helmich. See also A. Fötschl, [2001] *Versicherungsrecht Beilage Ausland* (VersRAI), 60.

[72] See OGH in [1995] ZVR, no. 46; [1997] ZVR, no. 75; [2001] ZVR, no. 52 with cmt. by E. Karner (see above, case 10). *Cf.* also E. Karner, Rechtsprechungswende bei Schock- und Fernwirkungsschäden Dritter? [1998] ZVR, 182 *et seq*; E. Karner/H. Koziol (*supra* note 30), pp. 5 *et seq.*

[73] F. Bydlinski, [1965] JBl, 246 and 251; K.-H. Danzl, in K.-H. Danzl/K. Gutiérrez-Lobos/O. F. Müller, *Das Schmerzengeld in medizinischer und juristischer Sicht* (7th edn. 1998), pp. 141 *et seq.*, *ibid.* Schmerzengeldansprüche für Angehörige der Opfer des Unglücks von Kaprun? [2000] ZVR, 398; R. Reischauer in P. Rummel (*supra* note 39), § 1325 no. 5, § 1327 no. 4. *cf.* also OGH in [1987] ZVR, no. 23; [1995] ZVR, no. 46. In favour of compensation for pure emotional harm: H. Koziol, (*supra* note 46), no. 11/11; E. Karner, Rechtsprechung bei Schock- und Fernwirkungsschäden Dritter? [1998] ZVR, 182 *et seq.*; *ibid.*, Schmerzengeld für Angehörige, [2001] ecolex, 37; *ibid.*, cmt. to [2001] ZVR, no. 52 (see *supra* case 10), [2001] ZVR, 208 *et seq.*; C. Huber, Antithesen zum Schmerzengeld ohne Schmerzen – Bemerkungen zur objektiv-abstrakten und subjektiv-konkreten Schadensberechnung, [2000] ZVR, 218, 229 *et seq.*

71 Now the Supreme Court argues that this forms a gap in the law to be closed by analogy. According to the Supreme Court it can be derived from § 1331 ABGB (damages for sentimental value in case of damage to property), § 1328 ABGB (compensation in cases of sexual abuse), § 1329 ABGB (compensation for deprivation of liberty) and § 213a ASVG (compensation for someone injured by an accident at work or an occupational disease, so-called compensation of integrity – *Integritätsabgeltung*[74]) that comparable immaterial damage not being a physical injury can be compensated only in cases of gross negligence or intent. Moreover, the extent of the duty of compensation is enlarged in cases of gross negligence or intent according to the general rule of § 1324 ABGB.

72 The Supreme Court therefore arrives at the conclusion that the grief about the loss of a near relative not leading to a physical injury according to § 1325 ABGB can only be awarded if the tortfeasor acted with gross negligence or intent. In cases of slight negligence or strict liability the grounds of imputation are not strong enough to award compensation for mere emotional damage.

73 As there was neither gross negligence nor intent involved in the case at hand, the plaintiffs were not compensated for their non-pecuniary loss.

c) Commentary

74 The Supreme Court's decision has been met with approval by commentators.[75] It is a consistent further development of the court's practice concerning mental shock of relatives. If the grief can be qualified as an illness, near relatives will be compensated according to § 1325 ABGB. If however, their grief can be qualified as a normal reaction, they will only be awarded damages in case of gross negligence or intent, *i.e.* if the grounds for imputation are very strong.[76] The decision, nevertheless, leaves some questions open: what is meant by near relatives; is contributory negligence of the person killed to be taken into account and will there also be compensation for near relatives in cases of very serious injuries? For the question of contributory negligence Karner[77] convincingly argues that it should be taken into account. Since the quality of being a near relative is decisive for the claim, it should also be taken into account for the question of the extent of the claim.

74 E. Karner/H. Koziol (*supra* note 30), p. 11.

75 E. Karner, [2001] ZVR, 287; L. Stärker, [2001] AsoK, 323; A. Fötschl, [2001] VersRAI, 60. Critical E. Helmich, [2001] ecolex, 668.

76 See E. Karner's cmt. in [2001] ZVR, 287.

77 [2001] ZVR, 289.

C. LITERATURE

1. P. Apathy, Deliktshaftung und Gesellschaft bürgerlichen Rechts, *Krejci-Festschrift* (Manz, Wien 2001), p. 427

Apathy examines the delictual liability of civil law associations (*Gesellschaften bürgerlichen Rechts*). Here, as in the case of legal persons, the question of interests pursued for the benefit of a separate estate is at hand. Because of this, Apathy arrives at the conclusion that civil law associations will be liable for their representatives. 75

2. E. Bernat, Unerwünschtes Leben, unerwünschte Geburt und Arzthaftung: der österreichische "case of first impression" vor dem Hintergrund der anglo-amerikanischen Rechtsentwicklung, *Krejci-Festschrift* (Manz, Wien 2001), p. 1041

Starting from the Austrian leading decision in this field,[78] Bernat discusses the 76
problem of compensation for wrongful birth and wrongful life. He discovers a pleasingly wide uniformity of results in Austrian and Anglo-American law and agrees with the Austrian Supreme Court that a claim for damages for wrongful life of a person born handicapped has to be rejected. Contrary to the Supreme Court, Bernat advocates a solution where parents cannot only recover the additional expenditure caused by a handicapped child but do so even if the birth of the child is not an extraordinary burden for the parents.[79] In conclusion, Bernat stresses that it should always be examined whether the protective purpose of the norm violated by the physician includes the pecuniary loss of the parents.

3. A. Kletečka, Tauerntunnelkatastrophe: Haftung nach dem EKHG, [2001] ZVR, 219

On 29 May 1999, a car-crash involving several cars and trucks led to a fire in 77
the Austrian Tauern-tunnel. The author analyses the liability according to the Statute on the liability of keepers of railways and motor vehicles (*Eisenbahn- und Kraftfahrzeughaftpflichtgesetz*, EKHG) for the vehicles involved in the accident. He examines if and under which conditions the EKHG applies to a stationary vehicle. Kletečka argues that the danger on which the liability according to the EKHG is based cannot be confined to the speed of a vehicle but stems from the vehicle's participation in traffic in general. After analysing the practice of the Supreme Court, he arrives at the conclusion that the EKHG will apply to a vehicle stopped in front of a red traffic light on a motorway.

[78] OGH 25 May 1999, 1 Ob 91/99k = [1999] JBl, 593 = [1999] *Recht der Medizin* (RdM), no. 23 = [1999] RdW, 781.

[79] For a divergent opinion see F. Bydlinski, Das Kind als Schadensursache im Österreichischen Recht, in: U. Magnus/J. Spier (eds.), *European Tort Law. Liber amicorum for Helmut Koziol* (2000), pp. 29 *et seq*

78 In order to establish whether liability is excluded according to § 9 EKHG because of an unavoidable event, Kletečka then examines the question if there was an "extraordinary operational danger", which would preclude an exclusion of liability. According to the Supreme Court in case of an "extraordinary operational danger", the danger regularly and necessarily connected with the operation of a vehicle is increased by further circumstances which are not due to the normal operation of the vehicle. Kletečka denies the existence of such an "extraordinary operational danger" if a vehicle has stopped in front of a red traffic light on a motorway. Moreover, the orderly haulage of dangerous goods can – according to Kletečka – not be considered as an "extraordinary operational danger". But if a vehicle is pushed into another vehicle, this will have to be considered as "extraordinary operational danger".

4. D. Kocholl, *Punitive Damages in Österreich. Über Schadensprävention und Privatstrafe im Zivilrecht* (Neuer Wissenschaftlicher Verlag, Wien 2001)

79 The introductory section of this dissertation from Innsbruck starts with a description of punitive damages (pp. 18 *et seq.*); the author then considers the separation of civil law and criminal law (pp. 19 *et seq.*), the functions of tort law (pp. 22 *et seq.*) and he explains his method and his premises (pp. 30 *et seq.*). Kocholl attaches special importance to the economic analysis of law and to the idea of prevention, which is emphasized by the economic analysis.

80 In the second section Kocholl somewhat briefly describes the present situation in Austria and Germany (pp. 39 *et seq.*), which is characterized by the idea that tort law has a compensatory function. Kocholl criticises the "dogma" of the compensatory function and proposes that punitive damages be accepted. He attempts to show that even existing legislation recognizes punitive damages and refers to § 87 *Urheberrechtsgesetz* (Copyright Act) and § 53 (3) *Markenschutzgesetz* (Trademark Act), which in case of violation of intangible property rights provide compensation amounting to twice the adequate fee for the use of the right. Moreover, he refers to the necessity of protecting personal rights effectively. According to Kocholl insufficient compensation of non-pecuniary loss and law enforcement costs speak for the introduction of punitive damages. However, it remains open why these problems should not be solved by a proper extension of damages for non-pecuniary loss and by the rules of unjust enrichment.

81 The third part (pp. 79 *et seq.*) focuses on EC law, the ECJ and the ECHR. Kocholl mentions state liability and argues that EC law demands of national courts to grant punitive damages in certain cases. Thereby, he somewhat neglects the prerequisite stressed elsewhere, namely that this only applies if the respective national law accepts punitive damages. To prove that EC law accepts punitive damages, Kocholl further mentions the rule providing for a minimum compensation in the case of overbooked scheduled flights; but this rule concerns the area of contract in which liquidated damages and penalty payments are generally known.

The fourth section (pp. 93 *et seq.*) is dedicated to the situation in England and Wales and is concluded by an excursus on punitive damages in the United States. 82

In the fifth section (pp. 123 *et seq.*), Kocholl examines the advantages and disadvantages of punitive damages. Again he stresses the idea of prevention and argues that the acceptance of punitive damages can also be justified through Wilburg's flexible system. He does however, not sufficiently take into account, that Wilburg only pointed out on which grounds *a damage that has already occurred* can be shifted to the wrongdoer. Moreover, Kocholl leaves open the fundamental question if there should also be punitive damages in cases where no damage occurred as the wrongdoer only attempted to commit a tortious act. Only if this is the case, can the purpose of prevention really be achieved. But this would mean that any connection with tort law would be lost. 83

The sixth section (pp. 143 *et seq.*) deals with the field of application of punitive damages. Kocholl in particular stresses the protection of intangible rights and personal rights. The sections seven and eight contain further legal policy proposals as well as a prospect for the revival of punitive elements and protection of legal interests through prevention of damage. 84

5. H. Koziol, Ein europäisches Schadenersatzrecht – Wirklichkeit und Traum, [2001] JBl, 29

Koziol points out that the directives of the EU and the decisions of the European Court of Justice are leading to a problematic harmonisation of legislation, being very selective and without overall idea. As a result, an unpleasant inconsistency of the legal systems is caused. Therefore, Koziol feels that drafting a fundamental concept of tort law is a necessity. For the realisation of such a project he recommends following the idea of a "flexible system" as suggested by Wilburg. 85

6. H. Koziol, Die Bereicherung des Schädigers als schadenersatzrechtliches Zurechnungselement? *Festschrift für F. Bydlinski* (Springer, Wien 2001), p. 175

Generally, a clear borderline is cut between the law of damages and the law of unjust enrichment. The law of damages deals with compensation of loss suffered, whereas the law of unjust enrichment focuses on skimming off benefits gained in an unjust way. Koziol however, tries to point out that enrichment is also of considerable importance for the law of damages. In doing so, he refers to Wilburg who considers the rule embodied in Austrian law (§§ 921, 1447 ABGB) that no one should be enriched by the loss of someone else, as being an argument of legal policy though not as a principle. Furthermore Koziol stresses that various legal systems contain indications of the importance of enrichment as a factor for the imputation of damage. He refers to the Caroline-judicature of the German BGH (*Bundesgerichtshof*, Federal Court of Justice), to the decision of the House of Lords in *Attorney General vs. Blake and* 86

Another as well as to art 6:104 of the Dutch BW (*Burgerlijk Wetboek*, Dutch Civil Code). Above all he underlines the importance of the treatise *Anspruch und Ausgleich* (1999) by Christiane Wendehorst, in which she demonstrates the interrelation between compensation of damage and the existence of benefits.

87 Koziol argues as follows: In the law of damages the imposition of a duty of compensation upon the wrongdoer requires significant reasons of imputation. However, much lower prerequisites are attached to the duty to restore benefits unjustly gained. According to Koziol this is justified, as skimming off benefits is a considerably milder legal consequence than the compensation of damage. If therefore, the indemnification is covered by a benefit gained by the wrongdoer through the act giving rise to liability, a duty of compensation could, according to Koziol, more easily be imposed.

88 This position could have several consequences of importance next to the skimming off of benefits under the law of unjust enrichment: If the wrongdoer has gained a benefit through a wrongful act, he would have to prove that the damage caused is lower than his benefits. Therefore, if the amount of damage cannot be established, this would be to the detriment of the wrongdoer. Moreover, there is a certain range in the assessment of damages, especially concerning the assessment of immaterial damage. This range could be used in favour of the person wronged as far as this would be covered by the benefits gained by the wrongdoer. Finally the borderlines of adequacy and of the scope of protection would have to be drawn wider as long as the benefits cover the damage.

7. H. Koziol, Schadenersatz für den Verlust einer Chance? in: *Festschrift für Hans Stoll* (Mohr Siebeck, Tübingen 2001), p. 233; also published in: [2001] *Zeitschrift des Bernischen Juristenvereins* (ZBJV) 137, 889

89 In this comparative paper Koziol first presents particular categories of loss of chance cases: of gain, of litigation and of recovery. By the example of lost chances of recovery he points out the basic problems: if the patient is able to prove the predominant probability of causation by the physician he will receive full compensation; if the patient fails to prove this, he will receive nothing. Therefore, minimal differences in probability lead to results which are completely opposite to each other. The theory of *perte d'une chance*, which is supported mainly in France, tries to avoid this unsatisfactory result. However, this theory has a decisive imperfection: chances are not independent objects of legal protection, the impairment of which would lead to a liability to pay damages. Referring to the theories developed by F. Bydlinski, Koziol proposes a solution based on alternative causation: If on the one hand, the conduct of the defendant was wrongful, culpable and to a high degree concretely dangerous for the impaired interests and if on the other hand, it is highly probable that the disadvantage can be attributed to an event to be borne by the plaintiff, there will be partial compensation according to the rules on joint responsibility.

8. H. Krejci, Amtshaftung für den Verlust BWG-widriger Investitionen in eine Bank? [2001] *Österreichisches Bank-Archiv* (ÖBA), 461

Krejci discusses a specific case on official liability of the Federal Republic for breach of the state's duty of banking supervision. The case particularly raises the question of the scope of the violated rule (*Rechtswidrigkeitszusammenhang*): A credit institution fighting to survive accepted an investor with dubious funding sources and the banking supervision authority tolerated "the saviour of ill repute". Nevertheless, the bank went bankrupt and "the saviour" now wants to recover its lost investments from the Federal Republic on the grounds that the supervision authority should have forbidden its engagement. Krejci rightly points out that such damage is not covered by the scope of the rule. 90

9. P. Schwarzenegger, *Staatshaftung. Gemeinschaftsrechtliche Vorgaben und ihre Auswirkungen auf nationales Recht* (Neuer Wissenschaftlicher Verlag, Wien 2001)

In the first part of the book (pp. 21–175) Schwarzenegger describes the development of state liability under EC law. He differentiates three phases in the judicature of the ECJ (Francovich–Faccini Dori, Brasserie–Denkavit, Comateb–Rechberger) and he points out clearly how the ECJ increasingly specified the conditions and consequences of liability. 91

In the second part of the book Schwarzenegger focuses on the regulating powers of the Member States (pp. 177–242). He discusses in which way the person harmed will have to be compensated and deals with procedural enforceability on the one hand and the substantive basis of the claim on the other hand. He points out that enforcement will in any case have to take place before national courts and according to the national procedural rules. Regarding the more difficult question of the substantive basis of the claim, he examines in which way the doctrine of state liability is binding on legislators and courts in the Member States. Schwarzenegger reaches the conclusion that both Community law and national law could be a possible basis of the claim. According to the subsidiarity principle, national law conforming to Community law could be used. Rules in breach of Community law would have to be adjusted; as long as this adjustment has not taken place, the relevant rules of Community law would form a directly effective legal basis of the claim. As far as there are no national rules, the Member States would – according to Schwarzenegger – be obliged to create such rules; Community law would then form the legal basis of the claim. In the course of the examination Schwarzenegger considers in particular, the normative basis of state liability (art. 288 EC), the admissability of this further development of the law, the qualification of state liability as primary or secondary EC law, the lack of democratic legitimation of the ECJ and the subsidiarity principle. 92

In the third part (pp. 243–303) Schwarzenegger examines the effects of the state liability judicature on Austrian law. As he points out, there are no special 93 difficulties as far as liability in the field of "private economic administration"[80], sovereign administration and judicative wrong are concerned. The reason for this is that the Civil Code or the Official Liability Act are applied. According to Schwarzenegger, jurisdiction, procedure and the law applicable are problematic as Austrian law does not know a liability for legislative wrong. The explicit exclusion of a liability for wrong of the highest courts would in any case be in breach of Community law. Schwarzenegger stresses that the existing unclarities urgently call for a regulation by law. He argues that at the moment there are stronger arguments for the jurisdiction of the courts of general jurisdiction. The Constitutional Court however, did not share this view in a recent decision[81], as it decided that cases of legislative wrong fall under its own jurisdiction. Schwarzenegger compares in detail the conditions of liability under EC law with those under Austrian law and comes to the conclusion that the latter do not always meet the requirements of Community law.

10. P. Schwarzenegger/R. Thunhart, Was kommt nach den fiktiven Heilungskosten? [2001] *Österreichische Juristen-Zeitung* (ÖJZ), 673

94 The authors discuss the consequences of a change of an established practice of the Supreme Court, now rejecting compensation for fictitious medical costs. Schwarzenegger/Thunhart examine the problems caused by the wrongdoer's duty, acknowledged by the Supreme Court, to grant the victim an advance payment for the therapeutic treatment. Especially the question of reclaim if the victim does not take medical treatment is at hand. The authors do not mention that under the condition that payment is secured, the problem might be solved by committing the wrongdoer to meet only obligations already accrued.

95 Moreover, the authors discuss if the person injured can choose between compensation for medical costs or compensation for the pain and suffering that would continue if he or she does not undergo medical treatment. According to Schwarzenegger/Thunhart the damages for pain and suffering should be diminished to a large extent even if these damages are lower than the medical costs in order to urge the person injured to take appropriate and reasonable treatment and in order to avoid a commercialization of health. This solution does however, have the questionable consequence of depriving persons injured of the free choice they would also have had in cases of injuries to be borne by themselves.

96 Finally they discuss if a person injured, who on his or her own demand received damages for pain and suffering first, can later claim compensation for medical costs instead. Schwarzenegger/Thunhart answer this question in the positive. This solution does however, lead to considerable difficulties because the claim for compensation for medical costs against the tortfeasor is passed to

[80] See *supra* note 57.

[81] 6 March 2001, A 23/00, (see *supra* case 12).

the social insurer by way of legal cession while it is the tortfeasor who can reclaim the damages for pain and suffering from the person injured, which means that a setoff is impossible.

11. R. Thunhart, Totalschadensberechnung bei Neuwagen [2001] ÖJZ, 270

Thunhart discusses the problem of assessment of damages in cases of total wreckage of a new-car. The loss of value of a new-car is disproportionately high in the beginning. In case of a total wreckage shortly after the purchase, the party wronged will only receive the market value of the car, which is considerably lower than the acquisition price. Thereby, the party wronged will be burdened with the disproportionately high loss of value. If the tortfeasor acted with gross negligence or intent, the subjective assessment of damages allows, according to Thunhart, to take into account that the party wronged intended to keep the car for a few years, which means that he or she would only have suffered a considerably lower loss of value. Thunhart argues that in cases of gross negligence or intent, damages have to be calculated by deducting the aliquot part of the loss of value until the planned date of resale. This means that the amount of damages will depend on the intended date of resale. According to Thunhart the owner of the car does not have to bring full proof concerning this date but it will suffice to show probability. 97

12. A. Wirbel-Rusch, *Telemedizin. Haftungsfragen* (Verlag Österreich, Wien 2001)

Wirbel-Rusch discusses the question whether possible claims in the field of tele-medicine can be solved satisfactorily within the existing Austrian legal system. First the author analyses the legal relationship between the tele-doctor and the patient as well as the treating physician or the hospital. If there is no contractual relationship between the tele-doctor and his patient, the tele-doctor acts as vicarious agent of the treating doctor/hospital. 98

Wirbel-Rusch deals in detail with the liability for giving advice as well as for the required care of the involved physicians. She points out that the necessary skills of the treating doctor in case of emergency should be such that he is able to perform the operation on his own or to seek the assistance of a qualified physician within due time. The tele-doctor as well as the treating physician have a duty of supervision over the hospital staff. Furthermore, it is necessary to inform the patient about possible technical faults and the resulting consequences. This duty can be fulfilled either by the tele-doctor or the treating physician. According to the author, the tasks of operating and supervising the instruments do not have to be performed by the tele-doctor. The responsibility for occurring faults lies with the technician and not the physician. If there is no individual negotiation, the parties must apply Art. 4 of the EC Convention on the Law Applicable to Contractual Obligations, which states that the question of liability is determined by the legal system of the country where the tele-doctor is located. Wirbel-Rusch comes to the conclusion that the existing 99 legal rules suffice for the carrying out of tele-medicine. The legislator does not have to pass new laws for dealing with liability cases.

II. Belgium[1]

Dimitri Droshout[2]

A. Legislation[3]

1. Compensation of Vulnerable Victims of Traffic Accidents[4]

Since 1995, the Belgian legislator has introduced a specific regime compensating vulnerable victims of traffic accidents in which a motor vehicle is involved.[5] With the exception of drivers of motorised vehicles, every victim of a traffic accident (either a passenger driving along a motorised vehicle, a cyclist or a pedestrian), as well as the victim's *ayants droit*, can invoke the newly introduced regime to obtain compensation for personal injury and death. Contributory negligence of the victim is hardly ever taken into account.[6] Compensation is due by the automobile liability insurer of each motor vehicle, which is involved (the French concept of *implication*) in the accident.[7] It is typical for this regulation that the legislator abandoned the clas- 1

[1] This report cannot be regarded as an encompassing case law overview which extensively covers case law and literature concerning Belgian tort law in 2001. It merely provides a brief summary of the most striking tendencies and evolutions observed during the past year. Consequently, it is confined to a discussion of recent legislative initiatives, accompanied by a limited selection of case law and literature. The reader should also be aware that many comments on late 2001 case law were not yet published at the time this report was compiled.

[2] The author wishes to acknowledge his sincere thanks to Prof. H. Cousy for his useful comments and suggestions improving this report.

[3] The vast majority of Belgian legislative acts is available at http://www.cass.be/e-justice, section *gecoördineerde wetgeving/legislation coordonnée*, containing both Dutch and French consolidated texts, as well as an archive with previous version of the current legislation.

[4] See also, C.4, nos. [47]–[52]. For the sake of clarity, case law of the *Cour d'Arbitrage*, which relates to the specific regime compensating vulnerable victims of traffic accidents, is discussed under this heading and not in part B of the present report which highlights some striking 2001 court decisions.

[5] Art. 29bis Act 21 November 1989 on the Compulsory Automobile Liability Insurance, inserted by the Act 30 March 1994 (which entered into force on 1 January 1995), as amended by Act 13 April 1995 (which entered into force on 1 July 1995) and Act 19 January 2001 (which entered into force on 3 March 2001).

[6] See *infra* no. [4].

[7] Under specific circumstances (*e.g.* an accident caused by a non-insured driver), victims will be compensated by the so-called Common Motor Guarantee Fund, financed by the automobile liability insurers.

sical and rather severe causal requirement that a certain set of facts must represent a *conditio sine qua non* for the occurrence of the damage. After the example of the French *Loi Badinter*, the fact that a vehicle is "involved" in an accident – no matter how or to what degree[8] – is sufficient to bring a claim. There is no need whatsoever to prove fault of the driver of the involved vehicle. One talks about "automatic compensation".

2 The newly introduced compensation regime was adapted by the Act 19 January 2001 on the modification of various provisions of the regime concerning the automatic compensation of damage, suffered by vulnerable road users and passengers of motor vehicles. The modifications aimed at enlarging the scope of protection offered by the regime and intended to clarify the initial objectives of the legislator by rewording parts of the article holding the regime.

3 Most importantly, the modified regime allows victims of traffic accidents involving vehicles moving on rails such as trains, tramcars, etc. to address the owner of the involved vehicle on the basis of the specific compensating regime. Claims should not be brought against the liability insurer of the vehicle, since the Act on the compulsory automobile liability insurance does not impose an obligation to take out liability insurance covering vehicles moving on rails.[9] Formerly, damage caused by accidents involving the latter category of vehicles did not qualify for compensation under the specific compensating regime (set aside the hypothesis in which another motorized vehicle was involved as well). The adaptation of the regime was rendered necessary by a 1998 decision of the *Cour d'Arbitrage* (the Belgian Constitutional Court), which considered the exclusion of vehicles moving on rails from the field of application of the new regime to violate the constitutional principles of equality and non-discrimination.[10]

4 The possibility to deny compensation to contributory negligent victims was further narrowed down. Thereto, the already severe rule, denying compensation to victims, aged 14 years or older, whose own unforgivable fault (*faute inexcusable*) was the sole cause of the accident, was rephrased. Actually, compensation can only be refused to victims, aged over 14, who have wanted both the accident and its consequences to happen. It is intended that this definition merely matches cases of suicide or suicidal attempts.

5 Claims can only be brought by victims and by their *ayants droit*, i.e. those suffering damage because of the victim's damage. Drivers and their *ayants droit* cannot appeal on the regime. By the 2001 amendment of the law, the legislator settled the discussion about the question whether a driver can claim compensation in his quality of *ayant droit* of another non-driving victim entitled to compensation under the regime. The current wordings of the regime imply

[8] *E.g.* even a car parked according to all regulations can be considered involved in an accident.

[9] Art. 1 Act 21 November 1989 on the Compulsory Automobile Liability Insurance.

[10] *Cour d'Arbitrage*, no. 92/28, 15 July 1998 (case law of the *Cour d'Arbitrage* is available at http://www.arbitrage.be).

that a driver can obtain compensation in his quality of *ayant droit* of another victim, unless he caused the accident intentionally.

The regime allowed compensation for personal injury, death and for what is called a "functional prosthesis". Since the modification, it also compensates damage to clothes. **6**

The current text explicitly prohibits application of the regime to accidents occurring on strictly private property. **7**

Other modifications were merely intended to clarify the *ratio* of the regime. The present provision clearly expresses that victims can address the insurer of each vehicle involved in the accident. The text explicitly describes a functional prosthesis as "all means used by a victim to compensate bodily injury". Furthermore, the current wording of the regime explicitly states that it applies also whenever a driver intentionally causes an accident. **8**

Less than one year after the recent adaptation, the regime compensating vulnerable victims of traffic accidents has once more become a centre of interest. The new discussion concerns the question whether it would be desirable to extend the protection offered by the regime to drivers. A leading author repeatedly advocated such expansion.[11] Several Members of Parliament put forward an amendment (to a proposed bill) intended to eliminate the exclusion of drivers of motorised vehicles.[12] **9**

Reference must also be made to the request to the *Cour d'Arbitrage* to assess the constitutionality of (the earlier version of) the regime. In a judgment of 19 January 2001, the Liège Police Court[13] submitted to the *Cour d'Arbitrage* the question whether the different treatment of drivers of motorized vehicles (and their *ayants droit*) and other road users violated the constitutional principles of equality and non-discrimination. The Liège Police Court also requested to clarify whether the difference between drivers of motorized vehicles and non-motorized vehicles (*e.g.* cyclists, horsemen) was reconcilable with the aforementioned constitutional principles. In a decision of 23 January 2002, the Court ruled that none of these differences in treatment violates the constitutional principles of equality and non-discrimination.[14] **10**

In 2001, Belgian politicians, the public opinion and the media paid great attention to the high number of fatal accidents and cases of personal injury due to traffic accidents. Likewise, the fact that a considerable and growing number of drivers no longer succeeds in obtaining the compulsory automobile liability **11**

[11] See D. Simoens, nos. [49]–[50].
[12] Chambre des Représentants, *Parliamentary Documents*, 50 1079/004, (parliamentary documents of the *Chambre des Représentants* are available at http://www.lachambre.be).
[13] Liège Police Court, 19 January 2001, *Belgisch Staatsblad* (B.S.) 6 April 2001, (the electronic version of the Belgian official state gazette is accessible via http://just.fgov.be).
[14] Cour d'Arbitrage, no. 23/2002, 23 January 2002.

insurance has become an issue of public interest. An explanation for the growing scarcity of available coverage lies in the next step towards liberalisation, which confronts the Belgian automobile liability insurance sector due to the abolition of the so-called *bonus-malus* system as from 2002. A related reason is to be found in the ever growing tendency to segmentation of the insurance market, ending up in the exclusion of whole segments characterised by bad risk profiles.[15] Indeed, under the pressure of competition, insurers do away with every form of subsidising solidarity so as to end up with a mere mutualisation based on equal chances within smaller groups showing almost homogeneous (and acceptable) risk profiles. The idea to oblige insurers to underwrite automobile liability insurance for drivers with a bad risk profile is gaining field. Thereto, certain Members of Parliament put forward a bill, complementing a driver's obligation to take out insurance with a right of access to the insurance market.[16] According to the proposal, losses caused by underwriting bad risks will be spread amongst all automobile liability insurers. Thereby, subsidising solidarity will be reintroduced into the system explicitly. However, the concept never really disappeared from a macro-economic point of view. It slips back into the existing system because damage caused by non-insured drivers is actually spread over all drivers taking out insurance, since the Common Motor Guarantee Fund, covering such damage, is financed by contributions on the premiums paid by all drivers taking out automobile liability insurance. Moreover, the idea of a right of access to automobile liability insurance can be founded on the idea of universal services, which should be accessible to everybody.

2. Access to the Industrial Accidents Insurance Market

12 The Act 10 August 2001 intended to open up the Belgian industrial accidents insurance market.[17] The act became necessary when the European Court of Justice sentenced Belgium[18] for failure to comply with the obligations imposed by the third non-life insurance Directive.[19] The standing legislation indeed prohibited foreign insurers to enter the market for compulsory industrial accidents insurances. The Belgian legislation held specific requirements concerning financial control applicable to every insurer providing compulsory industrial accidents insurance in Belgium, although such provisions, according to the third non-life insurance Directive, belong to the exclusive responsibility of the home country of the industrial accidents insurer.[20] As a defence,

[15] See H. Cousy, no. [61].

[16] See Proposal to insert art. 19bis into Act 21 November 1989 on the Compulsory Automobile Liability Insurance, Chambre des Représentants, *Parliamentary Documents*, 50 1079.

[17] Act 10 August 2001 on the adaptation of the industrial accidents insurance to the European directives concerning direct insurance other than life assurance, [2001] *Belgisch Staatsblad* (B.S.) 7 September, 30270, implemented by Royal Decree 10 November 2001.

[18] ECJ, 18 May 2000, case no. C-206/98.

[19] Council Directive 92/49/EEC of 18 June 1992 on the co-ordination of laws, regulations and administrative provisions relating to direct insurance other than life assurance and amending Directives 73/239/EEC and 88/357/EEC (third non-life insurance Directive). See J.-M. Binon/ B. Dubuisson, no. [59].

[20] Art. 55 Directive 92/49/EEC.

Belgium held that the Directive only applied to the optional complementary industrial accidents insurance, and that the compulsory industrial accidents insurance forms part of the statutory system of social security, which is explicitly excluded from the scope of application of the third non-life insurance Directive. However, the ECJ clarified that the Directive also applies if private insurers, who are operating at their own risk, function within the framework of the social security system, as is usual in Belgium. Consequently, the Act 10 August 2001 adapted the Belgian legislation to the European point of view and threw open the Belgian industrial accidents insurance market. Thereto, the act reorganised the competences of the supervisory authorities monitoring the industrial accidents insurance sector. At present, the Industrial Accidents Fund no longer exercises prudential control on the industrial accidents insurers. This competence was transferred to the *Office de Contrôle des Assurances* (which takes care of the home country control on the Belgian industrial accidents insurers). The competences of the Industrial Accidents Fund were narrowed down to technical and medical control of specific non-financial provisions allowed by art. 55 third non-life insurance Directive. The Belgian legislator felt obliged to require foreign insurers to have a branch or a representative in Belgium. Moreover, foreign insurers are obliged to provide a bank guarantee at the first request of the Industrial Accidents Fund.

3. Product Liability

The Act 12 December 2000[21] adapted the Belgian Product Liability Act to a European Directive aimed at improving the undermined consumer confidence in agricultural products by including primary agricultural products into its scope of application.[22] Consequently, the former sub-section of art. 2 *in fine* Product Liability Act, holding the exclusion of products of the soil, of stock-farming, of hunting, and of fisheries, which had not undergone initial processing,[23] was abolished. The act entered into force retroactively on 4 December 2000, in order to comply with the time limits imposed by the Directive. **13**

4. No-Fault Compensation in the Health Care Sector

Up till now, Belgium does not know any specific liability regime related to medical malpractice. For several years now, the introduction of a so-called no-fault compensation system in the health care sector has been the subject of discussion. During the first weeks of 2002, the federal government announced that it would put forward a proposal to introduce a no-fault compensation scheme. It is expected that victims of medical accidents will no longer need to prove a fault of a physician, at least if they are satisfied with a limited compensation. **14**

[21] Act 19 December 2000 modifying Act 25 February 1991 on liability for defective products, [2000] B.S. 12 December.

[22] Directive 1999/34/EC of the European Parliament and of the Council of 10 May 1999 amending Council Directive 85/374/EEC on the approximation of the laws, regulations and administrative provisions of the Member States concerning liability for defective products.

[23] See former art. 2, 3rd paragraph Product Liability Act 25 February 1991.

5. Compensation of Victims of Courageous Acts

15 Persons suffering damage while performing an occasional courageous act to save the life of a third person in peril of death, often had to bear their own damage. One thinks particularly of situations in which no one can be addressed in tort for causing the sticky situation rendering necessary the courageous act. It was considered morally unacceptable to leave these persons, who showed a profound sense of responsibility, without compensation. For that reason, the Act 24 August 2001 on the compensation of victims of courageous acts created a possibility thereto.[24] An additional provision was inserted to the sub-section of the Act 15 August 1985[25] which already dealt with the award of particular compensation in cases of damage suffered by members of the police or emergency services, and by persons who rendered assistance in their quality of volunteer. The new provision only applies to persons who render help on an occasional basis, *i.e.* persons who are not professionally involved with safety or cooperating with organisations aimed at providing assistance or aid to third persons. The latter categories were already protected by the Act 15 August 1985. Compensation can only be allowed for those kinds of damage which are explicitly mentioned in the Act 15 August 1985.[26] The compensation is limited to an amount of € 61,973.38.

B. Cases

1. *Cour de Cassation* – Breach of Causation

16 Under Belgian law, causation between a fault (or the required equivalent in cases of strict or vicarious liability) and damage is established if the damage, as appeared *in concreto*, would not have occurred (to the same extent) in the absence of the fault.[27] In other words: judges have to examine whether a certain fault can be considered a *conditio sine qua non* for the occurrence of the damage.[28] Each fault being a necessary cause of the damage equally entitles a victim to full compensation.[29] Consequently, when multiple faults cause the same

[24] Act 24 August 2001 on the compensation of victims of courageous acts, [2001] B.S. 24 October 2001. See L. Cornelis, no. [24].

[25] Chapter III, subs. III on the award of a particular compensation in case of damage suffered by members of the police and emergency services, and persons who voluntarily or occasionally render assistance, art. 42, § 2, 9° and § 4bis Act 15 August 1985 holding fiscal and other provisions.

[26] Art. 32, subs. 1 Act 15 August 1985 holding fiscal and other provisions.

[27] See *e.g. Cour de Cassation*, 30 May 2001, (case law of the *Cour de Cassation* is available at: http://www.cass.be).

[28] The decision in which a causal relationship is denied without explicitly stating that the damage would also have occurred in the absence of the fault will be quashed (see *e.g. Cour de Cassation*, 21 February 2001). The decision in which a causal relationship is denied because the damage could have occurred as well in an hypothesis which does not match the *in concreto* circumstances of the case will be quashed (see *e.g. Cour de Cassation*, 28 March 2001).

[29] A victim's right to full compensation will only be diminished in case of contributory negligence. See *e.g. Cour de Cassation*, 6 June 2001.

damage, the victim can address each tortfeasor to compensate the whole damage.[30] This very victim friendly tenet is known as the "equivalence theory".

In order to limit the effects of this very broad conception of causation, the *Cour de Cassation* accepted, since the late seventies, that a so-called "independent legal cause" cancelled the causal relationship between a fault and the related damage. An independent legal cause could take the shape of legislative, contractual or otherwise legally grounded obligations. The Court developed this doctrine for the first time in the so-called "Walter Kay" decision.[31] The river ship Walter Kay sunk due to a navigational error of the captain of another colliding vessel. The Court held that the authority, which complied with its legal obligation to clear the fairway, was not allowed to recover the accompanying costs from the captain who committed the fault. Contrary to the principles of the equivalence theory, the obligation to clear the fairway was considered to be an "independent legal cause", breaking through the causal relationship between the captain's fault and the damage consisting in the costs related to the clearing of the fairway. This doctrine of the *Cour de Cassation* was the subject of severe criticism, because it implied an inadmissible derogation from the equivalence theory.[32] Because of this jurisprudence, the legislator explicitly attributed the right to recover costs to several institutions (*e.g.* to the civil services). **17**

The Court mitigated its standpoint in a keystone decision dating from 13 April 1988. Since then, an independent legal cause was only considered sufficient to bring about a breach of causation if the obligation, representing the independent legal cause, could not be considered secondary to the tortfeasor's obligation to compensate the damage. **18**

In a series of decisions of 19 and 20 February 2001, the *Cour de Cassation* again changed its position.[33] These cases concerned situations in which governmental authorities or other public bodies continued to pay the salaries of staff members, although the latter were unable to work due to the fault of a third party.[34] In contrast to its former line of thought, the Court rejected argu- **19**

[30] Thereto, multiple tortfeasors will be declared liable *in solidum*. Afterwards, damages will be split up among the tortfeasors in accordance with the contribution of each fault to the occurrence of the damage (and not in accordance with the relative gravity of the faults).

[31] *Cour de Cassation*, 28 April 1978.

[32] During 1984–1985, the *Cour de Cassation* deviated from the Walter Kay doctrine. The Court held that an independent legal cause only broke through a causal relationship if the text or the *ratio legis* of the obligation undoubtedly made clear that the expenditure should finally be borne by the party on whom legally rests the obligation holding the independent legal cause. This evolution was warmly welcomed by legal doctrine. Nevertheless, the Court again changed its point of view (see no. [18]), until 2001 when it finally turned back to the clear standpoint dating from 1984–1985 (see no. [19]).

[33] *Cour de Cassation*, 19 February 2001, C.99.0014.N; *Cour de Cassation*, 19 February 2001, C.99.0183.N; *Cour de Cassation*, 19 February 2001, C.99.0228.N; *Cour de Cassation*, 19 February 2001, C.900.242.N and *Cour de Cassation*, 20 February 2001, P.98.1629.N. Thereby, the Court turned back to its 1984–1985 point of view (see *supra* note 35).

[34] See I. Boone, no. [37] and B. De Temmerman, no. [39].

ments relating to the primary or secondary character of the legal obligation imposing the continuation of payment of the salaries. Now, the Court considered that a legal obligation, even if it imposes continued payments, does not alter the possibility that a causal relationship between the damage, consisting in the continued payment, and a fault of a third party might exist. The Court added that such legal obligation can only break through the necessary causal relationship if the text or the *ratio* of the obligation makes undoubtedly clear that the expenditure should be finally borne by the party appointed by the obligation. Later on, the Court confirmed its revised point of view several times.[35]

2. *Cour de Cassation*, 27 March 2001

20 Mention should be made of a judgment of the *Cour de Cassation*,[36] because the press suggested that this decision held that the non-compliance to obligations imposed by tax law can cause damage to competitors complying with all legal obligations.[37] The Court indeed quashed a decision of the Gent Court of Appeal,[38] which did not allow a fishmonger to claim compensation for damage suffered because his competitors did not comply with many obligations imposed by tax law. The original claim was brought by way of a civil action before a criminal court, judging the infractions to the legal obligations violated by the competitors. However, the *Cour de Cassation* did not pronounce itself on the question whether the non-compliance to tax law can cause damage to competitors complying with all legal obligations imposed upon them, but only held that the fishmonger had a sufficient personal interest to bring such a claim by way of a civil action before a criminal court. Thereby, the *Cour de Cassation* pointed out that the claim of the fishmonger could not be considered to represent an inadmissible *actio popularis* and thus set aside the motivation of the Gent Court of Appeal stating that the interest of the fishmonger coincided with the public interest, which can only be taken care of by the Public Prosecutor.

3. Brussels Court of First Instance, 9 February 2001

21 The Belgian state was sentenced because it became clear that the secrecy of a criminal investigation was broken by an organ of the State.[39] Journalists were informed about the imminent arrest of a member of the bar. They photographed the suspect in the corridor of the court; they were informed about the indictment, etc. The Brussels Court of First Instance allowed compensation for both pecuniary and non-pecuniary loss suffered by the involved member of the bar, who was cleared of the charge afterwards. Damages were set at € 25,000.

[35] *Cour de Cassation*, 29 February 2001 and *Cour de Cassation*, 13 June 2001.

[36] *Cour de Cassation*, 27 March 2001. See G. Siffert, no. [33].

[37] See *e.g.* L. Arnou, no. [22].

[38] Gent Court of Appeal, 26 April 1999.

[39] Brussels Court of First Instance, 9 February 2001, [2001] *Jurisprudence de Liège, Mons et Bruxelles* (J.L.M.B.), 659.

C. LITERATURE

1. General

a) L. Arnou, Belastingontduiking is vergoedbare concurrentievervalsing, [2001] *De Juristenkrant* (Juristkr.) 29, 1.

The title of this article seems to overrate the importance of the discussed decision of the *Cour de Cassation*. See above, no. [20]. **22**

b) H. Bocken, Tort Law, in: H. Bocken/W. De Bondt (eds.), *Introduction to Belgian Law* (2000), pp. 244–273.

A basic introduction to Belgian tort law (introduction, tort and contract, the basis for liability, causation, damage, industrial accidents and traffic accidents). **23**

c) L. Cornelis, Hulp gevraagd, [2001] *Tijdschrift voor Privaatrecht* (T.P.R.), 489–495.

See above, no. [15]. **24**

d) H. Cousy/M. De Graeve, Belgian Country Report in: M. Faure/H. Koziol (eds.), *Cases on Medical Malpractice in a Comparative Perspective* (2001), pp. 84–101.

Six cases on medical malpractice, resolved under Belgian law. **25**

e) H. Cousy/D. Droshout, Non-Pecuniary Loss Under Belgian Law, in: W. V. H. Rogers (ed.), *Damages for Non-Pecuniary Loss in a Comparative Perspective* (2001), pp. 28–53.

A country report discussing the compensation of non-pecuniary loss under Belgian law. **26**

f) H. Cousy/C. van Schoubroeck, *Wetgeving Verzekeringen 2001* (7th edn. 2001).

A comprehensive collection of European and Belgian legislation related to insurance law. **27**

g) E. Dirix, Abstracte en concrete schade, [2000–2001] *Rechtskundig Weekblad* (R.W.), 1329–1335.

The Belgian law of damages classically requires damage to be assessed *in concreto*. Even when damage can only be assessed *ex aequo et bono*, judges are expected to respect the principle of compensation *in concreto*. However, in spite of these principles, damage is often assessed *in abstracto* under the current state of Belgian law.[40] Dirix puts forward convincing examples of both **28**

[40] See below, nos. [40]–[42] (indicative table).

legislation and case law illustrating such compensation *in abstracto*, *i.e.* on the basis of a normative or objective approach. He concludes that compensation *in concreto* (as required by the *Differenzhypothese* of Mommsen) should remain the leading principle of the Belgian law of damages, but advocates that compensation *in abstracto* can play a more important role with regard to the compensation of certain categories of damage (*e.g.* non-pecuniary loss, environmental damage, infringement of intellectual property rights). According to Dirix, judges should have the possibility to turn to an assessment *in abstracto* if they prefer to do so because of the nature of the damage or when a victim suffers difficulties to furnish proof. However, compensation of merely fictitious damage should be avoided. Therefore, the proposal holds that a normative approach can only be applied to establish the height of compensations and not to determine whether a victim effectively suffered damage. Victims will thus still need to prove the existence of damage, but will no longer be required to prove the extent of the damage, which, according to the author, can be assumed to correspond to the extent of the damage usually suffered in similar cases (*quod plerumque fit*). As far the height of damages is concerned, the burden of proof would thus be shifted to the tortfeasor, the latter having the possibility to prove that the actual damage does not run up to the commonly usual extent.

h) B. Dubuisson, Faute, illégalité et erreur d'interprétation en droit de la responsabilité, [2001] *Revue critique de jurisprudence belge* (R.C.J.B.), 28–72.

29 Under Belgian law, the violation of a legal rule is usually said to constitute the objective element of fault. The author thoroughly examines in which situations the violation of a rule can be considered to constitute a fault. More specifically, he pays attention to the application of the law by citizens, by the public authorities and by the judiciary. He discusses the different standards applied when assessing the conduct of each of the aforementioned categories.

i) T. Papart, Le dommage aux choses; J. Tinant/B. Ceulemans, Le préjudice naissant des incapacités temporaires; D. De Callataÿ, Questions spéciales sur le préjudice matériel résultant d'une incapacité permanente; M.-A. Lange/B. Prignon, Le préjudice né de déces; M. Vanderweckene, Nature et évaluation du dommage moral; J.-L. Fagnart, Le Fond commun de garantie automobile; O. Michiels, L'action subrogatoire de l'organisme assureur; N. Simar, Le recours de l'assureur loi; and M. Houben, De la subrogation au droit propre, in: J.-L. Fagnart/N. Simar (eds.), *Assurance, roulage, prejudice corporel* (2001), 336 pages.

30 A yearbook, holding different contributions, *inter alia* related to the compensation of personal injury (temporary and permanent incapacity for work) and death, recourse actions brought by insurers, the Common motor guarantee fund, etc.

j) **P. Lucas, La rationalisation de l'évaluation européenne des atteintes à la personne humaine, [2001] *Revue belge de dommage corporel et de médecine légale* (Con.M.), 53–82.**

The author discusses the compensation of personal injury in Europe (comparative overview, steps towards harmonization already taken, future developments, etc.). **31**

k) **G. Schamps, Le relâchement des liens entre les responsabilités pénale et civile. La mise en danger, distincte du principe de précaution, *Liber Amicorum Jean du Jardin* (2001), pp. 381–429.**

According to the author, causing danger (*la mise en danger*) can function as the decisive criterion if a general principle on strict liability is introduced under Belgian or French law. However, the introduction of such principle will cause problems under Belgian law, given the undesirable effects of the theory holding the unity of the fault concept under civil and under penal law. **32**

l) **G. Siffert, Niet alleen de fiscale administratie kan zich burgerlijke partij stellen in fiscale strafzaken, [2001] *Tijdschrift voor Fiscaal Recht* (T.F.R.), 871–875.**

See above, no. [20]. **33**

m) **H. Vandenberghe/M. van Quickenborne/L. Wynant/M. Debaene, Overzicht van rechtspraak aansprakelijkheid uit onrechtmatige daad 1994–1999, [2001] T.P.R., 1551–1955.**

Fourth edition of the leading and most comprehensive case law overview on Belgian tort law. **34**

n) **W. van Gerven/S. Covemaeker, *Verbintenissenrecht* (2001).**

Standard work on the Belgian law of obligations, which, in its second part, presents a clear and well-structured overview of tort law. **35**

o) **G. Wailliez, Chronique de décisions des juridictions militaires en matière de responsabilité civile (1999–2000), [2001] *Revue Générale des Assurances et des Responsabilités* (R.G.A.R.) no. 13360.**

A case law review discussing the judgments related to tort law given by the Belgian military jurisdictions during 1999–2000. **36**

2. Causation

a) **I. Boone, De arbeidsongeschikte ambtenaar en het regres van de werkgever op de aansprakelijke, [2001–2002] R.W., 217–233.**

See above, no. [19]. **37**

b) R. de Corte, Ommezwaai in causaliteit bij onrechtmatige daad, [2001] Juristkr. 26, 1.

38 See above, no. [19].

c) B. De Temmerman, Aansprakelijkheid, [2001] *Tijdschrift voor Belgisch Handelsrecht* (T.B.H.), 289–290.

39 See above, no. [19].

3. Indicative Table

a) National Federation of Magistrates in the Courts of First Instance and the Royal Federation of the Justices of the Peace and the Police Courts, Tableau indicatif/Indicatieve tabel, [2001] *Tijdschrift van de vrede – en politierechters* (T.Vred.), 194–209/210–225.

40 No statutory definition of pecuniary or non-pecuniary loss is given under Belgian law. Damage has to be defined as the negative difference between the actual situation of a victim and the situation wherein that person would have been if the damage-causing event had not occurred. Once tortious liability is established, a victim is entitled to a so-called *restitutio in integrum*. This general principle implies that a victim should be compensated for its entire damage though not for more and that only the damage as it appears *in concreto* must be compensated. If possible – and if claimed by the victim – damage should be repaired *in natura*. Otherwise, an indemnification will be paid. If the damage cannot be assessed adequately (*e.g.* non-pecuniary loss), it should be compensated *ex aequo et bono* (*i.e.* in fairness), but even then Belgian law holds that the principle of compensation *in concreto* should be complied with.

41 However, in practice damage which is difficult to assess is often compensated on the basis of a normative approach (*i.e. in abstracto*).[41] Already in the early nineties, the Antwerp Court of Appeal started circulating its own tariff. At a national level, the National Federation of Magistrates in the Courts of First Instance and the Royal Federation of the Justices of the Peace and the Police Courts drew up a first overview in 1995. This so-called *indicative table* provides an overview of categories of damage and listings of amounts considered appropriate to compensate for it. Updates of the indicative table were published in 1998 and 2001. The table has no statutory authority and does not have any obligatory effect towards judges (therefore it is called a "table" and not a "tariff"), but nonetheless it provides an overview of the common practice with regard to the compensation of damage which is difficult to appraise. The table was subject to profound criticism because it was reproached to cause an inflation of damages by listing the maximum amounts of compensation paid for specific heads of damage at its time of publication, rather than to reflect the averages. The increase of amounts caused by the publication of the Antwerp tariff was still welcomed positively because it corresponded to a real

[41] See E. Dirix, no. [28].

increase of the cost of living, which until then had not been taken into account. However, the repeated rises of the amounts of compensation caused by the indicative table were not always received the same way.[42] The insurance sector claimed that the 2001 update of the indicative table urges a 5% raise of premiums related to the compulsory automobile liability insurance.

The introduction to the 2001 indicative table *inter alia* describes damage as well as the basic principles of the law of damages, followed by a classification of different categories of damage due to personal injury and a guide to the use of the table. Part I suggests amounts and calculation methods with regard to damage following personal injury, which is divided into two major categories, viz. economic damage (temporary incapacity to work, the need for additional efforts, permanent incapacity, death, economic value of domestic work, aid by third persons, post-professional damage) and loss of well-being (non-pecuniary loss related to incapacity to work, non-pecuniary loss in case of death (including claims *ex haerede*), aesthetical damage, *pretium affectionis*, *pretium voluptatis*). Part II concerns the compensation of common forms of material loss (damage to clothes and luggage, unavailability of a vehicle, loss of a school year, administrative costs, medical cost after consolidation of the damage, funeral expenses). Part III holds guidelines with regard to the technical aspects of compensation (capitalization and the splitting up of damages in amounts related to the periods before and after the moment when consolidation of the damage took place, the applicable interest rate, mortality tables, the use of an indexed compensation, interest). Part IV gives an example of a declaration appointing an expert. Some concluding remarks on the table are made in part V "Comments" (the uncertain nature of damage, the history of the table, the motivation to draw up the table). **42**

b) Indicatieve tabel, [2001] *De Verzekeringswereld* (Verz.W.) Document no. 2, 1–15.

See above, no. [40]. **43**

c) Indicatieve tabel, [2001] *Tijdschrift voor aansprakelijkheid en verzekering in het wegverkeer* (T.A.V.W.), 166–176.

See above, no. [40]. **44**

d) J. Schryvers, De nieuwe indicatieve tabel revisited, [2001] T.A.V.W., 151–165.

See above, no. [40]. **45**

e) J. Schryvers, Nieuw indicatief tarief letselschade: semper altius, [2001] T.A.V.W., 15–17.

See above, no. [40]. **46**

[42] See J. Schryvers, no. [46].

4. Compensation of Vulnerable Victims of Traffic Accidents

a) B. Dubuisson, La loi de 19 janvier 2001, modifiant le régime d'indemnisation des usagers faibles de la route "Cent fois sur le métier", [2001] *Journal des Tribunaux* (J.T.), 585–592.

47 See above, nos. [1]–[11].

b) N. Estienne, La nouvelle réforme du régime d'indemnisation automatique des usagers de la route, [2001] R.G.A.R., no. 13392.

48 See above, nos. [1]–[11].

c) D. Simoens, Het verkeersongevallenartikel 29bis W.A.M., versie 2001: hoelang bestand tegen de nieuwe eew?, [2001] T.P.R., 637–701.

49 See above, nos. [1]–[11].

d) D. Simoens, Schendt het verkeersongevallenartikel 29bis W.AM. de grondwettelijke gelijkheidsbepalingen?, [2001] *Tijdschrift voor Belgisch Burgerlijk recht* (T.B.B.R.), 604–612.

50 See above, nos. [1]–[11].

e) H. Ulrichts, 29bis WAM: de automatische vergoeding van de zwakke weggebruiker… wordt vervolgd, [2001] T.A.V.W., 83–90.

51 See above, nos. [1]–[11].

f) C. Vanschoubroeck, Actualia Verzekeringsrecht – De vernieuwde vergoedingsregeling inzake verkeersongevallen met motorrijtuigen en recente rechtspraak betreffende de bepalingen inzake aansprakelijkheidsverzekering van de wet landverzekeringsovereenkomst, in: Centrum voor Beroepsvervolmaking in de Rechten (ed.), *Jaarboek* (2001), pp. 297–361.

52 See above, nos. [1]–[11].

5. Compensatory Interest on Damages *ex aequo et bono*

53 Many authors paid attention to the changing position of the *Cour de Cassation* with regard to compensatory interest on damages that are awarded *ex aequo et bono*. According to well-established case law of the *Cour de Cassation*, compensatory interest will never be due on the part of a compensation related to damage which will actualise after the date of the judgment.[43] Compensatory interest is only due with regard to damage which has already been suffered by the victim. Consequently, judges have to split up damages in an amount related to the period before the judgment and another part related to the period after the decision. In the late nineties, the *Cour de Cassation* stressed repeat-

[43] See *Cour de Cassation*, 13 June 1983, [1982–83] *Arresten van het Hof van Cassatie* (Arr. Cass.), 1261.

edly that splitting up damages was even necessary in the case of an assessment *ex aequo et bono*.[44] Assigning compensatory interest to the whole amount of a lump sum awarded *ex aequo et bono* was said to compensate future damage. Thereby, the Court tried to stick close to its 1967 decision which pointed out that, even if damage is assessed *ex aequo et bono*, damages should attach to the situation *in concreto* as much as possible. In a series of decisions of September and October 2000, the Court changed its point of view.[45] *E.g.* the judgment of 5 October 2000 did not quash a judgment of the Liège Court of Appeal which did not split up damages awarded *ex aequo et bono*, albeit compensatory interest was assigned on the whole amount of damages.[46] The *Cour de Cassation* motivated this turnaround abolishing the requirement to split up damages *ex aequo et bono* by stating that the court of appeal had taken into account the fact that compensatory interest may not relate to future interest while determining the amount of damages. Furthermore, the *Cour de Cassation* considered that, although the damage will be suffered gradually over the course of time, the damage can be compensated by a lump sum at the time of consolidation, since the damage was certain and fit to be assessed in its entirety.

a) D. de Callataÿ, Splitsing: le début de la fin?, [2001] J.T., 101–103.

See above, no. [53]. **54**

b) J. Schryvers, Ommekeer in de cassatierechtspraak inzake splitsing van een forfait, [2001] *Algemeen Juridisch Tijdschrift* (A.J.T.), 298–299.

See above, no. [53]. **55**

c) J. Schryvers, Revirement à reconsidérer?, [2001] R.G.A.R., no. 13.343.

See above, no. [53]. **56**

d) D. Simoens, Berekening van de compensatoire interesten als onderdeel van een gemeenrechtelijke schadeloosstelling die ex aequo et bono is begroot: een wijziging in de cassatierechtspraak? Draagwijdte van deze wijziging?, [2001] T.B.B.R., 444–454.

See above, no. [53]. **57**

e) B. Wylleman, Vergoedende intrest op forfaitaire vergoedingen voor in de tijd bestendige schade. Splitsen of niet? Het Hof van Cassatie brengt duidelijkheid, [2000] *Recente Arresten van het Hof van Cassatie* (R.Cass.), 295–303.

See above, no. [53]. **58**

[44] See D. Simoens, no. [57], 445 (*e.g. Cour de Cassation*, 8 December 1999, [1999] Arr. Cass., 1597).

[45] *Cour de Cassation*, 13 September 2000; *Cour de Cassation*, 5 October 2000, *Cour de Cassation*, 11 October 2001

[46] *Cour de Cassation*, 5 October 2000.

6. Insurance Law

a) J.-M. Binon/B. Dubuisson, Les implications de l'arrêt de la Cour de justice des Communautés européennes du 18 mai 2000 sur l'assurance contre les accidents de travail, [2001] R.G.A.R., no. 13350.

59 See above, no. [12].

b) Ph. Colle, *Handboek bijzonder gereglementeerde verzekeringscontracten* (3rd edn. 2001), 301 pages.

60 Manual discussing specifically regulated insurance contracts.

c) H. Cousy, De contractsvrijheid op de proef gesteld – van verplichte verzekering naar recht op verzekering, [2001] Verz.W.;/H. Cousy, La liberté contractuelle à l'épreuve – de l'assurance obligatoire au droit à l'assurance, [2001] *Le Monde de l'Assurance*.

61 See above, no. [11].

d) H. Cousy, De ontwikkelingen in het verzekeringsrecht (1964–2000), [2001] T.P.R., 23–54.

62 In this contribution to a special edition of the Belgian Review of Private Law, published at the occasion of the turn of the century, the author examines the evolution of insurance law from 1964 to 2000.

e) J.-L. Schuermans, *Verzekeringsrecht* (1st edn. 2001), 602 pages.

63 The most recent general manual on insurance law.

III. Czech Republic

*Luboš Tichý**

Development of Czech Law of Tort

1. Introduction

As can be seen immediately, the structure of this Report differs from other national reports inasmuch as it does not respect the rules set for the composition and content of individual national contributions. In lieu of an overview of the analysis of the latest development of the law of tort, the Czech report describes, frequently in a superficial manner, the entire history of the law of tort valid on the territory of the Czech Republic. If however we are to submit a contribution and not a mere statement that in recent times or development nothing of any substance has happened, particularly in the realms of case law and literature, the present structure of this Report was inevitable. The fact that the case law and literature have not afforded any special suggestions sufficient for presentation is certainly a striking point to which we shall devote ourselves at the end of our contribution, where we will assay an analysis of the causes thereof. 1

This Report functions primarily as a summary of the development of the law of tort in the Czech and, as appropriate, Czechoslovak Republic from the time of the creation thereof through to the present day (for brevity, we shall refer herein to the Czech Republic, Czech Law and Czech Law of Tort). Because this development has gone through several fundamental changes, the aim of this Report is to analyze certain grounds for these changes, and only then to appraise the changes themselves. Since the said substantial changes in development were of a legislative nature, it has not proved difficult to structure this Report into four chapters mapping out the individual developmental periods, being: the Austrian *Allgemeines Bürgerliches Gesetzbuch* (ABGB), the Civil Code 1950, the period of trial third way based on the Civil Code 1964 and finally the reform of this third way from 1991 (Reform) and the development thereof. 2

* In cooperation with Jiří Hrádek

3 This short statement already evinces one characteristic feature of Czech private law, which significantly differentiates the Czech conception not only from private-law systems of the traditional states of Central and Eastern Europe, but also from the majority of so-called socialist states. Indeed, only the development of the former GDR bears any comparison. This characteristic feature consists in changes made to the written legal arrangement, and the content and significance of these changes, triggering the loss or non-existence of a property belonging to every traditional legal conception – and Czech private law lacks stability and continual, evolutionary development of its legal arrangement. From the structural point of view of the legal system (and thus not from the perspective of content), as well as of the conception of Law of Tort, this feature expressed itself immediately in several ways. The decisive issue if written law, which to a considerable extent is counterpoised against the existing legal arrangement (the codex), which it supersedes. The new arrangement is founded on a new conception, which considerably "devalues" the existing case law and doctrine, which are henceforth utilizable frequently only as evidence of the opposite. Judges and practising lawyers are referred to the text itself of the law, since even before stable case law and quality doctrine have been able to sufficiently develop, they have already been surpassed once more by a variant legislative arrangement. This outcome is one of the causes leading to so-called positivism and formalism, which are evident in the fact that interpretative activity is in fact restricted purely to grammatical construction. Case law does not assay the creation of law or judicial law[1]. This non-existence of creativity leads to a state which reminds one of the denegation of law (*denegatio iustitiae*). This is attested to by, for example, a negative stance towards the interpretation of the general clause in sec. 420 Civil Code 1964, in the sense of grounding responsibility of a manufacturer for damage caused by a faulty good, etc. A further cause of this approach may be a certain level of passivity and restraint amongst the proponents of a doctrine which, with a few exceptions, lacks thorough research and confrontation with western trends, and does not therefore offer any inspirational conceptions. The apologies and explanations of legal theorists consisting in references to the insufficiency of case law are false. These lead to a vicious circle, whose actual cause is the impotence of the Czech legal community.

2. The Austrian *Allgemeines Bürgerliches Gesetzbuch* (ABGB) in the Content of Czechoslovak Tort Law

a) Introduction

4 Act No. 11 of 1918 carried over into the Czech legal code all the existing Austrian regulations, and thus also the ABGB, which was valid on the territory of the so-called historic lands (Bohemia, Moravia and Silesia), *i.e.* in essence on the territory of the present Czech Republic, whilst Hungarian law was valid in Slovakia (the present Slovak Republic) and the Trans-Carpathian Ukraine, which is now a part of the Ukraine. During the period of its validity, *i.e.* until 31

[1] See under 7 of this Report.

December 1950, the ABGB was amended several times, though not in the area of the law of tort. In 1920, work was commenced on a new Civil Code, which was to suppress the entire ABGB, including the law of tort. This attempt, which – as we shall see – did not differ from the ABGB in its conception of law of tort[2], was not successful. Work on the draft ceased in 1931, and the four volumes, 46 chapters, 1353 sections of the draft new Civil Code never became law.

b) Development

The conception of Austrian law is based on principles fundamentally exceeding contractual and extra-contractual liability for damage. Czech legal doctrine and judicial praxis unequivocally affirms this tendency. Both commentary and systematic literature place both types on the same level, or, in other words, reject any differences between the two principles. There is also a clear active tendency to reject the duality of systems of liability. This is evident for example from the critique of Sedláček[3] directed at the Vienna authors (Mauczka, Mataya, Swoboda). Krčmář[4] assayed a certain degree of differentiation, by pointing out the division or existence of the two principles side by side. He went no further, however, than that indication – failing to reach an explanation of the fact. All the less reason to consider elaborating this thought and providing a rationale for the existence of both principles side by side. 5

Judicial praxis seems to be clear. It does not differentiate between the said principles of liability. It does not attempt to differentiate or bring into question the principle incorporated in § 1295 subs.1 of the ABGB. According to the unified system, it was necessary to assess both the responsibility of the contractor according to a contract for work (compensation of damages for fungus on the walls of a house) and a defaulting debtor in the event of a drop in the exchange rate[5]. 6

3. Civil Code/1950, Socialist Law of Tort (1951–1964)

a) Sources

The main source for civil law in the Czechoslovak Republic after 1950 came to be the Civil Code of 25 October 1950, No. 141 Coll., which, as will be 7

[2] See the basic provision (sec. 1114) of the draft:
1) All shall have the right to seek compensation for damages from whomsoever shall have culpably caused such damage thereto, regardless of whether such damage be incurred as a result of breach of obligation ensuing from a legal act or extraneous to such obligation.
2) Whosoever willfully causes damage in a manner contrary to good morals, shall be liable therefore; should, however, harm be incurred during exercise of a rightful entitlement, such person shall be liable only in cases where said exercise of rightful entitlement could have no other purpose than to cause damage. In other cases, liability shall fall to such person as causes damage by exercise of a rightful entitlement only when the bounds set by law are exceeded.

[3] J. Sedláček, *Komentář k čsl. Obecnému zákoníku občanskému* (Koment./Sedláček), pp. 699 *et seq.*

[4] J. Krčmář, *Právo občanské, Právo obligační* (2nd edn. 1932), p. 301.

[5] See the decisions of the Czechoslovak Supreme Court (No. 6207 and No. 2398)

shown later, attempted to facilitate the transformation of the society from capitalist to people's democratic. The Code was composed of 6 parts, 37 chapters and 570 sections.[6]

8 As had been the tradition of civil law in the Czech lands, the new Civil Code did not constitute the isolated source of law, but was supplemented by a range of further promulgatory and supplementary laws. From the matter which is to be discussed hereunder, *i.e.* in reference to liability for damage, it is necessary to cite at least the following regulations: Act No. 63/1951 Coll., on Liability for Damage Caused by Means of Transport, Act No. 66/1950 Coll., on Employment and Salarial Relations of State Employees, wherein sec. 11 provides for compensation of damage caused to the state by employees of the state apparatus, similar provisions being found also in Act No. 88/1952 on Material Security for Members of the Armed Forces, and also liability for damage caused to goods, travel luggage or express parcels during rail transport, liability for damage caused by the state quality inspectorate, but also for example liability of operators of marine vessels. From the host of laws passed even prior to the effectiveness of the new codex, it is possible to cite Act No. 225/1947 Coll., on Gamekeeping, with provisions on liability for damage caused by hunting and game or Act No. 1771/1927 on Compensation of Damage During Cadastral Proceedings. In the context of these regulations, the Civil Code had a subsidiary validity – a set of fundamental rules which could in principle, during later interpretation, also be related to legal norms such as these.

b) Bases for Liability in the Civil Code

9 The introductory provisions of sec. 337 entitled Covenants on Compensation for Damage read: "Whosoever willfully or neglectfully damages another by breach of covenant or other legal obligation shall compensate such damage."

10 Here we find encapsulated the two major categories of liability for compensation of damage caused with culpability. On the one hand we have breach of contractual, covenanted obligation, and, on the other, breach of obligation ensuing from the legal regulations expressing some certain order or prohibition. There is no doubt from the language that liability relates both to breach of covenant and contractual liability, and liability for a wrong under law of tort. The concept of a wrongful act will thus have to include both categories.

11 In civil law, just as in criminal law, the merits of the case serve to determine who is liable. The merits of the case here will involve a collection of subjective and objective circumstances leading to the determination of civil-law liability.[7] These are the basic elements: Subject object, objective aspect, causal

[6] The structure of the Code was as follows: Introductory Provisions, which more or less reflected the new societal foundations, General Provisions with instituted procedures such as representation, legal force, calculation of time and statute-barring, Rights in Rem, Law of Covenant, Probate Law, and Final Provisions both interim and conclusive.

[7] Š. Luby, *Systém a základné tézy občianskoprávnej zodpovědnosti* (1954), p. 48.

connection, damage, and in addition culpability can also be counted amongst them, though this is not a condition for attaching civil-law liability to the subject. According to Knapp[8], the elementary assumptions for the creation of penalties are the existence of a covenant, breach of obligation and causal connection between the conduct of the subject and the breach of obligation. To these can be added the incurrence of damage and causal connection between the breach of obligation and the incurrence of damage.

The incorporation of a legal person is always tied either directly to the law or indirectly to the law in such a way that its incorporation necessitates an expression of will from a body of state administration pertinent thereto under the law. In addition there must be a guarantee that the incorporated legal person will fulfill its social role.[9] Should it fail to do so, it fails to be a legal person. In theoretical terms the question was greatly discussed whether a legal person is competent under the law of tort, whereto the answer was affirmative in view of the fact that a legal person can be viewed as a real company of people. The culpability (fault) which is attributed to a legal person is understood to be the culpability of its bodies and not its employees, since the bodies are liable for the employees under provisions on vicarious liability.[10] **12**

A further inevitable assumption of civil liability is a causal connection between the damage and the act of a given subject. This involves a relationship between conduct and effect, without which conduct the effect would not have occurred, or would have occurred differently than it did. One cannot however confuse the concept of causal nexus with the concept of culpability, since causal connection is an objective phenomenon which arises independently of the will of the subject of the conduct.[11] In order to reliably ascertain the cause of a given consequence it is necessary to isolate the individual causes and effects and thus determine the relevant phenomena for the occurrence of damage. **13**

A further assumption for liability is damage. This may involve either material damage or non-material damage, or, according to another division, material damage or personal damage, though in each case it is always necessary that the injury be expressed in monetary terms. This is also in accord with the definition of damage as all material injuries (losses) expressible in generally equivalent terms, *i.e.* in money. In the event of damage, it is necessary to distinguish actual damage – injury consisting in reduction, decrease, or other devaluation of hitherto existing property (*damnum emergens*) and lost profit – consisting in the injured party's failure to increase his property, which, all else being equal, he would have done (*lucrum cessans*) – pursuant to sec. 354, both forms of damage shall be compensated. Though this does not always have to be the case. In the case of arbitration proceedings on business agreements pur- **14**

8 V. Knapp, Některé otázky odpovědnosti [1957] *Právník*, 98, 69.
9 Reasoning report to act No. 141/1950.
10 Š. Luby (*supra* note 7), p. 210.
11 Š. Luby (*supra* note 7), p. 213.

suant to Act No. 99/1950 Coll., only compensation of actual damage is awarded, not lost profit, as ensues from the special relationship between socialist organizations.[12] Damage is compensated by restoration to the prior state, and, if this is impossible, in money.

15 Wrongfulness is understood by the theory of law to mean conflict with the entire legal codex, and any human conduct can be deemed wrongful, whether culpable or non-culpable. Wrongfulness is always understood to consist in discord with objective law. The Civil Code 1950 itself however recognizes so-called circumstances precluding wrongfulness of action, *i.e.* facts which, whilst they display the features of wrongfulness, do not involve wrongful activity. In sec. 342 we find provisions on necessary means of defence and in sec. 343 extreme emergency. The provisions on extreme emergency however assume that "such person as from himself or from others averts a clear and present danger shall compensate damage; though this obligation shall not pertain to a person that destroys or damages a thing threatening safety where said person did not himself cause such danger." In cases worthy of consideration, the court may then reasonably reduce compensation of damage pursuant to sec. 358. This will occur chiefly in cases where the damage occurred during the states of emergency dealt with under sec. 9 of the Penal Act, *i.e.* with regard to acts whereby some person averts a clear and present danger to the people's democratic republic, the socialist infrastructure, the interests of the proletariat and individuals. Further circumstances precluding wrongfulness of an act include performance of an obligation imposed by legal norm, performance of occupation, exercise of a right, self-help, consent of the injured party, order from a superior or official order.[13]

16 Culpability is not, in contrast to the hitherto described institutions, an obligatory element of every liability relationship. It will always depend on whether the legal code will require culpability itself for such a wrong. Culpability is a legal category dependent on two elements: both the free and rational aspect of the subject. Culpability is precluded even by the want of one of these elements. Legal theory however assumed an interesting stance in relation to legal error, when it declares that a basic knowledge of the law is on the one hand presumed, but if, for personal reasons, such knowledge was actually lacking, *ignorantia juris excusat*.[14]

c) Liability for Fault

17 Under the Civil Code 1950, liability for a culpable act or omission is divisible into three basis categories. Firstly, this involves general liability for a culpable act or omission either willful or even carried out with malice aforethought, secondly liability for chance occurrence, and thirdly presumed culpability of the owner or user of a thing.

[12] J. Blažke, *Náhrada škody v novém československém právu* (1954), p. 30.
[13] Š. Luby (*supra* note 7), p. 125.
[14] Š. Luby (*supra* note 7), p. 132.

The basic arrangement of the first category is set forth in sec. 337, which stipulates that *whosoever willfully or by negligence harms another by breach of covenant or other legal obligation shall compensate damage* and in sec. 338(1), *he shall be liable for damage that causes such by a willful act contrary to principles of good conduct.* The assumption for attaching liability thus consists in the case of the first citation in willfulness and negligence – whilst per contra, a non-willful act contrary to the principles of good conduct does not give rise to any liability. Though there does not exist in law any list of the principles of good conduct, these are adjudged from the general ethics of socialist man.[15] It will always therefore be incumbent upon the judge assessing a specific case to decide what is and what is not in accord therewith. The Act further details chicanery in exercise of a rightful entitlement – indeed in sec. 2 it states: *Whosoever shall injure another by exercise of a rightful entitlement shall compensate damage if he so did with the intention of causing such injury.* 18

Sec. 341 stipulates liability for damage caused by chance attaching to such person as induced such chance, in particular by breach of some regulation or established procedure which are designed to prevent chance damage. This case involves an abridged version of the former § 1311 of the ABGB. If we take a literal interpretation of the language *to induce*, then liability for a culpable act in the case of a chance occurrence is grounded on causal connection and it is therefore possible to attach liability thereto even in the case of a secondary and almost immaterial cause, which however leads to fatal effects. An example could be the theft of a roof tile and the subsequent water logging and collapse of the roof.[16] There exist two exceptions from this principle, being Sections 351 and 480. In these cases liability is precluded provided that the damage was caused by *force majeure*. The principle of chance was interpreted: "An event of chance is an occurrence that is culpably caused and can neither be foreseen in advance.[17]" In a specific case which the court decided, it is not an event of chance if a hunter stumbles whilst firing, since the act of hunting itself requires that certain principles be met, as, for example, that a steady stance be assumed while firing. Therefore it is not possible to stumble and cause wrongful effects by chance. 19

The third category of liability for a culpable act involves primarily a shift of the burden of proof from the injured party to the owner or user of the thing. Such person may release himself from liability, *i.e.* exculpate himself, if he can prove that he exercised the necessary care and attention. The issue of what constitutes due care and attention will be dealt with in connection with liability for a third person. 20

[15] J. Blažke (*supra* note 12), p. 32.

[16] J. Blažke (*supra* note 12), p. 38.

[17] See the decision published under No. 116/1955 in the collection of Court Decisions in Civil Matters

21 In the text itself of the Civil Code one can find examples of strict liability. We refer to sec. 351, according to which "during operations of an especially dangerous nature, the operator shall be liable for damage caused by any such activity of the source of increased danger as externally manifests the danger of the operation." The legislative thus, in conjunction with special laws, provided for general liability for especially dangerous operations. Pursuant to Decision No. 116/1955 Coll., however, especially dangerous operation pursuant to the Civil Code is not understood to mean, for example, hunting with a rifle[18] – but involves only those types of operation where the danger of the operation itself is the source of the increased danger, whether it be because of the special nature of the production process, the hazardousness of the raw materials used, or the risky technical equipment, explosives etc., wherein the general arrangement of liability for damage caused by a culpable act is insufficient. One can also refer to liability pursuant to sec. 346, which treats liability for damage caused by incorrect official procedure. This section itself preempts the promulgatory legislation. The only two regulations which modified this material were the Government Ordinance on the State Quality Inspectorate in sec. 8 thereof and the Cadastral Act of 1927. sec. 346 did not survive to the special law on liability of the state – the promulgatory act was issued only in 1969 under No. 58.

22 Since norms elaborating sec. 346 did not exist, case law had to settle an important issue as to what is and when is it a case of official procedure. We find the solution (somewhat under the influence of its age) once more in the Collection of Court Decisions in Civil Matters under No. 30/1954. According to this interpretation, official procedure involves only that activity of state bodies consisting in the issue of decisions and orders to which all must submit.

23 The majority of the laws governing liability extraneous to the Civil Code are based on strict liability. Probably the clearest example from the period of this Civil Code is liability for damage caused by means of transport, provided for in Act No. 63/1951 Coll.

d) Differences as Against the ABGB

i. Culpability (Fault)

24 The Civil Code/1950 departed from the actual civil-law definition of culpability. Without expressly stating so, it relies on the criminal-law definition.

25 This tendency was then only emphasized by doctrine, which was considerably under the influence of Soviet Civil Law. As Luby[19] states, this question was set entirely unambiguously by Vyšinský, who, in his speech of 16 July 1938, delineated the need to purge the term culpability of its scholastic abstraction

[18] See *supra* note 17.
[19] Š. Luby, *Prevencia a zodpovednosť v občianskom práve* (1957), p. 449.

and all the deformations which ensue therefrom. From that time on, notes Luby[20], Soviet theory of civil law engaged itself with the concept of culpability together with the teaching of criminal law (!). Luby[21] himself makes a sharp tangent away from the traditional doctrine, and criticizes his predecessors, in particular Sedláček[22], who traditionally distinguished culpability according to whether a breach of criminal-law or civil-law norms is involved. Luby[23] even considers this differentiation to be deleterious, since it does not only entail distinguishing between civil-law and criminal-law culpability, but also between a civil-law and a criminal wrong. From the conceptual perspective there is thus no reason, says Luby[24], to distinguish between civil-law and criminal-law culpability – it suffices simply to distinguish willfulness and negligence pursuant to sec. 3 of the Penal Act, and under the concept of willfulness to distinguish direct and indirect willfulness and conscious and unconscious neglect. He repudiates the terms gross, ordinary, and slight negligence. Surprisingly, Blažke[25] assumes a milder stance.

ii. New Additions and Changes

Whilst the Civil Code took over its arrangement of acts in extreme emergencies from the ABGB (§ 1306a), it also introduced provisions on liability for acts of necessary defence (sec. 342), in which case whosoever meets the challenge of an attacker shall not be liable for injury caused to said attacker during necessary defence. It is only remarkable that compensation of damage is in no manner delimited and put into some connection with the acts of the attacker. Neither is there any sense here of the principle of proportionality. **26**

The Civil Code/1950 newly sets forth liability for especially dangerous operations (sec. 351) and liability during unfair competition in business relations (sec. 352). **27**

e) Appraisal

It is remarkable to what extent the communist code is loyal to the extant Austrian arrangement (§§ 1293–1341), and in particular to § 1295, which both ensues from the Austrian conception of liability for damage and takes over certain specific provisions from the ABGB, often word for word. **28**

The foundation of the Civil Code/1950 consists in overcoming the dichotomy between liability for damage due to a wrong and under an agreement: the language of sec. 337 is almost word for word the same as the provision of § 1295 subs. 1 of the ABGB. In the case of liability for an act contrary to good morals (§ 1295 subs. 2 of the ABGB), the Civil Code/1950 replaced the latter part of **29**

[20] Š. Luby (*supra* note 19), p. 450.
[21] Š. Luby (*supra* note 19), p. 495.
[22] J. Sedláček (*supra* note 1), p. 689.
[23] Š. Luby (*supra* note 19), p. 497.
[24] Š. Luby (*supra* note 19), p. 493.
[25] J. Blažke (*supra* note 12), p. 26.

the phrase will the collocation "principles of good conduct" – otherwise the language of sec. 328 is identical.

30 Just as with the ABGB, the Civil Code/1950 is structured upon liability for fault, whilst non-culpable liability is suppressed into the very margins of special provisions on liability (*viz.* liability for damage incurred during operation of means of transport [special act no. 63/1951 Coll.] and during an especially dangerous operation).

31 The Civil Code/1950 also takes over liability for chance and the specific solution of this case differs negligibly from the handling in the ABGB (compare § 1311 of the ABGB and sec. 341).

32 Likewise, the Civil Code/1950 issues from the principle of restitution, which is to precede reparation. It also issues from the principle of compensation of overall damage, including lost profit. In summary, one can then state that in contrast to other fields of provision under the Civil Code/1950, including in particular in comparison with the provisions on rights *in rem*, in the field of law of tort liability there were no fundamental changes in the law of tort in comparison with the traditional provisions in the ABGB.

4. Third Way Law of Tort (Civil Code/1964, 1964–1991)

a) Legal and Political Context

33 In 1960 Czechoslovakia declared in its new constitution that socialism had won in our country and that the country was heading for another historic milestone – communism. The new social establishment could not do with the old legislative system and new codes were gradually promulgated to regulate again all walks of life: the Penal Rules, the Penal Code, the Economic Code, the Labour Code. Also the Civil Code was revised by said Act no. 40 of 1964.

b) Principles of Liability in Civil Law

34 The theory[26] of civil law after the promulgation of the new Civil Code is also based on the following types of liability: a) liability for proprietary damage or liability without proprietary damage, b) contractual and extra-contractual liability, and finally, c) liability for fault and strict liability.

35 The prerequisites for the occurrence of civil law liability include: wrongful acts, existence of proprietary damage, *causal nexus* in regard to wrongful conduct, and sometimes, if no strict liability is involved, culpability, whether willful or in the form of negligence. Švestka[27] further defines entirely general prerequisites for the occurrence of legal liability, which include: a) the existence of a legal obligation, b) breach of such legal obligation, *i.e.* a wrongful

[26] J. Švestka, *Odpovědnost za škodu podle občanského zákoníku* (1966), pp. 46–52.
[27] J. Švestka (*supra* note 26), p. 46.

act or willful conduct against the rules of social coexistence, c) the existence of harm in the form of a breach of a legal relationship, and finally d) the existence of causality among all of the above conditions.

A wrongful act comprises two elements – illegality and act. Illegality means a breach of a legal obligation, a conflict with an objective law. A legal obligation may be stipulated in a legal regulation, *i.e.* in a law or other legal regulation of a minor legal force, but also in a contract in which an individual or an organization assumes a certain obligation, or it may ensue from some other legal fact, such as a unilateral act. A breach of contractual or extra-contractual relationships is thus involved. Wrongfulness may also be defined as an objectively existing relation between a certain act and an obligation imposed upon the addressee by statute.[28] **36**

Wrongfulness is not at issue if the act was permitted directly by an objective law. The following circumstances are included[29]: a) Acts which are an exercise of law. According to artt. VI and VII such acts must be in accordance with the rules of social coexistence and may involve a misuse of law. A justified use of a weapon under sec. 15 of the Penal Code is a special case[30]. b) Acts which represent the performance of obligations acknowledged or imposed by law. c) Necessary self-defence (sec. 418(2)) if used against a continuing or threatened assault and was not manifestly incommensurate with the nature and level of threat of the assault. d) Utter distress as regulated by sec. 418(1), if, under the given circumstance, the danger cannot be averted otherwise or unless the caused consequence is equally or more serious than the consequence that would have been threatened, and the threatened danger that was averted was not initiated by the acting party. e) A consent of the damaged party if not inconsistent with the interests of the society if given by the damaged party prior to the occurrence of the damage.[31] f) The final element referred to by the then existing theory is self-help contained in sec. 6, which is available to every individual in aid of averting an unjustified immediate interference with his rights. **37**

c) Damage

The term damage is not defined in the new act though it is amply used. However, it is generally accepted that damage means a proprietary damage objectively expressible by a general equivalent, *i.e.* money. This definition implies that damage within the meaning of civil law may only consist of proprietary harm occurring either with respect to a proprietary relationship or proprietary aspects of other protected interests.[32] **38**

[28] J. Švestka (*supra* note 26), p. 46.
[29] J. Švestka (*supra* note 26), p. 65.
[30] Z. Kratochvíl et al., *Nové občanské právo* (1965), p. 565.
[31] Such as Sections 130(1), 39.
[32] J. Švestka (*supra* note 26), p. 76.

39 Again, damage can be actual, *i.e.* proprietary damage expressible in money terms and consisting of diminution of property of the damaged as a result of an event and representing property values that need to be expended to restore the thing into its original condition, or lost profit, *i.e.* proprietary damage expressible in money terms and consisting of the fact that, due to the damaging event, proprietary values cannot be reproduced though it might be expected in view of the ordinary course of events.

40 The new code introduced several changes as compared to the original regulation. First, it differentiates between damage to things and damage to property. The novelty in respect to damage to things is that only actual damage is indemnified whereas lost profit is taken into account only in exceptional cases. It will be so in the case of willfully caused damage, when the court may award other damages provided that the failure to do so would be in conflict with the rules of socialist coexistence. The term "other damages" may raise certain doubt, but it is clear that the legislator thought of an equivalent for the previously used term "lost profit".

41 As far as actual damage is concerned, the legislators abandoned the practice of determining the value of a thing based on a specific value of the thing to the damaged party, and determined that the amount of damage shall be given by the price of the thing at the time of the damage, *i.e.* the actual price determined based on comprehensible rules which the thing has at the relevant time. The amount of damage shall be determined based upon the price of the item at the time of the damage. In the case of a theft of old or used items, circumstances diminishing the value shall be taken into account.

42 In the case of damage to health, the compensation will include the cost of medical treatment, lost wages, as well as compensation for pain and suffering and impairment of the social role. In the event of death of the damaged individual, the compensation will cover the cost of alimentation of the survivors and the cost of a funeral.

d) Causality

43 Causality must be addressed on a case by case basis. In each case all factors important for the determining of the case must be evaluated and subsequently it must be determined what was the relevant cause.[33]

e) Third-Way Law of Tort

44 Differences as against the Civil Code/1950:

aa) On the one hand, the Civil Code/1964 is based on liability for fault for damage in the same way as the Civil Code/1950, but in contrast to its predecessor it introduced presumed culpability.

[33] Z. Kratochvíl *et al* (*supra* note 30), p. 565.

bb) The Civil Code/1964 omitted liability for chance, evidently as residual from the Austrian Civil Code.

cc) The third-way Civil Code omits further meritorial elements which were either taken over into the Civil Code/1950 from the ABGB or lost their justification as a result of the socialist development of the law in general. So, for example, the merits of liability for damage caused by an object and liability for damage during unfair competition in business relations were omitted.

dd) New is the introduction of a whole special Division (Chapter I(6) of the Civil Code) on prevention (sec. 415–419). This part contained several specific provisions and one general. The Civil Code/1964 introduced a general duty of prevention (*viz.* sec. 415), pursuant to which each shall be obliged to act in such a way as to avoid damage to health and property, and to avoid wrongful property benefit to the detriment of society or an individual. The rule on prevention has the character of a principle valid for the entirety of civil law (the entire then valid field of application of the Civil Code) and not for the field of law of tort. This provision evidently has its substantiation in those fields where damage is incurred by breach of obligation which are not set forth by specific provisions of legal norms. Specifically this involves sporting activities, where activity is regulated by rules which do not have the character of legal provisions and whose breach does not constitute a breach of legal obligation, unless it would be the general clause of sec. 415 of the Civil Code/1964. As a special-nature penalty, the Civil Code also stipulated in sec. 416 a reporting duty which is incumbent upon all and which related purely to significant damage.

Otherwise, the preventative provisions included rules familiar from the ABGB or the Civil Code/1950 on liability for damage due to acts in emergencies and necessary defence.

ee) The Civil Code/1964 did take over liability for a third party, respectively the rule on responsibility of the injured party, *i.e.* the provision which was already familiar from the ABGB and which was taken over by the Civil Code/1950. Similarly, it took over from the Civil Code/1950 liability for especially dangerous operations, and added to the Civil Code a provision on liability for damage caused by operation of means of transport, which it took over from Act No. 63/1951.

5. Law of Tort of the Transition Period (Amendments of 1991, 1992–2000)

The amendment to the Civil Code/1964 was markedly hurried. As a result of this, the original idea of a new codification of civil law was abandoned. The purpose of the codification of 1991 was to adapt the existing socialist third-way civil code to the needs of capitalist development and the creation of the necessary mandatory framework of private-law relations. 45

Even though the modifications made by the amendment removed the most significant obstacles to economic development, it could not bring about the rebirth of the conception of the Civil Code. The bulk of the Civil Code 46 remained untouched, despite the fact that the content of the still-valid provisions is regulation of the private-law relations of the new conception, which is to serve in entirely different relations. In the context of the proverbial conservatism of the Czech courts, the brief meritorial elements of the socialist conception cannot operate with any great success.

47 The law of tort, or, as the case may be, the law of liability for damage, was amended in the following respects:

- Duty of prevention was modified by repealing reporting duty.
- In addition to the general principle of liability for fault, the Civil Code was supplemented by a principle of strict liability as a second pillar. These principles function alongside one another in the provisions of sec. 420 and 420a.
- In addition to the provisions on liability for damage, the Civil Code was supplemented by certain explicit provisions of contractual liability, involving liability for damage caused to objects taken into custody, liability for damage caused during the provision of services using machines and instruments or other objects used during the performance of obligations. The principles of this strict liability also relate to the provision of health-care, social, veterinary and other biological services (sec. 421 and 421a).
- The principle of the damages was changed. Reparation is to precede restitution, unless the injured party request restitution and provided restitution be feasible and reasonable.

6. Draft New Civil Codes

48 In 1996 and 2001 two attempts were made at a new codification of private law. The first attempt did not meet with success and not even the detailed language of the individual sections was submitted in the form of a government bill. This effort evidently became the victim of political change and/or political development. The second attempt initiated in 2001 by the issue of principles of foundations of a new code is still underway. The stated principles, which were approved by the Government, were published and form a basis for the government bill on the new Civil Code.

a) Draft Civil Code from 1996

In the sixth part of the contemplated Civil Code modification were made to obligations with liability for damage.[34]

49 Chapter 40 has six [sic!] divisions. The first contains joint provisions, the second provides for liability for fault, the third contains strict liability, the fourth contains liability for damage due to breach of contract, the fifth relates to liability for damage caused to valuables in trust, the sixth amends liability for damage caused by defective products, the seventh provides for liability for damage caused by an unlawful decision, and the eighth compensation for damage.

[34] See Právní praxe (1966) 5–6, 346 *et seq.*

The basis principle of liability is liability for fault. Strict liability is recognized only in certain cases, which are frequently not cases of strict liability, as we shall go on to describe. Liability for damage precludes in whole or in part other forms of liability only in the cases stipulated by law. In other words, the draft principles allow liability to be claimed for example for a defect in addition to liability for damage. In contrast to its predecessors, including the ABGB, the draft makes a significant differentiation between law of tort liability and contractual liability, the principles of which are provided for in a special division. **50**

The draft defines the fault and does not leave it to the provisions of criminal law. The draft itself also sets forth the forms of negligent culpability. Liability for fault is deemed to be liability with the presumed fault. **51**

New provisions are set forth on liability for damage caused by an object or by natural forces. At present, the owner is liable, unless he can prove himself inculpable of the damage. Instead of said owner however, liability shall be held by whosoever released under contract or took possession of such object or natural force. **52**

The principle of strict liability is ground down. It permits a broad range of excuses, including grounds consisting in taking efforts which may be justifiably requested. **53**

Liability for damage during breach of contract on a general level is provided for in a special manner. This involves strict liability with excuses, consisting in an obstruction which arose independently of the will of the wrongdoer, which said wrongdoer could not foresee or avert or overcome. Such obstacle may not consist in the wrongdoer's business relations nor may it occur at the time of his default. The draft has illogical provisions in a special division on liability for damage to valuables in trust, since this case itself also involves contractual liability. Liability for damage caused by a defective product is a special modification of the arrangement contained in the European Directive. **54**

The draft leaves valid the provisions on prevention, liability for presumed culpability, liability for the unable and other persons, just as with liability for damage caused by unlawful decision, the provisions on which are taken over from a special law. **55**

b) Draft Principles from 2001

The draft principles denote the entire field as obligations in tort, wherein this liability is understood to mean not only liability for damage, but also liability for defects and for defaults, *i.e.* contractual liability.[35] **56**

[35] See K. Eliáš/M. Zuklínová, *Principy a východiska nového kodexu soukromého práva* (2001).

57 The draft intends to make new provision for the entire conception of liability for damage. This is to be based on general liability and special provisions, where general liability will rest upon liability for fault. Liability for fault is to be built upon presumed liability for negligence. Differentiation needs however to be made between an entrepreneur and a consumer (non-entrepreneur) in the construction of their presumed negligence. In the case of acts of a person who is not an entrepreneur, negligence will be found in a breach of such care and caution as can be required from every ordinary person. In contrast, negligence in the acts of an entrepreneur will be deemed to consist in such acts as shall not comply with the requirements placed on persons with special knowledge, experience or care, with regard to that particular profession. The same quality will also be required from a person who, without being coerced to do so, performs acts necessitating specialist knowledge or experience or exceptional care.

58 The draft intends to offer new provision for liability for chance events.

59 The draft wishes to newly include an incontrovertible conception of the solidarity of wrongdoers who are entrepreneurs. Solidarity shall apply likewise to wrongdoers who are not entrepreneurs, though the court will be able to decide in cases which are justified and worthy of special consideration that it shall not apply solidarity.

60 It is to be newly stipulated that the conception of damage will be broadened and will allow the injured party to seek satisfaction to compensate non-property injuries.

61 Under the terms of liability for damage caused under contract the wrongdoer will not be able to reap the benefit of accessory culpability of a creditor if the exculpatory grounds arose at the time when the debtor was in default with performance.

62 The draft intends to take over the provisions on liability for a person who is incompetent, or as the case may be a third person, liability for damage caused by means of transport and transport activity. Liability for damage caused by especially dangerous operations is not yet to be specially provided for. The Civil Code will also take over contractual liability for valuables in trust, liability for damage caused by a defective product, and a new division will be included providing for wrongs of unfair competition and liability for damage incurred as a result thereof.

7. Conclusion

a) Lack of Relevant Decisions

63 As indicated in the introduction, and as is evident from the entire content hereof, it has not been possible to comment upon the latest development of the

law of tort for 2001, since there is a shortage of sources. This phenomenon is remarkable for the very fact that the Czech law of tort thereby differs from comparable legal codes or arrangements in western Europe. This difference provokes commentary and calls for explanation, which we have done in a form and to an extent which are certainly generally insufficient, since these issues would require a separate treatment. For the given theme, it is however possible to sketch very briefly the causes for this phenomenon.

(i) The Low Population, and Therefore an Objective Restriction on Sources (Absolute Restriction)

This cause can only partially explain the given phenomenon. In comparison with comparable jurisdictions (Austria, Belgium, Portugal, Greece), we can also perceive a variant conception and significant differences.

(ii) Limited Accessibility or Publicity of Decisions (Technical Constraints)

This reason is no longer founded – the majority of court decisions are now accessible, whether on the Internet (all decisions of the Supreme Court) or in various collections of records or magazines. The author had an opportunity to go through the decisions adopted in the past thirty years and limited accessibility as grounds for the lack of relevant decisions can be limited to 5%.

(iii) Objective Limited Occurrence of Cases (The Unsaturatedness of Market and Life)

This cause may be one of the objective explanatory reasons for said phenomenon. It is a result of general scarcity existing here 12 years ago. Material and consumption scarcity could explain the relatively minor occurrence of damage or conflicts with law in general. It is worth noting that even after the elimination of this reason due to the unprecedented supply of new products and services on the market we see no widespread occurrence of damage and court proceedings.

(iv) Insufficient Number of Court Proceedings (Limited Tendency Towards Enforcement of Rights, and Compromise)

It is true that this "cultural" feature or phenomenon may be the cause of a lack of court decisions. This is seen when we compare it with other European jurisdictions in other areas. However we cannot say that Czech entities would be inclined to a compromise or to a preliminary court settlement. It is difficult to judge the average tendency towards law enforcement.

(v) Comprehensible Legal Environment (Transparent Rules) Reduce the Number of Disputes

A lack of interesting decisions could indicate the need for transparent law or existing case law. However, this is not the case and the opposite is true. Lack of case law was a phenomenon typical for the period starting in the mid 50s

Until then, thanks to the generational continuity, very interesting decisions could be found and their quality corresponded to those issued prior to 1950 though the legal regulation was different. The legal regulation is not detailed and clear enough not to provide grounds for interesting court interpretation.

(vi) The Lack of Inventiveness and Creativity of Lawyers and Particularly Judges and the Inadequacy of the Legal Doctrine (Main Reason)

This factor must be the main cause of said phenomenon. We have already discussed the matter in the introductory part of this contribution.

b) Evaluation

(i) Legal Concept

The regulation of the law of tort as it has evolved through the three stages since 1950 is not basically different from the traditional concept of the law of tort liability. Unlike other provisions on obligations and particularly the regulation of the rights *in rem*, the liability concept in the law of tort has not been exposed to any major change as compared to the regulation in effect in 1950, *i.e.* the concept contained in ABGB. It is interesting to see that changes were introduced by the Civil Code as late as in 1964 and these differences were not compensated for in the traditional concept, not even by the change in 1991. The regulation adopted during socialism, and, valid even to date, have the following typical features:

(ii) Damage, Indemnification, Statute of Limitations, Fault

Damage is necessarily understood narrowly and indemnification follows the same line. This is manifest particularly in absolute measures. Statute of limitations is typical of short periods. Culpability is typically based on penal law and this concept is silently followed.

(iii) Prevention

Provisions regarding prevention are rare only at the first sight, mainly because they can be arrived at even without any explicit regulation by interpreting basic principles governing private law.

(iv) Strict Liability

Strict liability as a basic principle is rare, and was introduced as late as 1991.

(v) Austrian Concept

The Austrian concept of liability law prevails. This is seen both in the understanding of the basic prerequisites of liability and in the specific form.

(vi) Unified Regulation of Strict Liability in Other Laws

This regulation follows up on the regulation contained in the Civil Code and directly refers to it.

(vii) The Doctrine

The doctrine is a watered-down version of the first republic doctrine, which however copies the Austrian school of the 19th century and early 20th century.

(viii) Court Practice

The case law fails to achieve, as already said, even the basic qualities of the case law in effect till the mid 50s of the 20th century.

IV. Denmark

Henrik Sandell

A. Legislation

1. *Erstatningsansvarsloven* (The Liability for Damages Act, EAL)[1]

1 In 2001 a bill was passed regarding amendments of *Erstatningsansvarsloven* (The Liability for Damages Act, EAL)[2]. EAL is the general law of torts in Denmark and it has been discussed for some years now, especially the amounts of damages stated in the act. EAL actually contains, among other rules, rules for assessment of damages, and maximum amounts. In year 2000 an expert report proposed some modified statutes and significantly raised amounts[3]. Most of the proposals have now been passed and the modifications will come into force during the summer of 2002, therefore this presentation is restricted to some of the major issues.

2 Concerning permanent personal injury: Compensation for permanent injury is fixed at a capital amount calculated with due consideration of the medical nature and scope of the injury. The injured person's lifestyle is also considered, his or her spare-time interests etc. Compensation/disability benefit for 100% injury was earlier DKK 200,000, about € 20,000. This is now changed to DKK 573,000 – 687,500, about € 57,000 – 68,000. The higher amount in very special cases of a 100% injury. In case of lesser injuries the amount is reduced correspondingly. No compensation is payable for a handicap less than 5%.

3 Concerning permanent reduction of ability to work: If a personal injury has caused a person's incapability to earn a living through work, the damage is of course fixed depending on the injured person's previous annual income. The maximum amount is now set to DKK 6,020,000, about € 600,000. That is about € 250,000 more than in the previous rule.

[1] Ministry of Justice Promulgation Order No. 599 of 8 September 1986, Act No. 228 of 23 May 1984, with later amendments.

[2] Act No. 463 of 7 June 2001.

[3] Betaenkning 1383/2000, Revision af Erstatningsansvarsloven.

Concerning reconsideration of a closed case: It is now easier for an injured person to request reconsideration of a closed case relating to compensation for personal injury. Earlier an assumption of a considerably higher disability percentage was needed to have the case opened again. In the modified rule there is no necessary connection to the disability percentage. Other aspects are to be considered as well, for example if the ability to work has been reduced without a change in the health or actual disability percentage. **4**

Concerning pain and suffering, the maximum amount is set to about € 5,000. The rule is simplified and it is now supposed to be easier for an injured person to receive compensation for pain and suffering. In the previous rule the compensation depended on how many days the injured person was ill in bed. Now it is possible to receive damages even if the person is not home from work. **5**

The damages paid to a spouse or a cohabitant of a deceased is raised to a maximum to about € 64,000. The previous rule stated a maximum of about € 22,000. **6**

a) Commentary

Danish legislation lays down more specific rules on the assessment of damages compared to the legislation of the other countries in Scandinavia. **7**

Since the amount of compensation payable from the alternative compensation schemes is usually determined on the basis of the general law of torts (EAL), the amount of compensation will be higher after the modernisation of EAL, *inter alia, Faerdselsloven* (Act on Motor Traffic Damage)[4], *Lov om sikring mod folger af arbejdsskade* (Act on Protection against the Consequences of Industrial Injuries)[5], *Patientforsikringsloven* (Patient Insurance Act)[6], *Lov om erstatning for laegemiddelskader* (Act on Damages for Pharmaceutical Injuries)[7], *Lov om erstatning fra staten til ofre for forbrydelser* (Act on Compensation from the State to Victims of Crimes)[8]. **8**

Particularly motor traffic liability insurance will be affected heavily. Most damages paid by the insurance companies are paid through motor traffic liability insurance. Not surprisingly the Danish insurance companies have been quite negative to the proposed modifications of EAL. According to some voices from the insurance companies, they believe the premiums will be raised about 50%. The unions in Denmark have been positive to the modifications in EAL since it has an effect on the levels of compensations to injured employees. The gap between what is paid from the social security systems and the general law of torts has now increased. The unions in Denmark are very active in actions for damages to injured employees. **9**

[4] Act No. 735 of 24 September 1992, with later amendments.
[5] Act No. 1058 of 17 December 1998, with later amendments.
[6] Announcement of The Ministry of Health No. 228 of 24 March 1997, with later amendments.
[7] Act No. 1120 of 20 December 1995, with later amendments.
[8] Act No. 470 of 1 November 1985, with later amendments.

10 Despite the increase in the amounts in EAL, the compensation that can be paid is fairly low and standardised in an international perspective.

B. Cases

1. *Höjesteret* (The Danish Supreme Court); 21 August 2001; U.2001.2338H[9]: Product Liability

a) Brief Summary of the Facts

11 A patient was about to receive a new kidney, a kidney transplanted from the patient's brother. After the operation of the brother, the kidney was damaged before it was transplanted into the patient. A defective product damaged the kidney, a certain liquid, which was used to rinse/wash the kidney and the operation/transplantation was cancelled. The liquid was produced by a pharmacy that was run by the same municipality as the hospital, in connection to the hospital.

b) Judgment of the Supreme Court

12 The Court of Appeal judged no liability for the hospital/the municipality. *Lov om produktansvar*[10] (The Product Liability Act) is not applicable if the producer proves that the product had not been put into circulation on the market. During the procedure in the Supreme Court, the Court of Justice/the EC Court tried the case and the decision came in May 2001. The Court of Justice ruled that the exception in the EC Directive, art. 7[11] (that a producer is not liable if the product has not been put into circulation on the market) is not applicable in cases when a product is produced and used for medical use on patients and if the medical care is financed by the state or another public body and if the patient is not paying for the medical care. The defective liquid was therefore considered to have been put into circulation on the market.

13 After the decision of the EC Court the municipality hospital admitted that the kidney was damaged by the liquid/the defective product, and admitted that the Product Liability Act is a ground for liability. The Supreme Court confirmed this confession in its judgment. The public hospital, the municipality, was liable to damages according to the Danish Product Liability Act.

14 The issue in the Court of Appeal and the Supreme Court only concerned whether the Product Liability Act was applicable or not in this case. After the judgment by the Supreme Court the case was to be tried at the Court of Appeal.

[9] Judgments from the Supreme Court are published in *Ugeskrift for Retsvaesen* (UfR, U).
[10] Act No. 371 of 7 June 1989.
[11] Art. 7, EC Directive 857374/EEC.

c) Commentary

This was the only product liability case in the Danish Supreme Court during 2001. As in the rest of Scandinavia, there are quite few cases on product liability tried by the supreme courts. One may wonder whether a kidney damaged outside a person's body is considered to be a damage to property or personal injury. In this stage of the procedure the Supreme Court only had to rule whether the Product Liability Act was applicable to the case or not. Since the tortfeasor admitted that the Product Liability Act was applicable, the Court of Appeal shall judge regarding the assessment of damage. **15**

2. *Höjesteret*; 18 January 2001; U.2001.781H: Liability of Auditor

a) Brief Summary of the Facts

A bank had granted credits to a company. The company later went bankrupt. The bank held the auditor who was engaged by the company responsible for the damages. Before the bank granted the credits, the auditor had presented accounts of the company to the bank. The accounts were defective and the bank argued that the auditor should have done more investigations and included a clear reservation in the auditor's report. **16**

b) Judgments of the Supreme Courts

Both the Court of Appeal and the Supreme Court judged that the auditor was not liable. The bank was not able to prove that the missing information in the accounts was of vital/decisive importance for the bank in its decision to grant credits. **17**

c) Commentary

The liability of professional advisors is frequently discussed in Denmark. During 2001 there was another case where the Supreme Court found that the auditor was not liable, U.2001.1516H. A buyer of shares claimed that the auditor was negligent when the auditor had calculated on the value of the shares. According to the buyer, the auditor made a wrong valuation of the pensions in the company. Since the buyer was also the chairman of the board of the company, she had a clear insight into the decisions taken by the board and the work of the auditor. The Supreme Court found that the auditor could not be held responsible for the loss. **18**

During 2001 the Supreme Court tried a case where the Danish tax authority had sued a lawyer for not acting correctly during a period of suspension of payments of a company, U.2001.325H. The Supreme Court stated that the lawyer had disregarded his obligations. However, despite the negligence, the state could not prove that the loss was a direct effect of the lawyer's negligence and the lawyer was not liable for the damages according to the Supreme Court. The Supreme Court remarked that the lawyer was not grossly negligent and that the burden of proof could not be reduced. **19**

20 The cases mentioned above did not concern the advisor liability in connection with their clients' criminal activities. However, some years ago some persons committed frauds related to emptying companies of capital, leaving only bankrupt companies with great debts. Some of the persons who used gaps/ "grey zones" in the tax legislation were also found liable for damages to the state and to creditors[12]. The state, the tax authority, has also shown interest in the banks, auditors and lawyers involved in giving advice in these kinds of money transactions. There are some judgments where the courts have found that the advisors, often auditors, should have understood that their clients were about to swindle money out of companies. However, the judgments from the courts have shown that mistakes by advisors and banks seldom actually lead to liability.

3. *Höjesteret*; 15 November 2001; U.2002.333H: Liability of the Police

a) Brief Summary of the Facts

21 A car was stolen in November 1995. On 17 November 1995 the police received the information that the car was parked at a certain address. On the same day, the police tried to reach the owner of the car by telephone, but did not succeed. Contrary to the usual procedure, the police did not make any further attempts after that to contact the owner. According to the investigation, the car was stolen once again on 1 December. The insurance company claimed for damages from the police corresponding to the value of the car.

b) Judgment of the Supreme Court

22 The Supreme Court stated that there is a fault if the police do not make more efforts to try to contact the owner of a stolen car. However, the information to the car owner is considered to be a service to the citizens so that the owner can recapture the possession of the car and not with the aim of preventing new crimes such as a new theft of the car. The Supreme Court judged that there is no causal connection between the fault made by the police and the new theft of the car and the police was not liable to pay damages.

C. Literature

1. AIDA, B. v. Eyben (ed.), *Alternative Compensation Mechanisms for Damages, The Nordic Countries, Common Report and National Reports* (Dansk Selskab for Forsikringsret, Copenhagen 2001) [13]

23 In October 2002, the XIth World Congress of AIDA (the International Association for Insurance Law) will be held. One of the topics of the congress is the

[12] For example U.2001.138H, U.2001.634/2H, U.2002.116H.

[13] The report can be bought from *Det Danske Selskab for Forsikringsret*, (The Danish Section of the International Association for Insurance law) tel +45 33 12 11 33, contact person is advokat Torben Bondrop.

development of mechanisms for compensating injury or damage to third parties that are alternative or supplemental to traditional tort liability and liability insurance, motor traffic accidents excluded. Denmark, Sweden, Norway and Finland present the schemes in a common report concerning alternative compensation mechanisms for damages to the world congress. Iceland is not a member of AIDA. There are similarities between the Nordic countries in this field, both in the actual texts of the statutes and in the policy goals and the techniques used to implement the policy goals.

The book is 372 pages long and it is written in English. Prof. Bo von Eyben, Copenhagen University, Denmark, has written the common Nordic report with assistance from the other countries. The book also consists of national reports with answers to the questionnaire from AIDA. The following authors have written the national reports: Denmark: Prof. Bo von Eyben. Finland: Prof. Mika Hemmo, University of Helsinki. Norway: Peter Lödrup, University of Oslo. Sweden: legal advisor Mats Magnusson, The Patient Injury Claims Committee. Prof. Bill W. Dufwa, University of Stockholm and claims manager Eva Ulvefeldt, AON, also contributed to the Swedish report. **24**

The national reports correspond to the questionnaire and the common report sums up the similarities and differences between the countries. In the national reports there are direct answers on questions such as whether the different schemes are compulsory or voluntary, whether it is an obligation to invoke general law of torts first, how the schemes are financed, the amount of compensation, etc. **25**

The social security systems in the Nordic countries cover a large part of the damages. In order to fill the gaps of the social security systems, the issue of damages is interesting for the injured party, such as compensation for loss of income that is not paid by the state, non-pecuniary loss, etc. The amount of compensation to be paid through the different alternative compensation schemes is often based on the general law of torts. However, in some schemes there are exceptions to the rule, such as maximum limits, a deductible, etc. **26**

The patient insurance schemes and schemes covering pharmaceutical injuries are comprehensive and differ from the rest of Europe and the world. Concerning injuries in relation to medical treatment there are many similarities between the Nordic countries. **27**

The book contains schematic surveys of the alternative compensation systems in the Nordic Countries regarding industrial injuries, environmental damage, injuries to patients, pharmaceutical injuries and victims of crimes. The schematic surveys correspond to the questionnaire. **28**

In the appendix you will find statutes for the compensation systems in the Nordic countries in English. **29**

30 Though AIDA mainly deals with topics on insurance, this book is of great use for comparative studies regarding international tort law and it gives the reader a good overview of the alternative compensation schemes in the Nordic countries.

V. England and Wales

Ken Oliphant

A. Legislation

1. Damages (Personal Injury) Order 2001, Statutory Instrument (SI) 2001/2301[1]

a) Brief Summary

The Lord Chancellor, exercising the powers conferred upon him by sec. 1 of the Damages Act 1996, set the assumed rate of return on the investment of damages for future pecuniary loss in personal injury actions at 2.5%. The order came into force on 28 June 2001. 1

b) Commentary

In calculating damages for future pecuniary loss in a personal injury action, the courts use what is called the 'multiplier' method. To the assumed annual loss ('the multiplicand') is applied a multiplier which reflects the number of years the loss is expected to continue. Because the award generally involves replacing a continuing stream of income (*e.g.* future loss of earnings) or compensating for continuing expenses (*e.g.* the cost of medical care) with a single lump sum payable immediately, the multiplier must be adjusted to take account of the fact of accelerated payment. A lump-sum damages award invested properly will give a rate of return significantly higher than the rate of inflation, and a discount is necessary to ensure that the real value of what the claimant receives is equal to his or her loss. The crucial question is what rate of return is to be assumed when calculating this discount. In the 1970s and 1980s, the courts assumed a rate of return of some 4% to 5%,[2] but this was criticised as unrealistic: in practice, it was unlikely that the investment of damages would produce so high a rate of return, and there was therefore a risk that, especially in the case of claimants with long-term inju 2

[1] Noted by Davis & Hitchcock, Discount rates in personal injury awards [2002] 152 *New Law Journal* (NLJ) 251.

[2] See, e.g., *Cookson v Knowles* [1979] *Appeal Cases* (AC), 556.

ries, the fund created by investing the damages would be exhausted too quickly.

3 It was in response to this perceived problem that the Damages Act 1996 gave the Lord Chancellor the power to prescribe from time to time by order the rate of return on investment to be assumed by the courts for these purposes. But before he had exercised this power, the matter came before the House of Lords in *Wells v Wells*,[3] and their Lordships decided that it was necessary to depart from the previous approach of the courts. Although the ordinary investor with a balanced portfolio of investments might well achieve a rate of return of 4% to 5%, tort claimants were not ordinary investors. They were seeking to ensure a steady stream of income to cover their basic needs and necessary expenses, and could not afford to 'bide their time' in the pursuit of more speculative returns. Hence, it was to be assumed that they would invest in index-linked government stock (ILGS), offering a lower rate of return but greater security. On this basis, the House of Lords ruled that the courts should work on the assumption of a 3% rate of return on investment pending the Lord Chancellor's exercise of his statutory power. But Lord Lloyd, delivering the leading speech, made it clear that the matter was better resolved by legislation than caselaw: "the sooner the Lord Chancellor sets the rate the better. The present uncertainty does not make the settling of claims any easier."[4]

4 In March 2000, the Lord Chancellor's Department released a consultation paper, *Damages: The Discount Rate and Alternatives to Lump Sum Payments*, stating the Government's view that the power under sec. 1 of the Damages Act should be exercised: it would place an unreasonable burden on litigants and courts if it were left to the latter to decide in individual cases whether there had been a sufficient change in economic circumstances to justify adopting a new rate. When the consultation exercise was complete, the Lord Chancellor came to the conclusion that the *Wells v Wells* approach was broadly correct, as tort claimants who had suffered severe injuries could not be expected to take even moderate risks when they invested their damages, but that he was entitled to take account of the likelihood that those receiving large awards would invest in a mixed portfolio of equities and gilts (including ILGS), albeit one involving very low risks, and not in risk-free ILGS alone. Evidence presented to the Lord Chancellor suggested that the net average yield on ILGS was then in the range between 2% and 2.5%. Taking account of the higher returns that claimants with large compensation payments could be expected to make by way of a mixed investment strategy, the Lord Chancellor opted to set the discount rate at the higher of those two figures. He indicated that it was desirable to set a single rate to cover all cases, even though this meant ignoring the widely differing personal and financial circumstances of individual claimants, as this would promote certainty and facilitate the negotiation of settlements. The Lord Chancellor exercised his statutory power under sec. 1 of the Dam-

[3] [1999] 1 AC 345.
[4] [1999] 1 AC 345, 375.

ages Act on 27 June 2001. Subsequently, it came to light that the information upon which he had reached his decision was inaccurate in certain minor respects, but in a further statement on 27 July 2001 the Lord Chancellor confirmed the discount rate at 2.5%, having considered the matter again completely afresh.[5]

The effect of the decision will be a further increase in the sums recovered by tort claimants, and further pressure on the level of insurance premiums. According to insurance industry evidence presented to the Lord Chancellor, the reduction in the discount rate from 4.5% to 3% entailed by *Wells v Wells* had increased the amount paid out annually by way of compensation for personal injuries by some £ 115 million (approx. € 179,173,905).[6] If passed on to policy-holders, motor insurance premiums would have to rise by about 1%, employers' liability premiums by 2%, and public liability premiums by 7%. If the rate had been further reduced to 2%, as some claimants' lawyers had urged, the additional cost would have been around £ 100 million. However, these were matters which the Lord Chancellor was not permitted to have regard, as claimants are legally entitled to full compensation for their injuries and the discount rate had to be set accordingly.[7] **5**

It should be noted that the court is not precluded from using another rate if it is more appropriate in the case in question (Damages Act 1996, sec. 1(2)). In *Warriner v Warriner*,[8] the Court of Appeal ruled that the fact that the damages award was large and the claimant's life expectancy long did not make it appropriate to depart from the rate set by the Lord Chancellor. **6**

B. Cases

1. *Z v United Kingdom* (Application 29392/95), European Court of Human Rights, 10 May 2001: Liability of Social Services[9]

a) Brief Summary of the Facts

The four applicants were full siblings. In 1987, their parents were referred to the social services department of their local authority, Bedfordshire County Council, by their health visitor who was concerned about the children's well-being. Over the next few years, social services received several reports of ill-treatment of the children and insanitary conditions in the home. In 1989, the **7**

[5] 'Setting the Discount Rate: Lord Chancellor's Reasons' (http://www.lcd.gov.uk/civil/discount.htm).

[6] £ 1 = € 1.558 (July 2002).

[7] Lord Chancellor's Department, *Damages: The Discount Rate and Alternatives to Lump Sum Payments* (a consultation paper) (2000), § 14.

[8] [2002] *England and Wales Court of Appeal, Civil Division* (EWCA Civ), 81.

[9] [2001] 2 *Family Law Reports* (FLR) 612, (2002) *European Human Rights Reports* (EHRR) 97. Noted by Davies [2001] 117 *Law Quarterly Review* (LQR) 521, English [2001] 151 NLJ 973, and Gearty [2002] 65 *Modern Law Review* (MLR) 87

council assigned a social work assistant to the family but declined to put the children on the 'at risk' register, as the health visitor had requested, even after the social work assistant's further expressions of concern. In 1992, after the council had organised periods of respite care for the three older children, the applicants' mother told social services that the children would have to be placed in care or else she would batter them. The applicants were placed in emergency foster care and entered onto the Child Protection Register, and the council successfully applied for care orders to protect the children from further harm. In 1993, the Official Solicitor, acting as the applicants' next friend, brought an action for damages against the local authority, alleging amongst other things that the authority had been negligent in failing to act expeditiously and effectively when apprised of the children's condition and had thereby exposed the children to further ill-treatment with deleterious consequences for their health. At trial, the judge struck out the applicants' claims on the basis that they disclosed no cause of action and this ruling was upheld by the Court of Appeal and the House of Lords (*X and others (minors) v Bedfordshire County Council*[10]). In considering the applicants' claim for common law negligence, their Lordships ruled that it would not be fair, just and reasonable to find that the council owed them a duty of care.[11]

8 After the House of Lords ruling, the applicants commenced proceedings against the United Kingdom under the European Convention for the Protection of Human Rights and Fundamental Freedoms. They alleged that the local authority had failed to take adequate steps to protect them from severe parental neglect and abuse which they were known to be suffering, in violation of Artt. 3 and 8 of the Convention, and that their rights under Artt. 6 (access to a court) and 13 (effective remedy) had also been violated. In 1999, the European Commission for Human Rights expressed the unanimous opinion that there had been violations of Artt. 3 and 6 of the Convention, but that no separate issues arose under Artt. 8 and 13. The application was assigned to the Grand Chamber of the European Court of Human Rights, to be decided at the same time as the case of *TP and KM v United Kingdom* (considered below).

b) Judgment of the European Court of Human Rights

9 The Court ruled unanimously that there had been a violation of Art. 3 of the Convention. The State's positive obligations under the Convention included the taking of measures to ensure that individuals within their jurisdiction – particularly children and other vulnerable persons – were not subjected to torture or inhuman or degrading treatment. It was immaterial that such ill-treatment was administered by a private individual, provided that it was ill-treatment of which the authorities had or ought to have had knowledge. Here,

[10] [1995] 2 AC 633.

[11] To establish a duty of care in a novel case, *i.e.* one not covered by existing authority, the claimant must satisfy the three-stage test set out in *Caparo Industries plc v Dickman* [1990] 2 AC 605 by proving: (1) that damage to the claimant was foreseeable; (2) that there was a relationship of proximity between the parties; and (3) that it would be fair, just and reasonable to recognise a duty of care in the circumstances.

it was not disputed that the applicants' neglect and abuse amounted to inhuman and degrading treatment, and the matter was brought to the local authority's attention in 1987. Not until 1992, however, were the applicants taken into emergency care – and then only at their mother's insistence. Even allowing for the difficult and sensitive decisions which social services departments have to make, this constituted a failure on the part of the local authority to take reasonable steps to prevent ill-treatment of which it had knowledge. (In view of this conclusion, the Court considered that no separate issue arose under Art. 8 of the Convention.)

The Court ruled by twelve votes to five that there had been no violation of the right of access to court which was implicit in Art. 6 of the Convention. At the outset of the domestic proceedings, there had indeed been a serious and genuine dispute about the existence of the right asserted by the applicants under the law of negligence, and Art. 6 was therefore applicable to the applicants' claim. But there was no substance in the applicants' complaint that the striking out of their claims had deprived them of their right to a determination on the merits. There was no reason to consider that the striking-out procedure in itself offended the principle of access to court, as it merely addressed the question whether, on the assumption that the facts alleged in the statement of claim were true, the applicants had an arguable cause of action in law. The applicants had sufficient opportunity to submit arguments in favour of their view of the law, and their claims were properly and fairly examined. Once the House of Lords had ruled that they had no arguable case in law, the applicants could no longer claim any right under Art. 6 to a hearing on the facts. The Court declined to follow its previous decision in *Osman v United Kingdom* which it admitted was based on an understanding of the domestic law of negligence which had had to be reviewed. Although the applicants had correctly identified a gap in domestic law, it was one which gave rise to an issue under Art. 13, not Art. 6. **10**

The Court held by fifteen votes to two that there had been a violation of Art. 13 of the Convention. (This was in fact conceded by the United Kingdom government, but two members of the court, having reached the conclusion that there was a violation of Art. 6, found that no separate issue arose under Art. 13.) The State's obligation here was to make available a mechanism for establishing the liability (if any) of state officials or bodies for breach of Convention rights. Where there was found to be a breach of the fundamental rights under Artt. 2 and 3 of the Convention, compensation should in principle extend to the non-pecuniary consequences of the breach. Here, the applicants had no appropriate means of obtaining a determination of their allegations that the local authority failed to protect them from inhuman and degrading treatment and had been denied the possibility of obtaining an enforceable award of compensation for the damage suffered thereby. Although the applicants had received small awards of compensation from the Criminal Injuries Compensation Board, these related only to the effects of criminal acts of violence and not the consequences of the neglect that the applicants had endured. In addi- **11** tion, it was not enough that the applicants could have complained to the Local Government Ombudsman, as he only had the power to recommend the payment of compensation in cases of misfeasance, not legally to require it.

12 The Court awarded the applicants sums ranging from £ 40,000 to £ 132,000 by way of just satisfaction for the pecuniary and non-pecuniary damage which they had suffered as a result of the violation of their Convention rights.

c) Commentary

13 This decision was keenly-awaited by English lawyers, many of whom had been troubled by the implications of the Court's earlier decision in *Osman v United Kingdom.*[12] In *Osman*, the Court had ruled that the striking-out of a negligence action against the police on the basis that it would not be fair, just and reasonable to recognise a duty of care (the third stage of the *Caparo* approach[13]) amounted to a disproportionate interference with the right of access to a court which was implicit under Art. 6 of the Convention. There was considerable uncertainty on the part of English lawyers whether the problem the Court had identified in *Osman* was to do with the procedure employed (strike-out) or the substantive principles of negligence, or both. The present decision affirms that there is nothing in the nature of the striking-out procedure which renders it inconsistent with the right of access to a court. This is a matter of some relief, for there would surely be no point in insisting that claims without any arguable basis in law could only be dismissed after a full hearing on the facts. An interesting question is whether the courts, having become noticeably more reluctant to strike out dubious claims in the aftermath of *Osman*,[14] will embrace this procedure with any more enthusiasm now that the Court of Human Rights has given it the all-clear.

14 So what, according to *Osman*, was the problem with the substantive law of negligence? In a key passage, the Court criticised the domestic tribunal for proceeding on the basis that considerations of fairness, justice and reasonableness 'provided a watertight defence to the police and that it was impossible to prise open an immunity which the police enjoy from civil suit in respect of their acts and omissions in the investigation and suppression of crime' (§ 150). What it should have done was to weigh the considerations supporting the denial of a duty of care against 'other public interest considerations which pull in the opposite direction' (§ 151), taking account (it seems) of the 'degrees of negligence [and] of harm suffered' (*ibid.*). The implications of the Court's reasoning here were exceedingly disturbing to English lawyers, for the decision cast doubt upon basic notions about the role played by the duty of care concept in English law and the principles employed to determine whether such a

[12] [1999] 1 FLR 193, (2000) 29 EHRR 245.

[13] See *supra* note 10.

[14] See, *e.g.*, *Barrett v Enfield London Borough Council* [2001] 2 AC 550, *W v Essex County Council* [2001] 2 AC 592, *Jarvis v Hampshire County Council, sub. nom. Phelps v Hillingdon London Borough Council* [2001] 2 AC 619. *Cf. Palmer v Tees Health Authority* (2000) 2 *Local Government Law Reports* (LGLR) 69.

duty arose on particular facts. The concerns arising were well-summarised by Lord Browne-Wilkinson in the decision of the House of Lords in *Barrett v London Borough of Enfield*:[15]

The problems in applying this reasoning to the English law of negligence are many and various... In English law, questions of public policy and the question whether it is fair and reasonable to impose liability in negligence are decided as questions of law. Once the decision is taken..., that decision will apply to all future cases of the same kind. The decision does not depend on weighing the balance between the extent of the damage to the plaintiff and the damage to the public in each particular case.

It should be noted that these problems were not limited to litigation against public authorities, but arose also where the defendant was a private individual, as the right of access to a court applies to *every* determination of a person's civil rights and obligations.

These difficulties have not been wholly resolved by the decision of the European Court of Human Rights in the present case. The Court stated that its understanding of the English law of negligence has had to be reviewed since its decision in *Osman*, but it does not say that the result in that case was wrong. If Osman was indeed correctly decided, we must ask how it is to be reconciled with Z. One plausible view is that the difference between the cases is that, in Z, the House of Lords itself balanced all the relevant considerations, while in *Osman*, the Court of Appeal treated itself as bound by the authority of an earlier House of Lords decision, *Hill v Chief Constable of West Yorkshire*,[16] which it considered to have laid down a rule, based on the Law Lords' own weighing-up of the policy considerations, which was to apply in all subsequent cases of the same type. If this is indeed how the Court of Human Rights in *Z* distinguished its earlier decision in *Osman*, that would be very worrying for English lawyers, because it would effectively deprive an appellate decision on the question of fairness, justice and reasonableness of all precedential value, and require a re-balancing of the relevant policy considerations on the facts of each new case. This was precisely Lord Browne-Wilkinson's concern in the passage quoted above. 15

Of course, it is possible that the Court in *Z* gave as clear a signal as it could that *Osman* was wrongly-decided, but felt constrained for whatever reason from saying so explicitly. There are passages in the Court's judgment which support such an interpretation. In the passage immediately following the Court's admission that *Osman* was based on a misunderstanding of domestic law, we read (§ 100): 16

The Court is satisfied that the law of negligence as developed in the domestic courts since the case of Caparo... *includes the fair, just and reasonable criterion as an intrinsic element of the duty of care and that the ruling of*

[15] [2001] 2 AC 550, 559.
[16] [1989] AC, 53.

law concerning that element in this case does not disclose the operation of an immunity. In the present case, the Court is led to the conclusion that the inability of the applicants to sue the local authority flowed not from an immunity but from the applicable principles governing the substantive right of action in domestic law.

Previously, the Court had stated (§ 98): 'It is not enough to bring Art. 6 § 1 into play that the non-existence of a cause of action under domestic law may be described as having the same effect as an immunity, in the sense of not enabling the applicant to sue for a given category of harm.' These statements are potentially very significant. They suggest that the operation of the fairness, justice and reasonableness test *never* discloses an immunity, because it simply defines the scope of the right in domestic law, and hence *never* brings Art. 6 into play. Admittedly, the claimants had an arguable right at the start of their case, because theirs was a novel case in which the question of fairness, justice and reasonableness had not been resolved, but the effect of the House of Lords decision was to settle that issue and render their claim no longer arguable in law. From that moment on, Art. 6 had no purchase and there was therefore no right to a further hearing on the facts.

17 Yet it may be too hasty to jump to the conclusion that the resolution of duty questions by English courts will never attract the supervisory jurisdiction of the Court of Human Rights under Art. 6. The contrary is suggested by the fact that the Court thought it necessary to consider the fairness of the House of Lords' decision in any event. Its conclusion was that the applicants' claims had been 'properly and fairly examined in light of the applicable domestic legal principles concerning the tort of negligence' (§ 101): 'it cannot be said,' the Court opined, 'that the House of Lords came to its conclusion without a careful balancing of the policy reasons for and against the imposition of liability on the local authority *in the circumstances of the applicants' case*' (§ 99; emphasis added). What is striking is not so much this conclusion, as the fact that the Court felt obliged to address these questions at all. Clearly the decision that a finding of 'no duty' did not amount to an immunity did not preclude further scrutiny of the domestic court's decision under Art. 6. The precise juristic basis for this in Art. 6 appears rather obscure, but let us allow that to pass. Of more immediate interest to English tort lawyers is how domestic tort decisions can be rendered Art. 6-compliant. In this context, it is a matter of some concern that the Court of Human Rights talked of the House of Lords having balanced the relevant policy considerations 'in the circumstances of the applicants case' (see above). What of the domestic court that treats itself as authority-bound to accept that the policy arguments oppose the recognition of a duty in all cases of the same kind, irrespective of the particular circumstances? The implication is that such an approach could amount to a disproportionate interference with Art. 6 rights, yet, if it is, it seems that we are right back to the position in *Osman*, and *Z* does not represent a retreat from the earlier case at all.

On the facts of *Z*, the decision on Art. 6 was immaterial to the final outcome, as the applicants won on Artt. 3 and 13 anyway. It must be said that it appears far more satisfactory to base such decisions on violation of a 'substantive' Convention right, such as that under Art. 3, rather than upon the ostensibly-procedural rights in Art. 6. With the coming into effect of the Human Rights Act 1998, English courts are required by domestic law to act consistently with the rights under Artt. 2 to 12 and 14 of the Convention (and certain of the protocols), and it seems that, if the facts of *Z* were repeated today, an English court might very well conclude that the local authority did owe the vulnerable children a duty of care, having regard to the children's rights under Art. 3 in deciding the question of fairness, justice and reasonableness. Art. 13 is not a 'Convention right' under the Human Rights Act, but that would not matter if there was a remedy in negligence – and the court has, in any case, a statutory discretion to award compensation to the victim of a public authority's violation of Convention rights. These issues are considered in more detail, below, in the commentary on *TP and KM v United Kingdom*. **18**

2. *TP and KM v United Kingdom* (Application 28945/95), European Court of Human Rights, 10 May 2001: Liability of Social Services[17]

a) Brief Summary of the Facts

The applicants' local authority, Newham County Council, suspected that the second applicant, the first applicant's daughter, was being sexually abused and in 1987 placed her on the Child Protection Register. She was then four years old. In November of that year, in a video-taped interview with a local authority social worker and a consultant child psychiatrist employed by the local health authority, the second applicant said that she had been the victim of sexual abuse and identified her abuser as 'John'. John was the name of the mother's then partner, and the interviewers concluded that he was the John in question. They decided that it was necessary to remove the second applicant from the care of her mother immediately, and the local authority successfully applied to a magistrates' court for an order permitting it to detain the child and put her in a place of safety for a period of up to 28 days. Before that period had expired, the High Court made the girl a ward of court and granted care and control of her to the local authority, with her mother retaining only limited access rights. At no time during this process was the first applicant shown the video-tape of the interview with her daughter, or a transcript of the interview, as the local authority took the view that this would not be in the best interests of the child. It was not until November 1988 that the first applicant saw the transcript of the interview for the first time. This revealed that what the girl had said was inconsistent with the identification of the abuser as the mother's partner in certain key respects. In fact, it transpired that the girl had been speaking of a cousin, also named John, who had previously lived at the same address. In these circumstances, the local authority was willing to allow the second applicant's return to her mother for a trial period: although she had suf- **19**

[17] [2001] 2 FLR 549, (2002) 34 EHRR 42.

fered a seriously damaging experience from which her mother had been unable to protect her, there was evidence that her mother had matured and that her domestic situation was more stable than before. This course of action was allowed by leave of the court, and the second applicant remained with the first applicant from this time onwards. A year later, in November 1989, the High Court discharged the second applicant's wardship, there being no longer any concerns that required her to be a ward of court.

20 In 1990, the applicants brought proceedings against the local authority, the local health authority and the consultant child psychiatrist, claiming that they had both suffered a psychiatric disorder as a result of negligence and breach of statutory duty. Their main allegation was that the social worker and psychiatrist who had interviewed the second applicant had failed to investigate the facts with proper care and thoroughness, and to discuss their conclusions with the first applicant. The defendants sought to strike out the claims as revealing no cause of action and their application to this effect was granted by the High Court, whose decision was upheld by the Court of Appeal and House of Lords (reported as one of a number of consolidated appeals *sub. nom. X and others (minors) v Bedfordshire County Council*[18]). The social worker and psychiatrist owed no duty of care to either applicant as they were retained by the local authority to advise the local authority, and assumed responsibility only to the authority. It followed that their employers could not be held vicariously liable to the applicants for any mistake they had made. Even if this had not been the case, the policy arguments which precluded the recognition of a duty of care in the *Bedfordshire* case also applied to the present facts, and that it would not be fair, just and reasonable to impose a duty of care on the employees. Furthermore, with regards to the claim for breach of statutory duty, it was not possible to discern any Parliamentary intention to create a remedy in damages in passing the various Acts of Parliament which laid down the powers and responsibilities of local authorities in respect of children at risk. Their purpose was to establish an administrative system in the interests of social welfare, not to create a private law cause of action. The applicants subsequently commenced proceedings in Strasbourg under the European Convention for the Protection of Human Rights and Fundamental Freedoms.

b) Judgment of the European Court of Human Rights

21 The Court accepted that the second applicant's removal from her mother, the first applicant, although it disclosed an interference with the applicants' right to respect for their family life under Art. 8 of the Convention, was in accordance with the law, pursued a legitimate aim, being clearly aimed at protecting the 'health or morals' and the 'rights and freedoms' of the child, and could be regarded as necessary in a democratic society. As regards the last of these requirements, the court noted that the decision to remove the child from her mother was 'supported by relevant and sufficient reasons, namely, the strong

[18] [1995] 2 AC 633.

suspicions that she had been abused and the doubts which existed as to the first applicant's ability to protect her' (§ 74). It found that the mistake made by the psychiatrist and the social worker in assuming that the second applicant was referring to the first applicant's partner was not of such a nature as to deprive the decision of a legitimate basis, as interpreting the child's responses had been a difficult and delicate task. The interference therefore complied with the requirements of the second paragraph of Art. 8 and did not constitute a violation of the applicants' right to respect for their family life.

It was the Court's unanimous opinion, however, that there had been a violation of the applicants' right to respect for their family life in that the transcript of the interview which induced the authorities to take the second applicant into care was not disclosed to the first applicant until a year after the event. It was essential that parents should have prompt access to the information relied upon by the authorities in reaching such decisions or at least, if there were doubts as to whether this posed a risk to the welfare of the child (as here), that the matter should be referred to a court at the earliest possible stage in the proceedings. This was the responsibility of the authorities, even in the absence of any request by the parent. Here, the local authority's failure to seek a judicial ruling on the disclosure of the transcript to the first applicant had prevented her from being adequately involved in the decisions made about the care of her daughter, and had thereby deprived both applicants of the requisite protection of their interests in breach of Art. 8. 22

The Court also ruled unanimously that there had been a violation of Art. 13 of the Convention in that domestic law did not provide an effective remedy in respect of the breach of Art. 8. The Court considered that, where there was an arguable breach of a Convention right, the victim should be able to invoke some mechanism for establishing the liability of the state (if any) and, in appropriate cases, to recover compensation for the pecuniary and non-pecuniary damage flowing from the breach. In the present case, the right to apply to the court for the return of the child was insufficient, as it did not provide for redress in respect of psychological damage suffered during the period in which mother and child were separated. Similarly, the right of complaint to the Local Government Ombudsman, though it could result in a finding of maladministration, did not enable the applicants to obtain legally-enforceable compensation, as the Ombudsman was able only to recommend the payment of compensation and not to require it. 23

The Court held unanimously that there had been no violation of the right of access to a court under Art. 6 of the Convention for the reasons which it had set out in *Z v United Kingdom* (above). 24

The Court awarded the sum of £ 10,000 to each of the applicants by way of just satisfaction for the non-pecuniary damage which they had suffered as a result of the violation of their right to respect for family life under Art. 8. If the transcript had been made available at some earlier time, it may have been the 25 case that they would have been reunited more quickly. Although it was not certain that this would have occurred, the applicants had nevertheless suffered a loss of opportunity. In addition, the first applicant had suffered feelings of frustration and injustice. (The United Kingdom's judge on the court, Lady Justice Arden, delivered a separate concurring opinion in which she stated that she would have preferred to award only £ 6,000 to each of the applicants, as their psychiatric injury was minor and awards for comparable injuries in domestic law were likely to be in the region of £ 500 to £ 2,250.).

c) Commentary

26 On the Art. 6 point, the Court simply followed its earlier decision on the same day in *Z v United Kingdom* (above). For present purposes, the interest of the case lies in the Court's decision on Art. 8. The question arises how (if at all) this will be accommodated in English law under the Human Rights Act 1998. Under sec. 6 of the Act, courts are treated as 'public authorities' and as such are subject to the obligation not to act incompatibly with any person's 'Convention rights'. These are defined as the rights arising under Artt. 2 to 12 and 14 of the European Convention for the Protection of Human Rights and Fundamental Freedoms, Artt. 1 to 3 of the First Protocol, and Artt. 1 and 2 of the Sixth Protocol.[19] In proceedings in which a question arises in connection with one or more of these rights, the Act requires the court to take account of any relevant jurisprudence of the European Court of Human Rights,[20] though it is not bound to follow it.

27 It appears that the court's obligation under sec. 6 of the 1998 Act extends to the development of existing principles to ensure their compatibility with the Convention rights, if this can be achieved without undermining 'the measure of certainty which is necessary to all law'.[21] The question therefore is: can the common law of negligence be developed, without creating undue uncertainty, so as to provide the degree of protection of Art. 8 rights that was contemplated in *TP and KM*? There appears to be no principled reason why a duty of care should not be recognised in such circumstances–it is hard to see how this would create more uncertainty than already exists in this notoriously obscure area of the law–but it is problematic whether the injuries of which TP and KM complained could attract compensation in English law. The English law of negligence does not recognise liability for purely mental distress not resulting from physical injury (such as the first applicant's 'feelings of frustration and injustice') or, other than in cases of purely economic loss, for 'loss of opportunity'. It may be therefore that, in circumstances such as those arising here, the English courts would find that to award damages at common law would be a step too far, and that the only remedy would be that provided for by the Human Rights Act itself.[22] It is not yet clear what principles the courts will

[19] Human Rights Act 1998, sec. 1.
[20] Human Rights Act 1998, sec. 2.
[21] *Douglas v Hello! Ltd* [2001] 1 FLR 982, § 129, per Sedley LJ.
[22] Sec. 8. This provides that a court finding a public authority's act or omission to be unlawful may grant whatever remedy within its powers it considers 'just and appropriate', including, where necessary to afford 'just satisfaction' to the person to whom it is made, an award of damages.

adopt in awarding damages under the Act, though it is likely that they will adopt a more scientific approach than that of the Court of Human Rights, which here appears to have made its assessment of the compensation payable for loss of opportunity without any analysis of the sums normally payable for the injuries in question or the extent of the discount to be applied in respect of the probability that the injuries might have occurred anyway.

3. *Keenan v United Kingdom* (Application 27229/95), European Court of Human Rights, 3 April 2001: Treatment of Mentally-Ill Prisoner[23]

a) Brief Summary of the Facts

The applicant's son, K, committed suicide whilst serving a sentence of 4 months' imprisonment. For several years previously, K had undergone psychiatric treatment having displayed symptoms of paranoia, aggression, violence and deliberate self-harm; in the course of this treatment, he was prescribed anti-psychotic medication. The prison was informed of his medical history and, on admission, he was received by the prison's health care centre for observation and assessment. However, none of the prison doctors was trained in psychiatry. Whilst K was in the health centre, a prison doctor prescribed a change in his medication, and shortly afterwards he assaulted two hospital officers. K was placed in the segregation unit in the prison's punishment block, having been certified fit for cellular confinement, on the basis that he was behaving unpredictably and posed a threat to staff. Whilst in segregation, K was locked up for 23 hours each day, and had minimal contact with staff and none with fellow prisoners. He was periodically violent and abusive towards prison staff, and made several threats of suicide. On those occasions when he evinced signs of suicidal tendencies, he was placed under 15-minute watch. Some two weeks later, when there only 9 days to his expected release date, K attended a disciplinary hearing in respect of the assaults and was awarded 28 additional days in prison, seven of which were to be in segregation. The following evening, K was discovered dead in his cell, having hung himself from the bars of his cell with a ligature fashioned out of a bed sheet. K's medical notes contained no new entries for the eleven days prior to his death. 28

The applicant sought Legal Aid to pursue an action against the Home Office in respect of the treatment of her son and the conditions of his detention, but her Legal Aid certificate was discharged on counsel's advice that the action had no reasonable prospect of success. The applicant then brought proceedings in Strasbourg under the European Convention for the Protection of Human Rights and Fundamental Freedoms, alleging that her son had died as a result of the prison authorities' failure to protect his life, that he had suffered inhuman and degrading treatment due to the conditions of his detention, and that she had no effective remedy in respect of her complaints. The European Commission of Human Rights referred the application to the Court. 29

[23] (2001) 33 EHRR 913. Noted by De Prez [2001] *Tort Law Review* (Tort L Rev), 178.

b) Judgment of the European Court of Human Rights

30 The Court ruled unanimously that there had been no violation of Art. 2 of the Convention. The Court accepted in principle that state authorities have a positive obligation to adopt preventative measures to protect an identified individual whose life is, or ought to have been, known to be at real and immediate risk. It was immaterial whether the risk arose from the criminal acts of a third party (as had been the situation in *Osman*) or from the individual's propensity for doing injury to himself. Here the threat was real, and, although its immediacy varied – and it could not be concluded that he was at immediate risk throughout the period of his detention – the variability of his condition required that he be monitored carefully in case of sudden deterioration. The question was therefore whether, having regard to the nature of the risk, the prison authorities had done all that was reasonably expected of them to prevent him from taking his own life. On the facts, the Court concluded that they had. Though there had been deficiencies in K's treatment in the days before his death, their connection with his suicide was purely speculative, and they fell to be considered under Art. 3, not Art. 2.

31 The Court ruled by five votes to two that there had been a violation of Art. 3 of the Convention. The Court's jurisprudence established that the authorities were under an obligation to protect the health of persons deprived of their liberty, and that the lack of appropriate medical treatment could amount to inhuman and degrading treatment contrary to Art. 3. Whether it did so or not, was to be assessed in the light of the person's mental capacity, taking account of any vulnerability arising from mental illness. In this case, exposing K, who was mentally-ill and known to be a suicide risk, to additional stress by the imposition of disciplinary sanctions on him was inhuman and degrading treatment and punishment when considered in the light of significant defects in the medical care that he was afforded: the authorities had failed properly to maintain K's medical records and there had been insufficient input from trained psychiatrists into his assessment and treatment.

32 The Court ruled unanimously that there had also been a violation of Art. 13 of the Convention. As regards K, the United Kingdom had failed to provide an expeditious avenue of complaint for prisoners who required speedy redress, and did not have in place a system of automatic review of disciplinary decisions in respect of prisoners who were not in a fit mental state to make use of any complaints procedure provided. As regards K's mother, the United Kingdom had failed to provide any effective procedure to determine the liability of the authorities – the coroner's inquest that was held did not perform this role – or to ensure the payment of adequate compensation to his estate. The Court found that the domestic law of negligence was not capable of furnishing effective redress in such a case. First, the claim available to K's estate did not allow the payment of compensation for anguish and fear falling short of psychiatric illness. The Court considered that, in principle, compensation for non-pecuniary damage such as pain, stress, anxiety and frustration should be available

amongst the range of remedies for breach of Art. 3 which, with Art. 2, ranked as one of the most fundamental provisions of the Convention. Secondly, the applicant was unable to claim damages under the Fatal Accidents Act on her own behalf as she was the mother of an adult child and a non-dependent. It was the Court's view that the first applicant should have been able to apply for compensation for her own non-pecuniary damage under domestic law.

The court awarded damages of £ 7,000 in respect of the stress, anxiety and feelings of insecurity suffered by K as a consequence of the disciplinary sanctions imposed on him prior to his death, and £ 3,000 to his mother in respect of her anguish and distress at the circumstances of her son's detention and her inability to pursue an effective avenue of redress. 33

c) Commentary

It has already been accepted by the domestic courts that prison authorities, and those in an equivalent position, owe a duty of care to those in their custody, and that this duty extends to protecting the latter from self-inflicted injuries (see *Reeves v Commissioner of the Police for the Metropolis*[24]). In *Orange v Chief Constable of West Yorkshire Police*,[25] the English Court of Appeal found that English law was consistent with the *Keenan* decision in requiring there to be a foreseeable risk of suicide before the prison authorities could be held liable. There, the deceased asphyxiated himself whilst in police custody after arrest by looping his belt around the horizontal bar on the gate to his cell. He was apparently a 'run-of-the-mill drunk' and there was no reason to believe that he presented a suicide risk. As the court noted, suicides in police custody are much rarer than those in prison, whether on remand or after conviction. In the circumstances of the case, the police therefore owed the deceased no duty to take positive steps for his protection, for example, by taking away his belt. The court considered it immaterial that the cell in which he was held did not comply with a Home Office recommendation that structure and fittings should be such as to minimise risk of prisoners causing themselves injury. It may perhaps be doubted whether the Court of Human Rights would have been so forgiving, given the very clear link between the state of the cell and the manner of suicide. The Court's judgment suggests there might be basic precautions that the authorities should take in respect of every prisoner, not just those known to be particularly at risk (see, especially, § 91, where the Court talks of 'general measures and precautions… available to diminish the opportunities for self-harm', in addition to the 'more stringent measures' that might be necessary in respect of a particular prisoner). 34

These doubts aside, it seems that the present case does not require so fundamental a reconsideration of English law as do *Z v United Kingdom* and *TP and KM v United Kingdom* (above), both of which suggest that English law should recognise a duty of care where none was recognised before. But it goes beyond existing 35

[24] [2000] 1 AC 360.
[25] [2001] EWCA Civ, 611, [2001] 3 *Weekly Law Reports* (WLR) 736.

English law in allowing a claim for purely emotional harm not consequential on physical injury, both in respect of the primary victim, K, and the secondary victim, his mother. To an English lawyer, the mother's claim seems especially remote as her distress derived not from her own immediate perception of her son's ill-treatment but from hearing about it subsequently and being unable to pursue an effective avenue of redress. The question arises whether, with their new powers and responsibilities under the Human Rights Act 1998, the English courts will follow Strasbourg's example in allowing claims for such mental injuries and, if so, whether they will do so by extension of existing principles of negligence liability or by invoking their statutory discretion to award damages under the Act. The relevant provisions of the Human Rights Act are considered in more detail, above, in the commentary on *TP and KM v United Kingdom*.

36 There is also the question of the remedies available to the estate and relatives of the dead. In English law, a deceased's estate can in principle recover compensation for all loss, pecuniary and non-pecuniary, suffered in the period between injury and death.[26] However, in *Hicks v Chief Constable of South Yorkshire*,[27] the House of Lords ruled that no award at all should be made for non-pecuniary loss if death were to follow within seconds of injury, or if the deceased were to lose consciousness within seconds and die within minutes. In a separate concurring opinion in the present case, the British member of the Court, Lord Justice Sedley, noted that the *Hicks* decision made it 'extremely unlikely' that K's estate could have recovered damages in English law for the pain and suffering he endured during the period of his asphyxiation. The effect of this rule is compounded by the unavailability of damages for loss of life in English law.[28] Formerly, the fact of death attracted compensation indirectly in the form of damages for 'loss of expectation of life',[29] but such awards attracted much criticism because of their tokenistic nature,[30] and they were abolished by statute in 1982.[31] The same statute created a new claim for 'bereavement damages' in cases where death results from a tortious act, but this only benefits a bereaved spouse or, where the deceased is a child, the parents.[32] Where an unmarried adult without financial dependants suffers an instantaneous death, it therefore appears that the theoretical remedy in negligence is worthless. In *Keenan*, this consideration led to the conclusion that there had been a violation of Art. 13 not because the applicant was deprived of adequate compensation for her son's death, for the Court decided that the

[26] Law Reform (Miscellaneous Provisions) Act 1934, sec. 1.

[27] [1992] 2 *All England Reports* (All ER) 65.

[28] *Rose v Ford* [1937] AC, 826.

[29] *Ibid.* Damages under this head could be awarded even where the deceased had died the same day as the accident without recovering consciousness (*Benham v Gambling* [1941] AC, 157) and perhaps even where death was instantaneous (*Andrews v Freeborough* [1967] 1 *Queen's Bench* (QB) 1, 9, per Wilmer LJ, and 19, per Winn LJ).

[30] See, *e.g.*, *H West & Son Ltd v Shephard* [1964] AC, 326, 369, per Lord Pearce.

[31] Administration of Justice Act 1982, sec. 1.

[32] Fatal Accidents Act 1976, sec. 1A, introduced by Administration of Justice Act 1982, sec. 3. A fixed sum of £ 10,000 (recently raised from £ 7,500) is paid in every case, save where reduced by reason of the deceased's contributory negligence.

prison authorities were not in fact responsible for his suicide, but (it seems) because it was not reasonable to expect the applicant to sue in negligence if there was no prospect of obtaining compensation, and she therefore had no reasonable means of establishing where responsibility lay for her son's death. This unsatisfactory state of affairs can hardly be allowed to continue in English law, though it would appear that the necessary changes can only be effected by Parliament, not by the courts.

4. *Lister v Hesley Hall Ltd* [2001] *United Kingdom House of Lords* (UKHL), 22: Vicarious Liability[33]

a) Brief Summary of the Facts

Between 1979 and 1982, the appellants were residents of a school for boys with emotional and behavioural difficulties. The boarding annex of the school usually accommodated about 18 boys. The school and the boarding annex were owned by the respondent company, which employed Mr G. as warden and his wife, Mrs G., as housekeeper. On most days, they were the only members of staff present in the annex. As warden, Mr G. was responsible for supervising the boys when they were not at school, for example, by making sure they went to bed at night, got up in the morning, and got to and from school. Unbeknown to his employers, Mr G. systematically subjected the appellants to sexual abuse whilst they were resident at the school. The appellants made no complaint at the time, but in the early 1990s a police investigation led to the criminal trial and subsequent conviction of Mr G. for multiple offences involving sexual abuse. In 1997, the appellants brought claims for personal injury against the employers. At trial, the employers were found vicariously liable for the torts committed by the warden, but they appealed successfully to the Court of Appeal, which found that it was bound by the earlier Court of Appeal decision in *Trotman v North Yorkshire County Council*[34] to treat the sexual assaults as outside the scope of employment. 37

b) Decision of the House of Lords

The House of Lords upheld the appellants' appeal against the decision of the Court of Appeal. To establish vicarious liability, it had to be demonstrated that the employee's tortious acts were within the scope of his employment. In addressing this question, their Lordships found a useful starting point in the classic analysis of Sir John Salmond, originally advanced in the first edition of *Salmond on Torts* in 1907. According to Salmond, a master could be held liable for a tort committed by his servant if 'it is either (a) a wrongful act authorised by the master, or (b) a wrongful and unauthorised mode of doing some act authorised by the master.'[35] But he could not be held vicariously liable for 38

[33] [2001] 2 WLR 1311, [2001] 2 All ER 769. Noted by Feldthusen [2001] Tort L Rev, 173 and Hopkins [2001] *Cambridge Law Journal* (CLJ), 458.

[34] [1999] *Local Government Reports* (LGR), 584

[35] Sir J. Salmond, *Torts* (1st edn. 1907), p. 83. See now *Salmond & Heuston on Torts* (21st edn. 1996), p. 443

'an independent act'.[36] In the present decision, their Lordships recognised that no statement of general principle could determine which side of the line any individual case would fall as this was inevitably a matter of degree. In every case, it was necessary to inquire into the closeness of the connection between the employee's tort and the employment. Something more had to be shown than that the employment provided the opportunity for the commission of the tort. On the present facts, the crucial consideration was that the warden (unlike, say, the groundsman or the school porter[37]) had been entrusted with a general responsibility for the welfare of the boys: the sexual assaults could therefore be regarded as acts within the scope of his employment for which his employers were vicariously responsible.

39 The House of Lords overruled the decision of the Court of Appeal in *Trotman v North Yorkshire County Council*, where the facts were very similar. There, the Court of Appeal had reached the conclusion that the employee's acts could not fall within the scope of his employment because they amounted to the very negation of the employer's duty to the child and could in no sense be described as a mode of carrying out an authorised act. It now appears that the Court of Appeal, in both *Trotman* and the present case, had fallen into error because it had construed the relevant employment too narrowly. As Lord Clyde explained, it is 'inappropriate to concentrate too closely upon the particular act complained of. Not only do the purpose and the nature of the act have to be considered but the context and the circumstances in which it occurred have to be taken into account' (§ 43).

c) Commentary

40 It is clearly established that an employee's act can be within the scope of employment even if done exclusively for his own comfort or convenience[38] or in disobedience of express orders.[39] Insofar as criminal acts are concerned, it has been accepted for some considerable time that such acts may yet be regarded as within the scope of employment, for example, in the case of fraud by the solicitors' clerk acting as their agent in a particular transaction[40] or the commission of an assault in the unreasonably aggressive defence of the defendant's property.[41] In this context, the decisions of the Court of Appeal in *Trotman* and the present case were hard to justify: how, for example, were the assaults committed by the warden any more a 'negation' of his employer's duty than the fraud of the solicitors' clerk? And the decisions appeared even more anomalous when compared with another case decided before the Court of Appeal, *Morris v CW Martin & Sons*.[42] There, the court had ruled that the defendant dry-cleaners were vicariously liable for their employee's theft of a

[36] Sir J. Salmond (*supra* note 35), p. 84. See now *Salmond & Heuston* (*supra* note 35), p. 443.
[37] See [2001] 2 WLR 1311, § 62, per Lord Hobhouse, and § 82, per Lord Millett.
[38] See, *e.g.*, *Century Insurance Co Ltd v Northern Ireland Road Transport Board* [1942] AC, 509 (lighting a cigarette).
[39] See, *e.g.*, *Rose v Plenty* [1976] 1 WLR 141.
[40] *Lloyd v Grace, Smith & Co* [1912] AC, 716.
[41] *Poland v John Parr & Sons* [1927] 1 *King's Bench* (KB) 236.
[42] [1966] 1 QB 716.

garment left in their care. Set against this decision, *Trotman* appeared to espouse the unattractive doctrine that the care of people was less important than the care of chattels. That anomaly has now been removed.

5. *Kuddus v Chief Constable of Leicestershire Constabulary* [2001] UKHL, 29: Exemplary Damages[43]

a) Brief Summary of the Facts

The appellant alleged that, following the theft of property from his flat, he had reported the matter to a police constable who subsequently forged his signature on a written statement withdrawing the complaint. The respondent chief constable admitted the forgery and that the constable's conduct amounted to the tort of misfeasance in public office. However, he contended that the decision of the Court of Appeal in *AB v South West Water Services Ltd*[44] precluded the award of exemplary damages in respect of that cause of action, as it provided that they were only recoverable in respect of torts where their availability had been established by authority prior to 1964, the date of the House of Lords' decision in *Rookes v Barnard*[45] and of Lord Devlin's authoritative categorisation of the bases on which exemplary damages could be awarded. The chief constable applied successfully to have that part of the claim which was for exemplary damages struck out, and this decision was upheld by the Court of Appeal (Auld LJ dissenting). The appellant appealed to the House of Lords. **41**

b) Decision of the House of Lords

The House of Lords allowed the appeal, overruling the decision of the Court of Appeal in *AB v South West Water Services Ltd*. The claim for exemplary damages should not have been struck out on the basis that the claimant had had to establish that exemplary damages had been awarded for the tort of misfeasance in public office prior to 1964. The majority (Lord Slynn, Lord Mackay and Lord Hutton) found that this was consistent with the House's earlier decision in *Cassell & Co Ltd v Broome*,[46] notwithstanding certain dicta in the speeches of Lord Hailsham (with whom Lord Kilbrandon concurred) and Lord Diplock which could be read as supporting the *AB* approach. Lord Nicholls and Lord Scott, however, found it necessary to invoke the House of Lords' power to depart from the reasoning in *Cassell v Broome*, which they interpreted as providing firm support for the *AB* decision. With the exception of Lord Mackay, who based his opinion purely on an interpretation of *Rookes v Barnard*, their Lordships agreed that the 'cause of action' test had 'commit[ted] the law to an irrational position in which the result depend[ed] not on principle but upon the accidents of litigation.'[47] **42**

[43] [2001] 2 WLR 1789, [2001] 3 All ER 193.
[44] [1993] QB, 507.
[45] [1964] AC, 1129.
[46] [1972] AC, 1027.
[47] As is stated in W.V.H. Rogers, *Winfield and Jolowicz on Tort* (15th edn.), p. 746, in a passage cited by several members of the House of Lords.

c) Commentary

43 Exemplary or punitive damages are designed to punish the defendant rather than to compensate the claimant. Viewed by many as anomalous, they are limited at common law to the two categories of case identified by Lord Devlin in his classic analysis in *Rookes v Barnard*, namely, where there is oppressive, arbitrary or unconstitutional action by the servants of the government or conduct calculated by the defendant to make a profit for himself exceeding the compensation payable to the claimant. Not content with these restrictions on the availability of exemplary damages, it appears that the Court of Appeal in *AB v South West Water Services Ltd* had endeavoured to reduce the circumstances in which they could be awarded insofar as was consistent with authority. The results, as one commentator noted, were 'entirely arbitrary',[48] and it was no surprise that the Law Commission in its Report on *Aggravated, Exemplary and Restitutionary Damages* (1997) recommended the abolition of the 'cause of action' test adopted in *AB*,[49] nor that the House of Lords should take the first opportunity to overrule *AB* that arose.

44 The Law Commission in its Report of 1997 recommended statutory reform to make exemplary damages more widely available than was admitted by the House of Lords in *Rooke*. The test it proposed was whether the defendant was guilty of a deliberate and outrageous disregard of the claimant's rights.[50] The proposal has not yet been implemented, and indeed, in 1999, the Government stated that it had decided to defer consideration of legislative reform in the area, expressing the hope that further judicial development of the law might help to clarify the issues.[51] In the present case, the House of Lords was not asked to rule on the correctness of *Rookes v Barnard* – to the evident disappointment of Lord Nicholls, who thought that there was a case for going beyond *Rookes v Barnard* and allowing exemplary damages in respect of non-governmental oppression or bullying (§ 66) and Lord Scott, who argued that there was no longer any need for exemplary damages in English civil law (§ 107 and § 110).

45 The ruling of the House of Lords is ambiguous in one respect: did their Lordships intend to jettison the 'cause of action' test whatever form it might take, or only in the guise in which it appeared in *AB v South West Water Services Ltd*? Only Lord Scott seems to have appreciated that overruling *AB* merely entailed rejecting a 'cause of action' test based on the accidents of litigation, and did not preclude the adoption of a revised test which distinguished between causes of action on other grounds. His Lordship stated that he was in favour of 'a pragmatic solution' whereby exemplary damages would be allowed in respect of all torts except negligence, nuisance, breach of statutory duty (in the absence of express statutory authorisation), and all torts of strict

[48] Pipe [1994] 57 MLR 91, 101.
[49] Law Commission Report No. 247 (1997), § 5.49.
[50] § 5.46.
[51] *House of Commons Debates* (HC Deb), 9 November 1999, col. 502.

liability (§ 122). (It is not clear where this would leave defamation, where awards of examplary damages are more common than anywhere else, for liability in defamation is generally regarded as strict.) The matter was not directly addressed by the other members of the House of Lords, though they certainly gave no impression that they would have supported such a move.

One question left expressly unresolved by the House of Lords was whether an employer might be made to pay exemplary damages for a tort committed by his employee in circumstances falling under one of Lord Devlin's two categories in *Rookes v Barnard*. Lord Scott stated his provisional view that such a liability would be contrary to principle and ought not to be allowed (§ 137), but Lord Hutton considered that making the employer vicariously liable might serve some purpose where the tort has evidently been committed by one of the defendant's employees but it cannot be proved which (§ 79). If such awards are to be allowed, then the question raised by Lord Mackay will no doubt have to be addressed, namely, whether the court would be entitled to take into account the financial means of the employer in fixing the level of the damages, or only, as Lord Mackay was inclined to think, the financial means of the employee (§ 47). **46**

6. *Parkinson v St James and Seacroft University Hospital NHS Trust* [2001] *England and Wales Court of Appeal, Civil Division* (EWCA Civ), 530: Negligent Sterilisation[52]

a) Brief Summary of the Facts

After a negligent sterilisation operation performed by an employee of the defendant health authority, the claimant conceived and gave birth to her fifth child, a boy. In the course of her pregnancy, she was advised that the child might be born with a disability, which was not attributable to the defendant's negligence, but she chose not to have the pregnancy terminated. After giving birth, the claimant sued the defendant for damages on the basis that her son had indeed been born with substantial disabilities. On the hearing of a preliminary issue, Longmore J ruled that the claimant could recover damages for the cost of satisfying any special needs attributable to the boy's disability, but not for the basic costs of his maintenance. The defendant appealed and the claimant cross-appealed. **47**

b) Judgment of the Court of Appeal

Dismissing both appeal and cross-appeal, the Court of Appeal ruled that the claimant could recover only the special costs attributable to her child's disabilities. The decision of the House of Lords in *McFarlane v Tayside Health Board*,[53] to the effect that there could be no liability for the basic costs of maintaining a healthy child born after a failed sterilisation, applied equally to **48**

[52] [2002] QB, 266, [2001] 3 All ER 97. Noted by Bickford-Smith [2001] *Journal of Personal Injury Law* (JPIL), 404.

[53] [2000] 2 AC 59.

the case of a child born with a disability and precluded recovery of normal child-rearing costs. But it was fair, just and reasonable that the mother should be awarded damages for the extra expenses associated with the upbringing of a child with a significant disability.

49 According to Hale LJ (with whom Nourse LJ agreed), the decision of the House of Lords had been based upon a theory of 'deemed equilibrium' by which the costs attributable to the birth of a healthy child were cancelled out by the benefits the child would bring to the parents. This analysis was binding upon the Court of Appeal, although to Hale LJ '[t]he notion of a child bringing benefit to the parents is itself deeply suspect, smacking of the commodification of the child, regarding the child as an asset to the parents' (§ 89). Hale LJ stated that there was no reason to take the consequent limitation on the damages recoverable by the parents any further than it was taken in *McFarlane's* case, and reasoned that the extra costs of raising a disabled child should be recoverable as these went beyond those that could be set off against the benefits of having a child. In her opinion, this was not to treat a disabled child as bringing less pleasure and fewer advantages than a normal healthy child: the Court's analysis 'affords him the same dignity and status. It simply acknowledges that he costs more' (§ 90). Hale LJ suggested that the same analysis would apply whether the disability was present at the time of conception or caused during the course of pregnancy (§ 92), though Brooke LJ stressed that the negligent surgeon could not be held liable if whatever occurred during pregnancy amounted to a new intervening cause (§ 54).

50 In answering the question, How disabled does the child have to be for the parents to be able to make a claim?, the Court of Appeal proposed applying the test for entitlement to special-needs provision under sec. 17(11) of the Children Act 1989: 'a child is disabled if he is blind, deaf or dumb or suffers from mental disorder of any kind or is substantially and permanently handicapped by illness, injury or congenital deformity or such other disability as may be prescribed.'[54]

c) Commentary

51 This case forms part of the Court of Appeal's ongoing efforts to grapple with the decision of the House of Lords in *McFarlane*. There, the House of Lords had been dealing with the birth of a healthy child, and reserved its judgment on the case of a child born with disabilities.[55] The present decision resolves the law applicable to such a case. For all the detailed analysis of authority and consideration of principle by the Court of Appeal, it appears ultimately to have been based on a perception that the general public would think it unfair if the parents of a disabled child were unable to recover for the additional costs resulting from the disability.

[54] See § 91, per Hale LJ, with whom Brooke LJ expressly agreed on this point (§ 52).
[55] See [2000] 2 AC 59, 84, per Lord Steyn, and 99, per Lord Clyde.

In the robust judgment of Hale LJ, one of only two female Lords Justices of Appeal, there appear a number of criticisms of the decision of the House of Lords in *McFarlane*. Posing the question of whether its effect would be to encourage some women to mitigate their loss by having an abortion, she stated: 'Realistically, some may think, the result of their Lordships' decision could well be that some will have no other sensible option' (§ 66). Furthermore, her graphic account of what is entailed by the invasion of bodily integrity caused by conception, pregnancy and childbirth can be read as an implied rebuke to those in *McFarlane* who treated the financial consequences of giving birth as a form of purely economic loss, *i.e.* economic loss not consequent upon physical harm. It has to be admitted that it seems odd to determine the extent of liability in a case of unwanted birth by the application of concepts, such as 'assumption of responsibility', developed in connection with the provision of financial services. And as Hale LJ notes, recourse to such concepts may only muddy the waters further. For example, '[g]iven that the doctor clearly does assume some responsibility for preventing conception, it is difficult to understand why he assumes responsibility for some but not all of the clearly foreseeable, indeed highly probable losses resulting' (§ 80). **52**

Assuming that Hale LJ was right to consider that the same analysis would apply whether the disability was present at conception or caused during pregnancy, it is clear that the courts will face difficult questions of causation in the future. It will no doubt have to be determined, for example, whether the negligent surgeon can be held responsible for costs associated with a disability arising during pregnancy because of the mother's illness or use of a pharmaceutical product, or the application of violent force to her body. **53**

7. *Fairchild v Glenhaven Funeral Services Ltd* [2001] EWCA Civ, 1881: Causation[56]

a) Brief Summary of the Facts

In a consolidated appeal bringing together six separate actions, the Court of Appeal was required to address amongst other things the question of whether, and in what circumstances, a claimant who sustains mesothelioma through exposure to asbestos dust can recover damages from an employer who is one of two or more employers each responsible for different periods of exposure. It was accepted before the court that mesothelioma is an 'indivisible' disease which is triggered on a single unidentifiable occasion when one or more asbestos fibres initiate a process whose effects only become apparent years later, and that it is quite unlike asbestosis, which is a progressive condition that becomes more and more severe in proportion to the total amount of asbestos inhaled. The claimants conceded that none of them was able to prove on the balance of probabilities where they had been employed when the mesothelioma was triggered, but contended that they were nevertheless entitled to **54**

[56] [2002] *Industrial Relations Law Reports* (IRLR), 129.

recover full damages from any employer responsible for any period of the exposure.

b) Judgment of the Court of Appeal

55 The Court ruled that it was necessary for each claimant to prove on the balance of probabilities that the mesothelioma was triggered by a period of exposure to asbestos that was the responsibility of a particular tortfeasor. It was not enough that any individual employer had contributed to the risk of contracting mesothelioma. Since it was common ground in each of the appeals that this burden could not be satisfied, none of the claimants was entitled to damages in tort. In the Court's opinion, it would be unjust if an employer for whom the claimant was employed for quite a short time in a long working life should have to bear full liability for the claimant's condition when the claimant was wholly unable to prove on the balance of probabilities that that period of employment played any causative role in the inception of the disease. Admittedly, Lord Reid in the case of *McGhee v National Coal Board*[57] had concluded that the plaintiff was entitled to full damages from his employer when part of his total exposure to the agent responsible for his condition was attributable to the employer's breach of duty, even though there was no way of deciding whether that condition was caused cumulatively or by a single incident. But that was a case where there was only one causative agent and only one possible tortfeasor, and it was distinguishable where, as in the present case, there was more than one possible tortfeasor.

c) Commentary

56 In *Holtby v Brigham & Cowan (Hull) Ltd*,[58] where the same question was addressed in respect of asbestosis, the Court of Appeal ruled that each employer's liability should be limited to a proportion of the full damages to which the claimant was entitled, each employer's share of responsibility reflecting the proportion of the total exposure that was attributable to his breach of duty. In the present case, the claimants adopted an all-or-nothing strategy, arguing that once liability was established, there was no question of discounting the award on a proportionate-exposure basis. This was inappropriate because mesothelioma was an indivisible injury. But there was nothing to stop the employer against whom the claimant was successful from seeking contribution from those who were responsible for the rest of the overall exposure. In the event, the claimants were hoist by their own petard. We can only speculate what would have happened if they had claimed, in the alternative, that they were entitled to damages on a proportionate-exposure basis. Curiously, the Court states it had to decide whether the *Holtby* approach was appropriate in the case of an indivisible disease like mesothelioma (§ 71), but (unless this reviewer has overlooked something) it appears that it neglected to do so.

[57] [1973] 1 WLR 1.
[58] [2000] 3 All ER 421.

The case represents a restatement of orthodox doctrine, and displays the unwillingness of the English courts to countenance the innovative solutions to problems of causal indeterminacy that have been adopted in certain other jurisdictions.[59] Rather disappointingly, the Court's trawl of comparative material was limited to two other Commonwealth jurisdictions, Canada and Australia, in both of which the orthodox doctrine has so far prevailed in circumstances such as those under discussion here, whilst there was no citation of academic literature at all. It appears that the case is now under appeal to the House of Lords, and it is to be hoped that their Lordships will grapple more thoroughly with the issues than the Court of Appeal felt able to do. **57**

For what it is worth, the present reviewer considers that there is something to be said for departing from orthodox doctrine in circumstances where several defendants have, in breach of duty, exposed the claimant to the risk of injury but it is not clear whose breach of duty was in fact the injury's cause. This is generally regarded as necessary in the 'two hunters' scenario often considered by textbook writers, and this is supported by the decision of the Canadian Supreme Court in *Cook v Lewis*;[60] the same concern underlies the 'market share' liability doctrine adopted in certain American jurisdictions.[61] There is even some evidence that the English courts are prepared to depart from conventional principles where a claimant who has undoubtedly suffered tortious injury would otherwise be unable to fix causal responsibility on any one of those who breached their duty towards him.[62] The fact that the House of Lords has ruled out innovation in the case of 'the indeterminate plaintiff'[63] does not mean that they are obliged to do so in respect of 'the indeterminate defendant'.[64] The distinction between these two categories of case certainly makes more sense than that made here between the circumstances of *McGhee* and those of the case before the Court of Appeal. **58**

8. *A v National Blood Authority* [2001] 3 All ER 289, High Court (Burton J): Product Liability[65]

a) Brief Summary of the Facts

The claimants were infected with the Hepatitis C virus when they received transfusions of blood obtained from the defendants. They sought damages under Part 1 of the Consumer Protection Act 1987, which implemented the European Community (EC) Product Liability Directive (Directive 85/374). The six test cases which were brought to trial were representative of various **59**

[59] See, for a general survey, A. Porat/A. Stein, *Tort Liability Under Uncertainty* (2001), *passim*.

[60] [1951] *Supreme Court Reports* (SCR), 830. See also *Summers v Tice*, 199 *Pacific Reporter, Second Series* (P 2d) 1 (1948).

[61] See, especially, *Sindell v Abbott Laboratories*, 607 P 2d 924 (1980).

[62] See *Baker v Willoughby* [1970] AC, 467.

[63] See, especially, *Hotson v East Berkshire Area Health Authority* [1987] AC, 750 and *Wilsher v Essex Area Health Authority* [1988] AC, 1074.

[64] See further J. Fleming, *The American Tort Process* (1988), pp. 252–63.

[65] Noted by Howells and Mildred [2002] 65 MLR 95, and Melville Williams [2001] JPIL, 238.

common issues arising in a group action consolidating 114 separate claims. These related to the period of approximately three years from the date on which the provisions of the Act came into effect (1 March 1988). Blood producers and medical experts had known since the 1970s that between 1 and 3% of transfused blood was infected with Hepatitis C, even though the virus was not itself identified until May 1988. It was only in mid-1990 that screening techniques allowed it to be detected in donated blood. The key questions for decision were whether the infected blood could be regarded as 'defective' and whether the development risks defence was open to the defendants. On the question of 'defect', the defendants argued that it could not reasonably be expected that every batch of their blood would be free from contamination, as contamination was an unavoidable risk in a small minority of cases. So the public was only entitled to expect that there had been 'legitimately expectable' testing and precautions; they should not 'expect the unattainable'. In respect of the development risks defence, the defendants' argument was that this should be construed so as to apply even where the risk of the defect was known, so long as the state of scientific and technical knowledge did not enable the producer to identify the defect in a particular product so as to prevent its supply.

b) Judgment of the High Court

60 Burton J ruled that the blood was defective according to the test in art. 6 of the Directive (sec. 3(1) of the Act). The question of what degree of safety the public was entitled to expect was to be assessed by the judge in the light of the information which was in the public domain at the relevant time. Here, there was at that time no public understanding or acceptance of the risk of the infection of transfused blood and the public was therefore entitled to expect that the blood would be safe. There could be cases in which the public at large accepted that a proportion of products of a particular kind would be less safe than the norm, but that was not so here. Burton J rejected the defendants' submission that the public was only entitled to expect that there had been 'legitimately expectable' testing and precautions. This was effectively 'to reformulate the expectation as one that the producer will not have been negligent or will have taken all reasonable steps' (§ 56) and hence to undermine the strict liability that the legislation was intended to introduce. In considering the question of defect, it was not appropriate to take into account the avoidability of the harmful characteristic, the impracticality, cost or difficulty of taking precautionary measures, or the product's utility (§ 68). The latter factor could only be taken into account in asking whether with full information and proper knowledge the public accepted or ought to have accepted the risk.

61 The defendants were not entitled to rely upon the the development risks defence under art. 7(e) of the Directive (sec. 4(1)(e) of the Act). If the existence of a defect was known to be theoretically possible, the producer could not rely upon the defence even if there was no known way of discovering the defect's presence in an individual product so as to prevent its supply. Here, the defendants had known of the risk that some batches of their blood might be contaminated by the Hepatitis C virus but claimed that contemporary screening techniques did not allow them to identify whether any particular batch was contaminated. Deciding that the development risks defence did not apply on such facts, the learned judge stated (§ 74): "Once the existence of the defect is known, then there is the risk of that defect materialising in any particular product."

c) Commentary

It has taken ten years for a really significant case to arise under the new strict products liability regime, and this is it. What is pleasing about the judgment is Burton J's evident determination not to let the strict liability of the EC Directive be so diluted in the process of interpretation that it becomes fault-based in all but name. But his judgment leaves a number of loose ends, and it is to be hoped that an appellate court will have the opportunity to tie these up in the near future. **62**

Burton J shows a sound appreciation of the difficulties consumers may face in proving that the manufacturer of a product was negligent, and this was clearly why he preferred an impressionistic approach to the question of defect, based upon the information that is actually in the public domain, rather than one which calls for an extensive (and expensive) inquiry into production processes. Given the emphasis upon generally-available information, it seems that it may be advisable for a producer to seek to educate the public about the risks in question, though how these particular defendants could have done this is far from clear. The normal course of action would be to inform consumers of the risk by means of a warning supplied with the product, but many 'consumers' of transfused blood must receive it in emergency procedures after accidents in which they have been left unconscious. Public expectations could well have been lowered if there had been extensive media coverage of the risk of infection, but it would surely be socially undesirable for the defendants to seek such publicity as this could unduly alarm those needing transfusions, and perhaps panic them into refusing treatment that is in their best interests. **63**

A case which may be explicable on the basis that the public *did* accept the risk of quality-variations in the product in question is *Richardson v LRC Products Ltd.*[66] Here, the action was brought against the manufacturer of a condom which fractured as the claimant had sex with her husband; the claimant conceived and claimed damages for the unwanted pregnancy. Ian Kennedy J ruled that the mere fact that the condom had split did not prove that it had been defective: although it was naturally enough the user's expectation that a condom would not fail, the manufacturer had never claimed that no condom would ever fail and 'no-one has ever supposed that any method of contraception intended to defeat nature will be 100 per cent effective.'[67] It seems, how- **64**

[66] [2000] *Personal Injury Quantum Reports* (PIQR), P164.
[67] [2000] PIQR, P164, P171.

ever, that the primary ground for the decision was that there was no evidence that the condom in question fell below standard in any way.

65 Burton J's remarks about the relevance of the avoidability of the risk, the practicality, cost and difficulty of precautions, and the product's utility give rise to considerable difficulty. It is possible to agree with him to the extent that, where the public reasonably expects there to be no risk at all, questions of avoidability, etc., simply do not arise. But this surely cannot be the case where the public *is* aware of a risk, whether arising from product variation or from the product's basic design. Whether the degree of variation or inherent risk is acceptable can only be assessed in the light of its avoidability and the product's utility. There is simply no warrant in the Directive for excluding these considerations–indeed the Directive expressly states that the question of defect is to be addressed 'taking *all* circumstances into account' (emphasis added). In fact, Burton J's approach leads him to some very strange contortions. He states, for example, that a claimant cannot invoke the Directive where his claim is that a dangerous product ought not to have been marketed at all, even with a warning, when a risk-free alternative was available (§ 70), or that a product should have incorporated safety improvements to be found in a later model, there being no good reason for the delay in their incorporation (§ 72). It is submitted that there is nothing in the Directive, or in the essential logic of the judge's own argument, that justifies this conclusion.

66 The development risks defence had previously been considered by the European Court of Justice in *European Commission v United Kingdom*.[68] There the Court ruled that, despite its ambiguous language, the Consumer Protection Act did not require the domestic courts to apply a test of whether or not a reasonable producer in the industry in question could reasonably have been expected to gain knowledge of the risk. It was still open to the domestic courts to give effect to the true meaning of art. 7(e) of the Directive. When this was properly construed, it was clear that the mere fact that the risk was identified in scientific literature that was accessible to the producer was enough to preclude reliance upon the defence. In the present case, Burton J offers a helpful analysis of the key requirement of 'accessibility', noting, for example, that unpublished research retained within the laboratory or research department which carried it out would not normally be 'accessible' in the relevant sense. Taking the hypothetical case considered by Advocate General Tesauro in the case before the European Court of Justice – the brilliant researcher in Manchuria who identified the risk in question in a Chinese-language scientific journal which was not disseminated outside the region at the relevant time – Burton J agrees that the defence would ordinarily be available in such a case, but adds the qualification that the contrary might apply if the product were one for which Manchuria were especially known (§ 49).

[68] Case C-300/95. [1997] ECR, I-2649.

An interesting facet of the case is that Burton J chose to go straight to the wording of the Directive, and refrained from detailed analysis of the equivalent provisions of the implementing Act. This appears to have been perfectly proper on the facts of the instant case, as there was no suggestion that the provisions of Act and Directive were in conflict. In fact, in relation to the development risks defence, it appears that this was the desirable course of action, for the European Court of Justice in *European Commission v United Kingdom* had apparently accepted that the natural interpretation of the implementing legislation might be at odds with the Directive, albeit that it allowed an alternative interpretation that was consistent with the Directive. In the Court's view, the domestic courts could be relied upon to adopt the latter interpretation. In other cases, where the Act unambiguously differs from the Directive, it appears that the proper course of action is for the domestic court to give effect to the former. Applying the Directive would render nugatory the distinction between the doctrines of direct and indirect effect in EC law. 67

9. *Grobbelaar v News Group Newspapers Ltd* [2001] EWCA Civ, 33: Defamation[69]

a) Brief Summary of the Facts

The claimant, Bruce Grobbelaar, was a well-known footballer who played in goal for Liverpool FC for several years in the 1980s and early 1990s. In 1994, one of his associates, V, told a journalist working for the defendants' newspaper, *The Sun*, that Grobbelaar had received money for fixing the result of matches in which he was playing. V alleged that the money came from a betting syndicate in South East Asia. He was paid for his story. Seeking corroboration, *The Sun* covertly video and sound-recorded a series of meetings between Grobbelaar and their informant. During these meetings, Grobbelaar confessed to having taken money for losing matches in the past and took £ 2000 offered by V in return for fixing matches in the future. In November 1994, Grobbelaar was confronted with the allegations of match-fixing by *Sun* reporters and photographers. He denied any wrongdoing. The next day, *The Sun* printed a front-page exclusive under the headline 'Grobbelaar took bribes to fix games'. In subsequent daily issues, *The Sun* gave massive and relentless coverage to the story. Soon afterwards, Grobbelaar issued a writ against the defendant publishers, claiming damages for defamation. He denied he had dishonestly taken bribes or sought to fix the result of games in which he was playing. Before his action could proceed, however, Grobbelaar was arrested by the police in connection with the allegations made by *The Sun* and charged with criminal conspiracy and acceptance of a bribe. He stood trial twice on these charges. At the first trial (January-March 1997), the jury could not agree on either count. At his subsequent retrial (June-August 1997), the jury unanimously acquitted Grobbelaar of conspiracy, but could not agree on the count of bribe-taking. The prosecution declined to pursue the charge further and the 68

[69] [2001] 2 All ER 437. Noted by Mullender [2001] CLJ, 460 and Robertshaw [2001] 64 MLR 923.

judge directed a verdict of not guilty. In December 1997, Grobbelaar pleaded guilty to a disciplinary charge of assisting in betting brought against him by the Football Association.

69 The trial of Grobbelaar's defamation action took place in July 1999. The defendants relied primarily upon the defence of justification (*i.e.* truth), the trial judge having ruled that the defence of qualified privilege was not available to them. In support of their plea of justification, they presented (amongst other evidence) their tapes of the covertly-recorded meetings between Grobbelaar and V. Grobbelaar's explanation was that his conduct in the meetings was part of an elaborate scheme of his own that was designed to expose V as a fraud; he was merely pretending to play along. The jury found unanimously in Grobbelaar's favour and awarded him £ 85,000 in compensatory damages. The defendant appealed on two grounds: first, that the trial judge had been wrong to rule that the defence of qualified privilege had not been available to them; secondly, that the jury's verdict was perverse.

b) Judgment of the Court of Appeal

70 The Court upheld the trial judge's ruling that the defendants could not rely upon the defence of qualified privilege. The availability of that defence had to be assessed by reference to the decision of the House of Lords in *Reynolds v Times Newspapers Ltd*,[70] and in particular the specific considerations set out there by Lord Nicholls, including the seriousness of the allegations, the extent of the public concern in them, the reliability of the defendants' source and the steps they had taken to verify their information. The consideration which was decisive here was the *tone* of the publication. The defence of qualified privilege was not applicable to what was a sensational newspaper exposé unambiguously asserting the criminal guilt of its subject. It was, according to Simon Brown LJ, absurd to suggest that newspapers would be discouraged from pursuing their investigatory role by such a ruling, particularly bearing in mind the obvious commercial benefits derived from the style of journalism practised here by *The Sun*. In fact, to allow the defence in such circumstances would give rise to the altogether greater risk that exposés would become even more sensational.

71 The Court further ruled, however, that the jury's verdict in favour of the claimant should be set aside as perverse. Such a conclusion was only to be reached with reluctance and on very strong grounds, as the court should not usurp the jury's function, but it was the only conclusion that was open to the Court on the facts. Grobbelaar's story that he was trying to entrap V was 'simply incredible';[71] it was 'so utterly implausible that no jury, acting reasonably, could have accepted it as true.'[72] The only rational conclusion was that Grobbelaar had indeed taken corrupt payments. Even though the jury's implicit

[70] [2001] 2 AC 127.
[71] See § 92, *per* Simon Brown LJ, and §116, *per* Thorpe LJ.
[72] See § 241, *per* Jonathan Parker LJ.

decision that Grobbelaar had not actually thrown matches in which he was involved was supported by reasonable grounds, the gravity of the proven allegation of corruption precluded him from succeeding in his action for damages.

c) Commentary

This appears to be a unique decision. Though there are cases in which an appellate court has set aside on grounds of perversity a jury's decision as to the meaning of the words complained of,[73] the Court of Appeal was referred to no precedent for this where the question was (as here) whether the defamatory allegation was true or false. Certainly, the facts of Grobbelaar's case look damning, but it is hard – for us as well as for the Court of Appeal – to reach a definitive conclusion without having seen how the evidence unfurled at trial, and it should not be forgotten that three separate juries have now declined to find Grobbelaar guilty of corruption (albeit that two of them had to apply the criminal standard of proof beyond all reasonable doubt). Seen in this light, the Court of Appeal's conclusion perhaps appears more questionable than it did at first glance. **72**

A small puzzle is the basis on which the Court of Appeal ruled that Grobbelaar could not succeed on the basis that he had not actually thrown matches if he was proved to have accepted bribes. Under sec. 5 of the Defamation Act 1952, a defence of justification may succeed in a case involving two or more distinct charges even though the defendant has not proved the truth of every charge, provided that 'the words not proved to be true do not materially injure the plaintiff's reputation having regard to the truth of the remaining charges.' This principle seems to provide a sound basis for the ruling in question, but the defendants abandoned any attempt to rely upon sec. 5 in the course of the trial. Another possibility is that the truth of the proven charge so devalued Grobbelaar's reputation that, following *Pamplin v Express Newspapers Ltd (No. 2)*,[74] he effectively had no reputation to lose and therefore could not recover substantial damages. But the *Pamplin* principle entails a verdict in the claimant's favour: it merely justifies the award of contemptuous, rather than substantial, damages. The only viable explanation for the court's ruling on this point therefore seems to be that the allegations of corruption and match-fixing shared a common sting, which was sufficiently drawn by proof that Grobbelaar had in fact taken bribes. But it has to be admitted that this matter did not receive the attention it was due in the Court of Appeal's judgments. **73**

The relationship between judge and jury in libel trials was also at issue in two other decisions last year: *Safeway Stores plc v Tate*[75] and *Alexander v Arts Council of Wales.*[76] In the former, the Court of Appeal ruled that the court's **74**

[73] See, *e.g.*, *O'Brien v Marquis of Salisbury* (1889) 6 *Times Law Reports* (TLR), 137; *Australian Newspaper Co Ltd v Bennett* [1894] AC, 284.

[74] [1988] 1 WLR 116.

[75] [2001] 4 All ER 193.

[76] [2001] 1 WLR 1840, [2001] 4 All ER 205. See also *McPhilemy v Times Newspapers Ltd (No. 2)* [2001] 4 All ER 861

jurisdiction to grant summary judgment under Civil Precedure Rules 1998, rule 24.2 did not curtail a claimant's right to have the jury determine the question of libel or no libel. But, in the latter case, a differently-constituted Court of Appeal re-asserted the orthodox position that it is for the judge to determine whether the words are capable of bearing a defamatory meaning, and, if they are, for the jury to decide whether or not they in fact bear that meaning. The Court expressed the view that its reasoning in the earlier decision could be interpreted as meaning that the right of a judge to withdraw a case from a jury was not as wide as was in fact the case.

75 The effect of *Reynolds v Times Newspapers Ltd* on the defence of qualified privilege was given further consideration in *Loutchansky v Times Newspapers Ltd (No. 2)*, which is summarised below.

10. *Loutchansky v Times Newspapers Ltd (No. 2)* [2001] EWCA Civ, 1805: Defamation[77]

a) Brief Summary of the Facts

76 The claimant, an international businessman of dual Russian and Israeli nationality, frequently visited the United Kingdom on business until 1994. In that year, the Home Secretary ordered his exclusion from the United Kingdom on the ground that his presence would not be conducive to the public good. In 1999, the defendant newspaper published articles alleging that he was a leading figure in the Russian mafia and involved in money-laundering and the smuggling of nuclear arms. Soon afterwards, the claimant brought proceedings for defamation. The articles in question continued to appear on the newspaper's internet site, and this was the subject of a further complaint by the claimant. In their defence, the defendants did not seek to prove that their allegations were true, or even to prove that there existed reasonable grounds for suspicion, and relied primarily upon the defence of qualified privilege as recently explained by the House of Lords in *Reynolds v Times Newspapers Ltd.*[78] They also argued that the complaint about the publication of the articles on the internet was time-barred because it was more than a year since their first posting on the *Times* website. The trial judge rejected that argument, finding that there was a new publication, and hence a new cause of action, on each occasion the articles were accessed. He also ruled that the defendants could not rely upon the defence of qualified privilege because they had been under no duty to publish the articles: it could not be said that their failure to publish the material would have exposed them to legitimate criticism. The defendants appealed against these rulings.

b) Judgment of the Court of Appeal

77 On the question of qualified privilege, the Court observed that the correct interpretation of *Reynolds* was crucial to this appeal. In its view, '*Reynolds*

[77] [2002] 2 All ER 652.
[78] [2001] 2 AC 127.

privilege… although built upon an orthodox foundation, is in reality sui generis' (§ 32); it was 'a different jurisprudential creature from the traditional form of privilege from which it sprang' (§ 35). Unlike the traditional form of the defence, *Reynolds* privilege attached not to the occasion of publication but to the publication itself, and depended upon the defendant satisfying the requirements of responsible journalism. Consequently, little scope remained for any further inquiry as to whether the privilege was to be withdrawn on account of the defendant's malice. In the Court's opinion, the requirements of responsible journalism did not apply to the more conventional situations in which qualified privilege arose: 'a person giving a reference or reporting a crime need not act responsibly: his communication will be privileged subject only to relevance and malice' (§ 36).

In the present case, the judge had imposed too stringent a test in limiting the scope of *Reynolds* privilege to situations where the publisher would have been open to legitimate criticism had he not published. It was perfectly conceivable that circumstances would arise where one newspaper would decide to publish, while another would decide the contrary, without either of them falling below the standard of responsible journalism. In the Court's opinion (§ 41): **78**

The question to be posed is… whether it was in the public interest to publish the article, true or false, rather than whether it was in the public interest to publish an untruth. Even, moreover, when the untruth of the article is established (or when, as here, it is not formally disputed), it is important to remember that the defence of qualified privilege tolerates factual inaccuracy for two purposes: first so as not to deter the publication sued upon (which might have been true); and secondly so as not to deter future publications of truthful information.

The Court ruled that the case should be remitted to the judge to enable him to reconsider the defendants' claim to qualified privilege in light of the present judgment.

On the question of the internet publication, the Court reaffirmed the orthodox rule that each new publication of defamatory material gives rise to a separate cause of action, subject to its own limitation period. There was no reason to believe that this rule was inconsistent with the right to freedom of expression under European Convention for the Protection of Human Rights and Fundamental Freedoms, Art. 10, to which the courts are required to have particular regard whenever they are considering the granting of relief which might affect the exercise of that right.[79] In the Court's opinion, the orthodox rule did not have a chilling effect upon freedom of expression that went beyond what was necessary and proportionate in a democratic society for the protection of reputation. The Court accepted that the maintenance of archives, whether in hard copy or on the internet, had some social utility, but considered that it represented a comparatively insignificant aspect of freedom of expression. In any **79**

[79] Human Rights Act 1998, sec. 12.

case, the Court did not believe that the law of defamation would necessarily inhibit the responsible maintenance of archives, because attaching an appropriate notice to archive material which is or may be defamatory, so as to warn against treating it as the truth, would normally remove any defamatory sting. Furthermore, although it could be said that permitting an action to be based on the accessing of archive material long after its general publication was at odds with some of the reasons for the introduction of a 12-month limitation period for defamation, the scale of the new publication and the injury resulting from it was likely to be modest when compared with the original publication. There was therefore no warrant for radically changing the law of defamation so as to introduce the 'single publication rule' for which the defendants had argued, by which the distribution of defamatory material is deemed to involve only one publication, occurring on the occasion of its first publication in a particular format.[80]

80 The Court also decided that, whether or not the initial publication of the articles naming the claimant as a mafia boss were protected by qualified privilege, that privilege would not extend to their continued publication on the defendants' website, since this made no reference to the fact that their veracity was disputed. That was not responsible journalism.

c) Commentary

81 In *Reynolds v Times Newspapers Ltd*, the House of Lords had recognised for the first time what may be termed a 'journalistic privilege' to publish matters of public interest to the world at large. Previously, publication to the general public appears only to have been permissible in rare cases, for example, involving a suspected terrorist attack or the distribution of contaminated food or drugs.[81] *Loutchansky (No. 2)* makes plain that the House of Lords' decision effectively creates a new form of qualified privilege with only a superficial resemblance to the defence as conventionally understood. Whilst conventional privilege applies unless there is proof that the defendant was actuated by malice, journalistic privilege only avails a defendant who acts in conformity with principles of journalistic responsibility. There seems to be much to commend this approach – not least, that there might be an undue 'chilling effect' upon free speech on those occasions to which qualified privilege has traditionally attached if the privilege were to be withdrawn simply because the defendant was irresponsible.

82 Given that sec. 3 of the Human Rights Act 1998 requires a court determining a question which has arisen in connection with a Convention right to take into account all relevant judgments of the European Court of Human Rights, it is very disappointing that the Court of Appeal did not refer to any of the Strasbourg caselaw on the right to freedom of expression, especially since several

[80] The rule has been adopted in a number of American jurisdictions. See, *e.g.*, *Gregoire v GP Putnams Sons*, 81 *North Eastern Reporter, Second Series* (NE 2d) 45 (1948).
[81] See *Blackshaw v Lord* [1984] QB 1, 27 per Stephenson LJ.

Art. 10 cases were cited to it by counsel. It is also disappointing that the Court makes no effort to address the argument that its duty under sec. 6 of the Human Rights Act requires it to develop the common law to ensure that it is compatible with the Convention rights (though it is not clear whether this argument was in fact put to the court by counsel). It is apparent that it will take some time before our judges truly become human-rights literate.

It is not known whether this decision will be appealed to the House of Lords, **83** but, if it is, it is to be hoped that the 'single publication rule' proposed by the defendants will be given more serious consideration. The only positive argument the Court of Appeal gave in support of the existing rule that every new publication of defamatory material gives rise to a new cause of action, other than that it was firmly entrenched in the law, was that it might produce injustice in a case where a claimant does not become aware of the material until more than a year after the initial publication. As counsel for the defendants pointed out, this problem could be simply addressed by the court exercising its discretion to allow an action to proceed out of time. If that is accepted, then it appears that there is nothing to set against the defendants' concern that the existing rule is bound to affect the media's willingness to maintain internet archives, and thus to limit freedom of expression. The Court's answer that attaching an appropriate notice to questionable articles might draw their defamatory sting does not appear wholly satisfactory, because it appears that liability may arise for repeating a defamatory imputation even if it is made clear that the veracity of the charge is disputed.[82]

In previous proceedings in the same action,[83] the Court of Appeal had ruled **84** that a publisher claiming qualified privilege could not rely upon facts unknown to him at the time of publication. If it turned out that the defendants had failed to make diligent enquiries before publication, that was the end of the matter, and they could not excuse that failure by pointing to material they had acquired subsequently. The Court accordingly upheld the judge's decision not to allow the defendants, in an attempt to strengthen their case, to amend their pleadings so as to refer to intelligence reports and other material which they had only obtained after the publication of the two articles.

11. *Venables v News Group Newspapers Ltd* [2001] *Family Division* (Fam), 430, High Court (Dame Elizabeth Butler-Sloss P): Human Rights, Confidence and Privacy[84]

a) Brief Summary of the Facts

The claimants were convicted as children of the shocking and well-publicised **85** murder of two-year-old James Bulger. At the time of the hearing, they had

[82] *Cf.* the 'repetition rule', on which, see A. Grubb (ed.), *The Law of Torts* (2001), § 25.9.
[83] *Loutchansky v Times Newspapers Ltd (No. 1)* [2001] EWCA Civ, 536, [2001] 3 WLR 404, [2001] 4 All ER 115.
[84] [2001] 2 WLR 992, [2001] 1 All ER 908.

served the tariff set by the Lord Chief Justice and it was likely that the Parole Board would reach a decision over their reintegration into the community over the coming year. The claimants alleged that they were at risk of serious injury or death from vigilante attacks if details of their identity, appearance, or whereabouts on release from prison became publicly-known, and that there was a real likelihood that the press in general, and the defendants in particular, would publish such details. Relying primarily upon the law of confidence, they sought injunctions prohibiting the publication of that information by any person.

b) Judgment of the High Court

86 Dame Elizabeth Butler-Sloss, the President of the Family Division (P), granted the requested injunctions, which were to apply against the whole world. Their legal basis lay in the 'tort' of breach of confidence. The publisher of a newspaper was not a 'public authority' within sec. 6 of the Human Rights Act 1998 even though operating in the public domain and fulfilling a public service, and the claimants therefore could not rely upon the remedy against public authorities established by sec. 7 of that Act. Nor did the Act allow for the judicial recognition of a free-standing cause of action for breach of the claimants' rights under the European Convention for the Protection of Human Rights and Fundamental Freedoms. The Act required the court to develop existing causes of action to give proper effect to Convention rights, but it did not authorise the creation of wholly-new causes of action.

87 The duty of confidence could arise independently of any transaction or relationship between the parties, and the media owed such a duty in respect of information it acquired with notice of its confidentiality. Although the courts had not previously granted injunctions to protect information about a claimant's identity or location, it was necessary to treat such information as confidential on the facts of this case in order to protect the claimants' rights under Artt. 2, 3 and 8 of the Convention. There was a serious risk that they would otherwise be the objects of revenge attacks and their lives put at risk. The injunctions would result in some interference with the rights of the defendants and others to freedom of expression under Art. 10 of the Convention – to whose importance the court was directed by sec. 12 of the Human Rights Act to have 'particular regard' – but the case fell within the exceptions set out in Art. 10(2): the interference was in pursuit of a legitimate aim, being to protect the claimants' rights to confidence, and it was in accordance with law, necessary in a democratic society to satisfy a strong and pressing need, and proportionate to the legitimate aim pursued. The learned judge was 'uncertain' whether it would have been appropriate to grant the injunctions had it been only Art. 8 that was likely to be breached, but it was not necessary for her to come to a conclusion on this matter because of the real and serious risk to the claimants' rights under Artt. 2 and 3.

c) Commentary

88 The decision can be seen an attempt to make up for English law's lack of any tort of invasion of privacy[85] by stretching the law of confidence. The present

decision certainly marks a significant extension of the scope of the law of confidence, not just in the respect noted by the learned President of the Family Division – that information of the sort in question here had not previously been classified as 'confidential' – but also in respect of the circumstances in which a duty of confidence will arise. Although the learned judge treats it as uncontroversial, it is far from settled that a duty of confidence can arise merely from the acquisition of information with notice of its confidential character.[86] There is indeed judicial support for such a view, but most of it derives from *obiter dicta*[87] or preliminary rulings in interim hearings.[88]

With the passage of the Human Rights Act 1998, it is the court's duty to act compatibly with Convention rights. The duty, arising under sec. 6(1) of the Act, applies to all 'public authorities', and the court is a public authority by virtues of sec. 6(3). What the court's duty entails has been the subject of some controversy, but the predominant view – embraced here by Dame Elizabeth Butler-Sloss P – is that it extends beyond matters of legal procedure and permits the development of the existing substantive law, while stopping short of allowing the creation of wholly-new causes of action.[89] This view entails the continued rejection of a tort of invasion of privacy, and will no doubt result in claims that are really about privacy being dressed up as actions for breach of confidence. **89**

Liability for breach of confidence is equitable in origin, but the President of the Family Division here describes breach of confidence as a tort.[90] The historical distinction between equity and common law, the latter being the traditional home of the law of tort, has long obstructed the rational classification of civil wrongs in English law, and the categorisation of the equitable wrong as tortious is therefore to be welcomed. But it remains to be seen whether breach of confidence can truly be assimilated into the law of tort, or whether it is condemned forever to be distinguished from those causes of action whose origins are at common law. **90**

C. Literature

1. Law Commission, *The Illegality Defence in Tort*, Consultation Paper No. 160 (The Stationery Office, London 2001)

The Law Commission proposes that 'the current rules applied by the court when considering the effect of illegality on a tortious claim should be replaced **91**

[85] See *Kaye v Robertson* [1991] *Fleet Street Reports* (FSR), 62.

[86] See, generally, M. Lunney/K. Oliphant, *Tort Law: Text & Materials* (2000), pp. 671–2.

[87] *E.g. A-G v Guardian Newspapers (No. 2)* [1990] 1 AC 109 at 282, per Lord Goff.

[88] See, *e.g.*, *Francome v News Group Newspapers Ltd* [1984] 1 WLR 892. In English law, the purpose of the interim hearing is to determine whether the claimant's case is 'arguable' in law, not whether it is legally correct.

[89] See, generally, A. Grubb (ed.) (*supra* note 82), § 1.14.

[90] See also *Douglas v Hello! Ltd* [2001] 1 FLR 982, § 117, per Sedley LJ, but *cf.* North, Breach of Confidence: Is There a New Tort? [1972] 12 *Journal of the Society of Public Teachers of Law* (JSPTL) 149.

by a structured discretion, under which the court would be directed to consider whether, in the light of the underlying rationales and taking into account a number of guiding factors, the claim should be allowed or disallowed' (§ 1.18). It found that there was a lack of clarity in the way in which the illegality defence has been applied by the courts, and that the scope of the defence was potentially too wide, particularly in the area of personal injuries. The Commission thought that the illegality defence should be available only very rarely in a personal injury action, for example, where it was necessary to deter unlawful or immoral conduct or to preserve the dignity and reputation of the courts, or where the award of damages would undermine the rule making the conduct illegal and thereby render the law inconsistent. If the defence was supported by one of these policy rationales, the court should then consider whether it should be applied on the facts, having regard to such factors as the seriousness of the illegality, the knowledge and intention of the claimant, and proportionality. Claimants should not, however, be denied compensation for personal injuries on the basis that this was necessary to prevent them from benefiting from their own wrongdoing, as such compensation is not properly regarded as a form of 'profit' (§ 4.47).

2. A. Grubb (ed.), *The Law of Torts* (Butterworths, London 2001)

92 This new practitioners' reference work appears in the Butterworths Common Law Series. It provides coverage of the principal causes of action in the law of torts, and of general principles such as those relating to vicarious liability and remedies. An introductory chapter deals with the nature of tortious liability. In his preface to the volume, the editor states that the aim is "to provide an analytical account of the frameworks of the many torts that protect the physical, property, economic or personality interests of the individual… with an eye to the future as well as the past." Contributors are: David Burnet, Vivienne Harpwood, Steve Hedley, David Howarth, Mark Lunney, Paul Mitchell, Alastair Mullis, Donal Nolan, Ken Oliphant, and Janet O'Sullivan.

3. H. Carty, *An Analysis of the Economic Torts* (Oxford University Press, Oxford 2001)

93 The author summarises the law relating to both the 'general' economic torts – conspiracy, inducing breach of contract, intimidation, and unlawful interference with trade – and the 'misrepresentation' torts – deceit, malicious falsehood, and passing off. She argues that both categories are best incorporated into the same analytical framework (into which she also fits the negligent infliction of economic loss), in order to highlight the interconnections between them. This also has the benefit of countering the false impression that the individual torts within each of the categories are underpinned by the same general principle of liability. The author's proposed framework divides the economic torts into four categories: the secondary liability torts, which involve inducing or conspiring with a third party to commit an actionable wrong; the unlawful act torts, where the defendant performed an act capable of being a tort or breach of contract to a third party with the intention of injuring the claimant; conspiracy; and passing off. (The author appears to concede that the tort of malicious falsehood does not fit very readily into this scheme, although it overlaps to some extent with the unlawful act torts.) In the first three of these categories, liability rests upon the defendant's intention to injure the claimant; in the last, a different approach prevails because the basis of liability is not fault but the need to protect a trader's 'goodwill'. In the author's view, this framework has the advantage of furthering the policy that 'economic behaviour should only be controlled by the common law on a narrow basis' (p. 288). In the past, a failure to identify the conceptual basis of the economic torts resulted in what the author sees as an unwarranted expansion of liability by the courts, which is best to be countered by a rigorous description of the circumstances in which liability may properly arise.

4. A. Porat/A. Stein, *Tort Liability Under Uncertainty* (Oxford University Press, Oxford 2001)

The authors deal with what they call 'the problem of uncertainty', namely, that 94
the indeterminacy resulting from lack of knowledge of causal processes can leave victims of torts under-compensated and wrongdoers under-deterred. They consider and reject (entirely or in part) a number of possible solutions to the problem before putting forward their own proposal: the 'evidential damage doctrine'. By this doctrine, the defendant is liable in damages where his wrongful actions have impaired the claimant's ability to prove the causal link required by orthodox theory or the extent of the defendant's contribution to the injury. For example, where two hunters negligently let off their weapons at the same time, and a stray bullet – it is not known who fired it – strikes the claimant, it can be said of the hunter whose bullet misses that he has caused the claimant evidential damage. If he had not fired his gun, it would have been clear who was the real culprit. Here, each hunter is liable for the entirety of the claimant's loss, for each must have caused either the injury itself or evidential damage of equal financial value. In other cases, where the missing information would not have provided definitive proof of a causal link, damages should be calculated on the basis of the probability that the claimant would have prevailed at trial. So where the defendant's factory wrongfully emits carcinogenic radiation, causing an increase in the local incidence of cancer of 25%, the defendant is liable to each of the cancer sufferers, having prevented them by his wrongful conduct from identifying the real cause of their cancer, and must pay damages discounted to reflect the one-in-five chance that he was responsible. What if the background risk of cancer were attributable to a number of possible causes and it would have been impossible to identify the true cause even without the defendant's involvement? The authors submit that the payment of compensation would still be appropriate, because the defendant has interfered with each cancer victim's entitlement to information that affects his legal position and the value of the missing information equals 20% of the injury (pp. 193–4).

The authors claim that the advantage of their theory over that by which liabil- 95
ity results from the claimant's loss of chance is that evidential damage can be

viewed as an actionable injury even where there is no loss of chance. Where the likelihood is that the claimant's fate was predetermined prior to the defendant's wrongful act,[91] the preponderance of evidence rule entails that the claimant had no chance to lose at the relevant time. It is only the evidential damage theory that can right the wrong done to the claimant in such a case and provide the appropriate level of deterrence against future wrongdoing.

5. J. Wright, *Tort Law and Human Rights: The Impact of the ECHR on English Law* (Hart Publishing, Oxford 2001)

96 The author submits that, with the coming into effect of the Human Rights Act 1998, English lawyers must now analyse and develop tort law from a human rights perspective. She seeks to identify those areas of Convention law which will prove most relevant to domestic tort law, and asks what changes will be required and how these will be accommodated in doctrinal terms. In her view, the Act necessitates a significant change in attitude as English courts have frequently ignored international human rights standards in tort cases – sometimes because the parties failed to appreciate that human rights arguments were relevant at all. The book contains a thorough examination of the provisions of the 1998 Act, which the author contends have both vertical and horizontal effect, in the limited sense that the courts will be bound to respect Convention rights in developing existing common law principles, and of areas of existing law that may require reconsideration. She highlights in particular: whether the English courts' approach to the duty of care concept in negligence is compatible with Art. 6 of the Convention (the issue raised by *Osman*); whether the Act will induce the courts to recognise a duty of rescue of general scope at common law; whether the English law of defamation is compatible with the right to freedom of expression under Art. 10 of the Convention; how English law will develop to ensure the degree of protection for privacy required by Art. 8 of the Convention; and whether principles of English tort law – in particular, the law of private nuisance – are compatible with those Convention rights which impose a positive obligation on the state to guard against environmental harm. A recurring issue is the extent to which the courts, instead of developing existing causes of action, will leave claimants to their statutory remedy under sec. 8 of the 1998 Act, under which awards of compensation are discretionary and may be less substantial than those governed by existing principles.

6. Coote, Damages, *The Liesbosch*, and Impecuniosity, [2001] *Cambridge Law Journal* (CLJ), 511

97 The author considers the proposition, generally taken to be established by the House of Lords' decision in *The Liesbosch*,[92] that loss caused by the claimant's own lack of financial means is too remote. The rule is capable of operating very harshly on the facts of individual cases, and it is this that appears to

[91] As in *Hotson v East Berkshire Area Health Authority* [1987] AC, 750.

[92] *Owners of Dredger Liesbosch v Owners of Steamship Edison* [1933] AC, 449 (owners of damaged vessel not having funds to buy replacement immediately; damages only for cost of new vessel, not for hire charges incurred in interim).

have induced the Court of Appeal to distinguish *The Liesbosch* on numerous occasions.[93] Coote argues that the decision in *The Liesbosch* has in fact been misunderstood, and that the crucial determinant of its result was actually the prevailing rule that damages for property damage were to be assessed as at the date of loss, not a special rule concerning impecuniosity. If the measure of damages was the value of the sunken vessel as a going concern at the date of the collision, the plaintiff's inability to afford immediately to purchase a substitute was strictly irrelevant. In the 1970s, he notes, the date-of-assessment rule was relaxed – at least where the claimant sought repair costs, not replacement value – so as to allow some other date to be substituted if justice required.[94] Given this change in the legal context, Coote submits that there is no longer any reason to maintain any special impecuniosity rule, and regrets that the Privy Council did not undertake a fundamental reconsideration of the relevant principles when the opportunity arose in *Alcoa Minerals of Jamaica Ltd v Broderick*,[95] opting instead merely to distinguish *The Liesbosch* again.

7. Fairgrieve, The Human Rights Act 1998, Damages and Tort Law, [2001] *Public Law* (PL), 695

The author considers a number of issues arising in respect of the award of damages against a public authority under sec. 8 of the Human Rights Act 1998, seeking guidance from the jurisprudence of the European Court of Human Rights and principles of domestic tort law. Amongst the issues discussed are: Should fault be a precondition of the award of damages under sec. 8? Is it legitimate to limit the liability by reference to policy considerations, as permitted in tort by the third stage of the *Caparo* approach? Does sec. 8 allow the award of punitive damages? Will the courts be able to award damages for 'mere' mental distress? and To what extent will damages be available for loss of a chance? **98**

8. Gearty, Unravelling *Osman*, [2001] 64 *Modern Law Review* (MLR) 159

Writing before the *Osman* decision[96] was unravelled by the European Court of Human Rights itself,[97] the author notes the consternation that the case had caused English tort lawyers, and traces the development of the various strands of reasoning which the Court brought together in its judgment. He finds that the Court's approach to the right of access to a court implied by Art. 6(1) has been confused and inconsistent, making the 'conceptual disaster' of *Osman* almost inevitable. In his view, the Court's principal error was to base its decision upon the implied right of access to a court rather than the substantive right to a fair hearing that is explicit in Art. 6(1). Having found that the appli- **99**

93 See, *e.g.*, *Martindale v Duncan* [1973] 1 WLR 574, *Dodd Properties v Canterbury County Council* [1980] 1 WLR 433, and *Perry v Sydney Phillips & Son* [1982] 1 WLR 1297.

94 See, especially, *Miliangos v George Frank (Textiles) Ltd* [1976] AC, 443, and *Johnson v Agnew* [1980] AC, 367.

95 [2000] 3 WLR 23.

96 *Osman v United Kingdom* [1999] 1 FLR 193, (2000) 29 EHRR 245.

97 See *Z v United Kingdom* and *TP and KM v United Kingdom*, summarised above.

cant did have an arguable civil right, and hence that Art. 6 applied, it was a mistake to proceed to the question whether the English courts had effectively applied an 'immunity' such as to impair the essence of the implied right of access to a court. Its affirmative answer to this question entailed the confusing result that the applicant's civil right was at the same time presented as both arguable (in deciding that the right of access arose) and non-arguable (in deciding that there was effectively an immunity in domestic law). In Gearty's view, this confusion would have been avoided had the Court recognised that the question of whether the essence of the right of access has been impaired arises only when the threshold question, Is there an arguable right?, has been answered in the negative. In other words, it represents a fallback position enabling the Court to exercise a general supervisory role over the recognition of civil rights in domestic legal systems.

9. Howarth, Three Forms of Responsibility: On the Relationship Between Tort Law and the Welfare State, [2001] CLJ, 553

100 The author argues that the liability of a tortfeasor is underpinned by 'social' individual responsibility, which 'means accepting responsibility for the consequences that one's actions have for others' (p. 554). This is to be contrasted with an 'asocial' view of individual responsibility, whereby the person suffering the harm is treated as self-reliant and left to bear the loss. Whenever misfortune arises, a choice must be made between the two. Howarth then introduces the idea of collective responsibility, which underlies, for example, state welfare provision. In his view, collective responsibility addresses the same question as does social individual responsibility – when should we be responsible for the misfortunes of others? – but is fundamentally inconsistent with the asocial view of individual responsibility: 'Since the asocial view says that one should not impose the burden of an obligation to give support on another person, and collective responsibility is precisely the acceptance of such a burden by a group, the two are incompatible' (pp. 564–5). He concludes from this that collective responsibility is only warranted in situations which could give rise to social individual responsibility, and makes the dramatic pronouncement that the state should only take responsibility for misfortune, for example, through the National Health Service (NHS), where that misfortune is the responsibility of another person. Before the reader can recoil in horror, however, Howarth immediately inserts the qualification that 'most illness is the result of human agency' (p. 566) and could *potentially* (my emphasis) be treated as a matter of social individual responsibility – so NHS intervention is warranted. Using this conceptual framework, the author develops various further arguments about the relationship between tort law and the welfare state, concluding with the warning that abolishing tort in favour of no-fault compensation could fatally undermine the notion of responsibility for others upon which the welfare state, like tort, is based.

10. McIvor, Liability in Respect of the Intoxicated, [2001] CLJ, 109

The author surveys English and Commonwealth authorities dealing with the **101**
issues of liability for failing to protect an intoxicated person from harm, and for harm caused by an intoxicated person to others. She notes that at present the English courts have only gone so far as to recognise a duty of care towards an intoxicated person, and then only where there is an assumption of responsibility to him. But she warns that a failure to make a clear distinction between the two types of case, and to develop rules appropriate to each, could lead to an uncontrollable extension of liability to the detriment of the notions of individual responsibility which underpin the law.

11. Morgan, Nuisance and the Unruly Tenant, [2001] CLJ, 382

The author surveys the liability of landlords for nuisances committed by their **102**
tenants or licensees. He submits that landlords' liability should rest upon their failure to do what could reasonably be expected of them to control those on their land, and not upon whether the creator of the nuisance was a tenant or merely a licensee,[98] nor upon whether the landlord had 'adopted' the nuisance or merely permitted it to continue.[99] Effectively this would be to apply *Sedleigh-Denfield v O'Callaghan*[100] to owners of land who were not in actual occupation at the relevant time. There would be no question of extending liability to those more remotely involved, for example, environmental health officers who had failed to take action against the perpetrators. Morgan notes that, while the landlord's ultimate sanction over unruly tenants or licensees is eviction, the ability to evict will be constrained in cases where the landlord is a local authority by consequence of the authority's statutory duty to house the homeless.[101] He submits that this should be taken into account in assessing whether in all the circumstances the authority has acted reasonably. The author then gives an overview of the common law and statutory remedies that may be available personally against a 'neighbour from hell', but concludes with the observation that it may not always be realistic to expect victims of what may be persistent harassment to bring their tormentors to court: how much better if they could force their landlords to take their social obligations seriously.

12. Stauch, Risk and Remoteness of Damage in Negligence, [2001] 64 MLR 191

The author considers the principle of remoteness of damage in negligence and **103**
contends that it is more than simply a cover for the concealed policy choices

[98] The basis upon which the Court of Appeal in *Lippiatt v South Gloucestershire County Council* [2000] QB, 51 reconciled *Smith v Scott* [1973] *Chancery Division* (Ch), 314 (tenants) with *Page Motors v Epsom and Ewell Borough Council* [1982] 80 LGR 337 (licensees).

[99] The basis upon which the Court of Appeal in *Hussain v Lancaster County Council* [2000] QB, 1 distinguished *Page Motors* (*supra* note 98): there the defendant had adopted the licensees' nuisance by its own positive acts.

[100] [1940] AC, 880.

[101] Housing Act 1996, Part VII

of judges, as has sometimes been argued. He acknowledges that the traditional risk theory, which asks whether the risk of the type of harm in suit was reasonably foreseeable, leaves much to judicial discretion in determining the relevant risk. Consequently he suggests that, rather than define the risk in terms of *what* damage was sustained, as is traditional, we should do so in terms of *how* it occurred (the 'revised risk theory'). Here the focus is upon the set of causal conditions necessary for the occurrence of the injury, and in particular upon those conditions which, added to the defendant's conduct, completed the relevant causal set. The question for the court is whether the possible completion of that causal set was a reason for regarding the defendant's conduct as a breach of duty. If not, the injury is too remote (subject to a few exceptions, as mentioned below). This approach, Stauch submits, is capable of withstanding the accusation that determinations of remoteness are entirely subjective or policy-driven. He concedes, however, that it may be legitimate to depart from the standard test for reasons of policy (*e.g.* in the 'thin-skull' scenario), so long as the circumstances in which this is permitted are regarded as exceptional and limited in scope.

13. Waddams, Joanna Wagner and the Rival Opera Houses, [2001] 117 *Law Quarterly Review* (LQR) 431

104 The author traces the course of proceedings in, and historical circumstances of, two leading cases in English law. In *Lumley v Wagner*,[102] the manager of Her Majesty's Theatre, Haymarket, succeeded in getting an injunction to prevent the singer, Joanna Wagner (Richard Wagner's niece), from singing for the Royal Italian Opera, Covent Garden, at a time when she was under contract to sing at Her Majesty's. It was conceded that the court could not award specific performance of a contract for personal services. In *Lumley v Gye*,[103] the Court of Queen's Bench accepted in principle that the same plaintiff could recover damages from the manager of the Royal Italian Opera on the basis that the latter had knowingly induced Wagner to break the contract. A jury later found for the defendant on the facts,[104] but the decision on the preliminary issue of law has become the foundation stone for the modern tort of inducing a breach of contract – albeit that it was not followed, as Waddams notes, for some 30 years.[105] Waddams argues that the case itself provides no justification for so broad a liability, as the contract in question was one in which the plaintiff had a special interest in performance that warranted giving it something like proprietary effect: Joanna Wagner was 'hot property' and the future of Her Majesty's depended on her. In his view, 'it is not desirable to treat inducement of every breach of contract as a wrong' (p. 454).

[102] (1852) 5 *De Gex & Smale* (DeG & Sm) 485.
[103] (1853) 2 *Ellis & Blackburn* (El & Bl) 216.
[104] See [1854] 23 *Law Journal Queen's Bench* (LJQB), 116n.
[105] The first case was *Bowen v Hall* [1881] 6 *Queen's Bench Division* (QBD) 333.

14. Witting, Distinguishing Between Property Damage and Pure Economic Loss in Negligence: A Personality Thesis, [2001] 21 *Legal Studies* (LS) 481

The author seeks to explain why purely economic losses are not generally recoverable in the tort of negligence, while losses associated with damage to property are. To this end, he develops what he terms a 'personality thesis': 'whereas an individual's personality is partly constituted by the property that he or she owns, so that property can be seen as essential to the ways in which individuals constitute and define themselves, no such claim can be made with respect to mere abstract holdings of wealth' (p. 481). In the author's view, this consideration better justifies the distinction the law makes between property damage and pure economic loss than other explanations that have been advanced, *e.g.* that purely economic losses are difficult to prove or liable to be indeterminate in nature. It does not entail, however, that purely economic losses should never be recoverable in negligence. 105

VI. Finland

***Jaana Norio-Timonen*[1]**

A. Legislation

1 During the year 2001 no major legislative reforms concerning tort law took place. However, important work in the field of tort law was done by the Personal Injury Committee appointed by the Ministry of Justice.

2 In Finland, parliamentary legislation applying to liability in damages is to be found in the *vahingonkorvauslaki* (412/1974; Tort Liability Act, VahL). It is based on Nordic co-operation, which is why the Finnish Act was originally very similar to the Swedish one. The VahL applies to tort liability and damages. In contrast, it does not apply to contractual liability or damages or to liability provided in another act, unless otherwise provided.[2]

3 The background for the work of the Personal Injury Committee is as follows: Since the enactment of the VahL, the sphere in which it is being applied has undergone numerous noteworthy changes. One of them is the enactment of specific legislation to supplement and, in part, to supersede the VahL, *e.g.* the *tuotevastuulaki* (694/1990; Product Liability Act) and the *potilasvahinkolaki* (585/1986; Patient Injury Act). Likewise, different social insurance schemes and voluntary insurance policies have been developed and their supply is being expanded. Advances in medicine have had an impact *e.g.* on the evaluation of psychological injuries. Provisions on compensation for personal injury, loss of maintenance, and suffering are included in chapter 5 of the VahL. Despite the changes mentioned above, the chapter has retained its original form, save for the insertion, in 1999, of a new section 4a on the right to compensation that a deceased person's close ones have on the basis of anguish arising from the death, where it is the result of a deliberate or grossly negligent act.

[1] English translation by Mr Sami Sarvilinna VT, MJur, FM.

[2] For more information on Finnish Tort Law in English see J. Pöyhönen, Compensation for damage, in: J. Pöyhönen (ed.), *An Introduction to Finnish Law* (2002), pp. 64–79 and L. Sisula-Tulokas (ed.), *Contract and Tort Law: Twenty Cases from the Finnish Supreme Court* (2001).

The Personal Injury Committee published its report[3] in December 2001. The Committee noted that, in its current form, chapter 5 of the VahL contains but scant and generalised provisions on the compensation of personal injury. These provisions ought to be clarified and made more specific, so as to improve the legal security of victims and tortfeasors alike. Moreover, there is scope for some expansion in the right of injury victims to compensation. This is the case especially as regards the victims of serious violent crime and such victims' close ones. Nevertheless, in the opinion of the Committee, the current provisions offer a solid structural and material legislative basis, which has served well also in practice, so that there is no need to carry out any fundamental reforms thereon. The main proposals of the Committee concern the following topics: 1) compensation to the injury victim (*infra* [5]–[9]); 2) persons close to an injury victim entitled to compensation for expenses and loss of earnings (*infra* [10]); 3) compensation for death (*infra* [11]); 4) compensation for suffering arising from violations of personal integrity (*infra* [12]); and 5) establishing a Consultative Committee on Personal Injury Matters (*infra* [13]). **4**

According to the proposal of the Committee, a person sustaining personal injury ("injury victim") is entitled to compensation for medical expenses, other costs, loss of earnings, pain and suffering, any other temporary handicaps and any permanent handicaps. **5**

Compensation for medical expenses and other costs is at present assessed in accordance with the principle of full compensation. This principle is retained also in the proposal. However, compensation would be due only for necessary medical expenses and for other necessary costs. The necessity requirement is intended as a manifestation of the general tort law principle according to which the injury victim is under the obligation to mitigate his or her loss. **6**

Also *the compensation for loss of earnings* is now assessed and should in the future be assessed according to the principle of full compensation. It is proposed that the general assessment principles relating to compensation for loss of earnings be specifically stated in the VahL. The starting point in the assessment would be an estimate of the earnings that the injury victim would have gained, had the injury not occurred. From these estimated earnings, a subtraction would then be made as to the earnings that the victim has gained in spite of the injury, could have gained in spite of the injury, or can be estimated to gain in the future, taking into account his or her work capacity, training and education, previous employment, chances for re-training, age, living conditions and other comparable relevant circumstances. The assessment of compensation for loss of earnings is especially difficult in the case of children who, owing to personal injury, will never have the capacity to enter paid employment and who prior to the injury did not yet have career plans, either. **7**

3 Committee Report 2001.11. The Report is in Finnish, but contains a summary in Swedish. This presentation of the Committee Report is mainly based on the Report summary.

In order to guarantee the equal treatment of injury victims in such cases, it is proposed that the VahL contain a specific provision to the effect that the compensation for loss of earnings can be assessed on the basis of a standard earnings level, as defined in the VahL.

8 Furthermore, it is deemed justified that injury victims are also in the future awarded *compensation for non-pecuniary loss*. The level at which such compensation is assessed at present is to a large extent appropriate as well. Nevertheless, it is proposed that the heads of non-pecuniary loss be clarified and, in order to improve the coverage offered to injury victims, also somewhat expanded. The objective is that the diminished quality of life that ensues, in various forms, from physical and mental problems arising from a personal injury, would be compensated for at a uniform level. Hence, it is proposed that the heads of compensable non-pecuniary loss be changed so that compensation be assessed separately for pain and suffering and other temporary handicaps, on the one hand, and separately for permanent handicaps, on the other.

9 *Compensation for pain and suffering and other temporary handicaps* would be based on the discomfort that the injury victim has suffered from the occurrence of the injury until such time that he or she has recovered from the injury or otherwise reached a stabilised state of health. Accordingly, the victim could be assessed compensation for non-pecuniary loss that is likely to remain permanent already quite soon after the event of the injury, and not only later, when it can be definitively stated that the injury has resulted in a permanent handicap. The compensation for temporary handicaps would be assessed taking into account the nature of the personal injury, its seriousness, the need for, and duration of, treatment, and the duration of the handicap. *Compensation for permanent handicaps* would be based on such consequences of a personal injury which, according to the prevailing knowledge at the time of the assessment, will diminish the quality of the rest of the victim's life. Compensation for a permanent handicap would be assessed taking into account the nature and the seriousness of the personal injury and the age of the victim. In addition, it would be possible to take an especially severe diminution of the quality of the life of an injury victim into account as a basis for assessing the compensation at an increased level.

10 Especially as far as serious injuries are concerned, it is often important that also persons close to the injury victim take part in the care and treatment of the victim. This, however, may cause both expenses and loss of earnings to these persons. Such expenses and losses have already to some extent been compensated. However, the Committee proposes that provisions concerning *the entitlement to compensation of persons close to an injury victim* be included in the VahL. Thus, persons who are especially close to an injury victim would be entitled to reasonable compensation from the person liable for the injury for their necessary expenses and loss of earnings, where these ensue from their taking care of the injury victim. The same would apply to other measures following a personal injury, where these are conducive to furthering the recovery or rehabilitation of the injury victim. The persons entitled to this sort of compensation would be the injury victim's parents, children and spouse, as well as another comparable person who is especially close to the injury victim. However, this latter sort of close person would be entitled to compensation only for a special reason, the existence of which would be determined by taking into account the nature and seriousness of the personal injury, the age of the injury victim and the closeness of the relationship between the injury victim and the person claiming the compensation. Thus, a special reason for liability to arise in this context could be that the injury sustained by the victim has been serious or that the injury victim is a child.

As far as *compensation for death* is concerned, the most important proposal is an extension to *the compensation for loss of maintenance*. In contrast to the current legislation, everyone whose livelihood has actually depended on maintenance from the deceased would be entitled to compensation for loss of maintenance. Thus, it would no longer be relevant whether the deceased had any legal obligation to provide for the maintenance of the person claiming compensation. In the future, therefore, such compensation would be available *e.g.* to the domestic partner of the deceased. It is also proposed that the bases for the assessment of compensation for loss of maintenance be made more specific in the legislation. In the assessment of how much maintenance the claimant would probably have received from the deceased, it would be possible, if a special reason exists, to take into account the maintenance in kind that the deceased had provided by way of domestic work. This would be possible *e.g.* in situations where the deceased had not been in paid employment, but had provided for the maintenance of the family at home by taking care of the children and the household. Another extension to the compensation payable to persons close to the deceased is proposed for situations where the death has been caused deliberately or through gross negligence and, as a result of the death, a person especially close to the deceased self sustains a personal injury. In this event, such a person would be entitled to *compensation for the medical expenses, other costs and loss of earnings arising from the personal injury.* One of the objectives of the proposed provision is to promote the close person's chances to seek treatment as quickly as possible, by ensuring his or her right to compensation for the costs arising from the treatment. **11**

An extension is proposed to *the compensation for suffering arising from violations of personal integrity.* According to the proposal, a person would be entitled to compensation for suffering where his or her personal liberty, peace, reputation or privacy has been violated by a punishable act, or where he or she has been discriminated against by a punishable act. In this respect, the proposal is in line with the current legislation and case-law. In addition, however, a person would be entitled to compensation for suffering if his or her human dignity has been violated, deliberately or through gross negligence, in another manner comparable to the violations referred to above. In this event, compensability would not turn on whether the act is punishable or not. This latter proposal is intended as a guarantee for the necessary flexibility in the law in **12** situations where rapid societal or technical development can lead to new types of violation of personal integrity which have not yet been rendered punishable. In order to gain uniformity in the assessment of the compensation, it is proposed that the VahL contain a provision on the issues to be taken into account in the assessment. Accordingly, due note would be taken of the nature of the violation, the status of the victim, the relationship between the violator and the victim and the publicity that the violation may have received.

13 One of the objectives of the proposal is to promote uniformity in case-law and in the assessment of compensation. Therefore, the Committee proposes that a special *Consultative Committee on Personal Injury Matters* be established. The terms of reference of the Consultative Committee would be to obtain data on the amounts of compensation in case law and other assessment contexts, and to publish, on the basis of its findings, periodical summary-like recommendations relating to the amounts of compensation for non-pecuniary loss. The Consultative Committee would not be competent to issue compensation norms that would be binding on the courts.

B. Cases

14 The main task of the *Korkein oikeus* (Supreme Court, KKO) is to hand down precedents on points of law that are important for the whole legal system and in this way to give guidance for the application of the law. In 2001, the KKO handed down 140 precedents, 15 of which dealt with tort law matters. All the precedents have been published in *Korkeimman oikeuden ratkaisuja – Avgöranden av högsta domstolen 2001 I* (2001) and *II* (2002). They have been published and commented in P. Timonen (ed.) *KKO:n ratkaisut kommentein I* (2001) and *II* (2002).

1. *Korkein oikeus*; 2 January 2001; KKO 2001:1: Liability of Landlord: Liability for the Safety of Premises Open to the Public

a) Brief Summary of the Facts

15 The plaintiff had been a customer in a shopping centre owned by B Ltd. In the shopping centre, tempered glass panes had been installed as a part of the wall structure of a restaurant; a pane had shattered and fallen on the plaintiff, causing injuries. The plaintiff sued B for damages, alleging on the first hand negligence, as the installation had in the view of the plaintiff been defective in a number of ways. Secondarily, the plaintiff stated that B had strict liability for the injuries sustained by him. In the very least, the event had occurred in conditions where the defendant had an increased duty of care, so that it can avoid liability only by proving that the plaintiff himself had brought the injury upon himself. B contested the claim, stating that the liability of a landlord can only be based on negligence, and denying that there was negligence in the case at hand. B considered that the pane had been properly installed and that the reason for it shattering had not been established.

b) Judgment of the KKO

The reason for the pane shattering had remained unclear. The case turned on whether B Ltd, which owns the property, was liable for the event. KKO noted that the premises owned by the company were intended for the general use of persons with custom at the shopping centre or otherwise on the move there. It was the duty of the company to ensure that the structures of the property do not cause a hazard to the safety of the public. The glass pane installation, which had broken, had been constructed on commission by the company, which had also seen to the design thereof. The evidence showed that similar glass was regularly used in such installations and that the installation had been proper, but that one pane had nonetheless shattered and fallen. There was no reason to believe that this had been a result of an independent reason, not attributable to the structure in question or the company responsible for its safety. As the reason for the pane shattering remained unclear, the company had not proven that this was due to a circumstance beyond its duty of care. Accordingly, it was held that the company was liable in damages for the injury sustained by the plaintiff when the glass pane fell on him. 16

c) Commentary

This case emphasises the relative strictness of the negligence liability of the owner of premises open to the public. It appears in the precedent that any doubt as to the proof is to the disadvantage of the party that should show the absence of negligence; hence, liability can arise also in this manner. 17

2. *Korkein oikeus*; 8 February 2001; KKO 2001:17: Carriage of Goods by Road: Gross Negligence of Haulier

a) Brief Summary of the Facts

A parcel given to a road haulier in Denmark for carriage to Finland had been lost after it had arrived at the haulier's terminal in Finland. The plaintiff, the addressee of the parcel, stated that the haulier had been grossly negligent and claimed damages of an amount corresponding to the value of the goods and the bank costs, plus interest. The haulier stated that its conduct had not been grossly negligent and claimed that its liability was limited in accordance with § 32 subpara. 3 of the *tiekuljetussopimuslaki* (345/1979; Act on Carriage of Goods by Road) to a maximum of 8.33 Special Drawing Rights, as defined by the International Monetary Fund, for each kilogram of weight missing from the goods in question. 18

b) Judgment of the KKO

The case turned on whether the haulier had forfeited its right to invoke the limitation provision in § 32 subpara. 3 of the Act, by having caused the loss of the goods with grossly negligent conduct, as referred to in § 38 of the Act. The latter section corresponds in substance to Art. 29(1) of the Convention on the Contract for the International Carriage of Goods by Road (CMR) The KKO 19 cited also its own earlier precedent 1995:71, in which it held to have established that gross negligence is in Finland deemed to mean especially serious incaution which is close to being deliberate and thus displays an unscrupulous and reckless attitude in the person in question.

20 The haulier stated that the loss of the parcel was probably due to the parcel having been mixed up with other goods and then delivered to the wrong recipient. The KKO held that this kind of loss does not in itself show that the conduct of the haulier has been grossly negligent. The proof submitted in the case did not show that the haulier had treated the consignment in question otherwise than in accordance with its regular procedures, or in breach of the duty of care normal to the carriage business. The KKO held also that the plaintiff had also otherwise not proven that the haulier had caused the loss of the goods through gross negligence. Accordingly, the KKO held that the haulier was entitled to limit its liability to the maximum provided in § 32 subpara. 2 of the *tiekuljetussopimuslaki.* Furthermore, as compensation was payable only in respect of the weight of the missing goods, the plaintiff was not entitled to damages in respect of the bank costs.

c) Commentary

21 In this case, the KKO set a relatively high standard for gross negligence. The precedent, and the cited earlier precedent KKO 1995:71, may lead to the conclusion that the threshold of gross negligence has been raised in cases pertaining to the carriage of goods by road. Another interesting point is that the regular procedures of the haulier itself are considered significant in general, and that the observance thereof was deemed relevant also in the present individual case.

3. *Korkein oikeus*; 27 February 2001; KKO 2001:28: Compensable Loss: Liability of a Criminal Mischief-Maker in Damages for the Time That Rolling Stock Is out of Service

a) Brief Summary of the Facts

22 A, together with others, had defaced train engines and rolling stock owned by VR Ltd (the company), by painting graffiti on them. A was convicted of criminal mischief and ordered to compensate the company for the costs of the removal of the graffiti and the repainting of the rolling stock. KKO was presented with the issue of whether A was liable in damages to the company also for the loss of the time that the rolling stock was out of service while it was being cleaned and repainted.

b) Judgment of the KKO

23 The KKO noted that the principle of full compensation is the starting point of the VahL in respect to property damage. The manner in which economic losses arise depends on the situation and on the circumstances of the victim.

The duty of the victim to mitigate the loss is likewise relevant in the assessment of how he should proceed in the event of damage and how the economic consequences of the damage come about. Loss to be compensated may be incurred *e.g.* by payments made to third parties, by loss of income or by a decrease in the value of property, and also by additional costs or unnecessary expenses internal to the company sustaining the property damage.

The KKO noted that in the case at hand it had not been proven that the company had lost business income or incurred compensation expenses to passengers for reason of trains having been cancelled owing to the fact that the rolling stock was out of service. In the case of a company which is the monopoly provider of railway passenger services, the lowering of the standard of service for reason of certain equipment being out of order, in the form of cancelled trains or otherwise, is in practice often to the detriment of the passengers, and not the company. In contrast, the fact that the rolling stock was out of service caused economic loss to the company itself in the sense that it was subject to capital costs and other overheads, but not available to the use for which the investment was made. Such unnecessary expenses are not an unforeseeable or uncommon consequence of a damage event such as that in the case at hand. Accordingly, the KKO held that A was liable in damages also for the economic loss arising from the rolling stock having been out of service. 24

c) Commentary

No concrete loss sustained by the company for the time out of service had been shown in the case. The KKO nevertheless ordered A to pay damages for the same, which can be seen as a relative extension in the definition of compensable loss, and a departure from the requirement that the loss should be realised as a direct loss of income. These trends have been evident also in certain earlier precedents by the KKO. There is no indication in the case as to whether the KKO had attached importance to the fact that A had caused the loss by a deliberate act. 25

4. *Korkein oikeus*; 4 April 2001; KKO 2001:36: Tort Liability: Liability of a Member of the Board of Directors and an Auditor Arising from the Non-Payment of Share Capital[4]

a) Brief Summary of the Facts

When the share capital of a limited-liability company was being raised, a subscriber paid for his shares in kind. The members of the board of directors of the company had signed an affidavit, and its auditors a certificate, to the effect that the raising of the share capital had been fully paid up and the assets were in the possession of the company. However, a part of the assets handed over as 26

[4] This precedent has been commented also by Seppo Villa, see [2001] *Lakimies* (LM) 99, 888 *et seq.* and Kaj Glantz, Korkeimman oikeuden ratkaisusta 2001:36, [2001] LM 99, 1319 *et seq.*

in-kind payment had been pledged as security for the debts of the subscriber, and was later liquidated in order to cover the same. The limited-liability company was declared bankrupt, and the estate claimed damages from the members of the board of directors and from the auditors. At the time of signing the affidavit, some members of the board of directors had known of the status of the in-kind payment as pledged security. Other members and the auditors stated that they had not known of the same.

b) Judgment of the KKO

27 The KKO, which voted on the ruling, held that the affidavit and certificate that had been given contributed to the raising of the share capital having been entered into the Trade Register to the amount noted in the documents, even though the company in fact was not in possession of the corresponding assets. Hence, there was a potential shortage of share capital; it was not certain to be covered, but instead was realised when the pledged assets were liquidated in order to make good on the security. Accordingly, the loss incurred by the company, that is, the non-paid share capital, had ensued from the actions of the board of directors and the auditors. The KKO held that the members of the board of directors should have made sure that the information on the affidavit was correct before they signed it. By failing to do so, they had through their negligence contributed to the loss referred to above. The KKO did not make a distinction between actual knowledge of the error in the affidavit and a failure to determine whether the affidavit was correct. The liability of the auditors, for their part, arose from their failure to determine whether the assets had been conveyed to the company in a manner safeguarding its rights.

c) Commentary

28 The KKO has held of old that the amount of non-paid share capital is loss for which a party contributing to the non-payment is liable (KKO 1991:25); in this sense the precedent merely reinforces the existing case-law. In addition, it goes to show that the sphere of persons liable in this manner is extensive, covering both those aware of their affidavit or certificate being erroneous and those failing to find out whether the document is correct or not. At the same time, the precedent shows that the board of directors of a limited-liability company has a pronounced duty of care in assessing the true value of assets that form the share capital of the company.

5. *Korkein oikeus*; 7 June 2001; KKO 2001:58[5]: Liability of Tobacco Company for Smoking-Related Illness

a) Brief Summary of the Facts

29 The plaintiff had been a smoker of the defendant companies' cigarettes between 1941 and 1986. During the 1980s, he had been diagnosed with laryn-

[5] This precedent has been commented also by Michael Saarikoski, see [2002] LM 100, 231 *et seq*.

geal cancer and certain other diseases which he stated to have been caused by smoking. According to the plaintiff, the defendant companies had imported, manufactured and marketed cigarettes in the knowledge that they cause illness. Under a manufacturer's general duty of care and the legislative provisions cited by the plaintiff, the companies should have notified consumers of this negative health effect. However, they had consistently denied that tobacco was hazardous. Moreover, the plaintiff alleged that the sale of tobacco had in fact been prohibited up to the entry into force of the so-called *tupakkalaki* (693/1976; Act on the Prevention of Tobacco Smoking) on 1 March 1977. The plaintiff alleged that the companies had deliberately caused his illness. They were barred from alleging that the plaintiff had known of the negative health effects and contributed to his illness by smoking, as they themselves denied any causal relationship between smoking and the diseases contracted by the plaintiff. The plaintiff claimed damages, as specified in the action, to a total amount of FIM 486,000 (€ 81,739), plus interest.

The defendant companies contested the action, stating that their conduct had **30**
been consistent with the applicable legislation and could therefore not be considered negligent. The position of the companies should be assessed both in terms of the general knowledge of the health effects of tobacco and in terms of the plaintiff's specific knowledge of the same. The alleged negligent conduct of the companies could not have a causal relationship with the diseases of the plaintiff, nor had it been proven even on a general level that there was a causal relationship between smoking and those diseases in the first place.

b) Judgment of the KKO

Extensive medical evidence was offered in the case, both on any general **31**
causal relationship between smoking and the diseases which had been diagnosed in the plaintiff, and on the question whether the specific causal relationship between the plaintiff being a smoker and him contracting the diseases was a medically established fact. The decision of the KKO was that there was no medical proof to the effect that the diseases of the plaintiff were caused expressly and exclusively by him being a smoker. However, in view of the nature of the plaintiff's illness, the duration and extent of his smoking habit and the circumstances of the case as a whole, the KKO deemed there to be sufficient proof of smoking having been a contributory factor in the illness of the defendant and that there therefore was a causal relationship between him being a smoker and him contracting the diseases.

Regarding the alleged concealment of the health hazards of tobacco and the **32**
provision of misleading information, the KKO began by noting that the manufacturer and the seller of a product must know that product, and that it was an aspect of their duty of care to publish the known hazards of the product so that any user can act with appropriate caution and any user not aware of the hazard is not injured. This principle has been laid down *e.g.* in the earlier case law of the KKO (1981-II-109 and 1982-II-187) and restated in the legislation on con-

sumer protection and product liability. The KKO discussed this matter at some length, and decided to base its ruling on the one hand on the extent that the negative effects of tobacco were manifest in the media and health education throughout the period covered by the action, and on the other hand on the fact that, in light of the evidence, the information provided by the tobacco companies on the hazards of smoking could not have presented an essentially more accurate picture of the same. On this basis, the KKO concluded that, while failing to give caution on the hazardousness of tobacco, the defendant companies had still not neglected to undertake such precautionary measures which would have had a discernible effect on consumer behaviour. The KKO noted also that the evidence did not indicate that this issue should be approached any differently in the specific case at hand.

33 During the period covered by the action, Finland operated a prohibition of misleading marketing, applicable also to tobacco advertising. In the assessment of the reprehensibility of the advertising and its connection to the plaintiff being a smoker, the decisive issue, in the opinion of the KKO, was the picture provided in the advertisements on the health effects of tobacco. Advertising that states that tobacco has positive health effects can be deemed misleading and hence reprehensible. Applying these criteria, the KKO noted that certain tobacco advertisements had indeed been misleading. Moreover, it considered it probable that the plaintiff had seen these advertisements. The KKO stated that tort liability would arise only if this reprehensible conduct by a tobacco company was in a causal relationship with the injury sustained by the plaintiff.

34 The plaintiff had taken to smoking in 1941, at the age of 16. When the warning on the health hazards of tobacco was introduced on cigarette packs in 1978, the plaintiff had, according to his own statement, not considered giving up smoking. He had continued, even though in 1980 he had been diagnosed with bronchitis and a condition identified as emphysema, and even though his doctor had at the time advised him for this reason to cut back on smoking. The plaintiff had continued to smoke up to the day before his operation of laryngeal cancer, which was detected in 1986.

35 The KKO noted that health education on tobacco had been offered throughout the period covered by the action in various societal contexts, such as schools and voluntary organisations. Even before taking up smoking, the plaintiff had been educated at school on the health hazards posed by tobacco. The KKO noted also that the manufacture and sale of tobacco had been legal throughout the period covered by the action. The procurement and smoking of tobacco is a matter of individual choice. For the 45 years that he was a smoker, the plaintiff had been aware of the health hazardousness of smoking. Under these circumstances, it was not a credible proposition that the plaintiff had continued to smoke because of the misleading advertisements referred to above and because he thereby could rely on tobacco being safe. By smoking, the plaintiff had assumed a conscious risk that this conduct may be seriously detrimental to his health. Accordingly, his contracting the diseases could not be deemed a consequence of the advertisements. The majority of the KKO ruled that the defendant tobacco companies were not liable to the plaintiff (the estate of the original plaintiff, who had died during the proceedings).

c) Commentary

In any discussion of the liability of tobacco companies for the illnesses of their customers, the first question is of course what has been the prevailing medical knowledge at the time and what is the prevailing medical knowledge now on the significance of smoking as a risk factor in, or the cause of, various diseases. The second question is, what sort of medical evidence on a causal relationship meets the standard of adequacy in the law of tort and liability. In the case at hand, the KKO held that the causal relationship between the plaintiff being a smoker and him contracting the diseases had been established. However, the tobacco companies were not liable, as certain admittedly misleading advertisements were not deemed to be the reason why the plaintiff continued to smoke. It would appear that, in practice, it is quite difficult to prove that misleading information in marketing has a causal relationship with the conduct of a smoker; hence, it is quite likely that compensation will not be obtainable on this basis in the future either. **36**

6. *Korkein oikeus*; 19 September 2001; KKO 2001:93[6]: Liability of a Public Corporation: Duty of a Municipality to Provide Statutory Public Services

a) Brief Summary of the Facts

Under the *laki lasten päivähoidosta* (630/1991; Child Day-Care Act), the municipality had the duty to see to ensure that the parents of a child below school age can procure a municipal day-care place for their child. The plaintiff had filed an application with her home town for the procurement of places for her two children as of 20 November 1996. But the town had been able to allocate places for the children only as of 2 December 1996. Owing to the lack of day-care places, the plaintiff had been absent from work between 20 and 29 November 1996. The plaintiff sought damages for the loss of income in this respect, as the town had neglected a statutory duty imposed on it. The town admitted that the plaintiff had a subjective right to day-care places for her children, but claimed that it had not caused the loss through an error or negligence. **37**

b) Judgment of the KKO

The KKO noted that, under the law, a municipality shall grant the benefit referred to in the case at hand to anyone who meets the criteria set in the legislation. Thus, for instance, the duty of the municipality is not affected by the funds that have been budgeted for the purpose. As the arrangement of day- **38**

[6] This precedent has been commented also by Suvianna Hakalehto-Wainio, see [2002] LM 100, 634 *et seq.*

care places was a statutory duty of the municipality, the fulfilment thereof was to be deemed an exercise of public authority.

39 Hence, the case turned on whether the municipality was liable under those provisions of the VahL that govern liability in the exercise of public authority. According to chapter 3, § 2 subpara. 1 of the VahL, a public corporation shall be vicariously liable in damages for injury or damage caused through an error or negligence in the exercise of public authority. Although, according to the principle in chapter 5, § 1, damages shall constitute compensation for personal injury and damage to property only, they shall constitute compensation also for economic loss that is not connected to personal injury or damage to property where the injury or damage has been caused in the exercise of public authority. The KKO noted that the negligence required for liability to arise can be manifested also as an omission in a situation where action would have been called for. The town had not met its obligations towards the plaintiff, and this failure was not due to circumstances that were not attributable to the town having been negligent. Hence, the loss of income suffered by the plaintiff was caught by the definition of loss that arises from an error or negligence in the exercise of public authority.

40 According to the restrictive provision in chapter 3, § 2 subpara. 2 of the VahL, the liability referred to in § 2 subpara. 1 arises only if the performance of the activity or task, in view of its nature and purpose, has not met the reasonable requirements set for it. The KKO held that the duty of the municipality imposed in the *laki lasten päivähoidosta* was materially such that if no day-care place is allocated to someone entitled to it, the reasonable requirements referred to in that provision have indeed not been met. The KKO did not attach relevance to the great variation in the need of day-care places, the measures undertaken by the town to improve the day-care situation, the attempts of the town to locate a day-care place near the home of the family, or the short duration of the failure to provide the service. As a result, the town was liable to compensate the plaintiff for her loss of income, less a part of the day-care fees that had been spared. The quantum of the damages was some € 465, including interest. One of the five Justices of the KKO considered that, in view of the nature and purpose of the municipal duty, the town had met its obligations to a reasonable degree; in addition, the delay had been short, for which reasons that Justice would have released the town from liability.

c) Commentary

41 This precedent is the first one where the KKO discussed liability issues when a municipality fails to provide day-care service. However, there is an earlier, similar precedent (KKO 1997:141), in which a municipality was held liable in damages for a failure to provide work for a long-term unemployed person, in violation of the *työllisyyslaki* (275/1987; Employment Act). These two precedents go to show that a municipality runs a relatively high risk of liability if it does not see to the realisation of the statutory subjective rights of its inhabitants.

It is a prerequisite for liability that the right of the person is absolute. If this is the case, neither the scarcity of resources that is a practical barrier to the realisation of the right nor the measures already undertaken by the municipality to remedy the situation prevent liability from arising. In contrast, the precedent does not mean that the municipality is always liable if some statutory right of an inhabitant is not realised; the prerequisites for liability are to be assessed with a view to the strength of the right that is to be established by way of the legislation. 42

C. Literature

1. L. Sisula-Tulokas (ed.), *Contract and Tort Law: Twenty Cases from the Finnish Supreme Court* (Kauppakaari, Finnish Lawyers' Publishing Company, Helsinki 2001)

The aim of this book is to give in English an insight into Finnish commercial and tort law. Although the Finnish legal system is a typical continental system, based on written law, the importance of other sources of law, especially Supreme Court cases, has become more prominent. Therefore, in this book an approach different from the traditional way of describing the principles of essential legislation is chosen, and the focus is on Supreme Court cases. The Supreme Court (*korkein oikeus*, KKO) is the court that exercises the highest jurisdiction in Finland. 43

The book is divided into three sections, the first of which is a brief introduction to the Finnish legal system. The second consists of twenty cases put before the Finnish Supreme Court in the 1990s. Eight of these cases deal with tort law. Either Professor Sisula-Tulokas herself or Professor Mika Hemmo comments each of them against an international backdrop. The last section includes unofficial translations of essential Finnish acts, *e.g.* the *vahingonkorvauslaki* (Tort Liability Act) and the *vakuutussopimuslaki* (Insurance Contracts Act). 44

2. Th. Wilhelmsson, *Senmodern ansvarsrätt. Privaträtt som redskap för mikropolitik* (Kauppakaari, Juristförbundets Förlag, Helsinki 2001)

In his book, whose title translates as "Late-Modern Liability Law: Private Law as a Means of Micro Policy", Professor Thomas Wilhelmsson presents an interdisciplinary analysis of the effects of changes of late-modern society on the law, and especially tort and liability law. Some of the most significant such changes are globalisation, europeanisation, privatisation, fragmentation, medialisation and grass-roots activism. The leading thesis in the work is that the various provisions of private law governing liability issues may be vested with new functions and thereby also more importance in the private law of late-modern society. 45

In the first part of the book, Professor Wilhelmsson analyses the arguments that form the basis of his thesis. One of his arguments is that liability law will 46 become more important *e.g.* because of the changes in the traditional, government-driven welfare state brought about by the ever-increasing emphasis on the privatisation of services and market-driven structures. In addition, the emergence of the "risk society" will increase the importance of liability law. Professor Wilhelmsson discusses the needs for a new, stronger liability law also from the point of view of the status of ethics and morality in late-modern society. In practice, the new liability law is significant *inter alia* because our society is now a mass media society where the makers and strategies of micro policy have an increasing important role.

47 Professor Wilhelmsson presents some of the new functions of liability law, pertaining to the characteristics of late-modern society referred to above. The market-oriented attitudes and the decrease in the importance of public authority make it necessary to use liability law for management purposes which are considered important as such but which no longer are seen to by the authorities. This is the *management function*, consisting firstly of the *control function*, the use of liability law to lay down norms. The management function covers also the *monitoring function*, whose focus is to monitor the compliance of private individuals, legal persons and public corporations with those norms. Moreover, the uncertainty prevailing in the risk society also calls for liability law to have a management function, as described above. In addition, the control function of liability law can be perceived as a forum for the pragmatic discourse of moral issues in the application of liability law. The market-oriented attitudes, for their part, are connected with the *mandatory service function* of liability law: When market-driven mechanisms lead to a decrease of public services, liability law can be used for the safeguarding of essential services. Professor Wilhelmsson argues further that liability law can be vested with a *social welfare function*, by using compensatory payments to cover for the social welfare gaps left behind by the market-oriented approaches. Of these functions, Professor Wilhelmsson attaches the most importance to the control and monitoring functions, which can be said to incorporate also the mandatory service function.

48 In the second part of the book, certain liability law provisions are analysed from the point of view of how they can be used as a means to control the exercise of power. Professor Wilhelmsson looks into the liability law control of economic power, political power and media power. Towards the end of the book, there is an analysis of the concept of loss, where Professor Wilhelmsson argues that a departure from a person's own interests as a prerequisite for the filing of liability claims would lay open new avenues for the realisation of the new functions of liability law.

VII. France

Olivier Massot

Civil liability is the obligation made to a person to answer for the damage caused to someone else in a liable way, *i.e.* to repair it. Two ideas have to be addressed at the same time: the damage and the reparation. Reading the case law, it seems that the will to repair, to indemnify, to compensate takes the first place; however, different discussions concerning the grounds of the damage took place, especially concerning medical damage. So, this year, the *Cour de cassation* (the French "Supreme Court" for civil and criminal matters) pays attention to medical liability cases (A), nevertheless, other hypotheses of liability were debated (B). 1

A. Medical Liability

Of course, we will look at the continuations of the decision taken by the *Cour de cassation* dated 17 November 2001, also known as the "Perruche case". But, before, we will examine some notions of medical liability[1]. 2

1. Notions of Medical Liability

Two questions have been discussed by case law. The first one concerns the damage (a), the second the person who asks for reparation (b). 3

a) Nosocomial Infections and Therapeutic Hazard

Nosocomial infection can be defined as an infection contracted following care or a medical act, without the commission of a fault. The state of weakness of the patient's immune system and his presence in an unhealthy milieu can cause this kind of infection. Therapeutic hazard is the possibility that a risk arises during or in succession to a medical act. 4

[1] Y. Lambert-Faivre, La responsabilité de l'accident médical Obligation de sécurité: oui; aléa thérapeutique: non, [2001] *Le Dalloz* 7, 570.

i. The Case of Nosocomial Infection

5 In the cases of nosocomial infections, doctors are debtors of a security obligation of result[2]; over and above, violation of this obligation can be sanctioned in a penal way because of "a deliberate violation of a particular prudence or security obligation prescribed by state law, causing, unwillingly, injuries to the patient"[3]. Consequently, it is a liability without fault. The decision of the *Cour de cassation* dated 27 March 2001[4] specifies: "it is to the patient to demonstrate that the infection he is suffering, shows nosocomial feature". Henceforth, a causality link is not presumed and must be proved by the "victim" patient, which is far from easy. Already, in a case dated 4 September 2000[5], the Court of Appeal of Toulouse recognised: "if the doctor and the clinic are presumed liable of the infection contracted by a patient during an operation, in a surgery room, and if it is to the doctor and to the clinic to demonstrate that they did not commit a fault; then it is incumbent on the patient to demonstrate that the infection has, effectively, been contracted on this occasion". Here the question is to know how to prove the lack of an infection pre-existing before the medical act, *i.e.* what evidence a sick person, who will undergo a medical act, has to produce. This asks the question of the previous information of the patient: will it be just to ask a person to bring the proof that he is not infected when he does not know and he is not placed in the condition to know that he could contract it? Therefore, it will be necessary to conciliate the following principle: *nul ne peut se constituer une preuve à lui-même*, with the possibility for the person to bring before the court evidence concerning him personally[6].

6 It is interesting to compare this case with the one given by the *Cour de cassation* on 9 May 2001 dealing with blood transfusions[7]. According to this particular case: "when a person demonstrates, on the one hand, that the viral contamination which she suffers has appeared after a blood transfusion, and on the other hand, that she does not present any particular kind of contamination, it is up to the centre of blood transfusion, where liability is sought, to prove that the blood products, supplied by the centre, were free from any defect". In fact, is the nosocomial feature which must be proved by the patient, limited, first, to the proof that the infection appears after a medical act, and, second, to prove that the patient did not present any particular kind of infectious contamination before the medical act? This method presents the advantage of indicating the elements which have to be proved. However, this does not bring any information about the quality of the needed evidence. It is necessary to indicate the position of the case law, when uncertainty and doubt

[2] C. Cass. Civ[1] (First Civil Chamber of the *Cour de cassation*), 29 June 1999, appeal no. 97–21.903.

[3] C. Cass. Crim. (Criminal Chamber of the *Cour de cassation*), 11 September 2001, appeal no. 00-85.473.

[4] C. Cass. Civ[1], 27 March 2001, appeal no. 99-17.672.

[5] C.A. (*Cour d'appel*) Toulouse, 4 September 2000, [2001] *Le Dalloz* 2, 179.

[6] C. Cass. Civ[1], 2 April 1996, *Bulletin Civil des arrêts de la Cour de cassation* (Bull. Civ.) I, no. 170.

[7] C. Cass. Civ[1], 9 May 2001, appeal no. 99-18.161.

remain after the production of proof. In this case, uncertainty and doubt have necessarily to be held to the detriment of the one who has the burden of proof[8]. Thus, without discharging the medical corps of its obligation, it is difficult to engage its liability. And this could produce, *de facto*, an exemption of liability.

The project of state law dated 4 October 2001, concerning sick persons' rights and the quality of the health system, in its title III concerning the reparation of sanitation risks' consequences, provides, in art. 58, which modifies the writing of the first book of the first part of the Public Health Code (P.H.C.), including a fourth title, medical liability only in case of practitioner's fault[9]. Would case law look ahead to this evolution in order to protect the patient by conserving a spreading out of medical liability which disappears in the new state law? In fact, the terms of the first paragraph of the P.H.C. art. L. 1142–4 are: "Each person victim or considering himself victim of a damage attributable to prevention, diagnostic or care acts or his entitled beneficiary if the person is dead, or, if necessary his legal representative, has to be informed by the professional, the health establishment, the health services or the concerned organism about the circumstances and the cause of this accident". This must allow the specification of fault which could be reproached, if necessary, to the specialist. Thus fault and causality would be constituted; it remains to estimate the value of compensation due to the entitled person. For this, we must refer to the P.H.C. art. L. 1142–8[10]. In all hypotheses will liability be split up depending on whether there is fault or hazard; in the latter case, the compensation would be effected by the community[11]. Thus we will see the therapeutic hazard. 7

8 C. Cass. Soc (Social Chamber of the *Cour de cassation*), 31 January 1962, Bull. Civ. IV, no. 105.

9 P.H.C. art. L. 1142-1: "I Out of the case where their liability is engaged because of a health product default, health professionals mentioned in the fourth part of the present Code and every establishment, service or organism in which personal acts of prevention, diagnostic or care are done, are not liable of the prejudicial consequences of prevention, diagnostic or care acts only in cases of fault or breach whatever are the nature or the mode of the proving of this fault or this breach, proved or presumed, according to the appreciation of the competent judge."
"II When the responsibility of a professional, a health establishment, service or producer of products is not committed, a medical accident or an iatrogen disease open right to the repair of the damages of the patient to the title of national solidarity, when they are directly ascribable with acts of prevention, diagnostis or care and that they have had for the patient abnormal consequences taking into consideration his health like foreseeable evolution of this one and present a character of gravity desribed in the first two paragraphs of the article L. 1142–8."

10 P.H.C. art. L. 1142–8: "When the undergone damage shows a seriousness feature, fixed by Order in *Conseil d'Etat*, evaluated by looking at the loss of functional abilities considering the temporary disability ratio, the commission gives advice about circumstances, causes, nature and extent of damages, and the indemnification applicable rules."
"The seriousness feature mentioned in the preceding paragraph is also evaluated by looking at the consequences concerning the private and professional life of the concerned person when those consequences have special seriousness."
"The commission refers to the competent authority if it notes breaches which could lead to disciplinary actions."

11 See P. Rancé, L'indemnisation des accidents médicaux Interview de P. de la Grange, [2001] *Le Dalloz* 33, 2685.

ii. The Case of Therapeutic Hazard

8 Judges decided that: "the doctor has to give to his patient honest, educated and appropriate information about the serious risks relating to the suggested investigations and care and he is not exempted from this obligation by the mere fact that those risks exceptionally come true"[12], further, "the practitioner held by this obligation of particular information has to prove, by every means, its execution"[13]. The *Conseil d'Etat* (French "Supreme Court" for administrative matters)[14] used a similar expression in a decision dated 15 January 2001. This decision specifies that: "this information is not necessary in emergency hypotheses, impossibility or refusal of the patient to be informed in conditions allowing the collection of his educated assent"[15]. It is necessary to indicate that doctors have to inform, but they "do not have to succeed to convince their patient of the danger of the medical act which he demands"[16].

9 By a court decision dated the 27 March 2001[17] and based on the Civil Code (C.C.) artt. 1135[18] and 1147[19], the *Cour de cassation* acknowledges, again, that: "reparation of therapeutic hazard consequences is not a part of obligations that doctors have to respect contractually towards their patients". We can note the opposition of first and second degree jurisdictions. In fact, these jurisdictions identify a more wide security obligation obliging practitioners to repair the damage their patients suffer. Those judges prefer the compensation way. We can confirm this by their method of verification: "the accomplishment, without any fault of the practitioner, of an accidental risk which is inherent in the medical act and which cannot be controlled". This decision will be better understood if it is read together with two decisions of the *Conseil d'Etat*. According to these two decisions[20]: "when a medical act, necessary to the diagnostic or the treatment of a sick person shows a risk; when the existence of this risk is known but its accomplishment is special; and when no reason leaves anyone to think that the patient is exceptionally exposed to it; public service liability is engaged if the performance of this act is the direct cause of the damage, without considering the initial status of the patient or the foreseeable evolution of this status, and shows an extremely serious feature". We must indicate, as far as administrative law is concerned, the importance of the precautionary principle[21]. In fact, the main will is to compensate the damage.

[12] C.A. Paris, 25 October 2001, [2001] *Le Dalloz* 43, 3492.

[13] *Ibid.*

[14] See P. Ega, note, under T. A. Amiens, 14 December 2000, [2001] *Le Dalloz* 41, 3310.

[15] C.E. 15 January 2001, appeal no. 184386 and note D. Dendoncker, [2001] *Le Dalloz* 36, 2925.

[16] C. Cass. Civ[1], 18 January 2000, appeal no. 97-17.716 and note M.-L. Mathieu-Izorche, [2001] *Le Dalloz* 44, 3559.

[17] C. Cass. Civ[1], 27 March 2001, appeal no. 99-13.471.

[18] C.C. art. 1135: "Agreements bind, not only by what is expressed, but also by all the results that equity, use or state law give to the obligation according to its nature."

[19] C.C. art. 1147: "The debtor is convicted, if necessary, to pay damages, either because of the non-performance of the obligation, or because of the delay in the performance, every time he does not justify that the non-performance comes from a foreign cause which cannot be attributed to him, although there is no dishonesty from him."

[20] See *Commissaire du gouvernement* conclusions and decisions, [2001] *Le Dalloz* 15, 1196.

10 Consequently, we have to specify that the project of state law concerning sick persons' rights and the quality of the health system foresees the compensation of the patient who is a victim of a therapeutic hazard. Then is applied the principle of entire reparation[22]. The idea is double. On one hand, the point is to make the victim's compensation of therapeutic hazard (a medical accident or an iatrogen infection, *i.e.* treatment consequences without a fault in the prescription) easier. On the other hand, the point is essentially to make judicial and administrative trials converge as explained by Sargos[23].

11 Thus, medical liability is rationalised and becomes more and more a compensation proceeding[24]. But, if doctors are liable without being guilty of a fault

[21] J.-M. Favet, Le principe de précaution ou la prise en compte par le droit de l'incertitude scientifique et du risque virtuel, [2001] *Le Dalloz* 43, 3462.

[22] P.H.C. art. 1142–17: "When the regional commission estimates that the damage justifies compensation as a result of art. L. 1142–1 II, the office addresses to the victim, within a four month period after reception of the opinion, a compensation tender aiming at the entire reparation of the torts which it justifies."
"If the victim dies without instituted proceedings in compensation or dies during them, the entitled beneficiary can ask for compensation under the same conditions as their author."
"The compensation tender indicates the held evaluation, if necessary as provisional, for each charge of tort and the sum of indemnities which are owed to the victim, deduction made of the benefit listed in art. 29 of the state law no. 85–677 dated 5 July 1985 ["Only the benefits listed below paid to the victim of damage arising from blows to the individual open the right to a claim against the one held to repair or his insurance: 1) Benefits paid by organisms, establishments and services managing an obligatory regime of social security and by those who are mentioned in artt. 1106–9, 1234–8 and 1234–20 of the Rural Code; 2) Benefits listed in art. 1st II of the Order no. 59–76 dated 7 January 1959 concerning actions in civil reparation of the State and some others public persons; 3) Sums paid for repaying the cost of medical treatment and re-education; 4) Salary and other contributions made by the employer during the inactive period resulting from the event which caused the damage; 5) Daily indemnities for sickness and infirmity benefits paid by the mutual pooling ruled by the Mutual Insurance Code, provident institutions ruled by the Social Security Code or the Rural Code and insurance societies ruled by the Insurance Code."] and more generally all nature indemnities paid or to be paid by other debtors in charge for the same tort."
"The tender presents a provisional feature if the office has not been informed about the status of the victim's recovery. The final tender has to be done within a two month period from the date on which the office was informed of this recovery."
"The acceptance of the office tender is equivalent to a transaction in art. 2044 of the Civil Code ["Transaction is a contract by which the parties end a birthed dispute, or prevent a future dispute./This contract must be written."]."
"The payments have to be made within a one month period from the reception by the office of the acceptance by the victim for its tender, its tender having a provisional or final feature."
"If the office which made the tender to the victim estimates that the liability of a professional, or a producer of products noted in art. L. 1142–14 §1 ["When the regional commission of conciliation and compensation of medical accidents, iatrogene complaints and nosocomial infections, estimate that damage coming under art. L. 1142–8 §1 involves the liability of a health professional or an organism noted in art. L. 1142–1 or a producer of health product noted in art. L. 1142–2, the insurer who guarantees civil or administrative liability of the person considered as liable by the commission, addresses to the victim, within a four month period since reception of the opinion, a compensation tender aiming at the entire reparation of the torts undergone."], is given, he has a subrogation claim against this one."

[23] P. Sargos, report about the appeal no. 99-18.161, [2001] *Le Dalloz* 27, 2149.

[24] See C. Russo, L'avance sur recours, une solution à l'indemnisation des victimes d'accidents médicaux, [2001] *Le Dalloz* 40, 3211.

towards their patients, they can also be liable with regard to the Sickness Insurance Primary Fund. In fact, the *Cour de cassation*, in a decision dated 26 April 2001[25], recalled that "doctors are held, in all their prescriptions, to observe, in the scope of the legislation and the regulation in force, the most strict money saving compatible with the effectiveness of the treatment". In this case, first degree and appeal judges were sanctioned because they had not specified how each prescription could be justified by this simple condition: treatment's effectiveness. So a question has to be asked: who decides about the therapy's chances? This can shake the important link of faith between a doctor and his patient. In fact, a juridical control of the economic point of view in a medical relationship, which justifies itself using budgetary reasons, could limit the idea of private medicine.

12 Such clarification leads us to study who are the plaintiffs in compensation of tort involving medical practitioners?

b) Plaintiffs in Compensation

13 The case of a plaintiff who undergoes direct damage does not raise any problem[26]. Judges, by using their sovereign power of judgment, could even substitute a link of juridical causality, which is certain, with a link of scientific causality, which is uncertain; *e.g.* in order to seek the liability of the producer of a defective product (in the case of a hepatitis B vaccine)[27]. So, the point presented will be about the third party's claims.

i. Third Party as Indirect Victim

14 The *Cour de Cassation* by a decision dated 13 February 2001[28], under Civil Code artt. 1165[29] and 1382[30], stated that: "third parties to a contract are well-founded by referring to every breach of the contractual debtor when this breach caused them damage, without proving anything else". The Cour admits liability of contractual debtors toward third parties who are victims of the non-performance of a contract. The condition is that contractual breach must be

[25] C. Cass. Soc., 26 April 2001, appeal no. 99-20.936.

[26] C. Cass. Ass. Plèn. (Union of every chamber of the *Cour de cassation*), 28 November 2001, appeal no. 00-11.197, decided: on the one hand, "the fault committed by the doctor during the execution of the contract concluded with Mrs. X had prevented her from exercising her choice to interrupt her pregnancy for therapeutic reasons, and, on the other hand, it was not disputed that medical conditions of such pregnancy interruption were put together, parents could ask for compensation of the material tort arising from the handicap in straight causality relation with the held fault."

[27] C.A. Versailles, 14 May 2001, [2001] *Le Dalloz* 20, 1593.

[28] C. Cass. Civ[1], 13 February 2001, appeal no. 99-13.589.

[29] C.C. art. 1165: "Agreements are efficient only between the parties; they are not prejudicial to third parties and they profit the third party only in the case provided for in art. 1121 ["In a similar manner, we can stipulate in benefit for a third party, when such is the stipulation condition that we make for ourselves or the donation that we make for someone else. The one who made this stipulation cannot rescind it, if the third party declared his will to profit it."]"

[30] C.C. art. 1382: "Any act of man, which causes damage to others, obliges the one by whose fault it happens to repair it."

doubled by a fault, exterior to the contract. This fault will express the autonomy of non-contractual fault towards the contract[31].

In the presented case, Mr. le Manchec had been contaminated by the H.I.V. virus during a blood transfusion in 1983[32]. He was compensated for his specific tort by the Haemophiliacs and Transfused Compensation Fund. After his death by A.I.D.S., his daughter instituted proceedings against the Blood Transfusion Regional Centre (B.T.R.C.) of Rennes which supplied blood, and its insurer to obtain reparation of the moral and the economic ricochet tort she suffered. The censured decision, given by the *Cour d'appel* (second instance trial for non administrative matters) of Rennes dated 25 February 1998, nonsuited Ms. le Manchec saying that: "she could not refer to the contractual obligation of result security weighing on the Centre [...] and [that] she did not prove the fault of the said Centre". For the *Cour de Cassation* the breach of the contractual obligation of result security in matter of blood products – sold by B.T.R.C. – can be used both by the direct victim and the ricochet one. **15**

It is enlightening to compare this decision with the state law no. 98–389 dated 19 May 1998 concerning the liability of defective products' facts[33]. In fact, this state law created artt. 1386–1 and following in the Civil Code. According to art. 1386–1: "Producers, linked or not by a contract with the victim, are liable for the damage caused by a defect of his product". Case law had already admitted, under Civil Code artt. 1147[34] and 1384 §1[35] (interpreted in conformity with the European Directive no. 85–374 dated 24 July 1985, concerning liability of defective products) that every producer is liable for damages caused by a defect of his product towards both direct victims and ricochet victims – without having to distinguish if they are parties to the contract or not. So the *Cour de cassation* had the possibility to repair the tort suffered by a husband and the children of an A.I.D.S.' victim [36]. Nevertheless, the *Tribunal de grande instance* (first instance trial for non-administrative matters) of Aix-en-Provence remarks that: "defect of which the plaintiff has to prove the existence, does not have to be confused with the fault by which the product could be affected so that the plaintiff should have to establish the exact cause of the damage, in which case the state law dated 19 May 1998 could not bring, about this point, any modification of the anterior juridical regime"[37]. **16**

[31] G. Viney, Responsabilité civile, [1998] *Jurisclasseur Périodique* (J.C.P.) 25, I, 144.

[32] See D. Arthus, Hépatite C post-transfusionnelle: des voies et des réponses contentieuses désormais clarifiées, [2001] *Le Dalloz* 22, 1745.

[33] See C.J.C.E., 10 May 2001, and P. Kayser note, [2001] *Le Dalloz* 38, 3066.

[34] See *supra* note 19.

[35] C.C. art. 1384 §1: "We are liable not only for damage we cause by our own fact, but also for those caused by the facts of persons whom we have to answer for, or things we have under our care."

[36] C. Cass. Civ[1], 28 April 1998, appeal no. 96-20.421.

[37] T.G.I. (*Tribunal de grande instance*) Aix-en-Provence, 2 October 2001, [2001] *Le Dalloz* 38, 3092.

17 We can note, with the introduction of this European Directive, the change of the legal ground of liability. Now, it is permitted to expect a certain prevention from producers in addition to the obligation of result security that weighs on him: it is possible to expect producers to have an active attitude which will permit a sanctioning, if necessary, of their lack of diligence. The essential point is the suffered damage. This damage has to be certain, *i.e.* real and serious. Moreover, it has to be direct. So, we have to specify that the ricochet victim, even if she does not personally suffer the event which produced the principal damage, suffers direct damage following the personal damage of the principal victim. And, finally, a just interest has to be violated. Thus, all happens as if the only damage had to answer for opening conditions of a proceeding[38] in order to permit the compensation, independently of any other consideration. So, damage, irrespective of its type, creates right. This is also observed in the next hypothesis.

ii. Third Party as Direct Victim

18 The *Cour de cassation* tackles this question in its decision dated 9 October 2001[39]. Under Civil Code artt. 1165 and 1382[40], the *Cour* quashes and annuls the submitted decision. By their decision, the first judges nonsuited the plaintiff of his claim against the doctor and the clinic. This claim grounds upon a complaint from the faults committed during the plaintiff's birth and an information breach to his mother. This breach of information concerned the inherent risks in a breech presentation when a natural delivery is preferred to a Caesarean.

19 Facts have to be indicated. Mr. Y, the doctor, supervised the pregnancy of Mrs. X since June 1974. In December 1974 Mr. Y suspected the baby was in the breech position and demanded, in consequence of this, a foetal radiography which confirmed his diagnosis. At the time of the delivery, because of the breech presentation, a raising up of the child's arms took place. During obstetrical working, a delivery anomaly of the baby's shoulders appeared resulting in a bilateral paralysis of the brachial plexus. Today, the child has some after-effects at the level of right superior member – his Physical Partial Incapacity (P.P.I.) after healing is 25%. After his coming of age, he brought an action which provoked the decision presented now.

20 The child, directly suffering the damage, is considered as a third party to the contract between his mother and the doctor. Besides, the *Cour* affirms that: "the liability consecutive to this obligation's transgression [*i.e.* information duty of the doctor in relation to his patient] can be sought both by the mother

[38] N.C.P.C. art. 31: "Proceeding is open to everyone who has a just interest to see a claim having success or being rejected, without prejudice of the cases in which state law assigns the right to sue only to persons which state law qualifies to establish or fight a claim, or to defend a determined interest."

[39] C. Cass. Civ[1], 9 October 2001, appeal no. 00-14.564 and D. Thouvenin note, [2001] *Le Dalloz* 43, 3474.

[40] See *supra* notes 29 and 30.

and her child". The legal ground on which the mother could sue is clearly in the Civil Code art. 1147[41], *i.e.* contractual liability. The legal ground of the child's claim is purely non-contractual. Thus, in order to establish the doctor's liability, we have to prove the damage, *i.e.* here the P.P.I., a fault of the doctor and a causality between the first and the second element. The presented case raises a problem. In fact, in 1974 doctors were not contractually held to give complete information about the complications relating to the proposed investigations and care; and this was also so, even if the risk was exceptional. In this time, medical ethics were ruled by the decree no. 55–1591 dated 28 November 1955 which did not provide for an information duty. Nowadays, since the decree no. 95–1000 dated 6 September 1995 concerning the Medical Ethics Code, a duty[42] is created from the mere prescription of the decree no. 79–506 dated 28 June 1979[43]. The *Cour de cassation* decided: "a same rule interpretation, in a given time, cannot be different according to the age of the considered facts and no one can take advantage of an established right to a frozen case law". In so doing, the Cour allows new rules to have a retroactive effect. As a pretext they use a case law evolution aiming to protect the respect of the constitutional principle of the safeguarding of human dignity. In fact, this jurisdiction grounded the doctor's duty of information upon the necessity to respect human dignity.

This solution can seem astonishing because it violates the principle of non-retroactivity[44]. In the presented case, the contractual "fault", reproached to the doctor, grounding the child's claim in non-contractual liability could not be used in 1974 and so should not be used nowadays. In fact, subsequent case law considered that and successive contracts have to be ruled by the prior state law to a new published one[45]. However, one could plead that Civil Code art. 2[46], in the strict sense, only concerns state law and not decree. But this decision, as just it is, goes against some juridical principles. 21

[41] See *supra* note 19.

[42] M.E.C. art. 35: "Doctor must give to the person who he examines, he cares for or he advises, a loyal, clear and adapted information about her status, the investigations and care he suggests to her."
"For the duration of the sickness, he takes the patient's personality into account in his explanations and watches over their understanding."
"However, in the sick person's interest and for just reasons which are conscientiously estimated by the practitioner, a diagnosis or a serious prognosis can be withheld from a sick person, except in cases where the complaint from which he suffers exposes third parties to a contamination risk."
"Fatal prognosis has to be revealed only with circumspection, but the close relations must be informed of it, notwithstanding exceptions or if the sick person forbade this revelation or designated the third parties to whom it has to be given."

[43] (old) M.E.C. art. 37: "Doctor has to write out his regulation with all the necessarily clarity. He has to ensure that this is understood by the sick person and his/her close relations."

[44] C. Cass. Civ^3 (Third Civil Chamber of the *Cour de cassation*), 3 July 1979, Bull. Civ. III, no. 149.

[45] J. Carbonnier, *Droit civil Introduction* (21st edn. 1992), p. 241.

[46] C.C. art. 2: "State law prescribes only for the future; it has no retroactive effect."

2. Doctors' Liability

22 We will not come back to the *Cour de cassation* decision dated 17 November 2000, also known as *arrêt Perruche*[47] even if its essential elements should be evoked briefly. In fact, this year, first degree judges applied this case law[48]. Nevertheless, we will study the clarifications brought by new cases dated 13 July 2001[49] and the new liability ground admitted to by the case dated the 28 November 2001.

a) From the Loss of Chance in not Birthing…

23 We will divide this part into factual elements and the juridical solution.

i. Factual Elements[50]

24 We will distinguish facts and procedure to gain a better understanding.

(i) Facts

25 The three cases, from July 2001, show many similarities and can be presented at the same time.

26 The first case's facts[51] are the following: In 1989 on 31 October, Mrs. X gave birth to a child, named Jessica, who suffered a spina-bifida provoking serious after-effects. In fact, Jessica presents motivity blow of the lower limbs and open anal sphincter which caused, in spite of numerous operations, a complete paraplegia of the lower limbs, an hydrocephalous, an anal sphincterian incontinence with neurological bladder which is secondary to the paraplegia. Reproach addressed to the gynaecologists, consulted by Mrs. X during her pregnancy, is to have performed scans in imperfect conditions, which did not permit the diagnosis of the spina-bifida. We will indicate that, statistically, the possibility of detecting a serious malformation as Jessica suffers, was only from 40 to 50%.

27 The second case's facts[52] are the following: In 1992 on 5 July, Mrs. Y gave birth to a child, named Pierrick, without a left arm and with a higher right limb reduced by 50% and devoid of a hand ending with a two-fingered stump.

[47] See: D. Mazeaud, note, [2001] *Le Dalloz* 4, 332; P. Jourdain, note, [2001] *Le Dalloz* 4, 336; J.-L. Aubert, Indemnisation d'une existence handicapée qui, selon le choix de la mère, n'aurait pas dû être, [2001] *Le Dalloz* 6, 489; L. Aynès, Préjudice de l'enfant né handicapé: la plainte de Job devant la Cour de cassation, [2001] *Le Dalloz* 6, 492; Y. Saint-Jour, Handicap congénital – erreur de diagnostic prénatal – Risque thérapeutique sous-jacent, [2001] *Le Dalloz* 16, 1263; A. Terrasson de Fougères, Périsse le jour qui me vit naître, [2001] *Revue de droit sanitaire et social* (R.D. sanit. Soc.) 1; F. Leduc, Handicap génétique ou congénital et responsabilité civile (à propos de l'arrêt Perruche), [February 2001] *Responsabilité civile et assurances* (Resp. civ. et ass.), chron. no. 4, 4.

[48] C. A. Bordeaux, 18 September 2001, [2001] *Le Dalloz* 34, 2805.

[49] P. Jourdain, note, [2001] *Le Dalloz* 29, 2326.

[50] See Mr. Blondet report.

[51] C. Cass. Ass. Plèn., 13 July 2001, appeal no. 97-17.359.

[52] C. Cass. Ass. Plèn., 13 July 2001, appeal no. 97-19.282.

Reproach addressed to the gynaecologist consulted by Mrs. Y during her pregnancy, is to not have detected malformations during the scan done in 1992 on 5 March, *i.e.* during the period of 19 to 21 pregnancy weeks (period where the malformation is easiest to detect), and not to have repeated the same examination on 6 April 1992, the date of the third medical act which was performed at the very beginning of the pregnancy's third quarter (a period where such exploration was keeping all its efficiency).

The third case's facts[53] are the following: In 1990 on 15 May, Mrs. Z gave birth to a child, named Thomas, suffering a malformation of his higher right limb. In fact, this limb combines a muscular atrophy of the lower 2/3 arm, an elbow dystrophy with a flexion ankylosis and a forearm atrophy – including only one bone; in addition, his hand is reduced to a single finger. Reproach addressed to the gynaecologist consulted by Mrs. Z during her pregnancy, is to have underestimated a precedent: the second child of Mrs. Z already suffered a congenital malformation of the right hand (Mrs. Z having exposed this case to her doctor), and not to have executed the requisite care to the foetal morphologic study with adequate care. **28**

In those three cases, the malformations are congenital and have not arisen as a result of the fault of the doctor. Finally, in the third case, the parents indicated their will, in case of anomaly, to have recourse to a therapeutic abortion. These are the facts which initiated the following proceedings. **29**

(ii) Procedure

In the three proposed cases, the parents sued in their own name, for a moral tort, and in the name of their handicapped child; in the third case, the parents also sued in the name of their other children as their legal representative. **30**

The first judges had different opinions. In the first and second cases, first degree judges admitted, at least in principle, Jessica's and Pierrick's torts, qualified as loss of a chance; second degree judges in those two cases and the first degree judges in the third case considered, in substance, that the congenital damage of a child had not been caused by the doctors' fault. Consequently this damage cannot be compensated by the said doctors. Thus, the three decisions taken by the *Cour d'appel* of Versailles (1st case), Metz (2nd case) and Aix-en-Provence (3rd case) did not admit the compensation right to the handicapped children and the decisions were based upon the fact that there is no link of direct causality between the doctors' faults and the children's handicap. **31**

In these three cases, the first judges did not admit the reasoning of the *Cour de cassation* in the "arrêt Perruche" according to which "faults, committed by the doctor and the laboratory in the execution of the contracts formed with Mrs. P, prevented the mother from exercising her choice to stop her pregnancy in order to avoid the birth of a handicapped child; this child can claim compensa- **32**

[53] C. Cass. Ass. Plèn., 13 July 2001, appeal no. 98 19.190

tion for the tort arising from this handicap and caused by the held faults"[54]. The married couples X (1st case), Y (2nd case) and Z (3rd case) petitioned for quashing.

ii. Legal Dispositions

33 We will show the form and the substance of the law.

(i) Form

34 The form of those decisions is important because they have been taken by the *Cour de cassation* brought in *Assemblée Plénière*, which gave to them a great solemnity. Moreover the main consideration is the same in all those three cases, clarifying the decision dated 17 November 2000 according to which: "the child, born with a handicap can claim compensation for the tort arising from his handicap if this handicap is in a direct causality relation with the committed faults of the doctor in the execution of the contract formed with his mother, which prevented the mother from exercising her choice to terminate her pregnancy; […] in the case of a therapeutic abortion, it has to be established that medical conditions prescribed by Public Health Code art. L. 2213–1[55] were fulfilled".

35 Everything in the form indicates the judges' will to provoke a leading case. We can note an important difference between form and substance: in what

[54] C. Cass. Ass. Plèn., 17 November 2000, appeal no. 99-13.701.

[55] The *Cour* seems to refer itself to the new legislative part of the P.H.C. because, in the old Code, the article dealing with abortion was L. 162–12.
P.H.C. art. L. 2213–1: "Abortion can, at all times, be performed if two doctors, members of a multidisciplinary staff, certify, after this staff gives its consultative opinion, that either the continuation of the pregnancy continuation would greatly endanger the woman's health, or a great probability exists that the child will be born inflicted with serious complaint known as incurable during the diagnostic."
"When the abortion is envisaged on the ground that the pregnancy continuation of the pregnany poses a great danger to the woman's health, the multidisciplinary staff charged with examining the woman's request, is made up, at least, of three persons – a qualified obstetric gynaecology doctor, a doctor chosen by the woman and a qualified person kept by professional secret who can be a social worker or a psychologist. The two doctors have to work in a public health establishment or a private one which satisfies the provisions of art. L. 2322–1 ["Without detriment of application of the present code part VI, book I provisions, opening and management of a private health establishment usually receiving, subject to certain liabilities or not, and whatever their number women in real, apparent or presumed pregnancy status, is subordinated to the previous authorisation of the State in the department./Opening and management conditions which have to fulfil those establishments are fixed by statutory way./A decree fixes the authorised installations which private health establishments have to have at their disposal when they want operate an abortion."]."
"When abortion is envisaged ground upon there is a great probability that the child to be born would be inflicted by a severe complaint known as incurable during the diagnostic, the multidisciplinary staff, charged to examine the woman's request, is the one of a prenatal diagnostic multidisciplinary centre. When the said centre staff meets, a doctor chosen by the woman can, at her request, be involved in the co-ordination."
"In both cases, prior to the competent multidisciplinary staff meeting, the concerned woman, or the couple can, at her/their request, be heard by all or a part of the said staff members."

concerns the form, judges used all the means to introduce a leading case, but in what concerns the substance they did not have the means to produce a major evolution by case law. Obviously, the aim is not to give rise to rule decisions which are forbidden by Civil Code art. 5[56].

(ii) Substance

Quash grounds proposed are taken from the violation of Civil Code art. 1147[57]. This article bases contractual liability of the doctor, especially when he failed in his duty of information with respect to the patient. Besides, a ground of pure law has been automatically taken up. By this ground there was no causality link between proved faults and pleaded torts of victims. In fact, their tort was nothing else than "a strong probability that the child to be born would be inflicted with a severe harm known as incurable during the diagnostic". This last ground can either lead to a substitution of ground for promising to reject appeals, or to a lack of legal base to quash the decisions.[58] **36**

The legal ground of the doctor's obligation is contractual. In the presented cases, this contract links the mother to the gynaecologist. The child, the third party to the said contract, can take advantage of the faulty execution of the contract, or the non-performance of the contract, in order to engage the non-contractual liability of the doctor. Indeed, this is not new. But, the presented cases show a particularity: the third party of the contract suffers physical "damage" (if we agree that handicap is damage, and its property of being a third party to the contract is particular). In fact, as a child to be born, the said third party is the cause of the medical proceedings, *i.e.* of the contract linking his mother to her gynaecologist, and, during the birth, this third party would definitely profit from the doctor's services; in fact, as obstetrician, the gynaecologist has to assist in the birth. So we can ask: is the child to be born, once born, always a *penitus extranei*? **37**

Definitively, the *Cour de cassation* ratifies, in an implicit way, the idea of loss of a chance, undergone by a child: on the one hand, by resuming the idea that the handicapped child directly undergoes contractual faults of the doctor, and, on the other hand, clarifying conditions of abortion realisation. In fact, in this case, the decision, if it is the mother's one, does not only depend on her: the certification of two independent doctors is needed, because it is a question of abortion as pregnancy interruption on therapeutic grounds. The case is not tackled where the pregnancy interruption is not based on therapeutic reasons but at the will of the woman,[59] and so occurs in the first 10 weeks (actually 12) of the pregnancy. So the hypothesis of a mixing of these two kinds of **38**

[56] C.C. art. 5: "It is forbidden to judges to give a decision in statutory and general disposition way about the cases which are submitted to them."

[57] See *supra* note 19.

[58] See *supra* note 50.

[59] P.H.C. art. L. 2212–1 §1. "Pregnant woman whose status takes in a grief-stricken situation, can ask a doctor for an abortion. This abortion cannot take place after the end of the twelfth week of her pregnancy."

interruption is redundant. In fact, the handicap of a child yet to be born could not justify the grief-stricken status of the mother opening the possibility of operating an abortion. On the contrary, the likely handicap seems to systematically indicate a medical interruption of the pregnancy.

39 In two similar cases, *i.e.* the "arrêt Perruche" and the third presented case, where the families indicated their will to have recourse to an abortion if there was, on the one hand, a German measles attack and, on the other hand, any anomaly, the *Cour* decided in two different ways. In fact, in the "arrêt Perruche", the question of the abortion's reasons is not asked, whereas it is debated in the third case. So, for one, the loss of a chance will be admitted, and not for the other. The clarification brought by the *Cour de cassation* cannot be interpreted as a clear sudden modification in case law but as a kind of limitation. This case law evolved moreover.

b) ...To the Tort Birthing from Handicap

40 We have to indicate that on the same day, the *Cour de cassation* brought in *Assemblée Plénière* gave two decisions[60] about similar facts. Only the second case will be studied. We will divide this part into factual elements and juridical solution.

i. *Factual Elements*[61]

41 For a better understanding, we will distinguish facts and procedure.

(i) Facts

42 In 1995 on 27 January, Mrs. X gave birth to a child, named Lionel, suffering trisomy 21. Mr. Y is the gynaecologist consulted by Mrs. X during her pregnancy. Mr. Y was associated to a detection programme of foetal anomalies and proposed his patient to undergo a blood test to value the beta-H.C.G. in the sixteenth week of pregnancy. The dosage discovered, as passed to the gynaecologist by the University Hospital Centre's laboratory of Brest, revealed a rate superior to the 95%, as alarming by the expert appointed by provisional order. Besides, this expert emphasised that the scan graph, established by doctor Y, showed a discordance between the measurements of the foetus' biparietal diameter and that of the femur length.

43 All this justified, for the expert, the communication of information from the doctor to his patient and the recourse to a geneticist and a specialist in scan exams, who could prescribe an amniocentesis. As this was not done, Mrs. X was only informed of these alarming indications after the delivery.

44 Mrs. X sued doctor Y in her personal name and in the name of her child. We have to see, now, the procedure.

[60] C. Cass, Ass. Plén., 28 November 2001, appeals no. 00-11.197 (*cf.* no. 26) and no. 00-14.248.
[61] See Mr. Blondet report.

(ii) Procedure

The first degree judges recognised the gynaecologist's fault in his contract with Mrs. X and evaluated the degree of probability that women, in this situation, would operate a medical abortion. In so doing, they judged the tort caused by the birth of the child. This is surprising because we can read this decision like the recognition, to the mother, of losing a chance to abort; in spite the fact that it was established that birth, lacking particular circumstances, does not give any right to compensation of tort[62]. From another source, those judges declared Lionel's claim unacceptable saying that existence of a tort presupposed a prior situation without tort and juridically protected. 45

Mrs. X lodged an appeal. 46

On the one hand, the *Cour d'appel* confirmed the first decision by what it recognised to Mrs. X as a tort consecutive to the loss of a chance. On the other hand, it annulled a part of the first decision declaring Lionel's claim acceptable in compensation of the tort he personally undergoes. The *Cour* indicates: "This tort is constituted by damageable consequences of the handicap and, more particularly, the necessity to provide for continuous help to the child such as it is recommended by the expert". In so doing, those judges applied case law produced by the decisions dated 17 November 2000 and 13 July 2001. 47

Nevertheless, the judges of the *Cour d'appel* used, for the mother, the reasoning about the probability to have recourse to a medical abortion. They noted that: "*loss of chance due to the practitioner's fault*" did not justify the entire compensation of the damage caused to the child. 48

Mrs X petitioned against this decision because it restricted the damages suffered by Lionel; Mr. Y petitioned against this decision because it has confirmed Lionel's claim. 49

ii. Legal Dispositions

We will show the form and the substance of the law. 50

(i) Form

The presented decision had been quashed under the *visa* of Civil Code artt. 1165 and 1382[63] and based on the principle: "*l'indemnisation du préjudice doit être intégrale*"; besides, this decision had been taken by the *Cour de cassation* brought in *Assemblée Plénière*. So, because of its solemnity, this decision looks like another "arrêt Perruche". It could be the leading case which will end the fast and recent case law evolution about this point. 51

[62] J. Roche-Dahan, note under decisions dated 26 March 1996, [1997] *Recueil Dalloz* 3, 35.
[63] See *supra* notes 29 and 30.

52 Nevertheless, we can doubt this idea as the legal ground is not really the same.

(ii) Substance

53 Rejecting the incidental appeal of the gynaecologist, the *Cour de cassation* argued that "it was not contested by Mr. Y that the medical conditions for an abortion for therapeutic grounds would be met". So, the *Cour* confirms its position. By such position, the only possibility for the mother was to claim an abortion on medical grounds and for the loss of "the possibility to appeal to an amniocentesis [considering that] such abortion was directly connected with the tort caused to the child by his handicap". Also, medical conditions from the Public Health Code art. L. 2213–1, especially §§ 1 and 3[64] are not recalled. In fact, the child would be born inflicted with an especially severe complaint known as incurable during the diagnostic, in this case, trisomy 21.

54 The *Cour* also considers that: "[the] child's tort is not constituted by the loss of a chance but by his handicap". So, for this jurisdiction, handicaps have to be entirely compensated.

55 The entire compensation itself is not shocking. What the *Cour de cassation* sanctions is: the fixation of the tort's amount, in equity, to a lump sum[65] or to a compensation superior to the tort's amount conceded[66]. Moreover, in another decision, the *Cour de cassation* indicated[67], in order to justify the entire compensation of a tort, the link of necessity between original fact (here a traffic accident) and second fact (here a surgery act) which is the origin of the final tort (in this case the loss of an eye), is enough to prove the causality link between this damage (to be blind in one eye) and the initial fact (the traffic accident which only generated a spinal column wound): entire compensation is, in non-contractual liability, understood by Civil Code art. 1382[68]. In fact, the reparation aim is to return each party to their prior status, *i.e.* as it was before the tort and its consequences. Here an important question is asked.

56 Actually, a prior status of reference has to exist. Now, in the presented case, a sickness, Lionel's handicap, is consubstantial to the sick person. So the question is: to which original status, juridically recognised, have we to refer to in order to ground the compensation? This question can be asked in different ways and, for example to know if a right to not to be handicapped exists, or even a right to be "normal". Has the child to be born, the potential individual, got subjective rights already during the pregnancy? Are we facing a praetorian extension of the adage

[64] See *supra* note 55.

[65] C. Cass. Civ[1], 3 July 1996, Bull. Civ. I, no. 296.

[66] C. Cass. Com. (Commercial Chamber of the *Cour de cassation*), 11 May 1999, Bull. Civ. IV, no. 101.

[67] C. Cass. Civ[2] (Second Civil Chamber of the *Cour de cassation*), 27 January 2000, appeal no. 97-20.889, and note L. Chakirian, [2001] *Le Dalloz* 26, 2073.

[68] See *supra* note 30.

"infans conceptu pro nato habetur…"[69]? Those questions are asked although notions of handicap and normality are not defined and this is paradoxical because it is by those notions that compensation due by doctors are justified.

Here, perhaps, we go beyond limits of law, of positive law. All these questions could open a large ethical and juridial debate. In fact, according to the *Cour de cassation* decision dated 29 June 2001[70] for which the incrimination of manslaughter cannot be extended to the case of a child to be born "whose juridical regime comes from particular texts about embryo and foetus". 57

This compensation will is confirmed in others areas of civil liability. 58

B. Other Kinds of Liability

Looking at case law during the year 2001, we can distinguish lawyers' liability and liability in general. 59

1. Lawyers' Liability

We have to separate the faults of the representatives of the law from the liability of justice as administration. 60

a) Representative of the Law Liability

Examining case law, barristers and notaries are the two representatives of the law whose liability is the most frequently involved. 61

i. The Barristers

We will note with Rancé[71] that "professional secret of barristers is the heart of a European Directive against money-laundering[72]. With the state law dated 15 June 2000 concerning presumption of innocence, those new dispositions will intensify the summoning of barristers' risks". In fact, barristers' liability gave rise to an important litigation relative to the notion of loss of chance we have to introduce. 62

By two decisions dated 14 February[73] and 4 April[74] 2001 the *Cour de cassation* had to give its opinion on the liability of barristers towards their clients when this liability is based on the loss of a chance. To agree the loss of a chance of a party to win its action – and so to recognise a right to compensa- 63

[69] See G. Avocat, Un fœtus ne peut être victime d'un homicide involontaire, [2001] *Le Dalloz* 31, 2523.
[70] C. Cass. Ass. Plèn., 29 June 2001, appeal no. 99-85.973.
[71] P. Rancé, La responsabilité de l'avocat Interview de D. Liger, [2001] *Le Dalloz* 18, 1397.
[72] More information at: http://europa.eu.int/comm/internal_market/fr/finances/general/99-498.htm
[73] C. Cass. Soc., 14 February 2001, appeal no. 99-12.260.
[74] C. Cass. Civ[1], 4 April 2001, appeal no. 98-23.157.

tion – does not signify a granting to this party of the benefit of having won its action; this only signifies that the chance lost is equivalent to something that the victim has been deprived of[75]. In the scope of barristers' liability, in case of loss of chance, the ground is contractual: the barrister is considered to have committed a fault in his proxy.

64 In the first case, a worker had been laid off (by an economic redundancy procedure) with the tacit authorisation of the factory inspector (in France this kind of redundancy is only possible with such authorisation by such inspector). The barrister petitioned without a special authorisation given by the worker (so called "pouvoir spécial"). This petition had been declared unacceptable by the *Cour de cassation*[76]. In consequence, the worker tried to involve the barrister's liability. Two problems had to be solved. First, what was the consequence of the lack of the "pouvoir spécial" of the barrister; second, if the barrister had not committed any fault, would the worker have had a chance of winning his trial? On demand of the worker, the *Cour de cassation* had to check up the reliable feature of dispute concerning the legality of the tacit administrative authorisation. This last judgment confirmed that the barrister's fault had deprived the worker of a chance to actually succeed in the administrative dispute." Consequently, the *Cour de cassation* considered that the *Cour d'appel* violated Civil Code art. 1147[77]. The question is to determine the possible future. This seems to be connected with Art. 6 §1[78] of the European Convention of Fundamental Liberties and Human Rights. Nevertheless, this valuation has to be mitigated.

65 In fact, in the second case, the *Cour de cassation* indicates: "when the damage consists in the loss of a chance of a judicial claim's success, the real and reliable feature of the chance has to be appraised by looking at the success probability of this claim". Besides the *Cour de cassation* specifies that a *Cour d'appel* violates Civil Code art. 1149[79]; its reasoning, which grounds upon the result of a posterior proceeding, when it appraises the loss of a chance for "victims" to see favourably received a claim whose conditions of exercise were different. It is the first time, according to annotators[80], that Civil Code art. 1149 is used in a case concerning loss of a chance by the *Cour de cassation* which indicated, the same day in another case, that the loss of a chance feature originated from a fictive reconstitution. Those clarifications lead us to think that the hypothesis draws near to the probability, the future eventuality. Thus, loss of a chance tends to become a missed opportunity; a reversal of words shows the priority inversion and the will to open possibilities to be seen to be compensated.

[75] F. Terré/Ph. Simler/Y. Lequette, *Droit civil Les obligations* (6th edn. 1996), p. 551.
[76] N.C.P.C., Chapter II: Procedure without an obligatory representation.
[77] See *supra* note 19.
[78] F.L.H.R.S.E.C. art. 6 §1: "Every person has the right to see his action heard fairly, publicly and in a reasonable time by an independent and impartial trial [...]"
[79] C.C. art. 49: "Damages owed to the creditor are, usually, from the loss which he made and the profit which he has been deprived of, with exceptions and except for modifications."
[80] See note, [2001] *Le Dalloz* 20, 1589.

A last detail has to be mentioned in connection with the loss of a chance for a barrister's client to see his claims acknowledged by a court decision. The *Cour de cassation* decision dated 25 April 2001[81], specifies: "failing to inform his clients of quashing grounds which he plans, in enough time for them to formulate potential suggestions, the barrister does not deprive them of whatever chance of success for their petition, even though he maintains, in their name, allowable grounds during the discussion in front of first degree judges". The particular fact that the barrister, whose liability was searched, was an *avocat aux Conseils*, would not involve the particularisation of such decision presented in its principle; even if we have to specify that the liability of avocats aux Conseils is specific due to the technical nature of their profession and the proceeding speciality. 66

In this case, clients of an *avocats aux Conseils* saw their petition rejected. They decided to search their barrister's liability, who, as they thought, would not sufficiently argue the grounds and would not take into account Community law concerning competition. Referred to the Order council, this jurisdiction considered that the duty of advice was not violated, even though the argued ground was not devoid of a chance of success. According to this case the parties, *i.e.* clients of a barrister claiming a loss of chance do not seem to be in a position to appreciate grounds of law argued by their barrister. So, if they cannot judge the law's pertinence, they cannot give an opinion about the probability of success of their claim. Consequently, we can wonder how they can consider having a loss of chance as they are not able to grasp this chance. Even though, two questions have to be asked. The first one is in relation to the scope of the duty to inform of a barrister. Because of the technical nature of law, a barrister ought to have not only the last word in forming the strategy he establishes with his clients, but also, he ought not to take into account his client's suggestions. This indicates an important evolution in case law which decided that a barrister fell short of his duty of advice when he failed to inform his client about the defensive grounds regardless of the received instructions[82]. The second one concerns the appreciation of a loss of chance: it is independent from duties of advice and information. So, the chance is, completely, only in the performance of the barrister. Thus, the loss of a chance of seeing the triumph of one's claims can be seen as the missed opportunity of the barrister to win. Consequently, we can ask if the obligation of means, to which barristers are usually kept[83], is not becoming an obligation of reinforced means even an obligation of attenuated result. 67

There is another kind of representatives of the law who are especially confronted with the problems of liability: notaries. 68

[81] C. Cass. Com., 25 April 2001, appeal no. 98-13.456.
[82] C. Cass. Civ[1], 9 May 1996, Bull. Civ. I, no. 191.
[83] C. Cass. Civ[1], 7 October 1998, Bull. Civ. I, no. 282.

ii. The Notaries

69 Notaries are professionally bound to enlighten parties on the scope of acts they formed and on the value of warranties which can be attached to them. Case law recognises that the extent and scope of the duty to advise ought to be appreciated, according to the circumstances, and depending on whether the notary directly takes part in dealings concerning agreement stipulations or only intervenes to authenticate agreements already concluded[84]. However, it is admitted that notaries cannot refuse their liability pleading that they limited themselves to providing an authentic form to an agreement already concluded. So, in a decision dated 21 February 2001[85] the *Cour de cassation* affirmed that a "notary who contributes to the writing of a bill of sale is bound by a duty of advice intended to ensure validity and efficiency of acts in which he brings his help". In this case, the agreement written by the notary was posterior to the conclusion of transfers between the parties. According to the *Cour d'appel* the conclusion of transfers linked the parties in a definitive way and the agreement written by the notary had no influence upon their conclusion. This approach is sanctioned by the *Cour de casssation* for violating Civil Code art. 1382[86].

70 Notaries' duty of advice is more extended. In fact, a decision of the *Cour de cassation* dated 22 May 2001[87], sanctioned a decision of a *Cour d'appel* by which it had not been examined if the notary had advised his clients about consequences produced by the absence of an agreement reiteration. In this case, the private agreement specified the necessity to reiterate the act in front of a notary who was not charged with summoning the parties to proceed to the establishment of an authentic act. In another case, the *Cour d'appel* of Paris[88] sanctioned the notary who failed to inform heirs that they had to subscribe a declaration in a legal delay and to alert them about the risks of undergoing a fiscal penalty because of the non-performance of this declaration. The grounds upon which the *Cour* based its decision were that it was up to the notary "to initiate this [to give this information] even if the heirs had not informed him about their options to face the payment of the rights [*i.e.* the fiscal penalty]". So, notaries' duty of advice appears ever-changing. This attitude tends to go hand in hand with a worsening of liability consequences in case of serious fault[89]. In fact, even when, in the old times serious fault permitted the avoidance of a too easy stacking professional liability, nowadays this serious fault seems presumed for some professionals, like public officers as notaries, who have, for the *Cour d'appel* of Paris[90]: "the obligation to ensure effectiveness to the act he receives and authenticates".

84 C. Cass. Civ[1], 7 February 1990, Bull. Civ. I, no. 37
85 C. Cass. Civ[1], 21 February 2001, appeal no. 98-20.817.
86 See *supra* note 30.
87 C. Cass. Civ[1], 22 May 2001, appeal no. 98-18.888.
88 C.A. Paris, 10 October 2001, [2001] *Le Dalloz* 39, 3171.
89 F. Terré/Ph. Simler/Y. Lequette (*supra* note 75), p. 449.
90 C.A. Paris, 7 June 2001, [2001] *Le Dalloz* 31, 2561.

b) Liability of Justice

71 First of all, we have to indicate that "the State is held to compensate damage caused by the defective functioning of the service of justice; this liability is engaged only by a serious fault or by a denial of justice; justice inaptitude to complete the mission with which it is invested, constitutes a serious fault"[91].

72 We have to distinguish between the magistrate fault and the liability peculiar to the defective functioning of justice which one can compare with the liability of public power.

i. The Magistrate Fault

73 We have to note that according to Justice Organisation Code art. L. 781–1[92] and magistrature status art 11–1[93], the State accepts, beforehand, to support liability of every dysfunction. According to Clay[94], this leads to a factual impunity which can be the origin of dysfunction. In other respects, always according to this author, the effect of this is to privilege the magistrate to the detriment of amenable because the said magistrate is not accountable for his behaviour. This can incite him not to practise his jurisdictional mission to the best of his abilities. Such an attitude is peculiar if we consider that liability is the corollary of power. So, it is surprising to ascertain that, in spite of the increase of summons of public service of justice, personal actions engaged against magistrates are still very scarce, indeed non-existent[95]. According to the Title VIII of the V Republic Constitution, dated 4 October 1958, it is only question of a judicial authority whose independence is guaranteed by the President in pursuance of art. 64.

74 The irresponsibility of magistrates, like the irremovability of the Bench or the free speech of the body of public prosecutors, aims to guarantee their impar-

[91] C.A. Paris, 14 June 2001, [2001] *Le Dalloz* 31, 2562.

[92] J.O.C. art. L. 781–1: "The State is held to repair damage caused by the defective functioning of the service of justice."
"This liability is engaged only by a serious fault or by a justice denial."
"Liability of judges, for their personal fault, is ruled by the magistrature status concerning magistrates of the judicial body and by special state laws concerning judges of attribution jurisdictions."
"The State guarantees victims from damage caused by personal faults of judges and other magistrates, except its recourse against this one."
"Nevertheless, rules of Civil Procedure Code art. 505 ["Every party can have itself issuing, by the secretary of the jurisdiction in front of which the recourse could be formed, a certificate certifying the lack of opposition, appeal, or quash petition or indicating the date of the recourse if one has been done"] continue to receive application to the entry into force of the legislative provisions concerning the responsibility for the magistrates at a rate of their personal fault."

[93] Order no. 58–1270 dated the 22 December 1958 concerning magistrature status art. 11–1:
"Magistrates of the judicial body are liable only for their personal faults."
"Liability of magistrates who committed personal fault being connected with public service of justice can be engaged only upon the recursive action of the State."
"This recursive action is brought in front of a civil chamber of the *Cour de cassation*."

[94] T. Clay, Petite chronique judiciaire: la faute du magistrat, [2001] *Le Dalloz* 30, 2420.

[95] *Ibid.*

tiality[96]. Baudot[97] summarises this idea as follows: "it is true that you [magistrates] enter in a profession where we will frequently ask you to have character but, by this, where we only understand that you have to be ruthless towards poor wretches. Feeble towards yours seniors, uncompromising towards their inferiors, this is the usual conduct of men. Attempt to avoid this pitfall. We dispense justice with impunity: be moderate with that". The question is to take into account the stability of the juridical institution and the complaints of ordinary individuals who ought always to have the opportunity to complain. In fact, as Contamine[98] notes, the authority of *res judicata* has not to be disputed in this way. Besides, we could be shocked by the fact that disciplinary recourses against magistrates are engaged by ordinary individuals even in an indirect way: discipline has to be distinguished from liability.

75 Personal fault is defined as: "damageable act done by a public agent outwards of his service or producing, although done on the occasion of the service, the feature either of an intentional fault, or an extremely serious fault, so showing, following Lafferrière's classical formula: 'man with its weaknesses, its passions, its foolhardiness.'"[99]. This fault is often assimilated to the intentional fault which is: "the fault committed with intention to be injurious to others, more generally with the intention to cause a damage"[100]. Nevertheless, a difference exists: the term "personal fault" comes from administrative law, whereas the term "intentional fault" comes from civil law. We have to note the decision of the *Cour de cassation* dated 23 February 2001[101] specifying the notion of the serious fault: "this which has been committed under the influence of a so crass mistake that a magistrate, normally concerned about his duties, would not be induced into it, or also, this which reveals the personal spite, the intention to be injurious, or at last, this which comes from an abnormally deficient behaviour." This case, which inscribes itself in the famous case of the child Grégory, concerns procedural faults committed by an examining magistrate and judicial police officers. According to annotators[102], this decision is located "in the scope of a deep change aiming to extend liability of the public service of justice".

[96] Order no. 58–1270 dated 22 December 1958 concerning magistrature status art. 4: "The Bench is irremovable."
"Consequently, one of the Bench cannot receive, without his consent, a new assignment, even if it is a promotion."
Order no. 58–1270 dated 22 December 1958 concerning magistrature status art. 5: "The public prosecutors are under the management and the authority of their hierarchical chiefs and under the authority of the Lord Chancellor, Minister of Justice. During the hearing, they have free speech."

[97] O. Baudot, La harangue de Baudot, *Justice*, no. 168, http://www.syndicat-magistrature.org/article/67html

[98] C. Contamine, Responsabilité et discipline des magistrats, [2001] *Le Dalloz* 35, 2838.

[99] G. Cornu, *Vocabulaire juridique* (1st edn. 2000).

[100] *Ibid.*

[101] C. Cass. Ass. Plèn., 23 February 2001, appeal no. 99-16.165.

[102] C. Debbasch, Le nouveau régime de la responsabilité de la justice, [2001] *Le Dalloz* 22, 1752.

ii. The Public Power Liability

We will indicate, with Debbasch[103], that Judicial Organisation Code art. L. 781–1[104] is triply limited. 76

In the first place, this article only concerns the functioning of the public service of the judicial justice, *i.e.* by opposition to what depends on legislative or administrative (we should not confuse this with the term "jurisdictional" which refers to the mission to judge: all that is judicial is not jurisdictional and all what is jurisdictional is not judicial – *e.g.* administrative trials practise, into their regular jurisdictional functions[105]). Following on, administrative jurisdictions have a special regime. The *Conseil d'Etat* has a permanent Mission of inspection of administrative jurisdictions at its disposal. This Mission is in charge of controlling the good functioning of various administrative jurisdictions. Those inspections aim to clarify choices of conduct taken by those jurisdictions, to value obtained results both in the quantitative and qualitative scopes, to take bearings with each member of the jurisdiction about its liabilities and its career progress[106]. In the second place, this article does not concern liability arising from organisation difficulties of judicial justice which is answerable to the competency of administrative jurisdictions, according to the Administrative Courts of Appeal and Administrative Trials Code and the Administrative Justice Code[107]. In the third place, this article does not concern the particular regime of *amicus curiae* liability, *e.g.* experts whose status is ruled by the decree no. 74–1184 dated 31 December 1974[108]. 77

We have to note that the evolution, which the studied decision consecrates, shows the rise of the consumerism movement. Thus, like Debbasch underlines: "French agreed until the last few years to be citizens in the political order and subjects towards public services. Today, they aspire to the conquest of a citizenship which permits them to require that daily functioning of public services answers to their aspirations"[109]. So, we can explain that the restrictive position adopted by the *Tribunal des conflits* as well as the administrative and judicial 78

[103] *Ibid.*

[104] See *supra* note 93.

[105] G. Cornu (*supra* note 99).

[106] http://www.conseil-etat.fr/ce-data/cons.htm

[107] A.C.A.A: T.C. Art. L. 3: "Administrative trials are, in the first competence and under the reservation of appeal, the common law judges of administrative litigations."
"Administrative trials practise as well a conciliation mission."
A.J.C. art. L. 211–1: "Administrative trials are, in the first competence and under the competence attributed to the *Conseil d'Etat*, the common law judges of administrative litigations."

[108] Decree no. 74–1184 dated 31 December 1974 art. 25: "The expert control is done at the same time by the First President and by the Attorney General."
"Each of those magistrates receive complaints and makes, at every moment, useful inquiries to verify that the expert satisfied his legal obligations and fulfils them with punctuality."
"If it appears to the First President or the Attorney General that there are presumptions, against a registered expert to have been lacking in his obligations, he makes collect his explanations. If necessary he refers to the general assemble of the *Cour d'appel* or the office of the *Cour de cassation* with a view to his being struck off."

[109] C. Debbasch, [2001] *Le Dalloz* 22, 1752.

jurisdiction, has changed. In fact, since 1997, the *Tribunal de grande instance* of Paris[110] has judged that the absence of a guarantee from the State to ordinary individuals of jurisdictional protection is equivalent to a denial of justice. In this case, such qualification was preferred to the qualification of serious fault; it is the organisation of the public service of justice which is sanctioned. Consequently, the risk to reduce serious fault will be to reject the State improvidence upon its public servants who would have to manage a situation without having the human and material means to do such work. Such configuration can remind us of the case of gynaecologists, *mutatis mutandis* of course.

79 We note, also, that the *Tribunal de grande instance* of Paris in a judgment dated 11 July 2001[111] applied the reduced notion of fault as the *Cour de cassation* defined it in its decision dated 23 February 2001[112]. In fact, the so-called Tribunal considers that the serious fault was constituted by the incapacity for the public service to accomplish its mission. Facts allowing such an analysis are the following: "misappropriating of their aim actions of interception of telephone communication, authorised by state law in conditions especially restrictive since they involved a barrister, the examining magistrate had seriously flouted principles which are applicable in the present case, interfering with the defence's rights which the cancelling of the actions, unlawfully done, with the help of the practice by the barrister of recourse which he has at his disposal, did not have for effect neither to suppress nor to repair"[113].

80 The different kinds of professional liabilities which we have presented, cannot hide the evolution of the "general regime" of civil liability.

2. General Regime of Civil Liability

81 We have to separate the liability for a personal fact from the liability for something else.

a) Liability for Personal Fact

82 It is the non-contractual liability, as we called it, for a proved fault which is incumbent on the author of the damaging fact for the tort caused by its fault, even non-intentional[114]. We will study cases which open lawsuits for liability and those which exempt.

i. Opening Cases

83 The most important element is fault, *e.g.* personal liability of an auctioneer can be grounded upon Civil Code art. 1382[115] when he commits faults in the writing of the auction catalogue; in fact, auctioneers are held to give precise

[110] T.G.I. Paris, 5 November 1997, [1998] *Recueil Dalloz* juris., 9, note M.-A. Frison-Roche.
[111] T.G.I. Paris, 11 July 2001, [2001] *Le Dalloz* 34, 2806.
[112] C. Cass. Ass. Plèn., 23 February 2001 (see *supra* note 101).
[113] T.G.I. Paris, 11 July 2001(see *supra* note 112).
[114] G. Cornu (*supra* note 99).
[115] See *supra* note 30.

information in these catalogues[116]. The *Cour de cassation* re-affirmed this in a famous case[117]: *après avoir relevé qu'il n'était pas prétendu que Mme. Y…, qui n'a jamais rencontré Mme. X… antérieurement à sa liaison ni au cours de celle-ci, aurait, par son attitude, créé le scandale ou cherché à nuire spécifiquement au conjoint de son amant, qu'il n'était pas davantage soutenu qu'elle aurait à la suite de manœuvres détourné M. X… de son épouse, la Cour d'appel a pu décider que le seul fait d'entretenir une liaison avec un homme marié ne constitue pas une faute de nature à engager la responsabilité de son auteur à l'égard de l'épouse.*

This notion of fault rapidly becomes complicated, *e.g.* in the co-ownership scope. In the presented case[118] an association representative of co-owners in a block (of flats or apartments)[119], was not considered liable for the impecunious **84**

[116] C. A. Paris, 28 September 2001, [2001] *Le Dalloz* 38, 3092.

[117] C. Cass. Civ^2, 5 July 2001, appeal no. 99-21.445.

[118] C. Cass. Civ^3, 16 May 2001, appeal no. 99-19.838, note, C Atias, [2001] *Le Dalloz* 33, 2706.

[119] Decree no. 67–223 dated 17 March 1967 taken for the application of the law no. 65–557 dated 10 July 1965 fixing the status of co-ownership of built landed property, art. 28: "Without prejudice of the provisions of the Habitation and Construction Code art. L. 443-15-1 ["Without prejudice of the provisions of Urbanism Code IV book III title, a building for the purpose of habitation being owned by an organism of Moderate Rental Habitation and built with the help of the State, cannot be demolished without the prior agreement of State representatives in the department, of the implantation municipality, and of the loan guarantor./A decree taken in Conseil d'Etat fixes loan refunding conditions and the State helps in case of total or partial demolition."] and special stipulations of the rules of co-ownership, the functions of representative of co-owners can be assumed by any physical or moral person. Outside the hypothesis foreseen in the so-called art. L. 443-15-1, the function duration of representatives of co-owners cannot exceed three years. Nevertheless, during the delay foreseen in the Civil Code art. 1792 ["Every constructor of a workmanship is in full right liable towards the workmanship master or buyer, for damage, even arising from a ground defect, which compromise the workmanship strength or which, having an effect on one of its constitutive or equipment elements, prevail it inappropriate for its purpose./Such liability does not take place if the constructor proves that the damage comes from a foreign cause."], it cannot go beyond a year when the representative of co-owners, his joint, their principals or employers, their agents, their parents or relations by marriage until third degree included, have, directly or indirectly, with some title that it is, even through intermediaries, taken part in the landed property construction." "General assemble can renew the functions of representative of co-owners in the provisions fixed by the state law date the 10 July 1965 art. 25 ["Are only adopted by the all co-owners' voice majority decisions concerning: a) Every power delegation to take one of the decisions aims in the previous article; b) Authorisation given to some co-owners to execute, at their own expense, works having an effect on common parties or the exterior aspect of the landed property, and consistent with its destination; c) Naming or removal of the representative(s) of co-owners and of the members of the association board; d) Conditions which are realised disposal acts upon common parties or their accessories, when those acts arise from legal or statutory duty like those concerning terrace of common courtyard, others easements or transfer of joint ownership rights; e) realisation and execution modes of works obligatory issued by legal or statutory provisions; f) Modifications of expense distribution aims by article 10 §1 above, necessarily issued by change of the use of one or several private parties; g) Unless they raise from majority foreseen in art. 24, works of energy saving concerning thermal insulation of the building, air renewing, heating system and hot water production. Are only concerned by this provision works which are redeemable in a period below ten years. Those works nature, their redeemable modes, more particularly, those concerning the possibility to guarantee the conformity putting of lodging with healthiness, security and equipment standards defined by provisions taken for state law no. 67–561 dated the 12th of July 1967 concerning accommodation

situation of the association[120]. But he is considered as liable for having committed a fault by placing important orders with a firm. In this case, the association representative said nothing about the financial situation of the association to the contracting partner and did not collect the necessary capital. We also have to indicate that the association's liability is presented as the pendant of the building administration power. As Terré and Simler[121] said: "the nature of the association liability stems from different regimes." In fact, according to those authors, there are certainly similarities with the liability instituted by Civil Code art. 1386 ["A building owner is liable for the damage caused by its ruin, when it happens consequently to a lack maintenance of a defect of construction."] But they underline two differences: first, that this liability does not weigh upon the owner and, second, that the condition of the ruin of the building is moved aside. Also, the association becomes the keeper, in the meaning of Civil Code art. 1384 §1 ["We are liable not only for damage we cause by our own fact, but also for that caused by the fact of persons who we have to answer for, or by things that we have the care of."], of the building. Moreover, depending on the cases, the liability of the association can be engaged towards a third party or a co-ownership either as a principal or as a moral person. Finally, the contractual liability of the moral person can be engaged in the relationship between the association and its members. Following those authors[122], the quality of association's component cannot exempt the association representative from his personal liability both to the association – and this is a contractual liability – and to the third parties or co-owners – and this is a non-contractual liability. In this last hypothesis, the presented case took place. In fact, like Atias[123] notes: "a professional legal representative, non-contractually liable, is sanctioned not to behave as the diligent debtor of a contractual debt. Everything happens as if he ought to substitute for defaulting representative". Nevertheless, as this author precisely stresses, the association representative, as an association's mandatory, profits from Civil Code art.

improvement application; i) Unless they raise from majority foreseen in article 24, works of accessibility to handicapped persons of reduced mobility, without prejudice they do not have an effect on the building structure or its essential equipment elements; j) Fitting up or modification of common antenna or an internal network to the building joined to a cabled network, established or authorised by state law no. 86–1067 dated the 30th of September 1986 concerning communication liberty article 34; k) Continuous authorisation allowed by the police or the state police force to penetrate the common parties; l) Setting up or modification of a public electricity distribution network meant to feed in electric current vehicle parking locations, notably to permit charge of battery accumulator of electrical vehicle; m) Installation of cold water divisional meter."], for the duration foreseen in the previous paragraph."

120 State law no. 65–557 dated 10 July 1965 fixing the status of co-ownership of built landed property, art. 14: "The community of owners is constituted in an association which has civil personality."
"The association can take shape of a co-operative association ruled by this law provisions. Co-ownership statutes have to provide expressly for this mode of management."
"It establishes, if necessary, and amend the co-ownership statutes."
"Its aim is the care of the landed property and the administration of common parties. It is liable for damages caused to co-owners or third parties by a defect of construction or a lack of maintenance of common parties, without prejudice to all recursive actions."

121 F. Terré/Ph. Simler, *Droit civil Les biens* (4th edn. 1992), p. 425.

122 *Ibid*. pp. 451–452.

123 C. Atias, [2001] *Le Dalloz* 33, 2706.

1999[124], of a recourse towards the association. But should not have committed a fault. Now, in the presented case, the association representative kept quiet; can we qualify this silence as fraudulent? This question would have to be settled by the *Cour de cassation*.

Besides, we notice that case law, by enforcement of Penal Procedure Code art. 4–1[125] took into account the end of uniqueness of civil and penal faults. In fact, in a decision from the *Cour de cassation* dated 30 January 2001[126] we can note: "declaration by the criminal court judge of the lack of non-intentional penal fault does not stand in the way of what a civil judge considers civil fault of foolhardiness or negligence". So, the civil judge is no more held to respect the authority of penal *res judicata*; the autonomy of civil jurisdictions and repressive jurisdictions increases with this. In another respect, we note that according to the terms used by the *Cour de cassation*[127]: "the principle according to which 'le criminel tient le civil en l'état' is not applicable as far as provisional claims are concerned" in front of an indemnification commission (concerning penal victims) in conformity with the provisions of the Penal Procedure Code[128]. We 85

[124] C.C. art.. 1999: "The principals have to pay back the agent for advances and expenses incurred in the execution of the proxy, and to pay his wages when they were promised.
"If there is no fault attributable to the agent, the principal can neither excuse himself from making those repayments and payments, even if the deal is unsuccessful, nor reduce the advance and expenses sums using as a pretext that they could be lower."

[125] P.P.C. art.. 4–1: "The lack of non-intentional penal fault in the meaning of Penal Code art. 121–3 ["There is no crime or misdemeanour without intention to commit it./Nevertheless, when state law foresees it, there is misdemeanour in case of putting in deliberate danger another in deliberate danger./Also, there is misdemeanour, when state law foresees it, in case of foolhardiness fault, negligence or violation of a prudence or security duty foreseen by a state law or a statute, if it is established that the author of the facts did not execute the normal diligence, taking into account, if necessary, his missions or nature of his functions, his competence and power and the means he had at his disposal./In the case foreseen by the previous paragraph, physical persons who did not directly cause the damage, but who created or contributed to creating the situation which permitted the realisation of the damage or who did not take the measures allowing the avoidance of it, are, for the penal law, liable if it is established that they either violated, in a manifestly deliberate way a particular duty of prudence or security foreseen by law or statutes, or committed a typical fault which exposed another to a particular serious risk which they could not have ignored./There is no contravention in case of *force majeure*."] does not stand in the way of suing in civil jurisdictions to obtain compensation of the damage ground upon Civil Code art. 1383 ["Each one is liable for the damage which he caused not only by his own fact, but also by his negligence or his foolhardiness."] if the existence of the civil fault foreseen by this article is established or by application of Social Security Code art. L. 452–1 ["When the accident is due to inexcusable fault of the employer or of those who he is substituted for him in the management, the victim or his/her entitled beneficiary have the right to a complementary compensation in the conditions defined in the next articles."] if existence of the inexcusable fault foreseen by this article is confirmed."

[126] C. Cass. Civ[1], 30 January 2001, appeal no. 98-14.368.

[127] C. Cass. Civ[2], 15 November 2001, appeal no. 00-12.506.

[128] P.P.C. art. 706–7: "When penal actions have been engaged, decision of the commission can intervene before a decision about the public action has been given."
"The commission can, for application of art. 706–3 last paragraph ["Redress can be refused or its amount reduced because of the fault of the victim."], suspend giving a decision until the definitive decision of repressive jurisdiction. In every case, it has to suspend giving a decision on the claim of the victim."
"Proceedings take place and decision is given in *chambre du conseil*."

can indicate, still according to the *Cour de cassation*[129], "action grounded upon facts known as defamatory, cannot constitute an abuse of a proceeding right". In the presented case, defamation[130] was characterised only in its material element, the moral element was not constituted: relevant documents, establishing good faith have been held. Therefore, penal fault cannot be reproached; but civil fault still seems to remain and allows the defamed person to proceed without any risk of being sued for an abuse of proceeding.

86 In other respects, we are reminded that civil faults are equally separate from disciplinary faults "characterised by the violation of the statutes and sanctioned so far as such by the entitled authority"[131].

ii. Exemption Cases

87 Liability exemption, which only takes place in cases of *force majeure*, victim's fault or third party's fact, seems to be hypothetical. Therefore, the point is an obligation of result security (and even a mean's obligation appraised more strictly, notably towards a dangerous sport coach[132]). It is, more particularly, the case for an aquatic toboggan's operator. In the presented case, the *Cour d'appel* of Paris[133] estimated: "exact circumstances of the accident are still unknown and notably the fact to know if the victim committed a fault sliding down the toboggan head first, in opposition to the instructions of security, the operator has to be found liable for the damage suffered". In the same way, the *Cour d'appel* of Versailles[134] estimated that the passenger's behaviour "in a highly frequented station and fitted out with underground passages constitutes an unforeseeable and irresistible event, in consideration of swiftness progress of the facts, in such a way that the fault of the victim constitutes a *force majeure* fact, totally exempting the S.N.C.F.". We will remind that the S.N.C.F. is only held by an obligation of contractual safety during the transport; outwith this time, its liability is non-contractual[135]. The *Cour de cassation* already decided[136]: "victim's fault does not totally exempt the keeper from his liability excepting the case in which this fault constitutes a case of force majeure". In other respects, the consistency thought of the *Cour de cassation* is beyond doubt as this jurisdiction admits[137]:

[129] C. Cass. Civ^2, 15 March 2001, appeal no. 99-15.165.

[130] State law dated 29 July 1881 concerning press liberty art. 29: "All allegations or imputations of a fact which interfere with the honour or consideration of a person or to the body to which the fact is attributed, is defamatory. Straight publication or publication by way of reproduction of this allegation is punishable, even if it is done in a dubious form or if it is directed at a person or a body not named expressly, but whose identification is made possible by terms of the offending speeches, cries, documents or printed papers, posters or placards."
"All offensive remarks, terms of contempt or invective which do not contain imputation of any fact is an insult."

[131] C.A. Versailles, 19 January 2001, [2001] *Le Dalloz* 11, 909.

[132] C. Cass. Civ^1, 16 October 2001, appeal no. 99-18.221.

[133] C.A. Paris, 23 February 2001, [2001] *Le Dalloz* 12, 982.

[134] C.A. Versailles, 2 February 2001, [2001] *Le Dalloz* 10, 832.

[135] C.A. Paris, 15 October 2001, [2001] *Le Dalloz* 42, 3399.

[136] C. Cass. Civ^2, 11 January 2001, appeal no. 99-10.417.

[137] C. Cass. Civ^2, 29 March 2001, appeal no. 99-10.735.

"third party's fact, constituted by the fall of another client in an escalator, cannot totally exempt the keeper from his liability excepting the case in which this fall has been to his regard unforeseeable and irresistible which has not been demonstrated"; in the same way this *Cour* decided[138] "unidentified third party's fact does not exempt the thing keeper [...] except the case in which this fact presents feature of force majeure". Thus, it appears, in fact, that the *force majeure* is the only cause of liability's exemption. Nevertheless, we have to specify that for the *Cour d'appel* of Paris[139] "the decision taken by a company management to close definitively an establishment [...] this event, being usual in company life, at the very least devoid of exceptional feature, was not impossible to foresee and does not constitute a *force majeure* case".

As a result, we assist in the limitation of exemption cases, *i.e.* the increase, for victims, in their possibility to engage the liability of someone else. This leads to further compensation cases, *i.e.* an "insurantial" system – *e.g.* state law no. 85–677 dated 5 July 1985, leading to the improvement of the situation of victims of traffic accidents and the acceleration of compensation proceedings, rules in its art. 2 that *force majeure* or the acts of third parties cannot be raised as a defense by the driver or the keeper of a vehicle mentioned in art. 1[140]. The discussion moves from the fault, juridically understood, to the risk, as it is understood by insurance law, *i.e.* the damageable event whose happening is doubtful as for its realisation or the date of its realisation[141]. **88**

b) Liability for Persons and Things

It is the non-contractual liability based upon Civil Code art. 1384 and notably in its first paragraph which applies: "One is liable not only for damage one causes by one's own fact, but also for this caused by the fact of persons that one has to answer for, or by things that one has the care of". So, we will show the liability for other persons and things. **89**

i. Liability for Someone Else

Firstly, we will mention the liability of parents for their children which is organised by Civil Code art. 1384 § 4 in the following terms: "Father and mother, as they exercise their right of custody, are jointly liable for the damage caused by their underage children living with them". We will remind that the notion of cohabitation is an abstract one[142] since the *Cour de cassation* indicated: "the exercise of a right to access and lodging does not put a stop to the child's cohabitation with the parent who exercises the right of custody". This jurisdiction con- **90**

[138] C. Cass. Civ^2, 15 March 2001, appeal no. 99-11.033.
[139] C.A. Paris, 30 March 2001, [2001] *Le Dalloz* 21, 1670–1671.
[140] State law no. 85–677 dated 5 July 1985 art. 1: "Present chapter provisions apply to, even if they are transported in application of a contract, victims of a traffic accident in which is involved an earthly motor vehicle like its trailers, or half-trailers, with exception to railway and tramways circulating upon their own ways."
[141] G. Cornu (*supra* note 99).
[142] C. Cass. Civ^2, 19 February 1997, appeal no. 93-14.646.

firmed such solution[143] in these terms: "presence of an underage child in a school educational establishment, even in a boarding regime, does not suppress the child's cohabitation with his parents". In so doing, this jurisdiction comes back to a solution already admitted: this legal presumption evidence of father's and mother's liability stops with the cohabitation if there is a legitimate reason for this cessation, notably when the child is in a boarding school[144]. This solution is surprising because Civil Code art. 1384 § 6 applies: "teachers and artisans [are jointly liable] for damage caused by their pupils and apprentices during the time they are under their supervision", being specified that in the terms of this article § 8: "for what concerns teachers, faults, foolhardiness or negligence pleaded against them, like having caused damageable facts, would have to be proved, according to the common law, by the plaintiff, during the process". The idea pursued by this jurisdiction seems to make easier the compensation of victims by favouring the engagement of the liability of the parents. In fact, because in this case we have to prove the fault of the parents, this liability is more easy to engage than the liability of teachers. Actually, case law acknowledged that teacher's liability for damages caused by their pupils during the time that the pupils were under their supervision, could not be used, except in the case in which the fault pleaded against them is proved, which excludes the application of art 1384 § 1[145]. In other respects, case law admitted to condemn the State to compensate for the damage caused by pupils during the time they were under the supervision of a teacher. So, we have to retain the liability of a determined teacher, author of a personal fault[146].

91 Nevertheless, according to the *Cour d'appel* of Versailles[147], cohabitation's cessation can be considered as just in some cases. Judges indicated, in this case, that law principles based upon Civil Code art. 1384 § 1 have to be applied to an association to which Children Social Help entrusted a minor. In fact, this association had received from the *Tribunal pour enfant* (trial specialised in proceedings concerning children) the mission and the responsibility to organise, to conduct and to supervise the way of life of the underage victim and of three others minors from the same lodging home. In this case, there is a presumption of liability against this association.

92 Finally, the *Cour de cassation* reminded[148] "full right's liability brought by father and mother because of the fact of damages caused by their underage child living with them is not subordinated to the existence of a fault of the child". The *Cour* takes back, here, the decision which it adopted in a decision dated 9 May 1984[149] which terms were: "in order to be presumed, grounded

[143] C. Cass. Civ^2, 29 March 2001, appeal no. 98-20.721.
[144] C. Cass. Civ^1, 2 July 2001, Bull. Civ. I, no. 224.
[145] C. Cass. Civ^2, 11 March 1981, Bull. Civ. II, no. 55.
[146] C. Cass. Civ^2, 17 July 1991,Bull. Civ. II, no. 232.
[147] C.A. Versailles, 8 June 2001, [2001] *Le Dalloz* 30, 2461.
[148] C. Cass. Civ^2, 10 May 2001, appeal no. 99-11.287 and note O. Tournafond, De la faute à la théorie du risque: l'exemple de la responsabilité des parents du fait de leurs enfants mineurs, [2001] *Le Dalloz* 35, 2854.
[149] C. Cass. Ass. Plèn., 9 May 1984, appeal no. 79-16.612.

upon Civil Code art. 1384 § 4, the liability of father and mother of a child who lives with them, it is enough that the child committed an act which was the direct cause of the damage pleaded by the victim". Besides, we will indicate that, for case law[150], first degree judges have not to examine if the minor, the author of the damage, was able to discern the consequences of his act – in the case, the fact that the child had the use, conduct and authority over a stick which was useful for causing the damage, sufficed to engage the liability of his parents. The child seems to be considered as a risk, as an "insurantial" risk. We have also to mention the specific peculiarities of a child largely exposed by Jacopin[151].

Secondly, we will mention the liability due to the fact of employees which is organised by Civil Code art. 1384 § 5 in these terms: "Masters and principals [are jointly liable] for damages caused by their servants and their agents in the functions in which they are employed", this liability comes from the subordination's link. Case law specifies[152]: "subordination's link from which the liability of the principal comes, proceeds essentially from the right of the principal to make acts of authority giving orders or instructions to the agent about the way to serve, in a temporary or permanent title, with or without payment, the job which it is entrusted for a determined time and object". Also, the *Cour de cassation* could decide[153] that "the agent who acted without exceeding limits of the mission which was entrusted to him by his principal is not liable vis-à-vis third parties". Nevertheless, the *Cour* has been obliged to specify the scope of this principle[154] when the agent commits a misdemeanour which profits his employer (in the presented case the use of forgeries and frauds made to obtain, fraudulently, some subsidies for his employer). The presented decision shows: "the agent condemned by penal trials for having, intentionally, committed, was it on the principal order, an offence inflicting injury to a third party, engages his civil liability towards this one". In fact, the respect of a subordination's link cannot be an excuse both penal[155] and civil, as this was shown above. Moreover, such an attitude seems to take into account the end of uniqueness of civil and penal fault, as we said. In fact, whether the fault committed by the agent is or is not penal, his liability will be, or not, engaged (the reverse is true for his employer). 93

Consequently, when a restaurant places a carter at his clients' disposal and when this carter is paid by an independent skilled worker to which the restaurant has recourse in the scope of a contract of provision of service, the *Cour d'appel* of Paris[156] can distinguish between the fault engaging the contractual liability of the restaurant towards its clients, insofar as the carter is juridically 94

[150] C. Cass. Ass. Plèn., 9 May 1984, appeal no. 80-14.994.

[151] See S. Jacopin, La mise en conjonction des diversités préservées en matière de minorité, [2001] *Le Dalloz* 34, 2768.

[152] C. Cass. Crim., 16 April 1975, [1975] *Gazette du Palais* (G. P.), Journal of 26 July, 506–507.

[153] C. Cass. Ass. Plèn., 25 February 2000, appeal no. 97-17.378.

[154] C. Cass. Ass. Plèn., 14 December 2001, appeal no. 00-82.066.

[155] See Penal Code artt. 122–1 to 122–8.

[156] C.A. Paris, 24 April 2001, [2001] *Le Dalloz* 21, 1671.

its agent, even lacking a contract of employment, and the quasi-non-contractual fault engaging the liability of the restaurant towards third parties who are victims of the accidents caused by the carter. A special mention has to be made in the case of the existence of a professional independence. This is the case of a doctor practising in a clinic. In this hypothesis, the doctor answers for the faults committed by those who assist him, even if it is the staff of the health's establishment in which he practises. However, the Cour de cassation specifies[157]: "it is not so when the victim is the practitioner himself; he can, in this case, seek the liability of the clinic for the fault committed by one of its agents". Again, the intention is to favour the compensation of the victim: thus the *Cour* prevented the doctor being judged liable of his own tort.

95 We have to note a change in case law which appears concerning the liability of the supplier of the subcontractor[158]. In fact, the *Cour de cassation*[159] admitted that: "the contracting authority, as subvendee, is in full possession of all rights and actions attached to the thing which belongs to its author; thus he has a direct contractual action, grounded upon the non-conformity of the delivered thing, towards the maker at his disposal". Already, the third civil chamber of the *Cour de cassation* admitted that the subcontractor was liable because of the defects caused by the defectiveness of material used, unless he accounts for a foreign cause which cannot be attributed to him[160]. Also, this jurisdiction admitted that the subcontractor of a subcontractor was held, towards the latter, of an obligation of result to execute workmanship free from defects[161]. We will indicate in the terms of Civil Code art. 1792 § 1: "Every constructor of workmanship is fully liable towards the workmanship master or buyer, from damages, even arising from a ground defect, which compromise the workmanship strength or which, having an effect on one of its constitutive or equipment elements, render it inappropriate for its purpose". Besides, we will specify that the *Cour de cassation*[162] noted: "constructor, notwithstanding the ten years' prescription period, is, excepting the fault exterior to the contract, contractually held towards the contracting authority of his fraudulent fault when, in deliberate words even without the intention to be injurious, he violates, by an underhand way or by fraud, his contractual obligations". This constitutes a change as to the nature of the liability for wilful misrepresentation and as to the notion of fraudulent fault. A virtual homogenous chain of contractual liability gets to apply itself.

[157] C. Cass. Civ[1], 13 March 2001, appeal no. 99-16.093.

[158] State law no. 75–1334 dated 31 December 1975 concerning subcontracting art. 1: "In the meaning of the present state law, subcontracting is the operation by which a contractor entrusts by a subcontract, and under his liability, another person called subcontractor, with all or part of the execution of the venture agreement or public contract concluded with the contracting authority."

[159] C. Cass. Ass. Plèn., 7 February 1986, appeal no. 83-14.631.

[160] C. Cass. Civ[3], 23 October 1984, Bull. Civ. III, no. 171.

[161] C. Cass. Civ[3], 21 March 1984, Bull. Civ. III, no. 75.

[162] C. Cass. Civ[3], 27 June 2001, appeal no. 99-21.017 and note J.-P. Karila, [2001] *Le Dalloz* 37, 2998.

96 The *Cour de cassation* changed its position in a decision dated 12 July 1991[163], declaring: "contracting authority has, against the subcontractor with whom there is no contractual link, only a quasi-non-contractual action". Therefore, all contractual obligations are put in question. We will specify the divergence of opinion between the first and the third civil chamber of the *Cour de cassation* towards this point. The key issue concerns procedure, namely either enforcement of the short delay from Civil Code art. 1648[164] or the decennial delay from Civil Code art. 2270–1[165]. It is this last position which is confirmed by the *Cour*[166] in those terms: "having been exactly indicated that the company Normacarde, subcontractor, engaged its liability towards the contracting authority upon an offensive ground, the *Cour d'appel* held, with good reason, that the supplier of this subcontractor, the company Haironville, had to, towards the contracting authority, answer for its acts upon the same ground"; this shows the change of the third civil chamber of the *Cour de cassation* and should let augur a stabilisation of case law – which seems paradoxical since this jurisdiction holds that the liability for misrepresentation of the constructor is a non-contractual one[167].

ii. *Liability for Things*

97 Liability for something else was built upon Civil Code art. 1384 § 1 providing: "We are liable not only for the damage we cause by our own fact, but also for that caused by the fact of persons whom we have to answer for, or by things that we have the care of". Case law[168] considered: "principle of liability for the fact of inanimate things finds its ground in the notion of care independently from the intrinsic feature of the thing and of any personal fault of the keeper; that the inherent defect in the thing which caused the damage does not constitute, towards the one who exercises on this thing powers of control, authority and use correlative to the duty of care, an act of God or of *force majeure* the nature of which should exempt him of his liability towards the third party". The case law recognised that inert things can be an instrument of damage only if we prove that it occupied an extraordinary position or it was in bad condi-

[163] C. Cass. Ass. Plèn., 12 July 1991, appeal no. 90-13.602.

[164] C.C. Art. 1648: "Action due to crippling defects has to be engaged, within a short time period, depending on the nature of the crippling defects, and the practice of the place where the sale has been done."
"In the case foreseen by art. 1642–1 ["The landed property to be built by salesperson cannot be relieved before the receipt of works, nor before the end of a one month period after taken possession of by the vendee, of defects of the construction so apparent./There will be no cancellation of the contract or decrease of the price if the salesperson binds itself to repair the defect."], action has to be engaged, under the sanction of foreclusion, in the year following the date in which the salesperson can be relieved of apparent defects."

[165] C.C. art. 2270–1: "Actions in extra-contractual civil liability prescribe themselves by ten years from the manifestation of damage or its aggravation.
"When damage is caused by torture and acts of barbarity, violence or sexual aggression committed against a minor, action in civil liability is prescribed by twenty years."

[166] C. Cass. Civ3, 28 November 2001, appeal no. 00-14.450.

[167] C. Cass. Civ3, 27 June 2001, appeal no. 99-21.017, op. cit. n. 162.

[168] C. Cass. Civ2, 20 November 1968, [1970] J.C.P. II, 16567.

tion[169]. But the *Cour de cassation*[170] quashed for the breaking of Civil Code art. 1384 § 1 the decision of a *Cour d'appel* which rejected claims of the victim grounded that: "it was not demonstrated that the thing was the instrument of the damage" holding that the glass wall, fixed, presented neither any extraordinary feature nor defect or flaw of maintenance. For the *Cour de cassation*, the fact, emerging from the verification of the *Cour d'appel,* that such a wall intervenes in the realisation of the damage was enough. In the same way, this jurisdiction[171] holds that the thing, here a mail box, was the instrument of the damage to engage the liability of its keeper and this without proving its causal role in the realisation of damage.

98 According to a continuous case law, started with the decision of the *Cour de cassation* dated 2 December 1941 known as "arrêt Franck", the responsibility for damage caused by a thing is linked "to the use which is done with it, as well as powers of control and authority exercised on it which characterise the care"[172]. We will note that the *Cour de cassation*[173] considered the S.N.C.F. as the keeper of a railroad train, to quash for breaking of Civil Code art. 1384 § 1 the decision of a *Cour d'appel* which held that S.N.C.F. "could not be found liable for damage which it could not prevent, a railroad train not having the possibility, by reason of its weight and its moving mass, to stop on the spot or nearby, exempts the S.N.C.F. of the liability presumption weighing up it by application of Civil Code art. 1384 § 1 when the behaviour of the victim does not present the feature of *force majeure*". The notion of care is understood in a very extended meaning and seems to ascendancy over special provisions of state law.

99 In fact, in a decision dated 23 March 2000, the *Cour de cassation*[174], under the visa of Civil Code art. 1386[175] and art. 1384 § 1, considers that: "the first of those texts [art. 1386] does not rule out that the provisions of the second one could be referred to towards the non-owner keeper". It is an appreciable modification of prior case law, indeed a change since case law considered that art. 1386 ruled out the application of extended meaning of the provisions of art. 1384 § 1 concerning liability for every movable or real things we have under our care[176].

[169] C. Cass. Civ^2, 11 January 1995, Bull. Civ. II, no. 18.
[170] C. Cass. Civ^2, 15 June 2000, appeal no. 98-20.510, and note G. Blanc, Le heurt d'une baie vitrée: un contentieux récurrent en matière de responsabilité du fait des choses, [2001] *Le Dalloz* 11, 886.
[171] C. Cass. Civ^2, 25 October 2001, appeal no. 99-21.616.
[172] C. Cass. Civ^1, 23 February 1977, [1978] *Gazette du Palais* (G. P.) Journal of 7 February, 90–91.
[173] C. Cass. Civ^2, 11 January 2001, appeal no. 99-10.417, (*supra* note 136).
[174] C. Cass. Civ^2, 23 March 2000, appeal no. 97-19.991, and note N. Garçon, Responsabilité du fait des choses et ruine du bâtiment, [2001] *Le Dalloz* 7, 586.
[175] C.C. art. 1386: "A building owner is liable for the damage caused by its ruin, when it happens consequent to a lack maintenance of a defect of construction."
[176] C. Cass. Civ^2, 4 April 1972, Bull. Civ. II, no. 128.

Art. 1385 of the Civil Code[177] remains special; even if the keeping of animals is ruled by the Rural Code, Civil Code art. 1385 has only a complementary role[178]. In fact, the *Cour de cassation*[179] sanctioned, upon this basis, the decision which did not hold the owner of a dog liable when this owner had not proved that his dog had not taken part in the realisation of the damage or the tort came from an exterior fact, unforeseeable and irresistible. In the presented case, divergent views of witnesses did not permit to determine if the defendant's dog bit the victim or not; this did not have to prejudice the interests of the victim, who found it impossible to establish which of those animals caused his damage. Nevertheless, the active role of the animal in the realisation of the damage is necessary[180]. 100

All those developments lead us to the conclusion that there is an increasing modification both quantitatively – *i.e.* case law increase – and qualitatively – *i.e.* contortions which law of civil liability underwent. The aim of this modification is to favour the compensation of the victim. All happens as if the person deemed liable was the insurer of the person who underwent damage which is the continuation of the realisation of a risk (this term understood in its "insurantial" way). So we can note that the *Cour de cassation*[181] decided "a guarantee exclusion clause cannot be formal and limited therefore it has to be interpreted". We will conclude explaining this. 101

We have to note that this problem concerning compensation tends to produce new mechanisms wished by some[182]. The basic principle is of entire compensation of the tort: Terré, Simler and Lequette[183] remind us of this in these terms: "damages amounts awarded by the judge have to cover the whole of the reparable tort, by the creditor, but do not have to exceed it. It is an essential rule which applies both to the contractual liability and offensive liability, even if, in contractual matter the unforeseeable tort is excluded from the notion of reparable tort". That is how damages have to cover both future, but sure, tort and actual tort, which is moral or material, in this case concerning a missed gain or an undergone loss. In brief, the victim patrimony – *i.e.* the whole of his assets and his recognisances (rights and charges appreciable pecuniarily), regarded as formatting a universality of rights, a whole which includes not only present assets, but also future ones[184]. We have to underline that only per- 102

[177] C.C. art. 1385: "The owner of an animal, or the one, while it is with its use, is liable for the damage the animal caused, when either the animal was under his care, or it was lost or had escaped."

[178] A. Bugada, Des paons sans-gêne… ou comment faire cesser une querelle de voisinage sans casser d'œufs?, [2001] *Le Dalloz* 34, 2778.

[179] C. Cass. Civ[2], 15 March 2001, appeal no. 98-22.078.

[180] C. Cass. Civ[2], 27 September 2001, appeal no. 00-10.208.

[181] C. Cass. Civ[1], 22 May 2001, appeal no. 99-10.849, and note B. Beigner, [2001] *Le Dalloz* 34, 2778.

[182] M.-D. Douaoui, La réparation du trouble médiatique, [2001] *Le Dalloz* 17, 1333.

[183] F. Terré/Ph. Simler/Y. Lequette (*supra* note 75), p. 474.

[184] G. Cornu (*supra* note 99).

sons can have patrimony, each person has a patrimony which remains linked to him for all his life, and a person has only one patrimony[185].

103 This preciseness permits the understanding of the mechanisms of subrogatory recourse, notably those of social organisms, against the person who caused the accident[186]. By this contentious we can see the true stakes of the whole civil liability law: the mechanism, the "insurantial" mechanic. We ought to be shocked seeing victims of damage using courts as casinos where it is possible to win in each bet. In fact, this could have as a consequence to make all individuals non-responsible to the detriment of part of a peculiar group of persons. Implications of such phenomena are deep and numerous.

104 To finish, it is interesting to underline the proposition of state law amended by the government concerning the national solidarity and compensation of congenital handicaps adopted on 10 January 2002[187]. In fact, this proposition seems to ratify the "insurantial" phenomena, establishing, by a juridical construction, a case of allocation of a sum which is not compensation (because the handicapped person is not considered a victim of damage) nor damages (the handicapped person is not creditor of the doctor who has to repair damage caused by non-performance, bad performance or belated performance of its obligation: what is the obligation linking the doctor to the handicapped person?) nor compensation (where are the two reciprocal obligations between the same persons which have to disappear?). It is a new concept: an assigned payment – *i.e.* payment of money in performance of a monetary obligation – whose assignment is to provide for the past, present and future needs of the handicapped person, the first monetary obligation being here, a legal one.

[185] F. Terré/Ph. Simler (*supra* note 121), pp. 6–7.

[186] Y. Lambert-Faivre, Avancées et trébuchements sur le recours des organismes sociaux, [2001] *Le Dalloz* 3, 248.

[187] Proposition of state law dated 10 January 2002, text no. 757 art. 1: "Nobody, even born handicapped, can be prevailed of a damage by the mere fact of its birth."
"The person born with a handicap caused by a medical fault can obtain compensation of its tort when the faulty act directly caused the handicap, or aggravate it, or did not permit to take the measures susceptible of attenuate it."
"When the liability of a professional or a health establishment is engaged towards the parents of a child who was born with an especially serious handicap which was not detected during the pregnancy and caused by a serious fault, those with parental authority can claim compensation intended for the handicapped person corresponding to special charges resulting, life-long, from his handicap, deduction done of the sums of allocations and benefits, whatever they are, which this person will gain from the national solidarity or social security systems. In this precise case, social organisms cannot exercise recourse towards the author of the fault to obtain repayment of paid allocations and benefits."
"Provisions of this case law are applicable in the current process, except those where it was ruled, in an unrecoverable way, on the principle of the compensation."

C. Literature from the Dalloz

1. Articles

N. Balbo-Izarn, Le professionnel face aux risques informatiques, [2001] *Petites affiches*, 16 February, 4. **105**

A. Batteur, L'application de la loi du 19 mai 1998 relative à la responsabilité du fait des produits dans les rapports entre professionnels, [2001] *Petites affiches*, 8 October, 5. **106**

P. Brun, La mise en œuvre de la responsabilité des commettants du fait de leurs préposés, [January 2001], *Droit et patrimoine*, 52. **107**

P.-Y. Gautier, "les distances du juge" à propos d'un débat éthique sur la responsabilité civile, [2001] J.C.P., I, 287, 66. **108**

G. Vieny, Brèves remarques à propos d'un arrêt qui affecte l'image de la justice dans l'opinion, [2001] J.C.P., I, 286, 65. **109**

2. Notes

Y. Dagorne-Labbe, Le montant d'une indemnité allouée au titre de l'assistance d'une tierce personne ne saurait être réduit en cas d'assistance par un membre de la famille, note ss. C. Cass. Civ 2, 4 May 2000, [2001] J.C.P. II, 10489, 550. **110**

C. Robasczewski, Responsabilité du tuteur du fait d'un mineur, note ss. C. Cass. Crim. 28 March 2000, [2001] J.C.P. II, 10456, 135. **111**

F. Violet, Rupture de manière délibérée et de mauvaise foi de pourparlers, note ss. C. A. Paris, 10 March 2000, [2001] J.C.P. II, 10470, 317. **112**

D. Addendum

On 4 March of this year (2002) a proposition of state law amended by the Government was adopted by the National Assembly in a more general state law dealing with sick persons' rights. So the first article of this state law was taken in reaction from the decisions of the *Cour de cassation*. **113**

The most important element in this first article are the first and the second points which apply: **114**

"I. No one can prevail himself of a tort by the simple fact of his birth."

"One born with a handicap caused by a medical fault can obtain compensation of its tort when the faulty act directly provoked the handicap or made it worst, or did not permit to take the measures likely to attenuate it."

"When the liability of a professional or of a health establishment is engaged towards the parents of a child born with a handicap not detected during the pregnancy in succession of a typical fault, the parents can claim compensation only for their tort. This tort does not include the peculiar charges coming from, during all its life time, its handicap. The compensation of the latter comes from the national solidarity."

"The clauses of the present are applicable to the outstanding suits, with exception to the ones where it was irrevocably ruled on the principle of the compensation."

"II. Each handicapped person has a right, whatever is the cause of its deficiency, to the solidarity of the whole of the national community."

VIII. Germany

Jörg Fedtke

A. LEGISLATION

The modernisation of the German law of obligations codified in the second book of the German Civil Code[1] (the so-called "Schuldrechtsreform"), certainly one of the most profound legislative reform projects initiated in Germany over the past five decades, passed parliamentary procedures after extensive political debate and much academic criticism in October 2001.[2] The reform, triggered by the need to give effect to the European directives on the sale of consumer goods,[3] late payment in commercial transactions[4] and electronic commerce,[5] came into force on 1 January 2002.[6] Though reaching far beyond the legislative agenda set by the Community and designed to bring the BGB into line with modern legal, commercial and scientific developments, the *Schuldrechtsreform* hardly affected German tort law – one exception being the new rules on prescription. § 852 BGB is largely repealed,[7] delictual claims now following the new general rule to be found in § 195 BGB. The time limit 1

[1] *Bürgerliches Gesetzbuch* (BGB) of 1 January 1900.

[2] *Gesetz zur Modernisierung des Schuldrechts* of 26 November 2001, [2001] *Bundesgesetzblatt Part I* (BGBl. I), 3138 *et seq.*

[3] Directive 1999/44/EC of the European Parliament and the Council of 25 May 1999 on certain aspects of the sale of consumer goods and associated guarantees.

[4] Directive 2000/35/EC of the European Parliament and of the Council of 29 June 2000 on combating late payment in commercial transactions.

[5] Directive 2000/31/EC of the European Parliament and of the Council of 8 June 2000 on certain legal aspects of information society services, in particular electronic commerce, in the Internal Market.

[6] For recent articles on the reform see, *e.g.*, J. Wilhelm, Schuldrechtsreform, [2001] *Juristenzeitung* (JZ), 861 *et seq.*; S. Lorenz, Schadensersatz wegen Pflichtverletzung – ein Beispiel für die Überhastung der Kritik an der Schuldrechtsreform, [2001] JZ, 742 *et seq.*; W. Däubler, Neues Schuldrecht – ein erster Überblick, [2001] *Neue Juristische Wochenschrift* (NJW), 3729 *et seq.*; B. Heß, Das neue Schuldrecht – In-Kraft-Treten und Übergangsregelungen, [2002] NJW, 253 *et seq.*

[7] The new provision only leaves § 852 subs. 3 BGB (old), but now includes a separate time limit for recovery based on the rules of unjust enrichment if claims based on tort are excluded due to prescription.

is unchanged for claims based on tort (three years), beginning at the close of the year in which the creditor gains positive knowledge of the claim including the person of the debtor *or* fails to have this knowledge due to gross negligence. The express inclusion of gross negligence (though already a rule under present case law) will thereby slightly tighten the standards of knowledge applied to victims.[8] A second change is the addition of the new § 208 BGB,[9] which now bars prescription for claims of minors based on the infringement of their sexual self-determination[10] for as long as they are under 22 years old or, beyond that age limit, until a mutual household of victim and tortfeasor is dissolved. The reform of §§ 823 *et seq.* BGB as well as the general rules of the Code affecting both compensation (*Schadensersatz*) for tortious acts *and* breach of contract,[11] which have remained practically untouched by the lawgiver for over a century, is left to a separate initiative, introduced to the *Bundesrat* (the federal legislative body representing the German states, the *Länder*) in September 2001 and – three months later – to the *Bundestag* (Federal Parliament) under the heading "Entwurf eines Zweiten Gesetzes zur Änderung schadensersatzrechtlicher Vorschriften" (SchadÄndG-E).[12] The Bill, based on a government draft first presented by the Federal Ministry of Justice in February 2001,[13] proposes numerous amendments not only to the BGB, but also, *inter alia*, to the Medicines Act,[14] the Federal Mining Act,[15] the Road Traffic Act,[16] the Liability Act[17] and the Air Traffic Act.[18] Originally envisaged to come into force together with the *Schuldrechtsreform*,[19] it received extensive discussion during the legislative process[20] and passed both

[8] R. Heß, Neuregelung des Verjährungsrechts: Auswirkungen auf das Verkehrszivilrecht, [2001] *Neue Zeitschrift für Verkehrsrecht* (NZV), 66, 67.

[9] § 208 BGB now declares: "Die Verjährung von Ansprüchen wegen Verletzung der sexuellen Selbstbestimmung ist bis zur Vollendung des 21. Lebensjahres des Gläubigers gehemmt. Lebt der Gläubiger von Ansprüchen wegen Verletzung der sexuellen Selbstbestimmung bei Beginn der Verjährung mit dem Schuldner in häuslicher Gemeinschaft, so ist die Verjährung auch bis zur Beendigung der häuslichen Gemeinschaft gehemmt". See thereon F. Egermann, Verjährung deliktischer Haftungsansprüche – Gesetzesentwurf zum Schutz von Kindern, [2001] *Zeitschrift für Rechtspolitik* (ZRP), 343 *et seq.*; T. Henne, Schmerzensgeldansprüche nach Sexualstraftaten – Anmerkungen zu den geplanten Reformen im Gesetz zur Änderung schadensersatzrechtlicher Vorschriften, [2001] ZRP, 493, 495.

[10] § 823 subs. 1 BGB, § 823 subs. 2 BGB in connection with criminal law or § 825 BGB.

[11] §§ 249 *et seq.* BGB, located in the general part of the BGB (*allgemeiner Teil*), contain a set of rules dealing with *Schadensersatz* in general. These rules are complemented by special rules dealing with compensation in tort law.

[12] *Entwurf eines Zweiten Gesetzes zur Änderung schadensersatzrechtlicher Vorschriften* of 7 December 2001, BT-Drucksache (printed matter of the *Bundestag*) 14/7752.

[13] *Gesetzesentwurf der Bundesregierung* of 28 September 2001, BR-Drucksache (printed matter of the *Bundesrat*) 742/01; an earlier draft of the Federal Ministry of Justice was circulated in February 2001.

[14] *Arzneimittelgesetz* (AMG) of 11 December 1998, [1998] BGBl. I, 3586 *et seq.*, (as amended).

[15] *Bundesberggesetz* (BBergG) of 13 August 1980, [1980] BGBl. I, 1310 *et seq.*, (as amended).

[16] *Straßenverkehrsgesetz* (StVG), BGBl. Teil III, Gliederungsnummer 9231–1, (as amended).

[17] *Haftpflichtgesetz* (HaftPflG) of 4 January 1978, [1978] BGBl. I, 145 *et seq.* (as amended).

[18] *Luftverkehrsgesetz* (LuftVG) of 27 March 1999, [1999] BGBl. I, 550 *et seq.*, (as amended).

[19] See art. 13 SchadÄndG.

[20] *Bundesrat Plenarprotokoll* (protocol of the plenary session) 769 S. 619D-620A (9 November 2001); *Bundestag Plenarprotokoll* (protocol of the plenary session) 14/208 S. 20655A (13 December 2001).

the *Bundestag* and the *Bundesrat* in April and May 2002 respectively.[21] Prior critique of the *Bundesrat* was thereby mainly focused on the proposed changes to the Medical Preparations Act (see [18] below), the failure to expressly mention compensation for the infringement of the general right of personality in the BGB (see [7] below) and the proposed deletion of the so-called "unavoidable event" as a defense in the Road Traffic Act (see [9] and [11] below). The changes outlined in this report will most probably take effect on 1 August 2002.[22]

Calls for a reform of the German law of torts have become more frequent over the past 20 years.[23] The last legislative initiative prior to the proposal presently under discussion was a draft introduced to parliamentary procedures by the Conservative government of *Helmut Kohl* in 1998,[24] which lapsed due to the political changes following the general elections held in September of that same year.[25] It is worth mentioning that the shift in the country's leadership did not have any significant effect on the legislative agenda as far as the compensation of damages is concerned. With differences in detail, both drafts focus on the same key issues, which will be explained in greater detail below: (1) The introduction of a general claim for non-pecuniary loss (*Schmerzensgeld*) in cases of personal injury and infringements of personal freedom or sexual self-determination, and the limitation of this claim to cases of intentional harm or injuries reaching a certain degree of gravity; (2) the scope of protection for infringements of the right to sexual self-determination granted by § 825 BGB; (3) the position of children participating in public traffic (both road traffic and trains); (4) the defences of train operators as well as holders of motorised vehicles under strict liability statutes; (5) the consideration of value-added tax (VAT) in the calculation of material damage; (6) claims arising from harm caused by pharmaceutical products (*Arzneimittelhaftung*); (7) the level of maximum compensation (*Haftungshöchstgrenzen*) in the field of strict liability (*Gefährdungshaftung*); and (8) the liability of court-appointed experts who submit erroneous reports (*Haftung für gerichtliche Sachverständigengutachten*). These striking similarities between both drafts find their 2

[21] BR-Drucksache 358/02. Though completed before the final decision of the *Bundesrat* was taken (31 May 2002), this report reflects the adopted version of the Bill.

[22] [2002] NJW, VI.

[23] See, *e.g.*, proposals of the *Verkehrsgerichtstage* (conferences on road traffic adjudication) in 1980, 1991, 1996, 1998 and 2000; G. Thüsing, Das Schadensrecht zwischen Beständigkeit und Wandel – 5 Thesen zur Fortentwicklung der §§ 249 ff. BGB, [2001] ZRP, 126 *et seq.*

[24] *Entwurf eines Zweiten Gesetzes zur Änderung schadensersatzrechtlicher Vorschriften*, BT-Drucksache 13/10435.

[25] For a discussion of this proposal see E. Deutsch, Über die Zukunft des Schmerzensgeldes, [1998] ZRP, 291 *et seq.*; K. Geiß, Konfliktbewältigung in Verkehrssachen durch die Justiz, [1998] *Deutsches Autorecht* (DAR), 416 *et seq.*; M. Kleine-Cosack, Systembruch zu Lasten des Geschädigten, [1998] DAR, 180 *et seq.*; G. Müller, Zum Entwurf eines Zweiten Gesetzes zur Änderung schadensersatzrechtlicher Vorschriften, [1998] ZRP, 258 *et seq.*; D.-U. Otto, Neue Grenzziehungen im Schadensersatzrecht – Zum Regierungsentwurf eines 2. SchadÄndG, [1998] NZV, 433 *et seq.*; Deutscher Richterbund, [1998] *Deutsche Richter-Zeitung* (DRiZ), 179; R. Greger, Nur zwei Worte – Ein Gesetzesvorschlag zur Eindämmung von Missständen bei der Schadensregulierung, [2000] NZV, 1 *et seq.*; Deutscher Verkehrsgerichtstag, [2000] NJW, 2331.

explanation in the fact that the lawgiver was noticeably passive in this dynamic field of law over the past decades and rather left it to the courts to interpret, develop and adapt the rules of tort law and the compensation of damages to a changing legal and social environment.[26] Beyond party-political differences, the initiatives reflect the expressed will of both government and legislature to bring the text of the BGB into line with these trends and to regain a more prominent role in the future development of German tort law and the compensation of damages in general.[27] Besides the common issues mentioned above, the new Bill also features additional reform proposals concerning the liability of vehicle holders for damage caused to passengers in the course of non-commercial and free transportation as well as the delictual liability of deaf mute persons. Finally, it must also be stressed that the SchadÄndG-E aims at changing German law on two separate systematical levels – the special rules of tort law (found both in the BGB and in special statutes) on the one hand and the general rules of the Civil Code regulating all forms of compensation regardless of their legal grounds on the other (§§ 249 *et seq.* BGB).[28] Any amendments to the general rules of *Schadensersatz* will thereby have a profound effect on the *whole* legal system.

3 1. *Compensation for Non-Pecuniary Loss.* One of the most important changes envisaged by the SchadÄndG-E is the introduction of a *general* claim for pain and suffering in cases of personal injury (bodily harm or harm to the health) as well as infringements of liberty or sexual self-determination. To explain the proposed changes, it is perhaps helpful to provide a brief outline of the present regime. As a general rule, § 249 BGB[29] allows full compensation for non-pecuniary loss (*Schaden, der nicht Vermögensschaden ist*) as far as restitution *in kind* is concerned (*Naturalherstellung*),[30] whereas § 253 BGB[31] presently excludes the compensation of such losses *in money* unless otherwise explicitly provided by statute.[32] Only few provisions do so, of which § 847 BGB – grant-

[26] D.-U. Otto, Große Reformen müssen reifen – Zum Referentenentwurf einer Schadensrechtsreform, [2001] NZV, 335.

[27] This is openly stated in the explanatory section of the draft presented by the Federal Government, see BT-Drucksache 14/7752, p. 11; U. Haas/M. Horcher, Überblick über das 2. Gesetz zur Änderung schadensersatzrechtlicher Vorschriften, [2001] *Deutsches Steuerrecht* (DStR), 2118 *et seq.*; S. Schnorr/V. Wissing, Reform des Schadensersatzrechts, [2001] ZRP, 192.

[28] R. Schulze in: H. Dörner et al, *Bürgerliches Gesetzbuch* (2001), vor §§ 249–253 no. 1.

[29] § 249 BGB declares: "A person who is obliged to make compensation shall restore the situation which would have existed if the circumstance rendering him liable to make compensation had not occurred. If compensation is required to be made for injury to a person or damage to a thing, the creditor may demand, instead of restitution in kind, the sum of money necessary for such restitution". English translations of the BGB given in this report are taken from L. Goren, *The German Civil Code* (1994), unless otherwise indicated.

[30] H. Kötz/G. Wagner, *Deliktsrecht* (9th edn. 2001), pp. 185 *et seq.*; R. Schulze (*supra* note 28), vor §§ 249–253 no. 3.

[31] § 253 BGB presently declares: "For an injury which is not an injury to property, compensation in money may be demanded only as provided by law." This translation is not quite accurate since "injury which is not an injury to property" does not reflect the notion of the German text, which refers to immaterial loss ("Schaden, der nicht Vermögensschaden ist").

[32] H. Kötz/G. Wagner (*supra* note 30), pp. 202 *et seq.*; H. Brox, *Allgemeines Schuldrecht* (27th edn. 2000), p. 187; R. Schulze (*supra* note 28), § 253 no. 3.

ing compensation for pain and suffering in cases of personal injury as well as infringements of liberty or the sexual self-determination of women[33] – is certainly the most important in practice.[34]

This reluctance of German law to grant money compensation for non-pecuniary loss especially in the area of strict liability[35] – but also on the basis of contract[36] – has been heavily criticised in the past.[37] The draft presented by the government aims at closing these gaps in the protection of victims by adding a second subsection to § 253 BGB, which would allow the plaintiff to claim equitable compensation *in money* for personal injury (bodily harm or harm to the health) as well as infringements of liberty or sexual self-determination in case two alternative conditions are met: (1) the injury is caused intentionally; or (2) the damage is of some gravity, taking into account both its nature and duration.[38] The present § 847 BGB would be repealed.[39] The effects of this 4

[33] § 847 BGB presently declares: "(1) In the case of injury to the body or health, or in case of deprivation of liberty, the injured person may also demand fair compensation in money for damage which is not damage to property. (2) A similar claim belongs to a woman, against whom an immoral crime or offense is committed, or who is induced by fraud, by threats or by abuse of a relationship of dependence to permit extra-marital cohabitation".

[34] Other areas in which compensation for pain and suffering is granted include sexual discrimination occurring in connection with the formation of employment contracts and decisions on job promotion (§ 611a BGB) – see thereon G. Thüsing, [2000] ZRP, 126, 127 –; ruined holidays under package tour contracts (§ 651f BGB); infringement of certain copyrights (§ 97 subs. 2 *Urheberrechtsgesetz*) – see thereon S. Hacks/A. Ring/P. Böhm, *Schmerzensgeldbeträge* (20th edn. 2001), pp. 14/15; damage caused by military aircraft (§ 53 subs. 3 LuftVG), nuclear facilities (§ 29 subs. 2 Nuclear Energy Act, *Gesetz über die friedliche Nutzung der Kernenergie* – AtG –) and allied troops in Germany after the Second World War (§ 20 *Gesetz über die Abgeltung von Besatzungsschäden*, BesatzSchG); federal border patrol (§ 52 subs. 2 *Bundesgrenzschutzgesetz*, BGSG); social aid (§ 77 subs. 2 *Bundessozialhilfegesetz*); veterans' pensions (§ 25d subs. 4 *Bundesversorgungsgesetz*) and wrongful prosecution measures (§ 7 subs. 3 *Strafvollzugsentschädigungsgesetz*).

[35] See thereon A. Slizyk, *Beck'sche Schmerzensgeldtabelle* (4th edn. 2001), pp. 22 *et seq.*

[36] H. Kötz/G. Wagner (*supra* note 30), p. 202; H.-U. Kolb in: G. Schlegelmilch (ed.), *Der Haftpflichtprozeß* (23rd edn. 2001), p. 168; for general background see E. Deutsch, Schmerzensgeld für Vertragsverletzungen und bei der Gefährdungshaftung, [2001] ZRP, 351 *et seq.*

[37] For the area of tort law see C. Ott/B. Schäfer, [1990] JZ, 563 (573); E. von Caemmerer, *Reform der Gefährdungshaftung* (1971), pp. 23 *et seq.*; H. Kötz/G. Wagner (*supra* note 30), p. 148; H. Kötz, *Empfiehlt sich eine Vereinheitlichung und Zusammenfassung der gesetzlichen Vorschriften über die Gefährdungshaftung im BGB?: Gutachten und Vorschläge zur Überarbeitung des Schuldrechts II* (1981), pp. 1824 *et seq.*; M. Will, *Quellen erhöhter Gefahr, Rechtsvergleichende Untersuchungen zur Weiterentwicklung der deutschen Gefährdungshaftung durch richterliche Analogie oder durch gesetzliche Generalklausel* (1980), pp. 305 *et seq.*; resolution of the *Bundesrat* of 19 July 1998, BR-Drucksache 554/98. For contract see F.-J. Braschos, *Der Ersatz immaterieller Schäden im Vertragsrecht* (1979), pp. 40/41 and 252/253; G. Hohloch, in: *Gutachten und Vorschläge zur Überarbeitung des Schuldrechts, Band I*, pp. 375, 438; Reichsgericht (RG) in: *Amtliche Sammlung der Rechtsprechung des Reichsgerichts in Zivilsachen* (RGZ) 65, 21.

[38] Art. 2 Nr. 2b SchadÄndG-E. The proposed § 253 (2) BGB declares: "Ist wegen einer Verletzung des Körpers, der Gesundheit, der Freiheit oder der sexuellen Selbstbestimmung Schadensersatz zu leisten, kann auch wegen des Schadens, der nicht Vermögensschaden ist, eine billige Entschädigung in Geld gefordert werden, wenn 1. die Verletzung vorsätzlich herbeigeführt wurde oder 2. der Schaden unter Berücksichtigung seiner Art und Dauer nicht unerheblich ist".

[39] Art. 2 Nr. 7 SchadÄndG-E.

proposal are threefold. First and foremost, victims suffering infringements of the enumerated interests would be in a position to claim non-pecuniary loss not only in the field of non-contractual fault liability, but also on the basis of contract and strict liability statutes. For contractual relationships, this follows from the systematical position of § 253 BGB itself, which is applicable to the Code as a whole.[40] In the case of strict liability, the same result is achieved by additional changes of the Medicines Act,[41] the Federal Mining Act,[42] the Road Traffic Act,[43] the Liability Act,[44] the Air Traffic Act,[45] the Act on Genetical Engineering,[46] the Product Liability Act,[47] the Environmental Liability Act[48] and § 29 subs. 2 Nuclear Energy Act.[49] In other strict liability statutes the reference to § 847 BGB is exchanged for a reference to the proposed § 253 subs. 2 BGB.[50] Interestingly, the initiative of the previous government was based on a general clause granting *Schmerzensgeld* in cases of strict liability only and did *not* expand the compensation of non-pecuniary loss to the area of contract law.[51] This considerable expansion of compensation for non-pecuniary loss, regardless of the legal grounds on which claims are based, is accompanied by an exclusion of such compensation for minor injuries which are caused by negligence. Finally, the list of protected interests qualifying for a compensation of non-pecuniary loss (which was taken from the present § 847 subs. 1 BGB) is adapted to the constitutional requirements following from the right to equality[52] by protecting the sexual self-determination not only of women,[53] but also of men. Case law has thereby clearly shown that men can very well be subject to infringements of their sexual rights.[54]

[40] See the explanatory section of the SchadÄndG-E (BT-Drucksache 14/7752), p. 24.
[41] § 87 AMG, see art. 1 no. 3 SchadÄndG-E (BT-Drucksache 14/7752).
[42] § 117 subs. 1 BBergG, see art. 3 SchadÄndG (BT-Drucksache 14/7752).
[43] § 11 StVG, see art. 4 no. 5 SchadÄndG-E (BT-Drucksache 14/7752).
[44] § 6 HaftPflG, see art. 5 no. 3 SchadÄndG-E (BT-Drucksache 14/7752).
[45] § 36 LuftVG, see art. 6 no. 2 SchadÄndG-E (BT-Drucksache 14/7752). § 53 subs. 3 LuftVG, presently one of the few provisions which explicitly grant compensation for non-pecuniary loss in cases of personal injury caused by military aircraft, would become superfluous and thus be deleted, see art. 6 no. 7 SchadÄndG-E (BT-Drucksache 14/7752).
[46] § 32 subs. 5 *Gentechnikgesetz* (GenTG), see art. 9 no. 2 SchadÄndG-E (BT-Drucksache 14/7752).
[47] § 8 *Produkthaftungsgesetz* (ProdHaftG), see art. 9 no. 3 SchadÄndG-E (BT-Drucksache 14/7752).
[48] § 13 *Umwelthaftungsgesetz* (UmweltHG), see art. 9 no. 4 SchsadÄndG-E (BT-Drucksache 14/7752).
[49] See art. 10 no. 4 SchadÄndG-E (BT-Drucksache 14/7752). § 29 subs. 2 Nuclear Energy Act presently provides fault-based compensation for non-pecuniary loss caused by nuclear facilities; the Federal Ministry of Justice proposes to transform this provision into strict liability, see the explanatory section of the SchadÄndG-E (BT-Drucksache 14/7752), pp. 43/44.
[50] These areas include federal border control – *Bundesgrenzschutz* – (§ 52 subs. 2 BGSG) as well as compensation of damage caused by allied forces after World War II – *Besatzungsschäden* – (§ 20 BesatzSchG).
[51] Art. 2 no. 2 SchadÄndG-E (BT-Drucksache 13/10435) proposed to insert the following § 253 subs. 2 BGB (new): "Ist in besonderen gesetzlichen Vorschriften vorgesehen, dass ohne Verschulden wegen eines Körper- oder Gesundheitsschadens Schadensersatz zu leisten ist, so kann der Verletzte im Falle einer schwerwiegenden und dauerhaften Beschädigung wegen des Schadens, der nicht Vermögensschaden ist, eine billige Entschädigung in Geld verlangen. Die Vorschriften über den Umfang der Haftung bleiben hierdurch unberührt".
[52] Art. 3 subs. 2 Basic Law (*Grundgesetz*, GG)
[53] Presently, these can already demand compensation for pain and suffering under § 847 subs. 2 BGB.
[54] T. Henne, [2001] ZRP, 493.

These proposed changes of the BGB are to be welcomed. As the explanatory section of the SchadÄndG-E correctly points out, it has become increasingly difficult to justify the restrictions presently imposed by § 253 BGB. The historical intention of the lawgiver – to prevent the equal treatment of immaterial interests and material goods (feared to result from a compensation of both types of losses in money) – was originally justified with the traditions and values of 19th century German society, which regarded monetary compensation for non-pecuniary loss as something inferior and potentially disreputable.[55] This approach was disputed from the outset,[56] and the past 100 years have seen compensation for pain and suffering develop into an accepted (and indeed important) head of damage under German law;[57] any stigma resulting from a claim for *Schmerzensgeld* is certainly a thing of the past. Today, compensation for pain and suffering performs a vital function as it provides the sanction necessary for an overall protection of the individual, which – especially in cases of severe personal injury – cannot be achieved with a compensation in kind alone. This development has been strongly supported by court decisions granting victims compensation in money for infringements of their so-called "general right of personality" (*allgemeines Persönlichkeitsrecht*[58]) *contra legem* on the basis of § 847 subs. 1 BGB.[59] A second argument brought forward in favour of a restrictive approach to the compensation of non-pecuniary loss in money is the more difficult assessment of pain and suffering, which can – admittedly – lead to large differences and even inequalities once the outcome of individual cases is compared. This problem, though, has been mitigated by a vast amount of court decisions, made accessible by tables which report the sums and general circumstances of decided cases (so-called *Schmerzensgeldtabellen*).[60] These tables have led to a considerable degree of standardisation[61] and have somewhat limited the discretion of the courts in awarding compensation.[62] On a more general level, the introduction of compensation for pain and suffering in the area of strict liability will also help to relieve the caseload of the judicial system. Presently, many cases occurring in fields governed by strict liability nonetheless reach the courts since victims must 5

[55] Protokolle der Kommission für die 2. Lesung des Entwurfs des Bürgerlichen Gesetzbuchs, Band I, p. 622; G. Thüsing, [2001] ZRP, 126, 128.

[56] O. von Gierke in: K. Binding (ed.), *Systematisches Handbuch der deutschen Rechtswissenschaft* (1883), p. 83; see thereon U. Magnus, *Schaden und Ersatz* (1987), p. 312.

[57] See the statistical material dealing with the different heads of damages in road traffic accidents given by H. Kötz/G. Wagner (*supra* note 30), p. 199; G. Thüsing, [2001] ZRP, 126, 128.

[58] The *allgemeines Persönlichkeitsrecht* is derived from artt. 1 subs. 1 and 2 subs. 1 GG.

[59] The leading cases are *Bundesgerichtshof, Entscheidungen in Zivilsachen* (BGHZ) 13, 334 (*Schacht-Leserbief* decision); 26, 349 (*Herrenreiter* decision); 34, 269 (*Soraya* decision); 35, 363 (*Ginsengwurzel* decision) and *Entscheidungen des Bundesverfassungsgerichts* (BVerfGE) 34, 269. For further details see U. Magnus/J. Fedtke, Non-Pecuniary Loss Under German Law, in W.V.H. Rogers (ed.), *Damages for Non-Pecuniary Loss in a Comparative Perspective* (2001), pp.120 *et seq.*; H. Kötz/G. Wagner (*supra* note 30), pp. 240 *et seq.*; M. Fuchs, *Deliktsrecht* (3rd edn. 2001), pp. 38 *et seq.*; R. Damm/K. Rehbock, *Widerruf, Unterlassung und Schadensersatz in Presse und Rundfunk* (2nd edn. 2001), pp. 7 *et seq.*

[60] S. Hacks/A. Ring/P. Böhm (*supra* note 34); A. Slizyk (*supra* note 35).

[61] U. Magnus/J. Fedtke (*supra* note 59), p. 117; E. Deutsch/H.-J. Ahrens, *Deliktsrecht* (4th edn. 2002), p. 229.

[62] See § 287 subs. 1 Civil Procedure Act (*Zivilprozeßordnung*, ZPO); see thereto G. Thüsing, [2001] ZRP, 126, 129; M. Fuchs (*supra* note 59), p. 180.

rely on fault-based rules in order to recover non-pecuniary loss. A general claim for *Schmerzensgeld* will further address existing deficiencies of the contractual regime and lead to an equal treatment of personal injury both in the delictual and contractual spheres. This is especially important in the case of contracts which are closely related to non-pecuniary interests (*e.g.*, hairdressing and burial services[63]).

6 The proposal to limit claims for pain and suffering to cases of intent and severe injuries caused by negligence follows along similar lines already developed by case law as far as minor corporeal injuries (so-called "Bagatellschäden") are concerned. Presently, court decisions limit or exclude claims for *Schmerzensgeld* by a restrictive interpretation of the scope of § 847 BGB, which demands *equitable* compensation ("billige Entschädigung") of non-pecuniary loss.[64] The wording of the previous draft ("schwerwiegend und dauerhaft") was thereby changed significantly and will allow a more flexible approach by focusing on the nature of the injury ("Art") and its duration ("Dauer") *without* turning these criteria into cumulative requirements.[65] This difference is emphasised in the explanatory section of the SchadÄndG-E.[66] In contrast to the 1998 proposal, these limitations will not be restricted to cases of strict liability, but will affect *any* infringement of the enumerated interests regardless of the legal background (fault liability, stict liability or contract). Without pinpointing a clear amount of money, victims who were thus far awarded sums below € 500 will – in most cases – not qualify for *Schmerzensgeld* under this limitation if they are injured through negligence of the tortfeasor. This is true, *e.g.*, for slight infringements of personal integrity such as headaches and superficial wounds (bruises or scratches).[67] The reform proposal thus aims at a reduction of minor claims and will help limit the inflation of non-pecuniary loss – hopefully to the benefit of the more serious cases.[68] The limitation also serves to equalise the additional burdens placed on the insurance system by the expansion of compensation for non-pecuniary loss to the area of strict liability and contract law.[69] If the injury was caused with *intent*, compensation for pain and suffering will also be awarded to give the victim some degree of satisfaction (*Genugtuungsfunktion*).[70] This justifies the exclusion of intentional harm from the limitations imposed by the new § 253 subs. 2 BGB.[71]

63 See G. Thüsing, [2001] ZRP, 126, 129; F.-J. Braschos (*supra* note 37), pp. 177/178.

64 BGH in [1992] NJW, 1043; BGH in [1992] *Versicherungsrecht* (VersR), 504; BGHZ 132, 341; BGH in [1998] VersR, 201; OLG Köln in [1999] VersR, 116; see thereon M. Fuchs (*supra* note 59), p. 180; H.-U. Kolb (*supra* note 36), p. 180; A. Slizyk (*supra* note 35), pp. 43/44; D.-U. Otto, [2001] NZV, 335, 338/339.

65 E. Deutsch/H.-J. Ahrens (*supra* note 61), p. 221.

66 BT-Drucksache 14/7752, p. 25.

67 H.-U. Kolb (*supra* note 36), pp. 183 and 187; A. Slizyk (*supra* note 35), pp. 43 and 508 *et seq.*

68 See the explanatory section of the SchadÄndG-E (BT-Drucksache 14/7752), pp. 11 and 25. For insights into the public debate on the issue see the *Frankfurter Rundschau* (Frankfurt am Main) of 13/14 June 2001, p. A1 ("Aus der Traum vom Gewinn bringenden Trauma").

69 See the explanatory section of the SchadÄndG-E (BT-Drucksache 14/7752), p. 25.

70 U. Magnus/J. Fedtke (*supra* note 59), p. 113; E. Deutsch/H.-J. Ahrens (*supra* note 61), pp. 217 *et seq.*

71 See the explanatory section of the SchadÄndG-E (BT-Drucksache 14/7752), p. 25.

A prominent feature of the proposed reform involving the rules on compensation for pain and suffering is the conspicuous absence of the "general right of personality", which is not mentioned in the new § 253 subs 2 BGB. This must not be misunderstood as a change of the law. As stressed in the explanatory section of the SchadÄndG-E, this omission is due only to the special constitutional background of the claim for compensation based on infringements of the *allgemeines Persönlichkeitsrecht*. The claim, which seeks to enhance the constitutional protection provided – and indeed *required* – by artt. 1 and 2 GG on the level of private law, was differentiated dogmatically as well as terminologically from the general claim for *Schmerzensgeld* based on § 847 BGB by the Federal Court of Justice (*Bundesgerichtshof*, BGH).[72] The Federal Ministry of Justice has decided to uphold this theoretical distinction between the two claims, thereby admitting that some clarification concerning its status in the Civil Code might have been preferable.[73] It must be stressed, though, that the *allgemeines Persönlichkeitsrecht* is regarded as a so-called "framework right" (*Rahmenrecht*), which does not have a clearly demarcated content.[74] Its inclusion as an interest explicitly enumerated in the BGB would therefore have required some definition of its private law content – a step which might have limited the present scope as well as the future development of the concept. The *Bundesrat* proposes to include the general right of personality in the Code, albeit (in accordance with the Federal Supreme Court[75]) as a right *subsidiary* to other remedies.[76] 7

2. *Infringement of Sexual Self-Determination.* A second amendment long overdue is the proposed reform of § 825 BGB. Presently granting compensation for damage resulting from the sexual harassment of women outside marital relationships,[77] the SchadÄndG-E proposes to transform the provision into a protection against infringements of sexual self-determination in general.[78] 8

[72] BGHZ 35, 363, 367/368; BGHZ 39, 124, 130; BGHZ 128, 1, 15.

[73] See the remarks in the explanatory section of the SchadÄndG-E (BT-Drucksache 14/7752), p. 25.

[74] BGHZ 24, 72, 78; H. Kötz/G. Wagner (*supra* note 30), p. 242; A. Staudinger in: H. Dörner et al, *Bürgerliches Gesetzbuch* (2001), § 823 no. 91; W. Fikentscher, *Das Schuldrecht* (9th edn. 1997), § 103 no. 1216.

[75] BGHZ 128, 1, 13.

[76] See the proposal of the *Bundesrat* (*Stellungnahme*) on a new § 847 BGB, BT-Drucksache 14/7752, pp. 49/50: "Im Fall einer Verletzung des allgemeinen Persönlichkeitsrechts kann der Verletzte auch wegen des Schadens, der nicht Vermögensschaden ist, eine angemessene Entschädigung in Geld verlangen, wenn die besondere Schwere der Verletzung sowie das Verschulden dies rechtfertigen und ein hinreichender Ausgleich für die Rechtsbeeinträchtigung auf andere Weise nicht zu erreichen ist".

[77] § 825 BGB presently declares: "A person who by cunning, by threats, or by the abuse of a relationship of dependence, induces a woman to permit extra-marital cohabitation, is bound to compensate her for any damage arising therefrom".

[78] Art. 2 Nr. 3 SchadÄndG-E. The proposed § 825 BGB (new) declares: "Wer einen anderen durch Hinterlist, Drohung oder Missbrauch eines Abhängigkeitsverhältnisses zur Vornahme oder Duldung sexueller Handlungen bestimmt, ist ihm zum Ersatz des daraus entstehenden Schadens verpflichtet". For the present application of § 828 subs. 2 BGB to cases of contributory negligence see H. Thomas in: Palandt, *Bürgerliches Gesetzbuch* (61st edn. 2002), § 828 no. 4.

This would extend the scope of protection to victims of both sexes including children and spouses. These changes are very appropriate, though it must be pointed out that § 825 BGB in its present form does not have much practical relevance anyway since claims resulting from sexual harassment are also covered by the general right of personality, which the courts have accepted as "other right" within the meaning of § 823 subs. 1 BGB. In severe cases, additional protection will be granted on the basis of § 823 subs. 2 BGB in connection with protective norms of criminal law and/or § 826 BGB.[79] Immaterial loss is recoverable under § 847 BGB. As the explanatory section of the SchadÄndG-E stresses, the amendment is motivated not for legal, but for political reasons. In view of the other protective norms mentioned earlier, § 825 BGB could be repealed altogether, but this might be interpreted as a relaxation of the standard of protection granted to women – an impression the lawgiver clearly wants to avoid.[80] If § 847 subs. 2 BGB is indeed repealed, *Schmerzensgeld* will then be awarded on the basis of the new § 253 subs. 2 BGB.[81]

9 3. *Children in Traffic and Deaf Mute Persons.* More importantly, a new § 828 subs. 2 BGB aims at strengthening the position of children participating in public traffic (both road traffic and trains).[82] § 828 BGB presently excludes the responsibility of minors who have not completed their seventh year of age (subs. 1) and contains a flexible standard of delictual capacity for minors who are above seven but under eighteen years of age, as well as for deaf mute persons (subs. 2).[83] The proposed amendments to the provision would introduce a three-tiered system: (1) The position of minors under seven years of age is left untouched (no delictual responsibility).[84] (2) The new § 828 subs. 2 BGB excludes the responsibility of children who have completed their seventh but not their tenth year of age in case they negligently cause damage in accidents with motorised vehicles and trackbound or suspended trains. This provision does not apply if the damage is caused intentionally.[85] As under present German law with respect to minors under seven years of age as well as children who do not have the necessary understanding for realising their responsibility

79 A. Staudinger (*supra* note 74), § 825 no. 1.

80 BT-Drucksache 14/7752, pp. 24 and 26.

81 See [5] above.

82 For earlier proposals concerning a reform of § 828 BGB see Chr. von Bar, *Gutachten und Vorschläge zur Überarbeitung des Schuldrechts, Band II*, pp. 1681, 1762 and 1774 *et seq.*; E. Scheffen, [1991] ZRP, 458 *et seq.*

83 § 828 BGB presently declares: "(1) A person who has not completed his seventh year of age is not responsible for any damage which he causes to another. (2) A person who has completed his seventh but not his eighteenth year of age is not responsible for any damage which he causes to another, if he, at the time of committing the damaging act, did not have the understanding necessary for realising his responsibility. The same applies to a deaf mute".

84 § 828 subs. 1 BGB.

85 Art. 2 Nr. 4 SchadÄndG-E (BT-Drucksache 14/7752) proposes the following wording for the new § 828 subs. 2 BGB: "Wer das siebente, aber nicht das zehnte Lebensjahr vollendet hat, ist für den Schaden, den er bei einem Unfall mit einem Kraftfahrzeug, einer Schienenbahn oder einer Schwebebahn einem anderen zufügt, nicht verantwortlich. Dies gilt nicht, wenn er die Verletzung vorsätzlich herbeigeführt hat".

(these are the requirements of § 828 subs. 2 BGB) *and* act without fault regarding their self-exposure to danger,[86] contributory negligence[87] will not be taken into account either in case children of this age group (seven to under ten) suffer damage caused by others in traffic situations.[88] These changes are accompanied by the proposal to amend § 7 subs. 2 StVG (strict liability of vehicle holders in motorised traffic) and § 1 subs. 2 HaftPflG (strict liability of the operator of railway services), which presently allow tortfeasors to defend themselves by showing that a traffic accident was an unavoidable event (*unabwendbares Ereignis*).[89] One group of cases thereby involves the behaviour of the victim – in traffic accidents often children – which contributes to the course of events.[90] Following academic criticism,[91] the Federal Ministry of Justice proposes to limit this defence to the stricter standard required by an act of God (*höhere Gewalt*).[92] (3) The flexible standard of delictual capacity for minors aged seven to under eighteen – based on their individual ability to understand their legal responsibilities in the concrete situation – is shifted to § 828 subs. 3 BGB (new) and remains applicable to traffic accidents caused by intentional behaviour of minors. Deaf mute persons of full age may then no longer invoke this standard.[93]

The proposed changes concerning the participation of minors in motorised **10**
traffic stem from scientific findings on the development of children and take into account that minors under the age of ten are generally unable to recognise and respond to the special dangers resulting from traffic situations due to their limited physical and psychological abilities.[94] Characteristic features of young children such as playfulness, the natural urge to experiment and explore their

[86] BGH in [1962] NJW, 1065; BGH in [1975] NJW, 133, 135; BGH in [2001] NJW, 152/153; H.-J. Mertens in: *Münchner Kommentar zum Bürgerlichen Gesetzbuch, Band 3, Schuldrecht – Besonderer Teil, 2. Halbband, §§ 652–853* (2nd edn. 1986), § 828 no. 2; H. Kötz/G. Wagner (*supra* note 30), pp. 128 and 216; critical J. Esser/E. Schmidt, *Schuldrecht I* (6th edn. 1984), 1 § 35 I 3b.

[87] § 254 BGB, § 9 StVG and § 4 HaftPflG.

[88] See the explanatory section of the SchadÄndG-E (BT-Drucksache 14/7752), pp. 16 and 26/27.

[89] § 7 subs. 2 StVG presently declares: "Die Ersatzpflicht ist ausgeschlossen, wenn der Unfall durch ein unabwendbares Ereignis verursacht wird, das weder auf einem Fehler in der Beschaffenheit des Fahrzeugs noch auf einem Versagen seiner Vorrichtungen beruht. Als unabwendbar gilt ein Ereignis insbesondere dann, wenn es auf das Verhalten des Verletzten oder eines nicht bei dem Betrieb beschäftigten Dritten oder eines Tieres zurückzuführen ist und sowohl der Halter als auch der Führer des Fahrzeugs jede nach den Umständen des Falls gebotene Sorgfalt beobachtet hat." For further details see H. Kötz/G. Wagner (*supra* note 30), pp. 155/156; E. Deutsch/H.-J. Ahrens (*supra* note 61), pp. 173 and 175.

[90] This is discussed, *e.g.*, in the recent decision of OLG Hamm in [2001] NZV, 303.

[91] See H. Kötz (*supra* note 37) pp. 1803 *et seq.*; H. Kötz/G. Wagner (*supra* note 30), p. 166.

[92] Art. 4 no. 1b and art. 5 no. 1 SchadÄndG-E (BT-Drucksache 14/7752)

[93] Art. 2 Nr. 4 SchadÄndG-E (BT-Drucksache 14/7752) proposes the following wording for the new § 828 subs. 3 BGB: "Wer das achtzehnte Lebensjahr noch nicht vollendet hat, ist, sofern seine Verantwortlichkeit nicht nach den Absätzen 1 oder 2 ausgeschlossen ist, für den Schaden, den er einem anderen zufügt, nicht verantwortlich, wenn er bei der Begehung der schädigenden Handlung nicht die zur Erkenntnis der Verantwortlichkeit erforderliche Einsicht hat".

[94] BT-Drucksache 14/7752, p. 11; E. Scheffen, Änderungen schadensersatzrechtlicher Vorschriften im Hinblick auf betroffene Kinder und Jugendliche, [2001] ZRP, 380; A. Slizyk (*supra* note 35), pp. 65/66, D.-U. Otto, [2001] NZV 335, 339.

environment, spontaneous and impulsive reactions as well as the lack of concentration are the frequent causes of traffic accidents that the lawgiver wants to address.[95] As a consequence, the other participants of motorised traffic and train operators would have to bear the financial burdens of the new rule – *both* as victims (no recovery of damages) *and* as tortfeasors (no reduction of claims on the basis of a minor's contributory negligence). The explanatory section of the Bill addresses this problem by reference to § 829 BGB (duty to compensate for equitable reasons),[96] which could gain more relevance if the new rules were adopted.[97] It is more likely, though, that the insurance sector would have to carry most of these costs. This is already indicated in the introductory section of the SchadÄndG-E, where the government concedes that parts of the Bill might lead to higher financial burdens for insurance companies and a consequential increase of insurance premiums.[98]

11 On a different level, the proposed changes of the Road Traffic Act and the Liability Act – justified with the need to improve the situation specifically of young children, but also that of ailing and elderly persons in traffic accidents[99] – would have a more profound effect on these specific areas of law since the limitation of defences to acts of God (*höhere Gewalt*) is not restricted to accidents involving these groups of victims. Due to the conservative interpretation of *höhere Gewalt* under German law,[100] the enactment of the SchadÄndG-E would thus shift both statutes deeper into the area of strict liability by generally denying holders of motorised vehicles and train operators recourse to the fault-related defense of an "unavoidable event" (so-called "Unabwendbarkeitsnachweis"). It must be stressed, though, that even the present rules do not allow exculpation for unforeseeable risk-related *technical* defects,[101] and leave it to the holder to show that every possible amount of care was taken to avoid the accident in the given case.[102] This amounts to the standard of care which an ideal driver – applying utmost care, concentration and skill – would have complied with in the critical traffic situation. This can rarely be shown in practice,[103] and the requirements will still increase if the

[95] BT-Drucksache 14/7752, pp. 16 and 26.

[96] § 829 BGB declares: "A person who in one of the cases specified in §§ 823 to 826, is not responsible, by virtue of §§ 827, 828, for any damage caused by him, shall, nevertheless, where compensation cannot be obtained from a third party charged with the duty of supervision, make compensation for the damage as is reasonable under the circumstances; in particular where, according to the relative positions of the parties, equity requires compensation, and he is not deprived of the means which he needs for his own reasonable maintenance and for the fulfilment of his obligations imposed on him by law to furnish maintenance to others".

[97] BT-Drucksache 14/7752, p. 16.

[98] BT-Drucksache 14/7752, p. 2 and then again on p. 18.

[99] BT-Drucksache 14/7752, p. 30; see also U. Haas/M. Horcher, [2001] DStR, 2118, 2122.

[100] The rich case law this has developed strict criteria for acts of God, *e.g.*, BGHZ 7, 338, 339; BGHZ 62, 351, 354; BGH in [1953] NJW, 184; BGH in [1986] NJW, 2313; BGH in [1967] VersR, 138, 139; BGH in [1976] VersR, 963; BGH in [1988] VersR, 910.

[101] A. Kunschert, in: G. Schlegelmilch (ed.), *Der Haftpflichtprozeß* (23rd edn. 2001), pp. 779 *et seq*.

[102] E. Deutsch/H.-J. Ahrens (*supra* note 61), p. 175; A. Kunschert (*supra* note 101), pp. 781 *et seq.*

[103] For a discussion of the defence see the recent decision of OLG Bremen in [2001] NZV, 345.

defence is limited to acts of God.[104] Remarkably enough, even supporters of the changes presently under discussion suggest that insurance companies should not increase the premiums of their clients in case vehicles are involved in accidents which even a perfect driver could not possibly have avoided.[105] The explanatory section of the SchadÄndG-E also stresses the fact that vehicle holders may still invoke contributory negligence of the victim (see § 9 StVG, § 254 BGB) – unless these are children under ten years of age – and that this may even lead to a complete reduction of their own share of responsibility.[106] Finally, the proposed departure from the "unavoidable event" codified in § 7 subs. 2 StVG and § 1 subs. 2 HaftPflG is justified for dogmatic reasons. Motorised traffic is regarded as dangerous in Germany, but the risk inherent to this lawful activity (the so-called "Betriebsgefahr") is nonetheless tolerated because any resulting damage (excluding non-pecuniary loss) is compensated on the basis of strict liability. § 7 subs. 1 StVG and § 1 subs. 1 HaftPflG thus aim at compensation *regardless* of fault and the fault-related idea of prevention.[107] This construction is compromised to some extent if the holder of the vehicle may invoke fault-related standards – as in the case of the unavoidable event, which even the most careful driver could not have prevented.[108] As the explanatory section of the SchadÄndG-E points out, other German strict liability statutes do not offer this defence.[109] It must be kept in mind, though, that motorised traffic is not regarded as dangerous throughout Europe, and that other objectives – such as the distribution of loss and the reduction of litigation costs – may well justify less strict regimes.[110] In a similar vein, the *Bundesrat* has taken a more cautious stance and recommends that the defence of an "unavoidable event" be left in the StVG.[111]

An important difference to the initiative of the previous government is the exclusion of § 828 subs. 2 BGB in case minors aged seven to ten cause *intentional* damage to other traffic participants (*e.g.*, by throwing stones at vehicles).[112] This addition follows from a suggestion of the *Bundesrat*.[113] **12**

104 E. Scheffen, [2001] ZRP, 380.

105 E. Scheffen, [2001] ZRP, 380.

106 BT-Drucksache 14/7752, p. 30. See, *e.g.*, the recent judgment of OLG Dresden in [2001] NZV, 378/379 (no liability on the basis of § 7 subs. 1 StVG if a heavily drunken pedestrian suddenly crosses a road without using a nearby pedestrian crossing – secured by traffic lights – and is subsequently seriously injured by an approaching vehicle).

107 This is highlighted as the principal justification of strict liability by E. Deutsch/H.-J. Ahrens (*supra* note 61), pp. 162/163.

108 U. Haas/M. Horcher, [2001] DStR, 2118, 2122.

109 BT-Drucksache 14/7752, p. 30; this is also stressed by U. Haas/M. Horcher, [2001] DStR, 2118, 2122.

110 Some German academics thus go beyond the notion of danger when analysing the justification of strict liability; see, *e.g.*, H. Kötz/G. Wagner (*supra* note 30), pp. 137 *et seq.*

111 See the position of the *Bundesrat* (*Stellungnahme*) on the SchadÄndG-E, BT-Drucksache 14/7752, pp. 50/51.

112 The previous initiative proposed to incorporate similar rules in a new § 9 sent. 2 StVG (dealing with contributory negligence of *victims* under ten years of age injured in motorised traffic) and a new § 12 subs. 2 HPflG (dealing with the liability of *tortfeasors* under ten years of age who cause train-related harm), see artt. 4 no. 3 and 5 no. 6 SchadÄndG-E (BT-Drucksache 13/10435).

113 BR-Drucksache 13/10766.

13 The proposal to remove deaf mute persons from the scope of § 828 subs. 2 BGB is a result of corresponding demands of interest groups who criticise this as a potentially discriminatory provision, which places deaf mute persons on the same level of development as children.[114] It must be pointed out that a repeal of § 828 subs. 2 sent. 2 BGB would not have a profound effect anyway, since the standard of fault applied to deaf mute tortfeasors by the courts (though basically objective, see § 276 BGB) is determined on the basis of their abilities as a distinct group of persons with certain – at least potentially limited – capacities (so-called "gruppenbezogener Maßstab").[115]

14 4. *Liability for Damage in Non-Commercial Traffic.* On the basis of proposed changes to § 8a StVG, holders of motorised vehicles will in the future also be liable for personal damage caused to passengers as well as damage caused to things in the course of non-commercial and free transportation.[116] Presently, the strict liability of holders is limited to any personal damage caused *outside* their vehicles (§ 7 subs. 1 StVG) as well as damage caused to passengers *within* the vehicle if these persons are carried on a commercial and professional basis (*entgeltliche, geschäftsmäßige Personenbeförderung*).[117] Equally, damage caused to things carried by the vehicle is only compensated if these things belong to a passenger who is in turn protected by the StVG.[118] In most cases, passengers seeking compensation from the holder of a vehicle will thus have to resort to the general fault-based rules of the BGB.[119] Identified as one of the key aspects of the legislative initiative, these changes take into account the strong criticism brought forward against the present § 8a StVG.[120] Beyond historical coincidence,[121] there is indeed little justification for a different treatment of a passenger who is injured in an accident on occasion of a free ride

[114] BT-Drucksache 14/7752, p. 27.

[115] H. Heinrichs in: Palandt, *Bürgerliches Gesetzbuch* (61st edn. 2002), § 276 no. 17.

[116] Art. 4 no. 3 SchadÄndG-E (BT-Drucksache 14/7752) proposes the following wording for § 8a StVG (new): "Im Falle einer entgeltlichen, geschäftsmäßigen Personenbeförderung darf die Verpflichtung des Halters, wegen Tötung oder Verletzung beförderter Personen Schadensersatz nach § 7 zu leisten, weder ausgeschlossen noch beschränkt werden. Die Geschäftsmäßigkeit einer Personenbeförderung wird nicht dadurch ausgeschlossen, dass die Beförderung von einer Körperschaft oder Anstalt des öffentlichen Rechts betrieben wird".

[117] On § 8a StVG see A. Kunschert (*supra* note 101), pp. 833 *et seq.*

[118] § 8a StVG presently declares: "(1) Ist eine durch ein Kraftfahrzeug beförderte Person getötet oder verletzt worden, so haftet der Halter dieses Fahrzeugs nach § 7 nur dann, wenn es sich um eine entgeltliche, geschäftsmäßige Personenbeförderung handelt. Ist eine durch ein Kraftfahrzeug beförderte Sache beschädigt worden, so haftet der Halter dieses Fahrzeugs nach § 7 nur, wenn eine durch das Kraftfahrzeug unter den Voraussetzungen des Satzes 1 beförderte Person die Sache an sich trägt oder mit sich führt. Die Geschäftsmäßigkeit einer Personenbeförderung im Sinne der Sätze 1 und 2 wird nicht dadurch ausgeschlossen, dass die Beförderug von einer Körperschaft oder Anstalt des öffentlichen Rechts betrieben wird. (2) Die Verpflichtung des Halters, wegen Tötung oder Verletzung beförderter Personen Schadensersatz nach Absatz 1 Satz 1 in Verbindung mit § 7 zu leisten, darf weder ausgeschlossen noch beschränkt werden. Entgegenstehende Bestimmungen und Vereinbarungen sind nichtig".

[119] H. Kötz/G. Wagner (*supra* note 30), p. 157.

[120] E. Scheffen, [2001] ZRP, 380, 381; H. Kötz/G. Wagner (*supra* note 30), p. 166; E. von Caemmerer (*supra* note 37), p. 22; E. von Hippel, [1973] ZRP, 29 *et seq.*; G. Hohloch, [1979] VersR, 199, 206 *et seq.*; H. Kötz (*supra* note 37), pp. 1812 *et seq.*

[121] R. Greger, *Haftungsrecht des Straßenverkehrs* (3rd edn. 1997), § 8a StVG no 1.

(*e.g.*, a friend of the vehicle holder), and a pedestrian who is injured in the course of the same event. The compensation of these victims should follow along the same lines since both injuries reflect the typical risks inherent to motorised traffic.[122] The same is true for the different treatment of commercial and non-commercial passengers prescribed by the present rule. Both groups freely choose to use a motorised vehicle (thereby accepting a certain degree of risk), though – admittedly – passengers paying for the service of a taxi or bus company do so on the basis of a contract. This factor alone does not justify different systems of liability, as payment will be made only for the mere service provided by the entrepreneur rather than for a stricter level of liability prescribed by a statute.[123] The higher insurance premiums which have to be paid by commercial carriers (and which they in turn pass on to their customers as part of the fare) *may* result from this strict liability, but are equally justified by the frequent use of these vehicles. With respect to the interests of victims who accept free transportation and are mostly oblivious to the legal implications, the proposed changes are to be welcomed. This is especially true for family members of vehicle holders, who certainly form the most important group of persons not protected by the StVG today.[124] It must also be pointed out that vehicle holders may continue to limit their liability by agreement with non-commercial passengers;[125] this mechanism can be used by insurance companies to adapt their premiums to the frequency with which private clients use their vehicles for carrying passengers free of charge.

5. *Value-Added Tax in the Calculation of Damage to Things.* Another proposal, which is aimed at lowering the costs of the tort system in general and which might also help to level the ground between the compensation of damage to things on the one hand and personal injury on the other, is the exclusion of value-added tax (VAT, so-called "Umsatzsteuer") in the calculation of damage caused to things. This is achieved by an addition to § 249 BGB,[126] which presently allows creditors[127] to choose payment of the amount of money necessary for medical treatment of personal damage or the repair/replacement of a damaged thing *instead* of restitution in kind. In doing so, the damaged party may – with respect to damaged or destroyed *things* – further choose to accept the damage and rather use the money (equaling the *fictitious* costs of repair or replacement[128]) for a *different* pur- **15**

[122] See the explanatory section of the SchadÄndG-E (BT-Drucksache 14/7752), p. 17.

[123] In BGHZ 80, 303, 306 *et seq.*, the Federal Supreme Court argued that payment was also made for the fact that an entrepreneur was strictly liable on the basis of § 8a StVG.

[124] E. Scheffen, [2001] ZRP, 380, 381; U. Haas/M. Horcher, [2001] DStR, 2118, 2123.

[125] U. Haas/M. Horcher, [2001] DStR, 2118, 2123; G. Kirchhoff, Haftungsfragen bei der Beteiligung Dritter am Verkehrsunfall, [2001] NZV, 361, 364.

[126] Art. 2 no. 1 SchadÄndG-E (BT-Drucksache 14/7752) proposes the following wording of § 249 subs. 2 (new), which incorporates the present sent. 2 of the provision: "Bei der Beschädigung einer Sache schließt der nach Satz 1 erforderliche Geldbetrag die Umsatzsteuer nur mit ein, wenn und soweit sie tatsächlich angefallen ist".

[127] § 249 BGB refers to "Gläubiger", following the terminology of the general rules on compensation.

[128] So-called "fiktive Reparatur- oder Wiederbeschaffungskosten", see R. Rixecker in: G. Schlegelmilch (ed.), *Der Haftpflichtprozeß* (23rd edn. 2001), pp. 77 *et seq.*; D. U. Otto, [2001] NZV, 335, 337.

pose instead, *e.g.*, payment of a holiday with money awarded for the repair of a car. The courts have given creditors this choice on the basis of the wording of the Civil Code, which does not prescribe a certain way of using the money as far as compensation for damaged things is concerned. This gives creditors discretion to spend money awarded under this head of damage as they please (so-called "Dispositionsfreiheit").[129] The amount of compensation awarded in the individual case is thereby estimated on the basis of the means which the repair or replacement of a thing would *usually* require ("die für die Behebung des Schadens üblicherweise erforderlichen Reparaturkosten"). This includes VAT and – in the case of labour – the costs of social security contributions.[130] The situation is different in the case of money awarded for medical treatment. Freedom to use such money in any way (*e.g.*, for a holiday instead of medical treatment) would potentially circumvent the idea inherent to the present § 253 BGB, which does not allow the compensation of non-pecuniary loss – here, the money can also be used for *any* purpose[131] – unless explicitly prescribed by statute.[132] The same restrictions apply to the compensation of expenses only *indirectly* connected to the damage of things (so-called "Sachfolgeschäden"), *e.g.*, the costs of expert opinions or the temporary substitution of objects by way of rental.[133] With enactment of the SchadÄndG-E, the amount of compensation granted for damage caused to things would thus often be reduced, since VAT (currently 16%) could only be demanded if and as it has actually resulted from repair or replacement. If the creditor rather chooses to leave a damaged or destroyed thing unrepaired/unreplaced, *e.g.*, by keeping or selling it, and spends the money on something else (which he may continue to do), he will not be able to demand the "fictitious" costs as far as they would have resulted from VAT.[134] This approach is justified with reference to the fact that the victim is not really burdened by VAT resulting from the damaging event. Even if he chooses to spend the money otherwise – paying the same percentage of VAT, but on a different thing –, this expenditure would not be linked to the event either. The explanatory section of the SchadÄndG-E thereby puts much emphasis on the function of compensation, which aims at restoring the previous situation rather than giving victims the opportunity to freely rearrange their assets.[135] Interestingly, the reform proposal of the previous government even went one step further by deducting *all* costs resulting from public levies (so-called "öffentliche Abgaben") *unless* the victim

[129] BGHZ 54, 82; BGHZ 61, 56; BGHZ 61, 346; BGHZ 63, 184; BGHZ 66, 239, 241; BGH in [1985] NJW, 2469; BGH in [1989] NJW, 3009; E. Deutsch/H.-J. Ahrens (*supra* note 61), p. 205; H. Kötz/G. Wagner (*supra* note 30), p. 189; D.-U. Otto, [1998] NZV, 433, 434.

[130] See, *e.g.*, BGH in [1973] NJW, 1647; BGH in [1985] VersR, 865; BGH in [1989] NJW, 3009; BGH in [1992] NJW, 1618.

[131] BGH in [1991] NJW, 1544; H. Thomas (*supra* note 78), § 847 no. 11.

[132] BGHZ 97, 14; H. Kötz/G. Wagner (*supra* note 30), pp. 200/201.

[133] See the explanatory section of the SchadÄndG-E (BT-Drucksache 14/7752), p. 22.

[134] In the example given above, the victim is allowed to spend the money on a holiday instead of having his damaged car repaired, but he will not be awarded the VAT which a garage would have charged him for the repair service.

[135] BT-Drucksache 14/7752, p. 23.

shows that the damaged thing was actually repaired or replaced.[136] This would have included not only VAT but also the costs of social security in case labour is required in the process (so-called "Lohnnebenkosten").[137]

The question of fictitious costs for the repair or replacement of things is a highly controversial issue, which is especially relevant in the area of traffic accidents. A large proportion of the compensation of damage caused to vehicles is not used for repair or replacement, because (1) the damage is simply accepted by the owner; (2) repairs are made privately (saving at least labour costs including VAT and social security contributions, which are regarded as part of the victim's loss[138]); (3) repairs are made unofficially by a repair service (under contravention of taxation and social security laws); or (4) repairs are made using smaller garages in the countryside (saving up to 17.5% of the repair costs the same service would require in the larger cities) or even abroad (with dramatically lower repair costs, *e.g.*, in Poland or the Czech Republic).[139] Any of these methods will result in substantial gains if the victim chooses to regulate his damage abstractly on the basis of an expert opinion,[140] which is already done in around 33% of all traffic-related cases today. The German Lawyers' Association estimates that the proposed change of § 249 BGB would result in a loss of € 500,000,000 annually for the victims of accidents involving motorised vehicles alone.[141] This estimate highlights the reasoning behind the legislative proposal. The lawgiver wants to reduce the danger of over-compensation following from the fictitious evaluation of damages in favour of the more restrictive principle of precise damage calculation (so-called "konkrete Schadensberechnung") traditionally underlying German law.[142] This method limits claims to the actual expenses of the victim (depending on the way he chooses to proceed) and could have the effect of reducing the proportion of money the system as a whole spends on the compensation for damage caused to things (*Sachschäden*) – money, which in turn could rather be spent for the benefit of victims suffering personal injury.[143] It must be stressed, though, that the position of victims who choose to repair or replace damaged things *without* resorting to the alternatives outlined above is left 16

136 See art. 2 no. 1 SchadÄndG-E (BT-Drucksache 13/10435) which proposed the following wording for § 249 subs. 3 (new): "Bei der Beschädigung einer Sache beläuft sich der Geldbetrag nach Absatz 2 auf die nachgewiesenen Kosten der Reparatur. Soweit der Geschädigte auf die Wiederherstellung durch einen gewerblichen Betrieb verzichtet, bleiben die in dem Betrag nach Absatz 2 enthaltenen öffentlichen Abgaben bei der Feststellung des Schadensersatzes außer Ansatz". For a discussion of this proposal see D.-U. Otto, [1998] NZV 433, 435.

137 See the explanatory section of the SchadÄndG-E (BT-Drucksache 13/10435), p. 13.

138 R. Rixecker (*supra* note 128), p. 75.

139 As reported by the *Frankfurter Rundschau* (Frankfurt am Main) of 4 October 2001, p. 10 ("Damit Autofahrer aus Schaden klug werden und nicht reich"); R. Greger, [2000] NZV, 1, 2.

140 See thereon R. Rixecker (*supra* note 128), pp. 71/72; R. Greger, [2000] NZV, 1.

141 Press statement no. V 06/01 of the *Arbeitsgemeinschaft Verkehrsrecht im Deutschen Anwaltsverein* (DAV) of 30.11.2001. Insurance companies annually regulate claims amounting to € 1,500,000,000 on the basis of expert opinions; see R. Greger, [2000] NZV, 1, 2.

142 See the explanatory section of the SchadÄndG-E (BT-Drucksache 14/7752), pp. 11 and 13.

143 See the explanatory section of the SchadÄndG-E (BT-Drucksache 14/7752), p. 11; E. Schiemann, [2001] ZRP, 380, 381.

untouched. Following the principle of complete compensation (so-called "Grundsatz der Totalreparation"), they will continue to receive the full amount of money necessary for compensation in kind (§ 249 BGB) and must only be able to show that VAT was actually paid for the purpose of restoring the previous condition by repair or replacement.[144] VAT is also compensated in case a damaged thing is repaired *privately*, but spare parts have to be bought in the process; VAT for fictitious labour costs will not be compensated in this case.[145] Although victims will generally only receive compensation necessary for restoring their situation in the economically most effective way (so-called "Wirtschaftlichkeitspostulat"),[146] they may also continue to choose repair instead of replacement, or replacement instead of repair. In these cases, VAT is only compensated as far as the economically best approach would have required its payment.[147] Full fictitious compensation is also granted in case victims receive money because repair or replacement is impossible or would require unreasonable measures on behalf of the debtor (§ 251 BGB). In these cases, money is granted as a direct compensation for a loss of property (so-called "Wertinteresse"),[148] whereas § 249 BGB aims at compensating an infringement of the victim's integrity (so-called "Integritätsinteresse").[149] Reductions only seem justifiable if victims actually have a choice to repair/replace a thing or to live with the damage in some other way.[150]

17 Finally, the explanatory section of the SchadÄndG-E points out that an even stricter approach to the compensation of material damage was debated during the preparation of the draft within the Federal Ministry of Justice. This approach, focusing on the precise damage suffered by the victim, would have generally excluded *any* form of fictitious calculation of costs by taking into account only the measures actually taken by the victim in the concrete case. Victims suffering damage to things would then be entitled to claim compensation *either* (1) for the costs of repair (if the thing is repaired); *or* (2) the difference between the worth of the damaged thing – the so-called "Restwert" – and a replacement (if the thing is replaced); *or* (3) the difference between the worth of the damaged thing before and after the damaging event (if the victim decides to live with the damage). This approach was not followed because it would have resulted in a large amount of legal uncertainty following from the necessary radical break with the present system as developed by case law. The lawgiver was not prepared to go that far.[151]

18 5. *Liability for Pharmaceutical Products.* The often difficult procedural situation of victims who have suffered personal injury through harmful pharmaceu-

[144] See the explanatory section of the SchadÄndG-E (BT-Drucksache 14/7752), p. 23.
[145] See the explanatory section of the SchadÄndG-E (BT-Drucksache 14/7752), p. 23.
[146] R. Rixecker (*supra* note 128), p. 79; D.-U. Otto, [1998] NZV, 433, 434.
[147] See the explanatory section of the SchadÄndG-E (BT-Drucksache 14/7752), p. 24.
[148] BGHZ 92, 85; R. Rixecker (*supra* note 128), p. 85.
[149] G. Schiemann in *J. von Staudinger's Kommentar zum Bürgerlichen Gesetzbuch mit Einführungsgesetz und Nebengesetzen* (13th edn. 1999), § 249 no. 211.
[150] See the explanatory section of the SchadÄndG-E (BT-Drucksache 14/7752), pp. 14 and 23.
[151] See the explanatory section of the SchadÄndG-E (BT-Drucksache 14/7752), p. 14.

tical products is addressed by two proposed changes to the Medical Preparations Act.[152] In view of the problems encountered by these victims in proving that harm was caused by inadequate research, production or information of the producer,[153] the burden of proof for defective research and production (*Entwicklungs- und Herstellungsfehler*) is shifted from the plaintiff to the pharmaceutical entrepreneur.[154] This includes situations in which a patient has used more than one product at the same time and it is unclear which preparation actually caused the harm;[155] here, recourse among the entrepreneurs is possible if only one producer is sued by the victim (§ 93 AMG). Victims who wish to invoke § 84 AMG will thus only have to prove an infringement of a protected interest (life, physical integrity and/or well-being) as well as facts which strongly indicate that the harm could have been caused by the pharmaceutical product in question. According to the explanatory section of the SchadÄndG-E, this amounts to more than a mere assertion but less than full proof of causation; the Federal Ministry of Justice obviously envisages a flexible standard based on the circumstances of each individual case.[156] The position of victims is further strengthened by the proposal to introduce a claim for information on the established effects and side-effects of the product in question as well as known reciprocal effects with *other* medical preparations. This new claim, directed both against the producer and public authorities charged with the supervision of the pharmaceutical sector, is subject to statutory provisions expressly protecting this information for the benefit of outweighing interests of the producer or third persons.[157] With respect to privacy rights – and since the victim must still show (albeit not in perfect detail) that the harm

[152] § 84 AMG, which was introduced in 1976 as a reaction to the *Contagan*-cases, presently declares: "Wird infolge der Anwendung eines zum Gebrauch beim Menschen bestimmten Arzneimittels, das im Geltungsbereich dieses Gesetzes an den Verbraucher abgegeben wurde und der Pflicht zur Zulassung unterliegt oder durch Rechtsverordnung von der Zulassung befreit worden ist, ein Mensch getötet oder der Körper oder die Gesundheit eines Menschen nicht unerheblich verletzt, so ist der pharmazeutische Unternehmer, der das Arzneimittel im Geltungsbereich dieses Gesetzes in den Verkehr gebracht hat, verpflichtet, dem Verletzten den daraus entstehenden Schaden zu ersetzen. Die Ersatzpflicht besteht nur, wenn 1) das Arzneimittel bei bestimmungsgemäßem Gebrauch schädliche Wirkungen hat, die über ein nach den Erkenntnissen der medizinischen Wissenschaft vertretbares Maß hinausgehen und ihre Ursache im Bereich der Entwicklung oder der Herstellung haben oder 2) der Schaden infolge einer nicht den Erkenntnissen der medizinischen Wissenschaft entsprechenden Kennzeichnung, Fachinformation oder Gebrauchsinformation eingetreten ist".

[153] See, *e.g.*, the decisions of OLG Düsseldorf in [1995] NJW, 3060 *et seq.* and OLG Hamm in [1997] *NJW-Rechtsprechungs-Report Zivilrecht* (NJW-RR), 217 *et seq.* (both on AIDS and blood-related products) and OLG Celle in [1998] VersR, 1023 *et seq.* (on hepatitis); M. Fuchs (*supra* note 59), p. 249.

[154] See art. 1 no. 1 SchadÄndG-E (BT-Drucksache 14/7752), which proposes the following new § 84 subss. 2 and 3 AMG: "(2) Ist das angewendete Arzneimittel nach den Gegebenheiten des Einzelfalls geeignet, den Schaden zu verursachen, so wird vermutet, dass der Schaden durch dieses Arzneimittel verursacht ist (...). (3) Die Ersatzpflicht des pharmazeutischen Unternehmers nach Absatz 1 Satz 2 Nr. 1 ist ausgeschlossen, wenn nach den Umständen davon auszugehen ist, dass die schädlichen Wirkungen des Arzneimittels ihre Ursache nicht im Bereich der Entwicklung und Herstellung haben".

[155] See the explanatory section of the SchadÄndG-E (BT-Drucksache 14/7752), p. 19.

[156] BT-Drucksache 14/7752, p. 20.

[157] See art. 1 no. 2 SchadÄndG-E which proposes a new § 84a AMG.

suffered could reasonably have resulted from the product of the defendant – the SchadÄndG-E refrains from the introduction of a corresponding claim for information of the pharmaceutical entrepreneur vis-à-vis the victim.[158] The *Bundesrat*, which has proposed extensive amendments to this part of the SchadÄndG-E, is strongly in favour of such a claim.[159]

19 6. *Maximum Compensation (Caps) Under Strict Liability.* Most German strict liability statutes contain fixed or flexible caps (so-called "Haftungshöchstbeträge") limiting the maximum amount of individual damages for specific injuries as well as the overall amount of damages resulting from one and the same event. This is true for the Environmental Liability Act,[160] the Nuclear Energy Act,[161] the Product Liability Act,[162] the Air Traffic Act,[163] the Liability Act,[164] the Road Traffic Act,[165] the Act on Genetical Engineering,[166] the Federal Mining Act[167] and the Medical Preparations Act.[168] These caps, which place limitations on liability and therefore enable potential tortfeasors to seek insurance under reasonable conditions, are supposed to reflect the average damage caused by a severe accident in the given sphere of risk. Compensation exceeding these amounts can only be sought on the basis of (unlimited) fault liability. The SchadÄndG-E seeks to adjust the present levels of maximum compensation to the economic development of the country in order to provide sufficient protection.[169] Whereas the general price level, medical costs and private income have increased substantially over the past 20 years (in some sectors by more than 50%), caps contained in the majority of German strict liability statutes were left unchanged in the same period of time. Adjustments are also required with a view to the introduction of non-pecuniary loss in the area of strict liability (which will substantially increase the amount of damage the caps will have to cover) and the change of currency at the beginning of this year (from Deutsche Mark to Euro). On a different level, the Federal Ministry of Justice also wants to harmonise the individual caps for certain forms of loss (death, personal injury and damage to property), so that the same injury suffered in different cases – *e.g.*, quadriplegia – may be compensated with equal amounts *regardless* of the cause (*e.g.*, by motorised traffic or a mining accident). Finally, some caps are at present simply not sufficient to cover the loss suffered in practice. This is true, *e.g.*, in the case of the *overall* limit for damage resulting from one and the same accident in motorised traffic, which pres-

158 See the explanatory section of the SchadÄndG-E (BT-Drucksache 14/7752), p. 21.

159 See the position of the *Bundesrat* (*Stellungnahme*), BT-Drucksache 14/7752, pp. 45–48.

160 § 15 UmweltHG.

161 § 31 AtG.

162 § 10 ProdHaftG.

163 § 37 LuftVG.

164 §§ 9, 10 HaftPflG.

165 § 12 StVG.

166 § 33 GenTG.

167 § 117 BBergG.

168 § 88 AMG.

169 For the Road Traffic Act see E. Scheffen, [2001] ZRP, 380, 381 and U. Haas/M. Horcher, [2001] DStR, 2118, 2123.

ently fails to cover even two seriously injured persons who both claim the maximum *individual* compensation provided by the Road Traffic Act.[170] The present government initiative would increase this number to at least five heavily injured victims.[171]

The enactment of the SchadÄndG-E would change the following existing caps: 20

(1) Medical Preparations Act (last changed in 1994) – increase of the maximum individual limits for death or personal injury from € 500,000 to € 600,000 (lump sum[172]) and, alternatively, from € 30,000 to € 36,000 (pension per annum);[173] increase of the absolute maximum for several cases of death and/or personal injury caused by the same medical preparation[174] from € 100,000,000 to € 120,000,000 (lump sum) and, alternatively, from € 6,000,000 to € 7,200,000 (pensions per annum).[175]

(2) Federal Mining Act (last changed in 1980) – increase of the individual limits for death or personal injury from a maximum of € 250,000 to € 600,000 (lump sum) and, alternatively, from € 15,000 to € 36,000 (pension per annum).[176]

(3) Road Traffic Act (last changed in 1977) – increase of the individual limits for death or personal injury from a maximum of € 250,000 to € 600.000 (lump sum) and, alternatively, from € 15,000 to € 36,000 (pension per annum);[177] increase of the absolute maximum for several cases of death and/or personal injury caused by the same event from € 375,000 to € 3,000,000 (lump sum) and, alternatively, from € 22,500 to € 180,000 (pensions per annum);[178] increase of the maximum compensation for several cases of damage to property caused by the same event from € 50,000 to € 300,000.[179] In addition to the increase of caps presently established by § 12 StVG, the SchadÄndG-E proposes to introduce a new provision (§ 12a StVG), which would establish even higher levels in case harm was caused by road transport of dangerous goods and substances. These caps would increase the maximum compensation for several cases of death and/or personal injury caused by the same event to € 6,000,000 (lump sum) and, alternatively, to € 360,000 (pensions per annum).[180] Several cases of damage to immovable property caused by the same event would be covered to a maximum of € 6,000,000.[181] Dangerous goods and substances are

170 E. Scheffen, [2001] ZRP, 380, 381.
171 See the explanatory section of the SchadÄndG-E (BT-Drucksache 14/7752), p. 32.
172 So-called "Kapitalhöchstbetrag".
173 § 88 AMG, see art. 1 no. 4a SchadÄndG-E (BT-Drucksache 14/7752).
174 So-called "globale Haftungshöchstgrenze".
175 § 88 AMG, see art. 1 no. 4b SchadÄndG-E (BT-Drucksache 14/7752).
176 § 117 subs. 1 BBergG, see art. 3 no. 2 SchadÄndG-E (BT-Drucksache 14/7752).
177 § 12 subs. 1 no. 1 StVG, see art. 4 no. 6 SchadÄndG-E (BT-Drucksache 14/7752).
178 § 12 subs. 1 no. 2 StVG, see art. 4 no. 6 SchadÄndG-E (BT-Drucksache 14/7752).
179 § 12 subs. 1 no. 3 StVG, see art. 4 no. 6 SchadÄndG-E (BT-Drucksache 14/7752).
180 § 12a subs. 1 no. 1 StVG (new)
181 § 12a subs. 1 no. 2 StVG (new).

defined by reference to the ADR Treaty of 1957; small quantities as well as the movement of dangerous goods and substances within the limits of clearly defined industrial sites involved in the production, use or destruction of such goods are thereby excluded from the scope of these higher caps.[182] This legislative proposal is justified by the additional severe risks attached to road transport of highly dangerous material, which can potentially cause much greater harm than is usually to be expected in road traffic accident situations. The special environmental dangers resulting from dangerous goods (cost intensive harm to soil and water) is thereby cared for by the increase of caps as far as immovable property is concerned. The amendment will also affect international road transport of dangerous goods (German law will often be applicable on the basis of international private law) since the CRTD Treaty of 1989, which specifically addresses these issues, is not yet in force.[183] Finally, the Federal Ministry of Justice also wants to introduce a new § 12b StVG, which seeks to exclude special military vehicles (not "usual" vehicles like cars, trucks or buses used by the army) from the caps established by the Road Traffic Act.[184] This exception is justified by the dangers resulting from vehicles such as tanks as well as the special character of this state-based activity.

(4) Liability Act (last changed in 1977) – introduction of an individual limit for death or personal injury of € 600,000 (lump sum) and, alternatively, increase from a maximum of € 15,000 to € 36,000 (pension per annum);[185] increase of the maximum amount for several cases of damage to property caused by the same event from € 50,000 to € 300,000.[186]

(5) Air Traffic Act – increase of the individual limits for death or personal injury of *third persons* (not passengers), last changed in 1977, from € 250,000 to € 600,000 (lump sum) and introduction of an alternative annual pension of € 36,000;[187] conversion to Euro and slight increase of the present maximum amounts for several cases of damage (all types) resulting to third persons due to the same event, which depend on the weight of the aircraft in question and were last changed in 1992[188] (with a view to further changes which expected developments in international and EEC aviation rules will necessitate, these levels were otherwise left basically unchanged[189]); increase of the individual limits for death or personal injury of *passengers*, last changed in 1977, from € 160,000 to € 600,000 (lump sum) and introduction of an alternative annual pension of

[182] § 12a subs. 2 – 4 StVG (new), see art. 4 no. 7 SchadÄndG-E (BT-Drucksache 14/7752). As the explanatory section correctly points out (p. 34), harm caused by the transport of dangerous material *within* the clearly defined limits of production sites will be covered by the provisions of the Environmental Liability Act.

[183] See the explanatory section of the SchadÄndG-E (BT-Drucksache 14/7752), pp. 33 and 34.

[184] § 12b (new), see art. 4 no. 7 SchadÄndG-E (BT-Drucksache 14/7752).

[185] § 9 HaftPflG, see art. 5 no. 4 SchadÄndG-E (BT-Drucksache 14/7752).

[186] § 10 subs. 1 HaftPflG, see art. 5 no. 5 SchadÄndG-E (BT-Drucksache 14/7752).

[187] § 37 subs. 2 LuftVG, see art. 6 no. 3 SchadÄndG-E (BT-Drucksache 14/7752).

[188] § 37 subs. 1 LuftVG, see art. 6 no. 3 SchadÄndG-E (BT-Drucksache 14/7752).

[189] See the explanatory section of the SchadÄndG-E (BT-Drucksache 14/7752), pp. 36 *et seq.*

€ 36,000[190] (the proposal would thus result in an equal treatment of third persons and passengers); conversion to Euro and slight rise of the present individual maximum compensation for damage to the property of passengers from € 1,600 to € 1,700. Other changes of the Air Traffic Act indirectly affecting the compensation of victims involve the introduction of compulsory insurance for injuries not covered by EEC Regulations 2407/92 and 2027/97.[191]

(6) Federal Data Protection Act – conversion to Euro and slight increase of the present maximum amount for several cases of damage caused by an infringement of personal rights by a public authority from € 125,000 to € 130,000.[192]

(7) Act on Genetical Engineering – conversion to Euro and slight increase of the present maximum amount for several cases of personal injury caused by genetically changed organisms from € 80,000,000 to € 85,000,000.[193]

(8) Product Liability Act – conversion to Euro and slight increase of the present maximum amount for several cases of personal injury caused by a defective product from € 80,000,000 to € 85,000,000.[194]

(9) Environmental Liability Act – conversion to Euro and slight increase of the present maximum amount for several cases of personal injury caused by certain technical installations from € 80,000.000 to € 85,000,000.[195]

7. *Liability for Court-Appointed Experts.* The Federal Ministry of Justice finally aims at the introduction of a liability of court-appointed experts who submit erroneous reports (*Haftung für gerichtliche Sachverständigengutachten*). These experts are presently liable neither on the basis of contract nor on the basis of state liability,[196] and *delictual* claims will differ according to whether experts deliver their reports under oath or not. Whereas § 823 subs. 2 BGB in connection with §§ 154, 163 of the Criminal Code (*Strafgesetzbuch*, StGB) will establish liability for any economic loss already on the level of negligence *if* an oath is taken, this is not the case if an expert gives evidence without taking an oath: § 410 subs. 1 of the Civil Procedure Act (*Zivilprozeßordnung*, ZPO) is not regarded as a protective norm (so-called "Schutzgesetz") within the scope of § 823 subs. 2 BGB,[197] so that damaged parties must prove intent to cause harm **21**

190 § 46 subs. 1 LuftVG, see art. 6 no. 4 SchadÄndG-E (BT-Drucksache 14/7752).

191 § 50 LuftVG – see art. 6 no. 5a and 5b SchadÄndG-E (BT-Drucksache 14/7752) – and §§ 102 *et seq. Luftverkehrs-Zulassungs-Ordnung* (LuftVZO) – see art. 7 SchadÄndG-E (BT-Drucksache 14/7752).

192 § 7 subs. 3 *Bundesdatenschutzgesetz* (BDSG), see art. 9 no. 1 SchadÄndG-E (BT-Drucksache 14/7752).

193 § 33 GenTG, see art. 9 no. 2.2 SchadÄndG-E (BT-Drucksache 14/7752).

194 § 10 subs. 1 ProdHaftG, see art. 9 no. 3.2 SchadÄndG-E (BT-Drucksache 14/7752).

195 § 15 UmweltHG, see art. 9 no. 4.2 SchadÄndG-E (BT-Drucksache 14/7752).

196 OLG Düsseldorf in [1986] NJW, 2891; W. Jacobs, Haftung des gerichtlichen Sachverständigen, [2001] ZRP, 489 (490).

197 OLG Düsseldorf in [1986] NJW, 2891; H. Thomas (*supra* note 78), § 823 no. 155; W. Jacobs, [2001] ZRP, 489 (490).

contrary to *bonos mores* (§ 826 BGB) if they want to claim compensation for economic loss.[198] Similarly, court decisions limit claims based on § 823 subs. 1 BGB (which does not protect mere economic interests and is thus seldom helpful[199]) to cases of intent and gross negligence.[200] The SchadÄndG-E seeks to find a common delictual solution to these situations without affecting the differentiations made by civil procedure and criminal law. According to a proposed new § 839a BGB, court-appointed experts would thereby have to bear responsibility for intent and gross negligence regardless of the procedure followed.[201] The claim is not given if the parties settle in court (even if they do so under the impression of the evidence given by the expert) or if the damaged party fails to seek legal remedies against the court judgment which is based on the erroneous opinion.[202] Though this proposal will give additional protection in a number of cases, the lawgiver may be well advised to expand the scope of the new § 839a BGB in order to include experts appointed by *administrative bodies*. This is highlighted by a recent decision of the BGH,[203] in which erroneous expert advice sought by a public administrative body resulted in subsequent delays and financial loss for the applicant of a banking licence. The applicant, who did not have contractual or delictual claims against the expert, was left without compensation.[204] Finally, it might be necessary to introduce caps in order to limit excessive liability of court-appointed experts.[205] This would provide a basis for reasonable insurance coverage and acknowledge the difficult position of experts, who must accept the appointment by a court of law unless they are biased.

B. Cases

1. *Bundesgerichtshof* (Federal Supreme Court, BGH)[206]; 4 December 2001; VI ZR 213/00: Wrongful Birth

a) Brief Summary of the Facts

22 The plaintiffs are parents of uniovular twins, of which one is perfectly healthy whereas the other is physically heavily impaired, missing her right leg alto-

[198] OLG Hamm in [1998] NJW-RR, 1686.

[199] See, *e.g.*, OLG Nürnberg in [1988] NJW-RR, 791 for a case of grossly negligent medical advice.

[200] BVerfG 49, 304; OLG Schleswig in [1995] NJW, 791.

[201] See art. 2 no. 5 SchadÄndG-E (BT-Drucksache 14/7752) on the introduction of the following provision: "(1) Erstattet ein vom Gericht ernannter Sachverständiger vorsätzlich oder grob fahrlässig ein unrichtiges Gutachten, so ist er zum Ersatz des Schadens verpflichtet, der einem Verfahrensbeteiligten durch eine gerichtliche Entscheidung entsteht, die auf diesem Gutachten beruht. (2) § 839 Abs. 3 ist entsprechend anzuwenden".

[202] See the explanatory section of the SchadÄndG-E (BT-Drucksache 14/7752), p. 28.

[203] BGH in [2001] NJW, 3115.

[204] See thereon B. Kannowski/P. Zumbansen, Gemeinwohl und Privatinteresse – Expertenhaftung am Scheideweg?, [2001] NJW, 3102 *et seq.*

[205] W. Jacobs, [2001] ZRP, 489 (492).

[206] [2002] NJW, 886 *et seq.*; see Pressemitteilung des BGH Nr. 90/2001 of 4 December 2001, [2001] NJW, IX.

gether and suffering from severe malfunctions of the other leg as well as her right arm. They demand the costs of maintenance for their impaired child. The mother was a patient of the defendants, both gynaecologists, who performed regular pre-natal check-ups involving both standard tests as well as a more comprehensive diagnosis of possible physical deficiencies. The defendants are held responsible for a failure to identify the severe impairments of the handicapped child. The plaintiffs thereby claim that they would have terminated the pregnancy had they been informed of the impairments; they maintain that abortion would have been legally possible. The defendants declare that it was medically impossible to identify the impairments of the handicapped child prior to the beginning of the 23rd week of pregnancy, which would have been the time limit for an abortion in this case. Apart from that, an abortion would not have been a legal option anyway due to the high danger such an operation would have brought on the healthy twin. The court of appeal did not decide on the question of medical malpractice, but rather rejected the claim of the parents on the basis that an abortion would have been unlawful under the given circumstances (§ 218a subss. 2 and 3 StGB 1992, BGBl. I 1398 in connection with the judgment of the Federal Constitutional Court of 28 May 1993, BGBl. I 820). The court argued that the pregnancy would not have endangered the mother sufficiently, barring the way to an abortion on the basis of § 218a subs. 2 StGB 1992 (so called "medizinische Indikation"). Equally, an abortion on the basis of the impairments of the handicapped twin (§ 218a subs. 3 StGB 1992, so-called "embryopathische Indikation") would not have been permissible – not only with respect to the merely physical impairment of the handicapped child, but also with a view to the severe dangers which would have resulted for the healthy twin in case of an attempted selective abortion. Though legally possible, an abortion of both children would have required severe hazards for the health of the mother, which had not been shown by the plaintiffs.

b) Judgment of the Supreme Court

The starting point of the Supreme Court is the contractual claim of parents for the full costs of maintenance if a heavily impaired child is born due to medical malpractice. The judgment is then based on the assumption that the mother – if informed – would have indeed wanted to abort both children and that the physical impairments of her daughter were overlooked due to medical malpractice of the defendants. The Supreme Court nevertheless rejects the claim, since an abortion would have been unlawful under the given circumstances. The judgment thereby stresses the fact that the psychical stress put on the mother (and perhaps aggravated by a depressive predisposition) would not have justified the prognosis of a danger of sufficient weight to meet the requirements of § 218a subs. 2 StGB 1992. The severe physical impairments of one of the twins is in itself equally insufficient to justify the abortion of both twins (which, as the plaintiffs agree, would have been medically necessary). The Supreme Court thereby takes into account the fact that the impaired twin is mentally fully capable and (with technical help) will be allowed to par- 23 ticipate in family life and in the general social context. In contrast to the usual situation covered by § 218a subs. 3 StGB 1992, the disadvantages on the side of the mother must not only be weighed against the protection of the life of the impaired child, but also against the right to life of the healthy twin. Here, a balancing of interests would have clearly ruled out an abortion of both children.

c) Commentary

24 Though involving a claim following from a breach of contract (medical malpractice), it seems appropriate to include this case in the German report since it adds a new constellation to the group of cases frequently discussed under the heading "wrongful birth". The decision of the Supreme Court in this difficult constellation thereby seems reasonable. The coherence of a legal system requires that rules on civil compensation correspond to the legal duties established by criminal law. The inquiry into § 218a StGB 1992 is certainly difficult, but it reveals an appropriate weighing of interests between the rights of the parents (who wish to avoid the mental, physical and financial burdens of a heavily handicapped child) and the constitutional right to life. This borderline case would have been yet more difficult to decide if an abortion of the handicapped child itself had been covered by the statute, but would have involved the same hazards to the life of the remaining twin.

2. BGH; 23 January 2001; VI ZR 70/00[207]: Employer's privilege I ("gemeinsame Betriebsstätte")

a) Brief Summary of Facts

25 The plaintiff was victim in a workplace accident. Unloading bottles of gas from a truck on the premises of another company, he was crushed between his vehicle and the vehicle of the first defendant (not employed with this company), who had subsequently arrived and was waiting for the plaintiff to finish his work. The plaintiff was thereby seriously injured. It is established that the first defendant had negligently released the clutch of his truck. The plaintiff claims damages for pain and suffering of at least € 20,000 plus interest from the first defendant as well as the holder of the first defendant's vehicle (second defendant) and the insurance company with which this vehicle was insured (third defendant), deducting € 3,400 already paid by the third defendant prior to the proceedings. He also seeks a declaratory judgment establishing that the defendants are jointly and severally liable for any further immaterial loss resulting from the accident. The defendants invoke the employer's privilege for accidents occurring on a common workplace established by § 106 subs. 3 no. 3 Social Security Act Part VII (*Sozialgesetzbuch*, SGB VII). The court of first instance held that the employer's privilege was not applicable to this case, awarded damages for pain and suffering (€ 21,550) and issued the desired declaratory judgment. On appeal by the defendants, damages were merely reduced.

[207] BGH in [2001] NJW-RR, 741 *et seq*.

b) Judgment by the Supreme Court

Emphasising the intention of the lawgiver to establish a fairly wide employer's privilege for harm caused to employees of different companies working on a mutual site (so-called "gemeinsame Betriebstätte"), the Supreme Court argues that a meaningful interpretation of § 106 subs. 3 no. 3 SGB VII must involve an element of mutual working activity. The court thereby stresses the wording of the provision, which requires a *mutual* rather than just the *same* site of work. This implies a minimum of factual (even ad hoc) co-operation between the employees of different companies. The activities of the plaintiff and those envisaged by the first defendant do not fulfil this requirement since they were (going) to be performed separately. They thus fail to constitute a common workplace within the meaning of § 106 subs. 3 no. 3 SGB VII. **26**

c) Commentary

For comments please see [33] below. **27**

3. BGH; 3 July 2001; VI ZR 198/00[208]: Employer's privilege II ("Tierarzt"-Decision)

a) Brief Summary of Facts

The plaintiff is an employee of her husband, who operates commercial stables and called upon the defendant – a self-employed veterinarian – to examine a pregnant mare. The defendant diagnosed a double pregnancy and took measures to abort one of the foals. The plaintiff, assisting the defendant by restraining the mare with a rope, was seriously injured due to a sudden movement of the animal. She claims material and immaterial loss suffered by the accident, arguing that the defendant should have employed a different method to restrain the mare or ordered her to leave the zone of danger during the operation. The defendant denies having acted negligently in the course of the abortion and stresses that any liability based on negligence was in any case excluded due to the employer's privilege for accidents occurring on a mutual worksite (§ 106 subs. 3 no. 3 SGB VII). The claim of the plaintiff was rejected both by the court of first instance and the court of appeal on the basis of the latter argument. Both courts interpreted the privilege to protect not only employees, but also employers who themselves work on a mutual worksite. **28**

b) Judgment by the Supreme Court

The Supreme Court has little difficulty in establishing that the plaintiff and the defendant had indeed worked on a mutual site in performing and assisting in the abortion. The judgment then focuses on the scope of § 106 subs. 3 no. 3 SGB VII, emphasising that the employer's privilege is not already activated by the mere fact that companies co-operate on a mutual worksite; an employer *himself* may rather invoke the privilege only if he *personally* participated in **29**

[208] BGH in [2001] NZV, 423 *et seq.* – BGH in [2001] NJW, 3127 *et seq.*

the harmful activity and was thus a member of the group of persons facing common dangers resulting from the working process (so-called "Funktions- und Gefahrengemeinschaft"). This interpretation is confirmed by the wording of the provision, which demands that harm is caused by "a person working for an enterprise" (*für ein Unternehmen Tätiger*). As in the case of the self-employed defendant, who participated in the mutual activity of performing the abortion, this can also be the employer himself.

c) Commentary

30 For comments please see [33] below.

4. BGH; 3 July 2001; VI ZR 284/00[209]: Employer's Privilege III ("Kranführer"-Decision)

a) Brief Summary of Facts

31 The plaintiff is a carpenter who was injured in a workplace accident when trying to attach building material to the hook of a crane. The driver of the crane suddenly lifted the hook, causing the material to tumble. The plaintiff in turn lost his balance and fell through a stairwell into the cellar of the construction. The driver of the crane and the plaintiff were employed with different companies, the driver being an employee of the second defendant, who owned and operated a construction company. The second defendant was not personally present at the time of the accident. Later, the second defendant established a company with limited liability (first defendant), which filed for insolvency after the case reached the Supreme Court. The plaintiff claims damages for material and immaterial loss, as well as a declaratory judgment establishing that both defendants are jointly and severally liable for any further material loss resulting from the accident. The proceedings against the first defendant are stayed due to the insolvency. The second defendant invokes the employer's privilege for accidents occurring on a mutual worksite (§ 106 subs. 3 no. 3 SGB VII) and is successful both before the court of first instance and the court of appeal.

b) Judgment by the Supreme Court

32 The Supreme Court does not uphold the judgment of the court of appeal, arguing that the employer's privilege for accidents occurring on a mutual worksite may not be invoked by the employer *himself* unless he is *personally* involved in the activities leading to the harmful event. Whereas the driver of the crane is thus protected from claims arising from the accident, the second defendant – though owner and operator of the company at the time and thus also "working" for a different company engaged in activities on this site – can potentially be liable on the basis of §§ 823 and 831 BGB, depending on the factual circumstances of the case (which are not yet fully established). The Supreme

[209] BGH in [2001] *Neue Zeitung für Versicherung und Recht* (NVersZ), 573 *et seq.* = BGH in [2001] NZV, 421 *et seq.* = BGH in [2001] NJW, 3125 *et seq.*

Court makes this distinction between employers who actively participate in the workplace activity and those who are not present in the light of the wording of § 106 subs. 3 no. 3 SGB VII (which implies some form of activity leading to the accident), the legislative history of the norm and its protective purpose, which mainly aims at preserving social peace within the working sphere and seeks to protect members of working teams who face mutual dangers resulting from the working process.

c) Commentary

The three judgments of the Federal Supreme Court outlined above mark important cornerstones in the interpretation of §§ 104 *et seq.* SGB VII, which deal with colleagues, co-workers and employers who are injured on the job (as opposed to injuries occurring on job-unrelated occasions, so-called "Teilnahme am allgemeinen Verkehr"). § 106 subs. 3 no. 3 SGB VII[210] thereby extends the privileges granted to tortfeasors in the previous provisions to include the injuries of persons employed with *other* companies if a workplace accident occurs in the same industrial plant or on the same site (so-called "gemeinsame Arbeitsstätte"). These rules, though reformed in 1996, left unanswered a number of questions, two of which the Supreme Court now had the opportunity to clarify – (1) the definition of the requirement of a common workplace and (2) the applicability of § 106 subs. 3 no. 3 SGB VII to employers *themselves*. The first decision (outlined under [25] and [26] above) thereby links up with a previous case of the BGH,[211] which had already established that some form of co-operation was required in order to trigger the employer's privilege if employees of different companies work together on the same site and one of them is injured by negligence of the other. This interpretation of § 106 subs. 3 no. 3 SGB VII fits well into the overall structure of the provision, which deals with situations characterised by co-ordinated activities; it also respects the declared political will of the lawgiver, who wanted to expand the protection granted to employees in workplace accidents. The case itself reflects the rationale of the Supreme Court well. A privilege of the tortfeasor's employer (especially barring claims for pain and suffering, which social security benefits of the employed victim will not cover) requires some additional justification, which distinguishes these occupational accidents from normal tort claims. The persons involved were not working together in any form, and the only connection between them was the accident itself. The justifications for excluding claims against co-workers and employers in *normal* workplace situations (protection of the working climate, the idea of solidarity among a group of persons facing common dangers – so-called "Gefahrengemeinschaft" – and the fact that compulsory accident insurance is financed by employers 33

[210] § 106 subs. 3 no. 3 SGB VII declares: "Wirken Unternehmen zur Hilfe bei Unglücksfällen oder Unternehmen des Zivilschutzes zusammen oder verrichten Versicherte mehrerer Unternehmen vorübergehend betriebliche Tätigkeiten auf einer gemeinsamen Betriebsstätte, gelten die §§ 104 und 105 für die Ersatzpflicht der für die beteiligten Unternehmen Tätigen untereinander".

[211] BGH, decision of 17 October 2000 (VI ZR 67/00), in [2002] NZV, 32 *et seq.* = [2001] NJW, 443 *et seq.* – [2001] VersR, 336 *et seq.*

alone) do not apply. The other two new decisions of the Supreme Court cited above extend the privilege to employers who *personally* participate in harmful workplace activities on common worksites. This development will be especially important for self-employed persons or small enterprises, where employers frequently work side-by-side with their employees and are in fact hardly distinguishable. This interpretation seems reasonable, though it is only supported by the argument that employers working with the employees of another enterprise are equally part of a group of persons facing common dangers.[212]

5. BGH; 16 February 2001[213]; V ZR 422/99: *Verkehrssicherungspflichten* in Agriculture

a) Brief Summary of the Facts

34 The parties are wine-growers with neighbouring hills in an area in which wine is traditionally cultivated in single-crop farming. In 1995, both vineyards were strongly affected by mildew. Since the defendant did not cultivate his fields in that year and failed to take measures aimed at pest-control, the parasite was – with the help of the wind – able to spread more strongly on the farm of the plaintiff. Intensive pest-control could not prevent the spread. The plaintiff suffered a loss both in quantity and quality of his annual produce and claims over € 35,000 in damages. The court of first instance rejected the claim. The court of appeal held that the plaintiff could claim compensation on the basis of §§ 823 subs. 2, 1004 BGB because the defendant had infringed duties resulting from his membership in a community of farmers facing mutual dangers (so-called "Gefahrengemeinschaft"). These dangers (in this case: mildew), which could in the worst case even destroy the economic existence of farmers in the region, could only be met effectively if all members of the community observed the safety measures generally regarded as necessary. The court stressed the fact that the defendant had contributed to these dangers by employing the technique of single-crop farming himself.

b) Judgment by the Supreme Court

35 The Supreme Court does not confirm the existence of a duty of care (so-called *Verkehrssicherungspflicht*) of the defendant resulting 1) from his *own* single-crop farming and the decision to leave this particular piece of land uncultivated (and thus without pest-control) for a period of twelve months *or* 2) from a legally enforceable responsibility based on the idea of a community (single-crop farmers) in need of a common response to a mutual danger. The defendant was thus under no responsibility to act. The judgment thereby argues that

[212] For further details see K. Gamperl, Die Haftungsbeschränkungen von Unternehmen und Arbeitskollegen gem. §§ 104 ff. SGB VII, [2001] NZV, 401 *et seq.*; D.-U. Otto, Die BGH-Rechtsprechung zur Haftungsbefreiung beim Unfall auf einer gemeinsamen Betriebsstätte, [2002] NZV, 10 *et seq.*

[213] BGH in [2001] NJW-RR, 1208 = BGH in [2001] *Zeitschrift für Wirtschafts- und Bankrecht, Wertpapiermitteilungen* (WM), 299.

it was the responsibility of the lawgiver to establish rules pertaining to the protection of certain groups of people facing mutal dangers. Though such rules existed in other areas (*e.g.*, with respect to sea emergencies or existing regional statutes on pest control, which require wine plants to be destroyed if left uncultivated for a period of at least *two* years), this was not the case in the situation at hand. The Supreme Court agrees that a duty to act may also result from the creation of a source of special danger, but this could not be argued in the case of the defendant. The use of a vineyard is not dangerous and the harm caused to the crops of the plaintiff resulted predominantly from forces of nature. The judgment thereby concedes that the neglect of pest-control had indeed contributed to the course of events, but stresses the fact that dangers resulting from single-crop farming had not been *created* by the defendant, who had merely *participated* in a potentially dangerous form of agriculture common to the whole region. Agriculture exercised within the generally accepted methods (as in this case) could not trigger claims of neighbours affected by the adverse effects of these methods. In a similar vein, the Supreme Court excludes claims based on the principle of good faith or custom. Finally the judgment discusses possible claims based on a duty to inform the plaintiff of possible dangers resulting from the defendant's vineyard. Such duties could exist in order to allow potential victims to care for protection themselves. The Supreme Court thereby stresses that the plaintiff was well aware of the obvious danger to his crops and could have reacted by asking to perform pest-control on the neighbouring piece of land himself.

c) Commentary

This decision is important for the whole area of agriculture, especially for plants which are cultivated in single-crop farming. Subsequently, the spread of parasites due to fallow farmland will not give rise to many claims based on tort law unless the lawgiver has explicitly established rules designed to protect the crops of neighbouring farmers. A problematic feature of this judgment is thereby certainly the failure to take into account at all § 906 subs. 2 BGB, which regulates interference from adjacent property and which has been discussed and applied – with the consequence of compensation – in similar cases involving other natural causes of harm emanating from land (*e.g.*, leaves, pollen, doves, bees, flies or rain water).[214] Apart from that, it seems at least debatable whether the fact that the defendant, belonging to a closely-knit community of farmers who face immense problems from parasites, did not in fact increase this danger by his decision not to employ methods of pest-control on his fallow farmland – and whether this increase in turn did not constitute an infringement of a *Verkehrssicherungspflicht*, paving the way for a valid claim of the plaintiff for compensation under § 823 subs. 1 BGB, § 823 subs. 2 with 1004 subs. 1 BGB or – if fault cannot be established – § 906 subs. 2 BGB. 36

[214] J. Eckert in H. Dörner et al, *Bürgerliches Gesetzbuch* (2001), § 906 no. 3; P. Bassenge in Palandt, *Bürgerliches Gesetzbuch* (61st edn. 2002), § 906 no. 13.

6. BGH; 12.12.2000; VI ZR 411/99[215]: Contributory Negligence Through Failure to Wear a Seat Belt

a) Brief Summary of the Facts

37 The plaintiff is an employee of a security company. As a driver of one of the company's armoured vehicles, he was injured in a traffic accident caused by the second defendant, driver of a large truck insured with the first defendant. The injuries suffered by the plaintiff led to an impairment of his sense of smell and taste. He was awarded compensation for pain and suffering (€ 15,000) by the court of first instance. On appeal, the defendants invoked § 254 BGB (contributory negligence) based on the fact that the plaintiff had not worn a seat belt at the time of the accident. The court of appeal did not make an attempt to find evidence to this effect, but rather dismissed the appeal on the (legal) grounds that the plaintiff's vehicle had not been in motion when hit by the second defendant. The court thereby interpreted the duty to wear a seat belt following from § 21a subs. 1 StVG restrictively, requiring passengers of motorised vehicles to secure themselves only if a vehicle is actually *in motion.*

b) Judgment by the Supreme Court

38 The Supreme Court points out that § 21a subs. 1 StVG has thus far received contradicting interpretations as far as the duty of passengers to fasten their seat belts when a vehicle is standing motionless is concerned. Reflecting on different possible meanings of the word "Fahrt" – to drive (*verb*) or a journey (*noun*) – the judgment thereby takes the view that passengers are required to keep their seat belts fastened at all times. This is justified with a view to the frequent stops occurring during a journey, which are statistically similarly dangerous as those parts of a journey where a vehicle actually moves. Special rules applicable, *e.g.*, to taxi drivers (due to the fact that many chauffeurs have managed to save themselves from the assault of passengers by letting themselves drop out of their vehicles) are not applicable to the plaintiff, who was not in such a danger when driving the armoured vehicle of his employer. The case was consequently referred back to the court of appeal, which will have to establish whether the plaintiff had actually fastened his seat belt or not.

c) Commentary

39 This decision of the Supreme Court only needs a brief comment, for it focuses on the very narrow (albeit practically important) question of contributory negligence (§ 254 BGB) in cases where the driver or passengers of a motorised vehicle fail to fasten their seat belts and are subsequently injured in an accident at a time when the vehicle is not in motion. The general question – whether the failure to make use of a seat belt constituted contributory negligence – was already decided by the Supreme Court in its decision of 20 March 1979.[216] Many subsequent decisions clarified additional aspects of the prob-

[215] BGH in [2001] NJW, 1485 *et seq.*
[216] BGHZ 74, 25.

lem, but the issue at hand remained controversial.[217] The Supreme Court has now finally closed the book on this dispute by interpreting § 21a subs. 1 StVG to demand the use of seat belts at *any time* during a journey. The case itself thereby proves the point. If vehicles are brought into traffic situations, their passengers will be subject to a high amount of danger even if the vehicle is not in motion at the time of a crash (*e.g.*, because it is standing at the end of a traffic jam, at a red traffic light, or at a road crossing). The general duty of an injured party to mitigate the damage must thus also include the duty to make use of such technical devices which effectively limit the amount of personal injury.

7. BGH; 30 January 2001; VI ZR 353/99[218]: Duty to Inform About the Risks of an Operation

a) Brief Summary of the Facts

The plaintiff, suffering from a deterioration of his intervertebral discs, under- **40**
went medical treatment by the defendant. The operation left the plaintiff with an impaired foot nerve (peronaeusparesis) and impotence. He subsequently gave up his employment as a locksmith. It is established that the defendant did not inform the plaintiff about the most severe possible risk of the operation (paraplegia), nor of the possibility of impotence. It is not clear whether the risk of peronaeusparesis was discussed prior to the operation. The court of first instance awarded € 20,000 for pain and suffering and gave a declaratory judgment to the effect that the defendant was liable for all future material damage following from the operation. The court of appeal upheld the decision and granted additional interest on the damages for pain and suffering.

b) Judgment by the Supreme Court

The Supreme Court points out that the plaintiff has a valid claim due to the **41**
fact that the defendant did not instruct him of the risk of impotence following from the proposed operation. Since the plaintiff had convincingly shown that he would not have given his consent had he known of this risk (and would thus have avoided the operation altogether), *both* impairments – impotence *and* paranaeusparesis – could be imputed to this failure. The judgment thereby stresses that it was not relevant whether the defendant had informed the plaintiff of the *worst* possible risk resulting from the operation; this so-called basic instruction ("Grundaufklärung") would only have been relevant to the case if the plaintiff had suffered a very remote impairment due to the realisation of a risk which is usually *not* covered by instruction.

[217] See, *e.g.*, the decisions OLG Celle in [1981] *Zeitschrift für Schadensrecht* (ZfS), 326; OLG Düsseldorf in [1972] *Verkehrsrechts-Sammlung* (VRS), 211; Kammergericht Berlin in [1970] VRS, 299; LG Hannover in [1989] NJW-RR 1510.

[218] BGH in [2001] NJW, 2798.

c) Commentary

42 The judgment of the Supreme Court seems reasonable as far as the failure to inform the patient of the risk of impotence is concerned. Liability for other impairment resulting from the operation (paranaeusparesis) seems at least debatable, since it is *not* established whether the defendant actually informed the plaintiff of this separate risk or failed to do so. In the first alternative, this could be regarded as a situation of consent as determined by the Supreme Court in its judgment of 15 February 2000[219] (no liability if an impairment is due to a risk which was discussed, even though other possible risks were not). The overall result nonetheless seems viable. The Supreme Court – stressing the special circumstances of this case – could leave the question open if it was absolutely certain that the patient would have opted against the operation if informed of the other risk (impotence). It must be pointed out, though, that the already complex system of solutions developed by the courts in this area of law is further complicated by this decision.[220]

8. OLG Hamm (Court of Appeal); 14 February 2001; 9 W 23/00: No Product Liability of Brewery to Warn of the Dangers of Alcohol Consumption

a) Brief Summary of the Facts

43 The applicant seeks subsidy for legal advice (so-called "Prozeßkostenhilfe") in order to file a claim against a brewery for infringing a duty to warn consumers of the harmful and potentially addictive effects of beer. He claims to have consumed beer produced by the brewery over a period of 17 years, during which he developed an addiction to alcohol. The consequences were a divorce, the loss of his job and a loss of his driving licence due to drunken driving. He claims compensation for pain and suffering (€ 15,000), as well as a declaratory judgment establishing that the brewery was liable for any further material and immaterial loss resulting from his addicton. The applicant argues that he would have refrained from drinking the beer if he had been informed of the addictive effects of the product. The brewery rejected the claim on the basis of the argument that it was under no legal duty to warn consumers of the potentially addictive effect of alcohol and stresses that the applicant would not have refrained from drinking the beer even if expressly informed. The court of first instance rejected the application, arguing 1) that the brewery was under no legal obligation to warn consumers; 2) that the addictive effects of alcohol were generally known to consumers; and 3) that any claim for compensation would in any case have to be reduced to nil due to the overwhelming contributory negligence on the side of the applicant.

[219] BGHZ 144, 1 = BGH in [2000] NJW, 1784.

[220] See Geiß/Greiner, *Arzthaftpflichtrecht* (4th edn. 2001), pp. 229 *et seq.*

b) Judgment by the Hamm Court of Appeal

Emphasising the general duty of producers to warn consumers of the harmful effects of their products, the Court of Appeal confirms the decision of the court of first instance. It thereby stresses that a warning is not necessary if a danger resulting from the use or consumption of a product is so obvious that any reasonable consumer immediately realises the harmful effects of a product. The judgment thereby argues that the addictive effects of alcohol were indeed commonly known to the public. The duty of producers to provide information is designed to provide a basis for informed choices and does not seek to prevent consumers from making potentially harmful decisions. Finally, the applicant could not show convincingly that he would have indeed refrained from drinking the beer if the information had been given by the brewery. The Supreme Court declined further review. 44

c) Commentary

This judgment of the Hamm Court of Appeal, dealing with both § 823 subs. 1 BGB and §§ 1, 3 ProdHaftG, reflects the conservative stance of German courts in cases involving the very obvious hazards resulting from the abusive consumption of alcohol. Similar lines of argument can be found in cases involving health problems resulting from smoking.[221] Much emphasis is thereby put on the duty of producers to inform consumers of the potential dangers of their products, but this duty is limited where these dangers are common knowledge. This is certainly true both with respect to the consumption of alcohol and cigarettes. The approach of the judiciary, which seeks to protect the freedom of *choice*, is thereby well founded. The consequences of informed choices should be allocated to the consumer. 45

9. *Landgericht München*; 29 March 2001; 19 O 8647/00[222]: Amount of Compensation for Pain and Suffering

a) Brief Summary of the Facts

The plaintiff, a 48-year-old school teacher at the time, was involved in a head-on collision with the car of the direct tortfeasor, who himself died in the crash. Apart from participating in motorised traffic, the plaintiff did not contribute to the accident. Suffering from severe injuries to the head and numerous fractures of the arms, hips, spine and knees, he is almost unable to move any of his limbs and cannot speak. The plaintiff has also lost the sight of his left eye. He is awake but practically unable to communicate, the exception being limited emotional responses towards his wife and developments in his family life. The personality of the plaintiff seems to be destroyed to a large extent, his life thereby reduced to a very basic level. He cannot eat by himself or in any other way care for his most immediate needs. 46

[221] See the recent decisions of LG Bielefeld in [2000] NJW, 2514 and OLG Frankfurt a. M. of 1 February 2001 (1 W 11/00).

[222] LG München I in [2001] NJW-RR, 1247 *et seq.*

Bound to the bed or a specially designed wheelchair, his overall condition is unlikely to improve in the future. The defendant (insurer of the actual tortfeasor) paid € 150,000 as compensation for pain and suffering prior to the court proceedings. The plaintiff claims additional damages for pain and suffering of at least € 100,000 (lump sum) as well as a monthly pension of € 250 to be paid every three months in advance.

b) Judgment of the *Landgericht*

47 The plaintiff is awarded the exceptionally high amount of just over € 500,000 for pain and suffering, the *Landgericht* granting a lump sum of € 325,000 in addition to a monthly pension of € 750. Going beyond the claim of the plaintiff and well aware of the fact that the judgment exceeds all thus far reported amounts for pain and suffering, the court places much emphasis on the exceptional gravity of the plaintiff's physical and mental injuries. The function of *Schmerzensgeld* as a compensation for the loss of enjoyment of life (so-called "Genugtuungsfunktion") is thereby stressed. In acknowledgement of the strong impairment of the plaintiff's mental capacity, the court addresses the difficulties related to the loss of personality, which is regarded as an exceptional form of injury demanding the award of damages for non-pecuniary loss disregarding the fact that the victim is unable to comprehend the changes brought about by the injury and can neither be restored to health nor feel satisfaction. In determining the amount of compensation, the *Landgericht* observes that victims of severe injuries tend to recover higher amounts for pain and suffering in out-of-court settlements than the victims in reported judgments. Further arguments offered by the court involve inflation (the last comparable judgment of the *Landgericht* granting a lump sum of € 150,000 and a monthly pension of € 300 was delivered 16 years ago and involved the quadriplegia of a 19-year-old victim) and the general tendency to award higher amounts of compensation in severe cases. Finally, the *Landgericht* argues that the community of the insured is not unreasonably burdened by these exceptional awards, which will not lead to a substantial increase of insurance premiums.

c) Commentary

48 This judgment by the *Landgericht* shows the difficulties still connected to the assessment of damages for pain and suffering in cases of severe personal injury. With a view to the exceptionally grave consequences of the accident in question, the high amount awarded by the court seems to be well justified in the given case. The judgment also reflects the need for a change in the compensation of lesser injuries (*Bagatellschäden*) in order to provide the funds necessary for an adequate compensation of grave cases. This shift, already under way on the basis of a stricter interpretation of the present § 847 BGB, will be intensified if the new § 253 subs. 2 BGB, proposed by the Federal Ministry of Justice within the framework of the SchadÄndG, is enacted. The argument that a higher level of damages in these rare cases of intense personal injury would *not* overburden the insurance system and lead to an increase of premiums, already brought forward by other courts[223] in response to a judgment of the BGH,[224] will then lose its economic relevance.

C. Literature

1. H. Kötz/G. Wagner, *Deliktsrecht* (9th edn., Luchterhand, Neuwied und Kriftel 2001)

One of the important books on German tort law, which has gained acknowledgement beyond the academic sphere, has now reached its 9th edition. With Kötz (Bucerius Law School in Hamburg) joining forces with Wagner (University of Bonn), it is now for the first time the combined achievement of two authors. The basic structure of the book was thereby left untouched. More than any other German textbook in this area of law, it seeks to explain the legal and factual problems arising from tortious acts with the help of case law, thereby adding valuable historical, social, economic and comparative information. Like many other recent publications, the authors are in a difficult position as far as the reform of German tort law is concerned. The task of keeping up-to-date with new developments is thereby mitigated by the delay of the present reform proposal. 49

2. E. Deutsch/H.-J. Ahrens, *Deliktsrecht* (4th edn., Heymanns, Cologne, Berlin, Bonn, Munich 2002)

In its 4th edition, this book on German tort law has changed its title and is now under the combined authorship of Deutsch (University of Göttingen) and Ahrens (University of Osnabrück), who is also judge at the Celle Court of Appeal. Still following along the characteristic lines of a German student textbook, the authors have widened the scope of their work and include many references to case law, which will meet the needs of practitioners. An interesting feature of this edition is the attempt to provide information on the reform of tort law presently under discussion in the *Bundestag*. This is achieved by the addition of separate sections in the relevant chapters of the book, which outline the legislative proposal of the Federal Ministry of Justice, indicate the major effects of the Bill on the present tort system, and give information on recent literature dealing with different aspects of the reform project. 50

3. G. Schlegelmilch (ed.), Geigel, *Der Haftpflichtprozeß* (23rd edn., C. H. Beck, Munich 2001)

Last revised four years ago, this book is certainly one of the most comprehensive compilations of the German law of torts. Partitioned into three main sections, it gives a very detailed picture of the general concepts underlying the German tort system, the relevant provisions from which tortious liability may 51

223 See, *e.g.*, OLG Koblenz (12 W 461/95) of 29 November 1995.
224 BGH in [1976] VersR, 967.

arise (both inside the BGB and in most strict liability statutes) and the special problems and questions connected to the procedural side of tort-based claims. Due to the extensive references to court judgments, it is of high relevance to practitioners who seek updates to very specific issues in this area of the law. As with other books presently published, the authors were confronted with the problem of dealing with the imminent reform of tort law. Though mentioned in the preface, reform proposals are not discussed in the book itself. A new edition will thus almost certainly be necessary once the *Schadensersatzänderungsgesetz* is enacted and first cases based on new rules – especially in the area of non-pecuniary loss, the compensation of fictitious costs of repair or replacement and the liability of children in motorised traffic – start reaching the courts.

4. B. S. Markesinis/H. Unberath, *The German Law of Torts* (4th edn., Hart Publishing, Oxford 2002)

52 Though published only in 2002, this comparative work of Markesinis (now co-authored by Unberath) needs to be mentioned. Written in English, the book is an excellent treatise of the German law of torts, combining in-depth commentaries on the various provisions of the BGB with over 150 translations of leading German cases. The authors give an introduction to the German civil court structure and the general background of the BGB, and cover many additional aspects to the understanding of the system, such as the constitutionalisation of private law. In the main chapters of the work, §§ 823 *et seq*. BGB, liability for others (including § 278 BGB), labour law and strict liability are discussed in detail. The most important aspect of Markesinis' work is thereby its comparative approach. Solutions achieved by German judges on the basis of the BGB are compared to judgments on the same issues, which can be found in Common law jurisdictions (especially the United Kingdom and the United States). Though under much time pressure, this new edition has managed to incorporate the changes introduced by the recent reform of the law of obligations.

5. K. Geiß/H.-P. Greiner, *Arzthaftpflichtrecht* (4th edn., C. H. Beck, Munich 2001)

53 Dealing with the special area of medical malpractice (*Arzthaftung*), Greiner has presented a new edition of this book in a very short period of time (the third edition was published only two years ago). The rapid developments in this area of law are thus well cared for, including cases reported as late as October 2000. Commenting on the routine of practitioners, who frequently resort to tort law before turning to contractual claims, Greiner emphasises the (obvious?) need to focus on both systems – contract *and* tort – in order to facilitate sound legal advice. Consequently, typical contractual situations and the relevant provisions of tort law are examined in equal detail. Much space is thereby devoted to the discussion of certain forms of defective treatment (*e.g.*, anaesthesia and prenatal treatment including abortion), the burden of proof in cases of medical malpractice and liability for insufficient information of the patient as far as the risks inherent to certain forms of medical treatment are concerned.

6. M. Meyer-Abich, *Haftungsrechtliche Erfassung ökologischer Schäden* (Nomos Verlagsgesellschaft, Baden-Baden 2001)

Addressing a fairly young aspect of tort law, this PhD thesis of Meyer-Abich examines different forms of ecological damage under the headings of damage to moveable and immoveable property (§ 823 subs. 1 BGB), damage to property-related protected interests (hunting and fishing rights, the right to use certain water resources), the infringement of protective norms (allowing compensation under § 823 subs. 2 BGB), as well as new theories of property rights developed from the perspective of an economical analysis of the law. The work of Meyer-Abich thereby focuses on the instruments of civil law, though strict liability established by German public law statutes in various specified areas (*e.g.*, for water resources or genetical engineering) presently plays the predominant role as far as the compensation of ecological damage is concerned. The author thereby argues in favour of a stronger protection of ecological interests under private law, which also performs a preventive function and may thus contribute to a better level of overall protection. From the practitioner's perspective, the discussion of possible forms of compensation for ecological damage (compensation in kind – § 249 BGB – and compensation in money – § 251 BGB –) may provide some groundwork for the difficult calculation of claims in this area of tort law. **54**

7. R. Damm/K. Rehbock, *Widerruf, Unterlassung und Schadensersatz in Presse und Rundfunk* (2nd edn., Beck, Munich 2001)

Clearly an area of high practical importance, this work by Damm and Rehbock expressly addresses practitioners dealing with the infringement of personality rights by the press and the media. Numerous court decisions are mentioned and discussed under three main headings – first, the protected interests (the general right of personality, honour, and the right of the established and operating business); second, the infringement of these interests; and third, possible remedies. Special emphasis is thereby put on the compensation of damages due to the infringement of the *allgemeines Persönlichkeitsrecht*, including an appendix covering a large amount of court decisions by order of the amount of damages awarded. As special aspects within this area, which have received much attention due to an increasing number of cases, infringements of the right to the image (*Bildnisschutz*) and infringements of the general right of personality (*allgemeines Persönlichkeitsrecht*) on the internet receive special attention. **55**

8. A. Slizyk, *Beck'sche Schmerzensgeldtabelle* (4th edn., C. H. Beck, Munich 2001)

Already mentioned as an important tool in the harmonisation of the amount of money granted for pain and suffering, this book is more than a mere compila- **56** tion of reported and unreported court decisions in the area of German tort law, providing basic information on over 2700 cases. Reflecting on recent developments in this area of law, the book also includes a concise commentary on § 847 BGB, thus far the backbone of compensation for immaterial loss. Presented in categories of injury and in order of the amount of compensation granted, the work includes separate sections on minor injuries and special forms of injury such as AIDS, psychic damage, injuries inflicted by animals, loss of enjoyment and sexual abuse.

9. S. Hacks/A. Böhm/P. Böhm, *Schmerzensgeldbeträge* (20th edn., ADAC-Verlag, Munich 2001)

57 Together with the book by Slizyk mentioned above, this second table of German cases on the amount of compensation for pain and suffering is equally voluminous. Ordered according to the amount of compensation awarded by court decisions and accessed with the help of an index, the authors give more detailed information about each decision, including a description of the injury, brief details on the type of medical treatment and duration, permanent impairments and any special circumstances of the case which are important for the judgment in question. The book also includes a very brief outline of the legal issues underlying the compensation of pain and suffering.

IX. Greece

Eugenia Dacoronia

A. Introduction

The Greek Civil Code (hereinafter GCC), in its 39th Chapter (artt. 914–938) – chapter devoted to "unlawful acts", the Greek equivalent to the concept of tort or delict[1] – follows as a rule the principle of "no liability without fault"[2]. 1

The first article of this Chapter (art. 914) is a general clause on delictual liability[3] and lays down: "A person who unlawfully and through his fault has caused prejudice to another shall be liable for compensation". This provision, one of the most fundamental in the GCC, stipulates one of the broadest sources of obligations, the act which is unlawful and due to fault, the civil delict, which on the fulfilment of the other conditions of the provision, *i.e.*, prejudice (injury, detriment, damage) and causal relation between this act and the prejudice, creates an obligation to compensate on the party responsible[4]. Only as an exception, does the GCC introduce strict liability[5] in two cases: in the case of non-domestic animals (art. 924 § 1) and in the case of liability for employees (art. 922); it also makes liability for fault to approximate to strict liability by means of reversing the burden of proof, in case of harm inflicted by a person under supervision (art. 923) or by a domestic animal (art. 924 § 2)[6] or in case of damage caused by the collapse of buildings or structures (art. 925) from natural causes and without the intervention of human force[7]. 2

[1] Ph. Christodoulou, in K.D. Kerameus/P.J. Kozyris (eds.), *Introduction to Greek Law* (in English) (2nd edn. 1993), p. 114.

[2] See among an abundant relative bibliography Ap. Georgiades, Introductory remarks to artt. 914–938, in Ap. Georgiades/M. Stathopoulos (eds.), *Civil Code* (1982), no. 21.

[3] General clauses on delictual liability are also found in the French Civil Code (art.1382) and in the Swiss Code of Obligations (art. 41).

[4] M. Stathopoulos, *Contract Law in Hellas* (in English) (1995), § 39, p. 47.

[5] For the notion of strict liability see, among others, Ap. Georgiades (*supra* note 2), nos. 21–38.

[6] According to the Athens Court of Appeal 1367/2000 [2000] *Elliniki Dikaiosini* (EllDni) 41, 798, the horse used for recreation in an urban area is not considered as a domestic animal.

[7] Athens Court of First Instance 284/2001 [2001] *Chronika Idiotikou Dikaiou* (ChrID) A', 321, 322. In the same decision it is stated that the leakage of a pipe also falls under the notion of "collapse of buildings or structures".

The supervisor, or respectively, the keeper or the owner, are then presumed to be responsible. The duty to make reparations does not arise only if they satisfy the requirements of the exculpatory proof under art. 923, or art. 924 § 2, or art. 925 respectively[8]. A *general* rule comparable to art. 914 and regarding strict liability is not provided in the GCC. No-fault liability is also found in special laws[9], which impose strict liability in certain cases. The most usual basis of justification for these cases is that the activity of the person causing the prejudice constituted a source of risk and, usually, a source from which benefits could be drawn for himself (in which case it seems even more justifiable that the beneficiary should also shoulder the losses stemming from the same source)[10].

3 After this general introduction we will proceed with the presentation of the jurisprudence of the years 2000 and 2001 and books and articles on the subject matter. Regarding legislation, no particular laws have been found.

B. Cases

1. Athens Court of Appeal 5359/2001[11], Athens Court of First Instance 2460/2001[12]: Concurrence of the Contractual and the Delictual Liability

a) Brief Summary of the Facts

4 *Athens Court of Appeal 5359/2001:* The plaintiff, a company limited by shares, claimed that the defendant issued a cheque to the order of G.L., who endorsed it to the company. The latter presented the cheque to the bank in due time, but the drawee bank refused to pay, because there were no available funds in the defendant's account. This was known to the defendant from the moment he issued the cheque. As a result the plaintiff suffered prejudice and claims from the defendant 1,480,000 drachmas[13] plus the legal interest.

5 *Athens Court of First Instance 2460/2001:* The plaintiff filled his car with petrol from the defendant's petrol-station. When leaving the petrol-station and at a distance very close to it (200 metres), the car stopped due to technical problems. The car was transported to a garage, where damages in the car's feeding-system were confirmed due to the adulterated petrol sold to him at the petrol-station. As a result the plaintiff had to spend 292,245 drachmas for repairs and he claims them from the defendant.

[8] Ph. Christodoulou (*supra* note 1), p. 115. For an analysis of the said artt. see from the latest bibliography, P. Kornilakis, *Law of Obligations, Special Part* (2000), §§ 117–119, pp. 384–394.

[9] For a list in English of these laws up to 1994 and their common features see E. Dacoronia, Mass Torts: a Greek approach in [1994] *Revue Hellenique de Droit International* (RHDI) 47, 94–96.

[10] M. Stathopoulos (*supra* note 4).

[11] [2001] *Dikaio Etaireion kai Epicheiriseon* (DEE) 7, 1010.

[12] [2001] *Nomiko Vima* (NoV) 49, 1473 *et seq.* with note of K. Christakakou, 1475.

[13] 340.75 Greek Drachmas (GRD)= 1 Euro.

b) Judgment of the Courts

6 It was repeated in the above decisions that in such a case, two *individual claims* are born (one from the delictual act and the other from the non-performance of the contractual obligation). These claims have the same aim, that is the compensation of the particular damage. The person that sustained the damage has the right to choose the one or the other claim as best serves his interests, with the only restriction that the exercise of the one claim and his relative satisfaction bear as consequence the extinction of the other claim ("free concurrence of claims").

c) Commentary

7 In Greece, it is accepted by Greek jurisprudence, and approved by commentators,[14] that when the act or omission which constitutes the contractual non-performance is simultaneously and in itself unlawful, the two liabilities, delictual and contractual, concur[15].

2. *Areios Pagos* (Greek Supreme Court, AP) 447/2000 [16]: The Violation of the General Duties of Providence and Care Constitutes an "Unlawful" Act

a) Brief Summary of the Facts

8 The second defendant was driving his taxi on the new motorway Thessaloniki – Athens, heading towards Thessaloniki, at a high speed (120 km/h), exceeding the driving speed limit of the area (60 km/h). When he came close to the crossing with the new ring road of Thessaloniki, he did not slow down, as he should have done, given that it was evening and, due to the strike of the personnel of the Public Electricity Company, there was no "external" lighting and the traffic lights of the crossing were out of order. He kept driving at the same speed and tried to pass the crossing at this velocity, but at the same time the first defendant G.P. was driving his car on the ring road, heading towards Kalochori, and having two passengers in his car, K.T. and his wife S.T.. G.P. (the first defendant), though he had a STOP sign on his road obliging him to stop and give priority to cars on the motorway, entered the crossing without the necessary control. The taxi-driver (second defendant) could not react due to his high speed and his car crashed into G.P.'s car. As a result, the car passengers K.T. and his wife S.T. were killed. The plaintiffs, members of the family of the deceased, claimed damages from both defendants for their moral harm; the children of K.T. and S.T. for their parents' deaths; K.T.'s mother for the death of her son and of her daughter-in-law.

[14] See for the relative decisions P. Kornilakis (*supra* note 8), § 104, p. 339, note 4.
[15] M. Stathopoulos (*supra* note 4), § 41, p. 49.
[16] [2001] NoV 49, 836 *et seq.*

b) Judgment of the Supreme Court

9 The Court held that both drivers were liable for violating the Highway Code. The Court also mentioned that the drivers of vehicles are obliged not only to abide by the Highway Code but to go even beyond what is dictated by the said Code when this is necessary in order to avoid a detriment or in order to diminish the detrimental consequences of an act.

c) Commentary

10 The Court, with the above decision, takes another step towards the existing tendency of broadening the meaning of the term "illegally" in art. 914[17], including therein also the violation of the *general duties of providence and care*. According to this broad interpretation of the term "illegally", not only the act that violates a prohibitory provision of the law is illegal, but also the act that violates the *general duties of providence and care* dictated by the principle of good faith. So, whoever does not take the appropriate measures in order to avoid the risk of provoking a detriment to the goods of other persons may be liable to damages for the damage caused.

3. *Areios Pagos* 5/2001[18]: The Omission as Illegal Behaviour According to Art. 914 of the GCC

a) Brief Summary of the Facts

11 The first defendant company was the owner of a supermarket, also operating an underground garage for its clients' cars and inviting the clients with special signs to park their cars in the garage while shopping. The plaintiff went shopping to this supermarket and parked in the above mentioned garage. There she was attacked by two persons on a motorbike, who smashed the car window, stole some things from the car, and then disappeared. The defendant had no security guards in the garage. The plaintiff suffered pecuniary damage, a shock, and as a result a moral harm and claims damages and moral compensation due to the unlawful act of the defendant, *i.e.* its omission to hire guards. According to the plaintiff, the defendant and its employees (the director and the person responsible for security) were under a legal obligation to hire guards in order to protect the clients who park their cars in the garage, as the said guards could have prevented the attack or arrested the criminals immediately after the act.

b) Judgment of the Supreme Court

12 The Court of Cassation held the defendant and its employees (the director and the person responsible for security) liable, because, out of negligence, they had not hired security guards. It ruled that illegal behaviour also exists when there is an obligation for protection dictated by the law or the contract or the

[17] See the very interesting note of Ph. Doris under the above decision AP 447/2000 [2001] NoV 49, 840, and P. Kornilakis (*supra* note 8), § 109 IV, pp. 354, 355.

[18] [2001] ChrID A', 310, 311. See also AP 1454/2001 [2001] ChrID A', 796, 797.

good faith according to the prevailing social understanding, and, more particularly, when somebody has created a situation of danger with his previous act, and he has not taken the necessary measures to avoid such a danger. Such an obligation for protection also exists when an enterprise has addressed to the public an invitation to visit or use a particular space of its premises; in this case the enterprise should have taken all necessary and appropriate measures for the security of the visitors.

c) Commentary

The behaviour that can lead to an obligation for damages according to art. 914 of the GCC can be either a positive act or an omission. An omission constitutes illegal behaviour when there was a special legal obligation for the protection of the right or interest that has been inflicted and for the avoidance of the detrimental result. The Supreme Court gives an illustration of such a behaviour. **13**

4. *Areios Pagos* 1504/2000[19], *Areios Pagos* 14/1999 (Full Bench)[20]: Direct Prejudice as a Presupposition for the Liability of Art. 914 of the GCC

a) Brief Summary of the Facts

Areios Pagos 1504/2000. E.A., who was killed in a car accident due to the defendant's fault, was a partner in a general partnership (the plaintiff), participating at the gains and losses at a percentage of 25%. The plaintiff claimed that E.A.'s death led to the dissolution of the partnership and that, from this dissolution, the partnership suffered pecuniary damages, as, from the commercial activity of the deceased, the said partnership had a net income of 100,000 drachmas per day, 75% of which belonged to the partnership. Consequently and because of E.A.'s wrongful death, it has lost and continues to lose 75,000 drachmas daily. For this reason the partnership claims from the defendant 135,000,000 drachmas as lost income for the 15 years since E.A.'s death. **14**

Areios Pagos 14/1999 (full bench): After a request of the National Bank of Greece (defendant), the company "Athens Paper-Factory S.A." was illegally submitted under the provisions of l. 1386/1983 regulating the "Organisation for the Economic Restructuring of Enterprises", since there were no legal presuppositions (excessive debts and obvious economic weakness) for its characterisation as a "problematic enterprise" (art. 7 §1 of l. 1386/1983). Its board of directors was replaced by an appointed administration and, as a result, the plaintiffs lost the management of the company. The plaintiffs' shares were representing at that moment about 60% of the share capital, but due to successive increases of capital this percentage was reduced to 33.24% after the first increase and finally to 0.003% after the second one. As a result, the real value of every share was radically devaluated and the 3 plaintiffs suffered damages **15**

[19] [2001] DEE 7, 497.
[20] [2000] NoV 48, 454 *et seq.*

of 86,177,842,000 drachmas, 41,885,681,000 drachmas and 1,373,301,000 drachmas respectively. For these amounts the plaintiffs asked to be indemnified from the State.

b) Judgment of the Court

16 *Areios Pagos 1504/2000:* The Supreme Court has considered that the general partnership has no right for damages against the person who has caused the death of a partner, from whose commercial activity the partnership also earned gains, because the said partnership was only *indirectly* prejudiced by the unlawful act. From artt. 914, 297 and 298 of the GCC[21] it is deduced that only the person who has been *directly* prejudiced may ask for reparations. To the contrary, the person who has been *indirectly* prejudiced, that is the one who has sustained a damage from the injury of a legal good appertaining to another person, has a right to damages only if such a right is specifically provided by the law[22]. Such a right is provided: a) in art. 928 subpara. b', according to which, in case of death, the person bound to pay damages is also bound to make reparations, for the loss of maintenance or services, to the person who is entitled by law to claim maintenance or the performance of services by the victim[23] and b) in art. 929 subpara. b' of the GCC, according to which, in case of injury to the body or the health of a person, the person bound to pay damages, must also compensate the third party, who, being entitled by law to claim the performance of services by the victim, is now deprived of the services because of the delict committed against the victim.

17 *Areios Pagos 14/1999 (full bench):* According to this very interesting decision related to the above stated issue, the illegal submission of a corporation to the provisions of art. 7 § 1 of the l.1386/1983 regarding the Organisation for the Economic Restructuring of Enterprises – to which all problematic enterprises were submitted –, though the said corporation was not a problematic one, and the illegal increase of its share capital without the prior decision of the general assembly of the old shareholders and without giving the latter the right of preference in acquiring the new shares, bears as consequence the devaluation of the real value of the old shares; thus the patrimony of the old shareholders is *directly* affected provoking not an *indirect* but a *direct* damage to them, who

[21] Art. 297 of the GCC states: "A person who is obligated to pay reparations shall use money. Nevertheless, the court may, taking into consideration special circumstances, order restitution to be made in kind in so far as this is not contrary to the interest of the creditor" and art. 298 of the GCC states: "The reparations shall include the decrease in the existing property of the creditor as well as lost profits. Profit is deemed to have been lost which could probably have been expected in the ordinary course of events or according to the special circumstances, especially in the light of preparations and arrangements made". [The translation of the said articles is taken from the book of K.D. Kerameus/P.J. Kozyris (*supra* note 1)].

[22] See relatively P. Kornilakis (*supra* note 8), § 124, pp. 407, 408.

[23] It has to be noted that, according to AP 857/2001 [2001] ChrID A', 704, 705, this obligation continues to exist even if the person entitled by law to claim maintenance cohabits later permanently with another person in free union, as the said obligation does not constitute a duty to alimony – which ceases, according to art. 1444 § 2 of the GCC, when the person entitled to it remarries or lives with somebody else in free union –, but it has a compensatory character.

may ask for damages according to the above mentioned artt. 914, 298, 297 of the GCC, also against the State, according to art. 104 of the Introductory Law of the GCC, in view also of the Art. 1 § 1 of First Additional Protocol of the European Convention on Human Rights, which states that all natural or legal persons have the right to be respected in their patrimony.

c) Commentary

The Supreme Court seems to overrule with the above mentioned decision 14/1999 (full bench) its previous decision 1285/1980[24] – followed steadily by the jurisprudence of the Courts of First Instance –, according to which the liability is towards the legal entity itself for the detriment to the assets of the company; the shareholders are third persons who bear only *indirect* damage and therefore they are not entitled to damages. 18

The above decision generated a lively scientific discussion at the Athens Bar last year, where the Attorney-at-Law G. Costopoulos presented an interesting paper on "The indirect injury of the shareholder and the decision 14/1999 (full bench) of the Court of Cassation"[25]. 19

The author of the said paper finds the recent decision of the Court of Cassation convincing. According to him, however, there is no overruling of the decision of 1980, as the two decisions do not interpret in a different way art. 22b of the l.2190/1920; they arrive at different conclusions only because the facts presented to them are different. In the one case money was embezzled by a member of the board of directors; through this embezzlement the legal entity was affected and the assets of the company were diminished; consequently the shareholders were also affected, due to their participation in a company that had its assets diminished because of the embezzlement. In the other case, always according to the said author, the company did not suffer any injury, as the increase of the share capital, the issue of new shares, without the right of preference does not seem to diminish the assets of the company, but only the value – internal value – of each share. So this increase affects the shareholder *directly* and not as a reflection of the diminution of the company's assets, as in the previous decision of the Court of Cassation. 20

5. *Areios Pagos* 1257/2001[26]: The Causal Relationship as a Presupposition for the Liability of Art. 914 of the GCC

a) Brief Summary of the Facts

A.P., 67 years old, trying to cross a road, was struck by a motorbike, which was driven by the first defendant. As a result, she sustained severe injuries. The accident was due basically to the driver's fault, but also to A.P.' s fault, as she did not cross the road carefully. The victim stayed in hospital for 10 days 21

[24] *Epitheorissi Emporikou Dikaiou* (EED) 32, 394.
[25] Published in [2001] DEE 7, 348–354.
[26] [2001] ChrID A', 699, 700.

and returned home. 2 days later she died, and it was confirmed that her death was due to a massive lung embolism. Doctors, who made the post-mortem examination, also certified that the severe injuries caused by the accident are not the main and direct cause of the lung trouble and that there is no causal relationship between the injuries and her death, since 12 days had intervened between the accident and the victim's death.

b) Judgment of the Court

22 According to the above decision of the Supreme Court, the causal relationship is not excluded if a special predisposition of the injured party also contributed to the occurrence or the extent of the injury. This causal relationship is not levied either, when, after the detrimental result, another event takes place, which augments the detrimental result already occurred, as long as the situation to which the injured person was reduced to, because of the previous detrimental act, contributed to this augmentation. Consequently, the first defendant's negligent act is causally related to the detrimental result (death of A.P).

c) Commentary

23 One of the presuppositions of art. 914 of the GCC is the existence of a causal relationship between the act or the omission and the damage[27]. Such a causal relationship exists when the act or omission is, according to the dictation of common usage, capable of entailing the prejudice and it has actually caused it.

6. *Areios Pagos* 619/2000[28], *Areios Pagos* 1071/2000[29], *Areios Pagos* 1128/2000[30]: Concurrent Fault

a) Brief Summary of the Facts

24 *Areios Pagos 619/2000:* A motorbike and a car collided. Responsible for the crash was the driver of the car (first defendant), because he was not careful and drove into a crossing with a speed exceeding 100 km/h. As a result of this careless driving he caused the fatal wounding of the motorcyclist. The motorcyclist, on the other hand, was found under the influence of alcohol and did not wear a helmet.

25 *Areios Pagos 1071/2000:* No facts are mentioned.

26 *Areios Pagos 1128/2000:* A motorbike driven by the plaintiff and a car collided. The driver of the car drove under the influence of alcohol and therefore he was unable to drive carefully, so he crossed the dividing line and passed to the opposite traffic route, causing the accident. The plaintiff did not have a

[27] According to Ph. Doris, NoV 49, 839, 840, it is better to speak about causal relationship between the damage on the one hand and the rule of law that has been violated on the other.
[28] [2001] EllDni 42, 73, 74 = [2001] NoV 49, 1010 *et seq.*
[29] [2001] EllDni 42, 392.
[30] [2001] ChrID A', 31

driving license nor the required capacity and experience of a motorcyclist and he was driving very close to the dividing line of the road.

b) Judgment of the Court

According to the jurisprudence of the Supreme Court, the violation of the provisions of the Highway Code by the injured party (*i.e.* the consumption of alcohol or the omission of the use of a helmet by a motorbike rider) as such does not mean that the injured party has contributed by his own conduct to the damage. It constitutes, however, an element, that is going to be taken into consideration by the Court. The latter will judge whether there is a causal relation between the particular behaviour in violation of the Code and the prejudice. **27**

c) Commentary

The GCC provides in its art. 300 that if the injured party has contributed by his own conduct to the causing or the extent of the damage he has sustained, the court may, at its free discretion, either not award compensation or reduce its sum. Art. 300 of the GCC applies in any case of damage, caused either because of non-performance of a contract or as a result of a delictual act. The above decisions correctly state that a causal relation between: i) the behaviour of the injured party, which is in violation of the provisions of the Highway Code, and ii) the prejudice is necessary in order to speak of concurrent fault. **28**

7. *Areios Pagos* 426/2000[31]: Additional Pecuniary Compensation

a) Brief Summary of the Facts

Areios Pagos 426/2000: By the defendant's culpable act the plaintiff suffered severe injuries, which caused his permanent disablement. The percentage of disablement (95%) was confirmed in 1992, so it was not known yet to the plaintiff, when he first brought his action against the defendant in 1989, and it could not have been foreseen by the court either. The plaintiff claims now 5,000,000 drachmas as an additional pecuniary compensation for the additional moral harm he suffered from the unexpected consequences of his injuries (an almost total permanent disablement). **29**

b) Judgment of the Supreme Court

The adjudication of pecuniary compensation for the moral harm of a person injured in a car accident does not preclude the possibility of this person to ask later, with a new court action, additional pecuniary compensation. **30**

In order to ask for such additional compensation, the injured party has to prove that the consequences of the unlawful act and the moral harm have been **31**

[31] [2000] EllDni 41, 1575, 1576 = [2001] ChrID A', 125, 126. See also AP 715/2000 [2001] EllDni 42, 98, 99.

manifested later and that the court that adjudicated the previous pecuniary compensation could not have foreseen these new consequences.

8. *Areios Pagos* 1056/2000[32]: Insurance Contributions and Damages

a) Brief Summary of the Facts

32 The plaintiff suffered severe injuries due to the defendant's culpable act; as a result he had to stop working. If he had continued to work regularly, he would have earned in total 7,720,753 drachmas as mixed salaries for the period from January 1995 – 31 December 1997. Instead he received a total amount of 6,327,175 drachmas as a disablement pension. The plaintiff claimed the difference, 1,393,578 drachmas (7,720,753 – 6,327,175 = 1,393,578), from the defendant.

33 According to the Court of Appeal's decision, the plaintiff lost only his *net* salaries, *i.e.* the money left from the amount of 7,720,753 drachmas after the subtraction of his insurance contributions amounting to 1,227,600 drachmas. As a result, the plaintiff had (always according to the Court of Appeal's opinion) a claim against the defendant amounting to 165,978 drachmas [6,493,153 drachmas (net salaries) – 6,327,175 drachmas (disablement pension) = 165,978 drachmas].

b) Judgment of the Supreme Court

34 The Supreme Court found that the Court of Appeal violated the law, when considering that the plaintiff was entitled only to his *net* salaries and ruled that he is entitled to the *mixed* ones, the ones he would have had, had he not been injured. More particularly, the Supreme Court ruled that, according to insurance legislation, if the employee has temporarily ceased to work because of an accident that has rendered him temporarily incapable of providing his services, the employer is exempted from his obligation to pay the insurance contributions that burden him. These contributions however continue to be a gain for the employee, who loses it for the above reason. So, if the employee wants to have the enjoyment of the insurance contributions, he will have to pay them from his own money, or he will have to work later for an equal amount of time. Therefore, the loss of the insurance contributions constitutes a loss for the employee, who can ask the said contributions as damages from the person who has caused the accident that rendered him incapable to work.

c) Commentary

35 Art. 929 of the GCC states that in case of injury to the body or the health of a person, damages include, in addition to medical expenses and the damage already accrued, the detriment which the act occasions to future earnings, and the additional expenses said person will have to bear because of an increase in his needs. The question that has arisen is if the employee who has been tempo-

[32] [2001] EllDni 42, 387.

rarily incapable of working due to an injury, may, according to this article, ask from the tortfeasor also the insurance contributions that the employer is not obliged to pay, as long as the employee does not provide his services. According to the jurisprudence of the Supreme Court, the injured person may ask from the author of the accident damages for his incapacity to work that amount to his total (mixed) salaries, that he would have had, had he not been injured (in which damages are included the insurance contributions that the employer must retain from the employee's salaries).

9. *Areios Pagos* 1073/2001[33]: The Function of the Independent Claim of Art. 931 of the GCC (Additional Compensation for Disfiguration)

a) Brief Summary of the Facts

Due to a car accident caused exclusively by the car driver's culpable act, the plaintiff suffered severe injuries, which led to the amputation of limbs of his body. The plaintiff was not able to work anymore and claimed damages (the amount of money he could have earned from his work if the accident had not happened). Moreover, he claims 10,000,000 drachmas as an additional compensation for his disfiguration according to art. 931 of the GCC. **36**

b) Judgment of the Court

Art. 931 of the GCC dictates that the invalidity or disfiguration caused to the injured party is particularly taken into consideration when adjudicating damages if this invalidity or disfiguration affects the future of the person who suffered such invalidity or disfiguration. The Supreme Court gives definitions of the terms "invalidity", "disfiguration" and "future". As "invalidity" is meant any lack of the corporal, mental or psychical integrity of a person; as "disfiguration" any substantial distortion of the external appearance of the person, which is not necessarily determined by the science of medicine, but by the notions of life. As "future" is meant the professional, economic and social evolution of the person. Certainty of a negative influence in the future of the person is not required. A simple possibility, according to the usual course of things, suffices. In the professional–economic field, the invalidity or disfiguration of the person, according to the dictations of common usage, constitutes a negative element in everyday competition for such a person's economic evolution and promotion. These negative consequences are, according to the Supreme Court, even more intense in periods of economic difficulties and tightness in the business market; those who have an invalidity or disfiguration have a disadvantage and therefore they bear a bigger risk than their healthy colleagues to be found without a job. **37**

The provision of art. 931 of the GCC introduces an independent claim for the compensation of a future pecuniary damage, that is not covered by art. 929 or art. 932 of the GCC. **38**

[33] [2001] ChrID A', 700–701, followed by a note of G. Iatrou, [2001] ChrID A', 701–703.

39 The aim of the provision is to offer the injured party a lump sum, in addition to the amount adjudicated for damages. This lump sum goes beyond the damage adjudicated according to art. 929 of the GCC, on the ground that the invalidity or disfiguration will in the future cause difficulties in the injured person's professional–economic progress.

c) Commentary

40 G. Jatrou[34], commenting the above decision, considers more convincing the prevailing in theory view[35], according to which art. 931 of the GCC does not introduce an independent claim for the compensation of a future pecuniary damage, that is not covered by art. 929 or art. 932 of the GCC. It only has an instructive character, intending to instruct the judge to take particular consideration of the disablement or disfiguration when determining the amount of damages to be adjudicated for pecuniary damage or moral harm.

10. *Areios Pagos* 21/2000 (full bench)[36], *Areios Pagos* 447/2000[37], *Areios Pagos* 1114/2000[38], *Areios Pagos* 97/2001[39]: Notion of the Terms "Family of the Victim" and "Pain and Suffering" in Art. 932 of the GCC

a) Brief Summary of the Facts

41 *AP 21/2000 (full bench):* E.E. was killed. Her sister's husband and her sister's son, *i.e.* E.E.'s brother-in-law and nephew, claimed pecuniary compensation for moral suffering, as belonging to the family of the victim.

42 *AP 447/2000:* See above, case 2, [8].

43 *AP 1114/2000:* S.P., negligently driving her husband's car, insured by the defendant (insurance company), collided with a lorry and caused the fatal accident, where both she and her husband as well as their two minor children in the car died. The plaintiffs (a son of the deceased couple and some uncles) claimed damages and pecuniary compensation for moral suffering, as belonging to the family of the victim.

44 *AP 97/2001:* K, still a foetus, when his father, A, was killed in a car accident, claims pecuniary compensation (10,000,000 drachmas) for moral pain and suffering.

[34] [2001] ChrID A', 701–703.

[35] Expressed by K. Beis, [1998] Diki, 281; Doris, [2000] NoV, 36; Ap. Georgiades, *Law of Obligations, General Part* (1999), § 62, no. 96; Vossinakis, in Ap. Georgiades/Stathopoulos (eds.), *Civil Code* (1982), art. 931, no. 1.

[36] [2001] NoV 49, 599 *et seq.* with a note of Ph. Doris, NoV 49, 600–602 = [2001] ChrID, A', 117 *et seq.*, with a note of L. Kitsaras, ChrID A', 118–120.

[37] [2001] NoV 49, 836 *et seq.*, with a note of Ph. Doris, (*supra* note 27).

[38] [2000] EllDni 41, 1593.

[39] [2001] ChrID A', 120, with commentaries by L. Kitsaras.

b) Judgment of the Court

AP 21/2000 (full bench): The claim was rejected. According to the Supreme Court, though it is not specially defined in art. 932 of the GCC, to the family of the victim belong, apart from the spouse, also the closest relatives of the deceased, as long as they are closely connected to him and suffered from his loss, irrespectively of whether they cohabitated with him or not. Among the said persons are not included the nephews and brothers-in-law, even if no other close relatives exist. So brothers-in-law and nephews do not belong to the family of the victim entitled to pecuniary compensation for moral suffering according to art. 932 of the GCC. **45**

Anyhow, the closest relatives, who are entitled to pain and suffering, are qualified for that only if they showed love and affection to the deceased whilst he was alive, and the deceased had the same feelings towards them. **46**

AP 447/2000: The children of K.T. and S.T., as members of their family, were entitled to pecuniary compensation for moral suffering for their parents' deaths according to art. 932 of the GCC; K.T.' s mother was also entitled to pecuniary compensation for moral suffering not only for the death of her son but also for the death of her daughter-in-law. **47**

AP 1114/2000: The son of the deceased couple, as belonging to the family of the victim, is entitled to pecuniary compensation for moral suffering. The uncles were not considered members of the family who can seek pecuniary compensation for moral suffering. According to the Supreme Court, though it is not specially defined in art. 932 of the GCC, to the family of the victim belong, apart from the spouse, also the closest relatives of the deceased, irrespectively of whether they cohabitated with him or not. So to the family of the deceased belong: the spouse, the descendants, the ascendants, the brothers and sisters, as well as the sons and daughters–in-law and the fathers and mothers-in-law. **48**

AP 97/2001: K, though a foetus when his father, A, was killed in a car accident, is entitled to pecuniary compensation for moral pain and suffering. The amount of money given as pain and suffering can also cover the *future* pain and suffering that the foetus or baby will certainly feel from the loss of his father or mother *later*, when he will be mature enough to feel he is an orphan. **49**

c) Commentary

(I) According to art. 932 GCC in case of delict, irrespectively of the damages for the pecuniary injury, the court may adjudicate a reasonable, according to its judgment, amount of money for the moral or non-pecuniary harm, which the plaintiff has suffered as a consequence of the unlawful act. In case of death this amount of money may be adjudicated to the *family* of the victim as pain and suffering. **50**

51 A lot of discussion has taken place regarding the meaning of the term "family" in order to fix the circle of persons who may be entitled to compensation for pain and suffering. The above mentioned decisions of the Supreme Court dictate that to the family of the deceased belong: the spouse, the descendants, the ascendants, the brothers and sisters, as well as the sons and daughters-in-law and the fathers and mothers-in-law. These persons can seek compensation for pain and suffering. Among the said persons are not included the nephews and the sisters and brothers-in-law, even if no other close relatives exist.

52 In the note of Ph. Doris, under the above mentioned decision 21/2000 (full bench), it is mentioned that the said decision correctly states that the meaning of the term "family of the victim" is deliberately not defined in art. 932 of the GCC "obviously because the legislator did not want to delimit in an obligatory way the boundaries of an institution, which, because of its nature, is submitted to the influence of the social differentiations in the course of time". L. Kitsaras, however, in his note under the same decision, points out that, though the Court of Cassation starts from the correct point stating that the legislator leaves free field to the judge to define the "family" in each particular case, nevertheless it tries to find out the "true" meaning of the term "family" not in relation to the facts of each particular case. This is, according to the author of the note, not compatible with the elasticity the legislator wanted to give to the term "family" in order to meet the needs of the changing social conditions.

53 According to our view, the Court of Cassation is correct in trying to find out the "true" meaning of the term "family", not connected to the particular facts of each case. The legislator has not defined the said term, so that the Court can take into consideration what society understands as "family" in a particular period of time. The "family" of the beginning of the 20th century is not the same with the "family" of the beginning of the 21st century, when unmarried couples, or even homosexual couples may be considered as families. This, however, does not mean that the notion of "family" changes depending on each particular case that is presented to the Court in the same period of time. The Court must give a definition of the "family", not according to the particular facts of the case, but according to what society considers as "family" at the time of the implementation of art. 932 of the GCC[40]. This is, according to our view, what the legislator wanted by not choosing to define the term "family" in the GCC.

54 (II) A very important decision is the decision 97/2001 of the Supreme Court. This is the first decision of the Greek Supreme Court, which, following the new scientific views related to the interpretation of art. 932 subpara. c' of the GCC and the numerous relative decisions of the Courts of Appeal of the last 15 years, states that compensation for pain and suffering can also be sought for the foetus[41] as well as for the baby of a very young age; and this

[40] See also Ph. Doris (*supra* note 27).

[41] *Contra* AP 583/1997 [1998] EllDni, 88. AP 1153/1993 [1995] EllDni, 321.

irrespectively of their incapacity to feel any pain already at the time of the death.

The Supreme Court for the first time recognizes that the adjudicated amount can be for *future* pain and suffering (argument from art. 298 of the GCC, which recognizes the restitution of the future patrimonial damage). The jurisprudence of the Supreme Court, before the decision 97/2001, did not recognize such a possibility, because on the one hand damages for pain and suffering were given only for *present and actual* pain and suffering and on the other because foetuses and babies have not yet a formed moral personality which would enable them to feel a grievance. 55

The decision 97/2001 is followed by a commentary of L. Kitsaras, who finds its ruling just and in accordance with the abundant jurisprudence of the Courts of Appeal and of First Instance. 56

11. *Areios Pagos* 1239/2000[42]: Beginning of the Prescription Period in Case of a Continuing Damage

a) Brief Summary of the Facts

Due to a fire caused on 19 July 1973 by a culpable act of the defendant's (the Public Electricity Company) employees, the plaintiff's house was completely burnt down. The plaintiff brought against the defendant: a) an action on 17 July 1978, claiming damages amounting to 850,000 drachmas and b) a new action on 19 May 1986, claiming the readjustment of the amount of damages claimed with the first action to the amount of 4,914,040 drachmas, due to the subsequent rise of the price index. The plaintiff had knowledge of the damage and of the person of the tortfeasor already in March 1974. 57

b) Judgment of the Court

According to art. 937 § 1 of the GCC, the claim based on tort is prescribed after 5 years have elapsed from the moment the injured party has knowledge of the damage and of the person of the tortfeasor. The Supreme Court ruled that by knowledge of the damage under the said article is understood the knowledge of the detrimental consequences of the act, not the knowledge of the exact extent of the detriment or of the amount of damages and that in case of a continuing damage, the claim of damage is not being reborn continuously; the claim for the future damage is also born from the beginning, from the moment the act has started to send out its detrimental consequences, given that, according to the usual course of things, such a future damage could be foreseen. From this moment the 5-year prescription period provided by art. 937 § 1 of the GCC starts running for the whole damage. Accordingly, when the plaintiff filed the new action in 1986, her claim had already been prescribed. The total damages (including the part claimed with the new action) 58

[42] [2001] ChrID A', 313, 314

could not be considered as unforeseeable, since, according to the usual course of things, such a rise of the price index could have been foreseen[43].

c) Commentary

59 The Supreme Court confirms the jurisprudence of the previous years[44], according to which, in order to find out if a new prescription period starts, it has to be determined whether the detrimental consequences of an act are unforeseeable and unexpected or foreseeable. Only if the detrimental consequences are *unforeseeable*, does a new independent prescription period for the claim start.

C. Selected Issues of Civil Liability – Civil Liability of Banks and of Their Clients

1. *Areios Pagos* 99/2000[45]: Civil Liability of Banks for Illegal Acts

a) Brief Summary of the Facts

60 The defendant (a bank) has exercised, in an abusive way, its right to choose the employees to be promoted each year. As a result, the plaintiff was not promoted and therefore, with the action filed, he claims his promotion and damages caused by the bank's abusive act.

b) Judgment of the Court

61 The abusive promotion of one of the bank's employees instead of another, who had such a right, is an illegal act and constitutes the delict of art. 914 of the GCC.

2. Court of Appeal of Nafplio 679/2000[46], Court of First Instance of Piraeus 1187/1999[47]: Civil Liability of Banks for Acts *Contra Bonos Mores* Against Their Clients and Against Other Banks

a) Brief Summary of the Facts

62 *Court of Appeal of Nafplio 679/2000:* The plaintiff claims with his action, that in 1991 the defendant bank granted him a loan of 40,000,000 drachmas, that

[43] It has to be noted here, however, that according to Ap. Georgiades, in Ap. Georgiades/M. Stathopoulos (eds.), *Civil Code* (1982), art. 937, no. 19, the rise by leaps and bounds of the price index, that is due to an extraordinary event, such as the declaration of a world war, may qualify the detrimental consequences as unforeseeable.

[44] See relatively Ap.Georgiades, ibid. P.Kornilakis, *Law of Obligations, Special Part* (2000), § 132, p. 437, note 91.

[45] [2000] EllDni, 1015.

[46] [2001] ChrID A', 227 *et seq*., followed by a note of E. Nezeriti, ChrID A', 229, for the relation between the two general clauses, the one of art. 919 of the GCC (behaviour against *bonos mores*) and the other of art. 281 of GCC (abusive exercise of a right).

[47] [2001] ChrID A', 322–325, which has adopted the legal opinion of Ap. Georgiades, published in [2001] ChrID A', 372–376, under the title "Liability of the Bank against third parties when exercising its credit policy – *Contra bonos mores* provocation of damage from a Bank by giving incorrect information to another in relation to the trustworthiness of a person".

he only made use of a part of the loan and that the bank, under the pretext that he did not make use of the rest of the loan, illegally terminated the loan agreement. That thereafter, the bank exercised an intolerable psychological pressure on him, obliging him, under the menace that, otherwise, it will proceed to the auction of his goods, to accept the detrimental to him change of the terms of the loan, without even drafting and notifying him of the relative document, so that the exact content of the terms of the loan remained unknown to him. As a result of these culpable and contrary to *bonos mores* and to good faith acts of the bank, the plaintiff sustained damages and asks to be indemnified by the bank.

Court of First Instance of Piraeus 1187/1999: The plaintiff, an international maritime bank, having its registered seat in Edinburgh, Scotland, with an office in Piraeus, Greece, claims that since 1991 the third defendant (also a bank), acting on behalf of two international credit establishments (the second and the third defendants), had developed a banking and credit relationship in favour of the maritime company "BF", with a giro of credit amounting to 65,900,000 U.S. dollars. That since 1994 "BF" went into default, and was unable to meet the conditions of the credit contracts. That the defendants, however, instead of exercising their rights that derived from the said contracts, tried to find another banking establishment in good faith to finance "BF" to their interest. That in 1996 the plaintiff, based on the gains (fares) of the ships of "BF"'s group and on "BF"'s collaboration with the first and second defendants, being two international credit establishments, that would grant "BF", according to their affirmations, a new loan for 100,000,000 U.S. dollars, opened a current credit account in favour of "BF" up to 6,000,000 U.S. dollars. That later, as this credit limit was used, the plaintiff proceeded to an advance payment of 500,000 U.S. dollars to "BF", to enable the latter to pay its creditors. The plaintiff claimed that it would not have proceeded to the financing of "BF" if the defendants had not intentionally deceived them, by ascertaining falsely and intentionally that "BF" was trustworthy and that they themselves intended to finance "BF", whilst on the contrary they had decided, due to "BF"'s untrustworthiness, to revoke the totality of their credits and proceed with court actions against "BF". This contrary to *bonos mores* behaviour of the defendants caused the plaintiff a damage of 528,840.04 U.S. dollars, amount given as credit to "BF", and asks to be indemnified by the defendants. 63

b) Judgment of the Courts

Court of Appeal of Nafplio 679/2000: This judgment is very interesting, as it analyses in detail when a financial institution, such as a bank, may be liable under art. 919 of the GCC, according to which, whoever intentionally, in a manner which violates the commands of morality, causes damage to another is bound to make reparation to the other for any damage thus caused. 64

According to the Court, in order to be liable for damage caused to their clients, the institution's organs must have shown behaviour contrary to *bonos* 65 *mores*. Such behaviour is shown, according to the above mentioned decision, when:

66 i) the financial institution, exploiting its monopolistic or dominant position against its client, undertakes, specially at a critical economic period for the client, measures, which, in substance, will destroy him, instead of offering him the usual to the banking transactions possible financial solutions, which will enable him to surpass the economic danger. These facilities must be substantial, that is they must aim not only at the provisional prolongation of the client's (usually being an enterprise) viability, but at his definitive survival;

67 ii) the financial institution, exploiting its monopolistic or dominant position against its client, threatens the latter that it will terminate the loan agreement and ask for the whole amount to be paid. This behaviour obviously violates the commands of morality, taken into consideration the above mentioned economic superiority of the financial institution. This threat does not constitute the threat of art. 150 of the GCC (that is a threat, which, under the circumstances, instills fear in a sane person and poses a serious and immediate danger to the life, physical integrity, liberty, honour or patrimony of such a person or of persons closely related to him, and which may render void the juridical act resulting from the declaration of will, based on this threat), but constitutes an abusive exercise of the contractual rights, as, with this behaviour, the financial institution excessively binds the client and suppresses his economic, commercial and contractual freedom;

68 iii) though the financial institution has repeatedly promised the debtor, using deceiving means, that, due to the latter's economic situation, it will reformulate the existing debt in a manner convenient to him, ultimately the bank does not live up to its promise;

69 iv) the financial institution does not show to all clients the same attitude, does not treat all of them in the same manner or does not exercise towards all of them the principle of proportionality. The principle of proportionality is violated when the financial institution takes hard measures for some of its clients and favourable measures for others, or when it takes against the client some measures, which exceed the necessary ones, in order to satisfy its legal interests and which are not taken for other clients.

70 *Court of First Instance of Piraeus 1187/1999:* The Court ruled that the bank violates the commands of artt. 914 and 919 of the GCC when it gives incorrect information to another bank in relation to the good standing of a client; the bank must have acted out of *dolus eventualis* (eventual wilful conduct)[48], that is it must have foreseen the unlawful result (damage of the other bank) as a

[48] About the meaning of "fault" in the Greek law (in English) see M. Stathopoulos (*supra* note 4), § 251, p. 169

likely (not necessary) consequence of its conduct (giving incorrect information) and in spite of this, it has accepted this result.

c) Commentary

Art. 919 of the GCC is a special provision that complements the provision of art. 914 of the GCC, as it extends the delictual liability also to cases where there is no direct offence of a particular right or of a protected interest. 71

3. Court of Appeal of Thessaloniki 1335/2000[49]: Civil Liability of Banks for Acts of Their Employees

a) Brief Summary of the Facts

The plaintiff asked an employee of the defendant bank to withdraw a sum of money (1,000,000 drachmas) from his account, convert it into dollars and then deposit it in a new account. The transaction took place regularly. After some days, the plaintiff visited the bank again and once again asked the same employee to convert into dollars an amount of money equal to the previous one (1,000,000 drachmas) and then deposit it in the above mentioned account in foreign currency and to convert also another sum of money (1,630,000 drachmas) into Deutsch Marks and then deposit it in another new foreign currency account. This time the bank's employee did not deposit the sums of money (2,630,000 drachmas) but embezzled them. 72

b) Judgment of the Court

The Bank was held liable according to art. 922 of the GCC for the embezzlement of amounts of money made by its employee, who acted in abuse of his task. According to the said article, a person who appoints another to perform a function is bound to make reparations to a third party for the harm caused by an unlawful and culpable act or omission committed by the other in the execution of his task. A harm caused by the other in abuse of this task also generates liability of the person who appointed the other. 73

There is an abuse of task, when the unlawful act was committed within the limits of the tasks delegated to the third party, but in violation of the orders given to the latter or in excess of his duties. 74

c) Commentary

The above decision is in conformity with the jurisprudence of the Supreme Court, when, while interpreting the said art. 922 of the GCC, it considers that the person, who appoints another, is liable for reparations not only for the harm caused by this other *in the execution* of his task, but also when the harm was caused *in abuse* of this task. 75

[49] [2000] *Armenopoulos* (Arm), 926, 927.

4. *Areios Pagos* 355/2001[50]: Civil Liability of Clients

a) Brief Summary of the Facts

76 The client of a bank collects a larger amount of money (3,950,000 drachmas) than what she should have (395,000 drachmas), due to a mistake of the cashier. The client, however, conceals the mistake and then refuses to return the money when the mistake was found out.

b) Judgment of the Court

77 It was ruled that, by this behaviour, the client violates the principles of good faith and mutual trust and is obliged to make reparations according to art. 914 of the GCC.

5. *Areios Pagos* 1043/2001[51], *Areios Pagos* 653/2001[52]: Civil Liability of the Press

a) Summary of the Facts

78 No special facts are mentioned in the above decisions, but they deal with cases of offense of the honour and reputation of a person that took place through the press.

b) Judgment of the Court

79 *Areios Pagos 1043/2001:* Art. 1 of the l. 1178/1981 regarding the civil liability of the press introduces strict liability for the owner of the printed matter in case of a published matter that offenses the honour and reputation of a person. This strict liability exists even if the elements of fault exist only at the person of the author, the publisher or the publishing director. These persons are all *in solido* liable with the owner according to art. 926 of the GCC.

80 According to the Supreme Court, the provision of § 4 of the only article of the l. 2243/1994 (that has replaced § 2 of the only article of the above mentioned l. 1178/1981), which states that the amount adjudicated as moral harm, according to the above mentioned art. 932 of the GCC, for certain illegal acts made by the press, cannot be less than 10,000,000 drachmas, is not contrary to art. 2 of the Greek Constitution, stating that the respect and the protection of the value of the human being constitutes a primary obligation of the State. It is not contrary either to art. 14 § 1 of the said Constitution for the protection of the Press, as, according to art. 26 § 1 thereof, the legislator, when regulating the relations of human beings and the sanctions and obligations that derive from their behaviour, has the right to fix maximum or minimum limits, within which the judge may act. Finally the said provision does not contravene either Art. 10 § 2 of the European Convention on Human Rights or Art. 19 § 3 of the

[50] [2001] ChrID A', 419, 420.
[51] [2001] ChrID A', 819, followed by a note of G. Iatrou, pp. 819, 820.
[52] [2001] ChrID A', 614.

International Pact for the civil and civic rights, as the right to the freedom of expression, which includes the right of transmitting information, is submitted to limitations and sanctions that are provided by law, and aim at the protection of the honour and of the rights of third persons. The Supreme Court, however, considers that the court, when judging the case, has to take *in concreto* into consideration whether the adjudication of the provided by the law minimum amount of 10,000,000 drachmas violates the principle of proportionality between the means used and the aim wanted, principle explicitly expressed in art. 25 § 1 of the Greek Constitution revised last year, and adopted steadily in the jurisprudence of the European Court of Human Rights.

Areios Pagos 653/2001: The liability of the publisher-director is not strict but a liability based on fault according to artt. 914, 919 and 920 of the GCC. The publisher-director is liable when he has included the offensive article in the material to be printed, out of his own fault and knowing that its content is offensive[53]. **81**

6. C. *Areios Pagos* 18/1999 (Full Bench)[54]: Civil Liability of Lawyers

a) Brief Summary of the Facts

The plaintiff brings an action against a lawyer and claims damages caused during the exercise of the lawyer's professional activity, in a manner contravening the provisions of l. 2251/1994, for the protection of the consumer. **82**

b) Judgment of the Court

Though the liability of persons rendering services stems from art. 8 of l. 2251/1994 for the protection of the consumer, the law that has incorporated the directive 85/374/EEC, and there is no unanimity on whether the legal ground for this liability is contract, tort, or the law, it is of a special interest to lawyers to mention here the decision 18/1999 of the Supreme Court (full bench) – though it is a decision of the year 1999 –, as it deals with their liability. The Supreme Court with this decision and with a large minority of 9 members decided that the special nature of the profession of lawyers on the one hand and the scope of the law 2251/1994 for the protection of the consumer, which has incorporated the Directive, on the other, allow lawyers to be exempted from the scope of the said law. Hence lawyers do not fall under the category of persons (architects, doctors, etc) that are liable towards their clients according to art. 8 of the above law. According to the view of the minority, however, lawyers should not be exempted, as, while exercising their professional activity, they offer services in an independent way. **83**

[53] AP 653/2001 [2001] ChrID A', 614.

[54] [2000] NoV 48, 465 – 469 = [1999] EllDni, 1290 = [1999] DEE, 1172 – [2000] *Efimeris Ellinon Nomikon* (EEN), 230.

c) Commentary

84 It has to be mentioned that although the EU has not yet issued a directive regarding the liability of persons rendering services, the Greek legislator has made a further step, introducing with the above mentioned l. 2251/94 not only provisions regarding the liability of producers, but also the liability of persons rendering services (art. 8 of the l. 2251/94). Said article[55] has been drafted in conformity with the draft of the EU directive on liability of persons rendering services (CONSOM 20/ECO 86/6378/92, 12.5.92). The issue presented before the Supreme Court was whether also lawyers belong to the circle of persons rendering services and being liable according to the said art. 8 of the l. 2251/94.

85 The view of the majority of the said decision has become the object of a lively criticism in an article by G. Arnokouros, Scientific Collaborator of the Institute of Private Law of Molengraaff (Law School of the University of Utrecht, the Netherlands), published in the Review DEE of 2001, 467 – 474. The said author adopts the above mentioned view of the minority.

D. Books and Articles

1. Books

86 New books or manuals related exclusively to the subject of "Torts" were not published in 2001. The latest important books including the subject matter are:

- the volume on "Law of Obligations" (General Part) of Ap. Georgiades, 1999,
- the volume on "Law of Obligations" (General Part) of M. Stathopoulos, 1999, and
- the Short Law of Obligations (Special Part) of P. Kornilakis, 2000.

In all these volumes the recent developments and the latest jurisprudence related to "Torts" are extensively presented by the above mentioned distinguished authors.

2. Articles Published in the Law Reviews of the Year 2001

a) Civil Liability in Case of an Earthquake by Ap. Georgiades[56]

87 The author deals with the tortious and contractual liability of the constructor, the landlord, the producer of defective products that were used for the construction of the building that collapsed because of the earthquake and with the

[55] For an analysis of which see M. Avgoustianakis, in M. Stathopoulos/Ar. Chiotellis/M. Avgoustianakis, *Community Civil Law I* (1995), § 4 V, pp. 156–170, I. Karakostas with the collaboration of D. Tzouganatos, *Consumer protection* (1997), pp. 127—148.

[56] [2001] EllDni 42, 1181–1197.

eventual liability of the State and its employees, to the point that the construction of the buildings is submitted to State control.

b) The Crucial Time for the Calculation of the Damage in Torts by N. Nikas[57]

Adding his own critical remarks, the author presents the two views expressed **88**
in theory and in the jurisprudence about which time is to be taken as a basis for the calculation of damage. The first one states that crucial time for the calculation of damage is the time that the damage occurred, and the second one states that crucial time is the time of the hearing of the case in Court and of the issuance of the decision (prevailing view). The author of the article, however, is of the view, that crucial is the time of the payment of damages[58] and only exceptionally the time of the issuance of the decision; the latter when future damages are adjudicated. As a rule, the time of the payment coincides with the time of the restitution of the damage, except if, before the payment of the damages, the person who has sustained the damage has proceeded with the restitution of his damage; in this case the amount of damages is stabilised at this last point of time.

c) The Liability of Stock Exchange Companies Rendering Services [in Greek *Etairies Parochis Ypiresion*" (EPEY)] Against the Investors for Omission of Information or for Giving Wrong Advice by G. Triantafyllakis[59]

According to the author, the tortious liability of the said EPEY can be based **89**
only on art. 919 of the GCC, in case the EPEY shows a *dolus eventualis*, that is when it foresees the damage that may be provoked to the investor from the incorrect information and accepts this result; the liability of the EPEY cannot be based on art. 914 of the GCC, as such behaviour (omission of giving information or giving incorrect advice) does not constitute a violation of an absolute right and, therefore, it does not constitute an illegal behaviour according to this article.

d) Liability of the EPEY Against the Investors for Omission of Information in the Contracts of Execution only Business. Thoughts Regarding the Decision of the German Court of Cassation of 5.10.1999 by V. Tountopoulos[60]

This article is related to the above subject. **90**

[57] [2001] Arm 55, 3–24.
[58] See also AP 1239/2000 [2001] ChrID A', 313.
[59] [2001] ChrID A', 17–28.
[60] [2001] DEE 7, 481–489.

e) The Above Mentioned Article (*supra* [85]) of G. Arnokouros on "Liability of the Person Rendering Legal Services"[61]

f) Environmental Liability. Philosophical, Historical and Legal Parameters by G. Balias[62]

91 In this article the author presents the concept of liability as a legal-philosophical category. According to thc author, who follows the typology of E. Ewald, *L'Etat providence*, 1986, the development of the notion and the content of liability has taken place in three successive phases, during which three respective examples have been established: a) the example of certainty (in the 19th century, when liability is based on fault, b) the example of solidarity (at the end of the 19th century, when liability became strict; at this period there is a move from personal liability to the socialization of the danger, *i.e.* to the insurance of the danger) and c) the example of uncertainty (at the end of the 20th century, when humankind entered a period of total impairment of health and of the environment). Ecological disasters can be avoided only if liability is based on the principle of precaution. According to this principle liable should be considered not only the person who should have known but also the one who should have doubted; even if there is no scientific proof about the occurrence of the impairment and the legal causation between the act and the result, liability has to exist following the old maxim "better to prevent than to cure".

[61] [2001] DEE 7, 467–474.
[62] PerDik 1/2001, pp. 21–34.

X. Ireland

Eoin Quill

A. Legislation

1. Mental Health Act, 2001

Sec. 73 is designed to replace sec. 260 of the Mental Treatment Act, 1945, governing the initiation of civil proceedings against persons purporting to exercise functions under the legislation. Sec. 260 of the 1945 Act requires a claimant to seek the consent of the High Court (HC) for the initiation of proceedings, and such consent may only be granted where 'there are substantial grounds for contending that the person against whom proceedings are to be brought acted in bad faith or without reasonable care.' The case law on this subject has provided an interpretation of the section that sets a high standard for an applicant to attain in order to get the necessary consent to initiate proceedings.[1] The interpretation of sec. 260 is considered in detail below in respect of the High Court decision in Lehany v Loftus and the Western Health Board.[2] Sec. 73 of the 2001 Act provides that leave to institute proceedings should be granted by the High Court unless the court is satisfied 'that the proceedings are frivolous or vexatious', or 'that there are no reasonable grounds for contending that the person against whom the proceedings are brought acted in bad faith or without reasonable care.' This shifts the burden of proof from the applicant to the respondent. Sec. 1(3) of the 2001 Act provides that the provisions of the Act will only come into force after the making of a ministerial order, or orders. A similar provision contained in the Mental Treatment Act, 1981 was never used, thereby preventing the Act from coming into effect. It is hoped that the 2001 Act will not suffer the same fate. To this end a private 1

[1] O'Dowd v The North Western Health Board [1983] *Irish Law Reports Monthly* (ILRM), 186; Murphy v Greene [1990] 2 *Irish Reports* (IR), 566; O'Reilly v Moroney unreported (unrep.) Supreme Court (SC), 16 November 1993; *noted* by A.M. O'Neill [1994] *Irish Law Times (new series)* [ILT (ns)] 12, 211; Bailey v Gallagher [1996] 2 ILRM 433; Kiernan v Harris unrep HC, 12 May 1998; Melly v Moran unrep. SC, 28 May 1998; see also D. Tomkin/P. Hanafin, *Irish Medical Law* (1995), at pp. 121–123; J. Spellman, Section 260 of The Mental Treatment Act, 1945 Reviewed [1998] *Medico-Legal Journal of Ireland* (MLJI) 4, 20.

[2] *Infra* [93].

member's Bill has been published – The Mental Health (Amendment) Bill, 2001 – proposing that the Act should come into force on 7 April 2002, if the minister has not made the relevant orders before that date. Private member's Bills are, however, rarely enacted.

2. Adventure Activities Standards Authority Act, 2001

2 This Act establishes a new national authority, whose principal functions under sec. 14 are 'to promote, encourage, foster, facilitate and regulate the safe operation of adventure activities in the State.' While sec. 19 provides certain persons with immunity from civil claims in respect of the conduct of inquiries and investigations under the Act, no general immunity is provided to the authority in the performance of its functions. There is, consequently, a significant potential for tortious claims against the authority by people injured as a result of the exercise of its functions, particularly its regulatory function. The general principles governing such claims are set out below in the discussion of the recent Supreme Court (SC) decision in Glencar Exploration plc v Mayo County Council.[3] Under sec. 34, the authority may prepare and publish codes of practice, or approve codes drawn up by another body, which adventure activities operators are required to follow. Subs.7 of the section provides that breach of such a code will not of itself render the operator liable to civil proceedings. Such codes could, however, be used by the courts in determining whether the operator was in breach of a duty owed under common law, or a statutory duty – *e.g.* in a claim under the Occupier's Liability Act, 1995. Sec. 35 of the Act permits the authority to make regulatory schemes in respect of the conduct of adventure activities; subs.4 requires operators to comply with such a scheme, but there is no equivalent of sec. 34(7) in respect of liability for breach. Consequently, sec. 35 may give rise to an enforceable statutory duty on operators, generating an independent cause of action for persons injured as a result of the breach.

B. Cases

1. Glencar Exploration plc & Andaman Resources plc v Mayo County Council; Unrep. SC 19 July 2001. The Chief Justice (CJ), Mr. Justice Keane, Mr. Justice (J) Murray, Mrs. Justice (J) McGuinness, Denham J, Fennelly J. Duty of Care in Respect of Pure Economic Loss; Public Authorities' Duty of Care; Breach of Statutory Duty; Breach of Constitutional Rights

a) Brief Summary of the Facts

3 The applicant companies were in the business of prospecting for and mining minerals and ores and held prospecting licences for gold exploration in Mayo. Further investment was required for the commercial mining of the gold and, to

[3] *Infra* [3]–[5].

that end, the applicants entered into a joint venture with a third company in November 1991. In early 1992 a mining ban was included in the respondent's development plan under the relevant planning legislation,[4] as a result of which the third party investor withdrew from the joint venture. The applicants instituted judicial review proceedings seeking declarations that the ban was *ultra vires*, an order of certiorari, quashing the relevant provisions of the development plan, and damages for negligence, breach of constitutional rights and breach of statutory duty.[5] The High Court (HC) granted a declaration that the mining ban was *ultra vires*,[6] but found that although the respondent had been negligent, it was not in breach of any duty of care toward the applicants.[7]

b) Judgment of the Supreme Court

The HC decision was upheld on appeal by the SC. The claim for breach of statutory duty was rejected because the statutory provision involved the exercise of a power for the benefit of the public as a whole and did not involve a duty for the protection of a specific category of persons of which the applicants were members; consequently a breach of the provision was not amenable to an action in tort. The claim for breach of constitutional rights was rejected on the basis that the applicants' rights were sufficiently vindicated by the order of certiorari granted in the HC.[8] The court also considered the decision of the European Court of Human Rights (ECHR) in Osman v UK,[9] but distinguished it on the grounds that it related to the right of access to justice, arising out of the rejection of a claim by way of a preliminary ruling, whereas the applicants in the present case had been given a full hearing on the merits of their claims. In respect of the negligence claim, the decision in this case departed from the use of Lord Wilberforce's two-stage test, propounded in Anns v Merton LBC.[10] Influenced in particular by the judgments of the House of Lords in Caparo Industries plc v Dickman[11] and Brennan J of the High Court of Australia in Sutherland Shire Council v Heyman,[12] Keane CJ held that the imposition of a duty should only occur if the damage to the plaintiff was reasonably foreseeable, that there was sufficient proximity between the parties and that it be just and reasonable that a duty should be imposed. **4**

[4] The Local Government (Planning and Development) Act, 1963 (as amended).

[5] A claim for breach of legitimate expectation was also raised, but rejected by the Supreme Court; the topic is beyond the scope of this discussion, as it is not a claim in tort.

[6] [1993] 2 IR 237, Blayney J.

[7] Unrep. HC, 20 August 1998, Kelly J. The damages claim had been adjourned at the earlier hearing before Blayney J.

[8] Relying on the earlier Supreme Court decision in Pine Valley Developments v The Minister (Min.) for the Environment [1987] IR, 23.

[9] [1999] 1 *Family Law Reports* (FLR), 193.

[10] [1978] *Appeal Cases* (AC) 728, at 751.

[11] [1990] 2 AC 605.

[12] [1985] *Commonwealth Law Reports* (CLR) 157, 424.

c) Commentary

5 The rejection of the claims for breach of statutory duty and breach of constitutional rights were on well-established grounds.[13] The grounds for the judgments in respect of the negligence claim involve the most searching review of the general criteria for the imposition of a duty of care in an Irish Court since the decision in Ward v McMaster & Louth County Council.[14] The two-stage test had been prominent in Irish tort cases over the past two decades, so this decision marks a significant departure in holding that it is no longer the appropriate test.[15] The third requirement of the three-stage test – the just and reasonable element – departs from the prior approach in that it emphasises a need for the plaintiff to establish positive policy reasons to support the imposition of a duty, whereas the two-stage test placed the onus on the defendant to raise negative policy considerations to displace the presumption that a duty was owed once proximity and reasonable foresight were established. It is also worth noting that the application of the two-stage test had a tendency to conflate proximity and reasonable foresight into a single issue, with the concept of proximity losing any distinct meaning. The application of the three-stage test in England has reinvigorated the role of proximity as a discrete requirement, constraining the development of duty purely on grounds of reasonable foreseeability of damage. It is clear that this is also intended by the Chief Justice, as he specifically refers to Lord Atkin's use of proximity as a curb on the development of duty.[16] The Chief Justice also emphasised that cases of pure economic loss would not give rise to the imposition of a duty of care as readily as cases of physical damage to persons or property.[17] In applying these principles to the facts of the case it was found that the nature of the statutory power in question (the drawing up of a development plan) was not such as to create sufficient proximity between the parties such that it would be just and reasonable to impose a duty of care on the respondent. The case is analysed by M. Peart in the Law Society Gazette.[18]

[13] For general consideration of the action for breach of statutory duty see E. Quill, *Torts in Ireland* (1999), chapter 3; B. M. E. McMahon/W. Binchy, *Law of Torts* (3rd edn. 2000), chapter 21. For breach of constitutional rights see Hanrahan v Merk, Sharp & Dohme (Ireland) Ltd. [1988] ILRM, 629; W v Ireland [1997] 2 IR 142; E. Quill (*supra*), pp. 320 *et seq.*; B. M. E. McMahon/ W. Binchy (*supra*), pp. 4 *et seq.*

[14] [1988] IR, 337.

[15] See E. Quill (*supra* note 13), pp. 23–24; B. M. E. McMahon/W. Binchy (*supra* note 13), pp. 123 *et seq.*

[16] Donoghue v Stevenson [1932] AC, 562.

[17] He expressly reserves his position with respect to the imposition of a duty of care in respect of economic loss outside of established categories of cases, such as negligent misstatement. The law in Ireland is still somewhat broader than in England, since the Chief Justice accepts that the imposition of liability for economic loss on local authorities in defective buildings cases, such as Ward v McMaster (*supra* note 14) is correct. This is in contrast to the rejection of liability in England in Murphy v Brentwood DC [1991] 1 AC 398. Fennelly J also contrasts the applicants' position with the plaintiffs in Siney v Dublin Corporation [1980] IR, 400 and Ward v McMaster.

[18] *Infra* [128].

2. Sinnott v Ireland; Unrep. SC, 12 July 2001, Keane CJ, Denham, Murphy, Murray, Hardiman, Geoghegan & Fennelly JJ. Breach of Constitutional Rights

a) Brief Summary of the Facts

The first plaintiff suffered from autism since early childhood and was 23 years of age when the present proceedings came before the HC. He and his mother sued the State for its failure to provide appropriate education and training for him. He had received limited, though inadequate education through a variety of special education projects up to 1997, but had not received any official education or training since then. The evidence showed that his physical and mental capacity, as well as his enjoyment of life, would have been greatly improved if he had received appropriate education and training. The absence of adequate provision in earlier life created a continuing need for appropriate education and training in his adult life, though this would not fully undo the effects of the earlier failure to provide appropriate care. The first plaintiff's claim was that the State failed to discharge its constitutional obligations under artt. 40 and 42, as it failed to provide for free primary education, failed to provide reasonable aid to private education initiatives and failed to provide free transport for a significant period to the limited facilities available to the plaintiff. The first plaintiff's mother also claimed that the State's failure involved a failure to respect, defend and vindicate her constitutional rights as a parent under artt. 40–42. Declaratory relief, damages and a mandatory injunction were sought. Barr J in the HC awarded the first plaintiff £ 222,500 (€ 282,516) and awarded his mother £ 70,000 (€ 88,881). The State appealed against parts of the judgment, specifically the finding that the first plaintiff was entitled to free primary education after the age of 18 as long as he was capable of benefiting from such education and the award of general damages to his mother.[19] 6

b) Judgment of the Supreme Court

The SC held that the right to free primary education under art. 42.4 does not extend beyond 18 years of age, as the right is applicable to 'children' rather than 'citizens', and the choice of 18 was not arbitrary, as it is the age of majority for many issues (Keane CJ dissenting). The court also held that a failure to make provision for education for a child does not involve an actionable breach of parental rights under artt. 40–42, as the parent has no distinct interest from that of the child (Denham J dissenting). 7

c) Commentary

The decision was partly clouded by the fact that the State accepted liability for the full award of £ 222,500 (€ 282,516) to the first plaintiff, even though this included damages up to the age of 23, whereas the constitutional obligation 8

[19] A government press release of 7 March, 2001 indicated the State would pay for the plaintiffs' costs in both the HC and SC and claimed that the purpose of the appeal was to clarify constitutional issues for the future.

was only conceded up to the age of 18. The State further accepted that it would have to provide for the education needs of the plaintiff and other similarly situated persons after the age of 18, but claimed that this obligation arose under the Education Act, 1998 and not under the Constitution. The distinction was of particular importance to the State, as a constitutional duty could have exposed the State to financial responsibility for the educational needs of adults, other than those suffering from a disability. The State's concessions meant that the meaning of 'education' for the purposes of the constitutional obligation on the State to provide for free primary education was not directly in question, thereby leaving open the question of the correctness of the landmark HC decision of O'Hanlon J in O'Donoghue v The Minister for Health & Others.[20] That decision had held that education was not confined to scholastic learning, but included training and therapy that would allow mentally handicapped persons to attain their full potential. Three of the SC judges – Keane CJ, Denham and Geoghegan JJ – expressed support for the decision; Murphy J regarded it as erroneous, while the remaining three members of the court – Murray, Hardiman and Fennelly JJ – reserved their positions on the issue. The decision in respect of parental rights suggests that any disruption to family members that is secondary to an interference with the rights of another family member does not create an independent cause of action. This suggests that the rights of family members are to be treated as convergent and denies the possibility of discrete interests worthy of independent acknowledgement and protection.

3. Crilly v T J Farrington Ltd. & O'Connor; Eastern Health Board v Crilly and FBD Insurance PLC; Unrep. SC 11 July 2001; Denham, Murphy, Murray, McGuinness and Fennelly JJ. Recovery of Costs for Medical Treatment

a) Brief Summary of the Facts

9 Mr Crilly successfully sued Farrington and O'Connor in respect of personal injuries arising out of a road traffic accident (RTA). Sec. 2 of the Health (Amendment) Act 1986 permits recovery of costs in RTA cases covered by insurance. The Health Board sought recovery of the cost of care based on the average daily cost (ADC) *i.e.* total annual costs divided by the number of occupied bed days in the year. The HC had held that this was not permitted, since the Act allowed the imposition of a reasonable charge and a general average would place the costs of vastly different treatments on the same cost per day, which would not be reasonable.[21] The insurers argued that the entitlement to make a charge should involve a charge similar to that under sec. 55 of the Health Act 1970 – a charge involving a contribution towards the cost of

[20] [1996] 2 IR 20. In D & Others v Min. for Education & Others unrep. SC, 17 December 2001, the SC discharged mandatory injunctions granted against the State in respect of providing suitable educational placements for the plaintiffs on the grounds that it constituted a breach of the separation of powers doctrine. This raises doubts about the availability in the future of any actions against the government for failure to meet special educational needs.

[21] [2000] 1 ILRM 548, Geoghegan J.

care rather than the full cost, with the levels being set by Statutory Instrument. This was also rejected in the High Court where it was held that the charge should be on a *quantum meruit* basis. The bill had already been paid and the case centred on an application for declaratory relief with the objective of avoiding future disputes.

b) Judgment of the Supreme Court

The SC decision on the appropriate charge was delivered by Denham, J. She held that, although the precise method of charge was not set out, there had to be a relationship between the charge and the service and that the Act had set out a 'basic policy for a pragmatic scheme.' The appropriate public law principles applicable to the exercise of such a power was to act reasonably which would be breached only where there was manifest arbitrariness, injustice or partiality.[22] She held that the section 'does not expressly require the charge to cover precisely the services given' and added that the Health Board has a degree of discretion with respect to determining the appropriate charge. The ADC was found to be reasonable and that individualised charging would not be practicable, particularly as those covered by the section represent less than 1% of users of hospital services. **10**

c) Commentary

This decision extends the ability of hospitals to recover the cost of services provided to the victims of RTAs and will change the basis on which special damages are calculated in such cases. The overall benefit to the hospitals will be slight, due to the small proportion of its activities that these cases represent. The decision also clarifies that reliance is not normally to be placed on a ministerial statement on the meaning of a statutory provision when a court is interpreting legislation.[23] **11**

4. Hill v Cork Examiner Publications Ltd.; Unrep. SC 14 November 2001; Murphy, Murray, McGuinness JJ. Defamation; Meaning of Impugned Publication; Evidence of Bad Reputation; Quantum of Damages

a) Brief Summary of the Facts

The plaintiff was imprisoned for three years in July 1994 for occasioning actual bodily harm, contrary to sec. 47 of the Offences Against The Person Act, 1861. The defendant published a photograph of the plaintiff in his cell, accompanying an article, which referred to the wing of the prison as being principally for sex offenders and others isolated for their own safety. A HC jury awarded the plaintiff £ 60,000 (€ 76,184) damages for libel in November **12**

[22] Relying on Cassidy v Minister for Industry [1978] IR 297, at 310–311 per Henchy J and McGabhann v Law Society [1989] ILRM 854, at 862 per Blayney J.

[23] For a detailed consideration of the use of parliamentary materials in the interpretation of legislation see R.Byrne/J.P.McCutcheon, *The Irish Legal System* (4th edn. 2001) at §§14.177 *et seq.*

2000. The defendant appealed to the SC. The key issues in dispute on appeal related to determining the meaning of an impugned publication, the admissibility of evidence of reputation and the quantum of damages.

b) Judgment of the Supreme Court

13 Based on the fact that one third of the article related to sex offenders and the headline was entitled 'Isolation of Cork Jail's C Wing', followed by a subheading reading 'Cork Prison's Prison Within a Prison', the SC held that the jury were entitled to conclude that a reasonable reader of the article would believe that the plaintiff was a sex offender, or was isolated for his own safety. The SC accepted that the test applied by the HC on the admissibility of evidence of bad reputation was correct – that specific acts of misconduct were not generally admissible, but that an exception existed in respect of criminal convictions for other offences.[24] A caution issued by the trial judge on the introduction of such evidence was found not to amount to a threat, prejudicing the fairness of the trial, but was an appropriate reminder of the delicate balance involved in the issue. The sum awarded was found not to be disproportionate to the injury to reputation and was therefore upheld.

c) Commentary

14 The 'reasonable recipient' test applied for establishing the meaning of the publications is well established[25] and raises no difficulties on the facts presented. The rule with respect to evidence of bad reputation is also well established, though it is unusual for the defence to be successfully invoked. While the quantum of damages awarded is significant, it would surely have been higher if the defendant's reputation had been better, so the defence may be regarded as successful in this instance.[26] The decision on quantum is based on established principles, though their application is difficult to predict.[27] In this instance a serious allegation, combined with a flawed reputation, produced an award that the SC found to be appropriate, though at the upper end of scale for such a case.

[24] Based on Scott v Samson [1882] *Law Reports, Queens Bench Division* (QBD) 8, 491 and Plato Films Ltd. v Speidel [1961] 1 AC 1090.

[25] Barrett v Long (1846) *Irish Law Reports, Common Law* (ILRC) 8, 331; see M. McDonald *Irish Law of Defamation* (2nd edn.) at chapter 2.

[26] In McEntee & McEntee v Quinnsworth, unrep. SC, 7 December 1993 the plaintiffs were awarded £ 60,000 (€ 76,184) and £ 75,000 (€ 95,230) in respect of a slanderous allegation of shoplifting. A libel that the plaintiff was a sex offender, or an offender requiring segregation for protection, would surely merit a higher award in the absence of countervailing factors.

[27] Barrett v Independent Newspapers [1986] IR, 13; de Rossa v Independent Newspapers plc [1999] 4 IR 6; O'Brien v Mirror Group Newspapers [2001] 1 IR 1.

5. O'Mahoney v Tyndale and Corr; Unrep. SC 13 July 2001; Keane CJ, Murphy, Hardiman JJ. Medical Negligence; Role of Appellate Court

a) Brief Summary of the Facts

The plaintiff suffered from severe mental handicap allegedly resulting from the treatment of his mother during labour. The claim against the first defendant, representing the hospital, was that the plaintiff's condition of pre-eclampsia was such that a consultant obstetrician or registrar should have been present in case an emergency arose, whereas the consultant did not arrive until a significant time after an emergency arose. The claim against the consultant was that he failed to detect intra-uterine hypoxia (a lack of oxygen to the brain) and actively participated in a defective hospital system. The claim was dismissed by the HC[28] and the plaintiff appealed. 15

b) Judgment of the Supreme Court

The SC dismissed the appeal. The HC had found the hospital to have been negligent in two respects – the failure to properly operate the system of care, due to a delay in delivery that was 7–12 minutes longer than necessary and inadequate nursing records for the period immediately after birth – but that these had not contributed to the plaintiff's disability. The SC found that these findings were supported by credible evidence and, as primary findings of fact, were not therefore open to appeal.[29] The defence argument that the burden of proof should have been reversed on the basis of the maxim *omnia praesumuntur contra spoliatorem* (everything is presumed against a wrongdoer) was also rejected. The consultant was found not to have been negligent in the HC, as the emergency did not arise until he was on the way to the hospital and he arrived within a reasonable time of being informed that he was required. Also the system operated by the hospital was found to be reasonable and he could not have been aware that it would fail to be implemented in this instance. Again, the SC found these findings to be supported by the evidence. 16

c) Commentary

The causal finding turns principally on the resolution of the conflicting testimony of expert witnesses. Once this was resolved against the plaintiff, there was no prospect of succeeding. The decision not to interfere with findings of primary facts on appeal is consistent with the established authorities on the issue. The maxim *omnia praesumuntur contra spoliatorem* arises extremely rarely and is principally concerned with the suppression of evidence. The maxim only applies in cases where the defendant's fault leads to the destruction or unavailability of crucial evidence. This was not the case here, because there was eyewitness evidence on the issues raised, which was sufficient to 17

[28] Quirke J, 7 April 2000.

[29] The relevant principles are set out in Northern Bank Finance Corporation v Charlton [1979] IR, 149, at 191; Hay v O'Grady [1992] 1 IR 210, at 217; see E. Quill (*supra* note 13) at pp. 409–411.

dispose of the matter. The plaintiff's suggestion that a finding of negligence should generally lead to a reversal of the burden of proof on other aspects of the case, such as causation of damage, was novel and certainly would have had far reaching consequences.

6. Ryan v Connolly; SC 31 January 2001; [2001] 2 ILRM 174; Keane, CJ, Murphy & McGuinness, JJ. Limitation of Actions

a) Brief Summary of the Facts

18 The plaintiff was injured in a collision between his motorcycle and the defendant's car in April 1995. The defendant's insurers settled the property damage claim and a number of letters passed between his solicitors and the defendant's insurers in respect of the personal injuries claim. The insurers indicated a willingness to negotiate a settlement, but the plaintiff's solicitors failed to reply to a number of letters. Proceedings were instituted in December 1998, outside the limitation period. The plaintiff asserted that the defendants were estopped from relying on the limitation period; Kelly J upheld this view in the HC.

b) Judgment of the Supreme Court

19 The SC disagreed with the interpretation of the evidence by the HC, concluding that the statements of the plaintiff's solicitor did not show any belief that a limitations defence would not be raised; also there was no justification for such an inference merely out of the fact that settlement by negotiation appeared likely. Settlement of the property damage portion of the claim between the two insurers could give rise to no inference in respect of the personal injury claim, since property damage claims were often settled on a 'knock for knock' basis. The appeal was, therefore, allowed.

c) Commentary

20 The judgment of Keane, CJ helps to clarify the approach taken to settlement negotiations. He noted that correspondence 'without prejudice' is generally not admissible on grounds of public policy in order to encourage settlements, but found that it may be used to explain the context of decisions taken during proceedings, in particular a delay in issuing proceedings. He further noted that admission of liability does not preclude reliance on the limitation defence if negotiations become dormant; the admission must be such as to give rise to a reasonable inference that instituting proceedings was unnecessary.[30] This decision demonstrates the danger of assuming that an estoppel will arise once negotiations have begun and will be likely to encourage practitioners to file claims early even where they believe settlement is likely.

[30] Relying on Doran v Thompson Ltd. [1978] IR, 223 and Low v Bouverie [1891] 3 *Chancery Law Reports* (Ch) 82. See E. Quill (*supra* note 13), p. 417.

7. Thomas v Leitrim County Council; SC 7 March 2001; [2001] 2 ILRM 385; (Keane, CJ; McGuinness & Hardiman, JJ). Occupier's Liability; Contributory Negligence

a) Brief Summary of the Facts

The plaintiff was one of a group of persons walking on a path in a scenic area near a waterfall. They came across a tree on the path and, noticing two worn tracks in the grass to the side of the path, they decided to walk around the fallen tree, despite the fact that the terrain was very steep. The plaintiff's husband slipped, but was not injured; the plaintiff slipped and suffered a serious ankle injury. The HC made a finding of contributory negligence against the plaintiff.[31] The plaintiff appealed and the defendant lodged a cross appeal as to the categorisation of the plaintiff as an invitee rather than a licensee, giving rise to a higher duty at common law. **21**

b) Judgment of the Supreme Court

The SC held that allowing the tracks to develop was sufficient to amount to a breach of the duty to exercise reasonable diligence not to let the premises mislead the plaintiff. This failure partially contributed to the accident. Therefore the cross-appeal was rejected. While the defendant slightly misled the plaintiff on 'the negotiability of the terrain', its main features 'continued to be obviously dangerous.' Consequently, the finding of contributory negligence was upheld. The criterion for apportionment in cases of contributory negligence is relative blameworthiness[32] and the HC apportionment of 2/3 to plaintiff and 1/3 to defendant was also upheld. **22**

c) Commentary

The case was governed by the former law on occupiers' liability, as the facts occurred before the coming into force of the Occupiers' Liability Act, 1995. While it contains an excellent consideration of the old law it will be of little future value on this subject. The contributory negligence principles do not raise any novel features; while the apportionment of a high proportion of responsibility to the plaintiff is relatively rare, it is not surprising on the facts, given the relatively slight fault of the defendant and the foolhardiness of the plaintiff. **23**

[31] [1998] 2 ILRM 74.

[32] Sec.34(1) of the Civil Liability Act,1961; O'Sullivan v Dwyer [1971] IR, 275; Carroll v Clare County Council [1975] IR, 211. See E. Quill (*supra* note 13), pp. 394–395; Ward v Walsh unrep. SC, 31 July 1991, noted in R. Byrne/W. Binchy, *Annual Review of Irish Law 1991* (1993) at pp. 441–442. B.M.E. McMahon/W. Binchy (*supra* note 13), pp. 123 *et seq.*

8. Cassells v Marks & Spencer plc; Unrep. SC 30 July 2001; Murphy, Murray, McGuinness JJ. Retailer's Duty of Care in Respect of Products Supplied

a) Brief Summary of the Facts

24 The plaintiff's mother bought a cotton dress for her in a Marks & Spencer store in Brixton, before moving to Ireland. The mother left the plaintiff for approximately three minutes in a room with an unguarded open fire. The dress caught fire, causing extensive burns to the plaintiff. The dress contained a permanent tag that included a warning sign in red capitals – "KEEP AWAY FROM FIRE" – in English and three other languages. On a detachable tag (approximately 1½ × 2 inches = 3.8 × 5 centimetres) there was another warning in large red capitals – "IN THE INTEREST OF SAFETY IT IS ADVISABLE TO KEEP YOUR CHILD AWAY FROM FIRE"; this was repeated in small red capitals on the reverse side of the tag in English and three other languages. The plaintiff's mother admitted knowledge of the permanent tag, stitched into the garment, but did not recall seeing the detachable tag. The detachable tag was found probably to have been there in accordance with normal practice in the defendant's shops. The HC ruled that the defendant had discharged its duty of care to the plaintiff.[33]

b) Judgment of the Supreme Court

25 McGuinness J issued the judgment of the court, upholding the decision of the HC that the warning provided by the defendant complied with the standard of care established for flammable garments, established in earlier cases.[34]

c) Commentary

26 While there are regulations governing flammability and tags on children's night wear, there are no equivalent statutory requirements for children's daywear (which this garment was). The permanent tag conformed to the requirements for tags on nightwear and the second tag, which was more prominent at the time of purchase, would not even be required on nightwear under the regulations. The defendant's own standards therefore exceeded any established standards and a finding against it would have involved a radical extension of supplier's obligations towards consumers. Evidence in the HC suggested that if the fire retardant used on nightwear was employed, the injuries would have been significantly less. Barr J, in the HC, acknowledged some of the practical difficulties involved in using flame retardant chemicals, such as increased costs, skin irritation, loss of fabric strength, loss of comfort and unreliability of the retardant effect. The difference between the fire risks with nightwear and garments of this type were found to be sufficient to warrant different treatment in law and that the defendant could take account of trade practice, public

[33] Unrep. HC, 25 March 1999. Barr J.

[34] Duffy (A Minor) v Rooney and Dunnes Stores (Dundalk) Ltd. unrep. SC, 23 April 1998; O'Bryne (A Minor) v Gloucester and Others unrep. SC, 3 November 1988.

demand for the product and the absence of a demand for tighter regulation from the independent bodies in Ireland and the UK on these garments. The findings on this latter issue were not appealed, but are worthy of note, as they demonstrate that the legal standard is sufficiently sensitive to market conditions.

9. Newell v Bus Éireann (Irish Bus); Unrep. SC 10 July 2001; Denham, Hardiman, Fennelly JJ. Quantum of General Damages

a) Brief Summary of the Facts

The plaintiff was injured as a result of smoke inhalation caused by an engine fire on the defendant's bus, on which she was travelling. She suffered respiratory problems and related psychological problems for several years after the incident and her long term chances of recovery from the respiratory problems were approximately 40%. The HC awarded £ 30,000 (€ 38,092) general damages to the date of trial and £ 25,000 (€ 31,743) for the future. The plaintiff appealed on the grounds that the award was too low. **27**

b) Judgment of the Supreme Court

The sum of £ 30,00 (€ 38,092) to the date of trial was upheld as being appropriate and principally related to the psychological effect of the incident. The award for future suffering was increased to £ 50,000 (€ 63,486) on the basis that the plaintiff was left with a condition akin to asthma, which could only be controlled by a comprehensive programme of treatment and that there was 'a very real possibility' that she would have this condition for life. **28**

c) Commentary

The award for future harm may seem high in light of the prospect of recovery, however the SC considered the estimation of the chance of recovery as conjecture, rather than a real evaluation of probability. **29**

10. Rossiter v Dun Laoghaire Rathdown County Council; Unrep. SC 31 October 2001; Murphy, Geoghegan & Fennelly JJ. Quantum of Damages

a) Brief Summary of the Facts

The plaintiff was struck in the eye by a piece of wire propelled from a lawnmower, operated by an employee of the defendant. The injury resulted in almost total loss of vision in one eye. He was awarded £ 120,000 (€ 152,368) by Johnson J in the HC and appealed on grounds of inadequacy of the award.[35] **30**

[35] £ 30,000 (€ 38,092) for loss of employment opportunities and £ 90,000 (€ 114,276) general damages.

b) Judgment of the Supreme Court

31 Due to the difficulty of assessing the employment prospects of the plaintiff, as he had just finished his primary education prior to the hearing, the SC held that the loss of employment prospects should be treated as part of the general damages and therefore treated the award as if it had not been itemised into discrete categories by the HC. The court applied the established test for considering the propriety of the award; the award was held not to bear a reasonable proportion to the compensation to which the plaintiff was entitled and a sum of £ 150,000 was substituted for the HC award.

c) Commentary

32 The calculation of lost future income is routinely calculated distinctly, as an item of special damages in Irish courts. This decision reflects the reality that such loss often cannot be calculated with the degree of precision required for special damages, particularly when there is a partial, rather than total disability and the plaintiff is too young to provide reliable data on career prospects.

11. Vesey v Bus Éireann; Unrep. SC 13 November 2001; Denham McGuinness & Hardiman J. Quantum of Damages Where Plaintiff Has Feigned Additional Injury

a) Brief Summary of the Facts

33 The plaintiff was injured in an RTA and was awarded £ 72,500 (€ 92,056) by the HC.[36] The appeal by the defendant on the quantum of damages focused on the extent of the plaintiff's injury, which had proved extremely difficult to ascertain in the HC. The principal difficulty stemmed from the paucity of reliable evidence of the plaintiff's medical condition (as he had lied to doctors for both sides) or of his employment history.

b) Judgment of the Supreme Court

34 The SC reduced the award to £ 30,000 (€ 38,092), applying the same principles as in Rossiter v Dun Laoghaire Rathdown County Council.[37] The defence argued that the plaintiff should be penalised for his dishonesty through a form of reverse punitive damages, but this was rejected. The Court recognised that there may come a point when dishonesty amounts to an abuse of process, but this was not such a case, given that some harm had in fact resulted to the plaintiff from the accident.

[36] 14 November 2000. £ 7,500 (€ 9,523) special damages; £ 35,000 (€ 44,440) for loss of income and £ 30,000 (€ 38,092) general damages.

[37] *Supra*, [30]–[32]. The £ 30,000 (€ 38,092) awarded by the SC in Vesey was made up of £ 7,500 (€ 9,523) special damages; £ 7,500 (€ 9,523) for loss of income and £ 15,000 (€ 19,046) general damages.

c) Commentary

The rejection of reverse punitive damages is consistent with the earlier decisions in Deans v Sheridan[38] and Fagan v Wong.[39] In the latter case it was held that, while the plaintiff should receive full compensation for the actual injury suffered, she should only recover that portion of the costs appropriate to the proper pursuit of that claim; additional costs incurred by bringing the cases in the HC, rather than the CC, and by unnecessarily increasing the length of the case, were not awarded to the plaintiff. 35

12. Pethe v McDonagh & MIBI; Unrep. SC 25 July 2001; Murphy, McGuinness, Geoghegan JJ. Quantum of Damages

a) Brief Summary of the Facts

The plaintiff was injured in an RTA in 1996, causing a broken femur requiring eight operations to repair. In addition the plaintiff suffered fractures to two fingers, damage to seven teeth, several cuts and abrasions and was trapped in the wreckage for four hours. He was awarded £ 190,000 (€ 241,250) in the HC.[40] The defendant appealed two aspects of the award – £ 60,000 (€ 76,184) loss of income and £ 85,000 (€ 107,927) general damages to the date of trial. 36

b) Judgment of the Supreme Court

The SC rejected the appeal. The ruling on loss of income in the HC was based on a resolution of a conflict of evidence as to whether payments were gross, or net of tax. As there was evidence to support the trial judge's findings, the appeal was rejected. The award of general damages to date was found to be generous but not excessive and, taken in conjunction with a relatively modest award for the future (£ 30,000, € 38,092), the total award of general damages was held to be satisfactory. 37

c) Commentary

The decision on special damages involves the application of the rule that an appellate court will not normally interfere with findings of fact by the trial judge. In light of the seriousness of the injuries, the award of £ 115,000 (€ 146,019) general damages is in line with previous practice in Ireland.[41] 38

[38] Unrep SC, 26 October 1993.
[39] Unrep SC, 7 May 1997.
[40] O'Sullivan J, 28 June 1999.
[41] For a detailed consideration of the quantum of awards see R. Pierse, *Quantum of Damages for Personal Injuries 1997* (1997); R. Pierse, *Quantum of Damages for Personal Injuries 1999* (1999).

13. O'Keeffee v Kilcullen & Others; Unrep. SC 23 October 2001; Murphy, Murray, Fennelly, JJ. Striking out Claim Against Expert Witness

a) Brief Summary of the Facts

39 The plaintiff instituted proceedings against, inter alia, a court appointed psychiatrist, who provided a report and gave evidence during nullity proceedings brought against the plaintiff by her husband. The proceedings were struck out by the HC as disclosing no reasonable cause of action.[42] The plaintiff appealed to the SC.

b) Judgment of the Supreme Court

40 The SC dismissed the appeal, based on Looney v Bank of Ireland and Morey,[43] distinguishing Hall v Simons.[44]

c) Commentary

41 The analysis of the HC judgment below is equally applicable to the SC decision.[45]

14. Cawley v Foley & Foley; Unrep. SC 20 December 2001. Denham, Geoghegan & Fennelly JJ. Causation; Quantum of Damages for Soft Tissue Injury

a) Brief Summary of the Facts

42 The plaintiff was awarded £ 25,301 (€ 32,125) damages in the HC for personal injuries arising out of an RTA. The defendants appealed, disputing the existence of any damage, the causal connection to their negligence and the amount awarded. The dispute as to the existence of injury centred on a difference of opinion between the parties as to the speed the cars were travelling at and whether braking suddenly to avoid a collision at low speed could cause any significant injury.

b) Judgment of the High Court

43 The HC finding that an injury had occurred was supported by evidence and was not amenable to appeal, even though the factual findings of the trial judge were not set out as clearly as was desirable. The award of £ 25,000 (€ 31,743) general damages for back and neck pains and headaches was held to be excessive and the SC substituted a figure of £ 12,500 (€ 15,871).

[42] O'Sullivan J, 24 June 1998 on grounds of lack of causation and again on 21 February 2001 on the basis of immunity; considered *infra*. [72]–[74].

[43] [1996] 1 IR 157.

[44] [2000] 3 All England Reports (All ER) 673, where the advocate's immunity from suit in negligence was abolished.

[45] *Infra* [74].

c) Commentary

The upholding of the finding on the occurrence of injury is based on the principles discussed earlier with respect to O'Mahoney v Tyndale and Corr.[46] On the question of quantum, the SC will only overturn an award if it is grossly disproportionate to the injury suffered. This usually requires a disparity of 25% between the appropriate award and the award made by the HC.[47] The SC will substitute its own award where a retrial on quantum would involve unnecessary or disproportionate costs.[48] The substituted award is within the normal parameters for a soft tissue injury. Given the level of damages involved, it would have been more appropriate for proceedings to be brought in the Circuit Court (CC), which has jurisdiction for claims up to £ 30,000 (€38,092). **44**

15. Wildgust and Carrickowen Ltd. v Norwich Union Ltd.; Unrep. HC 17 August 2001; Morris P. Negligent Misstatement

a) Brief Summary of the Facts

The first plaintiff and his wife obtained a policy of life insurance from the defendant, which was assigned to a third party – Hill Samuel Merchant Bankers – in connection with a loan obtained from Hill Samuel. In March 1992 the direct debit from the first plaintiff's bank was not paid and the life policy lapsed. The first plaintiff became aware of this in June 1992. In April 1992 Hill Samuel contacted the defendant, having become aware of the lapse in payment, but was incorrectly informed that an alternative payment had been made by the first plaintiff. Hill Samuel would have paid the premium in order to preserve the policy. The first plaintiff's wife died in early 1993, but the defendant refused to pay out on the lapsed policy. The plaintiffs sued, claiming that they suffered financial loss as a result of a negligent misstatement by the defendant. **45**

b) Judgment of the High Court

Morris P followed the Supreme Court decision in Glencar v Mayo County Council[49] and used the three-stage test to determine whether any duty of care was owed. On the facts he rejected the plaintiffs' claim because it would not be reasonable to impose a duty in respect of a plaintiff who was not the recipient of the statement, had no knowledge of the statement being made to a third party and had placed no reliance on the statement. **46**

c) Commentary

The High Court has moved closer to the House of Lords approach in Caparo v Dickman,[50] emphasising that the imposition of a duty of care must be just and **47**

[46] *Supra* [15]–[17]
[47] Reddy v Bates [1983] IR, 141.
[48] Gahan v Engineering Products Ltd. [1971] IR, 30; Holohan v Donoghue [1986] ILRM, 250.
[49] *Supra* [3]–[5].
[50] [1990] 2 AC 605.

reasonable; the decision does not go as far as adopting the Caparo redefinition of the requirements of an action for negligent misstatement.[51] On policy grounds the decision is correct, since the first plaintiff must carry primary responsibility for maintaining the policy. However, the implication that a plaintiff could never succeed where the statement is made to and relied on by a third party without the plaintiff's knowledge goes too far. There are surely circumstances where a person that is the subject of representations and reliance between third parties is owed a duty of care, *e.g.* a worker who is the subject of a reference given by a former employer to a prospective employer.[52]

16. L v The Minister for Health & Children; Unrep. HC 6 April 2001; O'Neill, J. Hepatitis C Compensation Tribunal Act, 1997, Sec. 6(3)(e) & Sec. 5(15)

a) Brief Summary of the Facts

48 The plaintiff, who was 33 at the time of trial, was infected with Hepatitis C prior to 1983 during treatment for moderate Haemophilia A. He worked in various jobs up to 1997, when he was involved in a serious road accident, resulting in the amputation of his right leg above the knee. This forced him to give up his job as a curtain fitter and he became a self-employed pelmet maker and upholsterer. With respect to the plaintiff's claim for loss of future earnings, a question arose as to whether the 1997 injury precluded a claim for losses after that point.

b) Judgment of the High Court

49 The plaintiff was awarded general damages of £ 300,000 (€ 380,921), as the effects of the Hepatitis C 'seriously compromised his enjoyment of life and are continuing to do so.' Due to the mild nature of his Haemophilia he would have enjoyed a relatively normal healthy life but for the Hepatitis C. With respect to lost earnings, O'Neill, J considered the House of Lords' decisions in Baker v Willoughby[53] and Jobling v Associated Dairies[54] on causation and the SC decision in Reddy v Bates,[55] which held that factors such as illness must be taken into account in calculating damages. He held that a tortious event should not be regarded as one of the vicissitudes of life, so the 1997 accident did not terminate the defendant's liability for income loss resulting from the loss of capacity created by the Hepatitis C. £ 125,000 (€ 158,717) was awarded in

[51] In Caparo, the requirement of a special relationship between the parties was interpreted so as to require that the plaintiff be identifiable as an individual, or as a member of a limited class of persons. Secondly, the purpose for which the defendant made the statement was required to be in connection with a specific transaction or a particular type of transaction. This contrasts with the more general requirements of the House of Lords position in Hedley-Byrne & Co. Ltd. v Heller & Partners Ltd. [1964] AC, 465, applied by the Irish courts.

[52] Spring v Guardian Assurance plc [1995] 2 AC 296.

[53] [1970] AC, 467.

[54] [1982] AC, 794.

[55] [1983] IR, 141.

respect of future loss of income and £ 17,500 (€ 22,200) was awarded in respect of the period from 1997 up to the date of judgment.

c) Commentary

The judgment offers no explanation as to why the cap for general damages[56] is exceeded. The later decision in McEneaney v Monaghan County Council[57] raises the cap to £ 300,000 (€ 380,921), thus the award by O'Neill J should be considered appropriate in the circumstances. O'Neill also held that where the supervening event is a naturally occurring illness it must be regarded as part of the vicissitudes of life, citing Jobling as authority for the point, though this is inconsistent with some of the judgments in that case.[58] He also held that where the supervening event is a tort there is no universal principle, but the causation approach in Baker was disapproved. He suggests, obiter, that the original act and the 1997 incident were concurrent wrongs. This suggestion that the tortfeasor in the second incident could be liable for the loss of income based on the plaintiff's capacity prior to the Hepatitis C is surely incorrect, as the tort is not a factual cause of the loss. While a finding of legal cause in the absence of factual cause may be made in exceptional circumstances, there is no justification for doing so in cases such as this. The dictum is also inconsistent with statements earlier in the judgment in support of the rule in Performance Cars v Abraham[59] that a second tortfeasor should only be liable for additional losses and not for losses already brought about by the earlier incident. **50**

17. McEneaney v Monaghan County Council; Unrep. HC 26 July 2001; O'Sullivan J. Quantum of Damages; Tariff on General Damages; Calculation of Lost Future Income; Contributory Negligence

a) Brief Summary of the Facts

The plaintiff suffered catastrophic personal injuries when his car slid out of control on a patch of black ice, which had formed on a road maintained by the defendant council. The ice formed from ground water that had seeped out from adjacent land, rather than from rainfall. The plaintiff alleged that the defendant was negligent in failing to provide a drain, given the obvious risk of an accumulation of water arising from the slope of the road and its position next to a vertical face in the land. The defendant alleged contributory negligence on grounds of alcohol consumption, excessive speed and failure to wear a seat belt. The plaintiff had been travelling at 70 miles per hour (MPH), **51**

[56] £ 250,000 (€ 317,434), set by Morris P in Kealy v Min. for Health & Children [1999] 2 IR 456 and reaffirmed in O'N v Min. for Health & Children unrep HC, 19 October 1999.

[57] *Infra* [51]–[53].

[58] Only two of the Law Lords found in favour of the interpretation relied on by O'Neill J – Lords Russell and Keith [1982] AC, 794 at 810–811 and 815 respectively. Lords Wilberforce (at 804) and Edmund-Davies (at 806–809) suggested that Baker was a correct decision on the facts of the case, but did not establish a general principle for all such cases; Lord Bridge (at 821) held that Baker did not establish any general principle, but left open the question as to whether the decision was correct on the facts of the case.

[59] [1961] 3 All ER 413.

exceeding the speed limit by 10 MPH, but not exceeding the design parameters of the road in wet conditions.

b) Judgment of the High Court

52 O'Sullivan J found the failure to provide a drain to be negligent. There was insufficient evidence to support the allegation of excessive alcohol consumption.[60] With respect to speed, O'Sullivan J held that driving in excess of the speed limit, without a 'particular justifying excuse' involved a want of care for his own safety; he went on to find that once this enhanced the risk of injury, it could be treated as a contributing cause of the injury.[61] Enhanced risk could be established by statistical evidence, but 'no special evidence is required in an obvious case.' One-third responsibility was apportioned to the plaintiff as a result of this finding. The issue of failing to wear a seat belt was inconclusive on the issue of causal contribution, as the plaintiff was thrown through the rear window and the defence failed to discharge the onus of establishing that the seat belt would have affected the plaintiff's trajectory. Special damages were assessed as £ 3,374,369 (€ 4,284,564); general damages were assessed as £ 200,000 (€ 253,947). This made a total of £ 3,574,369 (€ 4,538,512); less one-third for contributory negligence, left an award of £ 2,382,913 (€ 3,025,675).

c) Commentary

53 The reasoning behind the calculation of disputed items of damages is worthy of note. Extensive consideration was given to economic evidence in order to determine the capital value of special damages (loss of income, cost of care and medical appliances; the judgment also considers the cost of investment advice). Relying on the House of Lords decision in Wells v Wells,[62] the multiplier for calculating income loss is calculated by O'Sullivan J using a discount of 2.5% to the actuarial calculation, rather than the 4% that had been usual in Irish courts. In respect of medical costs, it is accepted by O'Sullivan J that the trend is that the rate of increase in costs is 3% above the rate of inflation. These rulings will increase the level of special damages awarded to plaintiffs, as the assumptions previously made by courts on these issues were more favourable to defendants. The principles governing the tariff for general damages are also considered in some detail.[63] The cap of £ 150,000 (€ 190,460) set in 1984 would be equal to £ 235,000 (€ 298,388) today if inflation is used as a guide to translating the figure into current terms, but other indicators of

[60] O'Sullivan J found that, although the plaintiff admitted to drinking four small bottles of Heineken, the period of time involved, coupled with evidence about the plaintiff's ability to negotiate earlier hazards on the journey, 'alcohol did not affect or impair the plaintiff's judgment or ability to drive.'

[61] Relying on Sinnott v Quinnsworth [1984] ILRM, 523, at 528 per O'Higgins CJ; Conley v Strain [1988] IR 628, at 632–633 per Lynch J and Hamill v Oliver [1977] IR, 73 at 76 per Griffin J; Reeves v Carthy [1984] IR 348, at 366–367 per Griffin J.

[62] [1998] 1 AC 345.

[63] Sinnott v Quinnsworth [1984] ILRM, 523, at 532 per O'Higgins CJ; Kealy v Min. for Health (*supra* note 56), at p. 459 per Morris P.

changes in living standards suggest a higher figure, approaching £ 600,000 (€ 761,842). O'Sullivan J concludes that £ 300,000 (€ 380,921) would be the appropriate figure. He also held that the situation of the plaintiff as a paraplegic is not the same as a quadriplegic, so he awarded 2/3 of the maximum tariff, taking account of the fact that significant specials had already been awarded.[64] The scaling back of the damages because of the lesser level of injury is slightly out of step with previous HC decisions, which tended to award the maximum amount of general damages in any case of 'catastrophic permanent disablement'.[65] The finding of contributory negligence and the apportionment of 1/3 responsibility to the plaintiff are somewhat harsh also. The plaintiff was only travelling slightly over the permissible speed limit and it is arguable that the injuries sustained would have been of a similar extent, even if he had been travelling at the speed limit. The causal principles used to attribute a contributory role to the plaintiff involve a lower standard than that generally demanded of plaintiffs when attempting to prove the causal role of the defendant's tort.[66] On the apportionment issue, the criterion applied is relative blameworthiness and a finding of one-third responsibility against the plaintiff seems disproportionate when compared with the defendant's failure to provide a safe road.[67]

18. Curran v Finn; Unrep. HC, 29 January 2001; O'Neill, J. Proof of Causation; Cost of Care

a) Brief Summary of the Facts

This case involved the assessment of damages, the defendant's liability having **54**
been established in an earlier SC hearing.[68] The key questions in dispute were first, whether the defendant's negligence caused a prolapsed thoracic disc. And, secondly, did this or the related surgery aggravate the plaintiff's Multiple Sclerosis (MS)?

b) Judgment of the High Court

Although there was conflicting medical evidence as to whether MS could be **55**
aggravated by injury and whether surgery could also be an aggravating factor, O'Neill J held that on the balance of probabilities it could be aggravated by both injury and related surgery. He also found on the balance of probabilities that this plaintiff's MS was aggravated by the injury, as the temporal proximity between the injury and the deterioration due to MS made the injury a more likely explanation of the acceleration in the plaintiff's MS than natural acceleration. The surgery was also found to have contributed in fact to the aggravation of the plaintiff's condition. Damages were assessed on the basis that the aggravation produced a level of debilitation that would have taken approximately eight years to occur naturally and the aggravation of the MS would

[64] Relying on Cooke v Walsh unrep. SC 16 March 1984.
[65] Connolly v Bus Éireann (Irish Bus) & Others unrep HC, 29 January 1996, per Barr J at p. 27.
[66] See Best v Wellcome Foundation Ltd. [1993] 3 IR 421.
[67] For detailed consideration of apportionment see *supra* note 32.
[68] Unrep. SC, 20 May 99.

cause a loss of life expectancy. General damages of £ 200,000 (€ 253,947) and special damages of £ 129,158 (€ 163,996) were awarded. The cost of equipment and house adaptation was disallowed, as they would have been incurred even if the injury had not occurred.

c) Commentary

56 The resolution of conflicting medical evidence on causal issues has arisen many times in the Irish courts and this decision follows the leading SC authorities on the issue.[69] While scientists may find the test disappointingly rudimentary, it is one routinely used by lawyers to decide matters of this nature. Most of the special damages were based on care provided by the plaintiff's family since the aggravation of the MS and for the future and the amount was approximately 60% of the cost of professional care. This is in line with regular practice in the Irish courts where care is provided by family members, rather than professional carers.

19. Molloy v Farrell; Unrep. HC, 11 December 2001. Finnegan J. Quantum of Damages

a) Brief Summary of the Facts

57 The plaintiff was a front seat passenger in a vehicle involved in an RTA in April 1996 and initially suffered neck, lower back and ankle injuries. He later complained of headaches and severe back pains, radiating down his leg. While the broken ankle healed normally, the back and leg pains did not respond to physiotherapy or medication and in May 2000 he was still suffering from them and he was unlikely to make any physical improvement. He would never be fit for his previous employment again, though he would be fit for light work. There was also a significant amount of stress resulting from the physical damage and loss of income. Liability was admitted but a dispute arose with respect to some aspects of the quantum of damages.

b) Judgment of the High Court

58 Finnegan J awarded £ 130,000 (€ 165,065) in general damages; some items of special damages amounting to £ 3,992 (€ 5,068) were agreed. In respect of the disputed items of special damages, the plaintiff was awarded £ 41,611.53 (€ 52,835) for hospital expenses and £ 3,000 (€ 3,809) in respect of travel expenses related to his medical treatment, £ 185,000 (€ 234,901) in respect of loss of earnings and £ 46,146 (€ 58,593) in respect of loss of employment related benefits.

[69] Best v Wellcome Foundation Ltd. [1993] 3 IR 421; O'Leary v Cork Corporation unrep SC, 4 July 1997. Finlay CJ in Best, at p. 462, stated that;
"The function which a court can and must perform in the trial of a case in order to acquire a just result, is to apply common sense and a careful understanding of the logic and likelihood of events to conflicting opinions and conflicting theories concerning a matter of this kind."

c) Commentary

The award of general damages is high, but not entirely out of line with such damages in cases of permanent reduction of physical capacity and discomfort. The items of special damages turn on a resolution of conflicting evidence and raise no special principles. 59

20. Sheehy v The Devil's Glen Tours Equestrian Centre Ltd.; Unrep. HC, 10 December 2001. Lavan J. Occupiers' Liability; Contributory Negligence

a) Brief Summary of the Facts

The plaintiff was injured in a trip at the entrance to a building, forming part of the defendant's premises in 1997. She tripped on a door saddle made of wood with a metal strip on top, which was approximately two inches (5.08 centimetres) above the ground. These are commonly used in domestic premises, but are not usually found in commercial premises and usually protrude no more than three quarters of an inch. Quantum was agreed between the parties, but there was a dispute as to liability and contributory negligence. 60

b) Judgment of the High Court

Lavan J held that the plaintiff was a visitor for the purposes of the Occupiers' Liability Act, 1995, as she was on the premises with her husband and children for the purposes of availing of the defendant's commercial facilities. The applicable duty was one of reasonable care in the circumstances, which had been breached by the defendant. On the basis that contributory negligence is not as readily available in cases of breach of statutory duty, as it is in cases of breach of a common law duty, the plaintiff's failure to look down was not found to give rise to contributory negligence. 61

c) Commentary

The ruling on the difference between contributory negligence in respect of statutory and common law duties is supported by the jurisprudence of the courts,[70] though it does seem anomalous in a case such as this where the statutory duty is framed in exactly the same terms as a common law duty. 62

[70] Higgins v South of Ireland Asphalt Co. Ltd. (1961) *Irish Law Times Reports* (ILTR) 101, 168 (SC); Dunne v Honeywell Control Systems Ltd. & Virginia Milk Products Ltd. [1991] ILRM, 595 (SC); Kelly v McNamara unrep. HC, 5 June 1996 Connell v McGing unrep. HC, 8 December 2000; see B. M. E. McMahon/W. Binchy (*supra* note 13), pp. 608–611.

21. Williams v T.P. Wallace Construction Ltd. & Others; Unrep. HC, 23 November 2001. Morris P. Occupier's Liability; Occupational Safety

a) Brief Summary of the Facts

63 The plaintiff was injured when descending a ladder after attempting to inspect guttering on a building site where the first defendants were the main contractors. The plaintiff was acting on behalf of a third party, a distributor of building materials that had supplied the guttering in question.

b) Judgment of the High Court

64 The plaintiff was found not to have permission to be on the site and, consequently, did not qualify as a visitor for the purposes of the Occupier's Liability Act, 1995. The duty owed, therefore, was not to act in reckless disregard for his safety. The presence of an unsecured ladder was found not to be a breach of this duty. The claim in respect of breach of sec. 8 of the Safety, Health and Welfare at Work Act, 1989 was rejected on the basis that the duty owed to persons other than employees was dependant on the place of work being 'made available to them' by the defendant and this criterion was not satisfied.

c) Commentary

65 The finding in respect of occupier's liability is satisfactory on the facts, but does not provide any clear guidance on the interpretation of the reckless disregard standard, on which the Act is unclear. Morris P makes it clear that the behaviour would have constituted negligence against a visitor and that something more is required to establish recklessness, but he does not clarify whether gross negligence would suffice. The treatment of the 1989 Act fails to have regard to sec. 60 subs. 1(a), which precludes civil claims for a breach of the duty contained in sec. 8.

22. Devlin v Min. for Justice, Ireland & the AG and Sheahan; Unrep. HC, 4 April 2001; Morris P. Limitation of Actions in an Action for Trespass to the Person

a) Brief Summary of the Facts

66 The plaintiff alleged that a Garda (Irish term for a police officer) hit him with a baton in August 1991. A preliminary issue arose as to the appropriate limitation period. Should it be the general six-year period for tort actions, or the reduced three-year period applicable to actions 'claiming damages in respect of personal injuries to a person caused by negligence, nuisance or breach of duty'?[71]

[71] Sec.11(2)(b) of the Statute of Limitations, 1957 as amended by sec. 3 of the Statute of Limitations (Amendment) Act, 1991.

b) Judgment of the High Court

Morris P adopted the approach of Lord Griffith in Stubbings v Webb[72] and held that assault [*sic.*] was not a 'breach of duty' for the purposes of the legislation. Actions of trespass to the person are, therefore subject to the general six-year limitation period, even though they may involve personal injury. **67**

c) Commentary

Treating trespass actions differently from other personal injuries cases is an appropriate interpretation of the limitations legislation, given the important intangible interests such as dignity and autonomy protected by the torts. Morris P uses the term 'assault' though the facts clearly indicate the tort of battery; this misdescription often arises, perhaps as a result of the difference in terminology in criminal and civil law. More significantly, Morris P twice describes trespass as involving a deliberate intention to cause injury. The established requirement is that intention to make contact, rather than intent to harm, is sufficient for the tort of battery.[73] It is submitted that such a profound change in the nature of the tort should not flow from statements that are clearly obiter. **68**

23. McDonnell v Walsh; Unrep. HC, 1 March 2001; Barr, J. Quantum of Damages

a) Brief Summary of the Facts

A back seat passenger in a car that crashed suffered cuts to the face and leg; she also suffered pains in her head, shoulder, ear and leg; furthermore she lost consciousness for a brief period (a minute or two). The plaintiff recovered well from the physical injuries, but suffered severe post-traumatic stress disorder (PTSD). Prior to the accident the plaintiff had suffered from a mild mental disorder. The main focus of the case is on a difference of medical opinion in respect of the degree of care the plaintiff would need into the future, based on the likely level of recovery she would make. The trial was adjourned for three months to determine the plaintiff's progress with a view to resolving the difference of opinion as to the future prognosis. The expert witness for the defence accepted the plaintiff's recovery would be less than his earlier estimation, but still disagreed with plaintiff's witness that she would require an average of six weeks hospital treatment per annum. **69**

b) Judgment of the High Court

Barr, J held that the plaintiff is likely to need three weeks hospitalisation per year for the rest of her life and is significantly more vulnerable to stress than she was prior to the accident. General damages of £ 140,000 (€ 177,763) were awarded. Barr, J noted that the plaintiff will be unable to manage the money and recommended the use of the wardship jurisdiction of the court. **70**

[72] [1893] AC, 498.

[73] See E. Quill (*supra* note 13), pp. 152–154; B.M.E. McMahon/W. Binchy (*supra* note 13), pp. 616–617.

c) Commentary

71 The amount of general damages is high for a PTSD case. This cannot be entirely explained on the grounds of the accompanying physical injuries, as more than half of the award – £ 80,000 (€ 101,579) – is for future loss and the plaintiff's physical injuries had healed. This is to be welcomed as previous awards for PTSD were somewhat low compared to other types of personal injury.[74] The concern for the management of the award is also to be welcomed and is a factor that has only recently begun to receive attention by the courts.[75]

24. O'Keeffe v Kilcullen & Others; Unrep. HC, 1 February 2001; O'Sullivan, J. Immunity of Persons Submitting Reports in Respect of Judicial Proceedings

a) Brief Summary of the Facts

72 The third defendant conducted a psychiatric examination of the plaintiff in respect of proceedings brought by the plaintiff's husband, on foot of which a decree of nullity was granted. The plaintiff sued for negligence, leading to loss of entitlement to maintenance and other statutory benefits and for infringement of constitutional rights under artt. 41 and 42. The case was initially dismissed in June 1998 on the basis that the report did not cause the damage. The SC remitted the matter to the HC to consider whether the defendant was entitled to immunity from suit as a witness. The defendant argued that the witness immunity should extend to expert reports because the policy behind immunity is equally applicable to the circumstances in which reports are given and that, in any event the HC was bound by SC decision in Looney v Bank of Ireland and Morey,[76] concerning the submission of an affidavit. The plaintiff argued that the decision in Looney is distinguishable because it only applies to witnesses and that the SC acknowledged that the immunity had limits (though such limits were not specified). The plaintiff further asserted that the primary duty to the court of a court appointed witness does not exhaust all duties. Finally the plaintiff suggested that the House of Lords decision in Hall v Simons[77] should persuade the court that the public policy of remedying wrongs should outweigh those relating to witness immunity.

[74] £ 75,000 (€ 95,230) was awarded in Mullally v Bus Éireann [1992] ILRM, 722 for an extremely serious case of PTSD, while the SC in Kelly v Hennessy [1995] 3 IR 253 reduced a HC award of £ 75,000 (€ 95,230) to £ 55,000 (€ 69,835) on the grounds that the plaintiff was expected to make a partial recovery.

[75] In Ward v Walsh unrep SC, 31 July 1991 the plaintiff was awarded a significant amount of damages, having been rendered paraplegic; the award included a modest amount of special damages in respect of the cost of financial advice on the management of the award.

[76] *Supra* note 43.

[77] *Supra* note 44.

b) Judgment of the High Court

O'Sullivan, J ruled that he was bound by Looney and that the limits referred to by the SC only applied to malicious and irrelevant witness statements, or flagrant abuse of the privilege granted to witnesses. **73**

c) Commentary

The judgment is correct, as the submission of expert reports must be considered to be of a similar nature to depositions by witnesses. The disincentive to provide such reports that would flow from the imposition of a duty of care would be equally disruptive of the proper conduct of a trial as a duty imposed on witnesses. **74**

25. Weldon v Fingal Coaches; Unrep. HC, 25 January, 2001; Ó Caoimh, J. Negligent Management of a Vehicle; Striking out Proceedings

a) Brief Summary of the Facts

The plaintiff climbed into the luggage compartment of a coach and was seriously injured when he fell out while the coach was driving. The defence applied to have the action struck out for failing to disclose a reasonable cause of action under Order 19 Rule 28 of the Superior Court Rules, or alternatively, to have it struck out as frivolous or vexatious under the inherent jurisdiction of the court. **75**

b) Judgment of the High Court

Ó Caoimh, J held that applications to strike out under Order 19 Rule 28 of the Superior Court Rules should be decided without consideration of evidence; only the pleadings are considered. Striking out under the inherent jurisdiction of the court may involve consideration of evidence. Negligence and the Occupiers' Liability Act 1995 were considered as potential causes of action; the defence of waiver was also considered. He concluded that first, the mere fact that the compartment is left open does not give rise to a claim in negligence; secondly, if the defendant knowingly permitted use of the luggage compartment a claim may be sustained. Consequently the application must be refused. The possibility of a cause of action based on occupiers' liability was left undecided and finally, Ó Caoimh, J held that the defence of waiver could not apply. **76**

c) Commentary

The decision on the nature of a negligence claim on the facts alleged is correct. It would be unfairly disruptive of the business of coach driving if the mere fact of leaving the luggage compartment open was sufficient to generate a finding of negligence; however, knowledge of the use of the luggage compartment for stowing away is a suitable criterion for making such a finding. The ruling on the defence of waiver is also in line with the leading cases on **77** the subject, as the defence cannot be sustained unless there is communication between the parties on the allocation of risk.[78]

26. Kelly v O'Leary; Unrep. HC, 22 June, 2001; Kelly, J. Dismissal of Stale Claims

a) Brief Summary of the Facts

78 The plaintiff sought damages for physical and mental suffering arising out of an alleged breach of duty by an order of nuns in running an orphanage in which she was placed between 1934 and 1937. The action was instituted on 26 March 1998, more than 50 years after the last act complained of. The defendant sought to have the action struck out on the grounds that it would not be possible to mount a proper defence due to the interval between the occurrence of the events complained of and the time of trial.

b) Judgment of the High Court

79 Having referred to the principles set out in O'Domhnall v Merrick,[79] Toal v Duignan (No.1)[80] and Primor v Stokes Kennedy Crowley[81] Kelly, J does not attempt to resolve the differences between the three cases, but applies the test from the third case, which is more favourable to the plaintiff. The first limb of that test asks was the delay inordinate? On the facts he answered this affirmatively. He then proceeded to the second limb of the test – was the delay inexcusable? Again he answered this affirmatively, as there were no special considerations justifying a delay of this length. The third limb of the test then asks – does the balance of justice require dismissal of the claims? This was also answered affirmatively, as most of the witnesses that the defence would have required were dead, the defendant would be at least 83 by the date of trial and the events in question would be between 55 and 68 years in the past.

c) Commentary

80 The finding that the first limb of the test was satisfied is uncontroversial, given the time lapse involved. The finding on the second limb of the test involved consideration of Guerin v Guerin.[82] In that case the delay was excused because the plaintiff and his parents failed to appreciate, due to their socially deprived background, that a cause of action might be available. In the present case no evidence was adduced to show that the plaintiff was in a comparable position. The ruling on the third limb is based on the clear prejudice to the mounting of an adequate defence in the circumstances and is not surprising.

[78] O'Hanlon v ESB [1969] IR, 75; McComiskey v McDermott [1974] IR, 75; Ryan v Ireland [1989] IR, 177; [1989] ILRM, 544; Regan v RIAC [1990] 1 IR 278; Baldwin v Foy & Forrest Way Riding Holidays Ltd. unrep HC, 1 July 1997.

[79] [1984] IR, 151.

[80] [1991] ILRM, 135; see J.P.M. White, The Limitation of Personal Injuries and Death Actions, [1991] *Gazette*, 37.

[81] [1996] 2 IR 459.

[82] [1992] 2 IR 287.

27. Breslin v Corcoran & MIBI; Unrep. HC, 17 July 2001; Butler J. Intervening Cause

a) Brief Summary of the Facts

The first defendant left his car unlocked and with the keys in the ignition as he went into a shop to get a sandwich. An unknown person stole the car and struck the plaintiff, causing damages agreed at £ 65,000 (€ 82,532). The issue was which of the parties was liable – if the first defendant were not liable the MIBI would be obliged to meet the plaintiff's claim, under an agreement with the government covering injuries by uninsured or untraceable drivers. **81**

b) Judgment of the High Court

Butler J held that the intervention of the third party amounted to a *novus actus interveniens* (new and intervening cause), breaking the chain of causation between the first defendant's admitted negligence and breach of statutory duty and the plaintiff's injury, following Topp v London Country Bus (South West) Ltd.[83] He also indicated that a person such as the defendant could be liable if 'the vehicle was left in an area where it should be known to the owner that people routinely stole cars for the purpose of driving them around in a reckless and dangerous fashion.' Consequently liability for the plaintiff's damages and costs fell on the MIBI. **82**

c) Commentary

The finding of a *novus actus interveniens* is difficult to understand in light of the suggestion that liability should arise if the area was one where cars were routinely stolen for the purposes of joyriding. Given that the incident occurred in a city centre street in Dublin, it is difficult to imagine when liability would be imposed if such a street is not an appropriate place to regard as being known for car theft. Avoiding the intervention of car thieves, because of the dangers they pose to the public, is the principal reason for imposing a duty of care. Why then should the very thing that a plaintiff must guard against be treated as a *novus actus interveniens*? The ruling is contrary to earlier authority.[84] **83**

28. F v Min. for Health; Unrep. HC, 9 November 2001; O'Neill J. Hepatitis C Compensation Tribunal Act 1997; Eligibility for Compensation

a) Brief Summary of the Facts

The appellant's mother contracted Hepatitis C and was unable to continue her business of wholesale cigarette sales; in 1990 the appellant left school and took over the running of the business. He claimed that but for his mother's **84**

[83] [1993] 3 All ER 448.

[84] Cunningham v McGrath Brothers [1964] IR, 209; Stansbie v Troman [1948] 2 *King's Bench Reports* (KB) 48.

hepatitis he would have finished school and trained as a carpenter, giving him a significantly greater income than he now has. His claim under sec. 4(1)(d) of the 1997 Act was rejected by the tribunal as he was not a person 'responsible' for the care of his mother and that the assistance rendered would not qualify as 'care' for the purposes of the Act.

b) Judgment of the High Court

85 O'Neill J held that the concept of responsibility for care under the Act included moral responsibility and 'a son providing care for his mother is manifestly included.' He also held that assistance with the running of a small family business constitutes 'care' for the purposes of the Act and it would be artificial to draw a distinction between this type of assistance and domestic assistance, which the SC had held constituted 'care' in O'C v Min. for Health.[85] He also found that the decision to try and maintain the business was reasonable and that it would not have been possible for the applicant to pursue an alternative career and maintain the business; nor would it have been possible to employ a third party to maintain the business. As evidence of proof of the loss had not been heard, the case was put back for hearing on that issue.

c) Commentary

86 The decision is to be welcomed as the Act was designed to offset the hardship arising from a major public disaster and a narrow and literal interpretation of the Act would unduly reduce the scope of the benefit provided. The acceptance of assistance in running a small business concern as 'care' seems appropriate in the circumstances, as the applicant's mother was deeply concerned about its survival. It is fair that the economic strength of the business should not be the only concern and that the court should place some value on its social and emotional impact on the family.

29. Cooper-Flynn v RTE, Bird & Howard; Unrep. HC, 5 April 2001; Morris P. Defamation, Costs

a) Brief Summary of the Facts

87 The plaintiff instituted libel proceedings against the defendants on the basis of a story broadcast by the first and second named defendants, which alleged that the plaintiff advised the third plaintiff to evade tax. The jury found that she had not done so, but that she had so advised a number of other people and, consequently, her reputation had not suffered so no damages were awarded. The plaintiff sought to recover her costs either on the basis that the first finding indicated that she had won her case, or alternatively that, even if she could be seen as substantially losing the case, it was a 'special cause' meriting departure from the normal rule that costs follow the event.

[85] Unrep. SC, 31 July 2001; the case was principally concerned with the procedural question of whether interest was payable on awards under the 197 Act.

b) Judgment of the High Court

Morris P held that the finding in the plaintiff's favour on the first issue was rendered meaningless by the subsequent findings and that it was not a special cause. The jury findings were essentially a victory for the defendants and costs were awarded in favour of the defendants. The decision approved dicta from the English Court of Appeal decision in Reynolds v The Times[86] on the issue of costs. **88**

c) Commentary

The jury decision is a rare example of a case where the defence of justification has succeeded upon proof of the partial truth of allegations. It is correct to regard such a case as having been won by the defendant and the partial untruth should not be seen as a technical victory by the plaintiff. **89**

30. Kelly v Min For Agriculture, Food & Forestry, Ireland and the Attorney General (AG); Unrep. HC, 1 May 2001; Butler J. Duty of Care; Breach of Constitutional Rights

a) Brief Summary of the Facts

This was a trial of preliminary issues ordered by an earlier HC decision.[87] The plaintiff was a supervisor in a beef processing plant at which officers appointed by the first defendant operated a scheme for deboning intervention beef. The plaintiff alleged that his signature was forged on documents relating to the scheme, leading to a criminal prosecution being brought against him. The plaintiff was acquitted by direction of the trial judge. The main questions for consideration were whether the defendants owed the plaintiff a duty of care at common law or under the Constitution and, if so, whether there had been a breach of duty causing damage; ancillary issues were also raised. **90**

b) Judgment of the High Court

The parties agreed that the duty of care at common law should be decided on the basis of the two-stage test and it was found that a duty was owed. Butler J found that there was sufficient proximity between the parties and the policy argument raised by the defendants – that the imposition of a duty would inhibit the initiation of prosecutions – was rejected. The constitutional issue did not, therefore, arise; however, Butler J noted obiter that the interference with the plaintiff's liberty would give rise to a constitutional duty if he were incorrect on the imposition of a duty at common law. If the facts alleged were true then there was a clear breach of duty causing damage for which the defendants would be vicariously liable. **91**

[86] [1998] 3 All ER 961.
[87] Unrep. HC 4 December 2000; Johnson J.

c) Commentary

92 The duty of care issue may need reconsideration in light of the SC decision in Glencar v Mayo,[88] but it could be argued that the constitutional rights issue would make the imposition of a duty of care just and reasonable. It is also worth noting that Butler J gave due consideration to the defence argument of a policy basis for not imposing a duty and rejected the argument raised, further demonstrating the reasonableness of the duty imposed.

31. Lehany v Loftus and the Western Health Board; Unrep. HC, 20 July 2001; Ó Caoimh J; Leave to Institute Proceedings

a) Brief Summary of the Facts

93 The applicant sought leave under sec. 260 of the Mental Treatment Act, 1945 to bring proceedings against the respondents arising out of his involuntary detention for one day in July 1996. The first respondent certified the applicant for involuntary detention based on information received from the applicant's brother, a brief discussion with the applicant and his personal knowledge of the applicant's medical history. A doctor at the hospital to which the applicant was brought decided to keep the applicant in overnight for observation. The following day the applicant was re-examined and further information was received from third parties, as a result of which the applicant was released. The applicant claimed that on the basis of the SC decision in Bailey v Gallagher,[89] that he was only required to establish a prima facie case on the balance of probabilities that the respondents acted in bad faith or without reasonable care. The respondents argued on the basis of the SC decisions in O'Dowd v North Western Health Board,[90] Murphy v Greene[91] and O'Reilly v Moroney[92] that something more than a prima facie case was required. There was also a dispute as to whether the action was statute barred in any event.

b) Judgment of the High Court

94 Ó Caoimh J held that the respondents had acted in good faith and the hospital staff had acted with reasonable care; he also noted that, while the first respondent's reliance on the truthfulness of the applicant's brother may be regarded as erroneous with hindsight, such hindsight could not form the basis of judgment and the evidence did not disclose substantial grounds for finding a want of reasonable care on the respondent's part. Ó Caoimh J noted obiter that he believed that the applicant's claim would be statute barred even if there had been sufficient grounds to establish a claim.

[88] *Supra* [3]–[5].
[89] [1996] 2 ILRM 433.
[90] [1982] ILRM, 186, at 194 per Griffin J.
[91] [1991] ILRM, 404, at 410 per Finlay CJ, at 416 per O'Flaherty J, at 418 & 420 per McCarthy J.
[92] Unrep. SC, 16 November 1993.

c) Commentary

The judgment does not resolve the conflict with respect to the standard of proof required to obtain leave. The conflict results from some difficult and at times conflicting SC judgments on the issue. If sec. 73 of the Mental Health Act, 2001 is implemented this issue will no longer arise. **95**

32. Peter McCourt v Dan Dooley Ltd.; Unrep. HC, 25 June 2001; O'Donovan J. Quantum of Damages

a) Brief Summary of the Facts

The plaintiff was the driver of a car, which was involved in a head-on collision in March 1998, caused by the other driver's negligence. Liability was admitted and the dispute concerned the quantum of damages. The plaintiff suffered injuries to his head, neck, shoulders, chest, back and both knees. Although no bone injury was suffered, the plaintiff was in considerable pain and received only marginal relief from 9–10 physiotherapy sessions. In July 1998 the plaintiff was referred to an orthopaedic surgeon, who detected a cervical nerve root irritation and an aggravation of pre-existing degenerative changes in the ankle joint, in addition to the soft tissue injuries for which he was already being treated. The plaintiff made a significant improvement under the orthopaedic surgeon's care. **96**

b) Judgment of the High Court

O'Donovan J awarded the plaintiff £ 15,000 (€ 19,046) for general damages to date; £ 50,000 (€ 63,486) for general damages in the future, on the basis that 'he has to look forward to chronic pain in the future and the possibility of further surgery.' Special damages were agreed at £ 2,225 (€ 2,825). **97**

c) Commentary

The judgment raises no significant issue of principle and is no more than a routine application of established principles. The case does, however, highlight the absence of a clear scale of general damages in Ireland. Such a scale might have avoided the need for a judicial resolution of the dispute. **98**

33. Elizabeth McCourt v Dan Dooley Ltd.; Unrep. HC 25 June 2001; O'Donovan J. Quantum of Damages

a) Brief Summary of the Facts

The plaintiff was a passenger in the car, which was involved in the accident mentioned in the previous case. She suffered soft tissue neck and back injuries. Under treatment from an orthopaedic surgeon her neck improved significantly, but her back injury made only slight progress, leaving her with inhibited mobility and disruption to sleep. Conflicting evidence was submitted by doctors for both sides on the plaintiff's future prognosis. **99**

b) Judgment of the High Court

100 O'Donovan J accepted that the plaintiff's future prognosis lay somewhere between the opposing views of the doctors for each side, accepting that she would have some continuing difficulties, but is unlikely to get any worse. He awarded £ 15,000 (€ 19,046) for general damages to date, £ 25,000 (€ 31,743) for general damages in the future and £ 2,135 (€ 2,710) special damages (agreed between the parties).

c) Commentary

101 As with the previous case arising out of the same accident, the quantum issue raises nothing special. The resolution of conflicting medical evidence involved a routine resolution, based on the principles raised earlier in Curran v Finn.[93]

34. Mackey v Iarnrod Éireann (Irish Rail); Unrep. HC, 31 May 2001; Kinlen J. Employers' Liability

a) Brief Summary of the Facts

102 The plaintiff was employed in the maintenance of the defendant's trains at a shed in Connolly station, Dublin. He alleged that he suffered injury due to inadequate ventilation, inadequate extraction of fumes and the lack of appropriate protective apparatus. The only ventilation provided was to open the doors of the shed, making the shed unduly cold. The plaintiff was also required to use cleaning fluids that were known to contain irritants.

b) Judgment of the High Court

103 Kinlen J found the defendant to be negligent in failing to provide adequate control of diesel emissions, inadequate ventilation and in not providing facemasks and gloves. The plaintiff was not found to be contributory negligent; although he knew he had a bad chest, he had a family to support, so he was not negligent in continuing in this employment. It was found that the defendant's negligence did not cause, but aggravated the plaintiff's asthma; in the absence of specific evidence, the court attributed 50% of the plaintiff's disability to his working conditions. Loss of income to date was agreed at £ 119,945.65 (€ 152,299.56), less deductions for social welfare, a health board rent subsidy and income from various jobs that the plaintiff undertook since accepting redundancy – these amounted to £ 79,139 (€ 100,485); further deductions amounting to £ 8,993 (€ 11,418) were later agreed. Kinlen J applied sec. 2 of the Civil Liability Act, 1964 to hold that the plaintiff's redundancy payment should not be deducted.[94] Future loss of income was assessed at £ 53, 025 (€ 67,327); general damages to date were assessed at £ 40,000 (€ 50,789) and future general damages were assessed at £ 20,000 (€ 25,394). The total dam-

[93] *Supra* [54]–[56].

[94] The statutory provision provides that collateral benefits, payable in consequence of the injury, are not to be deducted from the award of damages.

ages were £ 144,838.65 (€ 183,907) and the plaintiff was awarded half of that figure – £ 72,419 (€ 91,953).

c) Commentary

The apportionment of 50% responsibility to the defendant in the absence of clear evidence on the contribution is in line with apportionment principles generally applied in cases of multiple causes. The Law Reform Commission (LRC) has recently queried the principle of non-deductibility of collateral benefits and provisionally recommended the introduction of a general principle of deductibility with limited exceptions.[95] To date no legislative action has been taken on the matter. **104**

35. Rothwell v MIBI; Unrep. HC, 6 July, 2001; McCracken J. Burden of Proof

a) Brief Summary of the Facts

The plaintiff skidded on a patch of spilt fuel, causing his car to collide with another car, travelling in the opposite direction. The claim is based on clause 6 of the agreement of 21 December 1988 between the MIBI and the Minister for the Environment, which relates to personal injuries caused by untraced or unidentified drivers. **105**

b) Judgment of the High Court

The cause of the spillage was unlikely to be from a leaking tanker, due to the small quantity involved; it was held to probably come from a spillage from a vehicle with a defective, or missing, or improperly fitted fuel cap. McCracken J held that 'driving' for the purposes of the agreement included management and control of the vehicle.[96] On the issue of whether the driving was negligent, McCracken J noted that there was no evidence of what had occurred and one could envisage situations where it could result from either negligent or non-negligent behaviour by the driver; he refused to apply the *res ipsa loquitur* principle, but noted that in an ordinary case between two drivers the onus would shift to the defendant due to his superior capacity to show what had occurred. Despite the defendant not having this superior capacity to prove, McCracken J felt that the purpose of the agreement was to facilitate injured persons in obtaining compensation where none was otherwise available and the plaintiff should not be required to prove something that he would not have to prove in litigation against a known driver. £ 30,000 (€ 38,092) was awarded for a dislocated shoulder with permanent disfigurement and discomfort. **106**

[95] LRC, *Consultation Paper on Section 2 of the Civil Liability (Amendment) Act, 1964: The Deductibility of Collateral Benefits From Awards of Damages* (1999) at §8.80.

[96] Relying on sec. 3 of the Road Traffic Act, 1961.

c) Commentary

107 The reasoning on liability is unusual, as the reversal of the burden of proof ordinarily only occurs if the defendant has a superior ability to establish what occurred and the plaintiff is unduly prejudiced by the normal burden of proof.[97] The defendant in this instance does not have a superior capacity to prove, so the rationale for the change in the burden of proof is not satisfied on the facts. Furthermore, the decision will necessarily mean that the MIBI will in some instances have to make payment where no tort was committed because they will be unable to prove the absence of tortious behaviour.

C. Literature

1. R. Byrne/W. Binchy, *Annual Review of Irish Law 2000* (2001)

108 This comprehensive review of legal developments in Irish law during the year 2000 contains an extensive chapter on tort (pp. 411–476), covering all the superior court cases for the year. The authors of this established series provide extensive critical appraisal of the developments in the law, cross-referenced to the leading academic writings on the issues raised. The chapter on the limitation of actions contains an analysis of the Statute of Limitations (Amendment) Act, 2000 (at pp. 415–418). The legislation extends the definition of disability under the Statute of Limitations, 1957 so as to include psychological injury resulting from child sexual abuse, thereby providing claimants with an extended limitation period for the initiation of a tort action.

2. R. Byrne/J.P. McCutcheon, *The Irish Legal System* (4th edn. 2001)

109 Chapter 12, on the doctrine of precedent, includes a discussion of the development of the tort of negligence in the twentieth century as an example of precedent in action (pp. 375 *et seq.*). The principal focus of the piece is on the development of the concepts of duty of care and standard of care in respect of solicitors in Ireland.

3. N. Brennan/J. Hennessy, *Forensic Accounting* (2001)

110 Chapter 7 deals with the role of forensic accountants in civil litigation in personal matters, including an overview of the situations in which they may be involved in personal injuries litigation (pp. 192–204). Chapter 9 considers their role in commercial litigation, including a short section on product liability (pp. 314–318). Chapter 10 considers their role in corporate cases, briefly addressing negligent and fraudulent misrepresentation (pp. 399–404). Chapter 12 deals extensively with accountants' liability in tort. Chapter 16 deals extensively with the calculation of damages in personal injury cases. Chapter 17 deals with the calculation of damages in commercial cases in both contract

[97] Hanrahan v Merk, Sharp & Dohme (Ireland) Ltd. (*supra* note 13).

and tort. Finally, chapter 19 deals with discounting and interest in the calculation of damages.

4. J. Canny, *Construction and Building Law* (2001)

This text covers a variety of aspects of law related to the construction industry, **111**
presented in a manner which is accessible to the lay reader. Chapter 9 outlines the main instances of tortious liability of builders, covering general negligence principles, nuisance, the rule in Rylands v Fletcher, negligent misstatement, negligently inflicted economic loss and statutory liability for defective products. Chapter 10 deals with the Occupiers' Liability Act, 1995.

5. R. Arthur, Duty of Care To Children In Care, [2001] 19 ILT (ns) 38

The author examines the duties owed by Health Boards under sec. 3 of the **112**
Child Care Act 1991. The first section considers the position under public law, but the latter half considers the potential for civil liability in negligence, breach of statutory duty and vicarious liability for the acts of employees in the course of the performance of functions under the Act. The author expresses doubt about the availability of such actions, though he emphasises that the position may require review in light of the decision of the ECHR in Osman v UK.[98]

6. C. Noctor, Statute Of Limitations (Amendment) Act, 2000 – Implications For Parties to Actions Regarding Child Sexual Abuse, [2001] 19 ILT (ns) 126

This article analyses the implication of the Statute of Limitations (Amend- **113**
ment) Act, 2000, which extends the limitation period for tortious claims by victims of child sexual abuse. It considers the amended definition of disability under sec. 48A of the Statute of Limitations, 1957, as inserted by the 2000 Act and its implications for actions both against the perpetrators of abuse and against institutions where such abuse was suffered. The author offers views on the likely interpretation of a variety of practical issues arising out of the legislation.

7. G. Carey, A Critique Of The Development of Occupational Injuries Liability in Irish Torts Law – Parts I & II, [2001] 19 ILT (ns) 130, 146

Part I of this article deals with the historical development of occupational inju- **114**
ries law, particularly in the 19th century, and examines the socio-political forces underlying that development. It focuses in particular on the doctrine of vicarious liability, highlighting difficulties both in its theoretical underpinning and its practical application. Part II examines the policies and principles underlying modern developments in occupational injuries law, focusing on statutory duties and developments in respect of concurrent wrongdoers.

[98] *Supra* note 9.

8. C. Gardiner, The State Claims Agency – A New Role for the National Treasury Management Agency (NTMA), [2001] 19 ILT (ns) 179

115 This article analyses one specific aspect of the National Treasury Management Agency (Amendment) Act 2000 – the establishment of a State Claims Agency for the administration of claims against the state. It highlights two features of the new functions to be provided by the NTMA – the management of personal injury and property damage claims against the state and risk management to reduce the incidence of such claims. The author welcomes the development, highlighting the potential for greater efficiency, earlier settlements and a reduction of legal costs arising out of such claims.

9. E. M. Dee, Professional Negligence of Solicitors, [2001] 19 ILT (ns) 282

116 The author examines the law concurrent duties in contract and tort. The article particularly emphasises solicitors' fiduciary duties and the duty to non-clients, highlighting the theoretical basis for the imposition of a duty in tort. The standard of care is also examined, with a specific focus on the issues of a solicitor's reliance on counsel's advice.

10. M. McGrath, Trips and Falls on Foot and Mouth Mats, [2001] 6 *The Bar Review* (Bar Rev.) 491

117 This article considers the potential liability in negligence of persons for placing disinfectant soaked mats on land of which they are not occupiers. It raises the question as to whether the public policy goal of preventing the spread of foot and mouth disease would be sufficient to either negate a duty of care arising at common law, or to lower the level of precaution required to satisfy the standard of care. The author concludes that such an economically based policy should not override a plaintiff's interest in physical integrity and so should not provide a defence to a personal injuries claim.

11. Prof. N. Brennan/J. Hennessy, Forensic Accounting and the Calculation of Personal Injury Damages, [2001] 6 Bar Rev. 533

118 This article analyses a number of difficulties arising from the method by which damages are calculated in personal injury cases, highlighting a variety of issues raised in their textbook on forensic accounting. It focuses on assumptions that are made in the quantification process, particularly in the case of lost future earnings, pensions benefits, and lost years (shortened life expectancy); it also highlights a number of items of loss that plaintiffs routinely fail to include and also critiques the setting of the multiplier used to determine the present capital value of such future losses. The authors call for a clarification of key issues in the quantification process to promote greater precision in the calculation of damages.

12. A. J. Buckley, Employer's Liability and the Personal Liability of the Manager Behind the Corporate Veil, [2001] 8 *Commercial Law Practitioner* (CLP) 13

This is a case note on Shinkwin v Quin-Con Ltd. & Quinlan,[99] in which the managing director of a company, who was also the day-to-day manager of the company's factory, was held personally liable for injuries caused to a worker by his negligence. The author distinguishes piercing the corporate veil from direct liability for breach of a duty of care and considers the merits and flaws of the introduction of a manager's liability insurance policy. **119**

13. S. Dodd, Passing-Off, Domain Names and Injunctive Relief, [2001] 8 CLP 79

This case note on Localireland Ltd. v Localireland-Online Ltd.,[100] a passing off action between two providers of advertising websites for small businesses, considers the principles applicable to passing off and the principles applicable to interlocutory injunctions. The treatment of passing off examines both the traditional tripartite formulation of misrepresentation, goodwill and damage and the five-part formulation by Lord Diplock in Erven Warnink BV v J Townend & Sons (Hull) Ltd.[101] – a misrepresentation, by a trader in the course of a trade, to customers or ultimate consumers, calculated to injure the business or goodwill of another and causing, or immediately likely to cause such damage. **120**

14. G. Carey/S. Leonowicz, Litigating Settlement Contributions, [2001] 8 CLP 85

The authors compare the Irish and English provisions on contribution actions after the claimant has settled with the injured person – sec. 22 of the Civil Liability Act, 1961 and sec. 1(4) of the Civil Liability (Contribution) Act, 1978. They note that the Irish provision uses plainer language and deals more effectively with particularly troublesome cases; one such case is where D1 has settled with P and seeks a contribution from D2, but evidence suggests that D1 may not have been liable; secondly the Irish statute requires the settlement to be reasonable, whereas the English law requires it to be *bona fide* – the authors suggest that the English provision may be more difficult to apply in cases of collusive settlements. Sec. 17(1) of the Irish Act is also stated to be better as it provides that accord and satisfaction by one wrongdoer discharges all wrongdoers, provided it indicates such an intention; this point is left open by the English provision, which fails to expressly deal with the issue. They then review the common law principles on accord and satisfaction and conclude that the position under the Irish Act, though generally clear has some minor ambiguities that the common law rules may assist in clarifying. **121**

[99] [2001] 2 ILRM 154; (SC, 2000).
[100] Unrep. HC, 2 October 2000.
[101] [1979] AC 731.

15. G. Carey, Misrepresentation and the Avoidance of Liability, [2001] 8 CLP 131

122 The author considers liability for pre-contractual representations, covering *inter alia* deceit, negligent misrepresentation, and statutory recovery for innocent misrepresentations and also considers liability in negligence for failure to disclose information. In respect of negligent failure to disclose, the author notes the limited chances of recovery – a duty will only be imposed where there has been an undertaking of responsibility by the defendant. Finally, he considers the use of exclusion clauses as a means of avoiding liability.

16. G. Carey, Concurrent Liability in Contract and Tort – Parts I & II [2001] 8 CLP 183, 214

123 Part I examines the historical division of opinion on the imposition of concurrent duties in tort between parties to a contractual relationship and scrutinises the leading modern authorities in England and Ireland – Henderson v Merrett Syndicates Ltd.[102] and Kennedy v Allied Irish Banks plc (AIB) & AIB Finance Ltd.[103] Several English decisions post-Henderson are also briefly considered and the author concludes that, while the law has been greatly clarified by the cases, there is still scope for uncertainty, from which litigation is likely to spring. Part II examines the law in Canada and New Zealand and concludes that the approach taken by the SC in Ireland in Kennedy v AIB is satisfactory.

17. M. Kealy, Hold the Front Page!, [2001] March *Law Society Gazette* (Gazette), 8

124 The author considers some of the implications that incorporation of the European Convention on Human Rights and Fundamental Freedoms into Irish law will have for the law in respect of defamation, privacy and the right to life. The author notes that artt. 2, 8 and 10 in particular are likely to have a significant impact.

18. K. Doran, A Healthy Alternative, [2001] March Gazette, 16

125 The author highlights the benefits that mediation has brought in medical malpractice cases in the United States and argues that Ireland would benefit from a greater use of mediation rather than litigation in this field of practice.

19. J. Deane, Pressure Points, [2001] August/September Gazette, 14

126 This article examines employers' liability for occupational stress, focusing on the standard of care imposed on employers under recent cases, particularly Curran v Cadbury Ireland Ltd.,[104] McHugh v Ireland,[105] and McGrath v The Garda (Police) Commissioner.[106] The author calls for clearer guidelines on the

[102] [1995] 2 AC 145.
[103] Unrep. SC, 29 October 1996.
[104] [2000] ILRM, 343. Circuit Court, Judge McMahon.
[105] Unrep. HC, 28 January 2000, Budd, J.
[106] Unrep. HC, Morris J.

distinction between recognised psychiatric illness and other forms of mental strain and the evidence required in order to establish a claim.

20. G. Kelly, Haunted by Hillsborough, [2001] August/September Gazette, 18

This case note provides a critical analysis of the House of Lords decision in White v Chief Constable of South Yorkshire.[107] The author highlights the limiting effect of the decision on claims for negligently inflicted psychiatric harm in England and compares this with the position in Ireland. **127**

21. M. Peart, Neighbourhood Watch, [2001] December Gazette, 22

The author critically assesses the Supreme Court decision in Glencar v Mayo.[108] It is argued that the shift in approach to judicial discretion in respect of the imposition, or rejection of, a duty of care will lead to greater uncertainty in Irish tort law. **128**

D. Proposals for New Legislation

1. Courts and Court Officers Bill, 2001

It is proposed that the financial jurisdiction of the lower courts should be raised. The District Court (DC) presently has a financial limit of £ 5,000 (€ 6,348) for tort claims, but this Bill proposes an increase to € 20,000 (£ 15,751). The financial limit of the CC in tort cases is presently £ 30,000 (€ 38,092), but is proposed to be raised to € 100,000 (£ 78,756). This would have the effect of moving many tort claims from the HC to the CC and moving the lower value CC claims to the DC. It could also have the practical effect of pushing up the amounts sought by plaintiffs in minor cases. **129**

2. European Convention on Human Rights Bill, 2001

This Bill proposes to implement the European Convention for the Protection of Human Rights and Fundamental Freedoms into domestic law. Sec. 2 requires courts to interpret and apply national law in a manner consistent with the provisions of the Convention, as far as possible. Sec. 3 requires organs of the State to carry out their functions in a manner consistent with the State's obligations under the Convention. Sec. 4 requires courts interpreting the provisions of the Convention to take judicial notice of any declaration, decision, advisory opinion or judgment of the ECHR; any decision or opinion of the Commission and any decision of the Committee of Ministers. Sec. 5(1) gives the HC, or SC on appeal, the power to declare a statutory provision or rule of law incompatible with the State's obligations under the Convention, provided no other legal remedy is adequate and available. Sec. 6(1) requires a Court to **130**

[107] [1999] 1 All ER 1.
[108] *Supra* [3]–[5].

give notice to the Attorney General where a declaration of incompatibility is being considered and sec. 6(2) permits the Attorney General to become a party to the proceedings with respect to the compatibility issue. Sec. 5(2) provides that a declaration under sec. 5(1) will not affect the validity of the law so declared, but sec. 5(3) requires the *Taoiseach* (Prime Minister) to have a copy of the declaration laid before the Houses of the *Oireachtas* (Parliament) within 21 days. Compensation is provided for on an ex gratia basis in sec. 5(4).

3. Residential Institutions Redress Bill, 2001

131 This Bill proposes the creation of a Board to make compensatory awards to people who were victims of child abuse in institutions subject to state inspection or regulation (industrial schools, reformatory schools, orphanages and children's homes). An agreement has been reached between the Government and religious institutions, under which the institutions are to provide € 128 million towards the scheme. This is made up of a mixture of cash, property transfers and counselling services.

4. Railway Safety Bill, 2001

132 Part 2 of the Bill proposes the establishment of a Railway Safety Commission whose functions would be to foster, encourage, regulate and enforce railway safety and to investigate and report on railway incidents. Part 3 proposes to impose general duties on railway undertakings, their staff and any other person on or near a railway or railway premises similar to common law obligations of reasonable care. No specific exemption from civil liability is offered in respect of the duties created in Parts 2 and 3, but the imposition of criminal penalties for breaches of the obligations in Part 3 suggests that they may not be amenable to civil action for breach. A civil action for breach of the obligations in part 2 may arise. The commission may also, under sec. 77, be required to indemnify inspectors, members of staff and advisors for any civil liability arising out of a *bona fide* exercise of their duties.

5. Law Reform Commission, Report on the Statutes of Limitations: Claims in Contract and Tort in Respect of Latent Damage (Other Than Personal Injury) (LRC 64 – 2001)

133 The report recommends the introduction of a discoverability rule in respect of the running of time limits for actions in contract or tort involving claims in respect of property damage and economic loss. The report also recommends the inclusion of a 10 year long stop provision, in addition to several specialised provisions for special cases, such as incapacity and fraud. A draft legislative proposal to implement the recommendations is appended to the report.

XI. Italy

Emanuela Navarretta **and** *Elena Bargelli*

A. Legislation

1. Law 5 March 2001 no. 57[1]: *danno biologico* (Physical Injury)

a) Brief Description of the Law

The law concerns the figure of *danno biologico*, which was completely created by case law in the 1970s and is typical of the Italian legal system. According to the doctrine of *danno biologico*, damages are awarded in case of a physical or psychical injury which has been ascertained by a legal doctor and can be compensated regardless of the victim's ability to earn. The law (art. 5 subs. 3) adopts this same notion and defines *danno biologico* as "the injury to the physical or psychical integrity, susceptible of medico-legal assessment" and adds that it can be compensated independently from the victim's capacity of producing income. 1

Nevertheless law. no. 57/2001 is not a general law concerning *danno biologico*, but regards the mere damages for slight physical injuries, that is injuries below the percentage of 9%. 2

For such harms it introduces standardised economic reference values to calculate *danno biologico* for the whole national territory (*e.g.* a certain amount of damages for 1% of *physical* disability, another for 2%, and so on). It is necessary to point out that art. 5 l. 57/2001 confirms as legislative rule the method for evaluating *danno biologico* that is based on the so called *calcolo a punto* (*calcul au point*), already created by case law[2]. It means that *danno biologico* 3

[1] For general information and critical notes, see G. Ponzanelli, La nuova disciplina delle micropermanenti, [2001] *Danno e responsabilità* (DR), 453 *et seq.*, and A. Nannipieri, La legge sulle microinvalidità: una soluzione inadeguata da rivedere, [2001] DR, 573 *et seq.*

[2] Everybody knows that this method was at first adopted by the court of Pisa: compare Tribunale (Trib., Italian First Instance Court) Pisa, 10 March 1979, [1979] *Responsabilità civile e previdenza* (RCP), 356, with footnote of G. Ponzanelli, Fermenti giurisprudenziali toscani in tema di

is evaluated by a legal doctor, who determines a percentage of disability; then the judge gives a conventional value to each point of disability, which depends upon the age of the victim and the gravity of his/her injury.

4 The reason why this law concerns only disabilities below 9% is that it aims in the first instance at constraining the amounts of damages usually awarded by courts in such cases. In fact some scholars have, for some time, pointed out that courts usually allow higher damages in case of slight injuries if compared with serious physical ones. Therefore it would be necessary to constrain costs in matters of insurance, in order to assure damages case of gravest *danno biologico*.

b) Commentary

5 This law is the result of a disputed legislative affair. It was preceded by a *decreto legge* – bitterly criticised and then withdrawn (d.l. 17 March 2000, no. 70, art. 3) – which stated different amounts of damages within rigid brackets, and did not allow a variation in the point value for the age of the victim or the gravity of the injury[3]. This law, on the contrary, pursues the objective of rendering foreseeable the compensation for slight physical injuries and of containing the cost of such compensation and, where necessary, preserving a margin of fair assessment in the settlement which is entrusted to the judge's evaluation of the concrete case. It provides the increase of point values in a way that is more than proportionate to the variation of the already mentioned two factors (age of the victim, gravity of the injury). Furthermore, in view of the subjective conditions of the victim, the injured party is permitted to ask the judge for additional compensation to that obtained by application of the fixed parameters.

6 The law defines *danno biologico* as damage that can be compensated regardless of the victims' ability to earn. The definition has already been confirmed by a previous law (art. 13 law no. 38/2000), which has introduced the notion of *danno biologico* in the field of Work Accidents Social Insurance (INAIL) and which qualifies *danno biologico* as "the injury to the psychophysical integrity, susceptible of medico-legal evaluation", specifying that "the awards for the restoration of the *danno biologico* are determined regardless of the injured party's capacity of production of income".

valutazione del danno alla persona; this decision adopted the doctrine of F. D. Busnelli, Tutela della salute e tutela risarcitoria, in: F. D. Busnelli/U. Breccia (ed.), *Tutela della salute e diritto privato* (1978), pp. 568 *et seq.* After a short period, the method has been used also by the Supreme Court: see Cassazione (Cass., Italian Supreme Court) 18 February 1993, no. 2009, [1993] *Giustizia civile*, (GC), 2101, with footnote of G. Alpa, Vecchi e nuovi problemi concernenti il danno biologico; more recently, Cass. 4 December 1998, no. 12319, [1999] DR, 515, with footnote of E. Bargelli, Valutazione del danno alla salute: il "percorso" della giurisprudenza al capolinea?). At last it has been adopted also by the Court of Genoa, which created the different method so called of «triplo della pensione sociale» (based upon the amount of social pension): Trib. Genova, 28 September 1998 e Appello Genova, 1 April 1999, [1999] RCP, 1104, with footnote of E. Bargelli, Il *quantum* del risarcimento del danno alla salute fra parità di trattamento delle vittime e valutazione equitativa del giudice: a proposito di un recente *revirement* genovese.

[3] See G. Ponzanelli, [2001] DR, 455.

While the definition of *danno biologico* is convincing, perplexity has been aroused by the definition of *danno biologico* with the injury to the psychophysical integrity, instead of its identification with the consequences of the same. However, this provision is implicitly corrected by art. 5 subs. 2, which states that it is the concrete loss and not the injury itself that is paid off as *danno biologico*. **7**

Furthermore, we feel it convincing that the method of *calcolo al punto* is confirmed, because it is the most coherent with the doctrine of the Constitutional Court since the decision no. 184/1986[4], where it suggested two main issues to the basic courts. First, to ensure the respect of the constitutional principle of equality (and, therefore, to ensure a minimal pecuniary uniformity in calculating damages)[5]; moreover, an adequate flexibility to the circumstances of concrete cases, so that damages could remove "the economic and social impediments to the full development of the human person that have been introduced by the tort" [art. 3, subs. 2, and 32 *Costituzione* (Italian Constitution, Cost.)][6]. **8**

The need of standardising at a national level the damages "tables" (containing the values for each point of disability, in relation to the gravity of the offence and the age of the victim) is closely linked to the constitutional principle of formal equality, that is the guarantee of the victims' parity of treatment. Obviously, this need is equally valid for all victims – independently from the gravity of the injury[7] – but for injuries that exceed the percentages considered by law no. 57, this need is far from being met. In practice, in fact, every court is free to adopt whichever assessment table it prefers, so that the current situation of "anarchy" in the compensation process[8] should not cause surprise. And yet, in the past, there have been projects thought up to produce a complete and organic answer to this and other open questions in the field of personal injury[9], **9**

[4] Corte costituzionale (Corte cost., Italian Constitutional Court), 14 July 1986, no. 184, [1986] RCP, 520, with footnote of G. Scalfi, Reminiscenze dogmatiche per il c.d. danno alla salute: un ripensamento della Corte costituzionale, and of A. Gambaro, Appunti sullo stile della sentenza n. 184/1986, *ibidem,* 589 *et seq*.

[5] About the meaning of constitutional principle of Equality and its value in the context of personal injuries, see P. Rescigno, Relazione di sintesi, in: *Giornate di studio sul danno alla salute* (1990), p. 98; G. Alpa, *Il danno biologico* (1993), pp. 60–63; D. Messinetti, Danno giuridico, *Enciclopedia del diritto, Aggiornamento,* I, (1997) p. 501.

[6] See F. D. Busnelli (*supra* note 2), p. 567, and Ibid., Riflessioni sul "Project Tunc". Per una riforma del sistema di indennizzo delle vittime della strada [1981] RCP, 308.

[7] G. Alpa, Il danno alla persona oltre le esperienze nazionali. Una prospettiva europea, [1998] RCP, 330 *et seq.*; F. D. Busnelli, Il danno alla salute ad una svolta: legge sì? Legge no? Quale legge? [1998] DR, 305 *et seq*.

[8] As we shall point out better *infra,* no. 4.1.

[9] See, *e.g.*, the law project proposed by the Commission elected by ISVAP, published in: ISVAP, Il danno biologico e prospettive di riforma, *Quaderni ISVAP,* n. 4, (1998); the Governement bill concerning the «new rules about personal injuries» of 4 July 1999, is published in [1999] DR, 727 *et seq*., with comments of F. D. Busnelli, Il punto di vista del giurista, and of Bargagna, Il punto di vista del medico legale, and in [1999] RCP, 844 *et seq*. In this review see the comments of P. Ziziz, Una nuova disciplina in tema di danno alla persona: prime impressioni sulla proposta di riforma approvata dal Governo, 833 *et seq*. and of E. Bargelli, Il disegno di legge in tema di danno alla persona: soluzioni giurisprudenziali e modelli teorici a confronto, [2000] RCP, 200 *et seq*.

projects which, however, have not as of this moment been transposed into binding laws.

2. Law 24 March 2001 No. 89[10]: State Liability for Excessive Duration of a Trial

a) Brief Description of the Law

10 This law concerns the protection of human rights which are violated by an excessive duration of a trial. Until now such a right was protected merely by Art. 6 European Convention of Human Rights, therefore victims had to claim damages only to Strasbourg's European Court. Now also Italian courts are competent to award damages in case of harms caused by the unreasonable duration of a trial. Art. 2 in fact states that the victim can obtain damages in case of pecuniary and non-pecuniary losses if he/she proves that the duration of the trial violates Art. 6 subs. 1 European Convention of Human Rights.

11 Furthermore art. 2 subs. 3 states that damages are calculated according to art. 2056 *codice civile* (Italian civil code, cc): such article concerns losses that cannot be evaluated in an objective manner and provides that damages are calculated according to court's equity.

b) Commentary

12 This law has been criticized, inasmuch as it concerns the mere effects of the unreasonable duration of a trial and does not solve the causes of it[11]. Nevertheless it has been met with approval by other commentators, who have pointed out that the victim can obtain damages for non-pecuniary losses beyond the limits of art. 2059 cc[12]. This rule, concerning non-pecuniary losses, states that they can be compensated only in cases provided by the law: cases which consist till recent years in the hypothesis of crime (art. 185 *codice penale*, Italian criminal code, cp). Recently, however, there have been numerous laws in which the compensation of non-pecuniary loss in the absence of a criminal offence has been admitted.

13 In particular, art. 29, subs. 9[13] of the law concerning the protection of privacy rights (Law 31 December 1996, no. 1996) foresees that: "non-pecuniary loss can be recovered also in cases in which art. 9 is breached" (art. 9 is the general rule which states the standard of lawfulness and fairness in the use of personal information).

[10] The text is published in [2001] DR, 571 *et seq*. For general information and critical notes, see G. Ponzanelli, "Equa riparazione" per processi troppo lunghi, [2001] DR, 569 *et seq*.

[11] G. Ponzanelli, [2001] DR, 569.

[12] G. Ponzanelli, [2001] DR, 570.

[13] About this rule see the comment of E. Navarretta, in: C. M. Bianca/F. D. Busnelli (ed.), *Tutela della privacy, Le nuove leggi civili commentate* (1999), pp. 684 *et seq*.

14 Art. 44 of Law no. 289/1998, on the other hand, introduces a civil action against discriminatory treatment of persons: according to this rule, the plaintiff can also claim compensation for pecuniary and non-pecuniary losses.

15 Moreover Law no. 89/2001 adds another legal hypothesis of damages for non-pecuniary losses in our system and, therefore, confirms a model of tort law where non-pecuniary losses that are incommensurable, can be compensated beyond the case of the crime if there is a serious personal injury. This rule can become a general rule if we consider the serious injury to a personal right protected by the Constitution to one of the cases foreseen by the law according to the provision of art. 2059 cc. According to this assumption, art. 2059 cc should be held as the general rule about non-pecuniary losses by a previous loose interpretation[14]. Art. 2043 cc, on the other hand, should remain the general rule about economic losses.

3. Law 21 July 2000, No. 205: State Liability (Jurisdiction)

a) Brief Description of the Law

16 This law reforms the trial rules concerning the unlawful administrative acts of the State (*e.g.*, when a local Government denies a licence it ought to give to the citizen, or when a taking is unlawful). Concerning torts committed by the State, the law states that *Tribunali amministrativi regionali* (TAR) and *Consiglio di Stato* (Italian special courts concerning claims of citizens against State) are also competent to evaluate damages and, therefore, to condemn the State to award them.

17 Before this law only "common" courts (*Tribunali, Corti di Appello*, regarding actions of a citizen against another citizen) were able to do so. The first cited courts were only competent to evaluate if the actions of the State were lawful or unlawful.

b) Commentary

18 Italian courts have for a long time denied that a citizen could claim damages if the tortfeasor was the State; Scholars, on the contrary, have for a some time suggested to admit State liability[15]. This last doctrine has been only recently met with approval by the *Sezioni Unite of Corte di Cassazione* (Italian Supreme Court deciding a very debatable problem, Cass. SS. UU.)[16]. After this important decision it has become necessary to determine which rules govern State liability. Therefore this law introduces a new rule about the jurisdic-

[14] G. Ponzanelli, Danno non patrimoniale e danno alla salute: due sentenze della Corte costituzionale, [1979] *Responsabilità civile e previdenza* (RCP) 595 *et seq.*; E. Navarretta, *Diritti inviolabili e risarcimento del danno* (1996), pp. 376 *et seq.*

[15] F. D. Busnelli, Lesione di interessi legittimi: dal «muro di sbarramento» alla «rete di contenimento» [1997] DR, 269 *et seq.*; E. Navarretta, Forma e sostanza dell'interesse legittimo nella prospettiva della responsabilità, [1999] DR, 949 *et seq.*

[16] Cass. SS. UU. 22 July 1999, no. 500, in [1999] *Foro italiano* (FI), 2487, with footnote of L. Palmieri/R. Pardolesi, Nota alla sent. n. 500/99 S.U.

tion in order to reduce the duration of trials[17]. In fact if the "ordinary" courts were the only competent to calculate damages, it would be necessary to repeat the trial before them after TAR's decision.

19 Nevertheless we are of the opinion that this law is not convincing. In fact the duplication of jurisdiction seems to build a first step toward unreasonable differences inside State liability rules, that is toward a "special" State liability.

4. *Decreto Legislativo* 8 June 2001, No. 231: Corporate Persons' Liability

a) Brief Description of the Law

20 The law has introduced criminal liability of Corporate persons, liability which now becomes unquestioned in the Italian legal system. The law requires that a physical member of the corporate person has committed a crime in order to benefit it, and not himself (art. 5). Furthermore, it is not relevant whether the crime is committed by a director or by an employer. But rules concerning the proof of the fault are different in the first and in the second case (art. 6). The corporate person is not held as liable if it has elaborated and respected the compliance programme before committing the crime (art. 7). Moreover, the law introduces specific penalties, because a corporate person cannot be imprisoned. Therefore, it will have to pay fines (art. 12).

b) Commentary

21 The law has been met with approval because it introduces the possibility to ascribe a crime directly to a corporate person (the crimes of corporate persons are in fact numerous)[18]. Nevertheless it does not state the concurrent liability of the physical person who commits the crime ascribed to the corporate one[19].

B. Cases

1. *Corte di Cassazione* (Italian Supreme Court, Cass.), 3 July 2001, No. 9009[20]: A Case of Mobbing in Absence of Crime

a) Brief Summary of the Facts

22 The plaintiff was asked to work even on the weekly days of rest. Therefore he claims the amounts of money necessary to compensate for non-pecuniary losses. As a defence, the defendant puts forward that the plaintiff has already

[17] As pointed out by G. Visintini, Danno ingiusto e lesione di interessi legittimi, [2001] *Contratto e impresa* (C. i.), 12; S. Cacace, La responsabilità della P. A. per lesione di interessi legittimi negli anni '90: dieci tappe di un'evoluzione, [2001] DR, 136 *et seq.*

[18] C. De Maglie, Responsabilità delle persone giuridiche: pregi e limiti del d.lg. 231/2001, [2002] DR, 247 *et seq.*

[19] C. De Maglie [2002] DR, 252.

[20] In [2001] DR, 1207.

been fully compensated, because the National Work Contract (negotiated by National Trade Unions) provides for an adequate reward for such work.

b) Judgment of the Supreme Court

At first, the Supreme Court confirms the idea that *danno biologico* has to be distinguished from other personal injuries[21]. *Danno biologico*, in fact, is ascertained by a legal doctor according to the objective parameter of pathology and is then converted into pecuniary terms according to the estimated percentage of disability[22], while the other personal injuries are recovered regardless of an objective method to determine damages. **23**

Furthermore the Supreme Court suggests a loose construction of tort law, able to go beyond the strict limits stated by art. 2059 cc[23]. This construction must be based on Constitutional principles (art. 2, art. 36), which induce to recover the violation of privacy rights even if the tort cannot be qualified as a crime. The Supreme Court, however, points out that damages could not be provided for "mere discomforts that originate in the personal sensibility of the subject". Losses, in fact, must be serious and relevant, while there is no compensation for slight injuries or simple idiosyncrasies. Therefore it "quashes" the judgments of Pretore and Tribunale of Foggia and states that the plaintiff has to prove a concrete and real harm. **24**

c) Commentary

The Court's decision is based on a widespread doctrine for what concerns the distinction between *danno biologico* and other personal injuries. *Danno biologico*, in fact, is a physical or psychical injury which can be "measured" by forensic–medicine and, therefore, traduced into conventional pecuniary terms. The other personal injuries, on the contrary, are incommensurable and, as consequence, damages solve a satisfactory function or punitive role[24]. **25**

Furthermore it takes up a convincing position about the question on what (and when) non-pecuniary losses can be recovered in the Italian legal system. The Supreme Court in fact accepts the doctrine based on the seriousness of the injury[25] and rejects the idea that even very slight losses of amenities of life can be recovered. The Court, however, applies art. 2043 cc, which is held as decisive to admit compensation for non-pecuniary losses. We feel this last **26**

[21] F. D. Busnelli, Nuove frontiere della responsabilità civile, [1976] *Jus*, 53 *et seq.*; Ibid., (*supra* note 2), pp. 515 *et seq.*; E. Navarretta, Bilanciamento di interessi costituzionali e regole civilistiche, [1998] *Rivista critica diritto privato* (RCDP), 559 *et seq.*; Ead., Complessità dell'argomentazione per principi nel sistema delle fonti di diritto privato, [2001] *Rivista di diritto civile* (RDC), 789 *et seq.*

[22] Corte costituzionale (Corte cost., Italian Constitutional Court), 14 July 1986, no. 184, [1986] RCP, 520.

[23] E. Navarretta (*supra* note 14), pp. 376 *et seq.*

[24] F. D. Busnelli, *Interessi della persona e risarcimento del danno*, [1996] *Rivista trimestrale diritto e procedura civile* (RTDPC), 1 *et seq.*; E. Navarretta (*supra* note 14) pp. 376 *et seq.*

[25] E. Navarretta (*supra* note 14).

assumption is not convincing because art. 2043 cc concerns the strict pecuniary losses (and also *danno biologico*, a harm which can be exactly evaluated by legal doctors); it would be necessary, on the contrary, a loose construction of art. 2059 cc, which regards non-pecuniary losses other than *danno biologico*.

2. Cass. 21 February 2002, No. 2515: Environmental Damage Caused by a Criminal Conduct (Seveso Case)

a) Brief Summary of the Facts

27 The plaintiff suffered pecuniary and non-pecuniary losses caused by the chemical pollution in the area of Seveso in 1976. He claims damages for *danno biologico*, for pain and suffering (caused by the fear and the worries suffered by all the people living in the Seveso area) and for some economic losses (the value of his share in a company's capital were decreased). The defendant (Icmesa s.p.a.), on the other hand, puts forward that the losses are not causally consequent upon the chemical pollution and that, therefore, they have not been proved by the plaintiff.

b) Judgment of the Supreme Court

28 The Supreme Court states that neither *danno biologico* nor the economic loss could be compensated. In fact the basic courts could not ascertain whether they are causally consequent upon chemical pollution. Compensation for pain and suffering, on the contrary, must be awarded according to art. 2059 cc (non-pecuniary losses). In fact the defendant had committed a crime against public health, therefore the application of art. 185 cp (and, as consequence, art. 2059 cc) is unquestioned here. The Supreme Court, however, has to discuss the defence of the defendant that the plaintiff has not proved his loss; in particular, the defendant puts forward that, in order to reach a complete proof, it would not be enough for the victim merely to assert to live in Seveso area. The Court, however, points out that the plaintiff, who lives and works in the polluted area, has proved his non-pecuniary losses; in fact the basic courts have correctly ascertained his anxiety about his health.

c) Commentary

29 At first we have to point out that the main question faced by the Supreme Court concerns the proof of a concrete loss in case of environmental damage. A recent decision of the Supreme Court, in fact, denied compensation for such losses and stated that there was not the proof of a causal link between them and the environmental damage[26]. Furthermore, we have to point out that here the Court does not have to face the question whether to recover non-pecuniary

[26] Cass. 20 June 1997, no. 5530, and 24 May 1997, no. 4631, [1997] FI I, 2068. The basic courts, however, had admitted compensation: see App. Milano, 14 April 1994, and Trib. Milano, 11 July 1991, [1995] RCP, 136, with footnote of Feola, Il caso Severo e la risarcibilità dei danni non patrimoniali alla collettività vittima di un disastro ambientale.

losses or not, because the tort committed by the defendant is a crime: therefore art. 2059 cc (and art. 185 cp) can be applied.

This decision is convincing because it points out that the plaintiff is a person living in the polluted area and not a passer-by. Therefore it states that individuals living in the zone can claim damages, but they have to prove a concrete loss. In case of environmental damage, however, this loss can be proved by presumptions (*e.g.*, pain and suffering is deduced by the high number of check-up or medical examinations the plaintiff have decided to undergo after the event of pollution). 30

3. *Giudice di Pace di Roma* (Italian Basic Court, Giud. Pace), 14 January 2002[27]: *danno biologico*

a) Brief Summary of the Facts

The plaintiff suffered harm caused by a car accident and claims damages. The defendant, on the other hand, put forward that physical injuries are slight (below 9%) and that, therefore, damages have to be calculated according to law no. 57/2001. 31

b) Judgment of the Court

The Court states that art. 5 subs. 2 l. 57/2001 is inconsistent with the Italian Constitution (art. 32, concerning the protection of public and individual health). The court is of the opinion that art. 5 violates the right to health because it constraints damages for physical injuries below 9%, while for the other physical injuries (beyond 9%) the plaintiff can claim compensation according to the general rules created by case law. Therefore it refers the decision to the Constitutional Court, which will have to evaluate if art. 5 is consistent or not with the Italian Constitution. 32

c) Commentary

The Court's decision is based on the assumption that compensation for *danno biologico* must be awarded according to the rules created by case law and based on the reference values adopted by each *Corte d'Appello*. Commentators, on the contrary, have pointed out that a law cannot be criticized for the mere fact that it changes the rules created by the courts. The question in fact is: who decides – courts or legislative rules – the extent of the damages which have to be awarded in case of *danno biologico*?[28] Furthermore it is necessary to point out that – if the economic resources are not endless – it is better to compensate more serious injuries than slight ones[29]. 33

[27] [2002] DR, 309 *et seq.*, with footnote of G. Ponzanelli, Micropermanenti, «undercompensation» e censure di costituzionalità.
[28] G. Ponzanelli [2002] DR, 315.
[29] G. Ponzanelli [2002] DR, 315.

4. *Consiglio di Stato* (Italian Supreme Court for Unlawful Acts of the State, Cons. St.), 6 August 2001, No. 4239[30]: State Liability

a) Brief Summary of the Facts

34 A local Government denied planning permission to a citizen, but this decision was held as unlawful by TAR. The Government was condemned to pay damages but, as a defence, put forward that the plaintiff did not prove every element of the tort, because he failed to show its fault.

b) Judgment of the Supreme Court

35 The Supreme Court states that if a citizen requests a licence from the State (or the Local Government), the relationship between these two subjects becomes similar to a contractual one. Therefore also liability rules in case of State's (or Local Government's) tort have to be similar to the ones stated by artt. 1218 *et seq.* cc. It means that the plaintiff must not prove the fault of the tortfeasor, because this element is deduced from the violation of law. The defendant (that is the State or the Local Government), on the contrary, has to prove that the violation of law could not be avoided notwithstanding the diligence.

c) Commentary

36 This decision states that some State liability rules – in particular, fault rules – can be deduced by art. 1218 cc. This doctrine could solve some problems arising from the difficulty in proving the State's fault as element of its tort, but, on the other hand, confirms the risk that "ordinary" courts (*e.g. Tribunali*, *Corti d'Appello*) and "administrative" ones (TAR, *Consiglio di Stato*) can create different rules about State liability[31].

37 Although the decision referred to contract rules, it is not based on the doctrine of *contatto sociale*[32], according to which State liability rules are qualified as contract liability ones (artt. 1218 *et seq.* cc)[33].

[30] [2002] DR, 183 *et seq.*, with footnote of V. Carbone, Il giudice amministrativo adotta la responsabilità da «contatto procedimentale».

[31] See F. D. Busnelli, Dopo la sentenza no. 500. La responsabilità civile oltre il «muro» degli interessi legittimi, [2000] RDC, 335 *et seq.*

[32] This theory, on the contrary, is adopted by Cass. 22 January 1999, no. 589, [1999] RCP 661 *et seq.*, with footnote of M. Forziati, La responsabilità contrattuale del medico dipendente: il "contatto sociale" arriva in Cassazione.

[33] See C. Castronovo, L'obbligazione senza prestazione. Ai confini fra contratto e torto, *Le ragioni del diritto, Scritti in onore di L. Mengoni* (1995), pp. 147 *et seq.*

5. *App. Roma*, 10 July 2001[34]: Violation of Art. 6 of European Convention of Human Rights

a) Brief Summary of the Facts

The plaintiff claims 24 million lire (€ 12,000 Euro) to compensate for pecuniary and non-pecuniary losses caused by the excessive duration of a previous trial (11 years) in which he sought damages for a car accident in which he was involved. **38**

b) Judgment of the Supreme Court

In the first place, the Court examines whether the behaviour of the competent judge was unlawful (that is, whether the waiting time needed to obtain the judgment is to be held as "unreasonable", taking into account the complexity of the proceedings and of the conduct at trial of the victim, according to the assessment parameters already used by case law concerning Art. 6 par 1 European Convention of Human Rights). **39**

Furthermore the court considers whether the long duration of the trial has really violated a human right of the plaintiff and, as a result, states that "no room should be left to unjustified, unfair and speculative claims, concerning excessive amounts even without there being any loss or, in any case, with loss of only slight importance". In this case, the violation of Art. 6 European Convention is not held as very grave by the court, which takes into account the nature of the injury suffered by the plaintiff (he has waited excessively long for a decision concerning losses caused by a mere car accident, and not, *e.g.*, regarding a crime involving him). According to these guidelines, the court upholds the demand of the plaintiff, but it awards only 1,000,000 lire (€ 500) for non-pecuniary losses, and not the 24,000,000 lire (€ 12,000), as claimed by him. **40**

c) Commentary

The Court's decision is important because it is one of the first concerning damages for non-pecuniary losses suffered by the victim of an excessively long trial (Law no. 89/2001). **41**

The Court confirms here that compensation for non-pecuniary losses can be awarded only if there is a serious injury to the person. The violation of the right to a reasonable duration of a trial is not sufficient: damages are awarded only if the victim can prove real harm (also by presumptions) and not in case of a mere idiosyncracy or a very slight injury. **42**

[34] [2001] DR, 957, with footnote of G. Ponzanelli, Prime applicazioni della legge Pinto.

6. Cass. 4 April 2001, No. 4970[35]: Pain and Suffering of Unconscious Person

a) Brief Summary of the Facts

43 The child of the plaintiff suffered a grave brain injury caused by the obstetrician during the delivery. The parents claim damages for *danno biologico* and pain and suffering suffered by the son. The defendant – the U. S. L. (public sanitary structure) – puts forward that only *danno biologico* should be awarded to the child; damages for pain and suffering, on the contrary, could not be claimed because the encephalopathic child is unconscious and, therefore, he is not able to have any sensations.

b) Judgment of the Supreme Court

44 While basic courts (*Tribunale* and *Corte di Appello*) had denied damages for pain and suffering, the Supreme Court asserts that they cannot be excluded. In fact it observes that basic courts have denied damages without seriously verifying whether the encephalopathic child is really able to have sensations or not. Therefore, if the judge ascertained a certain degree of cognitive awareness, the demand of the plaintiff should be upheld according to art. 2059 cc, which can surely be applied in this case because the defendant committed a crime (*cf.* art. 185 cp). If, otherwise, the child were really conscious, damages could not be given to the victim.

c) Commentary

45 The decision is based on the traditional doctrine according to which non-pecuniary losses are identified with pain and suffering[36]. Therefore the *ratio decidendi* has to be found in the idea that damages are awarded only if the encephalopathic individual is conscious and, therefore, able to have sensations. This doctrine is not unquestioned in case law. On the contrary, other decisions have asserted that pain and suffering can be recognized even if a person is in a deep coma[37]. This last opinion is more convincing. Pain and suffering, in fact, is not the only non-pecuniary loss which has to be recovered whenever the tort causes a serious personal injury or the violation of a constitutional right. Therefore, even if a person is unconscious, he/she can obtain damages for non-pecuniary losses (a notion we hold as more appropriate than pain and suffering), if his/her dignity has been violated[38]. According to this last opinion, non-pecuniary losses can be recovered even if the victim is a corporate person[39], whenever a non-pecuniary interest of constitutional relevance is violated.

[35] [2001] RCP, with footnote of C. Favilli, Il danno non patrimoniale del soggetto non senziente.

[36] See Corte cost. 14 July 1986 no. 184 [1986] RCP, 520.

[37] See, e.g., Cass. 6 October 1994, n. 8177 [1994] *Giurisprudenza italiana* (GI), 1534 *et seq*., with footnote of Citarella Stato di coma e danno morale.

[38] E. Navarretta (*supra* note 14), pp. 328 *et seq*.

[39] See, *e.g.*, *Corte Conti* (Italian Administrative Court), Sez. giurisdiz. Umbria, 18 October 2000, no. 557/R/2000, [2001] DR, 1191, with footnote of G. Cassano, Il danno all'immagine della P.A. come danno esistenziale?

7. Cass. 3 March 2001, No. 3132[40]: Liability of the Public Body Which Controls the Financial Market

a) Brief Summary of the Facts

Some consumers underwrote an offer to the world at large concerning the purchase of a share of a "s. r. l." (that is a limited liability company). The company went bankrupt and the consumers demand damages to the *Consob* (that is the public body which is obliged to control the financial market). The plaintiffs point out that *Consob* has omitted to control the truthfulness of the informative prospect. The defendant, on the oher hand, puts forward that *Consob* has to protect the general (or public) interest to the fairness of the financial market and, therefore, the single consumer cannot claim damages. **46**

b) Judgment of the Supreme Court

The Court asserts that *Consob* could be held liable, because it was obliged to verify the truthfulness of the information given by the company, to supervise the financial market and, if necessary, to make inspections. Moreover, if *Consob* ascertained that the company did something wrong, it had to prevent the corporate person from striking the business transaction. Therefore it upholds the demand of the investors and "quashes" the decision of the basic court. **47**

c) Commentary

This decision is based on the doctrine of Cass. N. 500/1999 (already cited above)[41], which has for the first time affirmed State liability as a general rule in our legal system. The commentors have pointed out the importance of this decision in our system[42], because it has admitted Public Body's liability even if the plaintiff is only indirectly involved in its conduct. *Consob*, in fact, has to supervise the financial market in order to protect a public interest, while it offers only indirect advantage to the investors or the consumers. Nevertheless the most convincing opinion points out that such a decision broadens the field of State liability rules too much. As consequence, there is the risk of an over-deterrence inasmuch as the officers are liable to pay damages even if the causality link between their unlawful act and the victim's loss is very slight[43]. **48**

[40] [2002] DR, 505 *et seq.*, with footnote of E. Cristiani/D. Dimundo, La Cassazione afferma la responsabilità della Consob per falsità del prospetto: un'occasione mancata ed un vecchio principio?

[41] [1999] FI, 2582.

[42] See E. Cristiani/F. Dimundo (*supra* note 41); M. Clarich, La responsabilità della Consob nell'esercizio della funzione di vigilanza: due passi oltre la sentenza della Cassazione n. 500/99, in [2002] DR, 223 *et seq.*

[43] M. Clarich (*supra* note 43).

8. Cass. 11 December 2000, No. 15580[44]: *danno biologico* of the Housewife

a) Brief Summary of the Facts

49 A housewife, who was injured in a car accident, claims damages for *danno biologico* and pecuniary losses. While compensation for *danno biologico* is unquestioned, the tortfeasor puts forward that economic losses could not be recovered, because they should be held as included in *danno biologico*.

b) Judgment of the Supreme Court

50 The Supreme Court upholds the claim of the housewife and rejects the defence of the tortfeasor. It is of the opinion that *danno biologico* and pecuniary losses are different types of harm and that, therefore, the one is not able to include the other. Moreover, the work of the housewife inside her family has an economic value and, more generally, a constitutional relevance (artt. 4 and 39 Const.). Therefore it has to be compensated.

c) Commentary

51 As pointed out above, compensation for *danno biologico* is based on the physical injury, regardless of earning capacity. Therefore damages have to be awarded even to persons who do not have an earned income, as in the example given, minors or housewifes. We have to remember that thirty years ago Italian courts denied compensation if they could not calculate a loss of the victim's earning capacity. Therefore if, example given, the injured person were a minor, it would be difficult to prove a loss[45].

52 This decision arouses perplexity, on the other hand, because it does not clarify how pecuniary losses can be proved in case of housework.

C. Literature

1. F. D. Busnelli/M. Bargagna (ed.), *La valutazione del danno alla salute* (Cedam, Padova, 2001)

53 The editors – a law professor and a forensic medicine professor – collect essays and cases concerning the main questions on *danno biologico* in the Italian legal system and in a European perspective[46]. They regard the most recent developments in this field of tort law, such as how to calculate damages[47],

[44] [2001] DR, 587.

[45] As happened in the famous «Gennarino case» (*cf.* A. Galoppini, Il caso Gennarino, ovvero quanto vale il figlio dell'operaio, [1971] *Democrazia e diritto*, (DD), 225 *et seq.*).

[46] As pointed out by F. D. Busnelli, Il danno alla salute: un'esperienza italiana; un modello per l'Europa?, pp. 3 *et seq.*

[47] M. Bargagna, La medicina legale ed il danno alla persona oggi, pp. 19 *et seq.*; A. Nannipieri, La liquidazione del giudiziale del danno in generale, pp. 79 *et seq.*

which is the role of *danno biologico* in the field of social insurance[48], when third persons can claim damages for mental shock caused by the killing of a relative[49], which are the most relevant decisions of Italian Supreme Court[50], of basic courts[51], of Constitutional Court[52], concerning *danno biologico*.

This book shows that the definition of *danno biologico* and its method of evaluation – based on forensic–medicine – are unquestioned in the Italian legal system. There is, in fact, the tendency to confirm liability rules at first suggested by scholars and then stated also by the Italian Constitutional court in 1986[53]. Both have theorised the systematic placing of physical injury within the framework of art. 2043 cc. An indispensable logical step to reach this result is the possibility of "measuring" *danno biologico* with the criteria provided by legal medicine. This allows *danno biologico* to be traduced in pecuniary terms, as a damage that can be compensated, so that its place within art. 2043 cc is justified. **54**

Another unquestioned point is that *danno biologico* can be compensated independently of pecuniary repercussions, as also the Supreme Court has recently confirmed[54]: this point is strongly emphasised especially in cases in which the victim is a subject receiving no income, as for example a minor or a housewife[55]. **55**

As consequence, the book contains the main guidelines on *danno biologico*, which can be useful to orientate courts and literature concerning this field of tort law. **56**

2. F. D. Busnelli, *Il Danno biologico. Dal "diritto vivente" al "diritto vigente"* (Giappichelli, Torino, 2001)

The author describes the main stages of development of *danno biologico*, as figure of loss before created by case law and then acknowledged by recent acts (art. 5 l. no. 57/2001 and art. 13 d.lgs. no. 38/2000). This is the meaning of the subtitle "dal diritto vivente al diritto vigente" (from case law to law in force). **57**

The first part of this book describes the beginning of such an evolution: the protection of health in private law was strongly supported by scholars in the **58**

[48] D. Poletti, Danno alla salute e infortuni sul lavoro: dall'evoluzione giurisprudenziale alla riforma legislativa, pp. 215 *et seq.*

[49] E. Navarretta, Danni da morte e danno alla salute, pp. 261 *et seq.*

[50] M. Zana/E. Pellecchia/M. Gorgoni, Svolgimenti giurisprudenziali, pp. 169 *et seq.*; D. Poletti, Le sentenze della Corte di Cassazione, pp. 489 *et seq.*

[51] E. Navarretta/E. Bargelli, Le sentenze delle corti di merito, pp. 547 *et seq.*

[52] A. Giusti, Il danno alla salute nella giurisprudenza costituzionale, pp. 189 *et seq.*; D. Poletti, Le decisioni della Corte costituzionale, pp. 441 *et seq.*

[53] Corte cost., 14 July 1986, no. 184, [1986] RCP, 520.

[54] Cass. 11 August 2000, no. 10725, and Cass. 12 September 2000, no. 12022, [2001], DR, 946, and 949, with footnote of F. Pellerito, Ancora guidelines della Cassazione sul danno biologico.

[55] Cass. 11 December 2000, no. 15580, [2001], DR, 587, with footnote of P. Maninetti, Sempre risarcibile il danno patrimoniale per diminuzione della capacità lavorativa della casalinga.

1970s[56] and then affirmed by the decision 184/1986 of the Constitutional Court[57]. The first step of the evolution in case law is given by the loose construction of art. 2043 cc, as a rule which can include not only economic losses, but also losses that can be measured by objective methods.

59 The second part of the book collects the essays concerning the theoretical questions on *danno biologico*: its notion[58], its boundaries[59] and its relationship with other non-pecuniary losses (such as environmental damage)[60].

60 The third part contains critical notes on the main decisions of the Constitutional Court: the famous 184/1986[61], and 372/1994[62].

61 The fourth part collects answers to the questions on *danno biologico* raised by a Constitutional Law Professor[63], by a Private Law Professor[64], by a Comparative Law Professor[65].

62 The fifth part describes the evolution of *danno biologico* in the last ten years[66]: moreover the authors point out the distinction between this figure and other personal injuries[67] and supports the adoption of different rules for pecuniary and non-pecuniary losses[68].

63 The sixth part concerns the latest development of *danno biologico* in the legislation, in the field of social insurance included[69].

64 The seventh and last part contains interesting essays concerning *danno biologico* in a European perspective[70].

[56] See Il problema della risarcibilità del danno alla salute, pp. 3 *et seq.*

[57] Corte cost. 14 July 1986 no. 184 [1986] RCP, 520.

[58] See Danno alla salute, danno alla persona e concetto di danno, pp. 85 *et seq.*; Danno biologico e danno alla salute: «modelli giurisprudenziali» a confronto, pp. 101 *et seq.*

[59] See Danno alla salute e danno da morte, pp. 111 *et seq.*

[60] See Danno alla salute e danno ambientale, pp. 123 *et seq.*

[61] See Condivisibili *rationes decidendi* e pericolosi *obiter dicta* della sentenza no. 184/1986, pp. 133 *et seq.*

[62] The mentioned decision is Corte cost., 27 October 1994, no. 372, [1994] RCP, 976, with footnote of G. Scalfi, L'uomo, la morte e la famiglia, and of G. Giannini, La vittoria di Pirrone, of E. Navarretta, Dall'esperienza del danno biologico da morte all'impianto dogmatico sul danno alla persona: il giudizio della Corte costituzionale. In the book see Danno alla salute e danno da morte nella rimeditazione della sentenza n. 372/1994, pp. 141 *et seq.*

[63] See Dialogo con Alessandro Pizzorusso. Gli interrogativi del costituzionalista, pp. 167 *et seq.*

[64] See Dialogo con Paolo Cendon. Le domande del civilista, pp. 191 *et seq.*

[65] See Dialogo con Antonio Gambaro. Le questioni del comparatista, pp. 219 *et seq.*

[66] See Le antinomie degli anni '90, pp.231 *et seq.*

[67] See Progettare il futuro tornando al passato (remoto), pp. 245 *et seq.*

[68] See Il modello «bipolare» del sistema italiano di risarcimento del danno alla persona, pp. 269 *et seq.*

[69] See Il danno biologico e gli infortuni sul lavoro: verso la modifica del T.U. INAIL, pp. 339 *et seq.*

[70] See Principi e regole per la costruzione di un modello europeo, pp. 373 *et seq.*, and Verso l'armonizzazione europea?, pp. 387 *et seq.*

3. E. Navarretta, Il danno alla persona tra solidarietà e tolleranza, [2001] *Responsabilità civile e previdenza* (RCP), 789 *et seq.*

The author illustrates the main theories on personal injuries, legislation and the most recent developments in case law. She feels it as convincing that personal injuries can be compensated beyond the limits stated by art. 2059 cc, but it is necessary to adopt a loose construction of this rule. This proposal is based on a "constitutionally oriented" interpretation of art. 2059 cc, whose strict formulation is inconsistent with constitutional principle. As consequence, every non-pecuniary loss should be recovered (loss of amenity of life, pain and suffering) if a constitutional right is seriously violated. Therefore, *e.g.*, it would surely be possible claim compensation for the mental shock caused by the killing of a relative, but not for the one caused by the death of the dog. The author comes to the conclusion that art. 2059 cc is the general rule concerning non-pecuniary losses. 65

The author comes to the conclusion that it is necessary to take into account two main guidelines in the field of non-pecuniary losses: solidarity toward the victim on the one hand; a minimal degree of tolerance on the other hand. This position should lead one to bear very slight injuries without claiming damages, while compensation can be claimed for losses which are causally consequent upon serious injury to the person. 66

4. P. Cendon/P. Ziviz, *Trattato breve dei nuovi danni* (Cedam, Padova, 2001)

The authors have already asserted in other previous essays that it is possible to claim compensation for every personal injury, even if very slight (*e.g.*, the suffering caused by the killing of the cat, or the pain caused by the theft of the victim's new motorbike)[71]. They merely held as necessary that the tort has changed one's style of life, that is what the victim did before the event: *e.g.*, to enjoy life, to go on holiday, and so on. According to this opinion, such interests – inasmuch as they are defined as "personal" – take the shape of damage to constitutional rights. If they are violated, damages could be claimed according to art. 2043 cc, not on the basis of art. 2059 cc, which concerns non-pecuniary losses and can be applied only if the tort is a crime. Art. 2059 cc, on the other hand, should be applied to recover the mere *pecunia doloris*, considered not to be of constitutional relevance. 67

This book is based on this assumption, but centres on the review of the possible types of injury which can cause the changing of one's style of life. It contains several groups of cases, some of which are real, others fictitious. Even if lacking in scientific value, we must remark that the book is interesting because 68

[71] P. Ziviz, Alla scoperta del danno esistenziale, [1994], *Contratto e impresa* (C. I.), 845 *et seq.*, published also in: P. Cendon (ed.), *La responsabilità extracontrattuale. Le nuove figure di risarcimento del danno nella giurisprudenza* (1994), pp. 41 *et seq.*; at last, Ead., L'evoluzione del sistema di risarcimento del danno: modelli interpretativi a confronto, [1999] RCDP, 88 *et seq.*; P. Cendon, Non di sola salute vive l'uomo, [1999] RCDP, 569 *et seq.*

it contains a lot of cases and because it is an example of a new trend in the field of personal injuries which has had some reception in case law.

69 Nevertheless we hold the doctrine as not convincing for two main reasons. At first, the victim of a very grave tort may continue to lead the same life as before, but this mere fact should not lead to the denial of compensation for personal injuries. Furthermore, such a doctrine leads to paradoxes such as affirming that if a victim changes his living habits in his leisure time as a consequence of the death of a domestic animal, then this damage must be compensated (*ex* art. 2043 cc) inasmuch as it is of constitutional status; if the victim simply suffers for the death of a child, on the contrary, the damage is not to be recoverable unless a crime occurs (*ex* artt. 2059 cc and 185 cp), because the damage is not of a constitutional status.

5. F. Tortorano, *Il danno meramente patrimoniale* (Giappichelli, Torino, 2001)

70 The book concerns the purely economic loss, that is the financial loss that is not causally consequent upon physical injury to a plaintiff or to his or her property. In the Italian legal system the debate on purely economic loss must face the general rule of art. 2043 cc, which takes into account the notion of *danno ingiusto* ("juridically relevant damage"). The author deals with the topic from a comparative point of view: he compares in fact the main law traditions – common law and civil law – and analyses their solutions. The last part of the book centres on solutions given by several European legal systems

71 He comes to the conclusion that both legal traditions have the purpose to restrain the field of losses that may be compensated, but does not propose an original theory about purely economic losses.

XII. The Netherlands

Michael Faure* and *Ton Hartlief

A. Introduction

Every lawyer interested in liability and insurance in the Netherlands has noted that the evolutions in the domain of liability and tort law in the Netherlands move very fast[1]. 1

It is interesting to notice that the evolutions in liability law are considered that important that even the Dutch government has paid attention to it. In this respect, we can point to a letter of the Dutch government concerning the so-called claim culture. Also the Minister of Justice formulated a few interesting comments with his view on the future of liability law within the framework of the discussions concerning the budgets for the Ministry of Justice[2]. 2

One of the problems the Dutch government is facing is that victims increasingly turn to the government with a claim on compensation. The Netherlands has unfortunately been confronted with serious catastrophes such as an explosion of a firework factory in May 2001 and a spectacular fire in Volendam on the New Year's Eve of 2000–2001. In these cases, the legal situation is often rather complex, since victims turn to the government both on the basis of liability law as well as simply for compensation. One of the crucial questions is obviously whether the government should have any role at all in the absence of government liability *e.g.* for lacking control, in providing compensation outside of the usual social security schemes[3]. The Minister of Justice of the 3

[1] It is not even possible to discuss all of these developments within the framework of this contribution to the yearbook, neither can we discuss all authors who have described these evolutions in 2001. For a few articles discussing evolutions in liability law during recent years in the Netherlands see T. Hartlief, [2001] *Nederlands Tijdschrift voor Burgerlijk Recht* (NTBR), 20 and Sieburgh, *Weekblad voor Privaatrecht, Notariaat en Registratie* (WPNR) 6450, 580.

[2] See parliamentary documents of the Second Chamber of Representatives, [2000–2001], 27400VI, nos. 54, 6 *et seq.*

[3] See Second Chamber of Representatives, [2000–2001], 27400VI, no. 54, 6.

Netherlands, Mr. Korthals, claims that this increasing tendency to make more use of liability law may lead to an unmanageability of the amounts of compensation due by insurance companies. Hence, the Minister of Justice claims that the time is ripe for a reconsideration of the goals and structure of civil liability law and related insurance law[4].

4 This background is rather important for understanding the developments concerning liability law in the Netherlands. It means for instance that a proposal for a new act on traffic liability will not be introduced within the near future and that the minister is rather interested in alternatives for the liability system, such as the model of direct insurance.

5 This means that within this Dutch contribution to the yearbook 2001, it is not always possible to make a strict distinction between legislation/case law and doctrine. Some evolutions will have to be discussed in a more integrated manner. Moreover, although we shall of course focus on evolutions in 2001, in some cases these have already taken a start earlier. Some court decisions, *e.g.* in late 2000, can be considered that important that they still need to be mentioned briefly within the framework of this overview, since otherwise the evolutions in 2001 might be difficult to understand.

6 Given the framework and background we have just sketched, the reader will understand that the Dutch Minister of Justice is now considering a fundamental rethinking of liability law in the Netherlands. This also means that legislative changes are now relatively scarce. However, there are various government and policy committees which have formulated interesting proposals. Thus, we will not only focus on new legislation in the strict sense, but also on evolutions at the government level which are *e.g.* reflected in policy documents but which may have an important influence on liability law in the near future.

7 Within the scope of this paper, it is not possible to discuss all the evolutions in the domain of liability law. That is especially the case as far as case law is concerned, which is rather extensive. Therefore, we were forced to make a selection, which undoubtedly has a subjective character.

B. Legislation and Evolutions at Policy Level

1. Direct Insurance and the Proposals of the Donner Commission

8 Above we already indicated that the Dutch government is at this moment contemplating alternatives for liability insurance. One of these alternatives is direct insurance. The literature has, however, argued that if the introduction of such a direct insurance would be combined with an immunity of (employers)

[4] Second Chamber of Representatives, [2000–2001], 27400VI, no. 54, 7.

liability, this would be problematic[5]. Nevertheless, direct insurance seems to gain support at the policy level. A government commission, named after its chairperson Mr. Donner, drafted a report on problems of unemployment caused through disability[6]. The commission argues that a so-called *risque professionnel* insurance should be introduced on a compulsory basis, so that every employer would have to take insurance coverage to the benefit of his employees, covering the consequences of professional diseases and industrial accidents. The introduction of such a scheme of compulsory insurance would then be combined with a (partial) immunity of the employer from liability. The proposals of the Donner Commission would hence lead to the introduction of a scheme of direct insurance.

This report of the Donner Commission is highly interesting, also for aspects other than the issue of direct insurance. Indeed, the importance for tort law is that the proposals of the Donner Commission would imply that many victims who now receive compensation under the disability act[7] would no longer receive compensation. The bottom line is therefore that the government would increasingly reduce the provision of compensation for disability via the social security system. That may cause a need for victims to increasingly use tort law against the employer or a third party, at least in those cases where a liable injurer can be found who caused the disability or the industrial accident. In other words: a consequence of the proposals of the Donner Commission to reduce the intervention via the social security system may be an increasing tendency to use tort law. 9

2. Product Liability

The Netherlands' civil code has – in execution of the European Product Liability Directive of 25 July 1985 – introduced a strict liability for product defects. It can be found in art. 6:185 and following of the Dutch civil code[8]. Nevertheless, in practice the classic tort liability of art. 6:162 of the Dutch civil code is very often used for accidents caused by product defects as well. This is caused by the many limitations and conditions for the applicability of the specific product liability regime in art. 6:185. The recent evolution in this respect occurs at the European level. As is well known, the Commission launched a Green Paper on product liability in which it examines the possibility to extend the European product liability regime. One extension of the product liability regime is meanwhile already taking effect. As a result of the dioxin and mad cow crisis as well as many hormone scandals, the exception 10

[5] See in this respect for instance the criticism formulated on the proposals towards direct insurance by Frenk, [2000/0] *Aansprakelijkheid en Verzekering* (AV&S), 2 and J.H. Wansink, Onverzekerbare aansprakelijkheid: (verplichte) directe verzekeringen een aanvaardbaar alternatief?, in: T. Hartlief/M.M. Mendel (eds.), *Verzekering en maatschappij* (2000), pp. 407–421.

[6] See Advies van de adviescommissie Arbeidsongeschiktheid, werk maken van arbeidsgeschiktheid (The Hague, 2001).

[7] *Wet op de Arbeidsongeschiktheidsverzekering*.

[8] See on product liability in the Netherlands L. Dommering-van Rongen, *Productaansprakelijkheid* (2000).

for agricultural products disappeared from art. 6:187 of the Dutch civil code, so that agricultural products are now fully covered by the product liability regime of art. 6:185 of the civil code[9]. The Dutch government moreover has declared that it is prepared to consider an increase of the statute of limitations and an extension of the product liability regime to damage suffered professionally (whereas professional damage is excluded from the current scope of the product liability directive)[10]. However, it can be assumed that other changes are less likely since, moreover, the Commission itself made clear that, taking into account the reactions to the Green Paper, it is not considering formulating specific proposals to change the European product liability directive at this moment[11].

3. Compensation for Non-Pecuniary Losses

11 As is relatively well-known, Dutch tort law has never been generous as far as the compensation for non-pecuniary losses is concerned[12]. This is the case in the first place for the level of compensation, that is to say the damages awards themselves[13], but it is especially so if one looks at the position of third parties. Third parties (other than the victims themselves), such as relatives of the victim, are not entitled to compensation of their non-pecuniary losses under Dutch law. In a case of September 2000, an attempt was made to change this, but unsuccessfully[14]. As a result of that decision, critical questions were asked to the minister in the Dutch parliament. As a result of that discussion, the Dutch government indicated that it is planning to introduce a statute granting a right of compensation of non-pecuniary losses to specific victims[15]. There seems to be a majority in Dutch parliament now in favour of an increased right of compensation for non-pecuniary losses and this has, moreover, often been argued in the literature as well[16]. If such a right were introduced, the government is thinking about the system whereby compensation would be awarded to recognize the fact that not only the victim but also the descendants and relatives of the victim have suffered as a result of the tort. The idea, which is now being launched by the Dutch government, is to award specific descendants or relatives (in case of death or serious disability of the victim) an amount of

[9] Implementation of this extension to agricultural products had to take place by 4 December 2000 and it is exactly per that date that the change took effect in the Netherlands. See in this respect documents of the second Chamber of Representatives 1999–2000, 27051, nos. 1–2.

[10] See in this respect the documents of the second Chamber of Representatives 1999–2000, 22112, no. 134, pp. 6–7 for a reaction of the Dutch government to the Green Paper on product liability.

[11] See in this respect Com 2000 (893) final.

[12] See in this respect among others M.H. Wissink/W.H. van Boom, The Netherlands, in: W.V. Horton Rogers (ed.), *Damages for non pecuniary loss in a comparative perspective* (2001), pp. 155–172.

[13] See in this respect concerning art. 6:106 civil code Hoge Raad 27 April 2001 [2002] *Nederlandse Jurisprudentie* (NJ), 100 (CJHB).

[14] Hoge Raad 8 September 2000 [2000] NJ, 734 (ARP) Baby Joost.

[15] See documents of the second Chamber of Representatives 2000–2001, 27400, no. 70.

[16] See for instance Lindenbergh, [2001] *Nederlands Juristenblad* (NJB), 61, van Dam, *Verkeersrecht* (2001), p. 1 and Haak, [2001] NTBR, 211.

€ 10,000[17]. The government argues that it would be important to indicate clearly in advance who would be the descendants and relatives who could claim compensation for non-pecuniary losses in such a case and it is equally argued that it would be important to fix the amount that would be awarded. The government also argues that this amount can be kept relatively low (as mentioned at € 10,000) since the goal of awarding compensation would not be to remove the suffering that has been caused by the death or disability of the victim[18]. Of course, the government realizes that the consequence of the introduction of such a right on pain and suffering, also for relatives of the victim, might be that the total amount of liability (and hence the pressure on insurers) may increase. However, these consequences (including the possible light increase of the liability insurance premium) are considered acceptable since the government argues that compensation for these non-pecuniary losses may provide (additional) incentives for careful behaviour[19].

However, if this argument of providing incentives to potential injurers is taken seriously, then it seems rather odd to limit *ex ante* the number of persons who could claim this compensation and to provide only for a relatively low amount of compensation. This has therefore already been seriously criticized in the literature[20]. The criticism is especially directed against the fact that all claimants would receive a similar (relatively low) amount. In that case similar cases would be treated unequally (why does one relative receive compensation while another is not entitled to compensation?). The literature indeed holds that one can question whether € 10,000 is indeed in all cases, irrespective of the specific type of suffering, an acceptable amount. Thus many cases, which are in essence different (and thus unequal), are nevertheless treated alike, which may violate the equality principle. 12

The necessity of statutory intervention has been made clear recently once more. Indeed, on the one hand the *Hoge Raad* made clear by the end of 2001 that a mother of a boy who was killed by the father certainly has a right to compensation of her non-pecuniary losses[21]; on the other hand the Hoge Raad has not been prepared to move away from the statutory system under which only a limited circle of persons is entitled to claim under tort law[22]. It is up to the legislator to reconsider this restriction. It is apparently not seen as the task of the *Hoge Raad* itself to introduce a right to so-called "affection damages" (for the non-pecuniary losses suffered by third parties). In this case, an amount of damages that was awarded for the emotional shock suffered by the mother 13

[17] These proposals of the Dutch government are by the way in line with the proposals as formulated in the dissertation by Lindenbergh (S. Lindenbergh, *Smartengeld* (1998); see also his contribution in [2001] NJB, 61).

[18] Documents of the second Chamber of Representatives 2000–2001, 27400, no. 70, pp. 4–6.

[19] Documents of the second Chamber of Representatives 2000–2001, 27400, no. 70, pp. 6–7.

[20] See van Boom, [2001] NJB, 1301–1302 and Verhey, [2001] NJB, 1562 *et seq.*

[21] *Hoge Raad* 26 October 2001, [2001] *Rechtspraak van de Week,* 169 = [2002] NJ, 216 with case note by JBMV.

[22] See recently *Hoge Raad* 22 February 2002 [2002] *Rechtspraak van de Week,* 48 = [2002] NJ, 240 with case note by JBMV.

(consisting both of material losses and of non-pecuniary losses) remain supported by the *Hoge Raad*. But the introduction of so-called affection damages apparently needs to be done by the legislator.

4. Statute of Limitations

14 Furthermore, the government has introduced a proposal concerning the statute of limitations for personal injury. The proposed law, which has been introduced by the government, aims to prevent a victim's claim to receive compensation for personal injury or death already having expired at a time that the victim would not have been in a position to file the claim. This can especially be the case with so-called long tail damages, such as with asbestos related occupational diseases. Therefore, the bill proposes to introduce the rule that a claim for compensation for damage caused by personal injury or death would only expire five years after the day on which the victim is acquainted both with the damage as well as with the liable injurer. This proposal was introduced especially with a view on the problems that victims of occupational diseases were suffering. Asbestos victims, for instance, often only found out about their illness and the possibility to file a liable employer at the moment when the claim had already expired. The goal of the bill is *inter alia* to improve the situation of those victims.

15 However, the victims of today will not benefit from this bill. The new rules will only apply to harmful acts that take place after the entering into force of the new act. Many obviously dislike this particular aspect of the bill: the victims of the future will no longer have problems with the statute of limitations. For them, their interests will weigh heavier than the legal certainty for potential injurers. However, many authors have therefore argued that also the victims of today should benefit from the new regime[23]. However, the government has recently argued again that there is no reason to apply the new regime to "old" victims[24].

C. Case Law

1. Accidents as a Result of Coincidence or Unlucky Courses of Events

16 The Dutch Supreme Court has often to deal with situations where an accident is caused by coincidence. In this respect, we can refer to a case concerning the sisters Jansen where, as a result of bad luck during the moving from one house to another, personal injury was caused by one sister to another. The case concerned an accident during the moving of a cupboard. One of the sisters

[23] E.A. Dek, Asbestontwikkeling – oprechte tegemoetkoming of doekje voor het bloeden? [1999] *Tijdschrift voor Milieuaansprakelijkheid* (TMA), 61–62, Van Dort, De nieuwe verjaringsregeling en asbestslachtoffers – een loos gebaar van de wetgever? [1999] TMA, 177–179 and K. Aantjes, Verjaring: de sexueel misbruik- en kindermishandelingsarresten [2000] *Verkeersrecht,* 173–177.

[24] Documents First Chamber of Representatives 2001–2002, 26824, no. 128, 10.

engaged in a rather clumsy movement as a result of which the other suffered serious personal injury. Both the civil court and the courts of appeals held the other sister (partially) liable. The *Hoge Raad*, however, is of another opinion; the *Hoge Raad* argues that this course of events leads to the conclusion that the accident was caused by an unlucky cumulation of circumstances[25]. Thus the *Hoge Raad* suggests that the "unlucky course of events" is a separate category of tort. The literature has previously held that this should certainly not be so. It is only after the liability issue itself has been answered on the basis of the so-called "kelderluikcriteria" that the accident can be characterized as being caused by an "unlucky course of events". The reason this type of accident is qualified as such is of course that it leads to the conclusion that the accident was not caused by the injurer's behaviour, at least that the injurer did not take greater risks than was justified under the circumstances. Thus, the literature holds that in fact the *Hoge Raad* simply examines the behaviour of the injurer and holds that the injurer was not negligent and is therefore not liable. Thus it is not the "unlucky course of events" which should be considered as a separate category, but simply the fact that in these cases, the facts indicate that the injurer's behaviour cannot be considered as negligent. Both Hijma and Van Dam argue strongly against considering the unlucky course of events as a separate category of cases[26].

2. Liability for Non-Subordinates

There is a lot of case law concerning artt. 6:169 and 6:170 of the Dutch civil **17**
code. These provisions deal with vicarious liability. One of the conditions for vicarious liability is that a third person can only be made liable for the act of another if there is the necessary functional link between the third party and the tortfeasor[27]. A rather important decision of the *Hoge Raad* concerning art. 6:170 of the Dutch civil code dates from 9 November 2001[28]. The question that arose in that case was what the legal situation is concerning the issue of contributory negligence of an employee when the employer is held liable on the basis of art. 6:170 of the civil code for the negligent behaviour of a colleague, that is, another employee. The case dealt with the situation where a colleague of the victim had negligently forgotten to close a drawer of a cupboard as a result of which the victim suffered serious damage. In the case of the employer's liability of art. 7:658 civil code, contributory negligence of the employee would only be accepted as a defence in case of intent or gross negligence on the side of the employee, being the victim. In this case, it is again the relationship of the employer with the employee that determines the circumstances of the accident. The employer remains primarily liable for determining the working environment. Therefore the *Hoge Raad* holds that within the framework of this liability under art. 6:170 in combination with art. 6:101 of

[25] See *Hoge Raad* 12 May 2000, [2001] NJ, 300 (with case note by J.H.) and [2000] *Aansprakelijkheid & Verzekering* (A&V), 106–107 (with case note by Hartlief).

[26] See the case note of Hijma in [2001] NJB, 300 and see Van Dam in [2001] *Verkeersrecht*, 139 and following.

[27] See on this requirement C. Klaassen, *Schadeveroorzakend handelen in functie* (2000).

[28] *Hoge Raad* 9 November 2001, [2002] NJ, 79 with case note by P.A. Stein.

the civil code the same threshold should apply: except in the case of intent or gross negligence on the side of the employee is contributory negligence not a defence.

18 The scope of art. 6:171 of the civil code was determined in two decisions of the *Hoge Raad* in 2001[29]. The latter decision is the most interesting since the *Hoge Raad* indicates in that decision, using parliamentary history that the so-called "unity of enterprise" is important to determine liability. Indeed, these decisions of the *Hoge Raad* deal with the application of art. 6:171 of the Dutch civil code. This article holds that a superior can be held liable for the torts committed by a third party, even if that third party is not formally a subordinate of the superior. This applies *e.g.* to cases where the superior has engaged a third party to perform services for him[30]. The scope of liability under this provision is potentially pretty large. Some hold, referring to the parliamentary history of this provision, that liability of the superior under art. 6:171 of the Dutch civil code requires that there is a so-called "unity of enterprise" between the acts of the superior and those of the third party. This "unity of enterprise" should then also be visible for third parties. In that respect, one thinks about a case where a third party (who is not a subordinate, *e.g.* an employee of the superior) takes action showing that he engages in the undertaking or enterprise of the superior, which is also visible for third parties as well as for the victim. This position was also defended before the civil court and the court of appeals and the *Hoge Raad* held that this interpretation cannot be considered as incorrect. This interpretation therefore limits the potentially large scope of liability under art. 6:171 of the Dutch civil code.

19 The case of 11 May 2001 also dealt with another issue, which was not taken into account in the parliamentary history concerning art. 6:171. This concerns the question of the effect of a limitation of liability of the injurer. In this particular case, the injurer could benefit from a statutory limitation of liability. The question then arises whether the liability of the superior can also benefit from the statutory limitation of the injurer or whether this vicarious liability in fact reaches further. The *Hoge Raad* held that the liability of the superior does not reach further than the liability of this non-subordinated injurer.

3. Liability for Goods

20 The Dutch civil code holds specific provisions concerning the liability for damage caused by specific moveables, animals, dangerous substances and defective products. There is much case law dealing with art. 6:174 of the Dutch civil code. An interesting *Hoge Raad* case of 15 June 2001[31] dealt with the following facts. During a big fire in an industrial area, asbestos articles

[29] *Hoge Raad* 15 May 2001, [2001] NJ, 631 with case note by K.F. Haak and Hoge Raad 21 December 2001, [2002] NJ, 75.

[30] See *Hoge Raad* 11 May 2001, [2001] NJ, 631 with case note by K.F. Haak, EMO/Witchin Company Limited.

[31] *Hoge Raad* 15 June 2001, [2001] *Rechtspraak van de Week,* 114, Almelo/Wessels.

were released that came down in a residential area. The local community removed the asbestos particles and subsequently filed a claim against the owner of the buildings that burned down. This claim in recovery of the costs incurred for the asbestos removal was based *inter alia* on art. 6:174 of the Dutch civil code. However, this article provides for a liability for damage caused through *defective* buildings. Such a building will only be considered defective when it did not meet the safety requirements one could expect from such a building. In this case, the risk that material with asbestos would release in the atmosphere was considered relatively low. Moreover, it was not prohibited by law to possess a building with roofing, which contains asbest. As a consequence, it was held that the building concerned was not to be considered defective and hence there was no liability under art. 6:174 of the Dutch civil code.

However, the case was not only based on the strict liability provision of art. 6:174 of the civil code, but also on the general tort provision of art. 6:162 of the Dutch civil code. The community argued that the owner of the building had acted wrongfully against the community by not removing the asbestos particles that came down on the residential area himself. Hence, so the local community claimed, the proprietor of the building had continued a dangerous situation, which should be considered as unlawful. However, also this claim was rejected, although the *Hoge Raad* is relatively short on this point. Apparently the *Hoge Raad* judged it important that the buildings concerned corresponded with the safety requirements one could expect from them. Moreover, another aspect was that the community involved had incurred the costs for the clean up of the asbestos particles in the execution of its public duties. That would hence bar a subsequent claim in tort. The latter aspect obviously does not apply in the case that citizens remove the asbestos particles and incur costs. **21**

Several *Hoge Raad* cases deal with the question when there is "defectiveness" in the sense of art. 6:174 of the Dutch civil code. **22**

A *Hoge Raad* decision of 27 April 2001[32] deals with the cumulation of contractual and tort liability. A veterinary surgeon had incurred personal injury when treating a horse. The *Hoge Raad* held that, although there is principally a contractual relationship (for treating the horse), the victim could nevertheless bring a suit against the possessor of the animal on the basis of art. 6:179 of the Dutch civil code. In other words: contractual liability does not exclude liability in tort. **23**

[32] *Hoge Raad* 27 April 2001, [2002] NJ, 54 with case note by CJHB, Donkers/Scholten.

4. Medical Liability

a) Unlimited Liability in Case of Violation of a Medical Protocol?

24 Several cases of the *Hoge Raad* in 2001 dealt with the consequences of a violation of the duty to inform in medical cases, with causation issues and with the question who is entitled to claim in case of medical malpractice. An important case which deserves to be discussed within the scope of this Dutch report for the yearbook is a *Hoge Raad* decision of 2 March 2001[33]. This case dealt with the importance of the violation of so-called protocols (for the treatment of patients) that had been fixed within a hospital. Victim was a Mr. In't Hout, who had undergone surgery on his left knee in the hospital MCL. After a certain period of time, he got a thrombosis. However, on the basis of a protocol that was established within the MCL in case of this particular surgery on the knee, a product against thrombosis should have been administered to the patient. In the particular case, the health care providers had apparently "forgotten" to provide that particular medication. The question arose whether this mere fact gives rise to liability of the hospital. A particular issue that arose in this context was the causation question. Indeed, the hospital claimed that the particular damage would also have occurred if the particular medication had been administered according to the protocol.

25 If the specific protocol concerned should be considered as a so-called safety standard, this would almost inevitably lead to a liability of the hospital. This was indeed what the court of appeals had accepted and which led to great concerns in the medical world[34]. The *Hoge Raad* is more careful and clearly avoids to qualify the protocol as a safety standard. However, in the end, it does not help the hospital that much. Indeed, the *Hoge Raad* holds that, in the case concerned, it could be expected that the hospital MCL would at least follow the instructions concerning medically appropriate treatments that it had drafted itself; a deviation from those prescriptions in the protocol would therefore only be acceptable if this were desirable from the point of view of appropriate care for the patient. The result is of course that there is almost no difference with the regime whereby the protocol would be considered formally as a safety standard (whereby violation of safety standards almost immediately leads to liability, if causation can be proven as well). The *Hoge Raad* apparently rules that protocols have to be followed and have to be applied. Deviation is possible, but only if this is motivated. This is in fact not different if one considered the protocol as a safety standard[35]. Lawyers practising medical law have been extremely critical of this case law since they hold that too much attention is paid to these so-called protocols, which lead to a too far reaching liability of health care providers. We, however, believe that this

[33] *Hoge Raad* 2 March 2001, [2001] NJ, 649 MCL./In't Hout with case note by F.C.B. van Wijmen and JBMV.

[34] See for critical comments concerning the decision of the court of appeals for instance T.V.G. Vermaas, (2000), p. 381 and Hubben, [2001] NJB, 490.

[35] See *Hoge Raad* 1 October 1993, [1995] NJ, 182 with case note by C.J.H. Brunner (case Tamara van Uitert).

criticism is somewhat overstated. Indeed, neither the decision of the court of appeals, nor the decision of the *Hoge Raad* imply that every protocol would have automatically the same bearing or that one would have to decide that deviations of the protocol would only be an exception. The case law apparently holds that deviations from the protocol are allowed, on the condition that they are motivated. One should, moreover, warn that the interpretation by health lawyers of this case law should not lead to the conclusion that hospitals should in the future become more careful with drafting protocols. Indeed, one may not forget that drafting these protocols, which prescribe the state of the art concerning appropriate treatment, is of course primarily in the interests of the patient. However, the health care provider himself also has an interest in these protocols. Indeed, it may only improve his own position if the health care provider can prove (in case of problems) that he has at least followed the internal hospital instructions as they appear in the protocol. The application of a totally open norm, without any instruction such as is the case with a protocol, could lead to much more uncertainty for the health care provider.

It is, however, important to stress that the *Hoge Raad* has held that the rule of the reversal of the burden of proof in case of uncertainty concerning the causal link (which will be discussed in more detail below) is not applicable in case of the violation of the information duties by the physician[36]. **26**

b) Wrongful Life and Wrongful Birth

The so-called wrongful life claims probably show the limits of liability law. Dutch lawyers meanwhile are "used" to the so-called wrongful birth claims[37]. The wrongful life claims are still more debated. In that particular case, the plaintiff in fact holds that he would rather not have existed[38]. The civil court of The Hague dealt with the following issue in the so-called baby-Kelly case[39]. The plaintiff, Kelly, came into the world with a handicap as a result of a deviation in the chromosomes. It was held that the gynaecologist did not react adequately to indications concerning a genetic deviation. In line with the so-called wrongful birth case law, the claim of the parents for the costs of raising and taking care of Kelly was admitted. The same was the case for the claim concerning the extra costs for medical treatment as a result of the handicap. Remarkably, the civil court also recognizes a claim of compensation for non-pecuniary losses of the mother, but not of the father[40]. Kelly herself also claimed compensation for non-pecuniary losses. Her claim was that she did **27**

[36] *Hoge Raad* 23 November 2001 [2001] *Rechtspraak van de Week*, 188.

[37] See *inter alia Hoge Raad* 21 February 1997, [1999] NJ, 145 with case note by C.J.H. Brunner. Another approach is suggested by Van Boom and Janssen, [2000] NTBR, 276.

[38] For an elaborate discussion of these so-called wrongful life claims, see Stolker and Levine, [1997] A&V, 38.

[39] See civil court The Hague, 2 February 2000, [2000] NJ kort, 54. See for a discussion of this case Lindenbergh, [2000] *Tijdschrift voor Vergoeding Personenschade*, 31, Slabbers, [2000] *Verzekeringsrechtelijke berichten*, 61 and Stolker, [2001] NTBR, 40.

[40] See for a critical analysis particularly of this issue Lindenbergh, [2000] *Tijdschrift voor Vergoeding Personenschade* (TVP), 35.

not blame the defendant for the fact that she was born (in other words for her mere existence), but for the fact that she was handicapped. That fact, however, was, so the court held, not caused by the gynaecologist, but obviously by the deviation in the chromosomes. Hence, the simple result was that there was no causal link between the fault of the defendant and the damage. This means that as a result of the position taken by the plaintiff, the court did not really have to decide the wrongful life issue in the true sense. Meanwhile, this issue has been extensively discussed in the Dutch literature, which also takes into account evolutions in this respect in neighbouring countries[41]. A key issue which is discussed in many of these commentaries is whether there should be any role for liability law at all in these particular cases.

5. Liability of Public Authorities

28 Several cases deal with damage caused as a result of police actions. The interesting issue is that in such cases the damage is not always caused by wrongful actions of the public authorities. For instance, a *Hoge Raad* case of 30 March 2001 deals with the question whether there should be compensation when the police undertakes a search in the house of a third party who is not a suspect of a crime at all[42]. The *Hoge Raad* clearly makes a distinction between the question whether the search itself is wrongful or not and the question whether causing damage at the occasion of the search is wrongful. In many cases, the search may have been legal in the sense that it took place on the basis of the rules of criminal procedure. This means that the search as such is lawful, but that does not necessarily imply that causing damage to a third party at the occasion of a legal search is therefore not wrongful. The *Hoge Raad* relies on the principle of the equality of the citizens before the public burdens[43]. The *Hoge Raad* holds that from this principle it follows that causing a disproportionate damage at the occasion of a public act which is as such lawful (like in this case the lawful search) may be wrongful against the victim. In the particular case, the court of appeals held that the damage that had been caused by the lawful police search was disproportionate and that therefore the public authorities were liable. This judgment was not reversed by the *Hoge Raad*. The key of this reasoning is therefore that it is still unlawful to cause disproportionate damage at the occasion of an action, which is as such lawful (in this case the execution of a search). The consequences of this case law may be rather far-reaching for all those cases where innocent third parties suffer damage as a result of actions of the police.

[41] See for instance Van Maanen, [2001] NTBR, 57, Nieuwenhuis, [2001] RM Themis, 97–98 and Schoordijk, [2001] NTBR, 212.

[42] *Hoge Raad* 30 March 2001, [2001] *Rechtspraak van de Week*, 71. See the discussion by Van Maanen in [2001] TVP, 38.

[43] This is usually referred to by the French expression "Egalité devant les charges publiques".

6. Employer's Liability

a) Employer's Liability: Is There Any Escape?

Much case law deals with the liability of the employer on the basis of art. 7:658 of the civil code for the consequences of industrial accidents and occupational diseases. The case law of the *Hoge Raad* gives the employer very few possibilities to escape this liability. An example of this far-reaching employer's liability is also provided in a *Hoge Raad* decision of 19 October 2001[44]. In that decision, as is the case in many others in this field, the fact that the duty of care of the employer is also determined by the fact that employees are supposed not always to take the necessary care for themselves plays a crucial role. Against this background the employer had taken an original position in a *Hoge Raad* case of 15 December 2001[45]. The employer held that an employee who does not respect the instructions given by the employer no longer suffers damage in the execution of his work for the particular employer. In the particular case, the employee had been working on a roof other than the one that he was instructed to work on and had suffered damage. The *Hoge Raad*'s decision in this respect, however, provides little hope for employers that this would give them an adequate defence against their liability. The *Hoge Raad* clearly held that the fact that an employee does not fulfil the specific duty given by the employer does not mean that he no longer suffers damage in the execution of his work. If the *Hoge Raad* had taken another decision, this would have been an easy way for employers to circumvent the very stringent case law of the *Hoge Raad* concerning the contributory negligence of the employee (which is only accepted in exceptional cases). 29

b) Burden of Proof

On 1 April 1997, title 7.10 of the new Dutch civil code entered into force. As a result of this, the employer's liability from 1 April 1997 was determined by the new provision art. 7:658 of the civil code. The *Hoge Raad* reconfirmed on 15 December 2000 that this new provision concerning employer's liability has immediate effect and therefore also applies to cases where the accident dates from before 1 April 1997[46]. This has, as a consequence, that the employee merely has to hold that he suffered damage in the execution of his work. According to the previously existing provision, the employee additionally had to hold (and eventually prove) that the employer had acted wrongfully. Now the burden of proof has in fact been shifted. It is now up to the employer to hold and prove that he took appropriate care[47]. 30

A consequence of the regulation of the burden of proof in art. 7:658 al. 2 of the civil code is that it is the employer who has to prove the circumstances of 31

[44] *Hoge Raad* 19 October 2001, [2001] NJ, 663.

[45] *Hoge Raad* 15 December 2001, [2001] NJ, 198, with case note by P.A. Stein (Van Uitert/Jalas).

[46] See *Hoge Raad* 15 December 2000, [2001] NJ, 252, with case note by P.A. Stein (van Merkstelјn/Öztürk). See also the case note by Van Dijk in [2001] AV&S, 55–57.

[47] See on this issue also Bier, [2001] *Verkeersrecht*, 133.

the accident in case there is a dispute on that issue[48]. That obligation can of course be highly disadvantageous for the employer, especially in those cases where a longer time lapsed since the accident or where no adequate report concerning the circumstances of the accident has been made. Recently, the *Hoge Raad* held that equity could in specific circumstances require that this specific rule of evidence is not applied, so that the general rule of evidence of art. 177 of the code of civil procedure would be applied[49].

c) Low Threshold for Liability in Case of Occupational Diseases

32 We already indicated that the threshold for employer's liability is relatively low since it suffices that the employee holds (and in case of motivated discussion proves) that he suffered damage as a result of the execution of this work[50]. However, even this low threshold for liability can constitute a serious barrier with specific occupational diseases. Sometimes, the employer can, as a defence, argue that the damage has a cause other than the execution of his work by the employee. The employer could for instance hold that (a specific type of) lung cancer can be caused by working with asbestos, but could equally have other causes, such as smoking. The same is true in case of new health risks such as RSI (repetitive strain injury) and stress. An employer would of course suggest that these complaints are connected to a variety of other factors which have nothing to do with the work (like lifestyle, working at home, family situation, etc.).

33 This issue has played a role in an asbestos procedure. There was doubt whether a victim of mesotheliom had incurred the mesotheliom when working for the employer De Schelde. The *Hoge Raad* held that there is no reason to expand the liability of the employer in such a way that he would also be held liable for damage which the employee has suffered and for which it may be *possible* that this has been caused as a result of the execution of the work by the employee[51]. The key problem here is of course that there is uncertainty concerning the causal link. In the end, it will not be possible to hold with certainty that the damage was incurred at the occasion of the execution of the work for the particular employer. In those particular cases, it will usually suffice that the employee can argue that it is reasonably feasible that he did indeed incur his occupational illness in the execution of his work[52]. Recent case law (although not from the *Hoge Raad*) shows that this can lead to success for the employee. For instance the *kantonrechter* of Middelburg accepted

[48] This issue has, moreover, been confirmed in a *Hoge Raad* decision of 4 May 2001, [2001] NJ, 377 (Bloemsma/Hattuma).

[49] See *Hoge Raad* 29 June 2001, [2001] NJ, 476 (Industromontaza Odo/Banfic). The exception was, however, not applied in that particular case.

[50] This was equally reconfirmed in *Hoge Raad* 29 June 2001, [2001] NJ, 476.

[51] See *Hoge Raad* 26 January 2001, [2001] NJ, 597 (Weststrate/De Schelde). For a comment on this decision see Giesen, [2001] NTBR, 242.

[52] An alternative solution is a so-called proportional liability, whereby the liability is linked to the chance that the damage was caused in the execution of the work. See in that respect a well-known decision of the civil court of Middelburg, 11 March 1998, [1999] NJ, 41 (Schaier/De Schelde).

that complaints concerning repetitive strain injury could by their nature indicate a link with the execution of the work[53].

d) Far-Reaching Employer's Liability for Traffic Accidents?

A very important *Hoge Raad* decision relates to the question whether an employer can be held liable for traffic accidents caused by his employee. Art. 7:658 civil code (dealing with employer's liability) has in general little meaning for traffic accidents. At first sight, one could argue that employer's liability on the basis of art. 7:658 of the civil code is applicable in case of traffic accidents; for liability under that provision it is indeed sufficient that the victim has suffered damage in the course of his employment. However, in practice the meaning of this provision in case of traffic accidents is relatively limited. Indeed, in most cases the employer can successfully defend himself by arguing that he did not violate his duty of care. Obviously, this will not always be the case. One could imagine cases whereby liability is based on the circumstance that an accident would be caused by the fact that the employer provided the employee with a defective motor vehicle, or that someone who has insufficient driving experience is appointed as a driver or one could think of cases whereby the employer orders the employees to drive in places or circumstances which are rather risky whereby these risks could have been avoided. It was especially the latter case that gave rise to the recent *Hoge Raad* decision of 19 October 2001[54]. A postman was involved in a traffic accident after he had to leave his car to pick up a piece of mail that was blown out of his car by the wind. In this particular case, employer's liability was accepted. This was, however, based on the idea that the employer could have done more to reduce the risk that pieces of mail be blown away from the car (and hence the employer violated his duty of care), but not on the fact that the employer would generally be liable for all traffic accidents suffered by employees. 34

As a general rule, there will be no liability since there is no breach of a particular duty of care of the employer. Therefore, in a draft statute concerning traffic accidents an art. 7:658a was proposed. This contains a strict liability of the employer for the damage caused by his employees caused in the execution of their work when driving a motor vehicle. Although this draft statute has meanwhile been repealed by the Minister of Justice, the *Hoge Raad* seems to anticipate this art. 7:658a in a decision of 12 January 2001[55]. 35

[53] See Kantonrechter Middelburg, 4 December 2000, [2001] *Jurisprudentie Arbeidsrecht* (JAR) 5. See for a commentary Fluit and Geers, [2001] *Sociaal Recht*, 69–70 and see also Kantonrechter Haarlem, 14 March 2001, [2001] JAR, 88.

[54] *Hoge Raad* 19 October 2001, [2001] NJ, 663.

[55] *Hoge Raad* 12 January 2001, [2001] NJ, 253, with case note by P.A. Stein (Vonk/Vanderhoeven). For comments on this important decision see Leerink and Holthuis, [2001] *Advocatenblad,* 178, Van Dijk, [2001] *Tijdschrift voor Vergoeding Personenschade,* 20, De Laat, [2001] *Sociaal Recht,* 251, Lindenbergh, [2001] *Nieuwsbrief BW* (NbBW), 44 and Hartlief, [2001] AV&S, 237.

36 The background for this decision is an earlier decision in the case Schuitmaker/Bruinsma Tapijt[56]. In this case it was held that an employer can be held liable for the damage that an employee suffers in his car when driving his own car in the execution of his work. The legal foundation for this decision was found in equity, given the specific nature of the labour contract. This decision obviously also gave rise to the question whether the *Hoge Raad* would come to a similar judgment in case the employee suffers personal injury. In favour of this, it is generally considered that personal injury is more important than material damage (it would be surprising to compensate the material loss of the employee to his car but not to compensate his personal injury). On the other hand, it might also be considered strange that this liability, which is not based on any breach of a duty of care of the employer and is merely based on equity, would reach further than the employer's liability based on art. 7:658. In the *Hoge Raad* case of 12 January 2001, the situation dealt with the position of an employee who was driving a van in the course of his work and caused a unilateral accident (no other car was involved) whereby all passengers, including himself, suffered serious personal injury. The damage of the three passengers was covered by the liability insurer of the van, but the driver (employee Van der Hoeven) caused the accident himself and hence did not receive compensation. Nevertheless, the civil court accepted liability of the employer on the basis of a reasoning which is similar to the one in the just mentioned case Schuitmaker/Bruinsma: it is held that the legal foundation for the employer's liability is equity and thus finds its basis in unwritten law. The employer appeals against this decision to the *Hoge Raad* and holds, basically, that the employer's liability, as laid down in art. 7:658, is an exclusive rule, in the sense that an employer cannot be held liable if there is no violation of the duty of care as laid down in article 7:658. The *Hoge Raad*, however, rejects this reasoning: the employer can under specific circumstances also be liable towards his employee even if the conditions of article 7:658 are not met[57]. As a consequence, the decision of the trial court, which held the employer liable, is confirmed by the *Hoge Raad*.

37 Although it is, at this stage, probably difficult to provide an exact interpretation of this decision it seems probable to assume that an employer is apparently liable to a large extent for traffic accidents caused by his employees. Indeed, it is not very likely that the *Hoge Raad* wishes to limit this employer's liability to the case that the employee-victim is not compensated and the other injured persons are. A consequence of this important decision could hence be that employees, who are driving a motor vehicle during the course of their work and become involved in a traffic accident, can always claim compensation from their employer, irrespective of the question who is liable for the particular traffic accident. There would only be an exception in case of intent or gross recklessness on the side of the employee. This approach, although it may

[56] *Hoge Raad* 16 October 1992, [1993] NJ, 264, with case note by P.A. Stein.

[57] The *Hoge Raad* refers in this respect explicitely to the mentioned decision Schuitmaker/Bruinsma Tapijt and to the decision *Hoge Raad* 22 January 1999, [1999] NJ, 534, with case note by P.A. Stein.

be the consequence of the *Hoge Raad* decision, of course carries the disadvantage that employees who are driving a motor vehicle now benefit a further reaching protection than "normal" victims of an accident at work. The latter will indeed not receive any compensation in case there is no breach of a duty of care by the employer. Moreover, this *Hoge Raad* decision may also have important consequences for insurers. The employer, who now has employees driving for him in the course of their work, would be well advised to purchase, in addition to a liability insurance, also a first party insurance for passengers. The latter may be important in case the employee uses a company car, but also when the employee uses his own car in execution of his work. Moreover: it is not clear how far the *Hoge Raad* decision actually reaches. If employees can now claim compensation for injuries they suffer when driving a motor vehicle in the course of their work, one can equally ask whether they should be compensated as well when suffering personal injury when driving from or to work[58] or *e.g.* when riding a bicycle. These questions are already discussed in the literature and may in the future give rise to new case law as well.

7. Traffic Liability

a) Introduction

In the introduction of this contribution to the yearbook, we already mentioned that the Dutch government declared that in the near future there will be no new draft legislation concerning traffic accidents. This is remarkable in the light of the fact that during the past decades, various proposals had been considered. **38**

Looking at case law, it is interesting to mention that the far-reaching case law of the *Hoge Raad*, protecting non-motorized victims against the consequences of traffic accidents, is now also applied to accidents caused by tramways[59]. **39**

b) Case Law Concerning Art. 185 of the Traffic Act

In the period under review, there is one specific decision of the *Hoge Raad* that deserves special mention. It concerns a decision of the *Hoge Raad* of 4 May 2001[60]. The case deals with the so-called reflex effect of art. 185 of the Traffic Act. This reflex effect has to do with the question in what respect the specific provision of art. 185 of the Traffic Act, which provides a wide scope of protection to non-motorized victims, also applies to a claim whereby the motor vehicle driver is the victim who acts as plaintiff against the non-motor- **40**

[58] In the *Hoge Raad* decision of 16 November 2001, [2002] NJ, 71 the accident dealt with a situation where the employee was driving from or to his work, but this was dealt with under the heading of the employer's liability of art. 7:658. That decision held a denial of liability, but that obviously does not imply anything concerning the other possible grounds for liability in such a case, such as artt. 6:248 and 7:611 of the Dutch civil code.

[59] See *Hoge Raad* 14 July 2000, [2001] NJ, 417, [2000] A&V, 143 with case note by Van Dam and [2001] *Verkeersrecht*.

[60] *Hoge Raad* 4 May 2001, [2001] *Rechtspraak van de week*, 99 = [2002] NJ, 214 with case note by CJHB, Chan-A-Hung/Maalste with case note by Hartlief in [2001] AV&S, 73.

ized injurer. The *Hoge Raad* held that the motor vehicle is in all cases to be considered as a more dangerous object than the non-motorized (injurer). The effect is therefore that this increased danger will be attributed to the motorized victim, at least to an important extent.

41 Also when the owner of a motor vehicle is damaged by an unmotorized injurer and therefore sues the unmotorized one in compensation, art. 185 of the Traffic Act indeed still applies[61]. The consequences thereof are:

- That the burden of proof as regulated in art. 185 of the Traffic Act applies as well;
- That the question of liability is also determined by the issue of *force majeure* as determined by art. 185 of the Traffic Act;
- That outside of these cases, the case law will take into account the fact that the motorized traffic participants in principle create a higher danger which will be considered as contributory negligence. This, however, will not formally be dealt with under the heading of causation (when determining the respective parts of the motorized victim and the non-motorized injurer), but simply as a so-called correction based on equity[62].

As a consequence of this, it will be pretty difficult for a motorized traffic participant, who is injured by the fault of a non-motorized injurer, to receive full compensation from the non-motorized injurer. He can only be fully successful if he can prove that for him the presence of the non-motororized injurer was *force majeure*. If the motorized victim cannot prove *force majeure*, he will have to carry a part of the damage himself. In that case, however, the general rules of art. 6:101 of the civil code are applicable and not the burden of proof as regulated in art. 158 of the Traffic Act[63]. In these types of cases a so-called causal division will first have to be fixed. This means that the judge will have to decide in what respect the behaviour of both traffic participants created the accident risk[64]. Within the framework of this so-called causal division, the fact that the motorized traffic participants created a higher danger than the non-motorized ones is not taken into account[65]. The same is the case for factors such as the age of the non-motorized victim. These elements, as well as the seriousness of the various faults and the damage of the motorized victim, are taken into account within the framework of the correction based on equity. Within this equity correction obviously the fact that the motorized traffic participants creates a higher danger will be held against him. However, the seriousness of his damage may be to his advantage.

The same, complicated, regime in principle also applies to social security carriers who exercise a right of redress. However, for them in most cases the so-called causal division will be determining the result; the correction based

[61] *Hoge Raad* 6 February 1987 [1988] NJ, 57 (Saskia Mulder).

[62] *Hoge Raad* 10 November 2000 [2000] NJ, 719 (Levob/Van den Bos).

[63] *Hoge Raad* 4 May 2001 [2001] *Rechtspraak van de Week*, 99 (Chan/Maalsté). See on this decision Hartlief, T., [2001] AV&S, 173 and Van Dam, C.C., [2001] *Verkeersrecht*, 349–352.

[64] *Hoge Raad* 2 June 1995, [1997] NJ, 700 (Marloes de Vos).

[65] *Hoge Raad* 10 November 2000, [2000] NJ, 718 (Levob/van den Bos).

on equity can only lead to a minor amendment since the equity considerations obviously play a different role for social insurance carriers than for "real" victims[66]. An element like the seriousness of the damage will not lead to a change of the result of the causal division in favour of the social insurance carrier. Moreover, a *Hoge Raad* decision of 4 May 2001 also indicated that such a so-called equity correction in favour of the motorized victim will not be easily applied in case the latter suffered an insured material damage (and not physical injury)[67]. The mere fact that the non-motorized injurer carries liability insurance does in principle not play a role in determining liability within the framework of art. 6:101 of the Dutch civil code. It can, however, give rise to a limitation of the compensation by the judge on the basis of art. 6:109 of the civil code.

However, it still is not very easy to decide what the effect is of the fact that the *Hoge Raad* holds that the motorized traffic participant in principle creates a higher danger than the non-motorized one. This leads, as we showed, to an important presumption against the motorized and in favour of the non-motorized traffic participant, based on equity. Hence the final division of liability will not only take into account the extent to which the negligence of both participants contributed to the accident, but also all other circumstances of the accident situation (the so-called equity correction). This typically concerns situations where the owner of a motor vehicle suffers damage to his car (or even personal injury) as a result of negligent behaviour of a pedestrian or cyclist. An interesting issue is that one could also wonder whether the fact that the unmotorized injurer had insurance influences the liability issue or not. The *Hoge Raad* does not answer that question. It is, moreover, unlikely that the mere fact of having insurance should influence the liability issue. It might merely lead to a mitigation of damages. **42**

8. Causal Uncertainty

We already mentioned that in many cases, for instance in the medical malpractice case we discussed above, the defendant will argue that there is no causal link between his behaviour and the damage. Remember that in the case concerning the protocol of the hospital, the defendant argued that the fact that the protocol was not followed was not the *conditio sine qua non* for the accident. The *Hoge Raad* has formulated certain exceptions to the rule that the victim needs to prove a *conditio sine qua non* link between the wrongful behaviour of the defendant and his damage. Some argue that these exceptions become that important that there is in fact something which could be called a reversal of the burden of proving the causal link. This rule applies in cases where a certain person has created a risk which also materializes; in that respect case law seems to accept something like a presumption of causal link. **43**

[66] *Hoge Raad* 5 December 1997, [1998] NJ, 400 (Quafa El Ayachi).

[67] See *Hoge Raad* 4 May 2001, [2000] *Rechtspraak van de Week*, 99 (Chan/Maalsté).

44 However, the case law of the *Hoge Raad* in this area is not very clear and at least highly debated. In this respect, the *Hoge Raad* case of 19 January 2001 is rather interesting[68]. Ter Hofte, the victim, had an accident with his motorcycle: he fell and suffered damage. Ter Hofte files a lawsuit against his garage, called Oude Monnink, which had recently repaired the motorbike. Ter Hofte claims that the oil cooling was not repaired appropriately, so that the motorbike leaked oil. This leakage would have led to a reduced grip of the back wheel of the motorbike on the ground and this would subsequently have caused the motorbike to slip and thus cause the accident, so Ter Hofte claimed. During the procedure, it became apparent that Oude Monnink indeed did not repair the oil cooler according to the state of the art. Hence, Oude Monnink has undeniably been negligent. The crucial question was, however, whether this leaking oil cooler finally led to the accident. If Ter Hofte were able to rely on the presumption of causation, this would obviously improve his chances of winning the case. The question the *Hoge Raad* had to answer is whether this rule of the presumption of causation only applies in the specific case of traffic and safety or whether it has a broader application. The *Hoge Raad* decides that the latter is the case[69].

45 One can also understand this case law of the *Hoge Raad*, especially in cases like this where the violation of the specific norm could indeed lead to the accident as it occurred; there is, in this specific case, indeed a "logic" combination of the violation of the norm and the accident. Specifically in those cases it seems reasonable to attribute the consequence of causal uncertainty to the party that violated the norm. In this case that was clearly the owner of the garage, Oude Monnink. Hence, there seem to be arguments in favour of a wider application of this presumption of causation. However, the question arises whether the consequences are fair for all cases where an injurer created an increased risk. The Hoge Raad seems to be aware of the risks of a too far expanding presumption of causation; indeed the *Hoge Raad* at least requires that it is clearly indicated which risk the defendant created. Moreover it should be clear that it is that particular risk (which was created by the defendant) that did indeed materialize. That is, by the way, one of the problems of Ter Hofte in the particular case.

46 Still, one can argue that in many cases a violation of a norm will be established whereby it is not always very clear what constituted precisely the particular tort. In this respect, we can recall a remarkable decision of the *Hoge Raad* of 16 June 2000[70]. In that particular case, an institution (Sint Willibrord) was held liable for letting a particular (mental) patient escape which had created an increased risk for the safety of third parties. However, that increased

[68] *Hoge Raad* 19 January 2001, [2001] NJ, 524 (JBMV). For a discussion see Beenders, [2001] NTBR, 278, Hartlief, [2001] *Ars Aequi,* 452 and Klomp, [2001] NbBW, 26 (case Ter Hofte/Oude Monnink).

[69] Therefore one can also see that in a subsequent case (*Hoge Raad* 2 March 2001, [2001] NJ, 649 (F.C.B. van Wijmen and JBMV)) the rule of the presumption of causation is applied.

[70] *Hoge Raad* 16 June 2000, [2000] NJ, 584, with note C.J.H. Brunner (Sint Willibrord).

risk could have materialized theoretically in hundreds of possible ways and is therefore rather vague. Nevertheless, the presumption of causation was also applied in that case. It is in those types of cases difficult to argue that the risk, which was specifically created by the injurer, did not materialize. That shows that the potential for an expanding liability is rather large as a result of this presumption of causation.

Especially for the domain of medical liability is it important to stress that the *Hoge Raad* does not hold the rule of the reversal of the burden of proof in case of causal uncertainty applicable in case of a violation of the information duty by the physician[71]. In case of a violation of the duty of care by the physician, the risk that has been created by the physician is not the fact that *e.g.* surgery does not have the desired results or that complications occurred, but the fact that the patient now made a choice that he would probably not have made if he had received a proper disclosure of information. Therefore it is held that there is no causal relationship between the violation of the duty to inform and the subsequent negligence during the surgery or treatment. **47**

D. DOCTRINE

1. Introduction

It would not be possible, within the scope of this contribution to the yearbook, to discuss all literature that has been published in the area of tort law in the Netherlands in 2001. As we showed in the introduction, tort law is in full movement in the Netherlands and hence gives rise to a lot of literature. Most of this literature deals with recent case law and thus we have referred to this literature when discussing the cases. Some others deal with legislative proposals and have been referred to in the corresponding footnotes. In the introduction we quoted a few papers which provide a general overview of recent evolutions in tort law in the Netherlands. **48**

Within the scope of this contribution, we are therefore not going to provide an overview of other articles published in law reviews which we have not discussed. Instead, we would like to briefly mention a few recent dissertations and a few proceedings volumes which contain various contributions of tort lawyers from the Netherlands. These dissertations and proceedings volumes might provide a good impression of the state of the literature concerning tort law in the Netherlands. **49**

2. Dissertations

Various dissertations were defended at Dutch universities, dealing with issues of tort law.

[71] *Hoge Raad* 23 November 2001, [2001] *Rechtspraak van de Week,* 188.

a) **I. Giesen, *Bewijs en aansprakelijkheid*, (Dissertation Katholieke Universiteit Brabant, Boom Juridische Uitgevers, Den Haag 2001)**

50 The main objective of the thesis of Dr. Giesen is to establish a theoretical model for possible deviations from the Kaufman division of the legal burden of proof within the fields of tortious and contractual liability. In order to develop this model, for the Netherlands Giesen builds on a comparative analysis of Dutch, English, French and German law. After having developed this model and applied it to Dutch tort law, Giesen also makes an attempt to fit the current rules of Dutch law into his model.

b) **T. Vanden Borre, *Efficiënte preventie en compensatie van catastroferisico's*, (Dissertation Defended at the University Maastricht, Antwerpen/Groningen Intersentia 2001)**

51 This dissertation deals with the compensation of damage caused by catastrophic accidents. It discusses the catastrophic accidents by the example of the nuclear risk. The author provides an overview of the conventions dealing with nuclear liability and deals with the insurance of the nuclear risk as well. He discusses proposals for a reform of nuclear liability and insurance, whereby the economic analysis of law is used.

c) **O. A. Haazen, *Algemeen deel van het rechterlijk overgangsrecht*, (Dissertation Defended at the Katholieke Universiteit Brabant 2001)**

52 Olav Haazen provides a general theory concerning the question how judges should deal with changes in case law. Haazen argues that implicitly much new case law has a retroactive effect, in the sense that it applies directly to "old" situations. Hence, the well-known problem of the retroactive effect of new tort rules is extensively discussed in this dissertation. Haazen provides, on the one hand, a detailed analysis of many cases of the *Hoge Raad* in which he recognizes retroactive effect (also outside of the area of tort law) and he equally provides a legal theoretical framework for dealing with the retroactivity issue.

d) **M. van Dam, *Verkeersongevallen. Een rechtseconomisch, empirisch en positiefrechtelijk onderzoek naar de werking van aansprakelijkheid, verzekering en veiligheidsregulering in het verkeer*, (Dissertation Defended at the University Maastricht, Boom Juridische Uitgevers, Den Haag 2001)**

53 Martien van Dam provides, in his dissertation, an economic analysis of traffic liability. He, on the one hand, discusses the well-known economic theories concerning liability, insurance and safety regulation as applied to traffic accidents and argues that an optimal mix of these instruments should be applied to prevent traffic accidents. He, moreover, discusses the rich empirical literature in which the effectiveness of these various instruments has been tested. Finally, van Dam examines to what extent the findings of the theoretical literature need to be amended on the basis of the results of the empirical literature. Van Dam ends his dissertation with proposals for a reform.

3. Proceedings Volumes

a) T. Hartlief/M. M. Mendel (eds.), *Verzekering en maatschappij* (Kluwer, Deventer 2000)

In this volume, which was edited by Professors Hartlief and Mendel, many scholars deal with current topics of liability and insurance. For instance part VI of the proceedings volume deals with the insurability of the liability risk. Thus Lindenbergh discusses insurability of non-pecuniary losses, Hartlief examines in what respect insurability plays a role in tort law and Wansink examines whether direct (first party) insurance provides a workable alternative for uninsurable liabilities. **54**

But many other issues are discussed in this volume as well, for instance the interface between tort law, competition law and competition on insurance markets (by M. Faure and R. Vandenbergh) and the relationship between tort law and social security (discussed by K.P. Goudswaard and G.J.J. Heerma van Voss). **55**

b) E. R. Muller/C. J. J. M. Stolker (eds.), *Ramp en recht* (Boom Juridische Uitgevers, Den Haag 2001)

This volume is the result of a research project initiated by the law faculty of Leiden University and deals with the question how the law should react to catastrophes. It is a multi-disciplinary volume in which lawyers from various backgrounds (public law, criminal law, civil law) deal with legal instruments in relation to catastrophes. Although various legal disciplines (public law and criminal law) are presented in the book as well, some contributions deal with private law. For instance Stolker, Levine and The Bell examine whether the increasing occurrence of catastrophes will lead to a defensive bureaucracy, in the sense that tort law would have such a preventive effect on governments as well (in case of liability of public authorities). Faure and Hartlief discuss compensation of catastrophes; this topic is addressed by Van de Bunt as well. **56**

c) SaRO

The Dutch organization for scientific research (NWO) sponsors a research group with funds made available through a *StimuleringsActie Rechtswetenschappelijk Onderzoek* (SaRO). A network of tort lawyers from the universities of Maastricht, Tilburg and Utrecht deals with issues of liability, insurance and compensation. **57**

As a result of this network, a first book was published under the editorship of Arno Akkermans, Michael Faure and Ton Hartlief, *Proportionele aansprakelijkheid* (Den Haag, Boom Juridische Uitgevers 2000). This volume deals with issues of causal uncertainty and the question whether a proportionate liability rule could be an appropriate remedy for this problem of causal uncertainty. Various scholars such as Hartlief, Van Dijk, Van Maanen, Peeperkorn, **58**

Akkermans, Van, Spier, Faure and Rogers deal with the various legal aspects of causal uncertainty.

59 A next volume of this SaRO network was published under the editorship of Michael Faure and Ton Hartlief, *Schade door arbeidsongevallen en nieuwe beroepsziekten* (Den Haag, Boom Juridische Uitgevers 2001) and deals with occupational diseases and industrial accidents. Various scholars interested in social law and tort law deal with interactions between both domains and look for alternative compensation mechanisms for damage resulting from industrial accidents and new occupational diseases.

4. Other Publications

60 Of course, many other books in the area of tort law were published in the past year. In this respect, we just – more or less at random – select two:

a) L. Dommering-van Rongen, *Productaansprakelijkheid* (2000), Deventer

61 It concerns a second, revised, edition of the doctoral dissertation of Loes Dommering-van Rongen. She adapted her dissertation to new developments in the area of product liability.

b) C. Klaassen, *Schadeveroorzakend handelen in functie* (2000), Inauguration Address Katholieke Universiteit Nijmegen, Deventer

62 This is the text of the inauguration lecture of professor Carla Klaassen who obtained a chair in tort law at the Catholic University of Nijmegen. It deals with the question of vicarious liability.

E. Concluding Remarks

63 As we mentioned in the introduction, the evolutions in the field of tort law in the Netherlands are, on the one hand, characterized by an expanding liability. This is, however, certainly not the only development. Indeed, there are certainly future developments towards an even more expanding liability; in this respect we can mention the legislation which will be enacted to provide a right of compensation of non-pecuniary losses to parties other than the direct victims and the legislation concerning the statute of limitations in case of personal injury. On the other hand, one can also notice concerns and tendencies to limit liability. Indeed, we equally mentioned that the government is increasingly concerned with developments in the area of tort law. The government has even suggested a fundamental re-thinking of the goals and organization of civil tort law. One of the consequences of this call for a re-thinking is at least that a new act on traffic liability will (at least in the near future) not be introduced. Moreover, one can notice that the Minister of Justice is contemplating the pros and cons of various alternatives for the tort system, such as a system of direct insurance which could be applied for occupational diseases or even in case of traffic accidents. This tendency towards a more cautious approach towards liability law also becomes clear when reading the letter of the Dutch government explaining the main features of a right to compensation for so-called affection damages. Moreover, also the case law of the *Hoge Raad* shows that one can certainly not argue that liability is expanding in an unlimited manner. First, the *Hoge Raad* is still very careful to apply liability law to smaller accidents happening in the home sphere. Second, also the interpretation of the strict liability *e.g.* from art. 6:171 of the civil code shows that the *Hoge Raad* remains careful and is apparently not prepared to accept a too extensive interpretation of this provision.

It is definitely clear that tort law is an area which is of great public interest in **64**
the Netherlands today. We showed in this brief overview of evolutions during 2001 that indeed a lot is happening. Much more can be expected both as far as legislation as well as case law is concerned in the coming years.

XIII. Poland

Ewa Baginska

A. Legislation

1. General

1 In 2001 there were no changes introduced to the general rules on torts in *kodeks cywilny* (Polish Civil Code, KC). The new bill considering liability of a public authority for damage caused by its wrongful acts is in the legislation process (see below the commentary to the judgment of the Constitutional Tribunal of 4 December 2001).

2. Environmental Protection Law, Act of 27 April 2001[1]

2 Artt. 322 – 328 of the new environmental protection law constitute special rules of liability for environmental damage. The rules in KC apply unless the statute stipulates otherwise. With the exception of the sea, the environment (air, water, soil, forest) is protected by general tort provisions of art. 435 KC[2] and art. 415 KC[3]. According to art. 324 environmental protection law, if the damage is caused by an enterprise operating at an aggravated or major risk, art. 435 KC (*i.e.* strict liability) is applicable even if the enterprise is run without the use of natural forces. The fact that the detrimental to the environment operation of an enterprise has its basis in an administrative decision does not constitute a defence to the liability for damage. Art. 323 provides that anyone who is exposed to risk of damage, or who incurred damage through another's illegal influence on the environment, may demand from the person liable that he restores the lawful state and takes preventive measures, such as through

[1] *Dziennik Ustaw* (Journal of Laws, Dz. U.) 2001, no. 62 at 627, not yet in force.

[2] Art. 435 § 1 KC: "Anyone who runs his own enterprise or business set into motion by natural forces (steam, gas, electricity, liquid fuel, etc.) is liable for any damage to persons and property to whomever caused through the operation of the enterprise or business, unless the damage occurred due to *force majeure* or exclusively through the fault of the injured party or of a third person for whom he is not responsible; § 2. The above provision is correspondingly applied to enterprises or businesses producing explosives or utilising them".

[3] "Anyone who by his own fault causes damage to another person is obliged to redress it".

installing safety appliance or machines. Where the preventive action is impossible or unreasonably difficult, the claimant may demand that the actor abstains from the infringement. The State Treasury, a local government, or an environmental organization has legal standing if an infringement or exposure to damage relates to the environment as a common value (art. 323 sec. 2). The plaintiff has a right to ask the court to oblige the defendant to supply all the information necessary to establish the scope of his liability. The person who repaired the damage has a right of indemnity towards the actor who caused it, however it is limited to the reasonable expenses of the restoration of the previous state (art. 326).

3. Polish Atomic Law, Act of 29 November 2000[4]

According to Title 12 (artt. 100 – 108) a nuclear operator (*e.g.* of nuclear reac- 3
tor[5]) is exclusively liable for nuclear damage caused by a nuclear accident within a nuclear device or caused in connection with a nuclear device, unless the damage resulted directly from acts of war (art. 101 subs. 1). During the transportation of a nuclear material, the liability is borne by the operator who dispatched the material, unless the contract with the consignee stipulates otherwise (art. 101 subs. 2). This liability is almost absolute. If the injured person intentionally caused or aggravated the damage, the court may release the operator from the liability for this person's harm (art. 101 subs. 3). Nuclear damage is defined very broadly and includes injury to person and things, environmental damage, economic loss arising in connection with damage to person, things or the environment, as well as the costs of taking preventive measures or harm caused by the preventive action. Compensation of environmental damage may be demanded by a ministry for environmental matters.

The new law introduces a cap of 150 million SDR (IMF special computation 4
unit) for the liability for damage to things and the environment. A special fund for claims exceeding this cap may be established along the principles of *kodeks morski* (the Polish Code of Maritime Law). A nuclear operator is obliged to obtain financial security of his liability. From the amount of the security, 10% is devoted to ensure compensation of personal injury claims arising out of a nuclear accident. By virtue of art. 105 Polish Atomic Law, personal injury claims are not barred by the statute of limitations. They may be brought directly to the other party of the indemnity (security) agreement. The State Treasury guarantees payment of those claims if they could not be covered by the financial indemnity.

4. Industrial Property Law, Act of 30 June 2000[6]

In artt. 287 – 302 the new law on industrial property (regulating patents, 5
designs, trademarks and geographical names protection) gives the holders of industrial property rights claims for compensation in the case of infringement

[4] Dz. U. 2001, no. 2 at 18.
[5] At present, there is no nuclear power station in Poland.
[6] Dz. U. 2001, no. 49 at 508.

of those rights. In addition to a claim for refraining from an unlawful activity and removal of its effects, a patent holder may demand that the person who committed the infringement returns unlawful gains and pays damages according to the general rules (*i.e.* on the basis of KC). Thus, a patent holder (or licensee), whose rights have been infringed, may seek pecuniary damages and non-pecuniary losses. If a person who registered an invention or got a patent unlawfully was at fault, the claimant might demand a proper sum be paid to a suitable social organisation, for the purpose of supporting industrial property.

5. Act of 25 May 2001 on the Financial Liability of Soldiers[7]

6 The statute replaces the old decree of 1955 regulating the financial liability of soldiers for damage done to their military unit. The new model of liability resembles the system of employees' liability for damage caused to the employer. A soldier who fails or negligently performs his duties is liable for damage caused to any State property remaining at the disposal of the military organizational units (art. 3). The compensation is limited to real losses (*lucrum cessans*), but if caused by unintentional fault of a soldier, it may not exceed a sum equal to his three-month pay. In the case of intent, the compensation covers full damage.

7 If a soldier caused damage to a third person while carrying out the service, the State Treasury is solely obliged to repair it. The Treasury has a right of recourse against the soldier. It is a special rule of the State liability. The State is liable provided all the conditions of a delict are proved[8].

B. Cases

1. *Sad Najwyzszy* (Polish Supreme Court, SN); 26 September 2000, III CKN 1089/00[9]: State Liability, Soldiers' Compensation

a) Brief Summary of the Facts

8 An army officer was injured during parachuting training exercises. By reason of the commander's fault he fell on the ground and broke his spine. He was partially compensated on the basis of art. 20 Act of 16 December 1972 on Payments for Accidents and Sickness Arising Out of Service (Act of 1972)[10]. He brought a tort cause of action against the State pursuant to art. 417 KC and won his claim for additional compensation in the first two instances. Defendant appealed to the Supreme Court claiming that the special compensation scheme precludes further claims by a soldier whenever he incurred damages due to negligent conduct of another soldier or officer.

[7] Dz. U. 2001, no. 89 at 967.

[8] See art. 421 KC.

[9] [2000] *Orzecznictwo Sadu Najwyzszego* (Decisions of the Supreme Court Civil Chamber, OSNC) 3, at 37.

[10] Dz. U. 1972, no. 53, at 342 as amended.

b) Judgment of the Supreme Court

At first, the Court analyses the 1972 Act and concludes that if the accident or sickness was caused by negligent conduct of soldiers or other functionaries in the line of duty, art. 20 should be interpreted so as to preclude claims for additional compensation brought by an injured soldier on the basis of the civil code. The Court relies on its precedent of 24 May 1990[11]. Next, the Court compares the soldiers' compensation and the workers' compensation systems (Act of 12 June 1975 on Payments for Work Accidents and Sickness, Act of 1975[12]). It points out that since the change of the political system (1989/1990) there has been a strong tendency in law to remove statutory barriers and limitations to the civil justice system. In 1990 the legislator annulled art. 40 of the Act of 1975 eliminating the barrier to achieving full compensation by injured workers (or relatives in the case of death) from the employers who are then held liable according to general principles of tort law (fault, strict liability or equity). 9

The Court moves on to declare that art. 20 of the 1972 Act violates the provisions of the Constitution concerning the principle of the rule of law (art. 2), the principle of equal treatment and non-discrimination (art. 32 subs. 1 and 2), the right to compensation for any harm caused by wrongful conduct of an organ of public authority (art. 77 subs. 1), and the right to access to the judicial system in pursuit of claims alleging infringement of freedoms or rights (art. 77 subs. 2). According to SN, soldiers are discriminated by law in comparison to other workers, because they may not seek full compensation of their injuries, but only compensation according to the low tariffs set in the 1972 Act. Due to the character of the military service, they are also more prone to inflicting personal injuries. Thus, the Court holds that art. 20 should not be applicable to the case because it violates the said constitutional provisions. 10

The Court rules that art. 20 Act of 16 December 1972 on Payments for Accidents and Sickness Arising Out of Service (Dz. U. Nr 53 at 342 as amended) violates the Constitution because it precludes or limits the right of an injured soldier to pursue a claim for compensation of pecuniary and non-pecuniary damages according to the principles of civil law and in common courts. 11

c) Commentary

The judgment met partly with criticism and partly with approval of the commentators[13]. As to the general outcome, there is an agreement that the soldiers' compensation system is old, insufficient because it does not allow for full compensation, and should be changed. But there is a dispute as to the proper practice by the courts before the legislator takes action. The main problem concerns the question whether common courts may refuse to apply a legal 12

[11] [1990] OSNC 10–11, at 123.
[12] Dz. U. 1983, no. 30 at 144 as amended.
[13] Critical note A. Szpunar [2001] *Przeglad Sadowy* 6, 130, approved of by A.Zielinski [2001] *Orzecznictwo Sadow Polskich* (Decisions of the Polish Courts, OSP) 4, at 65.

provision because in their judgment it violates the Constitution, or rather they should refer to the Constitutional Tribunal for the decision on its unconstitutionality. The Supreme Court itself is divided, as well as the legal writers. This Court took the more progressive position, but it is rather confusing why at the same time it reversed the verdict of the Court of Appeals that actually awarded the compensation on the civil law basis. It should be noted that eventually the case was re-tried and the Court of the first instance refused to apply the Constitution directly and dismissed the claim. As a consequence, the Ombudsman recently asked the Constitutional Tribunal to rule on the inconformity of art. 20 Act of 1975 with the Constitutional principle of equal treatment[14].

2. *Trybunal Konstytucyjny* (The Constitutional Tribunal, TK); 4 December 2001, SK 18/00[15]: Liability in Tort of Public Authorities

a) Brief Summary of the Facts

13 The Tribunal heard two joint cases brought by individuals[16]. In the first one, the tax and revenue office denied the plaintiffs the reimbursement of the execution fee that had been claimed and paid without a legal ground. The office kept the money for 1503 days. The plaintiffs sued for damages, but in two instances the claim was dismissed on the grounds that the plaintiffs did not prove the public servant's qualified fault (art. 418 KC[17]). In the other case, a policeman was made redundant in 1974 for the reason of concluding a Roman Catholic marriage. After the political change in 1989 his unemployment period was taken account of for social and pension benefits purposes according to the Act of 1989 on Rehiring Workers Dismissed On The Grounds Of Their Political Views, Religious Beliefs, and Activity In Independent Trade Unions[18]. In 1993 he brought a claim for damages for non-pecuniary loss and lost income, but was finally denied compensation by the Supreme Court on the grounds he did not prove damages and the fault of the State functionary.

b) Judgment of the Tribunal

14 Before ruling on the cases, the Tribunal sought opinions from the Ombudsman, the *Sejm* (Polish Parliament's lower chamber) and the Commission on

[14] *Rzeczpospolita* (Polish newspaper) 11 January 2002.

[15] Available at http://trybunal.gov.pl/.

[16] According to art. 79 subs. 1 Constitution "In accordance with principles specified by statute, everyone whose constitutional freedoms or rights have been infringed, shall have the right to appeal to the Constitutional Tribunal for its judgment on the conformity to the Constitution of a statute or another normative act upon which basis a court or organ of public administration has made a final decision on his freedoms or rights or on his obligations specified in the Constitution".

[17] According to art. 418 § 1 KC "If the damage was caused by a state functionary as a result of issuance of a decision or order, the Treasury is liable only when, in issuing the decision or order, there occurred a breach of law subject of criminal or disciplinary prosecution, and the fault of the person causing damage was affirmed by a criminal sentence or a disciplinary decision or was recognized by an organ superior to the person causing the damage".

[18] *Ustawa o przywróceniu praw pracowniczych osobom pozbawionym zatrudnienia za dzialalnosc zwiazkowa, samorzadowa, przekonania polityczne i religijne* (Dz. U. no. 32, at 172).

the Codification of Civil Law. To begin with, the Tribunal confirms that art. 77 of the new Constitution gives Polish citizens a right of protection of their personal rights and freedoms. According to art. 77 "everyone shall have the right to compensation for any harm done to him by any action of an organ of public authority contrary to law". The Tribunal highlights that art. 77 of the Constitution is not just a proclamation of a general principle. It constitutes a norm that has material contents and establishes the conditions for liability of public authorities. The scope of the liability marks a huge change to its very concept by making the liability strict and dependent only on the wrongful exercise of public authority, regardless of any person's fault.

The Tribunal discusses briefly the legal issue of the direct effect of the norms of the Constitution (art. 8 subs. 2 Constitution). It holds that common courts may not refuse to apply a statutory norm (*i.e.* KC) and adjudicate the cases on the basis of the Constitution until the norm has not been pronounced unconstitutional[19]. The courts should rather use their right to ask the Tribunal for the interpretation of the norm in question (artt. 188 and 193 Constitution). **15**

The Tribunal emphasises that statutory provisions may not limit the constitutionally guaranteed claim for damages. It briefly analyses the civil code provisions dealing with public authority liability and assesses them against the Constitution. Pursuant to art. 417 "the State Treasury is liable for damages occasioned by a servant of the state in carrying out a delegated function". However, this rule as interpreted by the courts, requires either a functionary's negligence or an "anonymous fault" of the state unit in order to hold the State Treasury liable. According to the Supreme Court's panel decision of 1971, art. 417 should be read in conjunction with the general clause of liability for faulty infliction of damage (art. 415 KC): liability must be predicated on fault of the servant. Another KC provision, art. 418 KC, makes it impossible for the injured to get any compensation from the State by requiring a prior prosecution of the guilty official when the exercise of public authority takes the form of issuing decisions (*actes de pouvoir*). **16**

The Tribunal agrees with the view that the present interpretation of art. 417 KC narrows down the liability of the State Treasury significantly. After having considered different views expressed in the legal writing[20], the Tribunal decides to follow the approach that suggests that art. 417 KC should be read as not to require proof of a public servant's negligence. The Tribunal states that the thirty year old interpretation of art. 417 has lost its validity and legal grounds with the enactment of the new Constitution, as far as it requires the **17**

[19] Compare the commented judgment of SN 26 November 2000.

[20] See: E. Letowska, W kwestii zmian przepisów KC o odpowiedzialnosci za szkody wyrzadzone dzialaniem wladzy publicznej, [1999] *Panstwo i Prawo* (PiP), 7; M. Kepinski/R. Szczepaniak, O bezposrednim stosowaniu artykulu 77 ust. 1 Konstytucji, [2000] PiP, 3; P. Granecki, Odpowiedzialnosc cywilna Skarbu Panstwa za szkode wyrzadzona dzialaniem swojego funkcjonariusza (wybrane zagadnienia), [2000] *Palestra*, 11 12; M. Safjan, Odpowiedzialnosc panstwa na podstawie art. 77 Konstytucji RP, [1999] PiP, 4.

proof of negligent act or omission of the functionary. Thus, the Tribunal holds it contrary to art. 77 and not contrary to art. 64 of the Constitution. The verbatim interpretation of art. 417 reinstated by the Tribunal is binding on all courts (art. 190 of the Constitution).

18 As to art. 418 KC, in the Tribunal's opinion it conflicts not only with the Constitution but also with the established case law that accepts evidence of an "anonymous fault" or organizational fault of the state unit sufficient to hold the State Treasury liable. It is also obviously contrary to the European standards of the liability of public authorities for damage. Therefore, the Tribunal finds art. 418 KC unconstitutional.

c) Commentary

19 The long awaited ruling of the Tribunal is groundbreaking. The problem concerns both the liability of the State Treasury and of appropriate territorial municipalities for damage to persons and property, as well as the question on which grounds compensation should be paid if the damage has been caused through enactment of a legal act or rendering of an individual decision in proper legal proceedings.

20 Strict liability of public authorities was first introduced in the Polish Constitution of 1921, but after World War II, under the new political regime, the scope of state liability was narrowed down[21]. The constitution of 1997 reintroduces the modern standard of liability of public authority into the civil law[22]. The statutory provisions should have been adjusted to the new Constitution within 2 years after it entered into force. However, in the matter at hand the proposed amendments to KC have not yet been enacted. This has caused confusion in the practice and theory of law. The current case law is far from consistent, since for some courts artt. 417 and 418 KC are binding regardless of the constitutional shape of the claim for damages, while for others art. 77 of the Constitution is self-executing and may be the ground for awarding damages.

21 After having considered the dominant view expressed in legal writing, the Tribunal decided to follow the less radical approach and, instead of pronouncing art. 417 unconstitutional, it rejected the SN's controlling interpretation of the norm, and directed a new interpretation, based on the literal meaning. The latest SN decisions seem to suggest this solution[23].

[21] For reference in English see W.J. Wagner, Recent developments in State Tort Liability in Poland, [1971] *The American Journal of Comparative Law* 20, 247.

[22] M. Safjan, Konstytucja a odpowiedzialnosc wladzy publicznej, *Rzeczpospolita* 24/25 December 2001.

[23] SN 26 September 2000, III CKN 1089/00, and SN 15 May 2000, II CKN 293/00. In the judgment of SN 8 January 2002, the Supreme Court already ruled according to the interpretation of art. 417 KC set by the Constitutional Tribunal and awarded damages occasioned by an illegal administrative decision. Plaintiff did not have legal standing in the administrative proceedings and could not claim damages on the grounds of art. 418 KC.

The need for reforming the old provisions has recently been discussed intensively in legal doctrine. The Commission for the Codification of Civil Law advocates that strict liability in tort should derive from wrongful conduct of public authorities. Thus, it has proposed a new wording of art. 417 KC. It would provide for the Treasury, or an appropriate territorial municipality, possessing legal personality, or other appropriate person exercising public authority be liable for damage caused in the course of the exercise of public authority. In the case of entrustment of the exercise of a right arising from public authority to another person, this person shall also be liable for the damage (art. 417 KC § 1). The liability of the person mentioned in the preceding paragraph arises if the damage has resulted from wrongful conduct of its functionary, employee or other person participating in the exercise of public authority (art. 417 § 2). If the damage has been caused through enactment of a legal act or rendering of an individual decision in proper proceedings, compensation may be demanded only when the legal act has been declared void on the ground of its unconstitutionality or non-conformity with an international agreement or a statute, or when the individual decision has been rendered unlawful according to the statutory rules. If the damage resulted from an individual decision that had been rendered on the basis of a legal act that was later declared unconstitutional or contrary to an international convention or a statute, compensation may be paid after the decision has been rendered unlawful according to the statutory rules (art. 417 § 3). 22

The new regime of the liability without fault needs further explanation and definition of the notions like "public authority", "organ of public authority", "exercise of public authority" and "contrary to law" (and its relation to wrongfulness). All the notions may have different meanings in public law and in civil law. 23

3. *Sad Apelacyjny w Katowicach* (Court of Appeals in Katowice, CA); 26 July 2001[24]: Public Authority Liability

a) Brief Summary of the Facts

The plaintiff wanted to build a trade centre near the former Nazi camp in Auschwitz in 1996. He got the required permission for construction works, issued by the city mayor. When strong protests from the Jewish national and international communities followed, the province governor (*voievode*) cancelled the building permission. The plaintiff had already taken an investment loan for which he made monthly payments. He claimed his damages from the province governor who settled for a part of it (PLN 500,000; € 138,900). Then the plaintiff filed a claim for additional PLN 1,464,000 (€ 406,666) of damages against the State (the province governor) and the local government (commune, *gmina*). The Court held that the plaintiff's cause of action lies only against the State, and dismissed the claim against the local government. The defendant 24

[24] *Rzeczpospolita* 27 July 2001.

governor maintained that the liability should be borne by the authority whose organ had issued the wrongful decision (that is by the local government unit).

b) Judgment of the Court of Appeals

25 According to the Polish Code of Administrative Procedure, if a decision was declared void because it was unsupported by legal grounds, or made in violation of the law, an appropriate organ may award damages (artt. 153, 160). However, in most situations only real losses (*damnum emergens)* may be compensated, but not the lost profits (*lucrum cessans*). A common court may adjudicate the lost profits on the basis of art. 418 KC if the conditions of the liability are fulfilled. The Court points out that in 1996, under the regulation of the former Constitution, the local self-government units (reintroduced in Poland in 1990) were not subject to the above regulation. In other words, positive law did not recognize the civil liability of the territorial municipalities for damage caused by their wrongful decisions. The rules of the liability of the State Treasury (art. 417 KC) are applicable *per analogiam*. The Court emphasizes that in a democratic political system the rule of law calls for the liability of the public authority despite the legal gaps. Art. 77 of the Constitution also supports this position.

c) Commentary

26 The Civil Code was amended by the Act of 23 August 1996 (Dz.U. 114, at 542) to introduce, among other things, the rules on the civil liability of the local government units. They were shaped according to the model of the State Treasury liability. The ruling of the Courts of Appeal shows the new approach to the problem of liability of the public authority for damages caused by wrongful conduct of its organs.

4. CA in Warsaw; 5 March 1999, I ACa 1386/98[25]: State Liability for Animals, Environmental Law

a) Brief Summary of the Facts

27 The plaintiffs sued the State claiming indemnity for damage done to their fishing farm by otters. In 1995 otters became a protected species, and that year the catch of fish at the plaintiffs' ponds showed a decline of 94%. The plaintiffs claimed that the Council of Ministers failed to issue a regulation by which the liability of State would be extended to the compensation of losses caused by otters and therefore compensation should be awarded on the grounds of the Constitution.

b) Judgment of the Court of Appeals

28 Liability for wild animals is regulated in game law (Act of 13 October 1995, Dz.U. no 147, at 713) and environmental protection law (Act of 16 October

[25] [2001] *Orzecznictwo Sadów Apelacyjnych* (Decisions of the Courts of Appeals, OSA) 3, at 17.

1991, Dz.U. 2001 no 99 at 1079). Art. 52 sec. 1 of the environmental protection law provides for the claim for damages against the State in cases where harm was caused by certain protected animals (*e.g.* wild boars, bison). The Council of Ministers may issue a regulation that expands the group of animals for which the State bears liability (art. 52 subs. 3 environmental protection law). The Council of Ministers did not use its prerogative to cover otters by such regulation. The Court emphasizes that the Constitution does not support the view that the State should be liable for failure to issue a legal act, had it not been obliged by law to do so. However, even if there are no special provisions, besides art. 44 of game law, the State Treasury may be still liable according to the general rules (artt. 417 and 418 KC), either in tort or in contract. The provisions of game law or environmental law do not pre-empt claims that may be brought on the basis of the civil code. Nevertheless, in the Court's judgment, the plaintiffs did not prove any negligence of a state servant, thus the cause of action based on art. 417 KC (or art. 418 KC) cannot stand. Finally, art. 77 of the Constitution of 1997 may not be invoked because the facts of the case occurred under the regime of the old Constitution.

c) Commentary

The Court's holding, which allows for a general cause of action in order to get 29
compensation for harm done by wild animals, is noteworthy. In the absence of a special rule in environmental or game law, the claimant will still have a cause of action, provided he proves all conditions of liability. In the case of contractual liability the debtor's negligence in performance or failure to perform the contract will be presumed. In the tort liability system, art. 417 KC, as now interpreted by TK, in fact provides for strict liability of the State for damage caused by wild animals (though it did not apply to the facts of the commented case). The cause of action based on art. 417 KC is more advantageous to the plaintiff, because he may claim full damages (art. 361 § 2 KC).

5. CA in Bialystok; 30 November 2000, I ACa 340/00[26]: Product Liability

a) Brief Summary of the Facts

A consumer organisation filed a claim for compensation on behalf of a con- 30
sumer who was injured while using the canned foam "Tytan" to tighten his bathtub. The consumer had read the instructions on the product and had opened all the windows to ensure better ventilation before he started work. One of the four cans he used exploded when his wife switched on the washing machine. The cause of the explosion was an ignition of the propane gas that had been leaking from the cans. The consumer suffered burns on his hands and his washing machine was destroyed. Defendant seller and producer maintained that the product conformed to the special labelling requirements set by law and had received a quality certificate.

[26] [2001] OSA 6, at 33.

b) Judgment of the Court of Appeals

31 The Court found the defendant producer liable for failure to provide adequate warnings (art. 415 KC). The manufacturer is a professional who, being aware of foreseeable risks linked with the use of his product offered on the market, has a duty to give clear warnings. The fact that the product got a certificate of a proper State agency and fulfilled the labelling standards set in the regulation concerning dangerous chemical substances is not a defence to the producer's negligence. The plaintiff sprayed the foam at the wrong angle, which was contrary to the instruction of use given on the label. Nevertheless, the producer did not warn of the negative effect of such a foreseeable manner of using the can, namely that the propane would leak. Therefore, the instructions were inadequate. Moreover, the producer did not give any warnings about the dangerous gas component and the possibility of fire due to any electric spark. The information and warnings given on a product should be complete and adequate to release the manufacturer from liability.

c) Commentary

32 The Court relied in its holding on the well-approved doctrine of the liability for failure to warn[27]. The general clause of liability (art. 415 KC) was applicable to the facts at hand because the harm caused by a dangerous product occurred before the new law on producer's liability came into force (Act of 2 March 2000 on The Protection of Some Consumer Rights and Products Liability[28]). In Poland, until the passing of the regulation on products liability implementing the EEC Directive 85/374, producer's liability was not strict, but based on fault. In the circumstances of the case, the "old law" was more favourable to the consumer as it comes to the compatibility of the product with binding technical standards. Under the new regime of product liability (artt. 449.1–449.11 KC), if the product conformed to the compulsory technical standards set by an appropriate state agency as binding law, the manufacturer may use it as a defence to the strict liability (art. 449.3 § 2 *in fine* KC). The plaintiff may only question the level of the legal standards as old and not meeting the ordinary consumer expectation test, and base his claim on the cause of action for negligence (art. 415 in conjunction with art. 449.10 KC)[29].

33 The old rules will remain the legal basis for all compensation claims that arose before 1 July 2000, provided the limitation time has not expired (at the maximum ten years from the day on which the event causing the damage occurred, art. 442 § 1 KC).

[27] See M. Jagielska, *Odpowiedzialnosc za produkt* (1999). M. Nesterowicz, Odpowiedzialnosc cywilna za szkody wyrzadzone wprowadzeniem do obrotu rzeczy niebezpiecznych z wadami, [1983] *Palestra*, 11.

[28] Dz. U. 2000, no. 22 at 271.

[29] See E. Letowska, *Prawo umów konsumenckich* (2nd edn. 2002), p. 123.

6. *Sad Okregowy, Rzeszów* (RC in Rzeszów, RC); 18 April 2001[30]: Product Liability

a) Brief Summary of the Facts

The plaintiff, a six-year old girl, was injured when an airbag unexpectedly exploded in a parked Ford Mondeo. Even though there had been no car keys left in the ignition, an explosion took place when she moved from the back seat to the driver's seat and touched a lighter. The girl was hit in the head and lost consciousness for 8 days. She has suffered serious physical and mental injuries, and despite several operations she remains hemiplegic and needs constant rehabilitation and psychotherapy. The plaintiff's parents sued Ford Distribution, the Polish importer of Ford cars, and the dealer who sold the car. They claimed PLN 500,000 (€ 138,900) for non-pecuniary loss, in addition to pecuniary damages and a monthly annuity. As a defence, the defendant importer pointed at the producer as the person liable for damage and maintained that the cause of the injury was purely accidental. 34

b) Judgment of the Regional Court

The Court states that an airbag's function is to ensure safety of the passengers and it should not work to the contrary. Then it points out that Ford Motor Co. delivered to its dealers and service stations product information concerning the foreseeability of an uncontrolled explosion of an airbag under certain conditions (such as a strong electromagnetic field). This information was not transferred to the buyer (the plaintiff's parents). The Court finds that both the importer and the seller were negligent in failing to warn of a risk they knew about, and so holds them jointly and severally liable for the damages (art. 415 KC). The award for pain and suffering in the amount of PLN 200,000 (€ 55,555) takes account of the severe mental shock experienced by the girl, as well as the loss of joy in life and of life prospects. The Court also establishes the defendants' liability for future harm that may occur in connection with the accident. 35

c) Commentary

This is the first case that has dealt with dangerously defective airbags in Poland. As in the above-cited judgment, the law applicable to the facts was the old regulation of the seller/producer liability based on fault (art. 415 KC). The liability of an importer of cars was established in SN decision of 26 March 1984[31]. In the commented case the actual cause of the explosion of the airbag was not established at trial. The judgment is in line with the new strict liability regime, under which the outcome of the case would be the same, except for the burden of proving the negligence of the producer. An importer of a product is responsible to the same extent as the manufacturer, but in certain situations 36

[30] *Rzeczpospolita* 19 April 2001.

[31] [1982] *Orzecznictwo Sadów Polskich i Komisji Arbitrazowych* (Decisions of the Polish Courts and Arbitration Panels, OSPiKA), 7/8.

he might not make use of defences available to the producer, such as the development risk defence (when the producer does not facilitate access to its documents). Therefore, his liability may occasionally be "stricter" than the producer's.

37 In general, compensation covers incurred damage as well as future harm that is certain to occur or can be foreseen at the moment of adjudicating the case. A final court ruling may not be modified or reconsidered since it is subject to the principle of *res judicata*. Thus, in case of further decline of the victim's health, no additional award is allowed unless a new injury appears that could not have been foreseen based on the facts of the adjudicated case.[32] If the court held in its judgment that the defendant is liable for damages that may occur in the future, the limitation period of three years for new claims will begin to run on the day when the injured person learned of the new damage[33].

7. SN 16 February 2000, II UKN 416/99[34]: Non-Pecuniary Loss

a) Brief Summary of the Facts

38 While working the plaintiff was hit on his neck by a bale of fabric. He did not suffer physical injuries, but only the pain. He sued his employer for non-pecuniary loss. The Court awarded PLN 1100 (€ 305), but the plaintiff claims that the award is too low.

b) Judgment of the Supreme Court

39 In the case where non-pecuniary loss is the only harm suffered by plaintiff, the court may award damages with reference either to the provisions on the minimal compensation for work related accidents set in the Act of 1975 on Payments for Work Accidents and Sickness, or to the average monthly salary.

40 SN emphasises that awards for non-pecuniary loss purport to make the injured person whole. At times it is the only type of damages that an aggrieved party is given. Art. 445 KC provides no guidance on the question of what constitutes adequate non-pecuniary loss damages. In the assessment of damages, courts must take into consideration all circumstances of the case, such as the degree and period of physical and mental suffering and the permanence of the effects of the tortious conduct. The Court confirms the well–established case law saying that damages for non-pecuniary loss serve the purpose of compensation, thus they may not be symbolic, nor excessive in relation to the damage inflicted. The quantum of damages must be reasonable and correspond to the current living conditions of an average member of society[35].

[32] SN Panel of 7 judges, 27 November 1967, [1968] OSN, 113.
[33] SN 17 February 1972, [1972] OSN at 149.
[34] [2001] OSNAP 16, at 520.
[35] SN 24 June 1965, [1966] OSPiKA, 92.

c) Commentary

The holding reaffirms the dominant position in legal doctrine and case law[36]. Polish jurisprudence says that because of their compensatory role, damages for non-pecuniary loss should be suitable, relate to the injury and take into account all the relevant circumstances, in particular the gravity of pain, duration of disease and permanent effects of the damaging act[37]. **41**

In 2001 a significant increase of the number of personal injury lawsuits was reported. The general pattern of awards shows their constant rise. For example, in a case where the plaintiff lost his leg because the doctors failed to diagnose artery damage occasioned in a motorcycle accident, RC in Krakow awarded PLN 50,000 (€ 13,890) for non-pecuniary loss. Plaintiff suffered a severe mental shock that led to suicidal attempts, depression and alcoholism[38]. The same amount of damages for pain and suffering was calculated in the case of a woman who was injured during natural childbirth. The physicians did not perform a caesarean section although it should have been the case and they did not inform the mother about the damage she had incurred due to the natural delivery process. Plaintiff has to undergo lengthy treatment and possibly surgery in the future[39]. **42**

In another case involving an infant's injuries at childbirth due to the erroneous decision of continuing a natural delivery, the plaintiff demanded PLN 325,000 (€ 90,278)for pain and suffering. The baby suffered irreversible brain damage. RC in Lublin held the defendant hospital liable for its organizational fault at the maternity ward and concluded that PLN 200,000 (€ 55,555) as non-pecuniary loss damages reflect the gravity of fault and the scope of suffered injuries[40]. **43**

In yet another case the District Court in Bialystok[41] awarded compensation to parents for the wrongful death of their son. A flagrant negligence of the ER doctor and the physician on duty in the ward for the intoxicated persons caused the death of an assaulted and beaten up student. Without any diagnostic testing, such as an X-ray of the head, he had been treated as a drunken man and diagnosed with an alcohol poisoning. Finally, he was sent back to the hospital where he was diagnosed with haematoma and died after delayed surgery. Both physicians were sentenced by the criminal court and deprived of the right to practise medicine for 2–3 years. As to the civil claim, the court found that under the circumstances of the case, the standard of care required an X-ray of the patient's head. The physicians have to pay PLN 30,000 (€ 8,333) and PLN 20,000 (€ 5,555) to the student's parents for the wrongful death of their **44**

[36] See E. Baginska/M. Nesterowicz, Non-pecuniary loss under Polish law, in W.V.H. Rogers (ed.), *Damages for Non-Pecuniary Loss in a Comparative Perspective* (2001), pp. 173–191.
[37] SN 15 July 1977, IV CR 266/77.
[38] *Rzeczpospolita* 3 April 2001.
[39] *Rzeczpospolita* 12 April 2001.
[40] *Rzeczpospolita* 26 September 2001 and 11 January 2002.
[41] DC 7 September 2001, *Rzeczpospolita* 8 September 2001.

son. This kind of compensation is based on art. 446 § 3 KC that allows for a claim for adequate damages to the nearest members of the deceased's family if, as a result of his death, they suffered a considerable deterioration of their situation in life.

45 The amounts of awards for non-pecuniary loss in the cases of violation of personality rights are also tending to increase. The cases adjudicated in 2001 are based on the new art. 448 KC. It provides for claims for non-pecuniary loss in every case of infringement upon personal interest. For example a Polish Olympian sports champion won a case against a stationery manufacturer that had used his picture in an advertising campaign without having obtained his consent. Plaintiff claimed that the publicity misled the public as to his sponsorship and caused hardship in negotiating his business contracts. The court held that defendant had breached the copyright provisions and awarded PLN 50,000 (€ 13,890) as well as obliging him to publish a statement of suitable content and form[42].

8. RC in Wroclaw 20 September 1999 IC 708/96, affd CA 1 June 2000 I A Ca 323/00[43]: Medical Malpractice, Non-Pecuniary Loss

a) Brief Summary of the Facts

46 Plaintiff was a 22-year old woman who had undergone heart surgery in 1983. Afterwards she experienced discomfort connected with her heart and was examined and tested by the same medical clinic (defendant) several times. These examinations never disclosed any information about the presence of any foreign objects in her heart. Two needles were discovered in plaintiff's heart in a routine X-ray taken in 1996, which was followed by two other invasive procedures aiming to precisely identify the location thereof. At present, a cyst has grown around one, but the other poses a danger to the patient because it is capable of moving inside the tissue when subject to electro-magnetic waves. Plaintiff consulted with the cardiologists in the defendant clinic and elsewhere, and found out that the removal of the needles creates a too high risk for her and that she has now to live with them. Plaintiff filed her claim in 1996 demanding PLN 200,000 (€ 55,555) as non-pecuniary loss for the stress she has been suffering and the constant threat to her life posed by the needles in her heart. Plaintiff may not be diagnosed with any modern medical device involving electro-magnetic fields because it would endanger her life. Defendant asks for the dismissal of action because the time limit for the claim has expired and maintains that there is no actual need to remove the needles since they remain rigid in the plaintiff's body.

[42] *Rzeczpospolita* 25 October 2001.
[43] [2001] *Prawo i Medycyna* 9, 115.

b) Judgment of the Regional Court

The court finds that leaving the needles in the patient's heart during the surgery denotes defendant hospital's negligence in the form of an "organizational fault". The evidence clearly shows the doctors must have seen the metal objects in plaintiff's heart on X-rays dating before 1996, however they failed to inform plaintiff about them. The surgical team did not count the used needles after the operation, which amounts to a breach of ordinary care and caution. The Court points out that plaintiff may be reasonably anxious concerning the possibility of negative consequences appearing in the future, which has led to a permanent mental trauma. 47

Referring to the defence, the Court first invokes art. 442 KC providing that a three-year period of limitation begins to run from the day on which the information about the loss and the person liable for it was acquired, and not on the day when the victim learned of the extent of damage or permanent consequences thereof. In any case, the three-year period stops running with the passage of ten years from the day of the tort[44]. The ten-year period is a maximum one and must always be counted from the day of the tort (*a tempore facti*), and not from the day of the awareness of the damage (*a tempore scientiae*). In this case, however, the Court overrules on the grounds of art. 5 KC defendant's plea of limitation of action. By virtue of art. 5, the use of one's right may be denied legal protection because of the consideration about the principles of community life. The court holds that art. 5 KC may be applied to the facts of the case because, for 13 years, the defendant hospital maintained that there was no negative outcome of plaintiff's heart surgery and that her discomfort and throbbing were not linked to the operation. Awarding PLN 80,000 (€ 22,200) from the State Treasury (art. 417 KC), the Court reaffirms SN's opinion that moral suffering may well be enhanced by the tortfeasor's insensitive behaviour after the tortious conduct or by his failing to undertake any actions aimed at diminishing the damage.[45] 48

c) Commentary

The system of compensating injuries caused by medical accidents and errors does not function well in Poland. The judicial protection is costly and lengthy, and there is no proper way of ensuring the victim's return to full well-being and normal life. This should be subject to change, for example by a revision of legislation and introducing a new regulation of compensating injuries regardless of the fault of the physicians or hospitals. 49

The case is an example of a flagrant medical error. The court reaffirmed its commitment to the widely accepted doctrine that a health care institution is liable in tort for personal injuries to its patients, even if the direct tortfeasor may not be identified, but the damage is causally linked with some breach of 50

[44] SN 17 February 1982, [1983] OSN, 8.
[45] SN 9 January 1978, [1978] OSN, 210.

professional duties and happened in the course of the performance of the entrusted tasks (anonymous fault). It is mostly used in medical malpractice cases in which it is often difficult to prove whose negligence (of which physician or nurse) caused the patient's harm[46].

51 The application of art. 5 KC to personal injury cases has been recognized in SN case law dealing with work accidents[47]. This decision is just because it allows for a flexible application of rigid rules of prescription of claims in unusual factual situations. Along these lines, CA in Cracow[48] awarded damages to a young boy for a hepatitis C infection in his infancy. He was treated in several health care institutions where he underwent surgery, a blood transfusion and diagnostic tests. Plaintiff's mother learnt of the infection after 8 years and she was told that there had been no possibility of diagnosing it at the time it had happened (1985). The Court ruled that the State was liable for the acts of all medical institutions involved. It overruled the plea of limitation of action on the grounds that plaintiff should not bear the consequences of being infected with an unknown and incurable virus.

9. CA in Krakow 9 March 2001, IACa 124/01[49]: Non-Pecuniary Loss, Medical Malpractice

a) Brief Summary of the Facts

52 During a procedure of removing a tonsil, the laryngologist did not secure the cut off tissue mass in the child's throat. The six-year-old plaintiff choked on the tonsil and stopped breathing. When he did so the laryngologist called the reanimation team but he did not inform them about the lost tonsil for 5 minutes. Only when the fourth and chief anaesthesiologist was called to the dying patient, did she manage to remove the tonsil in parts. The child was intubated but did not regain consciousness due to the broad and severe brain damage. As a consequence plaintiff has become quadriplegic, lives in a vegetative state comparable to infancy, experiences a few epileptic incidents per day and he has no prospects for improvement. He is declared 100% disabled. The physician's fault was determined by a criminal court. Plaintiff sued the State for PLN 300,000 (€ 83,300) of pecuniary and non-pecuniary damages. In the second instance defendant claimed the trial court's award of PLN 200,000 (€ 55,555) for non-pecuniary loss was excessive.

b) Judgment of the Court of Appeals

53 The State is vicariously liable for the doctor who was employed at the time of surgery in the public hospital (art. 417 KC). The condition of the State liability

[46] SN 21 November 1974 [1975] OSPiKA at 108; SN 17 April 1974 [1974] OSPiKA at 207, finding the State liable for damages.
[47] SN 11 September 1997, [1997] UKN II, 250, [1998] OSNAP 13, 406.
[48] *Rzeczpospolita* 27 September 2001.
[49] *Rzeczpospolita* 10–11 March 2001

is the functionary's negligence, which in this case was also proved in the criminal proceedings (see art. 11 KPC).

The Court holds that the laryngologist who performed the surgery breached the prescribed standards of medical procedure. Doctors are required to conform to a higher standard of care and diligence because the objects of their activities are human beings and the results are often irreversible. The Court points out that the criminal character of the doctor's conduct is significant and together with the degree of his negligence may increase the non-pecuniary loss. Moreover, in this case the hospital has not undertaken any steps to alleviate the results of the damage. Taking consideration of the circumstances, the total disability, plaintiff's age and lack of positive prognosis, he has been awarded adequate non-pecuniary damages (art. 445 KC). **54**

c) Commentary

The judgment the Court of Appeals reaffirms a widely accepted case law that requires taking into account all circumstances of the case and the compensatory function of damages for non-patrimonial loss (see also SN 29 September 2000, [2001] OSNC 3, 42). The conduct of the doctor in this case was particularly reprehensible, in fact, by failing to inform others of his error, he delayed the effective reanimation of the plaintiff and did not prevent further brain damage. The award is one of the highest in the practice of Polish courts, and, at the same time, well-justified. **55**

10. SN; 27 April 2001, II CZP 5/01[50]: Right of Contribution

a) Brief Summary of the Facts

A Sickness Insurance Fund filed a contribution claim against the criminal offender for the costs of the victim's treatment. The patient was insured under the universal health insurance scheme. **56**

b) Judgment of the Supreme Court

The Court held that neither a Sickness Insurance Fund nor a public health care institution may seek contribution from the tortfeasor for the costs of the treatment of the injured person. The Court first analyses legal provisions providing in specific situations for the right of contribution of the Social Insurance Office against intentional wrong doers. The Court points out that the right of recovery from a direct perpetrator is usually expressly provided for by law. If the legislator did not give that right to the Sickness Insurance Funds, it may not be implied *per analogiam.* Even though social insurance and universal health insurance systems are both financed from the citizens' obligatory premiums, recovery payments are not listed as a financial resource of a Sickness Insurance Fund, nor of a public health care establishment. The Court adds that these institutions are not destined to exercise a preventive function in the form **57**

[50] [2001] *Wokanda* 10, at 3.

of contribution claims. Finally, the funds and medical institutions would have to bear the costs of seeking contribution and maintaining a special administration. The Court concludes that the legislator should regulate the problem.

c) Commentary

58 Seeking contributions by the Sickness Insurance funds creates a new challenge for the courts. Since the health care reform that entered into force on 1 January 2001[51], the newly created 16 Sickness Insurance funds are financed from the premiums paid by the insured and are separate from the State budget. Since they have to manage the limited resources, they are inclined to seek alternative (to statutory) sources of income. Contrary judgments of lower courts have been reported[52].

11. RC in Gdansk; 25 April 2001[53]: Liability in Tort of Church Entities

a) Brief Summary of the Facts

59 A couple got married in a Roman-Catholic church in K. The priest failed to notify the act of this "concordat marriage" to the secular registration office in due time. The information was given after 66 days. According to Polish family law, the "concordat marriage" became void and the registration officer refused to register the act. After having learnt of the priest's failure, the couple had to marry again in front of the State official. The wife became pregnant and she claims to have experienced a mental shock that endangered her pregnancy. She claims compensation for non-pecuniary loss from the Roman Catholic Church in K.

b) Judgment of the Court

60 The Court opinion notes that plaintiff's cause of action is based on the general provision of liability for damage caused by one's fault (artt. 415, 416 KC). Thus, plaintiff should prove wrongful conduct on which liability may be based, the fault of the actor, the damage and the causal connection. The Court finds convincing the evidence of the priest's negligent conduct and the extent of non-pecuniary loss. The causation between the negligent failure to notify of the canon marriage by the priest and plaintiff's mental distress was established according to the court of the first instance, but the Regional Court reverses. The evidence presented at trial does not show the cause-in-fact because, as

[51] Act on Universal Health Insurance of 6 February 1997, Dz. U. 1997, no. 28 at 153 as amended.

[52] RC in Olsztyn; 16 May 2001, in *Gazeta Wyborcza* 17 May 2001. In summer 1999 the defendant bakery produced cakes that contained salmonella, which resulted in the food poisoning of over 150 consumers, 40 of whom were hospitalised. Contaminated raw eggs were used for the production instead of a required egg concentrate. The Sickness Insurance Fund claimed PLN 3,000 (€ 833) from the bakery for the costs of treatment of a single family of 4. The Regional Court held the defendant bakery liable for the contaminated food on the basis of art. 415 KC. The fault of the producer was without question. The Sickness Insurance Fund had a valid claim for indemnity of the costs of medical treatment (art. 441 KC).

[53] *Rzeczpospolita* 26 April 2001.

said by the expert witness, other reasons could endanger plaintiff's pregnancy. The evidence has not excluded the possibility that plaintiff's natural conditions caused the risk of miscarriage, taking account of the fact that the physical ailments occurred two months after she had learnt of the void act of her canon (concordat) marriage. The court holds no recovery for plaintiff.

c) Commentary

It is the first published case that deals with the liability of church juristic persons for damages caused by breach of the duties imposed by the Concordat signed between Poland and the Vatican in 1993[54]. The Concordat granted legal validity to a marriage contracted in the Roman Catholic church according to canon law (art. 10 Concordat). This triggered changes to *kodeks rodzinny i opiekunczy* (Polish Family Code, FC) of 1964. A religious marriage is legally binding if registered in the prescribed time, provided that international agreements provide so (art. 1 §§2–3 FC). Before the Concordat, Roman Catholics in Poland had to attend two ceremonies, because a legal marriage could only be concluded in front of the State official in the registry office. The parish officials have a duty to notify of the canon marriage within five days (art. 8 § 3 FC), otherwise the effects of the act in the sphere of (secular) civil law will not ensue (art. 1 § 2 FC). Church entities are juristic persons and so they may be held liable in tort for the fault of their organs on the basis of art. 416 KC. 61

C. Literature

1. M. Nesterowicz, *Prawo medyczne* (Medical law) (5th edn. Torun 2001)

The fifth edition of the treatise on medical law thoroughly and comprehensively presents the liability in tort of physicians, hospitals and sickness insurance funds towards patients. It deals in detail with the liability for medical malpractice, lack of informed consent, and lack of safety during hospitalisation, as well as with medical experiments, cosmetic surgery etc. The author advocates the concept of "anonymous fault" (*la faute anonime)* developed by Polish courts to deal with unidentified tortfeasors and organizational negligence of health care institutions. He suggests that the liability for medical accidents (*e.g.* infection with HIV during a blood transfusion, other hospital infections), medical experiments and vaccinations should be detached from fault and borne by the State. This guarantee – like liability – should be based on a special scheme designed upon the models introduced in the USA and some European countries. According to the author, the Swedish *No Fault Patient Insurance* scheme could be relatively easily introduced in Poland. The contributions to the fund would come from the liability insurance premiums paid by doctors and medical establishments, and partially from the State budget. In this way, the injured patients of public medical institutions, for which 62

[54] Ratified in 23 February 1998, in force 25 April 1998 (Dz.U. 1998 no. 51 at 318).

the State holds no vicarious liability since they have become incorporated, could obtain compensation.

2. M. Nesterowicz, Odpowiedzialnosc cywilna zakladu opieki zdrowotnej za zakazenia wirusowym zapaleniem watroby (Hospital Liability for Hepatitis Infection) [2001] *Archiwum Medycyny Sadowej i Kryminalistyki* LI, 1–9

63 The author discusses the judgments of Appeal Courts and of the Supreme Court dealing with harm caused to patients through a hospital hepatitis infection. Hospital infections lead to 75% of all medical lawsuits in Poland per annum (approx. 1300 cases). Nesterowicz approves of the practice of the courts that accept a high probability of infection coming from the defendant hospital to adjudicate the claim. He also advocates the use of the presumption of fact (art. 231 *kodeks postepowania cywilnego*, Polish Civil Procedure Code, KPC) that the hepatitis infection was acquired in hospital, the evidence to the contrary having not being submitted by the defendant. It is a presumption of culpability and causality advantageous to the injured. As a comparison, the author presents the French jurisprudence that created a hospital's "obligation de sécurité de résultat".

3. I. Dyka, Zasady przyznawania i ustalania wysokosci zadoscuczynienia pienieznego w razie naruszenia dobra osobistego (Principles of Adjudicating and Assessing the Non-Pecuniary Loss for the Infringement of Personal Interests), [2001] *Kwartalnik Prawa Prywatnego* (Private Law Quarterly, KPP) 3, 591–638

64 This article is a comprehensive study of principles for awarding non-pecuniary loss developed by Polish case law and legal doctrine. In the Polish legal system, damages for non-pecuniary loss perform an important compensatory function. The recently growing number of provisions allowing their recovery in new situations (especially for the violation of personal rights) shows the dynamic development in this area. The actual wording of art. 448 KC permits redress for non-pecuniary loss for the infringement upon personal interests. The norm contains an alternative that excludes a concurrence of claims. An aggrieved party may demand payment of damages either for his benefit or for the designated social purpose. Art. 448 KC gave rise to a dispute amongst scholars about the conditions for indemnity. Contrary to the majority view, Dyka takes the position that it should not be dependent on the perpetrator's fault.

65 The awarding of non-pecuniary loss is discretionary and arbitrary. It does not mean the court's freedom of action in adjudicating. The author analyses cases entitling to recovery of non-pecuniary loss and comes to the conclusion that, in the assessment of damages, courts must take into consideration all circumstances that influence the extent and gravity of the damage incurred. According to Dyka, the sums awarded by Polish courts as compensation for non-pecuniary loss are rather reasonable (average). In non-personal injury cases they have usually been lower and not exceeding the amount equal to a few average salaries in Poland. She also cites several personal injury cases in which the courts awarded quite different sums in similar or comparable situations.

4. M. Safjan, Odpowiedzialnosc odszkodowawcza kas za nienalezyta jakosc swiadczen medycznych (Liability for Damage Assumed by Local Health Authorities for Inadequate Quality of Medical Services rendered), [2001] *Prawo i Medycyna* (Law and Medicine) 9, 5–16

The author deals with the problem of quality in health care and liability for **66**
medical services that do not meet the required level of quality. Safjan suggests that a medical quality standard should be established objectively, by taking into consideration available resources, and according to the state of the art in medicine, however not by reference to the newest technology. Scarce resources do not justify limiting access to more modern procedures and the average national (or regional) level of the quality of a medical service is not the basis for the evaluation of the service *ad casum*. In Safjan's opinion, public authorities have the duty to establish and realize the required quality standard in health care. He advocates that the regional sickness funds should be liable in tort for breach of this duty on the basis of art. 417 KC. Public medical institutions may be held liable on the same legal ground, and private institutions on the basis of artt. 416 and 430 KC. Physicians should be regarded as servants rather than independent contractors when it comes to liability for low quality medical service, since they are dependent on the organization and financing of the services upon the institution and regional sickness funds.

5. M. Nesterowicz, Odpowiedzialnosc cywilna zakladu leczniczego za bezpieczenstwo pacjenta podczas hospitalizacji (Hospital Liability for the Safety of Patients), [2001] *Panstwo i Prawo* (State and Law, PiP) 3, 40–51

This article deals with legal bases of hospital's liability for breach of the duty **67**
to ensure patient safety during hospitalisation. The liability arises for damages that are unforeseeable to the patient; independent of treatment and not falling within the risk he consented to. Most often, it is a case for anonymous fault of an unidentified person or for organizational fault of the hospital. The author poses the question whether a hospital could be held liable if there is no fault at all and how the plaintiff's burden of proof could be eased when he learnt of his infection some time after the hospitalisation. Other cases concern the use of low quality or dangerous medical equipment or instruments. The comparative approach to the problem shows that Polish courts could follow the develop ments of the French case law. It would be possible if the obligation of hospitals was characterized not as a duty of due diligence but as the obligation of the effect. This is an auxiliary obligation, independent of the duty of due care in the provision of treatment. The author analyses several cases of Polish courts trying to shift the burden of proof from the plaintiff to the defendant hospital in order to facilitate the pursue of claims.

XIV. Portugal

André Gonçalo Dias Pereira

A. Legislation

1. *Decreto-Lei* (DL, Decree-Law) No. 131/2001 of 24 April – Defective Products Liability

1 This DL implements into national law, Directive 1999/34/EC, of the European Parliament and of the Council, of 10 May, on defective products liability.

2 The safety of products and the compensation of damages caused by defective products are considered important social needs. The European Community aimed to safeguard these values through Directive 85/374/EEC on defective products[1], and Directive 1999/34/EC.

3 This Directive aims to extend the principle of strict liability provided by Directive 85/374/EEC to all kinds of products, including agricultural products, namely agricultural raw material and hunted animals. Therefore, the producer or the importer of these products has the duty to compensate *without fault*. This circumstance increases the level of consumers' protection and aims to restore the trust in the safety of agricultural production, thus, encouraging producers and importers to respect the norms and regulations and to adopt a responsible attitude towards the safety of agricultural raw materials.

4 On the other hand, the Directive imposes the regime of strict liability within all the Member States, and eliminates the risk of unfair competition within the internal market.

5 In order to achieve improved consumers' protection, the law also eliminates the limits of compensation.

[1] Transposed by DL 383/89, 6 November.

2. *Lei* (L, Law) No. 78/2001 of 13 July (Regulates the Organization, Competence and Operation of the "Ward Courts" [*Julgados de Paz*])

Aiming to simplify the operation of justice, this Law created the "Ward Courts". These courts (that are long known in Brazil) tend to deal with matters of justice more quickly, closer to the citizens and the community and promote the mediation and the non-judiciary resolution of conflicts. 6

These courts are competent for actions, the value of which is under approx. € 400 (art. 8), and they are called to decide, among many other subjects, the "cases on tort and contractual liability" (art 9, subs. 1, sent. h)). 7

When there is no complaint, or there is a withdrawal of it, these courts are also competent to decide the civil compensation emerging from *soft* crimes like: bodily injury, negligent bodily injury, defamation, theft, fraud, and others (art. 9). 8

This procedural law will have, thus, some impact in the way people experience tort law and compensation. 9

3. DL No. 276/2001 of 17 October – Regulates the European Convention on the Protection of Pets

This DL creates another case of *compulsory insurance*.[2] 10

According to art. 63, the holder of any 'potentially harmful animal'[3] is obliged to have liability insurance for its actions. 11

The Civil Code already provided *strict liability* for the damage caused by animals on the part of those who in their interest use any kind of animals since the damage is linked to the special damages resulting from the animal's use (art. 502). Those who assume the duty to watch any animals are liable on the ground of fault for the damage the animals cause; nevertheless, art. 493, subs. 1, provides an *inversion of the burden of the proof.* 12

4. Draft Bill 95/VIII (State and Public Bodies Tort Liability) – Revokes DL 48051 of 21 November 1967

In Portugal, as well as in France, there is a special regime for State tort liability, emerging from deeds of *gestion publique*. In the field of substantive law, DL 48051 of 21 November 1967 applies. In cases of *gestion privée* the Civil Code applies. On the procedural side, the administrative courts are competent for these actions. 13

[2] For other cases of compulsory insurance, see Maria C. Lopes, *Responsabilidade Civil Extracontratual* (1997).

[3] 'Potentially harmful animal' is defined in art. 2, sent d) DL 276/2001 of 17 October, as "any animal, which due to its physiological, racial, aggressive behaviour, size or mandible power, may cause harm or death to people or other animals or damage goods".

14 Draft Bill 95/VIII had its roots in the law in force and jurisprudence. The novelties were the improvement of the Administration's liability. According to the present regime, following the best doctrine[4], we can only demand compensation from the State, who subsequently may recover the expenses from the civil servant who acted with *grave negligence*. Alternatively, we may demand compensation from both the State and the civil servant, if he acted with *dolus*.[5] The draft Bill advocated the solidarity regime also when the civil servant acted with grave negligence.

15 For the first time there would be general provisions to regulate the liability of the jurisdictional activity, and there would be a very innovative regime, also at the comparative level, for the political and legislative function's liability.

16 There was also a duty on the State to compensate all those, who – for public interest reasons – suffered *special* and *abnormal* damages.

17 This Draft Bill was rejected. Nevertheless, it was one of the most interesting legal debates in 2001, which will probably continue[6].

5. European Convention on Human Rights and Biomedicine

18 Portugal entered the new Millenium opening its law to the biomedical challenges. In fact, our country ratified the European Convention on Human Rights and Biomedicine and its additional Protocol at the beginning of this year[7].

[4] See Sinde Monteiro, Aspectos Particulares de Responsabilidade Médica, *Direito da Saúde e da Bioética* (1991), pp. 138–145; Canotilho/Moreira, *Constituição da República Portuguesa Anotada* (3rd edn. 1993), p. 953 (art. 271°) and Margarida Cortez, *Responsabilidade Civil da Administração por Actos Administrativos Ilegais e Concurso de Omissão Culposa do Lesado* (2000), pp. 27 *et seq.*.

[5] Following the other doctrine, see, *Sentence of STA of 3 May 2001* (http://www.dgsi.pt). It says that artt. 2 and 3 of DL 48051 shall be in accordance with the Constitution of 1976 (artt. 22 and 271). It means, that the civil servant would be the sole person responsible for his/her acts. The public bodies would be liable *in solidum* when the civil servant committed the wrongful act (with *dolus* or simple negligence), but the State should, afterwards, require the civil servant to reimburse the expenses in any case.

[6] Among various reports on the renewal of this Bill a special mention is due to the Colloquium organised by the Minister of Justice's Office (Lisbon, 8 March 2001), where several professors, judges and lawyers, experts on this field took part (see: http://www.mj.gov.pt/). See, also: R. Medeiros, A responsabilidade civil pelo ilícito administrativo no quadro da reforma do Decreto-Lei no. 48051, [2001] JA 27, 20–33; S. Correia, Da Sede do Regime de Responsabilidade Objectiva por Danos Causados por Normas Emitidas no Desempenho da Função Administrativa, ROA 61, III, 1313–1348; in *Liber Amicorum Rogério Soare* (*Estudos em Homenagem ao Prof. Doutor Rogério Soares*, Studia Iuridica 61, 2001): J. Miranda, *A Constituição e a Responsabilidade Civil do Estado*, pp. 927–949 and V. Cura, *Responsabilidade Civil da Administração por factos lícitos – Algumas considerações sobre o prazo de prescrição do direito à indemnização e a sua interrupção, quando a acção é antecedida da interposição do recurso contencioso de anulação do acto administrativo*, pp. 1221–1267.

[7] President's Decree 1/2001, DR 2 1ª-Série-A, 3 January and Parliament's Resolution no.1/2001, DR no. 2, 1ª-Série-A 3 January.

This ratification is considered to be of great importance for our health law, because, for the first time, some important aspects are more specifically regulated *e.g.* the value of professional standards (art. 4), the previously expressed wishes (art. 9), the right not to know (art. 10,2) and the juridical implications of genome knowledge (Chapter IV), research on embryos (art. 18) and the utilisation of part of the human body (Chapter VII). **19**

On the other hand, some particular norms are not in accordance with our legal system. Therefore, according to our constitutional norms, the Convention changes our law in fields like organ and tissue removal from living donors for transplantation purposes (Chapter VI)[8]. **20**

With regard to legislative development, there has been some degree of delay in certain matters, such as assisted procreation and the status of the embryo. In areas like the autonomy of the dying, euthanasia and assisted suicide, the debate is more or less stagnant and there has been no political incentive to encourage further discussion. **21**

The National Ethics Committee for Life Sciences has published Opinion 30/CNECV/2000, in which it said that the Portuguese ought to ratify the Convention on the Human Rights and Biomedicine[9]. **22**

It is highly positive for Portugal to ratify the Convention. Nevertheless, the Portuguese State should have first legislated on matters such as research on the embryos, both going ahead with the radical solution to ban non-therapeutic experimentation or regulating the circumstances in which it may take place. **23**

With respect to the human genome, the thinking of the Portuguese scientific community is in complete harmony with the norms outlined in Chapter IV of the Convention. The inertia of our legislator is the aspect that could lead to problems in the future, particularly in the areas of pre-implantation diagnosis (where there is no criminal protection for the embryo) and in the insurance business and labour relations. We believe that ratification of the Convention should be accompanied by legislative and supervisory measures that aim to guarantee the principles of non-discrimination and the protection of our genetic heritage. However, the recent ratification of the Convention and the additional Protocol is a very important step forward to a new juridical approach to the bio-ethical problems in Portugal. **24**

[8] See Law no. 12/93 22 April – Organ and tissue removal and transplantation.

[9] Parecer 30/CNECV/2000 on the ratification of the Convention for the Protection of the Rights of Man and the Dignity of the Human Being in the light of Application of Biology and Medicine, (www.cnecv.gov.pt). The National Ethics Board points out that certain provisions of the Convention (concerning consent, the human genome, research on embryos and the utilisation of part of the body) lack weighting in the revision of Portugal's domestic legislation. In those areas where domestic regulations already exist, the rules on consent by incapable persons for the conduct of clinical trials and the transplantation of organs and tissues should be re-examined.

25 The number of countries that did not ratify the Convention is losing its weight while those where the Oviedo Convention is part of law is increasing. It is, indeed, a signal that the Convention is and will be a very important international standard in bio-law.

B. Cases

1. Sentence of *Supremo Tribunal de Justiça* (STJ, Supreme Court) 22 May 2001 (*Colectânea de Jurisprudência* (*Acórdãos do Supremo Tribunal de Justiça*) [CJ] STJ, IX, 2001, T- II, 102–105)

a) Brief Summary of the Facts

26 The defendant was guilty of an accident that caused physical injuries to J. Santos, which were the necessary cause of his death. Afterwards, although he perceived the accident, the driver drove away and did not provide for any help to the victim.

27 The insurance company compensated the damages to the family, and sued the driver to reimburse the company.

28 According to art. 19 DL 162/84, 18 May (Compulsory Insurance against Civil Vehicle Liability) the insurance company has the right to reimburse against the driver in cases of intentional accident; authors or accomplices of robbery, thieves, or *furtum usus* of the vehicle, driving without license, driving under the influence of alcohol or drugs, falling of load due to negligent packing, suspension of the insurance guarantee, non-presentation of the vehicle to the compulsory periodic inspections (Only in this case, does the law explicitly allow the driver to prove that the accident had no causal link with it, and thus he may put aside the company's right of reimbursement).

b) Judgment of the Supreme Court

29 The STJ decided that, as the accident was due to the guilt of the defendant, who immediately abandoned the injured, without searching for help, the plaintiff (the insurance company that paid the compensation) has the right to be reimbursed against the defendant. In addition, the plaintiff needs neither to allege nor to prove that the abandonment was the cause of any damage or any aggravation.

c) Commentary

30 The STJ did not follow, in this sentence, its previous case law, according to which the insurance company has to allege and to prove that the abandonment of the injured person are the adequate cause of the aggravation of the damages

2. Sentence of the *Relação de Coimbra* (RCb, Court of Appeal in Coimbra) 20 February 2001 (CJ, XXVI, 2001, T-I, 42–44)

a) Brief Summary of the Facts

The defendant had exclusive fault in causing an accident. The vehicle ran out of control and collided head-on with the other vehicle causing material damage. The defendant was driving with 1.58g/l alcohol in blood. The defendant alleged, but did not prove, that the bursting of a tyre was the real cause of the accident. **31**

b) Judgment of the Court of Appeal

The Court of Appeal in Coimbra holds that, although the defendant was driving with more alcohol than accepted by law, he may not be condemned to pay the reimbursement to the insurance company if he proves that there is no causal link between the alcohol abuse and the accident. **32**

In this case, it was not proved that the abuse of alcohol had worsened the capacities of the driver, that he was over-confident in his driving skills or could not respond appropriately. On the other hand, the defendant proved neither that he had perfect control of his intellectual capacities nor that the bursting of a tyre was the real cause of the accident. **33**

Thus, the Court decided to condemn the defendant to reimburse the insurance company. **34**

c) Commentary

This sentence deals with the problem of the burden of proof when the insurance company wants the reimbursement from the driver who exceeded the legal limits of alcohol consumption (0.5 g/l). **35**

There are three different opinions in the jurisprudence **36**

1) The insurance company has the burden of proof that there is a casual link between the alcohol abuse and the accident;
2) If one proves that the driver was exceeding the legal limits of alcohol consumption, the insurance company automatically has the right to be reimbursed;
3) If it is proved that the driver was violating the legal limits, the driver does not pay the reimbursement only if he proves that the alcohol had no causal interference in the accident.

This sentence followed this last doctrine[10]; but the defendant did not prove that the alcohol abuse had no causal link with the disaster. **37**

[10] See in the same direction, Sentences of RCb of 23 January, 13 March and 15 May 2001 (at http://www.dgsi.pt)

38 In those two sentences, one can notice that this is a very controversial issue in the Portuguese courts and the sentence may be somewhat uncertain.

3. Sentence *Relação do Porto* (RPt, Oporto's Court of Appeal) 5 February 2001 (CJ, XXVI, 2001, T-I, 205–208)

a) Brief Summary of the Facts

39 The plaintiffs and the defendant agreed to an organised tour contract to the United States. Because of bad planning of the plane schedules (Vigo-Madrid-New York), the plaintiffs did not arrive in time in Madrid in time to catch the plane to New York. They only flew the following day, but consequently they could no longer entirely use the programme. The plaintiffs suffered great frustration and anxiety; they lived two days of intense stress in Madrid as well as the last day in New York. They were nervous, angry and emotionally disturbed.

b) Judgment of the Court of Appeal in Oporto

40 The Court condemned the defendant to compensate the plaintiffs for non-pecuniary damages. The anxiety, frustration and discomfort caused by living in an airport, due to the bad organization of the plane schedules; the consequent disorganisation and shortening of the tour are damages, for the gravity of which, compensation is deserved. One uses these organised tours exactly to avoid these kinds of problems.

41 Anyway, in this case, there is only slight negligence and the damage is transitory. Thus, the fair compensation shall not be comparable to the violation of physical integrity or honour, for loss of a relative, or other cases where the damage is hard and long lasting.

42 So, the Court of Appeal lowered the compensation from € 1250 (first instance) to € 250 for each of the plaintiffs (father, mother and two children).

c) Commentary

43 There are some doubts in the Portuguese doctrine whether non-pecuniary damages can be compensated in contract liability.

44 Anyway, organised tours are regulated by DL 209/97 of 13 August (amended by DL 12/99, of 11 January). According to art. 39, "travel agencies are liable towards their clients for due execution of the contractual obligations". In order to protect the client, art. 41, subs. 1 provides that the travel agency must contract a civil liability insurance. Subs. 2 determines that the insurance must obligatorily guarantee "sent. c) the compensation of pecuniary and non-pecuniary damages caused to clients or third parties, for acts or omissions of the agency or its agents." This means that this law clearly admits compensation of non-pecuniary damages in these cases.

On the other hand, Portuguese jurisprudence accepts, in a broad way, the compensation of non-pecuniary damages in contractual liability. 45

4. Sentence RCb 8 May 2001 (in CJ, Ano XXVI, 2001, T-III, 9–10)

a) Brief Summary of the Facts

The plaintiff was a victim of a traffic accident on the highway because the vehicle hit a dog, which suddenly appeared on the road. In the area where the accident took place, the fence was in a bad condition, allowing the entry of a dog. It was not proved where the dog came in nor if the defendant was guilty of that fact. 46

b) Judgment of the Court of Appeal

According to Portuguese law, the concessionaire of the highway has the duty to "fence the highway in all its extension" (Basis XXIII, subs. 11, sent a) do DL 315/91, 20 August and Basis XXII, subs. 5, sent. a) DL 294/97, 24 October). In this case it was proved that the fence near the accident was damaged. 47

The Court decided that, when access to the highway depends on the obligation to pay the toll as a counterpart of a safe and comfortable utilization by the client, one shall apply the rules of contractual liability. Thus, the concessionaire had the burden of proof to demonstrate that it could not be faulted for the presence of the dog (art. 799, subs. 1 Civil Code). 48

According to this, the Court condemned the defendant to compensate the plaintiff. 49

c) Commentary

Jurisprudence is starting to accept Prof. Sinde Monteiro's[11] doctrine, according to which "between the user and the concessionaire of the highway there is a *sui generis* contract, the main duties of which are the payment of the toll and its utilisation with comfort and safety" (see Sentence STJ of 17 February 2000). Thus there is a reversal of the burden of proof due to the contractual regime. 50

Traditionally, the jurisprudence considered that the payment of the toll was a tax for using a *public service*. Thus one could not affirm that there was a contract. Therefore, they applied the provisions of tort law, which are less advantageous for the user of the highway, notably in terms of *onus probandi*. 51

These few recent sentences are thus a very important reversal of case law. 52

[11] *Cf.* Sinde Monteiro, Acidente na Auto-estrada provocado pelo atravessamento de um animal, and Acidentes na auto-estrada – natureza e regime de responsabilidade da concessionária, *Revista de Legislação e de Jurisprudência* (RLJ), Ano 131, 132 and 133.

5. Sentence of *Supremo Tribunal Administrativo* (STA, Administrative Supreme Court) of 1 February 2001 (in [2001] *Justiça Administrativa* JA, March/April, No. 26, 77, only the Summary Available)

a) Judgment of the Court of Appeal

53 The Portuguese State is liable for pecuniary damages caused by the defective functioning of its justice organs if it wrongfully and faultily violates the right to execute a court sentence (art. 205, subs. 3 Constitution), namely the right to realize the seizure in a "reasonable time" (according to Art. 6, subs. 1 European Convention on Human Rights, and art. 10 of the Portuguese Constitution).

54 To determine the "reasonable time" one must consider the concrete lawsuit, notably the time taken by the diligence, its circumstances, its complexity and the conduct of the Court services.

b) Commentary

55 After several lawsuits and condemnations at the Commission and the European Court on Human Rights[12], our Courts are starting to find the Portuguese State liable to compensate the damage caused to citizens by the delay in the administration of justice

C. Literature

Books

1. Mário Júlio de Almeida Costa, *Direito das Obrigações*, (Law of Obligations), (Coimbra, Almedina, 9th edn. 2001)

56 Prof. Almeida Costa's handbook is one of the most important edited in Portugal, and it is also well-known in Brazil. In this 9th edition, the author offers us an up-to-date manual, regarding legislation, jurisprudence and doctrine.

[12] See Estima Jorge vs. Portugal, 21 April 1998 (16/1997/800/1003); Ferreira de Sousa e Costa Araújo vs. Portugal, 14 December 1999 (Petition no. 3657/97); Freitas Lopes vs. Portugal, 21 December 1999 (Petition no. 36325/97); Garagens Pintosinho, Lda, vs. Portugal, RLJ, Ano 123°, no. 3799, 293 *et seq.*; Guinhcho vs. Portugal, CJ, Ano IX, 1984, T-3, 17–22; Marques Gomes Galo vs Portugal, 23 November 1999 (Petition no. 35592/92); Martins Moreira vs. Portugal, 26 October 1988, Série A, no. 143, *Documentação e Direito Comparado*, 1988 (*Separata do BMJ*), no. 33/34, 1988, 412–436; Nunes Violante vs. Portugal, 8 June 1999 (Petition no. 33953/96); Santos vs. Portugal, 23 March 1994 (6/19993/401/479), Serie A, no. 286-A; Silva Pontes vs. Portugal, 23 March 1994 (6/19993/401/479). See, João Pereira, *A Responsabilidade Civil por Actos Jurisdicionais*, pp. 195–202.

2. Luís Menezes Leitão, *O Ensino do Direito das Obrigações*, (Law of Obligations and Its Teaching), (Coimbra, Almedina, 2001)

Proofs for Associated Professor, Faculty of Law – University of Lisbon.

The author presents the history of the teaching of the Law of Obligations in Portugal, since the reform of *Marquês de Pombal* (XVIII Century) and the reception of jus-rationalism, until our time. It allows the reader to follow the most important movements of contemporaneous European legal thinking: the Codification and *L'école de l'Exegèse* (XIX Century), from which resulted our first Civil Code in 1867; the arrival of the German *Pandekten* to Portugal (beginning of the XXth Century); the realization of the new Civil Code (in force since 1967) and, finally, the recent trend towards a European Civil Code. 57

Secondly, Leitão proposes a programme and a method of teaching the Law of Obligations that includes (as usual in Civil Law countries) torts, restitution and contracts. 58

3. João Álvaro Dias, *Dano Corporal–Quadro Epistemológico e Aspectos Ressarcitórios*, (Body Damage), (Coimbra, Almedina, 2001)

PhD in Civil Law at the Faculty of Law – University of Coimbra.

Dias analyses the *status* of bodily integrity, within the context of the *Risiko-Gesellschaft*. He looks at the historical evolution: from the fault's dogma to the socialization of the risks and damages. 59

The concept of 'body damage' ("dommage corporel", "danno biologico") is studied, taking into consideration, mainly, the Italian, French and Spanish experience and doctrine. He discusses various methods to evaluate the body damage, but the author discusses, above all, the advantages and disadvantages of the evaluation lists *(barêmes)*. 60

Afterwards he explains the pecuniary consequences of body damage, and analyses the doctrine of *perte de chance*. When the injured has no activity, or receives no income for his work, is a minor, who is still studying or is a high competition sportsman, the concept of body damage is of great importance, but, nevertheless, it is very hard to evaluate the damages. 61

Regarding the non-pecuniary consequences, Dias studies the damage of death. Furthermore he defends the application of the "quantum doloris", the aesthetical damage and the "loss of amenities of life" (*perte de joie de vivre, dano esistenziale, préjudice d'agrément*) 62

Finally Dias looks at particular situations, such as: clinical research, medical interventions, assisted reproduction, pre-natal diagnosis and the human genome. In the last chapter, he studies the 'wrongful life actions' and also neglected or sexually abused minors 63

4. Jorge Sinde Monteiro, *Relatório sobre o Programa, Conteúdo e Métodos de uma Disciplina de Responsabilidade Civil (para um Curso de Mestrado)*, (Tort Law-Programme of an LL.M. Course), (Coimbra, 2001)

Proofs for Cathedratic Professor.

64 The author shows how in different countries, different systems of tort law have been developed. As in England we find particular torts, in France we find a general clause of compensation of damages caused with fault (art. 1382 *Code Napoleon*), and in Germany the BGB was more strict and demanded wrongfulness. The Portuguese Civil Code followed the German model.

65 Monteiro offers us the novelties that are showing up all over Europe. At the national level, in Switzerland and in Germany, there are important renewals in their domestic tort law. At an international level, one learns about the important projects of unification of European private law: "The Principles of European Contract Law" (LANDO Commission) and the UNIDROIT Principles for International Commercial Contracts. In the field of tort law there is the European Group on Tort Law and the European Civil Code Group. The author, among many dogmatic changes, points out that the abstract-objective criteria of fault will probably be given up (see the draft bill of the law of obligations in Switzerland and the results of the research groups).

66 Monteiro pronounces the requisites of tortious liability: wrongful act or omission, fault, causation and damages. But, the novelty in the Portuguese doctrine is that he defends that the scope of protection of the norm should also be considered as an autonomous requisite.

67 In our law, besides the general clause of liability (art. 483 Civil Code), there are two particular cases: offence against consideration and credit (art. 484) and damages caused by following advice and recommendations. A new special tort is related with the certification service providers (bill on electronic signature and the Directive 1999/93/EC) and others will come for the online service providers with the Directive 2000/31/EC (Directive on electronic commerce)[13].

5. Pedro Caetano Nunes, *Responsabilidade Civil dos Administradores perante os Accionistas*, (Managers' Liability Towards the Shareholders), (Coimbra, Almedina, 2001)

68 This book is divided into 3 parts. Firstly, there is a comparative law study, with special attention given to the law in the United States. The author analyses

[13] Monteiro studies this issue in: Assinatura electrónica e certificação (A Directiva 1999/93/CE e o Decreto-Lei no. 290-D/99, de 2 de Agosto), in [2001] RLJ, 261–272. The author analyses the regime of the Directive on a Community framework for electronic signatures. He compares it with the Portuguese law (DL 290-D/99 of 2 August), and the model of the United States. One should note that art. 6 of the Directive creates a regime of presumed fault for the certification service provider.

managers' liability in the cases of transactions in control and explains the business judgment rule.

Secondly, Nunes explains the general regime of managers' liability towards the shareholders, and finally, he concentrates upon the cases of transactions to control the corporation. 69

In terms of tort law dogmatic, this book explains some situations where one can compensate pure economic losses. 70

6. Alexandre Dias Pereira, *Informática, Direito de Autor e Propriedade Tecnodigital*, STVDIA IVRIDICA 55, BFDUC, (Coimbra, Coimbra Editora, 2001), § 45.7, pp. 516–527

The author addresses an important copyright issue of electronic commerce and information society services: the liability of online service providers within the European legal framework established for by Directives on electronic commerce and copyright in the information society. In particular, the author analyses how the "three-step test" provided for under the new WIPO treaties (December 1996) has been applied at community level to the definition of the right of reproduction concerning activities of "mere conduit" (carriers and access providers), "system caching" and "hosting"; moreover, the provision of information location tools ("browsers", "crawlers", "hyper-linking" and "meta-tags") and the "no monitoring obligation" are also addressed, comparing the European legal framework with the regime of the U.S. Digital Millennium Copyright Act of October 1998. 71

7. João Aveiro Pereira, *A Responsabilidade Civil por Actos Jurisdicionais (Tort Liability for Jurisdictional Acts)*, (Coimbra Editora, 2001)

The author analyses the concept of jurisdiction. Then he presents several kinds of responsibility: the political, the constitutional and the social. The legal liability is analysed in the criminal, disciplinary and civil perspectives. This last one is developed and the book has historical and comparative law elements. 72

There was a modification of the "Judges Statute" *(Estatuto dos Magistrados Judiciais)*. Nowadays judges are also liable when they acted with grave negligence[14] (and not only in the traditional cases of *dolus*). However, one can sue the State, who pays the compensation to the citizen; afterwards the State may demand reimbursement from the judge. 73

In cases of judicial mistake, there are only few cases where it is possible to sue for compensation. Those are the cases of pre-trial detention and unfair condemnations. However, in the first case, the law imposes a strong limitation: the judge must have made a grave mistake when applying the law. In practice, 74

[14] See L 143/99 of 31 August.

there are very few cases where the plaintiff obtains compensation. In the second situation, one can only claim for compensation after a revision sentence.

75 The author also discusses whether this regime may be applicable to other entities such as: arbitrators, jurors, social judges, substitute judges and experts.

76 The last chapter develops the issue of mal-functioning of the justice system, especially by violation of justice in due time. The European Court on Human Rights has condemned the Portuguese State several times for violation of the "the reasonable time" in the administration of justice.

8. João Vaz Rodrigues, *O Consentimento informado para o acto médico no ordenamento jurídico português (Elementos para o estudo da manifestação da vontade do paciente)*, (Informed Consent in Medical Interventions), (Coimbra, Coimbra Editora, 2001)

77 This book addresses the issue of patient's informed consent on medical interventions.

78 The author pays special attention to the cases where Portuguese law requires a written consent: pre-natal diagnosis, abortion, medically assisted procreation, transplantation of tissues and organs among living human beings, clinical research in human beings, some surgical interventions on persons suffering from mental illness and genetic tests.

79 The validity of consent is analysed. The most relevant issues are the patient's competence, the duty to inform, and the respect for the *bonos mores* ("gute Sitten") and the *public order.* Afterwards, J. Rodrigues also studies the cases of treatments not requiring consent; the therapeutic privilege and the "living wills".

80 Finally, the author analyses the (scarce) Portuguese Jurisprudence on the informed consent issue.

9. A.G. Soares/J.M. Santos/M.J.R. Mesquita, *Seguro Obrigatório de Responsabilidade Civil Automóvel, Direito Nacional, Direito Comunitário, O Sistema de Carta Verde, Anotados e Comentados, (Compulsory Vehicle Insurance Liability: National, European and International Law with Comments)*, (Coimbra, Almedina, 2nd edn. 2001)

81 This book is a compilation of laws and international conventions, with notations and comments. This deals with the regime of automobile tort liability and the compulsory insurance scheme.

82 The book is divided in three parts. The first, is dedicated to the national law, and includes legislation, the regulations and the norms of the Portuguese Insurance Board.

The second part deals with the European law: the Directives, the Decisions and the Recommendations of the Commission, and the Jurisprudence of the European Union Court of Justice. Finally, it explains the system of the International Motor Insurance Card, the Geneva Recommendations, the Multilateral Agreements between the national insurance services and the reference to some foreign domestic legislation. **83**

It is a practical book, but the author addresses, at the same time, the theoretical problems. **84**

10. Dário Moura Vicente, *Da Responsabilidade Pré-Contratual em Direito Internacional Privado*, (Culpa in Contrahendo in International Private Law), (Coimbra, Almedina, 2001)

PhD, Faculty of Law, University of Lisbon.

This is a PhD thesis in the subject of Private International Law. Nevertheless, the author conducts very important research in the fields of tort and contractual liability and *culpa in contrahendo*. **85**

In Chapter I (pp. 93–237), Vicente offers a rich analysis of civil liability in contemporaneous private law. The comparative study includes Germany, France, Italy, England, the United States and Portugal. With this book one can understand the different tort law systems and the difficulties that exist in the process of the unification of European private law. **86**

Journals and Law Reviews

1. António Menezes Cordeiro, Os Direitos de Personalidade na Civilística Portuguesa, (Personality Rights in Portuguese Civil Law), [December 2001] *Revista d Ordem dos Advogados* (ROA) 61, III, 1229–1256.

As Cordeiro writes, "the XXth Century was the period of the contracts and its refinement, through "Treu und Glauben", and the XXIst Century can well be the time of the rights of the person…" This article drafts the historical evolution of personality rights in the legislation, doctrine and jurisprudence in Portugal. **87**

The author points out that the 1867 Civil Code was one of the Codes that gave more value to "personality rights". One should note that this Code came into force the same day of the abolition of the death penalty.[15] **88**

The XXth Century was, thus, dominated by a dictatorship that lasted approximately 50 years and jurisprudence was not very audacious. For the past 20 years – following the general development and opening of society – there has **89**

[15] Portugal was one of the first countries in the world to abolish the death penalty, 1 July 1867.

been an increasing study and implementation of tort liability for the violation of personality rights. In the last 10 years, it became common ground. One should point out the sentences recognising: the right to life, namely to compensate the death (a); the consecration of the right to a good environment (b); the right to health, to rest and to tranquillity (c); and the reinforcement of right to honour, reputation and credit, mostly by offences perpetrated by the mass media (d).

2. Joaquim Sousa Dinis, Dano Corporal em Acidentes de Viação, (Body Damage in Vehicle Accidents), CJ (STJ), Ano IX, 2001, Tomo I, 5–12

90 This article provides a very efficient and practical method of evaluation of body damage.

91 Concerning non-pecuniary damages, in case of death the court must compensate the damage "lost of life" (1), the damages suffered by the victim before death (2) and the damages suffered by the relatives (3) [art. 496º, subs. 2 and 3 Civil Code[16]].

92 The compensation of the damage-death shall be fixed at highest rank (in Portugal it is around € 25,000)[17].

93 The second damage depends on the subjective suffering and its duration. The third shall never be higher than the first (the lost of life), and we shall take into

[16] Art. 496 *Non-material damage*
For the determination of compensation, regard must be had to non-material damage which, because of its seriousness, deserves the protection of law.
Where a victim dies, the right to compensation for non-material damage shall be available, jointly, to a spouse who is legally separated… and to the children or other descendants; failing the latter, to the parents or the ascendants; and, finally, to the brothers and sisters or nephews and nieces representing them.
The amount of compensation shall be fixed equitably by the court, having regard in any event to the circumstances mentioned in art. 494; in the event of death, regard may be had not only to non-material damage suffered by the victim but also to such damage suffered by the persons entitled to compensation by virtue of the foregoing paragraph.

[17] After the tragic downfall of the Bridge in the Douro (Entre-os-Rios), the Government immediately assumed its liability and asked the Ombudsman to give its opinion on the criteria one should use to compensate the relatives of the victims (See, Resolution of the Council of Ministers no. 29-A/2001, 9 March). In those *Criteria presented by the Ombudsman* (see *www.provedor-jus.pt)* the following was defined: a) to establish global compensation for the death-damage and the non-pecuniary damage suffered by the victims of € 50,000. The Ombudsman defends that every human life has the same dignity and that implies the same compensation to everyone, and it is not possible to evaluate the different suffering of the victims as they were drowning in the River Douro. Subjective circumstances are irrelevant (such as the "social value of the victim" or the "affection of the victim to life").
The Ombudsman defended the following compensation for non-pecuniary damages suffered by third parties (the relatives): € 20,000 for the consort, descendants and ascendants in first degree; € 15,000 for ascendants and descendants in 2nd degree and € 5,000 for the other relatives.
In this document the Ombudsman also defines the criteria that shall apply to calculate the patrimonial damages suffered by the relatives (above all, the right to alimony and support) [see art. 495º, no. 3 Civil Code].

account the grade of the relatives, their relationship, the subjective suffering, and so on. Dinis defends that, in cases of an intense relation, the judge shall establish, as a minimum, € 5,000 for each relative.

In cases of total or partial incapacity, he follows the traditional criteria of *quantum doloris*, aesthetical damage, the "loss of amenities of life", the sorrow and the hospital reclusion.[18] 94

To compensate patrimonial damages, he defends that one should take into consideration the age of the victim, the life expectancy, the income, and the cost of living. The same applies to the situations of partial incapacity, but we should add the degree of incapacity and the possibility of changing activity. 95

Dinis defends the introduction of the computerized reconstitution of the accident and the system of *Barèmes*. This model aims at promoting the equality principle and allows the courts to compensate more precisely for the body damage. 96

Finally, he studies the case of impotency, due to traffic accidents (or others). The author thinks that, not only the injured has a right to be compensated, but also the spouse. The ground therefore would be the fact that, according to matrimonial law, there is a "conjugal duty" that corresponds to a right of the consort to keep a normal sexual relationship. "Thus, the sexuality, at least within a marriage, can be seen as a personality right". He also questions if this same doctrine should be applied to unmarried couples or even friends. 97

3. Luís Menezes Leitão, A responsabilidade civil na *internet*, (Tort Law in Internet), ROA 61, I, 171–192

Leitão presents several situations which can lead to liability in the internet, especially, the liability of online service providers in view of the Directive on electronic commerce (Directive 2000/31/EC). 98

[18] See, for example, Sentence of RCb 29 May 2001. The following compensations were decided:
(1) € 10,000 to the victim who suffered an "important" *quantum doloris* during 5 months of incapacity, a "moderate" aesthetical damage and the sequel and suffering that resulted from a fracture and a crane-encephalic traumatism and having fixed a partial permanent incapacity of 20%;
(2) € 3,500 to a 16 year-old injured for the "moderate" *quantum doloris* during 2 months of incapacity and the "moderate" aesthetical damage;
(3) € 7,500 to a 12 year-old child who suffered a "considerable" *quantum doloris* during 5 months of incapacity, medium aesthetical damage and the sequels and suffering that resulted from an abdominal traumatism and the right perineum fractures and the left tibia;
(4) € 12,500 to a 59 year-old woman who suffered "important" *quantum doloris* during 9 months of incapacity, the "medium" aesthetical damage and the sequels and suffering that proceed from a traumatism trans-thoracic with a fracture of the pelvis, a sacra-iliac dislocation, a retro-pernea haematoma and ravage of the left leg, a partial permanent incapacity of 25% was fixed.

99 These problems arise from the violation of copyright and industrial property rights. The author examines European and American jurisprudence and he discusses the possibility of imposing restrictions on the access to the net.

100 Secondly, he defends the application of the regime of liability for defective products[19] (strict liability) for the online products, when they are functionally equivalent to those transmitted outside the net (*e.g.* on discs).

101 Afterwards, Leitão analyses the Directive's liability regime. He considers the cases of content provider, the access providers, intermediary service providers and the hosting provider.

102 He gives special importance to the fact that there is no general obligation to monitor, since this means the exclusion of the *vicarious liability* (be it strict liability or even in case of *culpa in vigilando*). In this regard the Directive represents an important safeguard of the development of online services.

[19] DL 383/89, 6 November and DL 131/2001 of 24 April, on Defective Products Liability.

XV. Spain

María Paz García Rubio and *Javier Lete*

A. Legislation

1. *Real Decreto de 12 de enero de 2001, por el que se aprueba el Reglamento sobre la responsabilidad civil y seguro en la circulación de vehículos a motor*[1]

The Royal Decree contains the new regulation on the Road-Traffic Liability, and replaces the previous legislation of 1986. 1

2. *Decreto de 12 de junio de 2001, modificando el Decreto de 22 de febrero de 2000, por el que se establecen las normas sanitarias aplicables a las piscinas de uso público*[2]

This is a regulation which forms a part of the legal system in Catalonia. It refers to the health measures in the public use swimming pools. Although it is not a norm about tort, its purpose is the prevention of accidents. 2

B. Cases

1. *Tribunal Constitutional* (Spanish Constitutional Court, TC); 24 May 2001[3]: Noise and Fundamental Rights

a) Brief Summary of the Facts

The plaintiff of the defence (*amparo*) before the Constitutional Court was a woman who lived in a noisy area of the city of Valencia. She claimed PTA 649,280 (€ 3,902) from the Town Council to compensate for non-pecuni- 3

[1] *Boletín Oficial del Estado* (BOE) no. 12, 13 January 2001.

[2] *Diario Oficial de la Generalitat de Cataluña,* no. 3092.

[3] www.tribunalconstitucional.es/Stc2001/STC2001-119.htm (cmt. by J. Egea Fernández, Ruido ambiental, intimidad e inviolabilidad del domicilio: STC 119/2001, de 24 de mayo, 1/2002, www.indret.com.

ary loss for infringement of the fundamental rights to health, invasion of privacy and immunity of the domicile. The Town Council did not respond, and the woman claimed to the Administrative Court through the special way of the jurisdictional protection of the fundamental rights (*Ley Orgánica de protección jurisdiccional de los derechos fundamentales de la persona de 26 de diciembre de 1978*). As the Courts refused the appeal, the plaintiff has recourse to the Constitutional Court.

b) Judgment of the Constitutional Court

4 The Constitutional Court confirms the opinion of the European Human Rights Court saying that some environmental torts could mean an invasion of the privacy of people. The Court added that as the case of the noise implied a danger to the health of the people, this situation would mean an interference with the constitutional human right to a physical or moral integrity.

5 However, in this case, the Constitutional Court considered that the plaintiff had not proved the personal injury and that it had been impossible to establish the causal relationship between the noise and the health problem of the plaintiff.

c) Commentary

6 This constitutional decision is not a decision about tort. It is a case in which the person who had suffered personal injuries caused by excessive noise claims the liability of the Town Administration. As a consequence of the passivity of the Administration, the plaintiff claimed to the Administrative Court, through the special way of the jurisdictional protection of the fundamental rights and the claim finished before the Constitutional Court.

7 The Constitutional Court refuses the constitutional protection (*amparo*), because it did not consider that the fundamental rights to physical and moral integrity (art. 15 of the Spanish Constitution) and to privacy (art. 18 of the Spanish Constitution) had been violated. There is not an infringement to physical and moral integrity – the Court believes that the plaintiff did not prove that the noise existing in the area where she lived caused the personal injuries suffered by her. There is not an infringement to privacy, since the woman did not prove the level of noise suffered in her home. In this case, the Constitutional Court refused that there had been an infringement to the right to judicial protection (*tutela judicial efectiva*) and emphasized that the right to enjoy a proper environment (Article 45 of the Spanish Constitution) could not be covered by constitutional protection. In our opinion, the protection of the constitutional human rights is not a good way to get reparation of environmental damages.[4]

[4] J. Egea Fernández, January 2002.

2. TC; 17 September 2001[5]: Infringement of Rights of Personality (Privacy)

a) Brief Summary of the Facts

This decision ends a long process started by a person very well-known in Spanish society life, Isabel Preysler, against a magazine that published an interview with a former employee of the plaintiff. **8**

The plaintiff considered that the interview was an infringement of her privacy and claimed compensation for non-pecuniary loss from the journalist, the director of the magazine and the publishing company. The Court of First Instance (*Tribunal de Primera Instancia*) recognized compensation of PTA 5,000,000 pesetas (€ 30,050), and the Court of Appeal (*Audiencia Provincial*) accorded PTA 10,000,000 (€ 60,101). The Supreme Court cancelled the previous decisions and dismissed the claim of the plaintiff, who appealed the protection of the Constitutional Court. The decision of the Constitutional Court recognized the invasion of privacy and ordered to the Supreme Court the restoration of the fundamental right (Judgment 115/2000). The Supreme Court pronounced a new judgment fixing the compensation by the invasion of plaintiff's privacy at PTA 25,000 (€ 150,253). The plaintiff appealed to the Constitutional Court again and the Court declared the nullity of the second judgment of the Supreme Court and the revival of the compensation fixed by the Appeal Court (PTA 10,000,000/€ 60,101). **9**

b) Judgment of the Constitutional Court

The Constitutional Court confirms its opinion about the fundamental right of privacy, recognizing that any invasion of privacy has constitutional significance and it demands compensation in accordance with the importance of the interest and values that are at stake. **10**

c) Commentary[6]

This decision and its consequences have been very important in Spanish law for two reasons. First of all, the merits of the case about the amount of the compensation for non-pecuniary loss flowing from infringement of reputation, invasion of privacy and infringement of the right to image. In the second place, the conflict of jurisdictions between the Supreme Court and the Constitutional Court about who is the competent Court in the determination of the remedies in the case of infringement of constitutional human rights, and particularly infringement of reputation, invasion of privacy and infringement of the right to image. **11**

[5] www.tribunalconstitucional.es/Stc2001/STC2001-186.htm.

[6] P. Salvador Coderch/C. Gómez Ligüerre/A. Luna Yerga/S. Ramos González, *Libertad de expresión y luchas de poder en los tribunales*, Indret, 4/2001; F. Gómez, *El asunto Preysler y la teoría de los juegos*, Indret, 1/2002.

12 The first matter, compensation for non-pecuniary loss flowing from invasion of privacy, is governed expressly by the Act on the Civil Protection of Reputation, Personal and Family Privacy and Image (*Ley Orgánica de protección civil del derecho al honor, a la intimidad personal y familiar y a la propia imagen)*[7]. This Act contains the criteria that are applied to assess the quantum of non-pecuniary loss. These are "the circumstances of the case", "the importance of the infringement actually suffered, which will take into account, if applicable, the circulation or audience of the media through which the infringement was committed", and "the gains obtained by the wrongdoer through the infringement". In the opinion of the Constitutional Court there was invasion of privacy, although the Supreme Court did not recognize the fundamental right, or when it did, fixed very low compensation.

13 In a subsequent case the Supreme Court showed its disagreement with the criterion of the Constitutional Court[8].

3. Tribunal Supremo (Spanish Supreme Court, TS); 7 March 2001[9]: Liability of the Public Administration

a) Brief Summary of the Facts

14 The plaintiffs' son was killed in an accident at school, caused by a blow on his head. The event happened when boys were playing with football-posts, and the victim had hung on the horizontal post, which broke because of the weight of the boy. The school was a State (public) school.

15 The plaintiffs sued the State, the director of the school and the teacher who had to look after the children during the break. The plaintiffs presented their demand in the civil jurisdiction, that is to say before the First Chamber of the Supreme Court.

b) Judgment of the Supreme Court

16 Firstly, the Supreme Court confirms its opinion that a claim for damages can be directed against the insurance company and against the persons who caused the accident. Nevertheless, it is also possible that the claim be directed against only one of them.

17 Secondly, the Supreme Court confirms its opinion that the competent jurisdiction to deal with the claims of patrimonial liability of the Public Administration is the civil jurisdiction, in accordance with the legislation in force at the date of the accident, that is to say, the Act of the Legal System of the Administrative Jurisdiction of 26 December 1956 (*Ley reguladora de la jurisdicción contencioso-administrativa de 26 de diciembre de 1956*).

[7] BOE, 115, 15 May 1982.
[8] STS 5 November 2001, *La Ley-Revista Actualidad Civil*, 6/2002.
[9] [2001] *Repertorio Jurisprudencia Aranzadi* (RJA), 3974.

c) Commentary

The most important question of this judgment is the problem of the conflict between the civil and the administrative jurisdictions, in order to judge the questions of tort when the Public Administration is involved. The First Chamber of the Supreme Court confirms its own competence in the events of liability for damages which occurred in Public Schools, at least when the victim is one of the students in the school. **18**

The main reason of the First Chamber is that the applicable provision has to be the norm in force in the date of the accident, and in this case the norm was art. 41 of the Act for the Legal System of the Administrative Jurisdiction of 1956. This art. 41 awarded the competence to the administrative courts for the liability of the Public Administration only in the cases where the Administration performed with "imperium". **19**

An important group of authors as well as the Third Chamber of the Supreme Court did not share this opinion[10]. After the publication of the Act on the Legal System of Government Administration of 26 November 1992 (*Ley de regimen jurídico de las Administraciones públicas y del procedimiento administrativo común de 26 de noviembre de 1992*), and the new Act on the Administrative Jurisdiction of 13 July 1998 (*Ley reguladora de la jurisdicción contencioso-administrativa de 13 de julio de 1998*) the question is solved: in any case, the liability of the Public Administration must be sued before the administrative courts. **20**

4. TS; 16 July 2001[11]: Liability of the Public Administration

a) Brief Summary of the Facts

The plaintiff's husband, a young man who was 29 years old, was killed in an accident that happened while he was working. The man was an electrician, and he was putting up the Christmas Lights in the streets of a Spanish town, Vigo. Because of the bad state of repair of the public lights, the man was electrocuted, fell down the ladder on which he was working, and died. **21**

b) Judgment of the Supreme Court

The First Chamber of the Supreme Court confirms its opinion about the competence of the civil jurisdiction for the cases of patrimonial liability of the Public Administration. Only in the case that the damage was caused in a public service, would the competence be of the administrative courts. The First Chamber limits the concept of public service to the field of the administrative activity of the Public Administration. **22**

[10] L. Martín Rebollo, La responsabilidad patrimonial de las Administraciones Públicas en España: estado de la cuestión, balance general y reflexión crítica, January-June 1994 *Documentación Administrativa,* 11 *et seq.*

[11] [2001] RJA, 5229.

23 Concerning the prescription of the action for damages caused for the Public Administration in this case, the First Chamber of the Supreme Court applies art. 1.968(2) of the Spanish Civil Code for the delay of prescription (the action of civil liability prescribed by one year), and art. 1.969 for the determination of the *dies ad quo* (from the day on which the action could be put into practice).

c) Commentary

24 The Supreme Court is competent for the claim for compensation raised as a consequence of the death of the plaintiff's husband. The Supreme Court declared that the legislation to apply was the norm in force in the moment when the facts happened.

25 This legislation was very ambiguous. Nevertheless, in the opinion of the Supreme Court, those norms imputed the competence to the civil courts in the cases of liability of the Public Administration, when the acts were not a characteristic administrative activity. However, Spanish authors and courts have always debated this interpretation.

26 The matter is definitely solved with the Act on the Legal System of Government Administration of 1992 and the Act on the Administrative Jurisdiction of 1998. Both of them confer in every case the competence to decide the questions about the liability for damages caused by the normal or non normal operation of the public services to the administrative courts. This concept must include the whole activity of the Public Administration.

5. TS, 3rd Chamber, Administrative Law; 27 March 2001[12]: Liability of the State for Damage Deriving from Legislative Acts

a) Brief Summary of the Facts

27 The plaintiff was a commercial company that claimed the damage deriving from the payment of taxes to the Department of the Treasury, by the application of a statute of 1990 which, some years after, was declared unconstitutional by the Constitutional Court.

b) Judgment of the Supreme Court

28 In accordance with the system of the Administrative Procedure Act of 17 July 1958 (*Ley de procedimiento administrativo de 17 de julio de 1958*) the liability of the State for legislative acts only exists if the damage comes from an act of application of this law and if there is a particular patrimonial sacrifice of rights or a legitimate interest of the victim.

29 The Act on the Legal System of Government Administration expressly established the rule of the liability of the State for legislative acts. According to art.

[12] [2001] RJA, 2665.

139(3), "Public Administrations shall compensate individuals for those enforcements of legislative acts of a non-expropriating kind that they are not obliged to suffer, when it is thus established in the legislative acts themselves and in the terms specified by them".

If an Act is declared unconstitutional, the liability of the law-maker State can exist when the law has occasioned a privation of or injury to the rights or legitimate interests. **30**

c) Commentary

The matter of the liability of the State by legislative acts has been a very controversial question in Spanish law. **31**

When an Act has not been previously declared unconstitutional, both the Constitutional Court (judgments 108/1986, 99/1987 and 70/1988) and the Supreme Court (judgments of 11 December 1992 and 23 May 1995, but see judgment of 16 September 1997), have denied the above mentioned liability. Most of these judgments concern Acts affecting civil servants, like early retirement and incompatibility. **32**

On the other hand, if the law has been declared unconstitutional, the Constitutional Court has established the non retroactiveness of such declaration, thus negating any compensation deriving from damage previous to that declaration and confirming consolidated situations (judgment 45/1999, which declares unconstitutional some articles of the Income Tax Act of 1978). However, some decisions of the Courts believed that the liability of the lawmaker State could exist when the Act has occasioned a privation of or injury to the rights or legitimate interests. **33**

After the promulgation of the Act on the Legal System of Government Administration of 1992, art. 139(1) establishes the general rule for civil liability (strict) for the Administration. **34**

6. TS; 27 September 2001[13]: Non-Liability of the Teachers of a Primary School

a) Brief Summary of the Facts

The plaintiff's daughter was injured in a primary school. While the very young children were playing a non-dangerous game, some of them fell over the plaintiff's daughter, and the girl broke her elbow. Her parents sued the owner of the school, the teachers in charge of the surveillance and the insurance company. **35**

[13] [2001] RJA, 8155.

b) Judgment of the Supreme Court

36 The last paragraph of art. 1.903 of the Spanish Civil Code contains a presumption of negligence that did not need proof, but the defendant has the burden to prove his/her diligence. In this judgment, the result was produced unforeseeably and it excludes the liability for fortuitous harm.

c) Commentary

37 In Spanish law there is a general principle of liability for fault. The Spanish courts and authors think that very young children are generally incapable of negligence[14].

38 In this case, the Supreme Court recognizes that the accident was unforeseeable and so there is not negligence in the behaviour of the teachers who looked after the young children. The defendant has the burden to prove the diligence, but the Court did not consider the need of proof.

7. TS; 13 February 2001[15]: Vicarious or Personal Liability

a) Brief Summary of the Facts

39 The actors were the husband and the sons of a woman who was killed by a tree which fell while trees were being cut in a forest. The action was directed against the people who felled the trees as well as against the director and owner of the company charged with the job. The latter, as a defence, put forward that he was not the employer of the workers who were felling the trees. According to him, he only marked the trees that should be felled.

b) Judgment of the Supreme Court

40 The defendant is the owner of the trees, the administrator of the company and the boss of the group of the workers. Therefore, he is the main individual liable for the tort of the employees, when it was committed without the necessary security measures.

41 This person is liable for his own negligence in not adopting the right precautions for preventing the damage.

c) Commentary

42 The main topic of this sentence is the distinction between the vicarious liability and the personal liability. In this case, the Supreme Court thinks that it is not very important for the problem of the responsibility if the defendant has a labour relationship with the workers. It is most important that he was in charge of the work and had the power of control, and he must be liable for the torts committed by the workers.

[14] L. Díez-Picazo, [1999] *Derecho de daños*, 364 *et seq.*
[15] 4–10 February 2001 *Actualidad Civil*, 23.

However, the Supreme Court says that the boss is liable for his own negligence in failing to adopt the necessary security measures. Such liability is not a vicarious liability – it is not based upon own fault of the defendant. **43**

To recognize the personal liability, the Court prevents the matter of the "relationship of dependence" between the employee and the employer. Nevertheless, this relationship is essential in vicarious liability. **44**

Personal liability for negligence is contained in art. 1.902 of the Spanish Civil Code. In this case, the plaintiff must prove the fault of the defendant. On the other hand, vicarious liability is contained in art. 1.903 of the Spanish Civil Code. In this judgment the defendant could prove his non-fault, but in practice this proof is not possible; vicarious liability is a strict liability. **45**

8. TS; 22 February 2001[16]: The Requirement of Causation

a) Brief Summary of the Facts

The husband and father of the plaintiffs worked for the defendant company. During the job the employee fell down from a height of fifteen metres and died. The defendant put forward that this company had not contracted the victim and moreover that in this case the requirement of causation did not exist. **46**

b) Judgment of the Supreme Court

Negligence is a conduct that includes acts or omissions. In this judgment the negligence was determinated by the actions undertaken without the necessary measures to prevent an accident in the circumstances of the concrete situation. **47**

Causation means a connection between the injury of the plaintiff and the acts which were in its origin. This judgment considers that the causation seems obvious and so it does not need specific proof. **48**

c) Commentary

In Spanish tort law, the element of causation is particularly complex. The requirement of "cause" requires the plaintiff to prove that the conduct of the defendant caused damages recognized legally. However, the Courts, implicitly or explicitly, have often recognised that it must be possible to make causal judgments as a result of its previous experience. In particular, in this case the conduct of the defendant was deemed negligent for the very reasons that it created a risk of the kind of harm suffered by the plaintiff. So it is plausible to infer causation. **49**

[16] 18–24 June 2001 *Actualidad Civil*, 25.

9. TS; 15 March 2001[17]: Amount of Damages

a) Brief Summary of the Facts

50 The plaintiff was a man who, with his son, suffered a car accident caused by the bad state of the road. The defendant was a public institution which had thrown a lot of water on the road. Because of the low temperatures, the car slid on the ice and the plaintiff and his son suffered very serious injuries.

b) Judgment of the Supreme Court

51 The plaintiff claims the damages in his name and in representation of his son, in accordance with art. 162 of the Spanish Civil Code that awards the legal representation of minors to their parents.

52 The situation of this case cannot be considered as a "fortuit" or "vis maior", because the temperature is foreseeable with sufficient exactness. The omission of adequate security measures to avoid the sliding of the vehicles on the road implies the liability of the public institution as a consequence of the fault contained in art. 1.902 of the Spanish Civil Code.

53 The amount of damages recognized by the Court of First Instance cannot be discussed before the Supreme Court. This amount of the compensatory damage is decided at the discretion of the judge of instance. As it is a question of fact, there is not an appeal before the Supreme Court.

c) Commentary

54 This judgment of the Supreme Court raises several questions. The most important of them is the problem of the amount of damages. Generally, as in this case, Spanish courts consider that the assessment of damages is a question of fact that is to be decided by the Courts of First Instance. This opinion is criticized by the authors, who think that this criterion is very arbitrary and also discriminatory.

55 Nevertheless, the Spanish Courts have considered that they can review on appeal or even on cassation when the Court of First Instance has not observed the parameters established by the law (whether they exist) or by "prudence and reasonability".

56 Legislative tariffs exist only in relation to personal injuries and death caused by car accidents, and they were recently introduced by the Road Traffic Liability Act. Some points of this system (but not the whole system of legal tariffs) have been declared unconstitutional by the judgment of the Constitutional Court of 29 February 2000.

[17] 9–15 June 2001 *Actualidad Civil*, 28.

10. TS; 2 March 2001[18]: Foreseeability of the Damage

a) Brief Summary of the Facts

The dead person was a young man who cut trees next to the defendant, who had contracted him to undertake the work with him. Both men intended to extract a large trunk, but they rejected the idea on the ground that it would be impossible. Unlike the employer, who took some firewood to another place with a tractor, the young man decided to cut the large trunk alone. When the defendant returned to the wood, he observed that the trunk struck the young man, killing him. The parent of the victim sued the employer. As a defence, the defendant put forward that he did not order the trees to be felled in his absence and the victim himself decided to do so without the consent of the employer. 57

b) Judgment of the Supreme Court

The Supreme Court reminds that the liability for negligence needs the concurrence of these elements: first, the action or omission of the agent; second, the negligence of the agent; third, the damage (pecuniary or non-pecuniary loss), and finally, the causation, or relationship between the action or omission and the damage caused. 58

The Court confirms its opinion that the action and the damage are two questions of fact that belong to the scope of the Court of First Instance. On the contrary, causation and negligence are two legal questions and the Supreme Court can examine them. For the test of causation, the foreseeability of the damage is essential. In situations in which the damage was unforeseeable, liability does not exist. In this case, the behaviour of the man who died and the resulting death were unforeseeable for the defendant, because he had not ordered the trunk to be cut down during his absence. 59

The causation is a problem of "imputación". The imputation demands that the damage derives from the action or omission of the liable person. In the opinion of the Supreme Court, in this judgment the negligence of the victim was the only cause of his death. 60

c) Commentary

In this judgment, the Court reduces the test of causation link to a question of foreseeability. In our opinion, it is a bad use of the last concept. 61

A person is liable for the damage caused to another person if three elements exist together: the action or omission of the first person, the damage caused to the second person and a special relationship between the action or omission ("cause", by most of decisions and authors). 62

[18] 25 June–1 July 2001 *Actualidad Civil*, 26.

63 The foreseeability of the damage is not an element of the liability. It is a key factor in determining the extent of harm, in according to art. 1.107 of the Spanish Civil Code. Perhaps, it could be interesting to look into the negligence of the defendant, which raises the relationship between negligence and intentional tort. However, we think that whether the damage was or not "foreseeable" is never a problem of causal link.

11. TS; 17 October 2001[19]: Assumed Risk

a) Brief Summary of the Facts

64 The son of the plaintiff died in an accident in a river when the victim practised rafting with a group. The young man had bought a ticket from a sport association in order to carry out the rafting in Gállego River. Because of the bad weather, the water of the river was very dangerous. However, the people participating in the activity were experts in this type of sport. The actor sued both the sport association that organized the activity and the instructor of the activity.

b) Judgment of the Supreme Court

65 In this decision, the Supreme Court remembers the idea of secondary duties of protection (*Schutzpflichten*) in the performance of the contract. Nevertheless, it resorts to issue its decision on the basis of the non-contractual liability. The Court confirms its opinion about the assumed risk. The plaintiff's son assumed the risk of the dangerous sport by contract. The formal defects in the contract documents do not have a causal link with the death of the victim. Furthermore, the defendant's conduct was not negligent.

c) Commentary

66 In many sport activities the risks are inherent in the sport and it is assumed that their participants accept the danger. The concept of "assumed risk" represents the consent of the victim to accept a risk created by the defendant. His consent, express or implied, is a defence (*causa de justificación*) which eliminates the liability of the defendant[20]. Nevertheless, the consent of the victim to accept the risk does not entirely eliminate the duty of care of the defendant, but it can alter the standard by which that duty is met.

12. TS; 31 October 2001[21]: *Culpa in contrahendo* and Tort Liability

a) Brief Summary of the Facts

67 The plaintiff is a bank that sued a pharmaceutical company. The company requested a cash loan of PTA 612,000,000 (€ 3,678,194). When the date of the redemption arrived, the company did not redeem the debt. The bank consid-

[19] Diario La Ley, 5444.
[20] [1999] *L. Díez-Picazo*, 304–305.
[21] [2001] RJA, 9639.

ered that during the contractual negotiations the company had hidden its bad financial situation and so it had committed *culpa in contrahendo*.

b) Judgment of the Supreme Court

The Court confirms its opinion[22] that the negotiations that prepare the conclusion of a contract must be guided by good faith. So, negotiations against good faith and fair dealing can give rise to liability by *culpa in contrahendo*. However, in this case the Supreme Court considered that the bank should have taken the appropriate measures to avoid the risk assumed. The bank could have asked for adequate securities. If it did not do so, it must support the damage arising out of the default. **68**

c) Commentary

The Spanish Civil Code does not expressly know the pre-contractual liability by *culpa in contrahendo*. Nevertheless, this liability can be based on the good faith principle laid down in art. 7 of the Spanish Civil Code. Therefore, according to the authors[23], in the last years some decisions of the Supreme Court recognize that liability caused by *culpa in contrahendo* can exist, at least when one of the parties of the negotiation of a contract breaches the rules arising out of good faith and fair dealing. Then, unlike in German law, the usual opinion is that under Spanish law the liability for *culpa in contrahendo* is considered like a case of non-contractual or tort liability (art. 1.902 of the Spanish Civil Code), however, if the liability is based on misrepresentation, the basis of liability can be contractual. **69**

Nevertheless, to consider a party liable for the losses caused to the other party by *culpa in contrahendo* one must value the action of the other party, too. The other party has to perform with self-responsibility and to care for his own matters. If the party does not do so, it is not possible to claim the damages. If a party is liable by *culpa in contrahendo*, the scope of liability usually remains within the limits of negative interest. However, in exceptional circumstances, the damages could cover the positive interest. **70**

13. TS; 12 January 2001[24]: Medical Liability

a) Brief Summary of the Facts

The plaintiff is a woman who suffered damage as a consequence of a surgical operation in her neck. Her claim of compensation of PTA 30,928,405 (€ 185,883) was rejected by the Court of First Instance, which absolved the doctor who operated on the woman. However, the Court of Appeal established compensation of PTA 7,000,000 (€ 42,071) with the legal interest accrued **71**

[22] TS 26 February 1994.
[23] Mª.P. García Rubio, *La responsabilidad precontractual en el Derecho español* (1999).
[24] [2001] RJA, 3.

from the date of the judgment. The Supreme Court confirms the opinion of the Court of Appeal.

b) Judgment of the Supreme Court

72 Firstly, the Supreme Court declares that the information provided by the doctor about the risks of an operation is necessary to allow the patient to decide whether or not to undergo the operation. Her freedom to decide is contained in art. 10.1 of the Spanish Constitution on the dignity of people, and specially in art. 1.1 of the Spanish Constitution which speaks of freedom as one of the main values of the Spanish legal system. Moreover, the Court reminds that the so-called informed consent of patients is also recognised in the Spanish Health General Act and the International Convention for the Protection of Human Rights and of the Dignity of Human Beings in relation to the Applications of Biology and Medicine.

73 On the other hand, the Court confirms that the onus of proof regarding the information provided lies with the doctor who operated on the plaintiff. He had to give the woman information regarding the risk that the operation could affect her right nerve. Provided with this information, the patient would be able to choose the best option for her.

c) Commentary

74 The fact that sufficient information was not provided to the patient who subsequently suffered the damage is the main reason for awarding her compensation. The doctor, or even the hospital where the operation took place, should have supplied enough information on the complications that could arise after the operation. In accordance with other decisions, the Supreme Court confirms that the doctor is the person responsible to prove that he informed the patient adequately.

14. TS; 5 February 2001[25]: Medical Liability

a) Brief Summary of the Facts

75 The plaintiff is a woman whose two month old child died some days after having been examined in a medical centre where the paediatrician did not observe anything strange, but only a common cold. The claim for damages was rejected by the Court of First Instance and this opinion confirmed by the Court of Appeal and by the Supreme Court.

b) Judgment of the Supreme Court

76 The Court states that the behaviour of the doctor who examined the child was correct and in accordance with the symptoms of a common cold that he showed. In consequence, there is not fault from the doctor, as the only alternative, a chest X-ray, is contra-indicated for children who are still on a milk diet.

[25] 18–24 June 2001 *Actualidad Civil*, 22.

Although the doctor was only a substitute, she was authorized by those responsible for the area, had experience in the work and acted correctly. Therefore, there is not a causal link between the damage and the health service provided. 77

c) Commentary

The Supreme Court applies the traditional doctrine of fault in order to absolve the doctor who examined the child. 78

15. TS; 6 February 2001[26]: Medical Liability

a) Brief Summary of the Facts

The plaintiff is a woman whose husband died in hospital because of a heart attack. He had come to the emergency service of the hospital when he started to feel severe pains in his chest. There, the doctor performed an electrocardiogram and she did not observe any sign of a heart attack; consequently, the patient went home. Some hours later, as he did not feel a sense of relief, the man returned to the emergency service and the doctor performed a new electrocardiogram, providing him with medicine, too. However, the man was sent to his domicile once again. When he went into the hospital for the third time, it was evident that he had suffered a severe heart attack, as a result of which the man died. The plaintiff, on behalf of her children and herself, claims PTA 18,000,000 (€ 108,182) for the death of her husband because of the negligence of the doctor who attended him. As a defence, the defendant put forward that she had acted correctly. The claim was rejected by the Court of First Instance (*Juzgado de Primera Instancia*) and this opinion was confirmed by the Court of Appeal. 79

b) Judgment of the Supreme Court

Unlike the opinion of the Court of Appeal, which considered that the pains of the patient did not have a cardiovascular origin, the approach of the Supreme Court is the opposite. According to the Court, the fact that the condition of the patient did not improve with the medicine supplied by the doctor was not considered adequately, and it was not put in connection with the oppressive nature of the pains and other relevant symptoms, especially the location of the pains and the perspiration of the patient. In view of the circumstances it would have been wise to have had a chest X-ray and the establishment in blood of the CPK enzyme. 80

The Supreme Court declares that it is necessary to take into consideration the professional nature of the obligations of the doctor who was in the emergency service. Therefore she had to act with special diligence in accordance with the circumstances of the people, the time and the place as art. 1.104 of the Spanish Civil Code says. Although the obligation of a doctor is of means, and not of 81

[26] 9–15 June 2001 *Actualidad Civil*, 22.

result, it implies, however, that the doctor must use every means necessary, within the possibilities of the hospital, to try to achieve the recovery of the patient. In this case it required, for example, the doctor who attended the emergency service to have requested the collaboration of the cardiology service.

c) Commentary

82 The decision of the Supreme Court is based on the doctrine of the special diligence which affects some professionals, *e.g.* doctors. The nature of their activities explains that they have to take a great deal of care over their work since it relates to the protection of health. In any case, the Supreme Court applies, by analogy, art. 1.104 of the Spanish Civil Code on the diligence which comes from a contract to the liability arising from tort. It means that professionals in health services have to act with sufficient diligence in accordance with the concrete circumstances that exist in the matter.

16. TS; 24 March 2001[27]: Medical Liability

a) Brief Summary of the Facts

83 A couple, whose newborn went blind after remaining in the incubator of a hospital, claims compensation for damages. The Court of the First Instance rejects the claim and absolves the doctor and the hospital. On the contrary, the Court of Appeal accepts the reasons used by the couple and this opinion is confirmed by the Supreme Court.

b) Judgment of the Supreme Court

84 The Supreme Court states that the blindness of the newborn was caused during his first weeks in the incubator. Surprisingly, the doctor failed to undertake ophthalmologist explorations of the newborn, when they are prescribed between six and nine weeks after the birth. Therefore, he did not act in accordance with *lex artis*, as he maintained a passive attitude without any justification.

85 The doctor and the hospital where the event happened are liable for the damages caused. In this sense, it is not relevant that the doctor was only a collaborator in the hospital, without a labour link with it; the doctor, as a specialist, was chosen by the hospital to attend to the woman in labour, a fact that justifies him being submitted to the internal discipline of the hospital. There is a functional dependence of the doctor and it means that the hospital is liable, directly and jointly with the doctor, for the damages in accordance with art. 1.903 of the Spanish Civil Code.

[27] [2001] RJA, 3986.

c) Commentary

The Supreme Court recognizes the *culpa in eligendo* of the hospital where the doctor worked. Therefore, it is also responsible for the damages caused, the plaintiffs have not to sue both of them jointly. 86

17. TS; 27 April 2001[28]: Medical Liability

a) Brief Summary of the Facts

The plaintiff, a woman who had several children, underwent an operation to be sterilised in order to avoid further pregnancies. Nevertheless, some years after the operation, she gave birth. Her claim of compensation was rejected by the Court of First Instance. Unlike it, the Court of Appeal accepted partly the claim by the woman and this opinion was confirmed by the Supreme Court. 87

b) Judgment of the Supreme Court

The Court declares that the information supplied to the patient was not sufficient. It only consisted of a document drafted by the hospital without any specification on the concrete operation and its consequences. In fact, the hospital itself recognized that it had not provided information on the possibility of new pregnancies. Although this is a case of voluntary medicine, it does not exclude the supplying of all information that can be useful for the patient in order to decide the more adequate operation or treatment. The duty to inform comes from art. 10 of the Spanish Health General Act and is also contained in the Code of Medical Practice; it implies that the information must be exhaustive and comprehensible for the patient. 88

The onus of proof on the information is on the doctor and the health system, as they have the means to do so. 89

c) Commentary

The main topic of this judgment is that complete information about an operation and its future consequences has always to be supplied, even when the treatment is not curative, but voluntary. If not, the consent of the patient will not be valid, and the doctor and the hospital are responsible for the damages. 90

18. TS; 19 June 2001[29]: Medical Liability

a) Brief Summary of the Facts

The plaintiff is a man who fractured one of his arms and, after having been examined by different doctors, suffers irreversible consequences in his right arm and hand. His claim for damages was accepted by the Court of First Instance and confirmed by the Court of Appeal and by the Supreme Court. 91

[28] [2001] RJA, 6891.
[29] [2001] RJA, 4974.

b) Judgment of the Supreme Court

92 The Court declares that the Spanish Consumer Protection Act of 1984 can be applied to damage caused in the course of the activities developed by the national health system. While art. 1 of the Spanish Consumer Protection Act of 19 July 1984 (*Ley general para la defensa de los consumidores y usuarios de 19 de Julio de 1984*) speaks of "user", and the patient is also a user of the health system, art. 28 of the Spanish Consumer Protection Act refers to the liability for the damage caused in the use of goods and services, including health services, in its scope. As all services must include some technical and professional control of quality, the health insurance company which rendered the services is liable for the damage caused.

93 On the other hand, the Supreme Court states that the health insurance company is responsible for the damages, although it can be entitled to claim against the concrete staff who provoked the damages.

c) Commentary

94 Perhaps, the most interesting question is the use of the mentioned artt. 1 and 28 of the Spanish Consumer Protection Act to condemn the health insurance company as responsible for damage caused to the patient as a result of defective attention and treatment. In fact, the health insurance company is considered as a professional in the sense used in consumer law (relationship between professional and consumer or user). The liability is objective, damage is caused without either fault of the patient or intervention of *force majeure*.

19. TS; 17 October 2001[30]: Medical Liability

a) Brief Summary of the Facts

95 The plaintiff is a woman who contracted the AIDS virus after receiving a blood transfusion after a Caesarean birth. The defendant, the hospital where she had been treated, put forward that it had informed the patient about the risks of the transfusion and its consequences. The Court of First Instance accepted the claim of the plaintiff and established compensation of PTA 24,966,396 (€ 150,051) with the legal interest accrued from 1 August 1990 and the paying of the costs. This opinion was confirmed by the Court of Appeal. The Supreme Court rejected the action raised by the defendant.

b) Judgment of the Supreme Court

96 The Supreme Court declares that the hospital did not fulfil its duty to inform. It should have explained the need for the blood transfusion with its risks and consequences clearly. Only in this way should the patient be able to choose among the different options, even not to undergo any treatment. Therefore, the patient's consent is not valid. The Court lays great stress on the fact that if in

[30] [2001] RJA, 8741.

this case the blood transfusion was absolutely necessary, then the hospital should have used blood donated by the patient's family or by any others; but not from the blood health service, since it was not the safest.

c) Commentary

The behaviour of the hospital was negligent, as it did not take into consideration that the patient could be infected with the AIDS virus. Its liability is based on the fact that it omitted to inform the patient about the consequences of the transfusion and also on the absence of precaution. The hospital has not complied with its minimal diligence in the course of its activities. 97

20. TS; 18 October 2001[31]: Medical Liability

a) Brief Summary of the Facts

The plaintiff suffered serious damage as a result of a high risk surgical operation. He was informed about the risks of the surgery, which took place in a private hospital. The result of the operation was caused by a sudden and unforeseeable event without connection to the surgical procedure. Nevertheless, the patient sued the doctor who treated him, the private hospital and the insurance company for damages, as he considered that the defendant had not fulfilled his duty of information, and had broken the *lex artis ad hoc*. The plaintiff claims PTA 250,000,000 (€ 1,502,503) for all damages, and also the legal interest and costs. The claim was rejected by the Court of First Instance (*Juzgado de Primera Instancia*) and by the Court of Appeal and the Supreme Court (*Tribunal Supremo*), as well. 98

b) Judgment of the Supreme Court

At first, the Supreme Court confirms the opinion of the Court of First Instance and of the Court of Appeal, because the assessment of the proof was correct. The Supreme Court, in accordance with its own case law, stresses that it is not a third instance, but only a Court able to value a mistake of law due to the Courts of Instance when they considered the facts. The Supreme Court points out that the plaintiff knew his serious condition perfectly and also the high risks of the surgical operation he was to undergo. Moreover, the Court declares that the plaintiff has not proved that the doctor had omitted the skills and knowledge of his profession (*lex artis ad hoc*). 99

On the other hand, the doctor who performed the operation was not incorporated into the staff of the private hospital which implies that there is not a dependence relationship in order to justify a claim for damages against the private hospital. The Supreme Court only applies art. 1.903 of the Spanish Civil Code on liability by acts or fault of another when a hierarchical or dependence relationship exists between the employee, who caused the damage, and the owner of the hospital where he worked as a doctor. 100

[31] [2001] RJA, 8645.

c) Commentary

101 In this judgment the first question is to determine if an informed consent on the part of the patient existed. His knowledge about his condition and the risk of his treatment (a surgical operation), both provided by the defendant, excludes the possibility of claiming damages for this concept. On the other hand, it is clear that medicine is not an exact science, so the plaintiff cannot claim when the damage was caused by an unforeseeable event without any connection with the behaviour of the doctor.

102 In accordance with art. 1.903 of the Spanish Civil Code, a hierarchical or dependence relationship between the doctor and the owner of the private hospital is necessary to sue the hospital for the damage caused to the plaintiff.

21. TS; 11 October 2001[32]: Product Liability

a) Brief Summary of the Facts

103 The plaintiff is a person who suffered damage due to the explosion of a cigarette lighter. He claims compensation against the manufacturer, which is accepted by the Court of First Instance and diminished by the Court of Appeal. The Supreme Court confirms the opinion of the Court of Appeal, although not the reimbursement of costs.

b) Judgment of the Supreme Court

104 The Court declares that the supplier of the product, the cigarette lighter which exploded, is the responsible for the safety measures of the product and that it should not cause damage on the market. The manufacturer did not manage to prove that it acted with all necessary diligence in accordance with the risks of the product. On the other hand, it was accepted that the user did not manipulate the lighter and so the duty to indemnify is on the manufacturer. Only a *force majeure* would have been a cause to declare that the manufacturer was not liable.

c) Commentary

105 This judgment contains the question of product liability and the principle of the objective liability of the manufacturer. The Supreme Court applies the provisions contained in the Spanish Consumer Protection Act, because at the time of the accident the Spanish Parliament had not approved the Act on Product Liability of 6 July 1994 (*Ley de responsabilidad civil por los daños causados por productos defectuosos de 6 de julio de 1994*), which implemented into Spanish law Directive 85/374.

[32] [2001] RJA, 8735.

22. TS; 22 February 2001[33]: Non-Pecuniary Damage

a) Brief Summary of the Facts

The plaintiff suffered damage when he fell to the ground from the room of a hotel. The balcony collapsed, causing the plaintiff serious injuries. He was treated in a hospital where he was operated on and had to be rehabilitated. However, he became paraplegic for the rest of his life. His claim for compensation was rejected by the Court of First Instance. The Court of Appeal partly accepted the demands from the plaintiff and this opinion was confirmed by the Supreme Court. **106**

b) Judgment of the Supreme Court

The Supreme Court defines the non-pecuniary damage (*daño moral*) as the damage caused in the intimate sphere of a person which usually cannot be expressed in economic terms. It refers to physical or psychical suffering and pain caused by an illegal act. It can be any frustration or damage caused by the temporal or definitive absence of a person as a result of an accident, as well (*e.g.* the loss of the father or mother with regard to the children). **107**

When a person suffers damage caused in an accident and he recovers completely, it is clear that the compensation of the damage includes the non-pecuniary damage. If not, the result would be abusive. However, in the case of this judgment, where the consequences of the accident are serious, forcing the plaintiff to stay in a wheelchair, the reasoning must be different. It is comprehensible that it generates frustration and suffering in the victim, who will be entitled to demand an economic amount as a compensation. **108**

c) Commentary

The notion of non-pecuniary damage has traditionally been recognized in Spanish law in the field of privacy of people with regard to interferences coming from outside. But in this judgment the Court uses the notion of moral damage in connection with physical damage that has been caused to a person. The possibility to indemnify it separately implies that the different feelings included in the concept of moral damage are serious and able to be valued. When the consequences of an accident do not disappear, it could be reasonable to recognize the right to claim special compensation for the moral damage caused to the injured person. **109**

23. TS; 2 February 2001[34]: Liability for Damage to the Environment

a) Brief Summary of the Facts

The plaintiffs are a couple who own a farm, which is affected by the activities of an arids company. They claim for compensation, as they believe that the **110**

[33] 18–24 June 2001 *Actualidad Civil*, 25.
[34] 28 May–3 June 2001 *Actualidad Civil*, 22.

contamination caused by the transformation and transport of the arids, and also the noise of the machinery and the trucks of the company not only affect the conditions of the farm, but the situation of the people living there as well. The claim was accepted by the Court of First Instance, and the amount of the compensation fixed was increased by the Court of Appeal. However, the total amount is not very high, because the Court of Appeal considered that the plaintiffs were aware of the situation when they bought the farm. The Supreme Court establishes a larger compensation.

b) Judgment of the Supreme Court

111 The Court thinks that the development of the activities of the company causes damage for the owners of the farm. They are affected in their quality of life, and Art. 8 of the European Treaty on Human Rights recognizes the right to enjoy the environment. Also art. 45 of the Spanish Constitution contains the same provision.

c) Commentary

112 The main topic of this judgment is the use of the concept of quality of life, and its non-fulfilment as a way to indemnify the damage caused to people affected by certain activities. Nevertheless, it is a bit strange that there is no proof of the damages suffered by the plaintiffs, and even the judgment of the Supreme Court declares that apart from the nuisances coming from the activities of the company, there has not been any disease caused by them.

C. Literature

1. J. Santos Briz, *La responsabilidad civil, Temas actuales* (Montecorvo, Madrid, 2001).

113 The author of this book is a well-known specialist in the law of tort. In this book he collects some articles about matters like negligence, liability for damage to the environment, liability of the Public Administration, professional liability, the liability of minors, compensation for road accidents or product liability.

2. F. Pantaleón (ed), *La responsabilidad y el derecho* (Universidad Autónoma de Madrid. Boletín Oficial del Estado, Madrid, 2001).

114 This book is a collection of works about the relationship between liability and the law. From the point of view of the law of tort, are of special interest the contributions by P. Salvador Coderch (Punitive damages, pp. 139 *et seq.*), L. Díez-Picazo (*Culpa y riesgo en la responsabilidad civil extracontractual*, pp. 153 *et seq.*), F. Pantaleón (*Cómo repensar la responsabilidad civil extracontractual. También de las Administraciones Públicas*, pp. 167 *et seq.*) y L. Martín Rebollo (*Ayer y hoy de la responsabilidad patrimonial de la Administración: un balance y tres reflexiones*, pp. 273 *et seq.*).

3. J. J. Marín López, *Daños por productos: estado de la cuestión* (Madrid, Tecnos, 2001).

The author studies the most important questions about product liability at present. For that purpose, he analyses the EC Green Book on Product Liability. The main objectives are to show a view of this document and offer the *status quaestionis* in the matter. **115**

4. C. Trabado Alvarez, *La responsabilidad civil del artículo 1905 del Código civil. Daños causados por animales* (Septem ediciones, 2001).

This book deals with art. 1.905 of the Spanish Civil Code. This norm refers to the strict liability for damage caused by domestic animals. The liable person is the possessor or the person who uses the animal. **116**

5. M. Martín Casals/J. Ribot/J. Solé, Non-Pecuniary Loss Under Spanish Law, in W. V. H. Rogers (ed.), *Damages for Non-Pecuniary Loss in a Comparative Perspective* (Springer-Verlag Wien New York, 2001), pp. 192–243.

The authors present the situation of non-pecuniary loss in Spain. Unlike what happens in other legal systems, in which non-pecuniary loss is treated restrictively, in Spain pecuniary and non-pecuniary losses stand on an equal footing. The authors deal with the theoretical basis for the award of damages in personal injury and death cases, and in non-personal injury cases, like invasion of privacy, assault and sexual misconduct, interference with freedom or constitutional and human rights or other situations like breach of contract, unfair competition and some specific cases. **117**

6. L. F. Barrios Flores, Responsabilidad por suicidio como consecuencia del tratamiento antidepresivo (el caso Tobin v. Smithkline Beecham), La Ley, 6 December 2001, 1–9.

With regard to a famous case in the USA, the author analyses the liability of a pharmaceutical company because of marketing defects in a medicament for depression. It deals with a problem of product liability; especially a question of warning defects. He studies the problem in American law, and then discusses the question in Spanish law in which the liability for development risks exists in case of medicaments or foods for human use. **118**

7. J. Manrique de Lara Morales, El deber de información y la responsabilidad civil médica en la reciente jurisprudencia del Tribunal Supremo (I y II). A propósito de la Sentencia del Tribunal Supremo de 11 de mayo de 2001, La Ley, 29–30 October 2001.

In Spanish law a doctor has an obligation of information in favour of the patient about the illness, the prognosis and the treatment. This obligation raises a lot of questions. The author of this article analyses some of them. **119**

8. P. del Olmo García, Responsabilidad por daño puramente económico causado al usuario de informaciones falsas, [2001] *Anuario de Derecho Civil,* 257–368.

120 The author analyses the problem of the nature of the liability for false information, opinions or advice in Spanish law. In his opinion, it is a case of delictual liability (*responsabilidad extracontractual*). Unlike other systems, it is not necessary to consider the existence of a contract of information between the party who gives the information and the victim.

9. E. Serrano Alonso, La protección medioambiental: especial consideración de la responsabilidad civil por daños al medioambiente (A propósito de la sentencia de la Audiencia Provincial de Asturias de 10 Abril 2000), [2001] *Actualidad Civil,* 273–301.

121 The author thinks that the law of tort is a good instrument for the prevention and compensation of damage to the environment, although he recognizes that sometimes it is very difficult to identify the causal link and also the amount of the damages. Nevertheless, the author defends the publication of a special Act about this matter.

10. F. Gómez Pomar, Carga de la prueba y responsabilidad objetiva, InDret, 01/2001, www.indret.com.

122 The author studies the judgments of the Supreme Court concerning the onus of proof in negligence claims and the use of some rules like *in res ipsa loquitur.*

11. F. Cerdá Albero, Responsabilidad civil de los administradores sociales, ¿sólos ante el peligro? InDret, 01/2001, www.indret.com

123 This article contains an extensive study about the rules governing the liability of the administrators of corporations. Pursuant to these rules, the author discusses several questions: the action of responsibility of the company or the action of responsibility put into practice by one of the partners or by the creditors of the company.

12. R. Ragués i Vallès, Proceso al buen samaritano, InDret, 02/2001, www.indret.com.

124 The author studies the relationship between the action of saving someone and the law of tort and the existence of a possible liability due to a failure to save someone.

13. C. Gómez Ligüerre, Jurisdicción competente en pleitos de responsabilidad civil extracontractual, 03/2001, www.indret.com

125 The author analyses the questions coming from the existence of four groups of norms and jurisdictions (civil, criminal, administrative and labour) to solve matters on tort.

14. J. M. Silva Sánchez, Ex delicto. Aspectos de la llamada responsabilidad en el proceso penal, 03/2001, www.indret.com

The present article deals, from a new perspective, with the question about the use of the action of liability in criminal procedure. **126**

15. M. Martín Casals/J. Solé Feliu, Anticoncepciones fallidas e hijos no previstos, 03/2001, www.indret.com

The authors deal with some of the questions derived from wrongful conception or pregnancy. In this situation, the mother (or the parents) asserts that the defendant physician was negligent when he performed a medical procedure to prevent conception and however the mother bore a child, which implied an added expense of child rearing. The article focuses upon the causal relationship and the limitations on economic and emotional damages. **127**

16. J. Ferrer Riba, Relaciones familiares y límites del derecho de daños, InDret, 04/2001, www.indret.com.

This paper deals with the relationship between tort and family. Its main concern is the use of the law of tort as a remedy against the non performance of the spousal or parental obligations. **128**

XVI. Sweden

Henrik Sandell

A. Legislation

1. *Skadeståndslagen* (1972: 207) (The Tort Liability Act); *Trafikskadelagen* (1975: 1410) (The Motor Traffic Damage Act); *Brottsskadelagen* (1978: 413) (The Criminal Injuries Compensation Act)[1]

1 The main rules in Sweden on tort are found in *Skadeståndslagen* (1972: 207) (the Tort Liability Act, SkL). SkL has been in force since 1972, with a few changes since then. In 2001 the Swedish Parliament passed bills with some modifications of SkL, *Trafikskadelagen* (1975: 1410) (the Motor Traffic Damage Act) and *Brottsskadelagen* (1978: 413) (the Criminal Injuries Compensation Act)[2]. Since those modifications came into force on 1 January 2002 I will only present some general traits of the modifications.

2 The new provisions strengthen the right to claim damages for non-financial damage (non-pecuniary damage). There is now a clearer provision concerning non-financial damage represented by violation of personal integrity in conjunction with crime. There are new provisions concerning non-financial losses suffered in conjunction with personal injury. For example:

- The right to damages for psychological distress resulting from the death of a close relative through an act constituting grounds for damages, not limited to cases in which the death was wilfully caused. The plaintiff does not have to witness the accident or the action of the crime to be able to raise an action in damages.
- A possibility to reconsider damages for costs and non-financial damages if it is later shown that the assumptions regarding the compensation for damage have not been reasonably correct.

[1] Swedish codes, statutes and ordinances has a notation with year and number in the register of the Swedish Code of Statutes (*svensk författningssamling*, SFS) *e.g. Skadeståndslagen* (1972: 207) (The Tort Liability Act).

[2] *Regeringens proposition* 2000/01: 68, *Ersättning för Ideell skada*.

- Right to damages for non-financial losses, pursuant to the terms of the Tort Liability Act, is transferred to the injured party's heirs if a request for such damages was submitted prior to the death of the injured party.

Commentary

Since 1988 a Governmental Committee worked with modifications regarding non-financial damage. The Committee has presented some Government Official Reports, SOU 1991: 34 regarding the right to damages for non-financial loss for HIV infected persons, SOU 1992: 84 regarding violation of personal integrity in conjunction with crime and the final report, SOU 1995: 33, regarding compensation for non-financial loss in conjunction with personal injury. It took some time after the final report before the modifications were adopted. The Swedish insurance companies have raised questions regarding the lack of investigation concerning the costs for this reform. It is still not clear how the modifications will affect the premiums. However, during the last decade Swedish case-law shows that the Supreme Court has taken the work of the Committee into account, *e.g.* the right to damages for psychological distress resulting from the death of a close relative[3]. 3

2. *Patientskadelagen* (1996: 799) (The Patient Injury Act)

Patientskadelagen (1996: 799) (The Patient Injury Act) is applicable when a person is injured in connection with healthcare and medical care. In *Patientskadelagen*, sec. 5, the legislator declares the scope of healthcare and medical care, the kind of activities that is regarded as healthcare and medical care, *e.g.* activities performed under the Health and Medical Services Act (1982: 763). 4

On 1 October 2001 a new act was added to *Patientskadelagen*, sec. 5, to exemplify the scope of health and medical care. *Patientskadelagen* sec. 5 now includes malpractice in conjunction with circumcision of boys according to *Lagen om omskärelse av pojkar* (2001: 499) (The Act on circumcision of boys)[4]. *Patienskadelagen* is only applicable when a registered doctor, with the qualifications for this kind of surgery, has performed the circumcision. 5

3. *Atomansvarighetslagen* (1968: 45) (The Nuclear Liability Act)

From 1 April 2001, there are some modified provisions in sec. 17, 31 and 31a of *Atomansvarighetslagen* (1968: 45) (The Nuclear Liability Act). The modifications mainly establish an increase of the maximum amount to be paid by an operator of a nuclear installation, *e.g.* the operator of a nuclear plant is now responsible up to 300 SDR (about 3,3 billion SEK or € 300 million). The Swedish Government's opinion is that the nuclear industry in the future shall 6

[3] *E.g.* [1996] *Nytt Juridiskt Arkiv* (NJA), 377, a boy killed in a car accident by a driver who was under the influence of alcohol and, since the driver hit the boy on the pavement, the driver was grossly negligent. The boy's parents and sister were entitled to damages for non-financial loss.

[4] *Regeringens proposition* 2000/2001: 81, *Omskärelse av pojkar.*

be fully responsible for payment of damages caused by nuclear incidents, and this is a step in that direction. The Swedish Government is now investigating how an unlimited responsibility is to be put into *Atomansvarighetslagen*.

B. Cases

1. *Högsta Domstolen* (The Swedish Supreme Court, HD); 22 February 2001; [2001] NJA, 65 I, II[5]: Assessment of Damages

a) Brief Summary of the Facts

7 In the first case (I) a cat died from the injuries after an attack from a dog. The cat had suffered severe injuries and the owner took the cat to a pet hospital. The veterinarian did all he could and the cat's injuries were almost healed. Because of some brain injuries the veterinarian recommended the owner to put down the cat since the cat would not be the same again. The costs for the care at the pet hospital were 6,086 SEK (about € 550). After the death of the cat, the owner claimed damages from the owner of the dog. The owner of the dog accepted liability for payment up to 725 SEK (100 SEK regarding the market value of the cat and 625 SEK for transport to the pet hospital) (about € 66).

8 In the other case (II) a dog was injured after an attack from another dog. After extensive aid by a veterinarian the dog's injuries were healed after a while. The costs for the veterinarian were about 4 times higher than the market value of the dog. The owner of the attacking dog had paid some of the costs for the aid. The owner of the injured dog however claimed for more expenses, about 4 times higher than the value of the dog.

b) Judgment of the Supreme Court

9 According to *Lag* (1943: 459) *om tillsyn över hundar och katter*, an act concerning liability for cat and dog owners for damages caused by their dogs and cats, there is a strict liability for damages caused by a dog or a cat. In the above-mentioned cases it was indisputable that the owners of the attacking dogs were liable to damages.

10 The issue in the cases was whether it is possible to receive damages of an amount exceeding the value of damaged property. The Supreme Court first established the principal rule that it is not possible to claim for damages regarding expenses exceeding the value of the object. But the opinion of the court in both cases was that, in some exceptional cases, the cost of repairs could be compensated as long as it is reasonable to try to repair the object and if the costs are reasonable. The Supreme Court also mentioned that injured pets are not a material damage in the usual meaning. The Supreme Court

[5] [2001] NJA, 65.

points out that, in cases of injured pets, the care of a veterinary surgeon, resulting in expenses exceeding the value of the pet, must be reasonably well grounded medically. The owners of the attacking pets were liable to pay damages in both cases.

c) Commentary

The cases are of course interesting since the Supreme Court deviates from the principle that the liable party is not liable to pay expenses for repairing an object exceeding the value of the object. Dr. Marcus Radetzki has published an article regarding the cases and he is quite critical of the judgments[6]. His opinion is that the damages to be paid by the owners of the attacking dogs are to be considered as damages of a non-financial nature. The principal rule is that liability for non-financial damages must correspond to a law. In Sweden there is no law regarding this kind of compensation for sentimental value. His point of view is that this kind of right to damages for pet owners should come through legislation. He also remarks on the brief opinions of the court. According to Radetzki, the Supreme Court should have been clearer regarding the scope of "pets". Probably he means that these kinds of judgments might lead to lawsuits from owners of other kinds of pets. He also mentions that the Supreme Court should make it clear that in these kinds of cases one must take into account whether the aid by the veterinarian surgeon can be reasonably successful or not. **11**

Whether this case will lead to more law-suits of this kind in the future is uncertain. Most pet owners have their pets insured and it is quite unusual that expenses for aid exceed the sum insured. **12**

2. HD; 23 April 2001; [2001] NJA, 269: Liability for Inspection of a Building

a) Brief Summary of the Facts

An inspector undertook an inspection on behalf of a buyer, a family, before an acquisition of a house. The parties used a standard form/model contract often used for these kinds of inspections. The inspector mentioned in his report that there might be a risk of damp and mould in the building. The inspector also mentioned in the report that there was no need for further technical investigations regarding this. The year after the acquisition the buyer had costs relating to damp and mould. The family/the plaintiff claimed for compensation and argued that the inspector was negligent when giving the family the advice that further investigations were not necessary. According to the outline of the standard form, the inspector was not obliged to inform whether further investigations were necessary or not since the inspector had mentioned the risk of damp and moisture in the building **13**

[6] M. Radetzki, Skadeståndsansvar för reparationskostnad utöver skadans värde, [2001] *Juridisk Tidsskrift* (JT) 2000-01 No. 4, 928 – 937.

b) Judgment of the Supreme Court

14 The Supreme Court found the inspector negligent when he mentioned in his report that there was no need for further technical investigations. The Supreme Court found the inspector liable for damages. According to the Supreme Court, the inspector would not have been regarded as negligent if he had not stated anything concerning the need whether further technical investigations were necessary or not.

c) Commentary

15 Inspectors, as consultants in general, have a duty to inform their clients in matters of importance for the client. However, in some cases the consultant and the client use a standard form with standardised questions for the consultant to answer after his/her investigations. In those cases the consultants' duty to inform is quite tied to the actual questions in the standard form, but in spite of that, the consultant can be responsible for incorrect information that he/she was not obliged to give according to the standard form.

16 During the last years there has been more focus in Sweden on the liability of trustees, such as lawyers, trustees in bankruptcy, accountants, consultants, advisors, etc. In the field of advisory services there have been several cases where banks have been defendants. In most cases the courts have found the banks not liable.

3. HD; 13 March 2001; [2001] NJA, 99: Liability of a Trustee in Bankruptcy

a) Brief Summary of the Facts

17 On behalf of a bankrupt's estate, a trustee in bankruptcy (a Member of the Swedish Bar Association) raised a loan on real estate owned by the company in bankruptcy. The construction of the building was not completed and the loan was used to finish building the house. The trustee in bankruptcy was of the opinion that raising a loan for the purpose of finishing the building of the house was an adequate measure. However, the real estate was heavily mortgaged. The real estate was later sold at an auction under writ of execution and the bank with first priority concerning an earlier loan did not receive full payment. The trustee in bankruptcy had not conferred with that bank, the bank with first priority, before he raised the above-mentioned loan. The bank with first priority in the real estate claimed for damages and argued that the trustee in bankruptcy should have consulted the bank before raising more loans.

b) Judgment of the Supreme Court

18 The Supreme Court found the trustee in bankruptcy liable to damages because he negligently caused the company in bankruptcy damage and the Supreme Court ordered the trustee in bankruptcy to pay damages. According to the Supreme Court, a trustee in bankruptcy shall confer with the bank in this situ-

ation. The Supreme Court found the trustee in bankruptcy liable despite the fact that he had hoped that the building would be valuable enough after finishing the building of the house.

c) Commentary

The duties of a trustee in bankruptcy (in Sweden he/she is always a Member of the Swedish Bar Association) are, among others, regulated in legislation. Some of the actions by a trustee in bankruptcy are not that well regulated. Also in this case the Supreme Court stresses the duty to inform the parties concerned. 19

4. HD; 19 December 2001; [2001] NJA, 878: Liability of a Valuer in a Non-Contractual Relation

a) Brief Summary of the Facts

The dispute concerned pure financial loss in a non-contractual relation between a bank and a valuer of real estate. Both parties agreed that the value stated in the certificate was too high. The valuation done by the valuer was to be used in a dispute between the owner of the real estate and another party and was not intended to be used in a situation where a bank needed a value for granting of credits. As a defence the valuer argued that he cannot be responsible towards a third party to whom he had no contractual relation and that his valuation was not meant for a bank to use. 20

b) Judgment of the Supreme Court

As mentioned above, both parties agreed that the value stated in the certificate was too high. The Supreme Court found however that the valuer was not liable for the banks financial loss because the bank should have understood that the valuer's certificate regarding the value of the property was not meant for/suitable for the granting of credits. 21

c) Commentary

Though there is no rule in the Swedish Tort Liability Act giving a party in a non-contractual relation a right to damages for pure financial loss (only in event of criminal acts), the Supreme Court earlier found a valuer liable in a quite similar case ([1987] NJA, 692). In that case the Supreme Court ruled that a valuer should take into account that a third party, *e.g.* a bank, has the right to assume that the value is correct. In the case from 1987, the valuer knew that his certificate was to be used by the owner in his contacts with a bank and, if the valuer is negligent in those cases, the bank is entitled to damages. 22

5. HD; 28 November 2001; [2001] NJA, 755: Liability of a Municipality

a) Brief Summary of the Facts

23 A female student in a school run by a municipality sued the municipality for damages after a long period of being harassed/bullied by other students. According to the harassed student and an opinion handed in from the Swedish School Authority, the school had not acted in an appropriate way to solve the problem during the period when the student was harassed/bullied. When the school acted the damage was already done. As a defence the school argued that the teachers actually had brought up the problem with the boys who had teased the student and that the "victim" had not told the teachers about the problem beforehand.

b) Judgment of the Supreme Court

24 According to the Tort Liability Act Chapter 3 sec. 2, the State or a municipality is liable for damages when they are caused by a public body when it is exercising its authority/public powers, but of course fault or negligence has to be established. The Supreme Court was of the opinion that the rule in Chapter 3 sec. 2 is applicable since the measures a school shall take in case of bullying are a form of exercise of the authority of the municipality.

25 The school/the responsible municipality was not considered to be liable for negligence and the Supreme Court rejected the demand for damages. The Supreme Court stressed the importance of actions against harassment among pupils in schools but the court found that the teachers at the school had actually tried to find out why the girl did not feel well.

c) Commentary

26 The liability of the State or a municipality in case of harassed/bullied students has been widely discussed in the last years in Sweden. In the case mentioned above, the District Court found the municipality liable and decided that the municipality was liable for damages. It is important to stress that the actual teaching in the school is, according to the preparatory works of the Tort Liability Act[7], not considered to be an exercise of a municipality's authority and in those cases the Tort Liability Act Chapter 3 sec. 2 is not applicable.

27 As in the case mentioned above, there are often several separate regulations involved when the courts shall decide whether a public body is negligent or not. The measures to be taken by schools in case of harassment/bullying among the students is regulated in *Skollagen* (1985: 1100) (The School Act), *Arbetsmiljölagen* (1977: 1160) (Work Environment Act) and guidelines from the Swedish School Authority.

[7] *Regeringens proposition* 1972:5, *Skadeståndslag*.

6. HD; 29 January 2001; [2001] NJA, 31: Liability of the State

a) Brief Summary of the Facts

A company got a license from an authority to act in a certain area. The license concerned the right to mine, dig, etc. in the ground. Other parties concerned, who did not want the company to get the license, appealed to the same authority. The authority decided that it was not possible to try the decision again. The plaintiffs took the case to *Regeringsrätten* (the Supreme Administrative Court) and the Supreme Administrative Court decided that the first mentioned authority should try the case again. The company sued the State since the Supreme Administrative Court had made some mistakes during the procedure. 28

b) Judgment of the Supreme Court

The State is liable for the negligence of courts according to the Tort Liability Act Chapter 3 sec. 2. But there is one exception, in Chapter 3 sec. 7, for damages caused by the national legislature and the Supreme Court or the Supreme Administrative Court. After a petition/move for a new trial in the Supreme Court or the Supreme Administrative Court, and if the court, after trying the case again, corrects its previous mistake, there is a possibility for an action for damages against the State. In the above mentioned case the plaintiff, a company, was not entitled to damages from the State since the company had not moved for a new trial at the Supreme Administrative Court before the company claimed for damages. 29

c) Commentary

In a Government Official Report, SOU 1997: 194, the Government has suggested a repeal of the rule laid down in Chapter 3 sec. 7 since there is an apparent disparity between Community law and Swedish law with regard to the exception in the rule. According to Community law, the Member State is also liable for negligence by a Supreme Court. A victim of a Supreme Court's negligence is now treated differently in Sweden depending on whether it is an infringement of Community law or of Swedish law. However, the rule is still a part of the Tort Liability Act and the Supreme Court therefore still uses the rule. 30

7. HD; 14 May 2001; [2001] NJA, 309: Product Liability

a) Brief Summary of the Facts

A company bought lubricating oil for trains from another company. The oil used in the motors of the train caused damage since the oil contained zinc. 31

b) Judgment of the Supreme Court

The Supreme Court discussed the legislation concerning the sale of goods. However, *Köplagen* (1990: 931) (The Sale of Goods Act) excludes damages 32 for damaged property other than the defective product itself. *Produktansvarslagen* (1992: 18) (the Product Liability Act) is modelled upon the EC Directive concerning liability for defective products (85/374/EEC). Since the injured party who suffered a damage of property (material damage) was a company and not a consumer, the company could not base its action for damages on the Product Liability Act. However, the Supreme Court found the seller liable and ordered the seller to pay damages. The Supreme Court found that the buyer had the right to take for granted that the oil was free from zinc and that the seller must have understood that the buyer wanted oil without zinc since zinc causes damage to these kinds of motors.

c) Commentary

33 There is no legislation regulating this kind of liability in Sweden. This case is considered to be a part of the ongoing development of product liability in Sweden. In the case mentioned above the Supreme Court remarks in the opinion of the court that there should be room for further development of product liability in the future through case-law. There are fairly few cases in Sweden regarding product liability in general and especially on product liability when the buyer is a company.

C. Literature

1. J. Mikaelsson/A. Wergens, *Repairing the Irreparable, State Compensation to Crime Victims in the European Union* (Brottsoffermyndigheten, Umeå, 2001)

34 The book is written in English and it is published by Brottsoffermyndigheten (The Crime Victim Compensation and Support Authority) and consists of 415 pages. It is the result of the Umeå Expert Meeting on Compensation to Crime Victims in the European Union, organised in Umeå October 2000, and reports based on a questionnaire written by the ministries responsible for compensation to crime victims in the Member States after the meeting. One purpose of the meeting and the book was to deal with those areas in which the Commission has called for better standards concerning compensation and treatment of crime victims. Another purpose was to increase knowledge of state compensation schemes in the Member States. The Umeå meeting discussed, inter alia, the minimum standards established by the 1983 European Convention and whether it was possible to agree to take further steps. The book is developed from November 2000 until July 2001 and is to be considered as a guide providing the basic features of the state compensation schemes in the European Union.

35 After a presentation of the thirteen Member States which have schemes in force for compensating victims of traditional crimes (Greece and Italy are not presented) there is an extensive chapter in the book with concluding observations, 100 pages. The authors point out that it is extremely difficult to compare legislation from countries of varying legal traditions. The solutions differ substantially between the Member States. The different social security nets influence the schemes for state compensation to crime victims. What is covered by state compensation in one Member State may thus be covered by public insurance in another. The authors have found that it is a common principle found in most Member States that compensation from the state is subsidiary to compensation from other sources. In most Member States the assessment of damages of compensation for criminal injuries has its basis in the law of damages but with a number of restrictions. Great Britain has a tariff scheme and the other twelve Member States have state compensation schemes. According to the authors, the relevant legislation in Austria and Germany is more complex than that in other Member States. The Nordic countries have similar legal traditions and there are several similarities such as providing compensation for damage to property and compensation for violation of personal integrity. The guide shows that several Member States offer compensation for loss of honour or dignity, often referred to as compensation for moral damage. The authors have found that, concerning the territorial scope of application, the Member States do not discriminate other citizens of the European Union injured on their territory. However, regarding crimes committed in other Member States there are provisions that distinguish between Member States' own citizens and other citizens of the European Union. The authors remark that there are very few features common to all Member States.

In a schematic way an appendix sums up the following main issues described **36**
in the book: The scope of application of state compensation schemes in each Member State, the territorial scope of application/crime committed in the Member State, the territorial scope of application/crime committed abroad, reporting the crime as a condition for the receipt of state compensation, advance payment of state compensation to victims of violent crimes.

A very useful part of the book is the appendix where the legislation of the thir- **37**
teen Member States are all translated into English. It is apparent that there is a need for common definitions of concepts in relation to compensation.

As the authors remark, comparing thirteen different countries implies a risk of **38**
either simplifying too much or of getting too detailed. However, the book gives the reader a very good overview of the systems in the thirteen Member States and, as far as I know, there are few similar works done in the last years[8]. The book is a useful guide for persons dealing with compensation in the European Union and it will facilitate the contacts between persons working in the field of compensation to crime victims. According to the authors, the guide is not aimed at giving a full comparison of the levels of compensation but rather to prepare the ground for a common standard regarding compensation in the European Union.

[8] D. Green (ed.), *Compensating Crime Victims – A European Survey* (1996)

2. J. Hellner/S. Johansson, *Skadeståndsrätt* (6th edn. 2001, Norstedts Juridik, Stockholm)

39 The book Skadeståndsrätt is considered to be the main standard work in Swedish tort law throughout the years. The courts often refer to the book and it is often used by practitioners in their work and by law faculties in different law courses. This is the sixth edition and the co-author Svante Johansson has added some texts concerning new legislation and summaries of new case-law since the last edition from 1995. Jan Hellner is the most important author in Swedish tort law during the latest decades and his opinions are still fully represented in the book – there are no such modifications done by Svante Johansson. The book is 512 pages long and contains all fields of non-contractual tort law and a smaller part of contractual tort law.

40 The book consists of an extensive part regarding the general principles of tort law, a comprehensive part on personal injuries and property damages and a quite thorough part on assessment of damages, both on personal injury and property damages. The necessary conditions for being responsible for damages are described in great detail and the book gives the reader an overview of the prevailing opinions. The book also deals with fields subject to special legislation, such as motor traffic damages, work related damages, patient injuries, product liability and environmental liability. The book contains a great number of summaries of the most important court decisions and it has a generous table of references regarding books and articles of good help for the reader who wants to do further research.

3. B. Bengtsson/H. Ullman, *Det nya produktansvaret – en översikt* (3rd edn. Iustus förlag, Uppsala 2001)

41 Bengtsson and Ullman present an overview of *Produktansvarslagen* (1992: 18) (the Product Liability Act, PAL). PAL is modelled upon the EC Directive on product liability from 1985 (85/374/EEC).

42 The authors also deal with questions regarding product liability in the field of sale of goods and services, such as *Köplagen* (1990: 931) (The Sale of Goods Act), *Konsumentköplagen* (1990: 932) (Consumer Sales Act), *Konsumenttjänstlagen* (1985: 716) (The Consumer Services Act) and *Lagen* (1987: 822) *om internationella köp* (International Sale of Goods Act), the Swedish implementation of The Convention on International Sale of Goods (CISG). The Swedish Sale of Goods Act excludes all damage to persons or property caused by the goods. The Consumer Sales Act and The Consumer Services Act covers product liability regarding damaged property owned by the consumer. CISG does not apply to the liability of the seller for death or personal injury caused by the goods, but does not exclude damage to property.

43 The book gives an overview of the different exceptions concerning product liability in the most common Swedish model contracts in different lines of business. Most contracts exclude product liability for damaged property. Since

the legislation on product liability has such strict provisions, the authors point out the importance of insurance covering product liability. The authors present an overview of the terms and conditions of general product liability insurance. There are, however, some differences between insurance products covering product liability among the Swedish insurers. Also *Produktsäkerhetslagen* (1988: 1604) (The Product Safety Act), based on the EC Directive on product safety, plays an important role in the field of product liability and the authors deal briefly with different provisions in that act.

The book only gives the outlines of product liability in Sweden and contains little detailed information. It is most useful for the reader who wants a survey of the most important differences between the different acts in Sweden dealing with product liability. **44**

PAL came into force in 1993 and there have been quite a few books and articles published regarding the act and product liability in general[9]. The legislator's preparatory works are a valuable source of information for practitioners and judges in Sweden. As in the case of PAL the preparatory works are often quite extensive. **45**

4. Scandinavian Studies in Law Volume 41, *Tort Liability and Insurance*, P. Wahlgren (ed.) (Stockholm Institute for Scandinavian Law, Stockholm University, Stockholm 2001)

The editorial board of Scandinavian Studies in Law (Sc.St.L.) is attached to the Stockholm University Law Faculty and this volume contains 23 articles written in English on tort liability and insurance.[10] **46**

In the article "Environmental Liability – Modern Developments", E. M. Basse, first presents an overview of environmental law, the concept of sustainable development and trends in environmental law. In the chapter called The International Law Concept the author deals with the Lugano Convention, different international initiatives and access to justice. In one chapter the author describes the concept of environmental liability in the European Union, policy programmes, green and white papers and so on. The author analyses the national liability concept in a longer chapter and she gives some examples of issues and problems related to national legislation, mostly Danish rules. **47**

In the article "Governmental Liability in Swedish Law", B. Bengtsson, gives the reader a survey of the rules in *Skadeståndslagen* (The Tort Liability Act, SkL) concerning government liability. If there is no contractual liability or when a loss is caused by a criminal act SkL excludes compensation for pure **48**

[9] Some examples: S. Blomstrand/P-A. Broqvist/R M. Lundström, *Produktansvarslagen – en kommentar till den svenska lagen i ett EG-perspektiv* (1993), J. Hellner/S. Johansson, *Skadeståndsrätt* (6th edn. 2001) and B.W. Dufwa, *Produktansvar* (1978).

[10] Sc.St.L series has presented articles in different legal topics since 1957. More than 400 articles have been published written by jurists and legal scholars. The objective is to present Scandinavian law and legal theory to a wide readership in the English language.

economic loss. But there is one exception; pure economic loss is treated in the same way as physical damage when a public body is negligent when exercising its authorities or gives misleading information. In those cases the state or a municipality is also liable to damages for pure economic loss. One of the most common problems using the provisions in SkL regarding governmental liability is to establish whether the negligence or fault occurs within the actual exercise of power of the public body or not. Ordinary liability rules should be applied if damage is caused in another way.

49 The article "Development of International Tort Law Till the Beginning of the 1990s From a Scandinavian Point of View", by B.W. Dufwa, is 100 pages. The article consists of chapters with the following topics: – Tort law in the present, with a survey of different topics of tort law, – Fundamental Legal-policy Thoughts, with themes like the injured party as the centre of attention, the function of damages, transactions costs. The last mentioned chapter consists of analyses regarding, *inter alia*, the prevention debate, general deterrence and moral prevention. The article is mainly focused on the legal-policy debate in the field of tort law through the years and in different legal systems. The author points out that modern international and Swedish tort law doctrine discuss legal-policy issues openly and that legislative action in some countries is conducted in the same spirit, but some countries are more reserved. The author remarks that the courts' tendency to discuss legal-political issues varies from country to country. The article deals with lots of topics interesting for readers outside Scandinavia. The author refers to and uses a great number of international books and articles.

50 The article "Tobacco and Tort Liability", by A. Kjönstad, deals with the Norwegian judgments regarding compensation for health damage caused by smoking and facts in general for assessment of liability and compensation relating to tobacco. There have been several cases in Norway in the last years concerning tobacco related health damages. One example is a decision from October 2000 where the Norwegian Supreme Court judged that a bartender was entitled to full compensation from her employer's insurance company, an industrial injury insurance. The woman was an active smoker during the years at the working place, a bar. Medical experts concluded that the passive smoking had contributed to her lung cancer to a minimum of 40% and a causal relationship was therefore declared to exist between the damaging influence of her working place and the cancer.

51 Some examples of other articles on tort law in volume 41 of Sc.St.L: – Diversity and Unity, In search of a pluralistic view on problems in Tort Law, H. Andersson. – Liability of members of the board of directors and the managing director, R. Dotewall. – Alternative Compensation Systems, B.v. Eyben. – Recent developments in the Danish law of tort, B. Gomard. – Compensation for personal injuries in Sweden, a reconsidered view, J. Hellner. – Is Finnish tort law in the process of being Americanized?, H. Honka. – Profession and function, S. Jörgensen. – Adviser's liability in connection with duty to inform –

a problem inventory, J. Kleinman. – The future of international unification of transport law, J. Ramberg. – Placing the burden of proof of a hypothetical cause, N. Nygaard.

XVII. Switzerland

Heinz Hausheer **and** ***Manuel Jaun***

A. Introduction

1 The legal scene on third-party liability in Switzerland was especially marked by questions of damage compensation in family matters.

2 On the one hand, special attention was given to another federal ruling on so-called *household damages* (BGE[1] 127 III 403 *et seq.*) [see *infra* nos. [5] *et seq.*] which more strongly embeds the effects of housekeeping in existing valid marital law. On the other hand, the year 2001 also saw a judicial ruling passed by the Basel Municipal Court of Appeal on liability for an unsuccessful termination of pregnancy which resulted in especially strong reactions. Subject of this debate in Switzerland was the legally unresolved question of whether a *child can lead to damage in the legal sense*.

3 In connection with household damages *new tables* have also been printed for the year 2001. These tables are based on a special evaluation of Swiss labour statistics (SAKE[2]) which the Federal Office of Statistics had officially and representatively carried out over several years. The SAKE serves mainly to record the Swiss earning structure and the earning behaviour of the Swiss population older than 14. Meanwhile, the number of people asked to give information on any nonremunerated tasks performed in various structured households has been increased with immediate effect from the previous 16,000 to a total of 45,000 people. These statistics divert in various ways from the previously used Schulz-Borck/Hoffmann tables and their purpose is to provide both up-to-date and reliable data on work performed in households.

[1] "BGE" is the German abbreviation for a "Bundesgerichtsentscheid", in English, a decision made by the Federal Court, and also stands for the official written compilation of Federal Court decisions.

[2] "SAKE" is the German abbreviation for "Schweizerische Arbeits-Kräfte Erhebung", *i.e.* "Swiss Surveys on the Labour Force".

In 2001 the theme of family-related damage compensation also struck a chord in *literature*. Especially worth mentioning is a relevant Freiburg Ph.D. thesis by Th. Mannsdorfer, "Pränatale Schädigung Ausservertragliche Ansprüche prenatal geschädigter Personen; unter Berücksichtigung der Rechtslage im Ausland", a study on noncontractual claims of persons injured prenatally, with a main focus on comparative law (AISUF[3] Volume 192) and various periodical contributions (see the latest compilation in HAVE[4], "Personen Schaden Forum 2002", pp. 115 *et seq.*). 4

B. Cases

1. The Swiss Federal Court's Most Recent Case Law Concerning Household Damages

a) The Most Typical Situation

In BGE 127 III 403 *et seq.*, the facts were as follows: Following the frontal collision of two motor vehicles the front-seat passenger in one of the cars suffered from so-called whiplash. This health problem permanently impaired the woman from, on the one hand, managing the household for a family apparently consisting of several members, and on the other from supporting her husband's (garage) business. Her contributions to the latter business would have been considerably extended in the near future had the accident which caused the permanent injury not occurred. 5

Two lower instances ruled in favour of the partial action, specifically for the period beginning in 1992 when the accident took place, until the ruling made by the first instance in 1999. No decision had yet been made on any possible further damages in the future. In the time period set aside for the ruling, two cantonal courts differentiated between the impairment experienced in taking care of the household on the one hand, and at the same time, the reduced ability to work and earn money on the other, and thus ruled that a payment of a just compensation amounting to approximately Fr. 180,000.– be made. Their decision was based on a so-called *second earner marriage*, *i.e.* a marriage in which one partner works full-time and the other partner spends a greater portion of time managing the household while simultaneously working part-time. Today, such a marriage is one of the most frequent in Switzerland and is likely to remain so in the near future. 6

The Federal Court then had to make a basic decision on this initial position. This has led – also from a dogmatic point of view – to a welcome clarification 7

[3] "AISUF" is the German abbreviation for "Arbeiten aus dem juristischen Seminar der Universität Freiburg Schweiz".

[4] "HAVE" is the German abbreviation of a magazine titled "Haftpflicht und Versicherung", *i.e.* "Liability and Insurance".

of the Federal Court's existing case law of *household damages* as a specific element under the Swiss civil law damage compensation system.

b) Household Damages Exceptionally Recognized by Courts as "Normative" Damage

8 For the time being, the Federal Court has confirmed the principle in BGE 127 III 403 *et seq.* according to which Swiss (civil law) liability bases a decision on *property or financial damage*. According to the *difference theory* established by MOMMSEN, damage compensation presupposes involuntary property or financial loss as a result of the damaging event. This may consist of a reduction in property or finances or in a reduction of expected profits, but in any case it is tied to available assets and earnings yet to be made and not to the "consumption of goods, resources and services" (loc. cit. 405). On the other hand, the adverse encroachment of personal intangible legally protected rights basically does not mean any liability to make compensation payments for damages incurred. "The deprivation alone of a person's ability to produce (or enjoy) can under certain circumstances be considered immaterial damage (OR Art. 24, 49), but it cannot be considered property or financial damage or loss" (loc. cit. 405). According to the Federal Court, this principle is retained in the initial draft of the revision and unification of the law on noncontractual liability. Besides, damage compensation also prescribes the specific proof of loss of property or money, *i.e.* the devaluation of existing property or finances, increasing expenses or reduced income flow.

9 An exception is made with "damages resulting in restricted or non-ability to work in the household", in short, "household damages", whereby third parties are not required to provide conclusive evidence of additional expenses for a household aid. "What must be compensated is more the economic depreciation resulting from the impairment of a person's ability to work in the household, independent of whether such depreciation leads to the employment of a substitute, to more efforts on the part of the partially disabled person, to additional demands on relatives or to the acceptance of quality losses" (loc. cit. 406). Only when measuring the "normative" damage to be replaced, namely from a legal point of view without conclusive evidence of any resulting specific property or financial loss, can this be based simply on a hypothetical price for a suitable replacement.

10 For the first time the Federal Court justifies this *hypothetical ascertainment of damage* by citing the circumstance that "to obtain an external person to work in the private framework of a (family) household does not appear altogether reasonable and that the impediment is usually compensated by nonremunerated extra or additional expenses either on the part of the injured person himself or other family members, *i.e.* household members" (loc. cit. 406). The reason for the exception is the intimacy of the household which does not require specific proof of damage.

Based on this hypothetical damage ascertainment, the objection cannot be made that the work previously done in the household by the spouse who suffered the damage was not only for the benefit of the spouse managing the household but also for additional household members, because this work was said spouse's contribution to the marriage pursuant to ZGB[5] art. 163. However, this contribution represents the cash contribution by the other spouse which flows to all household members, the extent of which is freely agreed upon between the married couple. In this respect, the *household work* performed as a supporting contribution is thus deemed of *specific value in marital law*. Although it does not take on the meaning of a proper consideration, it must be considered as the fulfillment of a legal obligation, similar to the contribution in a simple corporation which triggers liability on the part of the other partners to make analogous contributions for the benefit of all. **11**

In this way a cash value is attributed to the *household work* actually performed to the benefit of the family unit. This cash value is *based on family law and goes beyond personal, immaterial and legally protected rights* relating to an individual's own ability to work, which as such is not available without being specifically remunerated. Therein lies a difference to the merely hypothetical ability to work of a student or a retired or unemployed person. With regard to the actually furnished supporting contributions, this legal family value also has two further consequences: **12**

- Because family household work is only a (partial) appropriate contribution to be provided and ensured by the couple together for all household members, and thus pursuant to ZGB art. 163 § 2 goes hand in hand with a basically equal contribution of the other spouse, no *particular provision for so-called reflex damage* is needed analogous to OR[6] art. 45 § 3, namely, the simultaneously occurring right of additional household members for compensation of *maintainer damage* which occurs when the spouse working in the household is injured (loc. cit. 407).
- Thus, the fact that both spouses basically provide equal supporting contributions also leads to the fact that any damaging third party *cannot* plead basic marital law and the obligation of the non-affected spouse to render assistance (loc. cit. 407), as concerns the duty to mitigate damages upon reduction of the working capacity in the household. This is only valid within the internal relationship of the spouses, but not towards damaging third parties.

Residing in the principles of family law, this value is put into the same category as property or financial damages in connection with an impairment of a spouse to actually perform household jobs which thus does not simply connect with the hypothetical ability to manage the household. According to the Fed- **13**

[5] "ZGB" is the German abbreviation for the "Schweizerische Zivilgesetzbuch", *i.e.* the Swiss Civil Code.

[6] "OR" is the German abbreviation for "Schweizerisches Obligationenrecht", *i.e.* the Swiss Commercial Code.

eral Court, this must be differentiated from a possible additional supporting contribution which is provided by a spouse injured by a third party in the form of a claim to compensation – or *Assistance in the Occupation and Business of the Other Spouse* – although also supported by ZGB art. 163 and thus not yet covered by ZGB art. 165. This actually occurred in the case of BGE 127 II 403 *et seq.* in which one of the just mentioned specific features of damage compensation, namely the exceptionally allowed hypothetical proof of damage, could not be applied. With respect to proof of damage, this type of supporting contribution – which allows a correspondingly higher occupational income or accordingly higher trade profit to be added to the marriage support by the other spouse, such as when using labour to make income – must be based on the completely *normal property or financial damage situation*. The injured party must thus provide conclusive evidence of any property disadvantage. Such proof can either be brought by presenting evidence of any additionally incurred costs for a temporary replacement, or by showing that professional income has been reduced, *i.e.* that smaller profits have resulted thereof.

14 The Federal Court based its reasoning on the assumption that it is quite reasonable to resort to temporary replacement of a third party (loc. cit. 409) in this external minded gainful employment of the other spouse, as opposed to the performance of housework. However, this does not apply to the assessment of third-party damages. As with actually performed household management tasks, no special legal regulation is required analogous to OR art. 45 § 3 on compensation of *reflex damages* of additional household members due to the impaired ability to manage the household.

c) Changes in the Allocation of Marital Functions

15 In the opinion of the Federal Court, any foreseeable changes in the scope of household efforts must be taken into account: whether these be objective developments which cause such changes, such as the need to look after growing children who leave home later on, or when the married couple wishes to divide up its mutual functions in a different manner. In this case, it was apparent that shortly before the accident, the couple had agreed to increase the wife's collaboration in the husband's business. Accordingly, the first instances were reprimanded by the Federal Court for not taking into account *life experience* – in such circumstances known to the courts – which shows that any extension of gainful employment normally leads to a simultaneous *reduction in the amount of household management functions*.

16 In Switzerland it is currently relatively easy to calculate such proven changes – in this specific case apparently definite changes – using the statistically sufficiently ascertained SAKE tables which are updated at short intervals (more on this subject later on).

d) On Damage Assessment

The damage assessment, which exceptionally must be made hypothetically, leads – as already mentioned – to the fact that "the damage to be compensated must be measured against the possible costs ensued by hiring a temporary replacement" (loc. cit. 406), putting the individual, subjectively viewed ability to manage a household in the background. More emphasis is to be placed on the current hourly wage of a *replacement person* who will take over all different types of household chores and whose future wage is to reflect future developments. Since in this regard there is not a sufficient market, appropriate mixed calculations are currently being used which are based on compensation sums of various individual occupational activities. **17**

e) Acknowledgement

The latest specifications of the judiciary regulation of so-called household damages can have *indisputable* advantages: **18**

- The increased linkage of functions falling under housework with legal marital support makes it necessary to not only consider the impairment of a hypothetical job possibility as assets, but all the more to introduce a special legal family cash value as part of an interplay between equally important supporting contributions benefiting all household members. This allows certain, otherwise *not easy demarcations*, especially also to personal immaterial damages pursuant to OR art. 47 and 49, which give rise to reparation rather than damage compensation.
- The newly discovered, *i.e.* more often used legal supporting framework of household damages also allows a quite *clear assessment of third-party damages* for the benefit of the household members immediately affected by the damaging cause.
- The variable organization of rights to support thus also allows a relatively *flexible adaptation to foreseeable changes* germane to the scope of household management efforts, for example in connection with different efforts for looking after children, depending on their age. The SAKE tables which are based on clear and broadly supported statistics are quite capable of mathematically coping with changes which occur in the course of time.

Considering the mere partial judgment which was confined to changes in the actually continued marriage, the Federal Court only had to give *in petto* thoughts on the *adverse consequences* which this combination of rights to support could perhaps lead to in case of a divorce. Meanwhile, such a marriage dissolvement may occur by a relationship of 4 to 6, if not shortly 1 to 1. In this case, the temporary help of the divorced spouse who has dealt to a greater share with the housekeeping during the time the couple was living together should, however, be reassessed in accordance with his or her evaluation on the general labour market and in the sense of his or her hypothetically offset earnings, instead of based on the value of a temporary help remunerated in line with household management duties. **19**

20 The often widely diverging evaluations of the different chores of the previously married and then divorced spouse who was more active in the household should not remain an exclusive internal problem between the former spouses which is settled solely in post-marital support. But even if we begin with such post-marital support, in case of a divorce we must still always determine how reasonable it would be for the people to either resume work or increase the hours in an already existing part-time job, which when compared to household management is often better paid.

21 Nevertheless, as in connection with household damages one must also consider the probability of a divorce and thus of a possible obligation to resume or increase gainful employment, the question is what requirements must be fulfilled by the corresponding – again specific – proof of damages? It may no longer be considered correct that in this regard the same high demands are put on future requirements as those generally specified by BGE 99 II 226 in view of a changeover from housework to gainful employment. At that time (1983) it was recorded: "The sheer possibility that a woman engaged in housework who does not have an accident could again pursue a job later on does not suffice to substantiate an additional (loss of income) claim. On the contrary, specific indications must be presented which, in accordance with living experience, not only make this objectively possible but also probable. But that is out of the question until reliable signs provide the *almost certain* impression that the injured party would really have become gainfully employed." However, it is impossible to clarify the probability of divorce in every case of household damage, including the calculation of a hypothetical income. On the other hand, it would be conceivable to expect a special generously established rectification reservation set up by the courts. This would have to discern itself distinctly from the legally valid OR art. 46, § 2 with its two-year limitation calculated from the day of the ruling.

22 It is thus with great suspense that we will keep a close eye on the continuing mosaic of case law which in the end should lead to a (more) comprehensive specific ruling on household damages.

2. Abortion as an Obligation to Reduce Damage?

23 Larger discussions were triggered in the year 2001 by a ruling of the Court of Appeals of Canton Basel City dated 23 October 1998 (in [2000] BJM[7], 306 *et seq.*) which was published only later on. Following two earlier successful terminations of pregnancy (1975 and 1982) using the suction currettage method, a woman experienced an additional undesired pregnancy in the 1990s. This pregnancy was to be ended in the same way as the previous two, but the same medical procedure did not lead to the same desired success this third time. This did not became apparent until the fifth month of pregnancy, at a time when the mother was no longer prepared to induce the birth in order to trigger

[7] "BJM" is the German abbreviation of a magazine titled "Basler Juristische Mitteilung", *i.e.* "Basel Law Review".

the certain death of the foetus. Thus following a lone judgment by a first instance of the District Court of Arbon on 16 October 1985, the Swiss judicial system was, after many long years, again called upon to answer the question whether the *undesired, but finally accepted birth of a healthy child could qualify as a justified reason to receive compensation for property or financial damage*.

The damage suit brought against the Canton of Basel City Hospital, among other counts with respect to child support, was dismissed by the first instance with the argument that because the mother refused to induce premature birth, one could no longer speak of an *involuntary occurrence of damage*. **24**

By comparison, the second cantonal instance viewed the matter from the point of view of a possible reason and stated that it would not have been unreasonable for the woman to have the birth of the child induced in order to initiate its death, in the sense of an obligation to mitigate damages to a minimum: "Even when looking at the matter from the plaintiff's point of view, *i.e.* an unvoluntary loss, there would be no reason to grant indemnification. The question would then arise as to whether the plaintiff (namely the mother) should not have agreed to undergo a renewed medical operation. Unreasonableness can be justified by religious, ethical or emotional reasons. ...[Still, the plaintiff] voluntarily agreed to an abortion in the years 1975 and 1982. Under these circumstances an additional interruption in pregnancy could not be considered 'an extremely unreasonable demand'". **25**

Left unchecked was whether or not a termination of pregnancy according to the still valid so-called indicative solution (grounds for a legal abortion) would still have been legally permissible in the 18th/19th week of pregnancy since two medical certificates confirmed that at least for this time period "the mother's life was not in danger, nor was she suffering from any great danger of serious and permanent injury to her health" which would justify a termination of pregnancy to save her life pursuant to art. 120 § 1 of the Swiss Penal Code StGB[8]. In any case, the circumstances prevalent at the time of the unsuccessful attempt to terminate the pregnancy cannot be concluded for the legal situation at the time of an advanced pregnancy which was only discovered much later. **26**

As long as there are no legal prerequisites for legitimate abortion, there is no case for any legal obligation to mitigate damages, regardless of whether the mother had at an earlier time actually applied for the then unsuccessful termination of pregnancy. **27**

Even if a serious emotional plight for the relevant period of the 18th/19th week of pregnancy as required by prevailing penal code could be adequately **28**

[8] "StGB" is the German abbreviation for "Schweizerisches Strafgesetzbuches" (Swiss Penal Code).

proven, the following, as already properly noted, would still have to be considered (F. Bommer, [2001] ZBJV[9], 667): "A termination of pregnancy is never permitted under criminal law without the permission of the plaintiff [*i.e.* of the pregnant woman]. By opposing to her that such termination would be a measure of mitigating the damage is thus nothing else except an unreasonable demand that she should have 'wanted to have an abortion', a request which is illegal for two reasons: First, the law only allows a termination of pregnancy to prevent a serious emotional plight, but not to avoid indemnification claims. And second, a termination using the loophole of mitigating damage is contrary to all legislative intent and would become a (soft) obligation instead of remaining a right."

3. Swiss Federal Supreme Court (*Bundesgericht*, BGer);126 III BGE *(Bundesgerichtsentscheide)* 14[10]: Liability for Animals, Duties of Care in Respect of Grazing Cows

a) Brief Summary of the Facts

29 A married couple by the name of M. was walking their two dogs on a trail which was not marked as a hiking path. The track led across grazing land which was fenced by a barbed wire. At a distance of approximately 100 metres, 25 milk cows and their calves were resting calmly. When the couple entered the meadow through the triangle entrance to the land, the cows started to move mooing. They approached the couple quickly and – being extremely incited by the dogs which were not kept on the lead – they trampled the couple, who were seriously injured thereby. According to the police report, mother cows typically show defensive behaviour to protect their calves when dogs are nearby. Apart therefrom, they do not show any aggressive behaviour towards humans. It was further established that the herd was checked twice a day by an experienced herdsman. The cows had behaved quietly on the morning of the day of the accident. Furthermore, there had never been any comparable incident until the respective day. The couple filed an action for damages in the amount of 67,365.90 Swiss Francs against the holder of the cows (the cantone of Berne). Their claim was denied in all court instances.

b) Judgment/Commentary

30 If animals owned by some public authority, but not used for public purposes, cause harm, such liability of the authority is determined according to art. 56 of the Swiss Code of Obligations (*Obligationenrecht*, OR)[11]. Therefore, the defendant authority can raise the defence that "all due care required for maintenance and inspection under the circumstances" had been observed. If no statutory or other written or at least commonly accepted rule of conduct (*e.g.* issued by private or semi-public institutions) is applicable, the standard of care

[9] "ZBJV" is the German abbreviation of a magazine titled "Zeitschrift des Bernischen Juristen-Vereins", *i.e.* "Journal of the Bernese Lawyers Association".

[10] *Die Praxis des Bundesgerichts* (Pra) [2000] 89, no. 48.

[11] See 115 II BGE 237 E. 2c.

is determined according to a weighing of the interests involved. Such examination therefore has to consider the efficacy of the contemplated measures as well as any costs and other efforts involved therewith on the one hand and the degree of the risk, as well as the probability and extent of possible harm, on the other hand (E. 1b).

In light of such criteria, the BGer considered the fact that grazing (mother) **31**
cows are not dangerous for humans in general as well as that the animals in question had never raised any problems before in particular. The Court therefore determined that no extraordinary measures of safety had to be taken. It particularly denied the plaintiffs' allegation that a herdsman should have been permanently present, or that the grazing land should have been completely locked. The latter was not considered to be an option since entrance to "forest and field" has to be open to the public according to art. 699 subs. 1 of the Swiss Civil Code (*Zivilgesetzbuch*, ZGB). The Court further rejected the plaintiffs' contention that the fencing had been inadequate so that the cows could have escaped at any given time. The injuries had been sustained within the fencing, so that the same harm had been incurred "even if such care had been observed" (as foreseen by the defence requirements[12] of art. 56 subs. 1 OR[13]). The plaintiffs finally failed to convince the Court that the keeper should have posted some warning of the danger. The Court came to that conclusion by way of an analogous application of the so-called follow-up argument: It thereby examined whether such a duty of care could prevail as a general rule, thereby leading to satisfactory results for those affected in future cases from the perspective of reasonableness and prevention of harm. This was denied in light of the extraordinarily low likelihood of harm as well as the very limited preventive effect of a jungle of signs on Swiss meadows.

The same result follows from looking at this case from the perspective of *risk* **32**
spreading as underlying art. 56 OR: Accordingly, the keeper of an animal has to take reasonable defence measures to ensure that the danger resulting from the unpredictable nature of his animal does not materialize in areas of regular social contact (*i.e.* in those places where contacts to this source of harm can hardly be avoided by the public[14]). The keeper of a dog which bites a passer-by can therefore not avoid liability by claiming that his dog had until then been entirely harmless so that it previously appeared unnecessary to keep him on a lead. If, however, the keeper of an animal has taken all necessary steps corresponding to the objectively justified safety expectations of the public and thereby fulfilled his duties of care, the risk is thereby shifted onto the victim. In any case, the latter has no claim for damages on the basis of art. 56 OR if it was his own behaviour which contributed to making it possible that he was

[12] See P. Widmer, Privatrechtliche Haftung, in: *Schaden – Haftung – Versicherung* (1999), no. 2.63.

[13] This article is not on the point, however, since it merely reflects the (self-evident) defence of lawful alternative conduct (*rechtmässigen Alternativverhaltens)*.

[14] *Cf.* Schmidt, Zurechnung, Zurechnungsprinzipien und Zurechnungszusammenhang, in: *Liber Amicorum Josef Esser* (1995), p. 154

harmed. This is the case, for example, if he approached the animal by his own free will, such as to pet straying cats or dogs on a lead, or by entering grazing land. The same were true if he had significantly raised the risk of being harmed by walking a dog which he had let off the lead. In that sense, art. 56 OR allows the keeper of an animal to avoid liability for harmful events which can predominantly be traced back to a conduct of the victim which remains within the latter's own responsibility according to the *ratio legis* even though such conduct may not be considered as severe as to have broken the chain of causation.

4. Federal Supreme Court, 126 III BGE 113[15]: Duty of Skiing Resort to Safeguard the Operation of Ski Lifts

a) Summary of the Facts

33 On 24 January 1993 around 12:30, Z. took the (single seat) ski lift operated by X. AG in order to access the skiing area of Thyon-Les Collon (Valais). On the seat immediately ahead of him was his daughter B. Just before pole no. 4, B. fell off the lift and slid backwards down the slope. Z. tried to get a hold of his daughter upon passing by, but failed to do so. He consequently let the shackle go and skied downhill alongside the lift track. He was so much focused on his daughter that he only realized pole no. 3 the very moment he collided therewith. He suffered several fractures leaving him with permanent injuries and forcing him to change his professional career. His action for damages against X. AG failed both before the cantonal court of Valais as well as on appeal before the Federal Supreme Court.

b) Judgment/Commentary

34 Let us first look at liability for *tortious acts* (art. 41 OR), which the Federal Supreme Court took as the basis of a possible claim as a matter of course: It is common court practice that whoever runs a skiing resort has to take all reasonable safety precautions in order to protect those who make use of the mountain railway and the slopes. This already follows from the general duty of care applicable to those who open or operate a source of danger[16]. It is questionable, however, whether a legal entity can be held liable directly and without any fault on the side of its officers since legal persons are only responsible for tortious acts within the limits of art. 55 § 2 *Zivilgesetzbuch* (ZGB)[17]. By answering this question in the affirmative (though not explicitly), the Federal Supreme Court has inadvertently added another basis of the claim next to a company's liability for its officers: Accordingly, a legal entity is liable for all harm resulting from a source of danger within its sphere that is not adequately safe (*Verkehrswidrigkeit*). Responsibility will thereby typically (though not

[15] [2000] Pra 89, no. 185.

[16] *Cf.* in particular 121 III BGE 358 E. 4a, commented in [1997] *Zeitschrift des bernischen Juristenvereins* (ZBJV) 133, 434 *et seq.*; see also 125 IV BGE 9; 122 IV BGE 193 *et seq.*; 118 II BGE 38; 113 II BGE 246.

[17] Artt. 722, 814 Abs. 4 and 899 Abs. 3 OR.

necessarily) follow from the fact that running a business (here: a skiing resort) raises certain safety expectations by those attracted by it[18].

Shifting the loss on the basis of such argumentation seems to lead to proper results, particularly in light of the advantage it brings to the victims who no longer have to take a complicated detour by construing some fault of a company representative which can hardly ever be proven. Furthermore, liability on this basis does not come entirely unexpectedly since legal entities are already strictly liable under several special tort law regimes which apply to natural as well as legal persons alike. In this case, for example, X. AG might as well have been liable as the owner of the ski lift based on art. 58 OR[19], which does not make any significant difference since the actual duties applicable in the instant case are the same under both lines of reasoning (E. 2a/bb and cc). **35**

The Court answered the question whether X. AG should have padded the lift pole for the safety of the skiers in reliance on the statement of the expert witness. The latter had testified that such measures were only customary and necessary in areas where the slope was very steep (at least 50 to 60 per cent), so that a skier falling from the lift would be in danger of hitting the pole at high speed. Since the hill between poles no. 3 and 4 was not steeper than 40 per cent (according to the facts ascertained in the court), the Federal Supreme Court could with apparent confidence deny that X. AG had violated a duty of care, even more so since it saw no further indication that the skiers were in any significant danger on said slope. According to the Court, the plaintiff, who had voluntarily left the lift and skied down the hill near its trail, had thereby made an uncommon use of the facilities contrary to regulations which the operators of the lift could not have expected. Consequently, there was no duty to provide for safety measures against such unpredictable behaviour (E. 2c). **36**

These arguments, however, are not entirely convincing. To begin with, it is quite surprising how easily the Federal Supreme Court sets aside its own prior rulings (on which the plaintiff had relied in vain). In 111 IV BGE 15 E. 3, for example, the Court held the following course of events – in blatant contrast to the present case – to be "not extraordinary enough so that one could not have expected it": A skier had fallen on the back of his head after the first swing. He unconsciously slid over the edge of the hard-frozen course which was about 35 to 40 per cent steep, then crashed into an unpadded pole of a ski lift. In that case, the Court had seen it as a matter of course that poles without padding on a slope of such steepness posed a significant danger to skiers falling off the ski tows (*cf.* E. 2 pp. 17 *et seq.*). There are hardly any doubts that the same Court would have held X. AG liable if it had not been the plaintiff who **37**

[18] *Cf.* 123 III BGE 306, where the tourist office of Colombier (who also runs the local swimming area) was held liable for failure to properly maintain a defective high-diving platform owned by the canton; [1998] ZBJV 134, 542 *et seq.*

[19] *Cf.* H.-K. Stiffler, Sportunfall, insbesondere Skiunfall, in: *Schaden–Haftung–Versicherung* (1999), nos. 13, 18; R. Brehm, *Berner Kommentar* (BK-Brehm) VI/1/3/1 (2nd edn. 1998) OR 58 no. 45.

had bumped into the pole but rather his daughter upon falling off the lift. For the sake of an adequate distribution of risk, one might in fact consider it obvious and reasonable to impose duties of care upon the operators of ski lifts under all those circumstances where the operation of the lift and the course predictably lead to a certain likelihood of harm, even if the potential victims themselves exercise all due and reasonable care under the circumstances. Seen in that light, the proper and predictable use of the facilities not only encompasses skiers who involuntarily fall, but includes other cases as well, be it a fallen skier who gets back on his feet and collides with the pole in the very moment he regains control, be it the instant case where a concerned father skies down the slope to rescue his child. The plaintiff had certainly not acted wilfully or carelessly, but in a certain predicament where it is somewhat unrealistic to require that he should have paid attention to everything ahead of him and skied in a way that he could have avoided any immovable obstacle on the course (E. 2d.). To call for a padding of the poles is certainly not asking too much, considering the Court's own words in 111 IV BGE 18 where it held such measures "reasonable since they could have been taken with little technical and financial effort".

5. Federal Supreme Court; No. 4C.53/2000 of 13 June 2000[20]: Hospital's Duties of Care Vis-à-Vis Suicidal Patients[21], Burden of Proof

a) Brief Summary of the Facts

38 In the early morning of 15 January 1991, A. was taken to hospital X. by an emergency psychiatrist who had diagnosed suicidal tendencies. After admission he was brought into a single room on the first floor of the protected ward where he had his breakfast and took some medication. Around 9:30 he opened a secured window of his room and jumped out, thereby suffering severe head injuries. On 31 May 1995, he sued hospital X. for damages for pain and suffering in the amount of SFR 175,000 (plus interest). The district court of Zurich denied his claim, which was confirmed by the cantonal court of appeals as well as the Federal Supreme Court.

b) Judgment/Commentary

39 On appeal, the plaintiff claimed that the lower court had failed to apply the so-called "*natural presumption*" test as developed in 120 II BGE 248 (in a case concerning an infection caused by the injection of some vaccine). According to this test, the mere fact that certain apparent risks of a treatment have materialized by itself leads to the presumption that these negative consequences have

[20] [2000] Pra 89, no. 155.

[21] There had been two prior cases before the Federal Supreme Court where it had to address the issue whether a hospital is liable for the (attempted) suicide of a patient who had suicidal tendencies. The first case concerned the issue whether such tendencies negligently had not been detected (120 Ib BGE 411 "Klinik Königsfelden", liability denied). While they were known in the second (as well as the instant) case, the key question was whether the patient was harmed due to insufficient safety precautions or supervision (112 Ib BGE 322 "Klinik Liestal", liability confirmed).

been caused by the lack of due care. Doctrine has almost *unanimously disapproved* of this test: Apart from the fact that such a factual presumption actually concerns the evaluation of evidence reserved to the cantonal courts and excluded on appeal, the significance thereof cannot be easily discerned[22]. Furthermore, the basis of these arguments is already problematic since it differentiates between risks of a treatment and the mere lack of its success. In light of the high standards required for a rebuttal of such presumption, which effectively leads to a "probatio diabolica" for the defendant doctor, this would lead to a redistribution of risks which can hardly be brought into accord with substantive law[23]. In the current laudable decision (which unfortunately has not yet been published), the Federal Supreme Court clearly states what it had previously only indicated in 120 II BGE 251: Not "any deterioration of the patient's health in the course of his treatment speaks in favour of a natural presumption of a lack of due care." The ruling of the prior decision is hereby clearly restricted to the particular kind of injection which was at issue. This excludes an analogous application of this test even in other cases of infections which occur in the course of some other kind of treatment (E. 2b).

For the time being, it is therefore still up to the victim to prove a lack of due **40**
care in the course of his treatment, no matter whether his claim is based upon contract law (such as in the instant case) or on the law of delict (including cantonal tort law)[24]. The failure to apply due care continues to be assessed on the basis of an *ex ante* perspective (which the Court underlines by following 120 Ib BGE 414 E. 4a); it is only confirmed if the conduct of the doctor appears to be no longer acceptable according to general standards of medical expertise. The Court started from the basic notion that suicidal patients only require control and restrictions of their freedom to the extent it is absolutely necessary, which is determined by the need for a lasting success of the therapy, which is questioned by measures that are too restrictive, such as tying him up or permanent supervision. In light of the medication, psychiatrist experts had raised no objections against accommodating the plaintiff in a single room or against the lack of a permanent warden (E. 3). It was further denied that the safety locks of the windows used in the plaintiff's room had not met the necessary standards. This was supported by the fact that only the application of considerable force could break such locks: The plaintiff had torn out the screws of the safety locks by forcefully pulling the window handle. The medical expert had testified that such a sudden and strong suicidal impulse, which had increased the plaintiff's muscle strength could not have been expected. The same type of window locks had been in use for several years without any hitch. Since the hospital could not have been expected to ensure abolute safety against any

[22] In particular H. Hausheer, [1996] ZBJV 132, 392.

[23] *Cf.* W. Wiegand, [1996] ZBJV 132, 330 *et seq.*; H. Honsell, [1995] *Aktuelle Juristische Praxis* (AJP), 227 *et seq.*; recently M. Gattiker, Kausalhaftung für medizinische Behandlungen – Realität oder Zukunftsmusik?, [2001] AJP, 652 *et seq.* (who criticizes that 120 II BGE 248 takes yet another step towards strict liability for medical malpractice).

[24] See *e.g.* 123 II BGE 583; 120 Ib BGE 414 E. 4a; *cf.* the overview provided by M. Gattiker (*supra* note 14) pp. 646 *et seq*

accident of the kind in question, there was no indication that the current safety locks of the windows should have been replaced by a newly developed system (E.4).

C. Literature

1. S. Weber, Von der Entstehung durch unerlaubte Handlung zur Entstehung durch Schädigung, in: *Die Rechtsentwicklung an der Schwelle zum 21. Jahrhundert, Symposium zum Schweizerischen Privatrecht* (Zürich 2001) pp. 253 *et seq.*

41 After pointing out the deficiencies of today's tort law, S. Weber addresses several modifications intended by the draft of a federal act on the revision and unification of tort law, such as the bases of the claim, the (highly disputed) merger of contractual and delictual liability, several issues of compensation (which have so far hardly been discussed in Swiss law), the weakness of the prevailing notion of damage (based on the balance theory), the distribution as well as the assessment of damages, colliding claims as well as recourse issues. The flaws of valuations detected in present tort law, which the author only partly sees cured in the draft revision, are primarily traced back to a presumed lack of clear notions of the functions as well as the basic ideas and principles of tort law.

2. J. Gross, *Schweizerisches Staatshaftungsrecht* (2nd edn. Berne 2001)

42 In his second edition, J. Gross has substantially revised his book first published in 1995. He provides comprehensive information on the state as well as future trends of the law of state liability in Switzerland, which in the last decades has evolved from liability of civil servants to primary and exclusive liability of the federation and the cantons for unlawfulness. Apart from borderline issues between private and public law, the book focuses in particular on wrongfulness, liability for lawful infliction of harm, contractual liability, enterprise liability as well as liability based on principles of reliance.

D. New Working Instruments

1. The New SAKE Tables

43 The already mentioned household damages rest, according to established administration of justice and practice, on the number of hours which the injured person spent in managing the household and on an estimation of the lost hours of household management following the damaging event. As already mentioned earlier, new tables are available to calculate household hours and to more closely characterize individual household tasks. They were compiled based on annual Swiss surveys on the labor force made since 1997

and include non-remunerated work in various households. The questioning of a large number of randomly selected people included a very detailed telephone survey in which individuals were asked what actual household tasks they performed on the specific day prior to the survey.

Based on these statistics, average values were then calculated for various specified household types. Of significance is the ability to dynamically show specific cases of household efforts and future changes on a time axis. The SAKE survey then allows us to obtain objective criteria to determine the amount of appropriate indemnification. This allows us to from now on drop the the previous Federal Court method of estimating the indemnification for housekeeping and from arbitrarily determining a quality surcharge for additional household activities. **44**

It now appears that these tables are also recognized by the Federal Court, following an extensive discussion on the methodical basis which apparently has eliminated various doubts. For more information on this subject see the next HAVE magazine "Haftpflicht und Versicherung" [*i.e.* Liability and Insurance, Schulthess Publishers, Juristic Media AG, Zurich 2002, 24 *et seq.*], V. Pribnow/R. Widmer/A. Sousa-Posa, Th. Geiser, on "Die Bestimmung des Haushaltsschadens auf der Basis der SAKE, [*i.e.* Determining household damages using SAKE tables]. **45**

2. LEONARDO: The New Calculation Programme

Together with the 5th edition of the cash value tables from Stauffer/Schaetzle which are also well-known outside of Switzerland, and the newer handbook Schaetzle/Weber on how to use these tables, M. Maurer/M. Schaetzle/St. Weber have developed a software program designed to simplify the very demanding and complex calculation of disability and support damages. This especially applies to the calculation of damages based on delayed and temporary pensions resulting from expected future income changes which cannot be taken directly from the cited cash value tables. The same applies to the capitalization of real wage increases which according to recent studies are to be given increased attention (also see the said handbook, "Kapitalisieren" [*i.e.* Capitalization], Zurich 2001, notes 4.4 *et seq.*). **46**

With the modulator "Assistant Calculator, expected income development" for any desired period can be made by entering a particular rising factor or an average annual percentual increase of income. A graphical illustration of income fluctuation serves to check the required plausibility compared to past income developments. The programme user can also separate a portion of household damages and income losses, based on a mixed calculation method. Furthermore, the programme easily distinguishes between various coexisting liability and insurance payments under private and public legal compensation systems. One can also choose between the calculation method still applied by the Federal Court and an alternative method which is being propagated by **47** scholars with special emphasis and good reason. Among other things, it becomes easier to handle out-of-court settlements. Finally, the programme is equipped with a new feature which also allows precise daily rather than annual calculations.

48 The calculation programme is enhanced by a relevant collection of rulings which will be updated regularly. This makes it easy to revert to the most important leading cases by the Federal Court and the upper cantonal courts. The same holds true for major legal regulations which show an increasingly short life span in Switzerland. Rounding the collection off are extracts from the most important literature on personal damages.

XVIII. European Union

Bernhard A. Koch

A. Legislation and Legislative Projects

1. Product Liability

1 On 31 January 2001, the Commission published its second report on the application of the Product Liability Directive.[1] The report was to a large extent based upon the various responses[2] to a Green Paper adopted in July 1999.[3] The latter had not only called for submissions on how the current product liability scheme worked in practice, but futhermore to what extent it should be modified. The report itself follows this two-partite structure in presenting the status quo in a comparative perspective (chapter 2) before outlining the range of views on desired amendments (chapter 3). In the final chapter, the Commission presents its conclusions drawn from this survey.

2 One of the major findings of the report was the fact that little can actually be found on the application of the Directive.[4] As in the first application report of 1995[5], the report summarises that "there is still limited experience", which it traces back to two factors: "the Directive was lately transposed in some Member States and, according to the possibility given to Member States under art. 13 of the Directive, national contractual or extra-contractual law or a specific liability regime is applied in parallel".[6] Furthermore, there seems to be hardly any reliable factual basis which would allow to identify any major problems

[1] COM(2000) 893 final (in the following: R-PL). The full text is available on the Internet: http://europa.eu.int/comm/internal_market/en/goods/liability/report-EN.pdf. All references to the Internet are current as of 1 February 2002.

[2] The responses are available at http://europa.eu.int/comm/internal_market/en/goods/liability/replies.htm.

[3] COM(1999) 396 final. The Green Paper can be downloaded at http://europe.eu.int/comm/internal_market/en/update/consumer/greenen.pdf.

[4] The Commission regrets "that only little information about the application exist and statistics, if available, are not complete" (R-PL p. 8).

[5] COM(95) 617 final (http://europa.eu.int/comm/internal_market/en/goods/liability/reporten.pdf) p. 2.

[6] R-PL p. 28.

that needed to be addressed. Consequently, the Commission finds it "premature to envisage any changes to the current liability system".[7]

3 Nevertheless, the process of information gathering shall be continued. The Commission therefore announced that it would institute an expert group which should serve as an "observatory" that continuously collects relevant data on the practice of product liability in all Member States.[8] It should further provide a "forum to continuously discuss issues related to product liability"[9]. The group should be composed of experts from national administrations as well as other interested parties.

4 The report also envisages additional studies and data-collection mechanisms, in particular on product safety as well as the economic consequences of the current liability system and possible changes thereof. Two specific alterations the Commission thereby has in mind include an extension of product liability to development risks as well as the abolition of caps on damages for serial incidents.[10] Another study shall "analyse and compare the practical effects of the different systems applicable in all the Member States on the bringing of claims for defective products".[11]

5 Finally, the Commission also vowed to undertake further actions in related areas such as amendments to the General Product Safety Directive 92/59[12] or initiatives regarding access to justice or environmental liability.[13]

2. Environmental Liability

6 In its strive for "a comprehensive Community scheme" based on the "polluter pays" principle[14], the Commission has prepared a draft "Directive on Environmental Liability with Regard to the Prevention and Restoration of Environmental Damage" (DD-EL)[15] for the Parliament and the Council. It was formally adopted by the Commission on 23 January 2002. At earliest (if at all), the proposal might be formally adopted in two years time.

[7] R-PL p. 28.
[8] R-PL pp. 28–29.
[9] R-PL p. 29.
[10] R-PL p. 29.
[11] R-PL p. 30. This study has just been awarded to the law firm Lovells.
[12] Council Directive 92/59/EEC of 29 June 1992 on general product safety, OJ L 228, 11. 8. 1992, p. 24. On 2 February, the Commission adopted a (revised) proposal for a revision of said directive: COM(2001) 63 (http://europa.eu.int/eur-lex/en/com/pdf/2001/en_501PC0063.pdf), which was amended on 28 June by Commission Opinion COM(2001) 376 final. The Council formally adopted the joint text on 27 September (http://europa.eu.int/abc/doc/off/bull/en/200109/p104060.htm).
[13] R-PL pp. 31–35.
[14] *Cf.* EC Treaty Art. 174 (2).
[15] COM(2002) 17 provisional version, available under http://europa.eu.int/eur-lex/en/com/pdf/2002/en_502PC0017.pdf

The background to this Draft Directive includes a 1993 Commission Green Paper[16] and seven years later a White Paper on Environmental Liability[17], which has instigated broad feedback[18]. The Environment Directorate-General also released a working paper on 25 July 2001[19], which asked for comments on the general outline of a future regime contained therein.[20] **7**

The proposal, which is not intended to have retrospective effect (art. 19 DD-EL), unfortunately covers only certain types of environmental harm, *i.e.* damage to biodiversity (as confined by existing protection under EU or national law[21]), waters (as regulated by the Water Framework Directive[22]), and land contamination creating serious potential or actual harm to public health. It does not extend to personal injury or damage to property, redress for which must still be sought under national tort law. Environmental harm covered by certain international conventions[23] is also excluded. **8**

The primary focus of the proposal is on certain risky activities as specifically listed in Annex I to the draft, which consists of cross-references to previous EU legislation.[24] There is, however, some limited extension of said scope inasmuch as other activities can trigger liability as well, but only if they are carried out negligently. **9**

The Draft Directive primarily aims at the prevention of environmental harm, but also requires the reparation of any damage actually caused. This has to be organised and controlled by administrative bodies. These "competent authorities" (art. 13 DD-EL) shall require the operator (art. 2 para. 1 no. 9 DD-EL) of a risky activity, who must be identifiable as such[25], to take or at least finance **10**

[16] May 14, 1993, COM(93) 47 final.

[17] February 9, 2000, COM(2000) 66 final, http://europa.eu.int/comm/environment/liability/el_full.pdf.

[18] Summaries thereof can be found at http://europa.eu.int/comm/environment/liability/followup.htm.

[19] http://europa.eu.int/comm/environment/liability/consultation_en.pdf.

[20] The numerous comments thereto have been published on the Internet: http://europa.eu.int/comm/environment/liability/wrkdoc.htm.

[21] The draft defines biodiversity as "natural habitats and species listed in Annex I to Directive 79/409/EEC, or in Annexes I, II and IV to Directive 92/43/EEC, or habitats and species, which are not covered by those Directives, for which areas of protection or conservation have been designated pursuant to the relevant Member States' legislation on nature conservation" (art. 2 para. 1 no. 2 DD-EL).

[22] Directive 2000/60/EC of the European Parliament and of the Council of 23 October 2000 establishing a framework for Community action in the field of water policy, OJ L 327, 22. 12. 2000, p. 1.

[23] Art. 3 DD-EL explicitly lists the relevant conventions, which renders this provision somewhat prone to continuous updating.

[24] The Commission thereby regrettably repeated the flaws of existing national environmental liability laws, in particular the German *Umwelthaftungsgesetz*.

[25] The draft therefore does not cover the most problematic areas of pollution, since it expressly holds itself "not a suitable instrument for dealing with pollution of a widespread, diffuse character, where it is impossible to link the negative environmental effects with the activities of certain individual actors." (9th recital of the DD-EL preamble).

all measures necessary to avoid or ultimately restore the harm caused (which not necessarily means that the original habitat must be reproduced at its prior location[26]). There are, however, certain exemptions and defences: In particular, liability is excluded if the activity causing the harm previously had been specifically authorised or if they were at the time believed to be safe according to the state of scientific and technical knowledge (art. 9 DD-EL).

11 The regime envisaged by this proposal is not based on tort law (at least as underlined by the Commission[27]), but is intended to introduce a public law scheme by channelling the execution of this legislation to administrative bodies. It is to be feared, however, that the interplay of this new regime and traditional tort law will work even less smoothly than the product liability model in light of the fact that – in contrast to the latter – it consciously deviates from present tort law systems without providing for adequate delimitations. Furthermore, it is worded (and officially explained) in tort law terminology, which might add to misunderstandings, to say the least.

12 There is at least some theoretical possibility for individuals likely to be affected by environmental harm as well as for public interest groups (in particular NGOs) to induce action by said administrative agencies if the latter should fail to do so. However, the proceedings outlined therefor by the Draft Directive seem to be too time-consuming in order to cope with any imminent threats to the environment.[28]

13 Furthermore, the proposal contains no alterations of traditional rules concerning the standard as well as the burden of proof[29], which makes it even more unlikely that any such initiative might be effective. Even the "competent authority" who should be "the driving force of the scheme"[30] has no options in that respect: "If a settlement cannot be found between the competent authority and the polluter regarding restoration of any damage established, the matter will be settled in court."[31]

14 Another downside of this draft is the fact that there is no sufficient requirement for financial cover. As art. 16 DD-EL currently reads, Member States shall merely "encourage the use by operators of any appropriate insurance or other forms of financial security".

[26] The Draft Directive therefore differentiates between "primary" and "compensatory restoration" (art. 2 para. 1 no. 16 DD-EL).

[27] See Memo/02/10 of 23 January 2002 ("Frequently asked questions on the Commission's proposal on environmental liability", http://europa.eu.int/rapid/start/cgi/guesten.ksh?p_action.gettxt=gt&doc=MEMO/02/10|0|RAPID&lg=EN).

[28] *Cf.* Artt. 14–15 DD-EL.

[29] Memo/02/10 (*supra* note 27).

[30] Memo/02/10 (*supra* note 27).

[31] Memo/02/10 (*supra* note 27).

3. Marine Pollution Liability

On 19 November 2001, the Commission adopted proposals for Council decisions authorising the accession to two recent IMO conventions, *i.e.* the so-called 'HNS' Convention of 1996[32] and the 'Bunkers' Convention of 2001[33]. The former[34] introduces liability for harm caused by certain hazardous substances when carried by sea; the latter[35] covers damage caused by spills of fuel oil carried in ships' bunkers. **15**

The HNS Convention provides for strict liability of the shipowner, which is limited by maximum amounts linked to the tonnage of his vessel. The shipowner is required to take out insurance cover to which claimants have a direct right of action. The liability of the individual shipowners is supplemented by a compensation fund system. **16**

The Bunkers Convention is modelled on the 1969 Brussels Convention on Civil Liability for Oil Pollution Damage[36]. It requires registered owners of vessels over 1,000 gross tonnage[37] to maintain insurance or other financial security to cover liability for pollution damage, again subject to limitations. It further allows for direct claims against the insurer. **17**

While both conventions are generally considered to be important additions to the existing international regime of liability for marine pollution, neither can be ratified as a whole by the Member States since they include provisions on jurisdiction as well as the recognition and enforcement of judgments that are in conflict with Council Regulation 44/2001. The Commission therefore proposes a Council decision exceptionally authorising ratification of those conventions, subject to making a reservation "whereby Member States undertake to apply Regulation 44/2001 in their mutual relations". This is only intended to be an "interim solution" in order to allow that these conventions can enter into force[38]. The Commission nevertheless recommends to re-negotiate both texts in the future in order to purge these existing incompatibilities. **18**

[32] International Convention on Liability and Compensation for Damage in Connection with the Carriage of Hazardous and Noxious Substances by Sea, adopted on 3 May 1996.

[33] International Convention on Civil Liability for Bunker Oil Pollution Damage, adopted on 23 March 2001.

[34] Commission proposal: COM(2001) 674 final (http://europa.eu.int/eur-lex/en/com/pdf/2001/en_501PC0674.pdf).

[35] Commission proposal: COM(2001) 675 final (http://europa.eu.int/eur-lex/en/com/pdf/2001/en_501PC0675.pdf).

[36] International Convention on Civil Liability for Oil Pollution Damage, adopted in Brussels on 29 November 1969 (1973 UNTS p. 3), as amended in 1976 and 1984.

[37] The insurance requirement of the aforementioned 1969 Brussels Convention only extends to ships carrying more than 2,000 tons of oil in bulk as cargo.

[38] As of today, the HNS Convention has been ratified by only two countries (the Russian Federation and Angola), the Bunkers Convention not by a single one.

4. Liability for Aviation Accidents

19 The EU Council for Transport Ministers decided on 5 April to ratify the Montreal Convention[39]. It also recommended that the Member States themselves should ratify the Convention at the latest by 31 December 2002. At their 29 June meeting, the Council further agreed to modify Regulation 2027/97 on air carrier liability[40] in order to align Community legislation with the 1999 Montreal Convention. It thereby followed the amended Commission proposal of 21 May 2001[41].

20 The most important change envisaged by the draft is the extension of air carrier liability beyond personal injury (as previously) to damage caused by delays or by the loss or deterioration of baggage. The scope of the amended regulation nevertheless deviates from the Montreal Convention inasmuch as it will (still) not cover cargo (which will also be reflected by a new title[42]). On the other hand, it will continue to apply to national air transportation as well, which is excluded by Art. 1 of the Montreal Convention.

21 The liability provisions of the Montreal Convention (Artt. 17, 19 *et seq.*) have not been incorporated by an express repetition of the respective wording. Instead, the Commission chose to include mere cross references to the relevant provisions of the Convention[43], which has been criticized in particular by consumer organizations.[44]

22 In contrast to the prior wording of Art. 6, the duty to make "adequate" information on liability requirements available to all passengers in advance has been specified and broadened by new draft Art. 6, which not only lists certain subjects that need to be covered, but also requires carriers to use a specific wording as provided by a new annex to the Regulation.[45] The mandatory noti-

[39] Convention for the Unification of Certain Rules for International Carriage by Air, signed at Montreal on 28 May 1999. It was recently also published in OJ L 194, 18. 7. 2001, p. 0039.

[40] Council Regulation (EC) No 2027/97 of 9 October 1997 on air carrier liability in the event of accidents, OJ L 285, 17. 10. 1997, p. 1.

[41] COM(2001) 273 final. See also the prior proposal of the Commission, COM(2000) 340 final of 6 June 2000.

[42] The new title will therefore be "Regulation (EC) No. 2027/97 on air carrier liability in respect of the carriage of passengers and their baggage by air".

[43] See only Art. 3 para. 1 of the proposal: "The liability of a Community air carrier for damage sustained in case of death or bodily injury of a passenger shall be governed by the provisions set out in Artt. 17, 20 and 21 of the Montreal Convention."

[44] See *e.g.* the comments of the European Consumers' Organization (http://www.beuc.org/public/xfiles2000/x2000/x101e.pdf), pp. 2–3.

[45] Art. 6 paras. 2 and 3 of the proposal reads as follows:
"2. All air carriers selling air transport services in the Community shall ensure that a summary of the main provisions governing liability of passengers and their baggage, including notification of deadlines for filing an action for compensation and the possibility of supplementary insurance for baggage, is made available to passengers at all points of sale, including sale by telephone and via the Internet. In order to comply with this information requirement, Community air carriers shall avail themselves of the notice contained in the annex to this Regulation.
3. In addition to the information requirements set out in paragraph 2, all air carriers shall provide each consumer in the Community who purchases air transport services with a written indication of:

fication of passengers in writing, however, is now restricted to the amounts of liability limits and no longer needs to be provided on the tickets themselves (as required by Art. 6 para 2 of the Regulation as in force), but only in (whatever) written form.

The minimum amount of advance payments, which is only optional under the Convention (Art. 28), but required by current Art. 5 of the Regulation, shall be raised to 16,000 SDR (Art. 5 para. 2 of the proposal). 23

As in the prior version of Regulation 2027/97, the insurance requirement of Art. 50 Montreal Convention will be introduced by reference to Art. 7 of Regulation 2407/92[46], whose "obligation of insurance … as far as it relates to liability for passengers shall be understood as requiring that a Community air carrier shall be insured up to a level that is adequate to ensure that all natural persons entitled to compensation receive the full amount to which they are entitled in accordance with this Regulation" (Art. 3 para. 2 of the proposal). 24

5. Compensation for Crime Victims

The Commission further adopted a Green Paper on "Compensation to Crime Victims" on 28 September, 2001.[47] The core issue thereby put on debate[48] is whether or not the European Union should introduce a minimum standard of state compensation for crime victims[49], particularly if someone is injured in a foreign Member State. The consultation period was scheduled to last until the end of January 2002. 25

The Green Paper starts out with an assessment of the current situation in the various Member States.[50] A study initiated by the Commission[51] has shown considerable differences among the various Member States in that respect, not 26

- the applicable limit for that flight on the carrier's liability in respect of death or injury, if such a limit exists;
- the applicable limit for that flight on the carrier's liability in respect of destruction, loss of or damage to baggage and a warning that baggage greater in value than this figure should be brought to the airline's attention at check-in or fully insured by the passenger prior to travel;
- the applicable limit for that flight on the carrier's liability for damage occasioned by delay."

[46] Council Regulation (EEC) No 2407/92 of 23 July 1992 on licensing of air carriers, OJ L 240, 24. 8. 1992, p. 1.

[47] COM(2001) 536 final (in the following: GP-CV). The full text is available on the Internet: http://europa.eu.int/eur-lex/en/com/gpr/2001/com2001_0536en01.pdf.

[48] Prior activities in that respect (as mentioned on p. 6 of the GP-CV) were *e.g.* the 1998 Vienna Action Plan of the Council and the Commission (OJ C 19, 23.1.1999, p. 1. Point 51.c), a communication by the Commission one year later (COM[1999] 349 final, 14.7.1999), as well as a call for drawing up such minimum standards by the European Council of Tampere (Presidency Conclusions, point 32).

[49] Direct liability of the actual offender was explicitly excluded; GP-CV, p. 7.

[50] The Council of Europe Convention on the Compensation of Victims of Violent Crimes 1983 is in force in nine Member States: Denmark, Finland, France, Germany, Luxembourg, Netherlands, Portugal, Sweden and the United Kingdom. The Convention has further been ratified by Azerbaijan, Cyprus, the Czech Republic, Norway and Switzerland.

[51] The study was conducted under the auspices of the Swedish Crime Victim Compensation and Support Authority: A. Wergens, *Crime victims in the European Union* (2000).

only as far as the extent of cover is concerned, but also when it comes to eligibility thereto.[52] The report concludes that the current situation in all Member States "leaves something to be desired"[53]. It particularly criticizes "the lack of convergence between the existing schemes"[54], which may lead to widely differing amounts of possible awards merely depending on the place where the crime was committed within the EU. This is even more true when it comes to the availability of state compensation in cross-border situations. "These effects, which must appear arbitrary from the individual's perspective, are clearly not satisfactory in view of the objective of establishing the EU as an area of freedom, security and justice for all."[55]

27 The Green Paper therefore introduces the three primary objectives for possible community action. The major goal therefore is to provide for a "safety net" for all community citizens who fall victims to a crime, thereby assuring their basic right to compensation as such. As a second step, the Green Paper proposes to harmonize the extent as well as the terms of availability of such compensation in all Member States. Thirdly, access to compensation in cross-border situtations should be facilitated in order to eliminate the mere fact where the crime took place as the decisive factor whether or not the victim can receive state payments.[56]

28 An important limitation to this strive for unification applies, however: As the Green Paper expressly states, "compensation levels expressed in pecuniary terms cannot be made uniform"[57] in light of different standards of living as well as deviating policies of the Member States in granting state relief payments in general. It is therefore only the "principles underlying compensation levels" that should be harmonized, but only inasmuch as a "minimum standard" can be achieved.

29 The opinions gathered in response to the Green Paper shall therefore focus primarily on the necessity as well as a possible definition of such a minimum standard of compensation. Such definition may, according to the questionnaire, include a combination of the following factors: the type of crime as well as the type of injury (including the question whether immaterial harm shall be recoverable), the degree of proof, further the victim's financial situation, her behaviour in particular or in general ("involvement in criminal activity"[58]), subsidiarity of compensation in light of other possible sources, finally aspects of justice or public policy. The specific concern of cross-border crimes shall be specifically adressed, in particular the choice of compensation in either the

[52] There is no such compensation scheme in Greece and Italy (the latter providing cover only to victims of acts of terrorists or of organised crime). See further the overview provided by the GP-CV on pp. 11 *et seq*.
[53] GP-CV, p. 19.
[54] GP-CV, p. 19.
[55] GP-CV, p. 19.
[56] GP-CV, p. 20.
[57] GP-CV, p. 21.
[58] Cf. GP-CV, p. 30.

home or the foreign Member State (or both) as well as procedural aspects such as harmonized claims forms.

The Commission mentions several preferred answers beforehand, however: Eligibility should therefore not be limited to citizens, but also extended to all legal residents in a Member State.[59] A minimum standard should at least include cover for intentional crimes causing personal injury.[60] The Commission also sees "strong reasons for including immaterial damages in a minimum standard"[61]. The victim's financial situation should not be a criterion when assessing the award.[62] The Green Paper further includes two proposals to solve cross-border cases, the so-called "mutual assistance model" (Member State in whose territory crime was committed pays, Member State of residence forwards applications)[63] and the "double responsibility model" (both *lex loci* as well as Member State of residence pay alternatively)[64]. **30**

B. Cases

1. European Court of Justice (ECJ) 10 May 2001 – C-203/99 *Henning Veedfald v. Århus Amtskommune*

a) Brief Summary of the Facts

The plaintiff was to undergo a kidney transplantation at a Danish hospital. **31** After a kidney had been removed from the donor (the plaintiff's brother), the organ was irrigated with a perfusion fluid that had been manufactured for this particular use in the laboratories of another hospital of the same carrier. Since this liquid was defective, the donor kidney could no longer be used for the transplant. The plaintiff subsequently claimed damages from the defendant, who owns and runs both hospitals. The defendant argued that it had not put the product into circulation and that the product had not been manufactured for an economic purpose in light of the fact that the hospitals were publicly funded. The Danish *Højesteret* asked the Court for a preliminary ruling on five questions on the interpretation of the Products Liability Directive[65].

b) Judgment of the Court

The first key issue under dispute was the question whether the liquid was "put **32** into circulation" as required by the Directive and the Danish products liability statute[66], since it had never actually left the sphere of the manufacturer and

[59] GP-CV, p. 21.
[60] GP-CV, pp. 21–22.
[61] GP-CV, p. 24.
[62] GP-CV, p. 26.
[63] GP-CV, pp. 33–35.
[64] GP-CV, pp. 35–36.
[65] Council Directive 85/374/EEC of 25 July 1985.
[66] *Lov n. 371 om produktansvar* (law on product liability) of 7 June 1989.

was only used in preparation of the services rendered by the hospital. The defendant further claimed that the mere use of a product in the course of providing some service were not within the scope of the Directive. The Court rejected these arguments by stating that it was nevertheless the product (*i.e.* the fluid) which was defective and not the services given in the instant case, where the person for whom the services were intended had to bring himself within the defendant's sphere of control. The exemption from liability contained in art. 7(a) of the Directive primarily applied to cases where it was not the producer himself who had caused the product to leave the manufacturing process. The Court therefore concluded that the fluid was indeed put into circulation even though it was only supposed to serve in the preparatory stage of a transplant surgery.

33 The defendant further tried to avoid liability by arguing that the entire operation (including the preparation of the liquid) was financed by public funds and not by the patient himself, so that the exemption of art. 7(c) of the Directive applied, which requires some economic purpose underlying the manufacturing or distribution process. The Court, however, denied that the operation was a charitable activity and confirmed that "the fact that products are manufactured for a specific medical service for which the patient does not pay directly but which is financed from public funds maintained out of taxpayers' contributions cannot detract from the economic and business character of that manufacture".[67]

34 As far as a uniform definition of damage was concerned, the Court argued that Member States may not restrict the types of recoverable harm, be it from death or from personal injury, or from damage to or destruction of an item of property. While they were free to specify the exact scope of reimbursement (and to decide about the availability of non-material damage), "full and proper compensation" for personal harm must as a minimum be provided for in all Member States in order to ensure the effectiveness of the Directive. National courts have to decide which category of damage listed by art. 9 is present in the case before them, but even if they should fail to do so, they are still not free to deny compensation at all by pointing at national law of damages if the conditions of liability as such are fulfilled.

c) Commentary

35 In its first preliminary ruling ever on the application of the Products Liability Directive[68], the ECJ significantly broadened its scope by shifting the boundaries between services and products closer to the latter. The Court thereby deviated from the opinion of Advocate General Ruiz-Jarabo Colomer.

36 The latter had argued that the Directive would only extend to movable goods which had been produced industrially. The liquid in the instant case had, how-

[67] Para. 21.

[68] Prior cases concerned the implementation of the directive; cases C-293/91 (1993) *Commission v. France* ECR I-1 and C-300/95 *Commission v. United Kingdom* (1997) ECR I-2649.

ever, been specifically prepared at the occasion of and only for the purposes of the transplantation.[69] Furthermore, a systematic view of the Directive would support his opinion that the liquid was not "put into circulation" since it was never intended to be used outside the hospital (and even there not for any other use than the operation to be performed in the instant case). Since it was also not meant to be used by a consumer within the meaning of the Directive, but only by the hospital's staff in the course of their services, the Advocate General held that it were rather these services as such that should be the focus of this case, which put it beyond the scope of the Products Liability Directive. He further supported this argument by pointing at the preparatory works for a Services Directive, which in itself showed that such a case should not be seen as a products liability issue.

While the opinion of the Advocate General seems very convincing, future prac- **37**
tice will have to live with the fact that the Court did not follow his arguments. It remains to be seen, however, if and how such position can be maintained if a Services Directive should ever make it through the legislative pipeline.

2. Other Cases[70]

In Joined Cases C-397/98 and C-410/98 (*Metallgesellschaft Ltd and Others,* **38**
Hoechst AG, Hoechst UK Ltd)[71], the Court confirmed *inter alia* that compensation for mere loss of profit cannot be excluded *per se* in actions for breach of Community law since such would render most litigation for liability in economic or commercial matters ineffective[72]. In the instant cases, subsidiaries of parent companies resident in another Member State were discriminatorily required to pay advance corporation tax. The sole financial loss suffered was therefore the interest resulting from such premature payment.

An Italian company's action for damages resulting from alleged harm to its **39**
reputation failed in Case C-315/99 P (*Ismeri Europa Srl*)[73]. Plaintiffs were expressly named in a report of the Court of Auditors without having had a chance to comment on the findings contained therein. The Court denied compensation by arguing that the defendant would not have changed the essence of its report even if plaintiffs had been heard in advance (which by itself was held to be a general principle of law whose observance should be ensured). Therefore, the necessary causal link between the contested behaviour and the damage was missing.

[69] The written observations of Austria, France, the United Kingdom as well as the Commission submitted in this case were against such argument, however, and therefore in favour of the plaintiff's position on this issue.

[70] This is not an exhaustive account of all cases involving matters of compensation before the ECJ; see *e.g.* joined Cases C-80/99 to C-82/99 *Flemmer and others*. Judgments of the Court of First Instance are not mentioned either; see *e.g.* Case T-196/99 *Area Cova, SA, and others* or Case 155/99 *Dieckmann & Hansen GmbH*.

[71] ECJ 8 March 2001.

[72] Paras. 91 *et seq.*

[73] ECJ 10 July 2001

XIX. South Africa

Johann C. Knobel

A. Cases

1. Carmichele v Minister of Safety and Security and Another (Centre for Applied Legal Studies Intervening) 2001 4 SA 938 Constitutional Court (CC): Liability of Organs of State for Omission on Part of Police and Prosecutors

a) Brief Summary of the Facts

1 C violently attacked the applicant, a 28-year-old woman, hitting her over the head with a pick handle, breaking her arm, and stabbing her in the chest with a knife so forcefully that the blade of the knife buckled in the process. C had previously been convicted on charges of housebreaking and indecent assault. At the time of the attack on the applicant, C was facing a charge of rape in the magistrate's court, but had been released from custody by the magistrate acting on the recommendation of the investigating officer. Soon after C had been released G, owner of a house in which the applicant frequently stayed and in which the attack on her eventually took place, learned of C's previous conviction and the alleged rape, and asked the police whether C could be kept in custody pending his trial. The police advised G to take the matter up with the public prosecutor, who in turn told G that nothing could be done unless C committed another offence. Shortly thereafter C attempted to commit suicide, and was interviewed by the prosecutor, revealing serious sexual deviation on the part of C. He was sent to a psychiatric hospital for observation, but the hospital reported that C was capable of understanding the court proceedings and had also been mentally capable at the time of the alleged rape. C again appeared in the magistrate's court and pleaded not guilty, whereupon he was released again pending a decision by the Attorney-General on whether the case should proceed in the High Court. There was no reference in the record to the question of bail having been raised. After C's release, the applicant saw him prowling around G's house. Both the applicant and G again spoke to the senior prosecutor, and were again told that the latter was powerless to do any-

thing. A few days later the attack on the applicant took place in G's house. After the attack on the applicant, the charge of rape came to trial and C was convicted of attempted rape, and later that same year C was prosecuted for the attack on the applicant and was convicted of housebreaking and attempted murder.

The applicant instituted a claim in delict (tort) against the respondents, alleging that the police officers and prosecutors, acting in the course and scope of their employment with the State, had owed her a legal duty to act in order to prevent C from harming her, and that they had negligently failed to comply with that duty. The case went on trial in the Cape Provincial Division (CPD) of the High Court, and then went on appeal, first to the Supreme Court of Appeal (SCA) and thereafter to the Constitutional Court (CC). 2

b) Judgments of the CPD and the SCA

The CPD held that there was no evidence upon which a court could reasonably find that the alleged legal duty had existed. An order for absolution from the instance was granted, and the applicant appealed to the SCA.[1] The judgment on appeal only dealt with the question whether the police and prosecutors owed the applicant a legal duty, and not with the elements of negligence and causation. 3

The SCA pointed out that the test for determining the wrongfulness of an omission had been settled in a number of previous decisions[2] of the Appellate Division (AD).[3] According to this test, the existence of a legal duty to avoid or prevent loss is a conclusion of law depending upon a consideration of all the circumstances of each particular case and on an interplay of many factors which must be considered. In essence the issue is one of reasonableness, determined with reference to the legal perceptions of the community as assessed by the Court. The interests of the parties and the interests of the community must be weighed, and a balance must be struck in accordance with what the court conceives society's notions of the demands of justice to be. There is a difference between morally reprehensible and legally actionable omissions, and a legal duty is not determined by the mere recognition of social attitudes and public and legal policy. The question must always be whether the defendant ought reasonably and practically to have prevented harm, in other words, if it is reasonable to expect of the defendant to have taken positive steps to prevent the harm. 4

Analysing the facts, the Court pointed out that the decision to release C was obviously taken by the Magistrate, so that the alleged legal duties had to be 5

[1] The judgment of the SCA was reported as *Carmichele v Minister of Safety and Security and Another* 2001 1 SA 489 (SCA).

[2] *Minister van Polisie v Ewels* 1975 3 SA 590 (A) 597; *Minister of Law and Order v Kadir* 1995 1 SA 303 (A) 317-318; *Knop v Johannesburg City Council* 1995 2 SA 1 (A) 27 and *Government of the Republic of South Africa v Basdeo* 1996 1 SA 355 (A) 367.

[3] As the SCA was known before the new constitutional dispensation.

confined to a duty on the police to provide the prosecutor with complete information, and a duty on the prosecutor to oppose bail and supply complete information relevant to C's being kept in custody or released to the court. Since the prosecutor was in possession of all the relevant information, nothing further was required of the police and no legal duty was owed by them. Therefore the only question to be decided was whether the prosecutors owed the applicant a legal duty to oppose C's release and secure his rearrest.

6 The Court stated that there was no absolute duty on a prosecutor to oppose bail in all cases. The prosecutor has a public duty to oppose bail in appropriate cases, but a breach of this does not necessarily constitute an omission legally actionable by any member of the public. Whether a duty is owed to a member of public would depend on what is reasonable, taking into account all facts and circumstances of the case, and the question whether the claimant stands in a special relationship with the defendant distinguishing the plaintiff from any other member of the public. In light of all the facts, particularly the fact that the psychiatric report had not declared C a danger to society and had not recommended keeping him in custody, the Court decided that it was not unreasonable for the prosecutor not to oppose C's release.

7 The Court was strengthened in its decision by finding that there was no special relationship between the applicant and the prosecutors indicating the need for a legal duty owed by the latter to the former. The appeal was dismissed.

c) Judgment of the CC

8 According to the CC the applicant had to prove that:

(i) the police officer or the prosecutors respectively owed a legal duty to the applicant to protect her;
(ii) the police officer or the prosecutors respectively acted in breach of such a duty and did so negligently; and
(iii)there was a causal connection between such negligent breach of the duty and the damage suffered by the applicant.

9 In respect of (i), the CC pointed out that the proceedings in the CPD and the SCA took place after the new Constitution of the Republic of South Africa, Act 108 of 1996, came into operation. Therefore, those Courts were obliged to take the provisions of sec. 39(2) of the Constitution into account when developing the common law. Sec. 39(2) requires all South African courts to promote the 'spirit, purport and object' of the Bill of Rights when developing the common law. However, both the CPD and the SCA assumed that the pre-constitutional test for determining the wrongfulness of omissions should be applied, and the demands of sec. 39(2) were overlooked.

10 The CC emphasised that the obligation of the courts to develop the common law in the context of the objectives of sec. 39(2), is not purely discretionary. There is a general obligation[4] on the courts to develop the common law if it is deficient in promoting the sec. 39(2) objectives. This does not mean that a court must, in each and every case where the common law is involved, inquire whether the common law is in need of such development,[5] but in given cases circumstances might be present obliging the court to raise the matter on its own and to require full argument from the parties.

The Court found that it was implicit in the applicant's case that the common law had to be developed beyond existing precedents. In such a situation there are two stages to the enquiry. The first stage is to consider whether the common law requires development in accordance with the objectives of sec. 39(2). The second stage concerns itself with how such development is to take place in order to meet those objectives. 11

The CC referred to the statement by the SCA that a weighing and striking of a balance between the interests of the parties and the interests of the community were necessary to determine whether there was a legal duty on the police officers to act. Branding this process a 'proportionality exercise', the Court stated that proportionality is consistent with the Bill of Rights, but the proportionality exercise must now be carried out in accordance with the 'spirit, purport and objects of the Bill of Rights' and the relevant factors must be weighed in the context of a constitutional state founded on dignity, equality and freedom and in which the government has positive duties to promote and uphold such values. Under the new Constitution, the Bill of Rights entrenches the rights to life,[6] human dignity,[7] and freedom and security of the person.[8] Therefore there is a duty on the state and all of its organs not to perform any act infringing these rights,[9] and in some circumstances there would be a positive obligation on the State and its organs to provide appropriate protection to everyone through laws and structures designed to afford such protection.[10] The Court was of the opinion that fears about the stifling effect such delictual liability might have on the proper exercise of duties by public servants, can be met by the proportionality exercise, and also by the requirements of foreseeability and proximity. This exercise will establish limits to the delictual liability of public officials. 12

The CC held that development of the common law under sec. 39(2) requires not only a proper appreciation of the Constitution and its value system, but also a proper understanding of the common law. This requires 'close and sen- 13

[4] In terms of sec. 39(2) read with sec.173.

[5] The CC also emphasised that judges should keep in mind that the major engine for law reform should be the Legislature and not the Judiciary.

[6] Sec. 11.

[7] Sec. 10.

[8] Sec. 12.

[9] The Bill of Rights applies to all law, and binds the Legislature, the Executive, the Judiciary and all organs of State (sec. 8(1)).

[10] The Court found it that it was not appropriate to restrict liability to positive actions as opposed to omissions; nor was it appropriate to grant public authorities like the police and local authorities an immunity against claims in delict by members of the public.

sitive interaction' between the High Courts and SCA (with their particular expertise and experience in common law) and the CC. Noting that the common law of delict as applied in South Africa spans many centuries, and that the debate regarding delictual liability, its elements and their relationship to one another remains lively, the CC stated that it was at a 'grave disadvantage' if saddled with the task to develop the common law without the benefit of a fully considered judgment from the High Court or the SCA.

14 Finding that the CPD misdirected itself in respect of the constitutional requirements of sec. 39(2), the CC proceeded to consider the issues relevant to legal liability in the context of the evidence given at the trial and the provisions of the Constitution. The Court pointed out that both the interim Constitution[11] and the Police Act[12] contained positive obligations on the police to prevent crime and maintain law and order and internal security, and when these obligations were considered in relation to the freedom and security of the person,[13] few things could be more important to women than freedom from the threat of sexual violence. South Africa also has a duty under international law to prohibit gender-based discrimination hindering the enjoyment of women of fundamental rights and freedoms, and to take measures to prevent the violation of those rights.[14] Again, the police is one of the primary agencies of the state responsible for the protection of the public in general, and women and children in particular, against the invasions of their fundamental rights by perpetrators of violent crime.

15 Referring to the view of the SCA that since the prosecutor had been in possession of all the relevant information, nothing further had been required of the police, and that the only question to be decided was whether the prosecutors had owed the applicant a legal duty to oppose C's release and secure his rearrest, the CC pointed out that this conclusion had not been challenged, and considered it prudent to deal with the matter on the basis that the SCA did.

16 As far as the case against the prosecutors was concerned, the CC held that prosecutors always have a duty to fulfil their functions independently and in the public interest. They have a duty to place before the court any information relevant to the magistrate's exercise of the discretion in respect of the granting or refusal of bail, and any conditions attaching to the granting of bail. While each case must depend on its own facts, there seems to be no reason why a prosecutor who has reliable information, for instance, that an accused person is violent, has a grudge against the claimant and has uttered threats of violence

[11] Constitution of the Republic of South Africa, Act 200 of 1993.

[12] Act 7 of 1958, replaced by the South African Police Service Act 68 of 1995.

[13] Protected by sec.12 of the Constitution.

[14] The Convention on the Elimination of all Forms of Discrimination against Women (CEDAW) was signed by South Africa on 29 January 1993 and ratified on 15 December 1995. The United Nations Committee on the Elimination of Discrimination against Women, which was established under the Convention, recommended in 1992 that "States may be responsible for private acts if they fail to act with due diligence to prevent violations of rights or to investigate and punish acts of violence, and for providing compensation."

against her, should not be held liable for the consequences of a negligent failure to bring such information to the attention of the court. If such negligence results in the accused being released on bail and then implementing the threat made, a strong case could be made for holding the prosecutor liable for the damage suffered by the claimant.

As far as causation was concerned, the CC thought it undesirable to express firm views without the benefit of the views of the relevant division of the High Court and the SCA. However, the CC found that the evidence was sufficient to justify a conclusion that if bail had been opposed and if all relevant information concerning C's background and sexual problems had been placed before the magistrate, bail might have been refused. That was sufficient, the Court said, to put the respondents on their defence in respect of that issue. **17**

Satisfied that the case for the applicant had sufficient merit to require careful consideration to be given to the complex legal issues raised, but not wishing to effectively act as a court of first instance in issues of fundamental importance to the development of the common law, the CC upheld the appeal, set aside the orders of the CPD and the SCA, and referred the matter back to the CPD to continue with the trial. **18**

d) Commentary

The decision of the CC in this case is very important in so far as it provides a model for future development of the common law where necessary to bring it into conformity with the provisions of the new Constitution. In my opinion the cautious approach of the CC in referring the matter back to the relevant provincial division of the High Court for developing the law in the greatest possible harmony with the existing common law, is a laudable one. See further the commentary on *Van Eeden v Minister of Safety and Security* below. **19**

2. ABSA Bank Ltd v Bond Equipment (Pretoria) (Pty) (Ltd) 2001 1 SA 372 Supreme Court of Appeal (SCA): Vicarious Liability of a Plaintiff Employer

a) Brief Summary of the Facts

The plaintiff was a customer of the defendant bank. S, an employee employed by the plaintiff, obtained cheques belonging to the plaintiff, deposited them into an account under the name of Bond Equipment (Pretoria), whereas the plaintiff's name was Bond Equipment (Pretoria)(Pty) (Ltd). The defendant bank collected payment for the cheques for Bond Equipment (Pretoria) instead of the plaintiff, notwithstanding the absence of any endorsement by the plaintiff. The plaintiff instituted an action for damages based on the defendant bank's negligent conduct. The bank's defence was that it was not liable for its negligence because the plaintiff was vicariously liable for the conduct of S. The Witwatersrand Local Division of the High Court (WLD) gave judgment in favour of the plaintiff, whereupon the defendant bank appealed to the SCA. **20**

b) Judgment of the SCA

21 The Court stated that the standard test for vicarious liability of an employer for the delict of an employee is whether the delict was committed by the employee while acting in the course and scope of his employment. In terms of this test an employer will only escape liability if his employee had the subjective intention of promoting solely his own interests and the employee, judged objectively, completely disassociated himself from the affairs of the employer when committing the act. The nature and extent of the deviation are critical. If the deviation is such that it cannot reasonably be held that the employee is still exercising the functions to which he was appointed, or still carrying out an instruction of the employer, the latter will cease to be liable. Whether that stage has been reached is essentially a question of fact. The Court said that it would not be sound social policy to hold an innocent employer liable or responsible to a third party, if his dishonest employee steals the employer's own property, especially if there is no suggestion that the employer was in any way negligent in selecting the employee. The Court then referred to a development in English law that theft by an employee to whom goods were entrusted is not regarded as an act outside the scope of his employment, but rather an improper mode of performing what he was employed to do. In this respect, the Court said, English cases seemed to confine the employer's liability to situations where the goods of a third party were in some way entrusted to the employee, in which case the employer could be liable to the third party. It would appear that there was no authority in English law for holding the employer vicariously liable in a case like the one before the Court. Applying these principles, the Court found that neither subjectively nor objectively could S be said to have acted within the course and scope of his employment. In the judgment of Zulman JA[15] it was said that S was on a 'frolic of his own', while Harms JA[16] said that it had not been a case of an improper execution of his duties; he had not performed his duties at all. In both judgments it was declared that the act of an employee who steals his employer's property whilst employed by the employer is the very antithesis of an act performed in the course and scope of his employment. Harms JA, with whom the majority of the Court concurred, added that he did not wish to lay down a general principle that an employer can never be responsible for the intentional wrongful act of an employee which causes harm to the employer.[17]

[15] Using the classic phrase said to have first been used in the English case of *Joel v Morison* (1834) 6 C&P (172 ER 1338).

[16] Quoting from *Mkize v Martens* 1914 AD 382 and *Columbus Joint Venture v ABSA Bank Ltd* 2000 2 SA 491 (W).

[17] In this context, Harms JA also added that it was not necessary to consider whether the judgment in *Greater Johannesburg Transitional Metropolitan Council v ABSA Bank Ltd t/a Volkskas Bank* 1997 2 SA 591 (W) was correct. In that case employees of both the plaintiff and the defendant had acted with intent, and the Court was prepared to make an apportionment of damages on that basis. Before that decision, damages were only apportioned if the plaintiff and the defendant had both been negligent.

c) Commentary

See the cmt. on the next judgment. 22

3. Ess Kay Electronics Pte Ltd v First National Bank of Southern Africa Ltd 2001 1 SA 1214 (SCA): Vicarious Liability of an Employer

a) Brief Summary of the Facts

W, an employee at the defendant bank (respondent) forged banker's drafts, 23
knowing that they would be presented to the plaintiffs (appellants) as payment for goods and that, upon the drafts being dishonoured, the plaintiffs would suffer damage as a result of non-payment. The main issue was whether the defendant bank was vicariously liable for W's actions.

b) Judgment of the SCA

The Court reiterated a statement in an old Appellate Division case[18] that an act 24
done solely for the employee's own interests and purposes, and outside the employee's authority, is not done in the course of employment even if done during such employment. Such an act would therefore not render the employer vicariously liable. Referring to the risk of harm created by the employer should the employee prove to be negligent, inefficient or untrustworthy, the Court emphasised that this 'risk theory' is a reason for the rule that employers are vicariously liable for the delicts committed by their employees in the course of their employment, but that it is not the rule itself. Unless the requirements of the rule are met, it cannot matter that it is the employee's appointment and work circumstances that place the employee in a position to commit the delict. It is also not decisive that the employee's acts in perpetrating the wrong are acts of a kind the employee is normally authorised to do and which appear to forge a close link between the wrong and the employee's duties. The question is always whether the acts were in fact authorised; and whether they were in fact performed in the course of the employee's employment. The Court found that W's conduct was outside the scope of his actual authority and the course of his employment. Answering the plaintiff's contention that fairness required the defendant bank to be held liable, the Court said that fairness and reasonableness do not require that an employer should, in effect, be an insurer for the employee's wrongs in a situation such as the one before it. Accordingly, the defendant bank was not liable.

c) Commentary

The *Ess Kay* and *Bond Equipment* cases are important decisions on vicarious 25
liability of employers for wrongs committed by their employees. It has become very difficult to predict in given instances whether an employee would be held to have acted within the course and scope of his employment (albeit, perhaps, performing the work in a so-called "improper mode"), or

[18] *Mkize v Martens* 1914 AD 382.

whether he would be held to have been on a so-called “frolic of his own”. Hopefully these judgments will bring more consistency and predictability to this part of the law.

4. Cape Metropolitan Council v Graham 2001 1 SA 1197 (SCA): Omission of Local Authority to Close Dangerous Mountain Pass

a) Brief Summary of the Facts

26 The plaintiff (respondent) was severely injured while driving along a mountain pass when his vehicle was struck by a landslide. There were traffic signs warning motorists of the possibility of falling rocks on both approaches to the pass. The plaintiff instituted a claim for damages against the local government body entrusted with the management and maintenance of roads in the particular area. The Cape of Good Hope Provincial Division of the High Court (CPD) found in favour of the plaintiff, and the case went on appeal to the SCA.

b) Judgment of the SCA

27 The defendant (appellant) did not dispute that it had been under a legal duty to take reasonable precautions to prevent or minimise injury to users of the road. Only the question of negligence was placed in dispute. The Court found that the risk of rockfalls or landslides had increased to such a degree that the ‘falling rocks’ road signs were no longer sufficient, and the proper course of action would have been for the defendant to close the road temporarily. For this finding, the Court relied on expert evidence concerning the steepness of the slope above the pass, the relative instability of much of the rock, and especially the fact that a period of abnormally high rainfall had preceded the accident, and that high rainfall had always raised the probability of major rock falls or land slides considerably. The defendant had not contended that there had been contributory fault on the part of the plaintiff, and the appeal was dismissed.

c) Commentary

28 This decision is in line with previous cases dealing with liability for omissions.

5. Road Accident Fund v Russell 2001 2 SA 34 (SCA): Does Suicide Break the Chain of Causation?

a) Brief Summary of the Facts

29 R sustained severe injuries, including brain damage, in a motor collision. He was not only disabled physically, but underwent a complete personality change, becoming severely depressed. On two occasions he appeared to have attempted suicide. On one of these occasions he had apparently crawled up a staircase to reach the roof of his house, since he was unable to walk. His wife thereupon had him admitted to a nursing home. There was no meaningful change in his personality after his admission to the nursing home. R’s wife regularly visited him, and she sometimes took him on excursions. She once took him for a medical assessment to determine his prospects of recovery and future working capabilities, but he was informed that he had no such prospects. Later that same day R committed suicide by jumping from a second storey parapet of the nursing home. R's wife instituted action against the Road Accident Fund (RAF) in terms of the relevant third party compensation legislation, claiming compensation for loss of support on behalf of her minor children.

The trial court found in favour of R's wife (the respondent), but granted the RAF (the appellant) leave to appeal to the SCA. **30**

b) Judgment of the SCA

The SCA found that the evidence had established that the brain injury had probably caused, or had been the major factor inducing, R's depression. R was not *non compos mentis*, but he could clearly not be regarded as a person with all his mental faculties intact. The appellant conceded that a factual causal link existed between the collision and the eventual suicide, but contended that the deceased's decision to terminate his life was an informed and voluntary act on his part, and as such constituted a *novus actus interveniens* breaking the chain of causation. Relying on English case law,[19] the SCA adopted the principle that a person who is not of sound mind cannot be said to have acted with unimpaired volition in forming a decision to commit suicide, and that such a suicide does not constitute a *novus actus interveniens*. The Court found that whilst R's act of suicide could be said to have been deliberate, his mind had been impaired to a material degree by the brain injury and resultant depression, and that his ability to make a balanced decision had been deleteriously affected. Therefore, his suicide was not a *novus actus interveniens*, and the appeal was dismissed. **31**

c) Commentary

Even accepting that R's ability to make a balanced decision had been impaired, I think it could be argued that his two previous suicide attempts (one of them necessitating the strenuous activity of dragging his disabled body onto a roof) show an advanced level of premeditation and planning on R's part. In view of his deliberate act of suicide, I am reluctant to agree that it would be reasonable and equitable (as the test for legal causation requires) to hold the Fund liable for the damage arising from R's death. I think that an unarticulated policy consideration behind the decision might have been a desire to ensure compensation by the Fund for the widest possible range of victims of motor car accidents. The decision can perhaps also be regarded as an application of the rule that "you must take your victim as you find him", in the sense that if the wrongdoer's victim is unusually prone to suicidal tendencies, and he com- **32**

[19] *Reeves v Commissioner of Police of the Metropolis* [1999] 3 All ER 897 (HL); *Kirkham v Chief Constable of the Greater Manchester Police* [1990] 3 All ER 246 (CA).

mits suicide after being seriously injured by the wrongdoer, the wrongdoer cannot escape liability for the suicide. Nevertheless, in a situation like the present one, where the deceased could evidently exercise a choice whether to live or terminate his own life, I am inclined to think that the damage caused by the suicide is too remote. In the final instance, furthermore, I think it was not necessary for the Court to find that R's suicide did not constitute a *novus actus* in order to award damages for loss of support to R's dependants. While still alive, R had no prospects of ever working again, and his dependants should have been entitled to damages for loss of support on that basis.[20]

6. Van der Berg v Coopers & Lybrand Trust (Pty) Ltd 2001 2 SA 242 (SCA): Defamatory Remarks in Court Documents

a) Brief Summary of the Facts

33 The plaintiff (appellant), a senior advocate, instituted an action against the trustees of an allegedly insolvent estate for defamatory statements made in certain court documents. In the relevant documents, the trustees had alleged that the plaintiff had manipulated attorneys (with whom the trustees had been dealing) to conduct themselves in a way inappropriate to their duties as officers of the Court. The CPD held that the defamatory remarks were privileged because they were made in the course of legal proceedings, whereupon the case went on appeal to the SCA.

b) Judgment of the SCA

34 The SCA emphasised that a defendant can only rely on the defence of privilege in the case of defamatory statements made in the course of legal proceedings if the defendant can prove that the statements were relevant to an issue in the proceedings. Stating that the SCA had never before determined whether the test for relevance is subjective or objective, the Court said that it was not necessary to decide the point since the parties were prepared to accept that the test was essentially objective. The accepted simple objective test for relevance was whether the defamatory matter could be regarded as reasonably necessary to protect the interest or discharge the duty which was the foundation of the privilege. Applying this test, the Court found that the defamatory remarks were not relevant and therefore not privileged. The plaintiff had not been a party to the litigation between the trustees and the attorneys, and it was not reasonably necessary for the trustees to speculate on the precise nature of the plaintiff's conduct or his motives. They need only have mentioned that the

[20] There is one old decision of the Transvaal Provincial Division (*De Vaal v Messing* 1938 TPD 34) in which it was held that where a breadwinner had been injured but not killed, the dependants had no claim for loss of support because the breadwinner had to institute a claim for loss of future income himself, which could then be used to support the dependants. However, this case has been criticised since it ignores the reality that the dependant's rights have also been infringed, and there is more recent authority in case law and statutory law for a contrary view (see J. Neethling/J. M. Potgieter/P. J. Visser, *Law of Delict* (4th edn. 2001), pp. 289–290. The only evil to be guarded against in such a situation is the awarding of double damages, *i.e.* to award compensation to the breadwinner as well as the dependants for the same damage.

attorneys had acted on the advice, or perhaps even insistence, of the plaintiff. Concerning the quantum, the Court took into account that the allegations had been serious, implying a deliberate perversion of the course of justice on the part of the plaintiff. Publication had been limited to a restricted class of persons, but it had been made in the very field in which the plaintiff's reputation rested. There was no evidence that the plaintiff had in fact been lowered in the esteem of law-practising colleagues or others. In fixing the quantum, the Court said, care must be taken not to award large sums of damages too readily lest freedom of speech be inhibited, or intolerance encouraged and litigation fostered. These considerations do not, however, detract from the fact that a person whose dignity has unlawfully been impugned, deserves appropriate financial recompense to assuage his or her wounded feelings. An award of R 30,000[21] in damages was made.

c) Commentary

The judgment appears to be correct. In defamation cases, evidence of a factual lowering of the plaintiff's esteem is irrelevant to establish the presence of wrongfulness,[22] but I do not think there should be any objections to considering this issue when fixing the quantum of damages. **35**

7. Sheriff, Pretoria East v Meevis 2001 3 SA 454 (SCA): Liability for Goods Stolen While Unlawfully Attached by Sheriff

a) Brief Summary of the Facts

S was arrested on suspicion that he was going to flee from certain court proceedings which had been instituted against him by H. M, who lived with S, handed certain items of her jewellery to the sheriff as security for the due appearance of S before the court. After judgment was given against S, H's attorneys instructed the sheriff to attach the jewellery in partial satisfaction of S' judgment debt. An armed robbery took place at the sheriff's office and the jewellery was amongst the items taken. The jewellery was never recovered. M subsequently instituted a claim for damages against the sheriff. The Transvaal Provincial Division (TPD) held that the sheriff was liable to compensate M for the damage she had suffered as a result of the attachment of her goods. The sheriff appealed to the SCA. **36**

b) Judgment of the SCA

The SCA found that there was no lawful basis for the attachment of M's jewellery, and that the attachment had been wrongful. Next it had to be decided whether the sheriff's wrongful conduct was the cause of the damage suffered by M as a result of the loss of the jewellery. Noting that the element of causa- **37**

[21] 1 South African Rand = 0.1002 Euro, (July 2002).

[22] All that is required, is that the allegedly defamatory remarks would have the tendency to lower the esteem of the plaintiff in the eyes of a fictional reasonable person. See J. Neethling/J. M. Potgieter/P. J. Visser (*supra* note 20), p. 340.

tion entails two inquiries, namely factual causation and legal causation, the Court said that it was only concerned with the first inquiry because it was common cause that if factual causation had been established, the requirements for legal causation had been satisfied. The majority of the Court found that had the jewellery been returned when it should have been, the jewellery would not have been in the sheriff's possession on the day of the robbery and would not have been stolen. Accordingly, the majority held, the sheriff's wrongful attachment of the jewellery caused or materially contributed to M's loss, and the sheriff was therefore liable. The minority judge argued that it had not been proved that if there had been no attachment, the loss would not have occurred anyway, because the sheriff would have been obliged by certain Rules of Court to keep the jewellery in his possession awaiting the outcome of interlocutory proceedings. The minority judge therefore did not agree that the appeal had to fail.

c) Commentary

38 I find it most unsatisfactory that the issue of legal causation was not considered in this case (it was apparently not placed into dispute by the defendant). If the majority decision that factual causation was present was correct, an inquiry into legal causation could arguably have led to a finding that the conduct of the robbers constituted a *novus actus interveniens*, and that the loss was accordingly too remote.

8. Michael v Linksfield Park Clinic (Pty) Ltd 2001 3 SA 1188 (SCA): Medical Negligence

a) Brief Summary of the Facts

39 The plaintiffs' son, aged 17, underwent corrective nasal surgery. He suffered cardiac arrest while under general anaesthesia. By the time his heart function had been restored by resuscitation he had sustained major brain damage, leaving him in a permanent vegetative state. The plaintiffs sued for damages in the Witwatersrand Local Division of the High Court (WLD), alleging negligence on the part of the anaesthetist in respect of the cardiac arrest, and joint negligence between the anaesthetist and the clinic in respect of the resuscitation process. The WLD dismissed the claim, and the plaintiffs appealed to the SCA.

b) Judgment of the SCA

40 Noting that the governing test for professional negligence is usually said to be the standard of conduct of the reasonable practitioner in the particular field, the Court added that this must be qualified. What is required, is an evaluation of the expert evidence to determine whether and to what extent the opinions advanced are founded on logical reasoning. The Court is not bound to absolve a defendant from liability for allegedly negligent medical treatment or diagnosis just because evidence of expert opinion, although genuinely held, is that

the treatment in issue accorded with sound medical practice. The Court must be satisfied that such opinion has a logical basis, in other words that the expert has considered comparative risks and benefits and has reached a defensible conclusion. A defendant can properly be held liable, despite the support of a body of professional opinion sanctioning the conduct in issue, if that body of opinion is not capable of withstanding logical analysis and is therefore not reasonable. However, it will very seldom be right to conclude that views genuinely held by a competent expert are unreasonable. Only where expert opinion cannot be logically supported at all, will it fail to provide the benchmark by which the defendant's conduct must be assessed. Furthermore, the fact that scientific and judicial measures of proof tend to differ, must be borne in mind.[23] After analysing the evidence, the Court found that the WLD had correctly dismissed the claim.

c) Commentary

The principles enunciated in this case appear to be fair and sensible. The law reports do not contain a complete record of the Court's analysis of the obviously very technical evidence, making it impossible to comment on that aspect of the judgment. **41**

9. Olitzki Property Holdings v State Tender Board 2001 3 SA 1247 (SCA): Suitability of Delictual Damages for Infringement of Constitutional Rights Resulting in Pure Economic Loss

a) Brief Summary of Facts

The government of Gauteng province invited tenders for office space to house government departments. The appellant obtained an option to purchase a certain building and tendered to provide office space in that building to the provincial government. The tender was not accepted. The applicant instituted a claim for damages against the State Tender Board and the provincial government, alleging that the provincial government, as an interested party, influenced the tender board in its decision, as a result of which the tender was awarded to someone else. The appellant based its claim on two alternative grounds: first, that the respondents had breached the appellant's right to a fair, public and competitive system of tendering as required by sec. 187(2) of the interim Constitution; and second, that the respondents infringed the appellant's fundamental right to administrative justice enshrined in sec. 24(a), (b) and (c) of the interim Constitution. The TPD held that both claims were untenable, and the appellant appealed to the SCA. **42**

b) Judgment of the SCA

In respect of the first claim, the Supreme Court of Appeal said that it raised the "not unfamiliar" question as to when a breach of a statutory duty (in this **43**

[23] The principles set forth in this judgment were derived from a decision of the English House of Lords in *Bolitho v City and Hackney Health Authority* [1998] AC 232 (HL (F))

case a statutory duty embodied in the interim Constitution) gives rise to a civil claim for damages. Dealing with the question whether the relevant provisions imposed a legal duty on the defendants to refrain from causing the plaintiff the kind of loss it had allegedly suffered, the Court stated that the inquiry involved applying a general criterion of reasonableness, taking into account the legal convictions of the community and the norms, values and principles contained in the Constitution. When dealing with a breach of a statutory duty, the focal question is one of statutory interpretation. The statute may on a proper construction itself confer a right of action, or it may provide a basis for inferring that a legal duty exists at common law. In both instances the process requires a consideration of the statute as a whole, its objects and provisions, the circumstances in which it was enacted, and the kind of mischief it was designed to prevent. But where a common-law duty is at issue, the outcome depends less on a formulaic approach to statutory construction than on a broad assessment by the court whether it is just and reasonable that a civil claim for damages be accorded. Wrongfulness in such a case does not follow from breach of a statutory duty *per se*, but rather from the reasonableness, in the circumstances, of compensating the plaintiff for the infringement of his right. In determining whether a delictual claim arises from breach of a statute, the fact that the relevant provision is embodied in the Constitution may (depending on the nature of the provision) attract a duty more readily than if it had been an ordinary statute.

44 Applying these principles to the facts, the Court pointed out that the primary and overriding import of sec. 187 was to impose legislative duties on the national and provincial legislatures in respect of the procurement of goods and services for the different levels of government. Such procurement had to be regulated by an Act of the central parliament and by provincial laws, and to this end provision was to be made for independent and impartial tender boards and a fair, public and competitive tendering system, free of improper interference by any organ of the State. Since the provisions invoked by the plaintiff entrusted the premise on which its claim depended to legislative action, and because such legislative action had not yet taken place, the plaintiff's contention that sec. 187 grounded a delictual claim for damages was unsustainable. Subsec. (3), imposing a general prohibition on improper interference with the decisions of the tender boards, at first glance offered a more promising foundation for the plaintiff's claim, and it would not be difficult to infer, even before the envisaged legislative action, that a member of the public aggrieved by its breach could base an application for review or an interdict directly on subsec. 3. The plaintiff's claim, however, went much further, and subsec. 3 had to be read in light of and subject to legislative directives contained in the rest of sec. 187. Since the applicable remedies had not yet been defined by the envisaged legislative action, a conclusion that subsec. 3 grounded a direct claim in damages for an aggrieved party's lost profit would be inappropriate.

45 In respect of the second claim, the question was whether an award of damages for lost profit was an appropriate remedy for breach of sec. 24 of the interim

Constitution, which granted every person the right to lawful and procedurally fair administrative action. On assumption that the alleged facts were true, the defendant's interference in the tender process certainly breached the plaintiff's rights in sec. 24. However, in a previous case[24] the Constitutional Court had held that a plaintiff assaulted by the police could not, over and above his entitlement to damages at common law, obtain 'constitutional damages' (including an element of punitive damages) to vindicate the constitutional rights violated by his assault. In the *Olitzki* case, it transpired that the plaintiff had been aware of the impropriety of the defendant's conduct nine days before the tender was awarded. He would therefore have been entitled to an interdict prohibiting the defendants from continuing with the tender process. What constituted appropriate relief, depends on the facts of each case, and the alternative remedies available to the claimant at all stages of the dispute must be a critical factor in the assessment. Furthermore, after award of the tender, the plaintiff's common-law entitlement did not encompass a right to be awarded the tender, but rather a right of review if it was aggrieved by the award of the tender. The grave financial impact on the government's scarce resources (the plaintiff's claim was for more than R10 million) further strengthened the Court in deciding that the plaintiff was not entitled to the constitutional damages it was seeking. The Court was at pains to point out that it was not necessary to decide that a lost profit can never be claimed as constitutional damages, but that in the circumstances of the particular case, including the availability of the alternative remedies of an interdict and by way of review, awarding such damages would have been inappropriate.

c) Commentary

The decision of the SCA appears to be logical and in line with an earlier judgment[25] of the CC. 46

10. Govender v Minister of Safety and Security 2001 4 SA 273 (SCA): Police Shooting a Fugitive

a) Brief Summary of the Facts

The plaintiff (appellant) instituted a claim for damages against the Minister of Safety and Security for serious injuries sustained by his son, J, who had been shot by a policeman. On the night in question J, who was 17 at the time, first spent some time with two friends drinking beer and looking for cannabis to smoke. At a shopping centre they met B, who had apparently just stolen the keys of a motor vehicle. They got into the car and drove off, well knowing that the car was stolen. J was the driver. B later got out of the car. Two police officers on patrol duty saw the stolen car veering off the road, hitting a water meter and the wall of a building. Thinking that the driver was drunk, the police officers switched on the sirens and blue lights of the police vehicle. J did not stop, 47

[24] *Fose v Minister of Safety and Security* 1997 3 SA 786 (CC).

[25] *Fose v Minister of Safety and Security* 1997 3 SA 786 (CC).

and a high-speed chase followed. In the meantime, the owner of the car had reported the theft, and when the police officers called the control room on the police radio they were informed that the car they were chasing had been stolen earlier that evening. Eventually J and one other boy got out of the stolen car and ran away. One of the policemen pursued them on foot. He twice shouted at them, identifying himself as a member of the police force and commanding them to stop, and also fired a warning shot into a grass bank. Convinced that he would not catch up with them, the policeman then fired at J, aiming at his legs. However, the shot struck J in the spine, as a result of which he became a paraplegic.

48 The Durban and Coast Local Division of the High Court (D&C LD) decided in favour of the defendant (now the respondent), whereupon the plaintiff appealed to the SCA.

b) Judgment of the SCA

49 The only question in dispute was whether the policeman had acted wrongfully. The respondent contended that the policeman's conduct was justified by his having acted within the scope of sec. 49(1) of the Criminal Procedure Act,[26] which provides, among other things, that someone who is authorised to arrest another may use such force as may in the circumstances be necessary to prevent the person concerned from fleeing. The trial court found that the force used was reasonable and necessary and proportionate to the offence of motor vehicle theft, in view of the seriousness of the crime, its increasing prevalence throughout South Africa, and the public's interest in the apprehension, prosecution and punishment of car thieves. The plaintiff argued that this approach lost sight of the constitutionally protected rights to which even a fleeing suspect is entitled. According to the interim Constitution, which was applicable at the time, these rights included a right to life;[27] a right to physical integrity;[28] a right to dignity;[29] a right to be presumed innocent until convicted by a court of law;[30] and the right to equality before the law and equal protection of the law.[31] The appellant did not attack the constitutional validity of sec. 49, but rather requested the Court to interpret it or 'read it down' to comply with the correct constitutional standard.

50 The Court pointed out that the threshold requirement laid down in sec. 49(1) was very low and had been criticised as making it too easy for police officers and even members of the public to use unspecified force simply to overcome a suspect's resistance or escape, and that the AD[32] had raised the threshold by requiring proportionality between the degree of force used and the seriousness

[26] Act 51 of 1977.
[27] Sec. 9.
[28] Sec. 11 (1).
[29] Sec. 10.
[30] Sec. 25(3)(e).
[31] Sec. 8(1).
[32] In *Matlou v Makhubedu* 1978 1 SA 946 (A).

of the crime of which the victim is suspected. However, the Court held, to comply with constitutional standards of reasonableness and justifiability, the threshold requirement had to be raised further. The existing test of proportionality between the seriousness of the relevant offence and the force used had to be expanded to include a consideration of proportionality between the nature and degree of force used and the threat posed by the fugitive to the safety and security of the police officers, other individuals and society as a whole. Applying this expanded proportionality test, and taking into account J's youthfulness and the fact that he had been unarmed, the Court found that the shooting of J was unlawful. The Court went further and formulated a general rule (while expressly allowing for possible exceptions) that sec. 49(1) of the Criminal Procedure Act must be interpreted to exclude the use of a firearm or similar weapon unless the person authorised to arrest a fleeing suspect has reasonable grounds for believing (1) that the suspect poses an immediate threat of serious bodily harm to him or her, or a threat of harm to members of the public; or (2) that the suspect has committed a crime involving the infliction or threatened infliction of serious bodily harm. The appeal was successful.

c) Commentary

This is yet another case where the law of delict was influenced by the new **51**
constitutional dispensation. According to pre-constitutional interpretations of the Criminal Procedure Act, the conduct of the policeman was arguably justified, whereas in light of the new constitutional values his conduct was found to be wrongful.

11. Norris v Road Accident Fund [2001] 4 All SA 321 (SCA): Liability of the Road Accidents Fund for Post-Traumatic Stress Disorder

a) Brief Summary of the Facts

The plaintiff was driving an armoured van transporting money in a rural area, **52**
when the van was flagged down by what appeared to be road construction workers. As he slowed down, a man with an automatic rifle shouted at him, and he realised that the van was being ambushed by a sizeable gang of armed robbers. He attempted to escape by driving the van in reverse gear. The robbers fired shots and a number of bullets struck the van. The robbers pursued the van in another vehicle, colliding with it and forcing it off the road and over an embankment. The van rolled over a few times and came to rest on its side. The plaintiff was pinned down by his two companions who had landed on top of him. The robbers broke into the back of the van and removed the money, while the smell of leaking petrol permeated the air in the van. The robbers called at them to get out of the van, but then fled the scene. The plaintiff and his companions waited for about five minutes, and then managed to get out of the van and summon help. The plaintiff claimed damages from the Road Accidents Fund (RAF)[33] for physical injuries and a psychological disorder descri-

[33] In terms of the Multilateral Motor Vehicle Accidents Fund Act 93 of 1989.

bed as post-traumatic stress disorder. The RAF accepted liability for the physical injuries but disputed liability for the post-traumatic stress disorder. The only question to be decided in the D&C LD was whether the post-traumatic stress disorder had been caused by or had arisen from the driving of the motor vehicle in question.[34] The Court held against the plaintiff, who thereupon appealed to the SCA.

b) Judgment of the SCA

53 Dealing with the defendant's contention that the stress disorder could have been triggered by any one part of the sequence of events preceding the collision rather than the collision itself, the Court held that to break the incident up into separate parts was artificial. The Court found that the harm suffered by the plaintiff was indivisible, and the collision had been a material cause of the stress disorder. The appeal was upheld.

c) Commentary

54 I think the SCA's approach in this case was a realistic one.

12. Marais v Groenewald 2001 1 SA 634 Transvaal Provincial Division of the High Court (T): Negligence as Fault Requirement for Defamation

a) Brief Summary of the Facts

55 A political party distributed a document which was defamatory of the leader of another political party.

b) Judgment of the Transvaal Provincial Division (TPD)

56 The Court held that the contents of the document would have lowered the plaintiff's esteem in the opinion of reasonable persons and that it was therefore defamatory of the plaintiff. Dealing with the fault requirement, it was clear that the defendants had been reckless concerning the truth or otherwise of their statements, and that unfounded conclusions had been made from unverified facts. The Court referred to the judgment of the SCA in *National Media Ltd v Bogoshi*,[35] in which strict liability of the media for defamation was abolished and replaced by liability based on negligence. Pointing out that the SCA had left open the question whether defendants other than members of the media could also be held liable for defamation committed negligently, the Court said that negligence must be recognised as a requirement for defamation. In this way a healthy balance between the constitutionally protected right to good name[36] and the right to freedom of expression is created. It accords with the legal convictions that a defendant who defames another, while negli-

[34] As required by art. 40 of the agreement contained in the Schedule to the Act.

[35] 1998 4 SA 1196 (SCA).

[36] The right to good name is not protected in so many words in the Constitution, but it is generally accepted that it falls within the ambit of the right to human dignity which is protected by sec.10.

gently under the impression that his conduct is lawful, should not escape liability. The Court found it unnecessary to decide whether *culpa levis* should have the same result. Applying these principles to the facts, the Court found that the defendants had not rebutted the presumption of fault.[37] The Court decided in favour of the plaintiff. In fixing the quantum, the Court took into account that politicians need to be less sensitive than other members of society, and that the Courts should not encourage litigation between politicians by making large awards of damages. The defendant's omission to make an apology was deemed to be aggravating. An award of R 20,000 was made.

c) Commentary

This is a very important decision. The general position in South African law has always been that *animus iniuriandi*, *i.e.* intent, on the part of the defendant is required for a defamation claim to succeed. In the case of the media, liability for defamation was later changed to strict liability.[38] The landmark decision in *Bogoshi* abolished strict liability of the press for defamation and introduced negligence as the requisite form of fault. The decision in *Marais v Groenewald* now extends this principle to other instances of defamation, where the defendants are not members of the media. In my opinion this is a healthy development, and I hope that this decision will be followed by other Courts. Elsewhere I express the opinion[39] that it might be expedient to extend liability based on negligence to other forms of personality infringement as well. 57

13. Dersley v Minister van Veiligheid en Sekuriteit 2001 1 SA 1047 (T): Failure of Police to Examine a Stolen Vehicle

a) Brief Summary of the Facts

The plaintiff took a motor vehicle to the police to ascertain whether it had been stolen. A policeman, who was not a member of the specialist vehicle theft unit of the police, fed certain details of the vehicle into a computer, and then assured the plaintiff that the vehicle had not been stolen. The vehicle was not physically inspected by any police officer, let alone a member of the vehicle theft unit. Thereupon the plaintiff bought the vehicle, but within 5 months it transpired that the vehicle had indeed been stolen, and it was repossessed. The plaintiff claimed damages to the amount of the purchase price from the Minister of Safety and Security. 58

b) Judgment of the TPD

The Court held that the police had owed the plaintiff a legal duty to assist him, especially since there had been a possibility of criminal activity and because 59

[37] The Court literally spoke about the 'presumption of intent', but in view of what it had said about liability based on negligence, it is submitted that this reference must be understood to pertain to fault in a broader sense, rather than only intent.

[38] See J. Neethling/J.M. Potgieter/P.J. Visser (*supra* note 20) p. 348.

[39] J.C. Knobel, Nalatige Persoonlikheidskrenking, to be published in [2002] *Journal of Contemporary Roman-Dutch Law/Tydskrif vir Hedendaagse Romeins Hollandse Reg* (THRHR), 24.

the plaintiff, as member of the public, had specifically approached the police for help. The police had furthermore negligently breached this duty. It would have been a relatively simple matter for a member of the vehicle theft unit, by physically inspecting the vehicle, to ascertain that it had been stolen. The plaintiff had not been contributorily negligent in respect of his own loss; on the contrary, he had done everything that could be expected of a lay member of public in his position. The claim was successful.

c) Commentary

60 I think the decision is correct. One could just add that this was an instance of negligent misrepresentation on the part of the police, a fact that was not specifically mentioned by the Court.[40]

14. Van Eeden v Minister of Safety and Security 2001 4 SA 646 (T): Liability of Organs of State for Omission on Part of Police

a) Brief Summary of the Facts

61 The plaintiff, a 19 year old woman, was sexually assaulted, raped and robbed of her car and other belongings by a prisoner who had escaped from police custody. The plaintiff instituted action against the Minister of Safety and Security, claiming damages for infringement of her dignity, emotional shock, past and future medical expenses, and patrimonial loss resulting from the theft of her possessions. The defendant conceded that the police had been negligent in so far as an open security gate had helped the prisoner to escape, and also conceded that harm was generally foreseeable. However, it denied that the police had owed a legal duty to the plaintiff and contended that the omission of the police was therefore not wrongful, and further contended that while the omission on the part of the police was factually the cause of the harm, legal causation was absent.

b) Decision of the TPD

62 The TPD relied heavily in its judgment on the decision of the SCA in the *Carmichele* case.[41] The Court found that there was no special relationship between the plaintiff and the defendant on the strength of which the plaintiff was a particular person or member of a particular class of people (in contrast to so-called faceless members of the public) in special danger of being harmed by the activities of the wrongdoer. The Court was of the opinion that the requisite special relationship was not dependent on the foreseeability of harm, but was rather a question of objective fact. Because of the absence of a special relationship, the TPD considered itself bound by the decision of the SCA in *Carmichele* to hold that the defendant did not owe a legal duty to the plaintiff. The Court was of the opinion that the Constitution did not influence the principles applied in the case. Interestingly, the Court said that it had little doubt that society, learning that a dangerous criminal, known to be able to cause harm

[40] Pointed out to me by Prof. J. Neethling.

[41] Discussed above.

again, had been apprehended but negligently allowed to escape, would cry out that those responsible for the escape should be held liable for each and every manifestation of foreseeable harm that ensued. To this the Court added that such a view could be accepted to be the legal convictions of the community (rather than mere moral indignation) insisting that the omission should be regarded as wrongful and the resulting harm should be compensated.[42] However, the TPD said, while always taking note of the voice of the people, the court cannot be blindly ruled by it. A person cannot be held liable for all the consequences of a wrongful act; policy considerations play an important part, and foreseeability alone is not sufficient. The plaintiff's claim was dismissed.

c) Commentary

Had the judgment of the CC in *Carmichele* been delivered before the proceedings in this case took place, the influence of the Constitution on delictual norms would undoubtedly have received much more attention in this case, and the outcome might conceivably have been different. In light of what the TPD itself said about the legal convictions of the community, the current prevalence of violent crime in South Africa,[43] and the number of escapes from prison,[44] and especially on the strength of what the CC said in *Carmichele* about the influence of the Constitution on this area of the law, one wonders whether the time is not ripe for the Courts to decide that, in principle, the police, jail services and other law-enforcement officials owe a duty to all members of society to prevent dangerous criminals from escaping or being released untimely, and causing harm. Perhaps such a duty should be independent of the question whether any special relationship between plaintiff and defendant existed. This would not mean that liability would necessarily follow each and every harmful consequence of a prisoner's escape or untimely release, since fault and legal causation should still be established. When dealing with legal causation, policy considerations of justice, fairness and reasonableness, combined with factors such as foreseeability, can be employed to determine whether the consequences are too remote for liability to ensue. 63

15. Van Duivenboden v Minister of Safety and Security [2001] 4 All SA 127 Cape Provincial Division of the High Court (C): Omission of Police to Remove a Dangerous Person's Fire-Arms

a) Brief Summary of the Facts

During a domestic quarrel, B shot and killed his wife and daughter. The plaintiff went to the assistance of B's son who had fled to the plaintiff's home, 64

[42] In this respect the Court quoted a well-known excerpt from *Minister van Polisie v Ewels* 1975 3 SA 590 (A) 597, a *locus classicus* on liability for omissions, as to when a legal duty to prevent harm will exist.

[43] In the *Van Eeden* case the court pointed out that the increase of crimes against women and children in the 1990s had caused the South African Police to declare such crimes to be a policing priority.

[44] In the *Van Eeden* case the following numbers of escapes from police holding cells were quoted: 3,595, 3,838 and 3,818 for 1996, 1997 and 1998 respectively.

whereupon B shot the plaintiff in the ankle and in the shoulder. The plaintiff instituted a claim for damages against the Minister of Safety and Security. He alleged that members of the police force had negligently breached a legal duty to prevent or reduce the risk of his being shot by B, through the employment of a procedure created by sec. 11 of the Arms and Ammunition Act,[45] in terms of which persons may be declared unfit to possess fire-arms on certain specified grounds.

b) Judgment of the Cape Provincial Division of the High Court (CPD)

65 Referring to English and Canadian case law and the decision of the SCA in *Carmichele*,[46] the Court proceeded to enquire whether a special relationship between the plaintiff and police had been created by sec. 11. Finding that the purpose of sec. 11 is to ensure that fire-arms are used responsibly by people who have obtained licences to own them, the Court held that a failure of the police to conduct a sec. 11 enquiry in circumstances where it would be unreasonable to ignore the licence holder's conduct, is a breach of a legal duty and constitutes wrongful conduct. Where circumstances exist indicating that a licence holder has a propensity to use the fire-arm in a manner dangerous to himself or other persons, the purpose of the Act is clearly to protect such other persons. Deciding whether the police had acted negligently, the question to be decided was whether a reasonable person in the position of the police officers would have foreseen the possibility of harm and would have taken steps to prevent it. In this respect the Court found it significant that two years before the shooting, B had pointed a fire-arm at his wife and thrown an ammunition box at her, and that a year later B had actually held his wife and children hostage. The "hostage incident", in particular, represented the kind of circumstance for which the sec. 11 enquiry had been designed, and a reasonable person in the position of a police station commander would have initiated such an enquiry. At the enquiry a picture would have emerged of a violent man who had assaulted his wife and children, abused alcohol, and who had been prepared to threaten his own family, the police, and members of the public with fire-arms. A reasonable person would thereupon have initiated action to remove B's fire-arms in terms of the Act. As far as factual causation was concerned, the Court found that a properly conducted sec. 11 enquiry would have led to B's fire-arms being taken away, and would have prevented the plaintiff's injuries. In regard to legal causation, the Court found that the failure of the police to remove the fire-arms by the procedure provided for in the Act was not too remote from the event that brought about the plaintiff's injuries.

66 In a minority judgment, Moosa J. disagreed, *inter alia* because there had been no special relationship between the plaintiff and the police; because in his opinion it was highly improbable that the police would have foreseen B shooting the plaintiff as a result of their failure to conduct sec. 11 proceedings; and because recognition of such a claim could potentially open the floodgate of litigation.

[45] Act 75 of 1969.
[46] Discussed above.

c) Commentary

Without having had the benefit of reading the judgment of the CC in *Carmichele*, the majority judges in this case delivered a judgment that appears to be in accordance with that trend-setting judgment. The minority judgment appears to be more in line with the judgment of the SCA in *Carmichele*, and in view of the decision of the CC the insistence on a special relationship as requisite for a legal duty is perhaps misplaced (see also the cmt. to the *Van Eeden* case). 67

16. Energy Measurements (Pty) Ltd v First National Bank of SA Ltd 2001 3 SA 132 Witwatersrand Local Division of the High Court (W): Negligence of Collecting Bank and Vicarious Liability of Plaintiff for Wrong Committed by Its Employee

a) Brief Summary of the Facts

An employee of the plaintiff stole two cheques made payable to the plaintiff. 68
The cheques were deposited into an account opened with the defendant bank, and the proceeds were withdrawn before the theft of the cheques was discovered. The plaintiff instituted a claim for damages against the defendant bank, alleging that the bank had owed it a duty of care when opening the account and had negligently breached this duty. The bank had taken the following steps: it had interviewed W (the person opening the account), had ensured that the necessary documentation had been supplied, and had done a credit risk check.

b) Judgment of the Witwatersrand Local Division of the High Court (WLD)

The Court held that it would be reasonable to impose a duty of care on a bank 69
when it received and processed an application to open an account. The standard of care required must be determined with reference to the practice of reasonable persons carrying on the business of bankers and endeavouring to do so in a manner calculated to protect themselves and others against fraud. Taking steps to safeguard owners of cheques would of necessity form part of the reasonable conduct of bankers. It was clear from the evidence that banks in practice foresee the reasonable possibility that when new accounts are opened, they may be used for fraudulent purposes to the detriment of owners of stolen cheques. As a minimum, a bank has a duty to ascertain the identity of a prospective client and to obtain some information to establish his bona fides. It was clear from the evidence that the only concern of the officials of the defendant bank had been to safeguard the bank against losses, and no apparent consideration had been given to the duty it owed to owners of cheques. The Court found that the Bank had acted negligently in opening the account. Since the opening of the account was the first and indispensable step to obtain payment on the basis of the stolen cheques (which had been marked "not transferable"), causation was also present.

The Court then proceeded to deal with the bank's contention that the plaintiff 70
was vicariously responsible for the conduct of its own employee, and that the

damages should accordingly be apportioned. When stealing the cheques and channelling them to his co-conspirators, the Court held, the employee's conduct had been the very antithesis of what he had been employed to do. Furthermore, the cheques had been the property of his employer and not the property of a third party which the plaintiff might have been obliged to take care of. The employee's conduct had not been a mode, albeit an improper one, of performing the work he had been employed to do. He had completely disengaged himself from the duties of his contract of employment. The plaintiff could not be held vicariously responsible for the conduct of its employee. To have held the plaintiff liable, would have implied that owners of property had a general duty to the public to prevent their property from being stolen on the basis that subsequent transactions involving the stolen goods could cause harm to the public. Such a decision would have opened the doors to a limitless number of potential claimants, and this could not be justified. Judgment was given in favour of the plaintiff.

c) Commentary

71 This decision of the WLD is in line with the recent judgments of the SCA in *Bond Equipment* and *Ess Kay Electronics*, discussed above.

17. Kgaleng v Minister of Safety and Security 2001 4 SA 854 (W): Police Shooting Man in Putative Defence

a) Brief Summary of the Facts

72 The plaintiff claimed damages from the Minister of Safety and Security for the allegedly wrongful killing of her husband, K, by a police officer, M. On the night in question, M was member of a patrol team that responded to a complaint that an electricity box was being broken into. On arriving at the scene, the police found a crowd of people, who dispersed quickly. M followed K, the last person to leave the vicinity of the electricity box, on foot. M's evidence, which was accepted by the Court, was that when he caught up with K, he saw projecting from K's hand what appeared to be the detonating mechanism of a hand grenade. Thinking that his life was in danger, M shot and killed K. A teargas canister was later found near K's body. Counsel for the parties later agreed that the detonating mechanisms of a teargas canister and a certain type of hand grenade respectively were indistinguishable at a distance of about three metres in the bright light of the Court room. The defendant pleaded that M had acted in self-defence, or alternatively, that M had not acted with intent or negligence.

b) Judgment of the WLD

73 The Court emphasised that the test to determine whether conduct could be justified by defence, was an objective one. The teargas canister had not objectively constituted a physical danger to M which would justify M in shooting K. The plea of defence could therefore not succeed. However, M had not acted with intent, since his subjective belief that shooting K was justified, excluded consciousness of wrongfulness on his part. Furthermore, a reasonable person in the position of M would have behaved no differently in the circumstances, and fault in the form of negligence was therefore also absent. The plaintiff's claim was dismissed.

c) Commentary

The Court's handling of so-called putative defence as a ground excluding fault, rather than wrongfulness, is perfectly in line with the treatment of this topic in eminent text books on the South African law of delict. **74**

18. Ntamo v Minister of Safety and Security 2001 1 SA 830 Transkei High Court (Tk HC): Police Shooting an Armed and Aggressive Civilian

a) Brief Summary of the Facts

N was a passenger on a bus in a rural area. En route the driver made an arrangement with the driver of another bus, altering the originally planned route in the process. Some passengers changed buses in accordance with this arrangement. N, however, was asleep when this happened. Upon waking up and apparently realising that the bus was not heading towards his intended destination, N became aggressive, gripping the driver's shoulder tightly and hurting him. Other passengers reprimanded N, and the driver offered to hire a taxi for N to take him to his village. N then confronted the passengers, shouting verbal abuse at them and pulling out a pistol. At that stage the bus reached the next village, and the driver stopped at the bus rank. N was slapping another passenger and pointing the pistol at him. N also cocked the pistol. The driver got out of the bus and rushed to the police station, hearing a shot go off before he arrived there. Four policemen went to the bus rank. The evidence about what happened thereafter was confusing and contradictory. Apparently one officer, M, was in civilian clothes while the other three were in uniform. M was armed with a pistol and the other policemen with automatic rifles. M went up to N, while the other three policemen stood about 16 paces away in a semicircle. M showed N his appointment certificate, told him that he was a policeman, and showed him the other three policemen. N was brandishing his pistol. M took N's arm that held the pistol, put it over his shoulder, and instructed him to drop the pistol behind him. Instead, N (who was a tall, well-built man) pushed M (who was a small, short man) away. M staggered and ran away. N fired in the direction of the police. All four policemen returned fire, killing N. None of the policemen were wounded. **75**

N's dependants instituted an action for loss of support against the Minister of Safety and Security. **76**

b) Judgment of the Transkei High Court (Tk HC)

The Court pointed out that N was behaving in an unlawful manner which threatened the lives and/or bodily integrity of other people. This entitled the **77** police to intervene and neutralise the threat. However, if threatened harm could be avoided without the use of force, private defence could not succeed as a ground of justification; and if force was necessary, the force used should not have been more than was reasonably necessary to achieve the purpose. The Court held that the defendant had failed to prove that the use of force on N's person was necessary. The facts did not reveal that he was about to shoot someone. On M's own testimony, the easiest way of disarming an aggressor was to give him instructions from a distance and watch his response. The police could easily have done this, using cars parked in the vicinity as cover. Warning shots could also have been fired. Consequently the Court held that the defendant had failed to prove the absence of wrongfulness. Although it could be argued that when N started to shoot at the police, they could not reasonably be expected not to shoot back, the point of the matter was that if the police had not acted wrongfully in the first place, there might not have been a life-threatening shooting at all. The Court said further that if it was wrong in deciding that the use of force was not reasonably necessary, it had to consider whether the force used by the police was proportional to the harm they were trying to prevent. The location of the bullet wounds suggested that the police had intended to kill, not just to neutralise. The Court said that whilst a life-threatening situation would affect one's judgment, the *boni mores* does not make light of the sanctity of life, and it can never be that any person who whips out a firearm and threateningly points it at the police apparently intent on shooting them is fair game to be shot and killed by the police. The police must justify their use of lethal force, with regard to factors such as (i) the imminence of the danger; (ii) how threatening the danger is to life or limb; (iii) the nature of the instrument, if any, the attacker is using; (iv) the proximity of the attacker and the attacked; (v) the mobility of the attacker and the celerity of his movements; and how easy or difficult it would be to apply force to a less delicate part of the body. The Court found further support for its decision in the new Constitution, enshrining the sanctity of life as a fundamental right[47] and influencing the *boni mores* of society in this respect, and also in the European Convention of Human Rights and decisions of the European Court of Human Rights.[48] Since only the issue of private defence had been placed into dispute, the Court found that the other elements of liability had been satisfied, and held that the defendant was liable.

c) Commentary

78 It is strange that the defendant did not argue that the police and N had acted as joint wrongdoers against the dependants in terms of sec. 2 of the Apportionment of Damages Act[49] (see the case discussion by J. Scott, mentioned under "Literature" below).

[47] Sec. 11.

[48] *McCann v United Kingdom* (1996) 21 EHRR 97; *Andronicou v Cyprus* (1998) 25 EHHR 491.

[49] Act 34 of 1956.

B. Literature

1. J. Neethling/J. M. Potgieter/P. J. Visser, *Law of Delict* (Butterworths, Durban 4th edn. 2001) Translated and Edited by J. C. Knobel

This book, now in its fourth edition, has established itself as one of the leading textbooks on the South African law of delict. The first edition was published in Afrikaans in 1989. *Law of Delict*, in its various editions, has been quoted as an authoritative source in numerous cases, and is a prescribed textbook at many universities. In this latest edition, special attention is given to the growing number of decisions on the application of the new Constitution to the law of delict. Several topics have been re-written in view of new case law, legislation or research, *inter alia* the place of wrongfulness and negligence in the hierarchy of delictual elements; the nature of the test for negligence; extension of the action of dependants; liability for psychological lesions or emotional shock; strict liability of an employer for intentional wrongdoing of an employee; and the vicarious liability of the owner of a motor car. The English and Afrikaans versions of this book now appear simultaneously (previously, they were updated and published alternately). In this latest English version, Afrikaans quotations from case law that used to appear untranslated in the main text, have been translated into English. The footnotes still contain quotations in Afrikaans. **79**

2. T. J. Scott/D. Visser (eds.), *Developing Delict: Essays in Honour of Robert Feenstra* (Juta, Cape Town 2000)

Although the date of publication of this work is 2000, it first became available in 2001. It is a compilation of papers which were read for the first time at a conference held at the University of Cape Town. The purpose of the conference and the resulting volume of essays was to honour Prof. R. Feenstra on the occasion of his eightieth birthday. Prof. Feenstra had forged valuable academic links between the university of Leiden and South African law faculties, and several South African jurists, among them the two editors of this volume, obtained doctorates under his leadership. The contributors to the volume include two justices of the SCA and several eminent academics. The contributions cover a wide range of topics, grouped by the editors under the following headings: "The structure of the Aquilian action: the general principles in perspective" (contributions by F. du Bois, A. Fagan, J. Potgieter, and J. R. Midgley); "The Aquilian action and the vicissitudes of pure economic loss" (J. Burchell, D. Hutchison and T. Davel); "The Aquilian action and intellectual property" (M. Loubser and J. Knobel); "The *Actio ad exhibendum*" (J. Neethling); "The *actio iniuriarum*" (D. McQuoid-Mason); "Vicarious liability" (T.J. Scott); and "The interface between delict and other areas of obligations: contract, enrichment and *negotiorum gestio*" (P. Olivier, D. Visser/D. Kleyn, D. H. Van Zyl). The volume also contains two personal tributes to Prof. Feenstra by A. van der Walt and Ph. J. Thomas. **80**

3. C. J. Davel, The Delictual Accountability and Criminal Capacity of a Child: How Big Can the Gap Be? [2001] *De Jure*, 605 *et seq.*

81 The author points out that the proposed Child Justice Bill raises the minimum age of criminal capacity of children from seven to ten years, whereas the current minimum age of delictual accountability is seven. According to the Bill, children who are at least ten but not yet fourteen, will not be prosecuted unless the Director of Public Prosecutions issues a certificate confirming an intention to prosecute the child, whereas the current position in delict is that children over seven but under fourteen years of age are rebuttably presumed to be unaccountable. The author is of the opinion that the discrepancies between the criminal capacity and delictual accountability of children, should the Bill become an Act of Parliament, will be untenable. She suggests that the most appropriate way to address the discrepancies would be to include and regulate the issue in the envisaged Comprehensive Children Statute.

4. J. C. Knobel, Trade Secrets and the Doctrine of Subjective Rights, [2001] *Journal of Contemporary Roman-Dutch Law/Tydskrif vir Hedendaagse Romeins-Hollandse Reg* (THRHR), 572 *et seq.*

82 The author argues that a trade secret is the object of an independent subjective right, and that the wrongfulness of trade secret misappropriation is best explained as an infringement of this right.

5. A. Kok, Delictual Liability in Case of Suicide, [2001] *Stellenbosch Law Review* (Stell LR), 156 *et seq.*

83 This contribution poses the question whether someone who could have prevented a suicide can be held delictually liable. The author argues that general delictual principles can be applied. He discusses possible defences, arguing that sec. 2 of the Apportionment of Damages Act,[50] dealing with joint wrongdoers, will probably be applicable.

6. A. Kok, Homosexuality, the Bill of Rights and the Unlawfulness Criterion in the Law of Delict, [2001] *The South African Law Journal* (SALJ), 102 *et seq.*

84 The author argues that, in the new Constitutional dispensation, a statement that someone is a homosexual is not defamatory, since the relevant person's esteem will not be lowered in the eyes of a reasonable person. A claim for defamation will therefore fail in such a case. However, claims based on an infringement of the person's dignity or privacy would be available in appropriate cases, and if patrimonial loss has been suffered as a result of such a statement infringing the dignity and/or privacy, such loss would be recoverable under the *actio legis Aquiliae*.

[50] Discussed above.

7. J. M. T. Labuschagne, Aanspreeklikheid vir 'n besering in die loop van 'n gholfspel, of -oefening of -vertoning opgedoen, [2001] THRHR, 46 *et seq*.

This contribution deals with liability for injuries sustained in the course of golfing contests, practice or demonstrations. After examining the position in German and American jurisdictions, the author concludes that ordinary negligence is a satisfactory basis for liability in South African law. Although non-compliance with the rules of the game are important to the enquiry into negligence, a golf player can also be negligent even if he has not broken any of the rules. 85

8. J. R. Midgley, Intention Remains the Fault Criterion Under the *actio injuriarum*, [2001] SALJ, 433 *et seq*.

The author discusses the implications of *Marais v Groenewald*.[51] He holds the opinion,[52] differing from a more generally held one,[53] that the *Bogoshi* case did not introduce negligence as fault requirement in media defamation cases, but rather reinstated intent after abolishing strict liability. In this contribution, he argues that the *Marais* judgment is in line with his view that intent is now a requirement for all defamation cases. 86

9. C. J. Nagel, Recent Case Law, [2001] *De Jure*, 214 *et seq*.

The author discusses *Absa Bank Ltd v Bond Equipment (Pretoria) (Pty) Ltd*.[54] He is intrigued by the possibility of the bank compensating the plaintiff in full, and then exercising a right of recourse against the thief in so far as the latter had been a joint wrongdoer.[55] 87

10. J. Neethling, Deelnemende elektroniese waarneming as dreigend - onregmatige privaatheidskending, [2001] THRHR, 131 *et seq*.

The author discusses the judgment in *Tap Wine Trading CC v Classic Wines (Western Cape) CC*,[56] which dealt with so-called participant electronic surveillance, *i.e.* where one of the participants in a conversation consents to the secret electronic recording of the conversation. The Court held that such recording by a private person (not the State) is not unlawful and evidence obtained in this manner is permissible in Court. The author agrees with this decision, but points out that revealing such recordings to other parties could be an invasion of privacy. 88

[51] 2001 1 SA 634 (T).

[52] See J. R. Midgley, Media Liability for Defamation [1999] SALJ, 211 *et seq*.

[53] See J. M. Burchell, Media Freedom of Expression scores as Strict Liability receives the Red Card: National Media Ltd v Bogoshi, [1999] SALJ, 1 *et seq*.; J. Neethling/J. M. Potgieter, Die Lasterreg en die Media: Strikte Aanspreeklikheid word ten gunste van Nalatigheid verwerp en 'n Verweer van Media-privilegie gevestig, [1999] THRHR, 442 *et seq*.; J. Neethling/J. M. Potgieter/P. J. Visser (*supra* note 20) p. 348.

[54] Discussed above.

[55] In terms of sec. 2 of the Apportionment of Damages Act 34 of 1956.

[56] 1999 4 SA 194 (C).

11. J. Neethling, Die regsplig van die staat om die reg op die fisies-psigiese integriteit teen derdes te beskerm: Die korrekte benadering tot onregmatigheid, nalatigheid en kousaliteit, [2001] THRHR, 489 *et seq.*

89 This is a case discussion of the judgment of the SCA in the *Carmichele* case[57] and a judgment of the CPD in *Moses v Minister of Safety and Security.*[58] The author comments on the way in which the Courts applied the delictual elements of wrongfulness, negligence and causation to factual situations.

12. J. Neethling/J. M. Potgieter, Die toets vir deliktuele nalatigheid onder die soeklig, [2001] THRHR, 476 *et seq.*

90 The authors discuss the application of the tests for negligence and legal causation in two decisions of the SCA.[59] They criticise the Court's tendency to decide whether negligence is present before wrongfulness of the act has been established. They also comment on the uncertainty created in some recent decisions concerning the boundaries of negligence and legal causation.

13. J. Neethling/J. M. Potgieter, Uitbreiding van die aksie van afhanklikes, [2001] THRHR, 484 *et seq.*

91 This contribution deals with recent extensions of the action of dependants in two decisions of the SCA. Before these two cases, only plaintiffs in respect of whom the breadwinner had had a recognised common law obligation of support, such as by legal marriage or blood relations, had a claim for loss of support against someone who had wrongfully and culpably killed the breadwinner. In *Santam Bpk v Henery*[60] the Court allowed a divorced woman, who had been entitled to support on strength of a Court order, to institute action against the person responsible for her ex-husband's death, and in *Amod v Multilateral Motor Vehicle Accident's Fund (Commissioner for Gender Equality Intervening)*[61] a plaintiff who had been married according to the Muslim faith, was allowed to claim for loss of support from the Fund after her husband had been killed in a motor accident. The authors welcome both cases, but express the opinion that interference with a purely contractual duty of support will, in the absence of special factors, not be actionable.

14. C. J. Roederer, Wrongly Conceiving Wrongful Conception: Distributive v Corrective Justice, [2001] SALJ, 347 *et seq.*

92 The author discusses the decision in *Mukheiber v Raath*,[62] in which a doctor had told a woman and her husband that she had been sterilised. The couple thereupon did not use contraceptives, resulting in pregnancy and the birth of a

[57] Discussed above.

[58] 2000 3 SA 106 (C).

[59] *Sea Harvest Corporation (Pty) Ltd v Duncan Dock Cold Storage (Pty) Ltd* 2000 1 SA 827 (SCA); *Mkhatswa v Minister of Defence* 2000 1 SA 1004 (SCA).

[60] 1999 3 SA 421 (SCA).

[61] 1999 4 SA 1319 (SCA).

[62] 1999 3 SA 1065 (SCA).

child. They instituted an action for patrimonial loss in respect of confinement costs and maintenance for the child. The SCA held that, in principle, they had a claim. The author is critical of the decision, arguing that the Court failed to deal with the real issues involved. He suggests several alternatives to the approach followed by the Court.

15. J. Scott, Deliktuele aanspreeklikheid vir veroorsaking van suiwer ekonomiese verlies: Die deur word wyer oopgemaak, [2001] THRHR, 681 *et seq.*

This is a discussion of *Dersley v Minister van Veiligheid en Sekuriteit*.[63] The **93**
author criticises the judgments in some respects, but finds himself in agreement with the result.

16. J. Scott, Re-Affirmation of the Doctrine of Immunity of Municipalities Against Liability for Wrongful Omissions Assessed and Rejected, [2001] THRHR, 502 *et seq.*

The author discusses one of the latest[64] in a long line of so-called "municipal- **94**
ity cases", being cases dealing with liability for omission, with municipalities in the role of defendant. The author is of opinion that the *boni mores* criterion, according to which the presence or absence of wrongfulness must be determined, succeeds in achieving justice between the parties, but fails to create legal certainty.

17. J. Scott, Recent Case Law, [2001] *De Jure*, 198 *et seq.*

This is a discussion of the then still unreported decision of the CPD in *The* **95**
Cape Metropolitan Council v Noel Raymond Graham.[65] The author concludes that the judgment will not be remembered for a systematic exposition of principles pertaining to negligence in the context of a wrongful omission, but that it does provide a good example of the way in which existing law is applied to a difficult factual situation.

18. J. Scott, Recent Case Law, [2001] *De Jure*, 404 *et seq.*

The author discusses the decision in *Ntamo v Minister of Safety and Security*.[66] **96**
He comments on the fact that poor evidence was a major stumbling block in this case. He finds it surprising that the defendant had not raised the defence that the deceased had been blameworthy in respect of his own death. On this basis, the deceased breadwinner and the police could have been regarded as joint wrongdoers against the dependants, in which case the defendant could have had a right of recourse against the deceased's estate. Such a right of recourse would have been of no use if the deceased's estate contained no or few assets, and the author speculates that this might have been the underlying

[63] Discussed above.
[64] *Cape Town Municipality v Bakkerud* 2000 3 1049 (SCA).
[65] Case no. 157/99 (C). The judgment of the SCA is discussed above.
[66] Discussed above.

reason why the defendant did not argue that the deceased had been a joint wrongdoer.

19. J. Scott, Recent Case Law, [2001] *De Jure*, 635 *et seq.*

97 This is a discussion of *Grootboom v Graaff-Reinet Municipality.*[67] According to the author, this case provides an excellent example of a practical application of the negligence test.

20. J. van der Walt, Progressive Indirect Horizontal Application of the Bill of Rights: Towards a Co-Operative Relation Between Common-Law and Constitutional Jurisprudence, [2001] *South African Journal on Human Rights* (SAJHR), 341 *et seq.*

98 The author discusses the horizontal application of the Bill of Rights, and a perceived difference in the approaches of the CC and the SCA in this respect. He contends that the only remaining significant difference between the indirect and direct horizontal application of the Bill of Rights concerns the need to create new causes of action where none exists at common law. Reference is made to several cases dealing with delictual questions. The author is critical of the decision in *National Media Ltd v Bogoshi*,[68] for allegedly obscuring the historical impact of the new constitutional dispensation and the horizontal application of the Bill of Rights on the law of defamation.

[67] 2001 3 SA 373 (E).
[68] *Supra* note 34.

XX. Comparative Remarks

Helmut Koziol

1. Introduction

The country reports contain a tremendous treasure of interesting legislation, cases and literature. The aim of this comparative report is not to merely provide a brief summary of these reports as, in my opinion, this would not be particularly constructive. I will, therefore only point out some trail-blazing developments and outstanding tendencies in European legal systems. 1

2. Environmental Liability

In the last years, one of the main topics under discussion has been environmental liability. In some European countries bills on environmental liability have been drafted, *e.g.* in the year 2001 in Poland, where a new Environmental Protection Law came into effect[1], and courts had to decide some cases[2]. Above all, the Commission of the European Union issued a Green Paper in 1993, a White Paper in 2000 and a Working Paper in 2001. All these papers designed regimes based on tort law. Therefore, it is rather surprising that the "Directive on Environmental Liability with Regard to the Prevention and Restoration of Environmental Damage", adopted by the Commission on 23 January 2002, introduces a public law scheme[3]. The Draft primarily aims at the prevention of environmental harm, but also requires the reparation of any damage actually caused. As Koch rightly points out[4], the draft unfortunately covers only certain types of environmental harm and does not extend to personal injury or damage to property. Therefore, for the future, national law will still be of great importance but Koch fears that the interplay of the new regime and traditional tort law will work even less smoothly than the product liability as it deviates from present tort law systems. 2

This example of European legislation emphasises once more the urgent need for European Principles on Tort Law. At the moment, the very selective legis- 3

[1] Poland no. [2].
[2] See *e.g.*, Spain nos. [110] *et seq.*
[3] See European Union nos. [6] *et seq.*
[4] European Union nos. [8] and [11].

lation of the European Union and with that the selective adjustment of the European legal systems leads to a double fragmentation of the law: On the one hand, the national legal systems are infiltrated with exotic insertions, on the other hand, even the directives themselves are not based on a consistent system and, therefore, are conflicting. One has to hope that we only face a brief difficult transitional phase, but one should strive to shorten this unpleasant period. I feel it a challenge to draw up a fundamental concept for the development of European private law, in connection with our area of European tort law. Only within the framework of general European principles will it be possible to avoid contradictions between directives of the European Union and to adapt the national legal systems in such a way that they correspond to the same fundamental ideas thus achieving a harmonious, consistent system of tort law which corresponds with the idea of justice. This is exactly the reason why the European Group on Tort Law is drafting principles of tort law.

3. Personal Injuries

4 In European countries there is a noticeable tendency to improve compensation in cases of personal injuries, especially compensation of non-pecuniary loss. Perhaps one can say that this is the mainstream in the development of European tort law in the year 2001.

5 For example, in *Austria*[5] courts have raised the rather low ceiling of compensation for pain and suffering and awarded in one case more than ATS 2 million (approx. € 150,000). Furthermore, the Supreme Court[6] not only confirms its opinion that a person who suffers an "emotional shock" by watching a severe accident involving relatives may have a personal claim if the shock amounts to bodily injury for compensation of pain and suffering caused by this injury, but rules that the same applies if the third person's injury was caused by the mere message of the death of a person with whom there is a strong emotional bond. Even more remarkable is that the Supreme Court[7] soon afterwards arrives at the conclusion that the grief for the loss of a near relative not leading to a physical injury can be compensated if the tortfeasor acted with gross negligence or intent.

6 The *Belgian* Indicative Table[8] proposed a rise in damages in cases of personal injuries.

7 The maximum amounts of compensation for personal injuries have been raised considerably by a *Danish* bill in 2001[9].

8 The *English* Lord Chancellor reduced the assumed rate of return on the investment of damages for future pecuniary loss in personal injury actions to 2.5%[10].

[5] Austria nos. [37] *et seq.*
[6] Austria nos. [51] *et seq.*
[7] Austria nos. [69] *et seq.*
[8] Belgium nos. [40] *et seq.*
[9] Denmark nos. [1] *et seq.*
[10] England nos. [1] *et seq.*

The effect of the decision will be a further increase in the sums recovered by tort claimants. Furthermore, in the case *TP and KM v United Kingdom,* the European Court of Human Rights recognised liability for purely mental distress not resulting from physical injury[11]. The same is true for *Keenan v United Kingdom*: The applicant's son, K, committed suicide whilst serving a sentence of imprisonment; the European Court of Human Rights awarded compensation for purely emotional harm[12]. But the country reporter Oliphant points out that it goes beyond existing English law in allowing a claim for purely emotional harm not consequential on physical injury, both in respect of the primary victim, K, and the secondary victim, his mother. He is of the opinion that to an English lawyer, the mother's claim seems especially remote as her distress derived not from her own immediate perception of her son's ill-treatment but from hearing about it subsequently and being unable to pursue an effective avenue of redress.

In *Finland* the Personal Injury Committee recommended improving the legal security of victims; further to clarify the heads of compensation of non-pecuniary loss and to expand them[13]. **9**

The *German* draft reform of the law of damages[14] plans a major step and allows the plaintiff to claim equitable compensation in money for personal injury as well as infringements of liberty or sexual self-determination not only under tort law but even in the area of strict liability and contractual liability. The victim will have such a claim on compensation if one of two alternative conditions are met: (1) the injury is caused intentionally; or (2) the damage is of some gravity, taking into account both its nature and duration. **10**

In *Greece* the family of the deceased can claim compensation for pain and suffering. In regard of the changing social conditions, the Court of Cassation defined the term "family" in a rather broad sense[15]. Even more important is the Court's ruling[16] that in case of the parents' death, damages for pain and suffering can also be asked for the foetus as well as for the baby of a very young age, irrespective of their incapacity to feel any grief already at the time of the death. The amount of money awarded for pain and suffering will cover the future pain and suffering that the foetus or baby will certainly feel from the loss of his father or mother later, when he will be mature enough to realise he is an orphan. **11**

In *Ireland* a plaintiff, who was infected with Hepatitis C, was awarded general damages of £ 300,000, as the effects of the Hepatitis C seriously compromised his enjoyment of life[17]. By this and also by a later decision the former cap of **12**

[11] See England nos. [19] *et seq.*
[12] England nos. [28] *et seq.*
[13] Finland nos. [4] and [8].
[14] Germany nos. [2] *et seq.*
[15] Greece nos. [41] *et seq.*
[16] Greece no. [49].
[17] Ireland no. [49].

£ 250,000 was raised significantly. Further, the country reporter Quill points out that in some cases[18] the amount of general damages has been rather high.

13 Personal injuries seems to be the prevailing topic under discussion in *Italy* and the legislator has introduced the category of *danno biologico* in the field of obligatory social insurance and has settled *danno biologico* caused by micro-disabilities[19]. Furthermore, courts have confirmed the rules on compensation for *danno biologico*[20]. On the other hand, the Italian Supreme Court is reluctant to award compensation for pain and suffering in case the victim is unconscious[21].

14 In the *Netherlands* the government indicated that it is planning to introduce a statute granting a right of compensation of non-pecuniary losses not only to the victim but also to the descendants and relatives of the victim who have suffered as a result of the tort[22].

15 According to the *Polish* country report[23] there has been a significant increase in the number of personal injury lawsuits and the general pattern of awards shows their constant rise.

16 As under *Spanish* law damages usually include compensation for non-pecuniary loss, it is remarkable that the Supreme Court ruled that the victim may have a separate claim for compensation for serious and lasting moral damage[24].

17 In *Sweden* new provisions strengthen the right to claim damages for non-pecuniary loss, among other things the right to compensation for psychological distress resulting from the death of a close relative[25].

18 In summary one may say that there is a tendency in Europe to extend compensation for non-pecuniary loss in the area of personal injuries, on the one hand by increasing the amounts awarded, on the other hand by expanding the scope of persons who are entitled to claim in cases of the victim's death.

4. Wrongful Life

19 Sensational are the decisions of the French *Cour de cassation* passed in *Assemblée Plénière*, which continued the "*arrêt Perruche*": A child born with a handicap can claim compensation for this handicap if the doctor negligently prevented its mother from exercising her choice to terminate the pregnancy[26].

[18] *Cf.* Ireland nos. [59] and [71].
[19] See Italy no. [2].
[20] Italy nos. [31] *et seq.*
[21] Italy nos. [43] *et seq.*
[22] Netherlands no. [11].
[23] Poland nos. [38] *et seq.*
[24] Spain nos. [106] *et seq.*
[25] Sweden nos. [2] and [3].
[26] See France nos. [40] *et seq.*

These decisions raise fundamental questions, especially whether there exists a right not to be born deformed or disabled, a right to be aborted or killed. The London Court of Appeal[27] asked: "How can there be a duty to take away life?" and further pointed out that a doctor is not under a legal obligation to a foetus to terminate its life. Therefore, it does not seem astonishing that the French *Conseil d'État* does not agree with the *Cour de cassation* but it is rather remarkable that the French legislator acted rather quickly and recently has been restricting compensation for "wrongful life"[28].

The Dutch *Hoge Raad* did not really have to decide the wrongful life issue in the true sense. The handicapped child claimed compensation for non-pecuniary losses, but she did not blame the defendant for her mere existence, but for the fact that she was handicapped. That fact, however, was not caused by the doctor, but obviously by the deviation in her chromosomes. Hence, the simple result was that there was no causal link between the fault of the defendant and the damage[29]. **20**

5. Pure Economic Loss

A very popular topic is the extremely complex problem of tortious liability for pure economic loss. It seems that even under those legal systems which have been rather restrictive in compensating such loss there is an increasing tendency to be more generous to the victim. In this report I can, of course, only highlight some examples. **21**

The *Austrian* Supreme Court awarded compensation for pure financial loss a bank suffered on account of a municipality's incorrect confirmation declaring a certain piece of land building ground[30]. This confirmation was presented to the bank by the purchaser of said real estate. Relying on the confirmation, the bank granted a mortgage loan to the purchaser. Consequently, the bank suffered loss as the purchaser was not able to pay back the loan. **22**

The *Finnish* Supreme Court[31] held that the members of the board of directors, who had signed an affidavit that the share capital had been fully paid up and the assets were in the possession of the company, should have made sure that the information on the affidavit was correct before they signed it. By failing to do so, they had, through their negligence, contributed to the loss of the estate and, therefore, the Court held them liable under tort law. **23**

The *German* Federal Ministry of Justice aims at the introduction of a liability of court-appointed experts who submit erroneous reports. Damage caused by such reports will nearly always be pure economic loss. According to the draft **24**

[27] *McKay and Another v. Essex Area Health Authority and Another*, [1982] 2 *Weekly Law Reports*, 890.
[28] Titre I Art 1er I of Act 2002–303 from 3 March 2002; see France no. [106].
[29] Netherlands no. [27].
[30] Austria nos. [10] *et seq.*
[31] Finland nos. [26] *et seq.*

and contrary to the valid law, court-appointed experts would have to bear responsibility for intent and gross negligence.

25 On the other hand, *Irish* courts seem to be reluctant to adjudicate compensation for pure economic loss[32]: The Chief Justice emphasised that cases of pure economic loss would not give rise to the imposition of a duty of care as readily as cases of physical damage to persons or property. He pointed out that in the case at hand the nature of the statutory power in question (the drawing up of a development plan) was not such as to create sufficient proximity between the parties such that it would be just and reasonable to impose a duty of care on the respondent.

26 The *Swedish*[33] Supreme Court found that the valuer was not liable for the bank's financial loss because the bank should have understood that the valuer's certificate regarding the value of the property was not meant for granting of credits. The valuer had issued the certificate for another purpose.

27 One can conclude from these examples that, at least in the field of negligent misrepresentation, quite some willingness to accept liability appears to exist.

6. Public Liability

28 Noteworthy seems to me the number of cases and legislation concerning the public liability[34]; in particular such development is pointed out by the Dutch reporters[35]. This cannot be explained by the relatively young possibility to sue the state for not transforming EU-directives into national law: Such claims are by far not the majority. Furthermore, Poland and South Africa are not Member States and the country reports from these countries mention quite a number of cases on public liability. Remarkable is, further, that many claimants argued that the public authorities have omitted protective measures. It seems that there is a growing tendency to accept duties of the public authorities to become active for the protection of the citizens.

7. Conclusion

29 By way of summarising one has to say that liability continues to expand. This is a phenomenon which has aroused the interest of the European Group on Tort Law from the beginning of its research[36]. Of course, from the point of view of the persons who suffer a loss, this development seems to be pleasing. But, on the other side, one has to take into consideration that a person who is a

[32] Ireland nos. [3] *et seq.*

[33] Sweden nos. [20] *et seq.*

[34] See *e.g.*, Austria nos. [10] *et seq.*, [16] *et seq.*; England nos. [7] *et seq.*; Ireland nos. [6] *et seq.*; France nos. [76] *et seq.*; Italy nos. [10] *et seq.*, [16] *et seq.*, [34] *et seq.*; Poland nos. [8] *et seq.*; Portugal nos. [13] *et seq.*, [47] *et seq.*; Spain nos. [14] *et. seq.*; South Africa nos. [1] *et seq.*, [6] *et seq.*, [47] *et seq.*, [58] *et seq.* and [73] *et seq.*; Sweden nos. [30] *et seq.*

[35] Netherlands nos. [3] and [28].

[36] See W.V.H. Rogers/J. Spier/G. Viney, Preliminary observations, in: Spier (ed.), *The Limits of Liability* (1996) pp. 1 *et seq.*; Spier (ed.), *The Limits of Expanding Liability* (1998).

victim in one case may subsequently be the defendant who has caused damage. It is not within the remit of this paper to point out all the pros and cons of expanding liability; this would be a topic in itself for a major conference. I would only like to emphasise one inconsistency which in my opinion is very striking and seems to be worthy of a thorough discussion[37]: We are already used to ever-growing duties of care in regard to one's fellow human beings and to an extension of strict liability in favour of victims. On the other hand there are quite some attempts to reduce the importance of contributory negligence or – in a broader perspective – contributory responsibility. For example, under the recent *Belgium* law[38] compensation can only be refused to victims, aged over 14, who have wanted both the accident and its consequences to happen; this definition merely matches cases of suicide or suicidal attempts. But would it not be more fair not only to increase the duties of tortfeasors but also to increase everyone's responsibility for his own interests?[39] In my opinion, this would contribute to prevention of damage with at least the same effectiveness as increasing the liability of the tortfeasor. Furthermore, I think it reasonable that one should not be able to shift the risk of one's own nonchalance entirely to other careless or strictly liable persons. Therefore, I advocate the line of the German seat belt-decision[40]: The German Supreme Court takes the view that passengers are required to keep their seat belts fastened at all times as passengers will be subject to a high amount of danger even if the vehicle is not in motion at the time of a crash. The topic of contributory negligence would perhaps be a suitable topic for one of the next annual conferences.

[37] The problem has been mentioned by G. Schiemann, Haftungsbeschränkungen, in: E. Lorenz (ed.), *Karlsruher Forum 1999. Haftungsbeschränkungen* (1999) p. 28.

[38] Belgium no. [4].

[39] The Dutch opinion seems to go in this direction, *cf.* Netherlands nos. [42] *et seq.*

[40] See Germany nos. [37] *et seq.*

Other Contributions

I. Liability and Liability Insurance in Large Loss Scenarios

Christian Lahnstein

A. Introduction

1 A reinsurer's annual review is a review of major losses: of earthquakes, windstorms, floods and other events which can usually be linked to a precise date; or of important developments in the run-off of long-tail claims complexes, *e.g.* strengthening reserves for asbestos or pharmaceutical losses.

2 The review of the year 2001 is dominated by the terrorist attack of 11th September. A loss event in New York gives rise to claims burdens of € 2 billion for a reinsurer in Munich: the function of reinsurance, which has always been global, continues to be of relevance, despite the increased financial strength of national insurance markets and of internationally operating primary insurers. As far as estimations of major loss scenarios are concerned, reinsurers have tended to concentrate on natural disasters in past years. This year it appears appropriate to take a more systematic look at the many types of man-made disaster, and it is in this context that the following considerations on large losses in liability insurance should be seen.

1. Concept of Large Loss

3 In the insurance industry, the term "large loss" seems to be clearest when it involves accidents, often spectacular scenarios which occur at a moment's notice, exceptional situations like industrial accidents, earthquakes or terrorist attacks. But when it comes to detail, the criteria are open to dispute. An earthquake in the Gobi Desert will not cause any damage, however strong it is: an event, not a loss event. On the other hand, the 1985 eruption of the Nevado del Ruiz volcano in Colombia, though relatively harmless on the basis of the Volcanic Explosivity Index, buried a town of 30,000. Nevertheless, the private insurance industry was affected much less by this than by the smashed roofs and dented cars caused by the July 1984 hailstorm in Munich. The UN Department of Humanitarian Affairs

defines a large loss (*i.e.* "national disaster") as an event which overtaxes the ability of the affected region to help itself. What if the region's ability to help itself is already overtaxed by everyday grievances? It must also be assumed that an exceptional situation will generate political pressure.[1]

2. Large Losses and Liability

In large loss scenarios, questions of liability are of interest in several respects. 4
They already play a part where natural hazard risks or political risks are to the fore. Flooding can also be caused as a result of zoning plans being faulty or not properly monitored. The causes of an earthquake cannot be attributed to anyone, but foreseeable or avoidable consequences of construction defects or poor disaster management can. The World Trade Center in New York, extolled as collapse-proof, was found to have construction weaknesses – the light, unprotected suspended construction and the unsafe connections between the floors and the vertical supporting members. "Failings" of this kind had also been discussed in a similar way following the sinking of "unsinkable" ships – the *Titanic* in 1912 and the *Andrea Doria* in 1956.[2]

3. Latent Losses and Liability

In what are initially less obvious large loss situations, public pressure builds 5
up in a process we may call "name, blame and claim". Such apportionment of blame may relate not only to exceptional but also to everyday situations, to familiar and long-accepted risks associated with production, consumption and transport. This is often what first creates acute public awareness of a large loss, transforming a latent or accepted grievance into a scandal. In the USA it became strikingly clear how industry and the unions, health authorities and workers' compensation insurers had ignored or hushed up the problem of asbestos for decades until it was picked up in the 1970s as a result of more strictly defined product liability and solved by the bankruptcy of the manufacturers.[3] Today, even though most asbestos processing has been stopped in the last 30 years, the wave of bankruptcies is still continuing to catch new groups of former manufacturers and their legal successors, though the attribution criteria are becoming increasingly questionable.[4]

4. Large Losses and "Event" Definitions in Insurance and Reinsurance

In insurance and reinsurance, terms like "event" or "loss event", "accumula- 6
tion loss" and "serial loss" form the subject of abstract, ambiguous contract

[1] *Cf.* Lahnstein, Großschaden und Haftungsrecht: Unternehmenshaftung im internationalen Überblick am Beispiel Asbest, in: Koch/Willingmann, *Großschäden – Complex Damages* (Rostocker Arbeiten zum Internationalen Recht, Bd.1 1998), pp. 117–127.

[2] The worst shipping disaster ever was the sinking of a German passenger ship carrying 10,000 refugees and marines in the Baltic Sea in 1945.

[3] Brodeur, *Outrageous misconduct: The asbestos industry on trial* (1985). Rosenberg, The dusting of America: a story of asbestos carnage, cover-up, and litigation, [1986] Harvard Law Review 99, 1693.

[4] *Cf.* Moser, *Mealey's Litigation Report* (11 December 2001), pp. 27–34.

clauses used to limit, in both contractual relationships, the deductibles and the retentions on the one hand and the sums insured or reinsured on the other. Far-reaching consequences are attached to "soft" preconditions that can be interpreted in different ways.

5. Large Loss as a Construct

7 The term "large loss" is therefore a construct – not only an object of observation but also a concept of observation, or glasses that are put on to identify a specific need for action. The same facts may be assessed for different purposes on the basis of different criteria by ecologists or medics, regional or central administrations, experts on social law and liability law, property and liability insurers, primary insurers and reinsurers, and also between liability insurers.

6. Large Losses and Mass Media

8 Large losses as the object and concept of observation: the influence and inherent dynamic force of the public comes into play here, and the role of the mass media with their specific criteria of perception. This includes the interest in scandal, in attributing fault to persons, companies and institutions in an often moralizing way, even if a most difficult evaluation of the consequences is involved; fitting things into a certain pattern or putting them under a certain heading so that, when the facts are complex, one particular aspect is emphasized and one of several possible interpretations made; the snowball effect of risk perception when the media reflect each other, when commentaries are commented on, and when statements of opinion are themselves scandalized.[5] In this way, pressure to take political action is exerted before there has been any opportunity to clarify the issue in factual terms. Then again, through this political action it may be possible to isolate the problem and to demonstrate initiative and efficiency in a state of emergency, instead of struggling with fundamental, commonplace, structural problems.

9 An overview of the different types of liability large loss scenarios follows (B.), along with thoughts on how transparency can be improved in an (individual) large loss complex affecting various countries (C.).

B. Large Loss Scenarios

10 A structured overview of large loss scenarios should differentiate between accidental causes of loss arising in the short term and those acting over a long period of time, and examine separately the liability scenarios associated with technological, natural and political risks. This results in six observation fields.

[5] *Cf.* Luhmann, *Die Realität der Massenmedien* (1996), pp. 53–81; Dunwoody/Peters, *The Mass Media and Risk Perception, in: Risk is a Construct: Perceptions of Risk Perception*, ed. by Bayerische Rück (1993), pp. 293–317.

Accidental risks 11

a. Technological risks, infrastructure (fire, explosion, escape of substances, business interruption), traffic (road, rail, bridges, tunnels, ships, aircraft, space), "crowd management" (hotels, shopping centres, stadiums)
b. Liabilities in connection with natural hazards (earthquake, flood/landslide, windstorm, fire/lightning)
c. Liabilities in connection with political risks (terrorism, riots, sabotage)

Long term risks 12

a. Technological and consumer risks: waste, emissions, noise; product risks (food, animal feed, chemicals, pharmaceuticals, tobacco), hazardous substances and technologies (asbestos, chlorine and chlorides, genetic engineering); service risks (planning, consulting, healthcare)
b. Technological risks in connection with natural (climatic, geological, hydrological) conditions
c. Political risks: restitution in relation to historical guilt (colonialism, discrimination)

The transitions are fluid: even accidents, events arising in the short term, can result in long-term damage, almost unlimited in the case of nuclear accidents, for example. A large number of individual accidents – such as leaks in industrial plants – can be seen as the result of one continued risky operation. The causes of an industrial fire may be specific to that industry, but they may also be sabotage or terrorism. 13

Nevertheless such a differentiation still appears to make sense. On the one hand, ecological and political aspects should each be looked at separately. On the other hand, typical structures should be perceived in large loss scenarios – each of which has a unique individual profile – and adequate claims management methods developed. 14

"Why does that make sense? What is the function of such a structuring venture? The diversity of complex damages incidents may resist a precise systematic categorization or even normative definition. But it seems fairly obvious that the traditional tort and liability rules are very much based in the individual bi-partisan constellation between tortfeasor and victim and are not very well equipped for multiple and more complex participation on either side – which is characteristic for our case scenarios. Hence the conclusion is near at hand that specific rules of liability are necessary in complex damages situations. These may pertain to causation, standards of attribution, of responsibility, to the notion of damages and the adjustment of claims."[6] 15

[6] Koch, Complex Damages and their Settlement: Liability principles, procedural economy, or law's retreat? In: *Munich Re, 6th International Liability Forum* (2002) (in print)

1. Accidents

a) Industry, Infrastructure, Transport

16 A topical example of explosion damage in production and storage facilities was the explosion of ammonium nitrate on 21st September 2001 at a plant in Toulouse belonging to the TotalFinaElf Group: over 80,000 claims, 27,000 damaged dwellings, 10,000 claims for bodily injury, including 4,800 industrial accidents and 30 deaths.[7] The total loss, largely insured, has been put at over € 2 billion. The suspicion of terrorism was neither proved nor disproved; debate about it has ended – a case of successful government risk management? A second terrorist attack ten days after 11th September would in fact have created further uncertainty in the global economy and motivated copycats. The problem of proving terrorism as an exclusion from liability or insurance cover is becoming clear.

17 The "explosion in production plants" category also includes the biggest civil technological disaster in recent decades, namely the escape of methyl isocyanate (MIC) from Union Carbide's plant in Bhopal (India). Here, in the early hours of 3rd December 1984, a toxic cloud blanketed a city in which most were sleeping and others were still awake in the railway station, teahouses and open-air cinemas, at wedding celebrations and a poetry festival. The case, which was not completely documented, is instructive in all too many respects. To start with, there was an incorrect estimate of the demand from Indian agriculture: an oversized production plant which after a brief period of euphoria was neglected. Unlike with drugs and pesticides, the health risks of an industrial chemical like MIC are not generally investigated as a priority. It was clear, though, that MIC quickly reacts with water, which meant that people's faces and breathing could have been protected with wet cloths. The company did not draw attention to this fact either preventively or when the crisis occurred. Whilst obvious prevention measures were not taken, a therapy remains unknown to this day. The number of victims was estimated at 12,000 to 16,000 dead and 200,000 injured. Experience gained from treatment was scarcely published. The US concern, which came off well with a settlement package of US$ 470 million (of which US$ 200 million was insured), has since been taken over by Dow, and its Chairman has disappeared. Indian legislation has reacted with laws on industrial accidents, information requirements and compulsory liability insurance.

18 The "utility companies" category includes nuclear power stations. Many lie close to large cities and a few in the surrounding areas of metropolises like Paris, Tokyo, New York or Los Angeles. What becomes particularly clear here is, on the one hand, the limits of disaster plans: evacuation cannot be carried

[7] Exactly 80 years earlier, on 21st September 1921, a similar explosion of ammonium nitrate at a plant belonging to BASF in Oppau caused the greatest civil accident in Germany's industrial history: 561 deaths and 1,952 injuries; 800 of the 1,000 buildings of the municipality were destroyed; windows even shattered 90 km away in Frankfurt.

out either as a practice drill or in an emergency. On the other hand, the underinsurance of the obligatory nuclear pools is notorious, their capacity barely exceeding that of the open liability insurance market for other major industrial risks. This is all the more disturbing in view of the fact that 11th September brought to light risks that had evidently been given little previous consideration.

In the "traffic risks" category, unlimited cover is usual in some motor liability insurance markets. This practice is under debate given the risk of large losses like the one at Selby in the UK in February 2001, with liability of around € 80 million, the transportation of dangerous goods, fires in tunnels (the cost of the accident in the Mont Blanc Tunnel in 1999 is put at some € 100 million) and, possibly, liability risks in connection with terrorism. **19**

b) Natural Hazard Risks

Liability associated with flood damage has always been of great concern to European public entity liability insurers. Generally, the question of public and private liability in the case of natural hazard risks is increasingly being raised, even in countries with less developed liability practice, like Turkey or Mexico. In the USA, it has long been a factor in earthquake accumulation scenarios, like those devised for San Francisco or Los Angeles by consultancy firms or the Federal Emergency Management Agency (FEMA). **20**

c) Political Risks

In the nineties, attention had already been drawn to a new trend towards large loss scenarios from international terrorism, particularly after the bomb attack aimed at destroying the World Trade Center already in 1993.[8] **21**

In connection with terrorism, a series of questions relating to liability law arises. What follows from the general and specific principles of liability based on fault and strict liability? And what follows from the rules relating to causality ("cause étrangère") which come into play with fault-based and strict liability alike? In detail, these questions are as follows: **22**

- How far does strict liability go in the case of traffic law (road, rail, air and shipping traffic) and as part of the various types of plant operator's, custodian's, environmental and nuclear liability? Does the risk for which strict liability may attach also include situations involving terrorism? In the case of American Airlines, the question remains open. The "September 11th Victim Compensation Fund", created on 22nd January 2002, established government liability for all bodily injury claims and retroactively limited recourse against the airline to the amount of the relevant aviation liability sums insured of US$ 1.5 billion in each case.
- How far does liability based on fault go in cases where there is negligent breach of event organizers', building owners' or employers' duties of care

[8] *Cf.* Hoffman, *Inside Terrorism* (1998), Chapter 7.

in general[9] or in particular in connection with wilful acts of third parties? It will often be possible to prove such breaches, especially in view of the fact that additional rules of conduct are being developed with respect to terrorism prevention.

23 It seems plausible to limit strict liability to typical operational risks and not to extend it to terrorist acts whose political motivation is directed less against the operator than against state or society. Liability based on fault can only be excluded by channelling liability through the state and expressly holding all other parties harmless by law, in the same way that nuclear liability is channelled via the operator. Hardly any initiatives of this kind are to be seen, with exception of the September 11th Victim Compensation Fund; which means that, overall, liability risks in connection with terrorism are considerable.

2. Long-Term Risks

a) Technology, Product and Service Risks

24 Because of the risks of change when dealing with the consequences of technology and the side-effects of products, this is probably the most complex category of large loss scenarios.

25 Risks of change arise from new technologies like genetic engineering,[10] from new hazardous substances or, more precisely, from new application of long-used substances: the latex problem of the 1990s as a result of the sudden massive demand for disposable gloves to prevent AIDS; the discovery of dioxin, notorious through the use of herbicides in Vietnam and the Seveso accident in 1976, in many industrial processes, thanks to more accurate detection methods in the 1980s. Extensively used substances become problems because of their persistence (like CHCs and PCBs in the 1980s, and currently MTBE in the USA), typically first of all in specialist circles, then among the general public, which in turn makes new research budgets possible and results in pressure to take political action.[11] A similar situation exists with respect to pharmaceuticals, when in the sea of side-effects and interactions certain relationships are spotlighted and attributed to certain manufacturers. One topical example of this is the case of the cholesterol-lowering drug Lipobay, with insured liabilities running into billions. Historical but by no means closed cases involve the damaging effect of pesticides on agricultural workers and the environment.[12]

[9] Thus following the collapse of the World Trade Center, responsibilities in connection with the initially suspected massive use of sprayed asbestos were discussed. After it became clear that the use of sprayed asbestos to protect steel girders had stopped from the 40th floor onwards of the first tower as early as 1971, the discussion shifted more onto the question of whether sprayed asbestos would have protected the steel structures for longer than the replacement product then used, and thus allowed more extensive evacuation.

[10] *Cf.* Munich Re, 5th International Liability Forum 2001.

[11] *Cf.* [8] above.

[12] *Cf.* Schinzler, *Zur Haftpflichtversicherung in einer vernetzten Weltwirtschaft* (Liability insurance in a worldwide business environment), in Munich Re, 1st International Liability Forum (1997), p. 25.

The biggest liability loss ever – personal injury claims due to asbestos – also falls into this category.[13] On the other hand, the comparably expensive cost of removing asbestos from buildings worldwide has so far had only a marginal effect on the insurance industry, whereas the cost of remedial work on middle- and lower-class dwellings in the US in connection with lead paints and the familiar old problem of toxic mould has placed a considerable burden on US homeowners and liability insurers. These examples only hint at the great number of relevant scenarios.

b) Liability in Connection with Climatic, Geological and Hydrological Processes

Despite the connection with a) above, it is advisable to take a separate look at **26**
long-term large loss scenarios arising from continuous emissions, waste or infrastructure projects in connection with climatic, geological and hydrological processes. Often it is a matter of historical liabilities like those found at production facilities in the oil or mining industries. Frequently the liabilities are latent or difficult to identify because of diffuse causal relationships. In the late 1950s, claims for compensation for asthma brought against oil companies in Yokkaichi were recognized on the basis of epidemiological proof of causality, one of the many Japanese environmental liability lawsuits of the time.[14] Many comparable "stormy" phases – where the attempt is made to simultaneously enforce state safety standards through spectacular liability lawsuits – can be seen today, and not only in new Asian industrialized countries, where the largest disaster potentials are to be found due to the risk exposure, general parameters and concentrations of value. Thus the City of Bogotá is currently being sued, together with utility companies and 76 industrial companies, by 3,600 families for damage amounting to US$ 1.5 billion caused by river pollution. As environmental protection and the protection of minorities are political topics, national and international liability lawsuits of this kind acquire additional impetus. There are overlaps with [27] below.

c) Liability in Connection with Historical Injustice

Finally, a new type of liability should not be ignored: the trend to rework his- **27**
torical injustice from earlier or more recent times with respect to liability law: the "sudden appearance of restitution cases all over the world",[15] consequences of war and colonialism, slavery and discrimination. History becomes a field for political struggle; immunities under public international law which protect not only states but also individuals and enterprises are increasingly being breached by criminal and civil liabilities.

[13] See Section C. below in this connection.

[14] *Cf.* Sawai, Soziale Probleme und Justiz in Japan – Die Wechselwirkungen von Gerichtsentscheidungen und gesellschaftlichem Bewußtsein, [1990] *Archiv für die civilistische Praxis* 190, 586–608.

[15] Barkan, *The Guilt of Nations* (2000), p. IX.

C. Analysis of a Large Loss

28 Loss events like the ones on 11th September in New York and 21st September in Toulouse affect different systems of social and personal insurance, different "first party" insurance coverage of property values and other assets, and different liabilities, with different involvement of the state and the national and international insurance markets: a large number of historically evolved structures with characteristic advantages and weaknesses.

29 In long-term technological large loss scenarios, the same consequences of technology – damage to health, damage to the environment – occur simultaneously or with certain time lags and are dealt with by different insurance and liability systems. The analysis can be carried out on a country-wide basis or be confined to a company's activity in a particular state. The following points outline the individual stages of such an analysis.

1. Spread and Economic Significance of Technology

30 The starting point is the history – rise and fall – of the product or hazardous substance. In what years was the drug in question licensed and what were the levels of sales involved? How much raw asbestos was processed in the individual years? Here, for example, the peak worldwide occurred around 1980; processing had already been reduced in the USA and the UK in the 1970s, in some European countries in the 1980s, and in others in the 1990s.

2. History of the Consequences of Technology

31 When, after what latency periods do what consequences manifest themselves? Among employees, among consumers, in the environment? With latency periods of 10 to 50 years and an average of 30 years, the number of new cases of asbestos-related cancer in the USA and the UK should gradually have reached its peak, whereas in the other European countries it is still likely to rise for 10, 15 or more years.

3. Perception of the Consequences of Technology

32 When and under what aspects are these consequences of technology perceived as a problem? When do traditionally accepted risks become a problem? Where are feared future risks anticipated – in the case of genetic engineering, for example, through the recall of genetically modified maize?[16] Where is there speculation about completely unknown risks, as in the long-standing debate around electromagnetic fields? Why was the amalgam health risk in Germany overestimated, at the expense of health insurers? Why is the environmental risk posed by asbestos overestimated – with excessive clean-up costs as a result – while the central problem of asbestos is a safety at work issue?

[16] *Cf.* Munich Re (*supra* note 10), pp. 168–172; the suspicion of an allergy having triggered the StarLink case has not been confirmed.

4. State and Private Safety Standards

Next comes the history of state and private prevention, from compulsory government licensing provisions, via the non-binding "recognized state of the art", to pure labelling requirements. On the one hand, inadequate prevention causes massive long-tail liability risks. On the other hand, overreaction to "phantom risks", anticipating liability, gives rise to a waste of society's resources. 33

As a result of 3 and 4 we find risks being relocated: production facilities are moved to, and products marketed in, places where less restrictive licensing regulations exist or where the risks are made less of a problem among the general public. US tobacco companies which in the USA showed themselves to be prepared to reach a settlement and undertook to pay compensation and to market their products more restrictively, even try – like Philip Morris – to change their name and thus shake off their tobacco past. At the same time they are increasing their exports by exerting pressure through the World Trade Organization on countries like China to open up their state tobacco monopolies. 34

5. State and Private Compensation Systems

One central point is the analysis of state and private systems of compensation: to what extent are personal injuries covered by social insurance, environmental damage remediated out of public funds, property and pure economic losses compensated by private property insurance and public aid programmes? What means of recourse and subrogation are provided for? 35

A large proportion of the victims of 11th September will be compensated by the US workers' compensation schemes and by the federal governments' involvement in the September 11th Victims Compensation Fund. The consequences of asbestos, on the other hand, will be paid without such involvement and to a far lesser extent by the workers' compensation systems in the USA. Some of the reasons are by no means convincing. A comparison with the different European compensation systems reveals the current US dilemma: the constantly expanding, vaguely defined groups of claimants and defendants. Whereas in Germany (via workers' compensation insurance), in the UK (mainly via employers' liability) or in France (via both routes) individual allocation to employers is practised, in the USA allocation to manufacturers (via product liability) is much more diffuse. This is the reason why "market share" rules, which could provide certain rules, are not recognized. At the same time, the link with workplace exposure is severed or loosened on the claimants' side as well, so that the notoriously overestimated environmental risk – unimpaired, low exposed claimants – is lumped together with high exposure safety at work risk. 36

6. Other Legal Parameters

Other legal parameters are the influence of constitutional law on liability law in many countries (protection of health and environment, protection against 37 discrimination); the influence of criminal law in Spain and Italy; "action directe" of injured parties against liability insurers in France, Spain and Poland; finally, procedural law in general, and especially in connection with mass torts, is of practical importance not only in the USA.

7. Different Liability Structures

38 1 to 6 above result in different liability structures: the same technological large loss problem has a different effect in each legal system. An example is the considerable variation in asbestos-related liabilities from country to country even within the EU, including differences in their temporal development. Then there are the specific differences in liability law in terms of both basic principles and special legislation, *e.g.* with regard to strict liability, causation, statutes of limitation or damages for non-pecuniary loss.

8. Liability Insurance, Reinsurance, Alternative Financing and Conflict Solution Models

39 At the centre of the insurance and reinsurance analysis lie the mechanics of national and international liability insurance programmes, multi-line covers, definitions of "event" and "serial loss", limits in terms of time, the differently delimited covers for gradual pollution, pure economic loss, loss minimization expenses and recall costs. Frequently, several coverage issues arise simultaneously in one claims complex, with various possible interpretations conceivable for each. If a claims complex extends over longer periods, conditions and parties involved change. This gives rise to different interfaces and overlaps in dealing with latent claims. So far "mega-coverage litigation" has developed into a "field of major legal and economic importance" only in the USA[17]. But everywhere there is the unsolved problem that whilst questions of liability law and insurance cover become too complex for detailed application in large loss scenarios, it has not yet really been possible – in the reality of extrajudicial *ad hoc* payments or fund arrangements – to develop satisfactory alternative solutions.

[17] Abraham, The Maze of Mega-Coverage Litigation, [1997] *Colombian Law Review,* 2102.

II. The Significance to the Insurance Industry of Damages for Non-Pecuniary Loss

Wolfgang Reisinger

1. Introduction

Although the institution of damages for non-pecuniary loss (chiefly pain, suffering and loss of amenity) has enjoyed great continuity in Austria (the wording and the substance of the relevant part of the Austrian General Civil Code have not been altered since 1811), the last few years have witnessed a lively running debate about the appropriateness of payments made in the past and about new forms of non-pecuniary loss. We will mention only the terms "mental anguish" and "compensation for the death of close relatives" at present. 1

This paper will discuss the economic significance to the insurance industry of damages for non-pecuniary loss and current settlement practice on the one hand, and the latest developments and their practical consequences on the other. 2

2. The Economic Significance of Damages for Non-Pecuniary Loss

When *Danzl*[1] says that such damages form the most significant practical compensation for bodily injury today, this is subjectively true from the point of view of the injured party, but incorrect from the overall, objective point of view. The material damages associated with the harm caused to the individual's health are many times higher than the compensation for intangible pain and suffering in all injury cases, considering in particular the many medical costs incurred, including physicians' costs, hospital costs, rehabilitation and nursing costs, but also the loss of earnings or its compensation by social insurance carriers. This is generally "forgotten" by both the injured and the injuring party, because Austria is a developed social state and these expenses are therefore not borne by the injured party him- or herself, but by others; as a rule social insurance carriers. 3

[1] In Danzl/Gutiérrez Lobos/Müller, *Schmerzengeld* (7th edn. 1998), p. 86.

4 The public at large is almost entirely unaware of the fact that these "invisible" costs are recovered from the party at fault indirectly through a number of legal provisions, that means they are normally recovered from that party's liability insurance company.

5 Although the insurance industry bears the full financial burden of the health damage, it cannot be denied that this burden – at least in comparison to others – is relatively moderate. The main parties affected here are motor third party insurance companies, firstly because a very large number of people are injured in traffic accidents, and secondly because a financially sound "payer" is always on hand because motor insurance is mandatory.

6 Almost exactly three quarters of the insurance industry's total expenses from motor third party liability insurance are incurred by compensation for material damage, only one quarter by the financial consequences of bodily injury. This, however, is primarily due to the fact that only around one in ten traffic accidents leads to bodily injury, and this rate has been dropping steadily for years.

7 The reasons for this fall remain largely unexplored, but there are probably several. In particular, the increased passive safety of vehicles and more efficient emergency rescue systems (rescue helicopters), but also the traffic-calming measures in the cities can be considered here. The increasing number of second and third cars with less mileage on the clock and the traffic situation on some roads, which makes speeding more difficult and thus reduces the risk of serious accidents, probably have a role to play as well.

8 Payments made under motor third party liability insurance break down as follows:

Material damage	75%
Repair costs	62%
Decrease in value	1%
Expenses	4%
Lawyer's costs	3%
Other material damage	5%
Bodily injury	25%
Non-pecuniary loss	12%
Social insurance carriers	8%
Loss of earnings	2%
Other bodily injury	3%

9 Only 12% of all expenses paid by motor third party insurance companies is for non-pecuniary loss, while more than 60% is for car repairs. This, of course, demonstrates clearly where the insurance industry's problems lie and where

worth-while savings potential is to be found. However, we should not conclude that the insurance industry does not care whether or how much damages are paid for non-pecuniary loss – that would be false. On the one hand, processing is more labour-intensive for bodily injury claims than for material losses, and on the other, claims department staff are not just commercially orientated but often also qualified legal experts, so that the debate on the development of damages for non-pecuniary loss is followed with interest.

3. Settlement Practice

Non-pecuniary loss claims take a great deal of time and effort to process, but are normally completed without major differences between the injuring and injured parties. One main reason is undoubtedly the fact that the injured parties are usually represented by lawyers, which not only ensures a professionally competent basis for discussion, but also means that the emotional component is more or less eliminated. **10**

In this context, it should be mentioned that the litigation rate in motor insurance, for instance, well known as a particularly sensitive area of the law of damages, is only 1% to 1.5%, in other words 98.5% to 99% of claims are settled out of court. The litigation rate is estimated much too highly by people who are constantly involved in court work. Some years ago when presenting a paper at a conference chiefly attended by judges, lawyers and automotive experts, I myself asked what the audience thought the litigation rate was. Estimates from the auditorium varied between 15% and 30%; the only probable explanation here is the selective perception of those groups who are constantly engaged in court proceedings relating to the area. **11**

The chronological sequence of processing a claim for non-pecuniary loss is as follows: **12**

1. The claim is filed with the injuring party or his/her liability insurance company.
2. A medical dossier is procured.
3. After the final stage of the healing process is completed, the amount is assessed:
   a. in the case of minor injuries (bruises, contusions, abrasions, slight cervical spine traumas) by the insurance company's claims officer;
   b. in the case of fairly serious injuries (fractures without complications, serious cervical spine traumas, slight cranial injuries and slight organic injuries) by obtaining a medical opinion on the dossier;
   c. in the case of serious injuries, by examination of the injured party by an expert and preparation of a medical expert report.
4. The periods of pain and suffering are converted into a capital sum, including an appropriate psychological component.
5. The final settlement is reached with the injured party or his/her lawyer.

13 The rates of damages for non-pecuniary loss which form a fixed component of our everyday practice today are dogmatically disputed and have recently, in particular, become the subject of passionate debate (most recently at the symposium "Kein Geld für Herz und Schmerz?", "No cash for pain and emotion?", of October 2001, organised by the Austrian traffic medicine association, the *Ärztliche Kraftfahrvereinigung Österreichs*). The principal criticisms raised here are the overly mechanistic application of these rates and failure to consider the specific conditions of the individual cases. In practice, however, it would be more or less impossible to do without such rates, because different cases have to be made comparable and considerable scope for negotiation is provided in any case, since individual extra allowances are granted.

14 At the above-mentioned symposium, a study was presented by the representatives of the victims according to which 78% of injured parties on a European average are dissatisfied with the financial compensation, presumably consisting mainly of the damages for non-pecuniary loss. This cannot be due to the level of compensation, since dissatisfaction is particularly high in Germany at 92%, although it is a well known fact that the highest non-pecuniary damages in Europe are paid in Germany. Rather, it is highly probable that the injured parties find the procedure described above difficult and, above all, long-drawn-out.

15 It is an empirical fact that obtaining the medical file and preparing a report by a medical expert takes some months even in relatively uncomplicated cases involving traffic accidents, and can take well over a year where more complex problems are involved (*e.g.* alleged medical malpractice). This is mainly because the number of experts available to write reports is relatively small, and, in addition, they normally perform this work as a sideline to one or more "main jobs".

16 The injured parties very often accuse the experts of drawing up reports "to order", in other words they claim that their rates for damages fall into the upper or lower range of discretion depending on whether the report has been commissioned by the injuring or the injured party. This frequently-raised criticism (most recently at the above symposium, on several occasions) is really nothing but an imputation which cannot be addressed in further depth here. However, it should be stated that a report written "to order", whomever it may be written for, is not a suitable basis for comparison and is therefore pointless. Insurance employees, who in contrast to the injured party do not have a personal interest in the level of damages, consider objective reports important, since only objective reports are recognised by the injured party or his/her lawyer and form the basis of further settlement discussions. A report "favouring" the liability insurance company would not only be a waste of money, but would minimise the possibility of an out-of-court solution.

4. International Claims Handling

The principle of *lex loci delicti*, which means that the injured party's claims are governed as a rule by the law of the place of injury, is of major importance in settling international damages claims. The Hague Traffic Accident Convention of 1971 applies to traffic accidents, which form the largest category of such cases. **17**

The maximum damages for non-pecuniary loss still vary widely in Europe, as shown by the following list of top sums paid in this area in western European countries: **18**

	(Former) local currency	**EURO**
Greece	Drs 1,500,000	4,500
Denmark	DKK 50,000	6,500
Portugal	Esc 1,300,000	6,500
France	FF 300,000	47,000
Switzerland	SFr 120,000	80,000
Sweden	SEK 1,000,000	120,000
Austria	ATS 1,800,000	130,000
The Netherlands	NLG 300,000	140,000
Belgium	BEF 7,000.000	175,000
Italy	Lit 500,000,000	250,000
England	GBP 175,000	275,000
Ireland	IRP 250,000	320,000
Germany	DM 700,000	350,000

Source: Pan European Organisation of Personal Injury Lawyers, Innsbruck seminar, February 2001

This list not only shows Austria occupying a good middle position, but also very drastic differences between the individual countries. Mediterranean countries do not pay high damages for non-pecuniary loss as a rule, with the possible exception of Spain (which, however, will not be discussed further here because of its complex regulations), so that the fairly small totals for Greece, Portugal and France come as no surprise. The maximum sums for these damages in Italy, England and Ireland are noteworthy, however, whilst Germany's leading position is less surprising, since it is well known for its particularly luxurious law of damages in favour of the injured party in all areas. **19**

Most former East Bloc countries make a very poor showing. For example, even Austria's neighbours, the Czech Republic and Hungary, do not provide for damages corresponding to the European standard. However, because the law to be applied following a traffic accident is that of the place of its occurrence, this leads to gross inequities. If, for example, an Austrian is injured in a traffic accident in Hungary, he will only be entitled to very low damages for **20** non-pecuniary loss as a rule. Conversely, if a Hungarian national is injured in a traffic accident in Austria, he will be entitled to a multiple of the sums payable in Hungary for an equivalent injury.

21 It is therefore hardly surprising that insurance customers often show little acceptance of the handling of such cases, since hardly anyone is aware of the existence of these differences, let alone of their amount.

22 At its first conference on European Traffic Law in June 2000, the EU discussed this issue at the Academy of European Law in Trier, Germany. This conference was intended to demonstrate whether it was basically feasible to develop homogeneous evaluation criteria for damage to health at the European level. In the recommendation to the European Commission, Parliament and Council formulated by the conference, it was explicitly stated that the principle of equality demanded an objective assessment of the intangible damage. A directive on this subject would have to aim to harmonise the regulations on damages for non-pecuniary loss in force in the Member States, and the evaluation criteria would have to be objective and uniform.

23 It is to be hoped that these efforts will be successful, all the more so because this is the first attempt at standardising the European law of damages.

5. Latest Developments – Example: OGH 2 Ob 84/01

24 If a near relative has been killed, the survivors are not entitled *per se* to separate damages, because on the one hand § 1325 ABGB (the Austrian Civil Code) only refers to injury to a claimant's own body, and on the other a claim for damages for non-pecuniary loss for surviving relatives is not mentioned in the exclusive list of § 1327 ABGB. Damages for the death of close relatives are nevertheless common in many countries, above all in France, Spain, Portugal and Italy etc. We will single out the Italian "danno biologico" as an example here, although please note that the legal systems of most of these countries explicitly provide for such compensation.

25 It was the spectacular cable-car accident in Kaprun in November 2000 that first sparked off discussion in Austria as to whether or not such compensation made sense. The fact that Austrian Civil Law does not provide for intangible damages in the case of the *de facto* immediate death of a victim is deemed by many to be unsatisfactory.

26 In its decision 2 Ob 84/01, the Austrian Supreme Court (OGH) ruled for the first time in favour of compensation for mental anguish about the loss of close relatives which did not lead to damage to the claimant's own health in the sense of § 1325 ABGB. At the same time, however, it restricted the justification of such damages to cases of gross negligence or intent on the part of the injuring party. This virtually invalidates the decision, since cases of gross negligence are extremely rare in the main area of application of such a ruling, *i.e.*

in road traffic, being largely confined to traffic accidents caused while under the influence of alcohol.

Although the vast majority of prevailing opinion welcomed the decision, the practitioner has some criticisms to make. Let there be no misunderstandings: the introduction of "danno biologico" in Austria is inevitable, not just because the current legal position is increasingly perceived as unsatisfactory, but mainly because Austria is one of the few countries in the European Union which does not yet have damages of this kind. The OGH's decision, however, raises a great many questions for practical claims settlement: **27**

- The term "gross negligence", which has not played any role whatsoever in the past, is thereby introduced into the handling of claims. On the one hand, § 61 VersVG, the Austrian Insurance Act, does not exempt the insurance company from performance because the insured event is brought about intentionally or by gross negligence except in the case of property insurance. On the other, the schedule of compensation does not depend on the degree of fault (disregarding those cases of intent which are irrelevant to insurance for lack of cover).
- In actual practice, the phenomenon was soon observed that almost all cases of fatalities with a background in the law of damages also involved claims for damages for relatives, even where there could be no question of gross negligence. Almost without exception, such demands are currently rejected by the entire insurance industry. As a result, these cases will not be easy to handle. In addition, court decisions will vary from region to region, since the OGH normally refuses to consider cases of gross negligence. Whether the assumption of gross negligence is justified by one particularly major error, or by a totality and frequency of single actions which would not constitute gross negligence individually "is basically not a legal issue in the sense of § 502 Para 1 ZPO (Code of Civil Procedure) where a judgment based each time on the circumstances of an individual case is justified"[2].
- The question of who is entitled to claim is entirely open. While in most countries a claim of this nature is restricted to the injured party's "nuclear family" (*i.e.* father, mother and spouse), some media (*e.g. Gewinn* magazine, September 2001, 215) are already mentioning life partners (including homosexual partners) in this context. The repeatedly-cited recommendation of the European Council also wants to include the fiancé(e) and children of the deceased among the claimant survivors, but only if "they were in a close emotional relationship with the injured party at the time of death". This will be difficult to prove in practice. Moreover, inequities are inevitable here as well: why should, for example, a father who pays no attention to his child apart from paying more or less regular maintenance be entitled to compensation if the child is killed, while his/her brothers and sisters are not?

[2] Standing Judicature of All Senates, *e.g.* 4 Ob 2010/96, 9 Ob 358/97, 7 Ob 8/99.

- At what level should such compensation be set? If it is too low it will have the nature of a meagre handout and therefore be pointless, if it is too high solidarity might break down, and the surviving relatives will soon be faced with the accusation of profiting from their relatives' death.
- Should the claim only hold up in the case of death, or also in the case of serious injury? Experiencing the long suffering of a relative, for example with apallic syndrome, must presumably be considered just as serious as the usually passing grief at the death of a close relative.

28 In any case, I agree with Danzl[3] that clear legal provisions would be desirable. It is to be feared, however, that the courts will soon be flooded with these claims in the absence of such clarity – and the development of standard practice is not to be expected under such circumstances.

6. Summary

1. The economic importance of payments of damages for non-pecuniary loss (compensation for pain, suffering and loss of amenity), while by no means negligible, is greatly overestimated.
2. Claims for such compensation under insurance cover take a great deal of time to process, but are uncomplicated on the whole.
3. In terms of the amount of compensation, Austria occupies a good middle position within Europe, standardisation at least within the EU should be given high priority.
4. Compensation for the death of close relatives is desirable, but its form should be a matter for the legislator and not for the courts.

[3] (*supra* note 1), p. 147.

III. Wilburg's Flexible System in a Nutshell

Bernhard A. Koch

More than 60 years ago, the Austrian *Walter Wilburg* started to build a comprehensive system of law (primarily focusing on tort law and unjust enrichment) which became known as the "flexible system" (*bewegliches System*) approach to law. Wilburg developed his concept based on the notion that there is hardly any area of the law (if at all) which can be perceived through the lens of a single guiding idea. Accordingly, the perspective must always be broader since legal rules are typically based on a *plurality* of valuations and underlying purposes. Inasmuch as these can be identified, they also have to be observed in the application of the law. 1

From that perception he inferred that those fundamental values (which he called "elements" or "forces") have varying degrees of influence on changing factual settings. Nevertheless, by recurring in alternate, but comparable circumstances, they can still be cited for a generalized description of the law as it is, as long as the extent of their impact can be considered in the individual case by way of *gradation*. 2

However, Wilburg was certainly not in favour of formulating sets of merely discretionary rules which can be either observed or ignored altogether in the decision-making process at random. On the contrary: All "elements" have to be considered in light of their specific interaction, and the choice of attributing more or less weight to one of them has to be justified on the basis of *balancing* all interests involved. 3

The overall goal has to be equal treatment of equal situations, which cannot be ascertained without a uniform yardstick. However, such yardstick has to be flexible enough to be adaptable to real life problems. Traditional legal theories apply a rigid ruler instead which at most can lead to one-dimensional results, but is certainly incapable of grasping the plurality of values that the law is founded upon. 4

5 Therefore, Wilburg opposed all attempts to trace, for example, delictual liability back to one single principle such as causation or fault or insurability alone. Instead, he identified four major "elements" that jointly help to decide who should bear a loss: (1) the extent to which the *cause* of an ensuing damage can be traced back to the sphere of a party, (2) some *defect* attributable to that party's sphere, (3) the degree to which some *risk* or *actual interference* encroaches on the other party's rights, and – as a subsidiary factor – (4) a balancing of the parties' *economic situation*. These four questions are not focused on the defendant exclusively: They all have to be raised for either side since justice may require that the plaintiff should, at least in part, bear the loss.

6 Even if considered alone, those examinations would hardly ever lead to the same outcome in any given case. This is particularly – but not only – true for the second element, since the defect mentioned might be anything from malice to slightest inadvertence, from acts under full physical and mental control to unavoidable reflexes due to a temporary or permanent incapacity. Since all four questions therefore lead to a range of answers rather than a uniform outcome even if assessed alone, it is unthinkable that there is a standardized overall result of the combined analysis applicable to every individual factual setting. If all results were scrutinized reversely, it is hard to imagine that there ever might be a single formula which could encompass this broad spectrum based on successive "yes or no" tests rather than an interaction of several "more or less" questions.

7 The introduction of a flexible system approach does not mean that such approach is floating freely in a sea of indetermination: In order to weigh an element "more or less" in light of a particular case, it is essential to have a *standard of comparison* which serves as a base-line for measuring the extent of deviation. Such base-line is drawn by the basic values (*Basiswertungen*) that the system is founded upon: If we take Wilburg's second element of tort law mentioned before, it is obvious that malicious intent to cause damage should weigh heavily in favour of liability, while entirely unavoidable minimal negligence might not be sufficient justification for shifting the loss. Even malice will not count, however, if the evil behaviour can in no way be connected to the cause of the damage, or if there was no damage at all. In light of these valuations (which can similarly be deducted from the other elements), one can formulate sample average cases which serve as guidelines for the application of the system.

8 It is perhaps helpful to consider the applicability of Wilburg's flexible system in an entirely neutral (*i.e.* fictional) context. Imagine the following example: There is a wall ahead of you that you need to climb over. However, there is no ladder lying around nearby. Instead, there are various boxes of all different kinds and sizes which you could use to pile up. Some of them are made of wood, some of them are made of cardboard. While you could stack cardboard boxes, they would not be sturdy enough to support you on your way up, so it only makes sense to use wooden boxes. Furthermore, let us assume you can-

not use more than five boxes since the tower would otherwise collapse. (These two caveats would correspond to the *Basiswertung*).

A rule under the traditional notion would be based on the presumption that all boxes are equal. If the wall were ten feet high, such a rule would therefore read something like: "Cross the wall by piling up and then climbing five wooden boxes which are exactly two feet high." However, there are hardly ever even-sized boxes lying around in the real world. Instead, you have to deal with various kinds and sizes, even though they are all boxes, even wooden ones. Wilburg would allow you to make your selection from all wooden boxes, as long as you can use them to reach the top of the wall. He would therefore not permit the use of cardboard boxes, just as he would not let you pick more than five. He would nevertheless not restrict you to an exact size, but let you choose from all boxes that are suitable for the final goal. Maybe the first box is smaller, but as long as all the other ones are slightly higher, you can still make it to the top. 9

A Wilburg rule would therefore certainly not be as vague as "Climb the wall!" or "Help yourself!" In fact, it would not be vague at all, since it would give clear and reasonable orders, but nevertheless make it easier for you to get over that wall. His rule would also be just as predictable as the classic alternative, even though it might be somewhat easier to compare boxes of equal height rather than measuring irregular ones. At any rate, it would be more practicable: In many cases, you will not find five boxes of exactly the required size. So you end up cheating – you need to pretend that the actual boxes you use correspond to the requirements of the traditional rule. Under the Wilburg variety, there is no need to "adjust" the rule this way. 10

If you needed to climb over the wall in order to determine the validity and binding force of a contract, for example, Wilburg would offer you a choice of four boxes to reach that goal, as Franz Bydlinski has elaborated in more detail: One box is private autonomy, whose size depends upon issues such as the extent of information available to the contracting parties, the degree to which they were actually able to use that information, and whether they were truly free to make up their mind. Another box is shaped by the reliance on statements or conduct by the other party, and the extent to which such confidence should be protected. A third box is determined by an objective evaluation of the intended exchange: The more balanced either party's rights and obligations are, the higher the box, while it would be almost flat in case of a donation. Bydlinski would label a fourth box "responsibility and self-reliance", since one of his contract law principles includes the duty to live up to one's promise and to abide by (at least) imputable promises. 11

While traditional contract law recognizes the impact of those forces on the validity of a contract by providing for problems such as mistake or incapacity, its singular rules cannot yet be combined to an overall concept. In the wording of the box hypothetical, it pretends that there is one single box which is occa- 12 sionally affected by erosion or other singular problems that affect its size. A flexible system could consider the same valuations that current contract law is founded upon, but still advance it by offering a balanced rule encompassing all influences on the binding force of a contract in advance: The relevance of mistake, for example, could be judged by considering the lower degree of private autonomy in comparison to the objective balance of the intended exchange as well as the other arguments listed above.

13 Admittedly, such a flexible system of contract law is an innovative approach that is only based upon, but not expressed in current rules. However, there are already formulas out there in the "real" legal world which actually use Wilburg's concept. Consider the following wording which explains a rule on strict liability: "[T]he factors listed in Clauses (a) to (f) ... are all to be considered, and are all of importance. Any one of them is not necessarily sufficient of itself in a particular case, and ordinarily several of them will be required for strict liability. On the other hand, it is not necessary that each of them be present, especially if others weigh heavily. Because of the interplay of these various factors, it is not possible to reduce abnormally dangerous activities to any definition." By the way – these words were not written by Walter Wilburg: They stem from the American Restatement, Second, of Torts (§ 520 cmt. f).

Selected Further Readings

- W. Wilburg, *Elemente des Schadensrechts* (1941).
- W. Wilburg, *Entwicklung eines beweglichen Systems im bürgerlichen Recht* (1950) = *The Development of a Flexible System in the Area of Private Law* (transl. by H. Hausmaninger, 2000).
- W. Wilburg, Zusammenspiel der Kräfte im Aufbau des Schuldrechts, [1964] *Archiv für die civilistische Praxis* 163, 246.
- F. Bydlinski *et al.* (eds.), *Das Bewegliche System im geltenden und künftigen Recht* (1986).
- F. Bydlinski, A "Flexible System" Approach to Contract Law, in: H. Hausmaninger *et al.* (eds.), *Developments in Austrian and Israeli Private Law* (1999) p. 9 (with further literature cited pp. 19–20).

Authors

Dr. Ewa BAGIŃSKA

Uniwersytet Mikolaja Kopernika
ul. Gagarina 15
87–100 Torun
Poland
Tel.: (+48–56) 662 3296
Fax: (+48–56) 611 4005
baginska@law.uni.torun.pl

Ewa Bagińska holds a PhD in law and is Assistant Professor in the Department of Civil and International Commercial Law, Faculty of Law and Administration, Nicholas Copernicus University (UMK), Torun. Fulbright Visiting Scholar (1998/1999) and NATO Science Fellowship grantee (2000/2001) at The Catholic University of America, Columbus School of Law, Washington, DC.
Areas of expertise: civil and commercial law – civil liability, contracts, consumer protection, products liability, unfair competition, health law, e-commerce, harmonisation of Polish laws with the EU legal system. Author of the book *Odpowiedzialnosc za produkt w USA* (Products liability in the USA), Torun 2000, and several articles.

Dr. Elena BARGELLI

Facoltà di Economia –
Universitá di Pisa
Via C. Ridolfi, 10
I-56124 Pisa
Tel.: (+39–050) 94 53 37
Fax: (+39–050) 54 03 40
e.bargelli@ec.unipi.it

Elena Bargelli got her Ph.D. degree in Private Law at Pisa Faculty of Law (Italy) in 1999 (mentors Prof. Breccia and Prof. Busnelli). She is currently Assistant Professor at the Faculty of Economics (Pisa University), where she has been working as researcher since 2001. Member of Pisa's Research Group concerning Physical Injuries ("Danno biologico") since 1998, she is author of several articles concerning Liability Law, Contract Law and Family Law.

Prof. Herman COUSY

University of Leuven
Faculteit Rechtsgeleerdheid
Afdeling Ekonomisch Recht
Tiensestraat 41
B-3000 Leuven, Belgium
Tel.: (+32–16) 325–134
Fax: (+32–16) 325–314
herman.cousy@law.kuleuven.ac.be

Prof. Cousy is currently teaching commercial and insurance law as well as a course on the legal aspects of credit transactions and European insurance law at the Catholic University of Leuven, where he has been a professor ordinarius since 1982. He was born in 1946 and graduated in 1969 with the degrees of Doctor iuris and Licenciaat in het Notariaat. He is also Master of Comparative Law (University of Chicago, 1970). Prof. Cousy has held numerous academic positions and for ten years he was the chairman of the Scientific Commission for Legal Sciences of the Belgian National Fund of Scientific Research (now: FWO-Flanders). Prof. Cousy is currently President of the "Commission de Assurance",

"Assessor" in the "Section Legislation" of the Belgian Council of State and Director of the Centre for Risk and Insurance Studies (C.R.I.S.). Prof. Cousy has published extensively in the field of private law, especially tort law and insurance law and lectures both nationally and internationally on these topics.

Dr. Eugenia G. DACORONIA

Attorney-at-Law, Lecturer of Civil Law at the Athens University Department of Law
312, Patission Str.
GR-11141 Athens, Greece
Tel. (+30–1) 201–0011
Tel./Fax: (+30–1) 223–7150
Dacoronia@yahoo.com

Dr. Dacoronia was born of Greek nationality in Cairo (Egypt) in 1958. She graduated with excellence in 1979 from the Athens Faculty of Law, where she also received her doctorate with excellence in 1994. She has attended several courses abroad (Amsterdam, King's College London, Tulane University).
Since 1980, Dr. Dacoronia has worked as an assistant at the Athens University Department of Law. Since her admittance to the Athens Bar in 1981, she has been practising mostly in civil (contracts and real property), intellectual property, commercial and administrative matters. She is a European Patent Attorney and a substitute member of the European Patent Office Board of Directors. Dr. Dacoronia has also been a lecturer of civil law at the Athens University Department of Law since 1995. She teaches, among others, General Principles of Civil Law, Real Property Law, Law of Environment, Torts in the legal system of the U.S.A.
She has participated in International Congresses as a National Representative and published various articles and notes on Court decisions in Greek legal periodicals and in the European Review of Private Law. Dr. Dacoronia participates in the Trento Common Core project as well as the Study Group on a European Civil Code as a member of the Advisory Council on Torts.

Dimitri DROSHOUT

University of Leuven
Faculteit Rechtsgeleerdheid
Tiensestraat 41
B-3000 Leuven, Belgium
Tel.: (+32–16) 325–134
Fax: (+32–16) 325–314
Dimitri.Droshout@law.kuleuven.ac.be

Dimitri Droshout is a research fellow who mainly focuses on tort and insurance law. Since late 2001, he has been employed at the Leuven Centre for a Common Law of Europe (Leuven CCLE) of the Faculty of Law of the Katholieke Universiteit Leuven and at the Maastricht European Institute for Transational Legal Research (METRO) of the Faculty of Law of the Universiteit Maastricht. He coordinates the Ius Commune Casebook Project, which is a joint initiative of both universities. In Leuven, he also functions as deputy director of Leuven CCLE. He studied law in Leuven (K.U. Leuven, lic. jur. 1999). From 1999 until 2001, he was employed there at the Institute for Commercial Law and Insurance Law.

He contributed to several reports for the European Group on Tort Law and ECTIL, delivered by the Leuven Centre for Risk and Insurance Studies (CRIS). He also took part in a EU-funded study dealing with Advanced Legal Aspects on Virtual Enterprises. He is preparing a Ph.D. in the area of tort and insurance law.

Prof. Michael FAURE

METRO, Faculty of Law
Maastricht University
P.O. Box 616
6200 MD Maastricht, The Netherlands
Tel.: (+31–43) 388–3028
Fax: (+31–43) 325–9091
Metro.Institute@facburfdr.unimaas.nl

Prof. Faure studied law at the University of Antwerp (licenciate in law 1982) and criminology at the University of Gent (licenciate in criminology 1983). He obtained a Master of Laws from the University of Chicago Law School (1984) and a doctor iuris from the Albert Ludwigs Universität Freiburg im Breisgau.
He was first a lecturer and then a senior lecturer at the department of criminal law of the law faculty of Leiden University (1988–1999) and became academic director of the Maastricht European Institute for Transnational Legal Research (METRO) and professor of Comparative and International Environmental Law at the law faculty of Maastricht University in September 1991. He still holds both positions today.
In addition, he is academic director of the Ius Commune Research School and member of the board of directors of ECTIL.
Since 1982 he is equally attorney at the Antwerp Bar.
He publishes in the areas of environmental (criminal) law, tort and insurance and economic analysis of (accident) law.

Dr. Jörg FEDTKE

University of Hamburg
Edmund-Siemers-Allee 1
D-20146 Hamburg, Germany
Tel. (+49–40) 42838–5711
J-FEDTKE@jura.uni-hamburg.de
University College London
Institute of Global Law, Faculty of Laws
Bentham House, Endsleigh Gardens
London, WC1-HOEG, United Kingdom
Tel. (+44–20) 7679–1474
j.fedtke@ucl.ac.uk

Dr. Fedtke obtained his doctorate at the University of Hamburg, Germany, where he worked as a researcher for private law at the *Seminar für ausländisches und internationales Privat- und Prozessrecht.*
Dr. Fedtke is currently teaching at University College London at the Institute of Global Law where he is a DAAD/Clifford Chance Lecturer.
He has published in the areas of tort and constitutional law.

Prof. María Paz GARCÍA RUBIO

University of Santiago de Compostela
Faculty of Law
E-15782 Santiago de Compostela, Spain
Tel. (+34–981) 563100–14648
dcdc007@usc.es

Prof. García Rubio graduated as a bachelor of law at the University of León in 1984, where she was awarded her doctorate in 1988. She worked as an assistant of civil law at this university until 1989.
She pursued extensive research abroad in Italy (University of Salerno), Germany (Bremen), Switzerland (Swiss Institute of Comparative Law) and France (Le Mans). She was a visiting professor at the Faculté de Droit et Sciences Economiques of the Université du Maine (France) in 1996.
She became a Professor Titular of Civil Law at the University of Santiago de Compostela in 1990, where she has held a chair since 2000 (*Catedrática de Derecho civil*).
Prof. García Rubio has published extensively in tort law and other areas of Spanish and Galician civil law.

Prof. Ton HARTLIEF

University of Maastricht
Postbus 616
NL-6200 MD Maastricht
Tel.: (+31–43) 388–3104
Fax: (+31–43) 325–8981
t.hartlief@pr.unimaas.nl

Ton Hartlief is professor of private law at the University of Maastricht.

Prof. Heinz HAUSHEER, M.C.L.

University of Berne
Zivilistisches Seminar
Falkenplatz 9
CH-3012 Berne, Switzerland
Tel. (+41–31) 631–3796
heinz.hausheer@ziv.unibe.ch

Prof. Hausheer was born in 1937. He graduated from the University of Berne in 1963. Two years later, he was awarded his doctorate at the same university. After practising in London, he pursued graduate studies at the University of Chicago (1963/64). After completing his habilitation in 1970, he became a professor at the University of Berne and has held a chair as a full professor since 1990. He has also worked at the Federal Office of Justice and practised as a judge at both lower court level as well as at the Swiss Federal Court.

Dr. Manuel JAUN

University of Berne
Zivilistisches Seminar
Falkenplatz 9
CH-3012 Bern
Tel. (+41–31) 631–3795
manuel.jaun@ziv.unibe.ch

Dr. Manuel Jaun is a lawyer and has been a Senior Assistant at the University of Berne since 2000.

Prof. Johann C. KNOBEL

University of South Africa
Postbox 392
Pretoria 0001, South Africa
Tel. (+27–12) 429–8352
Fax (+27–12) 429–3393
Knobejc@unisa.ac.za

Prof. Knobel has lectured in the law of delict at the University of South Africa since 1987. He obtained his doctorate in 1996 with a thesis entitled "The Right to the Trade Secret". He has published contributions on delict in South African books and legal journals and has acted as editor and translator of the latest English edition of the standard South African handbook on the Law of Delict by J. Neethling, J.M. Potgieter and P.J. Visser. His special research interests include the role of negligence in liability for personality infringements and the role of delictual elementology in liability for trade secret infringements. He is assistant editor of the Journal of Contemporary Roman-Dutch Law/Tydskrif vir Hedendaagse Romeins-Hollandse Reg.

Prof. Bernhard A. KOCH, LL.M.

European Centre of Tort
and Insurance Law
Landesgerichtsstraße 11
A-1080 Vienna, Austria
Tel. (+43–1) 40127–1610
Fax (+43–1) 40127–1685
koch@ectil.org
University of Innsbruck
Innrain 52, A-6020 Innsbruck, Austria
Tel. (+43–512) 507–8036
Fax (+43–512) 507–2821
Bernhard.a.koch@uibk.ac.at

Prof. Koch was born in 1966 in Feldkirch (Austria). He studied law in Innsbruck (Austria, Mag. iur. 1989), Tübingen (Germany, Dr. iur. *summa cum laude* 1992), and Michigan (USA, LL.M. 1993). He completed his habilitation for private law and comparative law in 1998. Prof. Koch started to work as an assistant at the University of Innsbruck in 1985. He was awarded tenure in 1999 and currently teaches Austrian and German private law as well as comparative law in Innsbruck. Since the academic year 2001/2002, he has been on leave for work at the European Centre of Tort and Insurance Law.
His current main fields of research are tort and contract law. He is a member of the European Group on Tort Law.

Prof. Helmut KOZIOL

European Centre of Tort
and Insurance Law
Landesgerichtsstraße 11
A-1080 Vienna, Austria
Tel. (+43–1) 40127–1680
Fax (+43–1) 40127–1685
koziol@ectil.org

Prof. Koziol is currently Executive Director of the European Centre of Tort and Insurance Law as well as Director of the Research Unit for European Tort Law of the Austrian Academy of Sciences. He was born in 1940 in Vienna and, after graduating (Dr. iuris) from the University of Graz in 1963, he worked as an assistant at the Law Faculty in Bonn. Prof. Koziol returned to Austria in 1967 when he became Professor of Private Law at the University of Linz (1967–1969), subsequently being offered a chair at the University of Vienna which he held until 2000.
His main fields of legal research include Tort Law and Banking Law.

Prof. Koziol is currently working on the drafting of European Principles of Tort Law as a founding member of the European Group on Tort Law and has contributed to the publications of the European Centre of Tort and Insurance Law both as editor and country reporter.

Christian LAHNSTEIN

Munich Re
Königinstraße 107
D-80791 Munich
Tel. (+49–89) 3891–9611
Fax (+49–89) 3891–9854
CLahnstein@munichre.com

Christian Lahnstein studied law in Tübingen, Geneva, Munich and Salamanca. He is legal counsel, expert for tort and insurance law, liability and accident insurance at Munich Re.

Dr. Javier LETE

University of Santiago de Compostela
Faculty of Law
Campus Sur S/N
E-15782 Santiago de Compostela
Tel. (+ 34) 981 563 100–14739
dcdcjla@usc.es

Dr. Lete was born in 1965. He graduated as a bachelor of law with honours at the University of Santiago de Compostela in 1988. He was first research assistant and then Profesor Titular de Escuela Universitaria of Civil Law at the same University from 1993 until 1998. He obtained a doctor iuris at the University of Santiago de Compostela in 1997 and became Professor Titular de Universidad of Civil Law at this University in 1998. After completing his research work at the Free University of Brussels (Institut d'études européennes) in 1995, he was a research scholar at the Department of Law of the London School of Economics, and also in the Institute of Advanced Legal Studies in 2000.
Dr. Lete has published in the areas of civil, contract, consumer and European Law, and also in Galician civil law. He is a member of the BIICL (British Institute of International and Comparative Law) and contributor to its Bulletin of Legal Developments. He is also a member of the German-Spanish Association for Lawyers (Deutsch-Spanische Juristenvereinigung e.V.) and of the Club du CIDIDAC (Centre du droit de l'enterprise de l'Université de Lausanne).

Olivier MASSOT

University of Geneva
40, boulevard du Pont d'Arve
CH-1211 Genève 4, Switzerland
Tel. (+41–22) 705–8640
Olivier.Massot@droit.unige.ch

Olivier Massot is assistant for legal philosophy at the University of Geneva. He is a Member of the Centre d'Etudes Politiques de l'Europe Latine (CNRS UMR 5112 University of Montpellier). Olivier Massot is writing his doctorate under the supervision of Louis Assier-Andrieu ("L'humain legislatif: du genre au genre. – Pour une relecture anthropologique des politiques legislatives en Europe"). He was awarded the D.E.A.: droit, institutions, societés, Mediterranée, Islam Afrique francophone and droits institutions, societés Catalogne et Andorre, and also the LL.M.: Master's Course in Legal Theory.

Prof. Emanuela NAVARRETTA

University of Pisa
Palazzo della Sapienza
Via Curtotone e Montanara 15
I-56100 Pisa, Italy
Tel. (+39–050) 2212–809/800
Fax: (+39–050) 2212 830
navarretta@ddpriv.unipi.it

Prof. Navarretta was born in Campobasso in 1966. She is a first level professor at the Scuola Superiore S. Anna where she taught as a second level professor before. She is currently lecturing private law at the Università degli Studi di Pisa.
Prof. Navarretta has been a member of the editorial Committee of the journal «Responsabilità civile e previdenza» since 1992. She is the holder of research funds, and coordinator of two research groups: one on the subject of damage to the person; the other on bioethics and private law.
She has published extensively in tort law as well as in other private law areas.

Dr. Jaana NORIO–TIMONEN

University of Helsinki
Institute of International Economic Law
P.O. Box 4 (Fabianinkatu 24 A)
FIN-00014 University of Helsinki, Finland
Tel. (+358–9) 191 23391
Fax (+358–9) 191 23390
Jaana.Norio-Timonen@helsinki.fi

Dr. Norio-Timonen is working as a researcher in the Institute of International Economic Law at the University of Helsinki. Her special field is insurance law. She has also been working at the Insurance Department of the Ministry of Social Affairs which is responsible for the drafting of most of the insurance legislation and which previously was also the supervisory authority in the field of insurance.

Prof. Ken OLIPHANT

Cardiff University
P.O. Box 427, Museum Avenue
Cardiff CF10 3XJ, United Kingdom
Tel. (+44–29) 2087–5365
oliphantka@cf.ac.uk

Prof. Oliphant was born in Glasgow but educated in England. He studied at St John's College, Oxford, gaining his BA (Juris) in 1987 and his BCL in 1988. For his BCL year, he was awarded a British Academy studentship. In September 1988, he took up a position as lecturer in law at King's College London, where he remained until moving to Cardiff Law School in September 1999. Prof. Oliphant has also held appointments as a visiting lecturer at the University of Passau (Germany) and as a visiting research fellow at the Institute of Australian and New Zealand Law in the Victoria University of Wellington (New Zealand). Amongst numerous other domestic and foreign engagements, he has delivered lectures and conference papers at the Universities of Bergen (Norway) and Uppsala (Sweden), and at the Academy of Arts and Sciences in Budapest.

His main field of research is the law of tort. He is the author of *Torts*, Macmillan, 1st edn., 1993, 2nd edn., 1997 (with Alastair Mullis) and of *Tort Law: Text and Materials*, Oxford University Press, 2000 (with Mark Lunney). He also contributed the chapters on 'The Nature of Tortious Liability', 'Injunctions and Other Remedies', 'Employers' Liability', and 'The Economic Torts' for the new title in the Butterworths Common Law Series on *The Law of Tort*, Butterworths, 2001 (ed. by Andrew Grubb). Amongst his other published output are numerous articles on the law of tort and on accident compensation.

André Gonçalo Dias PEREIRA

University of Coimbra
P-3004-545 Coimbra,
Portugal
Tel. (+35–1) 3985–9801 2
Fax: (+35–1) 23982–1043
andreper@fd.uc.pt

André Pereira graduated in Law (Faculty of Law, Coimbra University, awarded prize Prof. Manuel de Andrade for best student of the course 1992–1997). He is an Assistant Professor for civil law at the Coimbra Faculty of Law, where he also taught Criminal Law from 1998 to 2000. Moreover, he was Assistant Professor for Obligation Law, Contract Law and Law of Warrantees at the Moderna University. He has a Post-graduation in Civil Law and a Post-graduation in Medical Law. He is currently preparing his Ph.D. at the University of Coimbra. André Pereira has published several articles in Portugal, Germany and Brazil. He studied as Erasmus-student at the Georg-August Universität Göttingen in the academic year 1996/1997 and attended Summer Courses on Medical Law at the Utrecht University (1999) and Helsinki University (2000), and he was the coordinator of the summer course on the same subject that took place at the University of Coimbra (2001).

Eoin QUILL

University of Limerick
School of Law
Limerick, Ireland
Tel. (+353–61) 20–2220
Fax (+353–61) 20–2682
Eoin.Quill@ul.ie

Eoin Quill was born in Limerick in 1965. He studied law at University College Cork, a constituent college of the National University of Ireland, between 1982 and 1988 obtaining two bachelors and a masters degree – BCL; LLB; LLM.

He lectured at the School of Professional and Management Studies in Limerick from 1988–1990 and has been lecturing in the University of Limerick since 1991 in a variety of subjects including Tort, Commercial law and

Comparative Civil Obligations. His publications include a textbook – *Torts in Ireland* (Gill & Macmillan 1999) – and a variety of journal articles on issues in tort and contract. He was treasurer of the Irish Association of Law Teachers from 1997 to 2000 and is currently an examiner in Tort for the Law Society of Ireland.

Dr. Wolfgang REISINGER

Wiener Städtische Versicherung AG
Obere Donaustraße 49–51
A-1020 Wien
Tel: 01–53 1 39– DW 1500
Fax: 01–53 1 39– DW 3185
w.reisinger@staedtische.co.at

Dr. Wolfgang Reisinger was born in Vienna in 1952. He graduated with a Mathematics Degree in 1975 and in 1980 he completed his law studies. Dr. Reisinger began working for Wiener Staedtische Insurance Company/ Vienna (Assistant Manager in the Motor-Claims-Department) in 1980. From 1988 – 1992 he was Deputy Head of the Claims Department and since 1992 he has been Head of the Claims Department.

Henrik SANDELL

Advokatfirman Brunnéd
Sibyllegatan 43
S-11442 Stockholm, Sweden
Tel. (+46–8) 545–853 70
Fax (+46–8) 545–853 79
advokat.sandell@swipnet.se

Member of the Swedish Bar Association, Partner at Advokatfirman Brunnéd, Stockholm, Researcher, Tort law and Insurance law, Faculty of Law, Stockholm University Lecturer, Tort law and Insurance law, Faculty of Law, Stockholm University, Member of the EILI board, European Insurance Law Institute, Stockholm

Mag. Barbara C. STEININGER

European Centre of Tort and Insurance Law
Landesgerichtsstraße 11
A-1080 Vienna, Austria
Tel. (+43–1) 40127–1689
Fax (+43–1) 40127–1685
steininger@ectil.org

Mag. Steininger was born in Feldkirch (Austria) in 1977 and was brought up bilingually (German/Dutch). Between 1998 and 2000 she worked as a student assistant at the Institute of Roman Law, University of Vienna. She completed her law studies in Vienna in 1999. From 1998 to 1999. Mag. Steininger gained experience of a foreign university when she completed two terms at the University of Leiden, the Netherlands. Mag. Steininger is currently working on her doctoral thesis under the supervision of Prof. Helmut Koziol ("Verschärfung der Verschuldenshaftung"). Mag. Steininger has worked at the European Centre of Tort and Insurance Law in Vienna since its beginnings in 1999.

Prof. Luboš TICHY

Právnická fakulta University Karlovy
nám Curieových
CZ-Praha 1, Czech Republic
Fax: (+42–02) 248–104–72
ltichy@ssd.com

Professor of European, International Private and Civil Law, head of the European Community Law Department at the Faculty of Law of Charles University in Prague. Graduated from Charles University, further studies at Max-Planck-Institute for Foreign and International Private Law in Hamburg, the Swiss Institute of Comparative Law in Lausanne and University of Michigan Law School. Former President of the Czech Bar Association (1996). Former Partner of Squire, Sanders & Dempsey L.L.P. His main publications comprise law of obligations, private international law, law of arbitration, community law and law of consumer protection.

Prof. Bénédict WINIGER

University of Geneva
40, boulevard du Pont d'Arve
CH-1211 Genève 4, Switzerland
Tel.: (+41–22) 705–8642
Fax: (+41–22) 705–8468
Benedict.Winiger@droit.unige.ch

Prof. Winiger received bachelor's degrees in law (1978) as well as in philosophy (1985) and has held a doctorate of law since 1991. After working as an assistant and subsequently as a lecturer at the University of Geneva, he has been a professor of Roman Law and European Civil Law at the Department of Legal History of the Geneva Law Faculty since 1998. He was also a research fellow at the Università degli Studi "La Sapienza" at Rome from 1995–1996.
He currently teaches European Civil Law, Roman Law and Philosophy of Law.

European Centre of Tort and Insurance Law

1. Origins

In 1993 *Jaap Spier*, at that time Professor at the University of Tilburg in the Netherlands, called together a working group to discuss the fundamental questions concerning tort law on a comparative basis. The limits of liability were first examined. The results of these deliberations were published in two volumes. Subsequently, quite a demanding project was begun – the drafting of *Principles of European Tort Law* – which should serve as the basis for a future European tort law. This Group, in the meantime, has grown and today comprises over twenty members. It is also well-known under the name *European Group on Tort Law.*

The European Centre of Tort and Insurance Law (ECTIL) was founded in Vienna at the beginning of 1999 with a two-fold purpose – on the one hand to create a secure institutional basis for the drafting of the *Principles* and, on the other hand, to undertake further research projects in the field of tort law.

2. The European Centre of Tort and Insurance Law

Since November 2000 the European Centre of Tort and Insurance Law, based in Vienna, has been an association, whose purposes, as contained in the statutes, are:

- to undertake legal and comparative legal *research* in the field of *national, international and common European law of tort and insurance law*;
- to assist research work in this area, in particular the research activities of the *European Group on Tort Law*;
- to promote co-operation among researchers and research institutes of tort and insurance law as well as with other interested entities;
- to support scientific trainees in the area of tort and insurance law.

ECTIL is currently supported, among others, by the following institutions: the Austrian Ministry for Education, Science and Culture, the Austrian Ministry of Justice, the Swiss Federal Office for Justice, Munich Re, as well as the Austrian Association of Insurance Companies. It is hoped that further supporters will be included in the near future.

In addition to the members of the Board of Directors and the members of the Supervisory Board, scientists from almost all European Union countries as well as Switzerland, Poland, the Czech Republic, Israel, South Africa and the United States of America contribute to projects of the European Centre.

3. Cooperations

In 2002, the European Centre of Tort and Insurance Law entered a close cooperation agreement with the newly-founded *Research Unit for European Tort Law of the Austrian Academy of Sciences.*

Furthermore, ECTIL currently co-operates with: *Institute for Transnational Legal Research* (METRO, University of Maastricht, the Netherlands); *Swiss Institute of Comparative Law* (Dorigny, Switzerland); *Centre for European Private Law,* (Westfälische Wilhelms-University Münster, Germany); *European and Comparative Private Law Observatory* (University of Girona, Spain).

4. Research Activities

a) Principles of European Tort Law

The drafting of the *Principles of European Tort Law* is, without a doubt, the most extensive project of the European Centre of Tort and Insurance Law which will continue for several years. The aim of this broadly-based comparative research is the creation of a discussion foundation for a future harmonisation of the law of tort in the European Union, above all with respect to a possible codification of European Private Law. Further, the "Principles" to be drafted form a stimulus for both academics and practitioners and could serve as a guide for national legal systems, thereby leading to a gradual legal harmonisation. Not least, the present regulation of isolated tort law issues, which are at times themselves contradictory, requires a uniform concept from the European Union.

In order to attain the necessary overview of the various legal systems, written country reports on the tort law questions to be examined are prepared. These individual country reports address abstract issues as well as concrete cases. This methodology takes into account the legal systems of most of the countries of the European Union, some Eastern European countries as well as Switzerland which is currently involved in a reform of the law of tort. This work is positively supplemented by contributions from the legal systems of the USA, Israel and South Africa. South Africa in particular, with its mixed system, based on continental and English law, can provide valuable knowledge concerning legal harmonisation. With regard to a possible eastern expansion of the European Union in the future, a co-operation with these countries in the fields of legal integration is of particular significance.

A comparative report follows in which the similarities and differences between the tort law regulations in the individual countries is presented. This basis forms the starting point for the drafting of the Principles which could be acceptable for all of the legal systems examined. Due to the diversity of the legal systems under question, it is rarely the case that, in this work, uniform regulations already exist. Rather, existent solutions require further development or even new solutions have to be sought.

The work of the European Group on Tort Law on these projects has already led to concrete results, namely several publications in the *Principles of Tort Law* series which have been or will soon be published by Kluwer Law International Publishing House (The Hague):

- Spier (ed.), *The Limits of Liability: Keeping the Floodgates Shut* (1996)
- Spier (ed.), *The Limits of Expanding Liability: Eight Fundamental Cases in a Comparative Perspective* (1998)
- Koziol (ed.), Unification of Tort Law: *Wrongfulness* (1998)
- Spier (ed.), Unification of Tort Law: *Causation* (2000)
- Magnus (ed.), Unification of Tort Law: *Damages* (2001)
- Koch/Koziol (eds.), Unification of Tort Law: *Strict Liability* (2002)
- Widmer (ed.), Unification of Tort Law: *Fault* (in preparation)

The next volumes in this project will examine the areas of *Vicarious Liability* and *Contributory Negligence*.

b) Further Research Projects

The work of the European Centre of Tort and Insurance Law is, however, not limited to the drafting of the Principles. In addition, the Centre is involved in other comparative legal research studies, the results of which are published in the series "Tort and Insurance Law" by Springer Publishing House (Vienna/New York).

5. Projects Concluded

The project *Non-Pecuniary Loss* examines the pre-conditions for the compensation of non-pecuniary loss. The research project *Medical Malpractice* addresses the increasingly urgent issue of the liability for medical malpractice, in particular the future difficulty of the insurability of this risk. These two studies were published in autumn 2001 by the Springer Publishing House (Vienna/New York). *Tort Law and Social Law* deals with the difficult area of the distribution of risk between the individual inflicting harm and the public sector; the results will be published in the course of 2002.

6. Current Projects

The *Pure Economic Loss* study, to be completed in 2002, has met with great interest from the insurance industry as the rules regarding the compensation of pure economic loss are in the individual countries extremely diverse and the risks, especially those electronic risks created by the Internet, do not respect national borders.

On the initiative of the Dutch Ministry of Health and in co-operation with the Dutch Institute for Transnational Legal Research (METRO), the European Centre of Tort and Insurance Law dealt with the possibilities of a no-fault liability for medical malpractice in the project, *No-fault Compensation in the Health Care Sector.* A further project under the same frame of reference as just mentioned, *Liability for and Insurability of Bio-Medical Research* examines to what extent insurance can be expected to carry the risks of medical research on human subjects.

A further comparative study examines *Compensation for Personal Injury* in ten European legal systems and a project addresses the issue of *Children in Tort Law.* Due to recent events, a project on *Liability for Terrorist Acts* has been initiated.

Board of Directors

Michael Faure	Maastricht University	*Netherlands*
Attila Fenyves (Vice-Director)	Vienna University	*Austria*
Helmut Koziol (Director)	ECTIL	*Austria*
Ulrich Magnus (Vice-Director)	Hamburg University	*Germany*
W.V.H. Rogers	Nottingham University	*Great Britain*

Supervisory Board

Suzanne Galand–Carval	Paris University	*France*
Gerhard Hopf	Ministry of Justice	*Austria*
Ralph Kempkens	Munich Re	*Germany*
Konstantinos D. Kerameus (Vice-Chairman)	Athens University	*Greece*
Raoul Kneucker	Ministry of Science	*Austria*
Franz Lauer	Austrian Association of Insurance Companies	*Austria*
Reiner Schulze	Münster University	*Germany*
Pierre Widmer (Chairman)	Swiss Institute of Comparative Law	*Switzerland*

Members

All Members and Guests of the *European Group on Tort Law* (see below)

Fellows

Kenneth S. Abraham	Virginia University	*USA*
Arno J. Akkermans	Amsterdam University	*Netherlands*
Willem van Boom	Tilburg University	*Netherlands*
María Paz García Rubio	Santiago de Compostela University	*Spain*
Heinz Hausheer	Bern University	*Switzerland*
Monika Hinteregger	Graz University	*Austria*
Eoin O'Dell	Dublin University	*Ireland*
Giulio Ponzanelli	Brescia University	*Italy*
Willibald Posch	Graz University	*Austria*
Alexandra Rumo-Jungo	Freiburg i. Ue. University	*Switzerland*
Gottfried Schiemann	Tübingen University	*Germany*
Pierre Tercier	Freiburg i. Ue. University	*Switzerland*
Gerhard Wagner	Bonn University	*Germany*
Christiane Wendehorst	Göttingen University	*Germany*
Bénédict Winiger	Geneva University	*Switzerland*

EUROPEAN GROUP ON TORT LAW

Members

Francesco Busnelli	Scuola Sup. S. Anna, Pisa	*Italy*
Giovanni Comandé	Scuola Sup. S. Anna, Pisa	*Italy*
Herman Cousy	Leuven University	*Belgium*
Dan B. Dobbs	Arizona University	*USA*
Bill W. Dufwa	Stockholm University	*Sweden*
Michael G. Faure	Maastricht University	*Netherlands*
Suzanne Galand-Carval	Paris University	*France*
Israel Gilead	Jerusalem University	*Israel*
Michael D. Green	Wake Forest University	*USA*
Konstantinos D. Kerameus	Athens University	*Greece*
Bernhard A. Koch	Innsbruck University	*Austria*
Helmut Koziol	ECTIL	*Austria*
Ulrich Magnus	Hamburg University	*Germany*
Miquel Martín-Casals	Girona University	*Spain*
Jorge Ferreira Sinde Monteiro	Coimbra University	*Portugal*
Johann Neethling	South Africa University, Pretoria	*South Africa*
Edgar du Perron	Amsterdam University	*Netherlands*
W. V. Horton Rogers	Nottingham University	*Great Britain*
Gary T. Schwartz †	Los Angeles University	*USA*
Jaap Spier	Hoge Raad, Den Haag	*Netherlands*
Luboš Tichý	Prague University	*Czech Rep.*
Geneviève Viney	Paris University	*France*
Pierre Widmer	Swiss Institute of Comparative Law	*Switzerland*
Michael R. Will	Geneva/Saarbrücken (em.)	*Germany*

Guests

Miroslaw Nesterowicz	Warsaw University	*Poland*

ECTIL Publication List

Principles of European Tort Law

Volume 1: The Limits of Liability: Keeping the Floodgates Shut

Edited by Jaap Spier

Kluwer Law International, The Hague
Hardbound, ISBN 90-411-0169-1
1996, 162 pp.

Volume 2: The Limits of Expanding Liability. Eight Fundamental Cases in a Comparative Perspective

Edited by Jaap Spier

Kluwer Law International, The Hague
Hardbound, ISBN 90-411-0581-6
1998, 244 pp.

Volume 3: Unification of Tort Law: Wrongfulness

Edited by Helmut Koziol

Kluwer Law International, The Hague
Hardbound, ISBN 90-411-1019-4
1998, 144 pp.

Volume 4: Unification of Tort Law: Causation

Edited by Jaap Spier

Kluwer Law International, The Hague
Hardbound, ISBN 90-411-1325-8
2000, 161 pp.

Volume 5: Unification of Tort Law: Damages

Edited by Ulrich Magnus

Kluwer Law International, The Hague
Hardbound, ISBN 90-411-1481-5
2001, 225 pp.

Volume 6: Unification of Tort Law: Strict Liability

Edited by Bernhard A. Koch and Helmut Koziol

Kluwer Law International, The Hague
Hardbound, ISBN 90-411-1705-9
2002, 444 pp.

Tort and Insurance Law

Volume 1: Cases on Medical Malpractice in a Comparative Perspective

Edited by Michael Faure and Helmut Koziol

Springer, Vienna/New York
Softcover, ISBN: 3-211-83595-4
2001, 331 pp.

Volume 2: Damages for Non-Pecuniary Loss in a Comparative Perspective

Edited by W.V. Horton Rogers

Springer, Vienna/New York
Softcover, ISBN: 3-211-83602-0
2001, 318 pp.

In preparation:

Volume 3: The Impact of Social Law and Private Tort Law Concerning Personal Injuries

Edited by Ulrich Magnus

Springer, Vienna/New York
Softcover, ISBN 3-211-83795-7
2002, approx. 320 pp.

Volume 4: Compensation for Personal Injury in a Comparative Perspective

Edited by Bernhard A. Koch and Helmut Koziol

Springer, Vienna/New York
Softcover, ISBN 3-211-83791-4
2002, approx. 350 pp.

INDEX

The numbers refer to the marginal notes, the letters refer to the country reports; A stands for Austria, B for Belgium, C for the report of Herman A. Cousy, CH for Switzerland, CR for Comparative Remarks, CZ for Czech Republic, D for Germany, DK for Denmark, E for Spain, EU for European Union, EW for England and Wales, F for France, FIN for Finland, GR for Greece, I for Italy, IRL for Ireland, K for the report of Bernhard A. Koch, L for the report of Christian Lahnstein, NL for the Netherlands, P for Portugal, PL for Poland, R for the report of Wolfgang Reisinger, S for Sweden, W for the report of Bénédict Winiger and ZA for South Africa.